GLOBAL FINA
SYSTEMS

GLOBAL FINANCIAL SYSTEMS

STABILITY AND RISK

Jon Danielsson

Director, Systemic Risk Centre
London School of Economics

PEARSON

Harlow, England • London • New York • Boston • San Francisco • Toronto • Sydney
Auckland • Singapore • Hong Kong • Tokyo • Seoul • Taipei • New Delhi
Cape Town • São Paulo • Mexico City • Madrid • Amsterdam • Munich • Paris • Milan

PEARSON EDUCATION LIMITED

Edinburgh Gate
Harlow CM20 2JE
United Kingdom
Tel: +44 (0)1279 623623
Web: www.pearson.com/uk

First published 2013 (print and electronic)

ISBN: 978-0-273-77466-2 (print)
978-0-273-77471-6 (PDF)
978-0-273-77467-9 (eText)

British Library Cataloguing-in-Publication Data
A catalogue record for the print edition is available from the British Library

Library of Congress Cataloging-in-Publication Data
Daníelsson, Jón.
Global financial systems / Jon Danielsson.
pages cm
ISBN 978-0-273-77466-2
1. International finance. I. Title.
HG3881.D3266 2013
332'.042—dc23
2013012036

10 9 8 7 6 5 4 3 2 1
16 15 14 13

Print edition typeset in 9.25/13.5 Stone Humanist ITC Std by 75
Print edition printed and bound in Slovenia by Svet Print – Ljubljana d.o.o.

NOTE THAT ANY PAGE CROSS-REFERENCES REFER TO THE PRINT EDITION

CONTENTS

Errata and online chapter

For errata and an online chapter on the latest regulation and crisis development, please visit www.GlobalFinancialSystems.org.

AUTHOR'S ACKNOWLEDGEMENTS

This book is based on my lecture notes for my LSE course 'Global Financial Systems'. The course was originally developed by Hyun Song Shin, who taught it from 2001 until 2004 and generously gave me access to his lecture notes which formed the skeleton for the first time I taught the course in 2008.

I was fortunate to be able to employ two exemplary students, Jacqueline Li and Jing Zeng, who took the course in 2008, to work with me in the summer of 2009 to help me to develop the lecture material into what became this book. Their assistance was invaluable, and they made significant contributions both to the book version of the lecture notes and to the slides. Their ability to master the computational aspects of the course material (latex, mercurial, R) and the economic topics was impressive, as was the apparent ease with which they mastered all the technicalities. Their work was generously funded by the LSE Teaching Development Fund and the Department of Finance.

I was equally fortunate during the summer of 2010 to employ three former students of the course, Georgia Lv, Eric Pashman and Nick Zeifang. Since then, Kyounghwan Lee has been very helpful in developing some of the material. Several students have made valuable contributions, including Fan Gao, Radhika Saini, Yong Bin Ng, Murathan Kurt, Basak Yeltekin, Janis Sussick and Stefan Doykin.

Several friends made invaluable contributions to the book. Robert Macrae of Arcus Investment read the manuscript twice, and made innumerable comments. His insight into the subject matter and his keen understanding of financial markets from an investor's point of view made the book much better than it otherwise would have been.

Con Keating of EFFAS read the whole manuscript, and by identifying the places where my analysis and logic fell short, significantly improved the book.

Giovanni Bassini read the chapters on financial regulations and pointed out the most up-to-date developments. David Schraa from IIF read the chapter on future developments in regulations and gave me very useful insights into the fine points of the ongoing regulatory debate.

I would like to thank my wife Sigrun for her shrewd comments, her honest observations and, above all, her patience.

Without all of these people, this book would not have seen the light of day. Any inaccuracies and errors that remain in the book are the result of my not paying enough attention to their comments.

E·S·R·C ECONOMIC & SOCIAL RESEARCH COUNCIL

The author gratefully acknowledges the support of the Economic and Social Research Council (UK) [grant number ES/K 002309/1].

PUBLISHER'S ACKNOWLEDGEMENTS

We are grateful to the following for permission to reproduce copyright material:

Logos

Logo on page xi from Economic and Social Research Council.

Tables

Table 5.1 from On the measurement of Zimbabwe's hyperinflation, *Cato Journal*, Vol. 29, No. 2, 356 (Hanke, S. H. and Kwok, A. K. F. Spring/Summer 2009), Copyright © Cato Institute. All rights reserved; Tables 6.1, 6.2 after http://data.worldbank.org/, World Bank; Table 11.2 from Forty Years' Experience with the OECD Code of Liberalisation of Capital Movements, OECD Publishing. http://dx.doi.org/10.1787/9789264176188-en.

Photographs

The publisher would like to thank the following for their kind permission to reproduce their photographs:

Getty Images: Cate Gillon / Staff 173, Agus Lolong 147.

Cover images: *Front:* **Getty Images**

In some instances we have been unable to trace the owners of copyright material, and we would appreciate any information that would enable us to do so.

INTRODUCTION

The focus of this book is on how the world's financial system functions, the various policy choices governments have, and how the system has built-in vulnerabilities which lead to crises. Financial crises have been our constant companion from the very first time human beings created a financial system. This means that over time, we have accumulated deep knowledge and understanding of the economic forces enabling such crises. This experience shows that financial crises are all fundamentally the same, only the details differ. This is why financial crises are so hard to prevent and so costly to fight. Every time, we are faced with new details that enforce age-old vulnerabilities.

The various types of financial-system fragilities are systematically analysed in this book, lessons from past crisis events are used to study recent crises, and up-to-date research is employed for the analysis of crises long past. In doing so, we make use of the rich body of research that has emerged with the continuous crisis from 2007.

The focus of the book is on policy issues. It uses a number of case studies, aiming to create a unified theme linking all the cases. It is written from a point of view of economics, but does have relevance in other policy-oriented fields such as government, political science and law.

The target level is intermediate to advanced undergraduate students and masters students. Some knowledge of economics and financial markets is helpful but not essential.

Most of the chapters are non-mathematical, a few make some use of mathematics and one is essentially dedicated to formal models. It is an open question what is the best way to incorporate the technical material. It is quite helpful for students with the right background, but can be skipped by others.

The first part of the book presents basic concepts in financial stability, such as systemic risk, endogenous risk, the fundamental role of the central bank and the multi-faceted concept of liquidity. These chapters provide a foundation for more specialised analysis later in the book. One important case study is contained in this first part, the Great Depression of the 1930s, which is the worst financial and economic crisis we have ever seen and, hence, has had a huge impact on financial and economic policy. The response to the ongoing crisis is significantly shaped by the Great Depression.

After this, we provide more specific analysis of the various parts of the financial system, and how they relate to financial stability. We start with a detailed case study of the Asian crisis of 1997 which clearly demonstrates the various dimensions of modern financial crises. This is followed by discussion of banking crises and bank runs. Thereafter the book focuses on financial markets, speculation, trading and the market for credit. The final part of the financial system that is discussed is currency markets, which are the focus of two chapters, the first focused on policy issues and the second currency crisis models.

Governments have various ways of intervening in financial markets, and the next chapters in the book discuss financial regulations and bailouts. Financial regulation is a rich topic that is easily the subject of its own book, but here we limit the discussion to the main arguments for regulating, some of the challenges faced by the authorities and finally international regulations on bank capital. The last part of the book focuses on the ongoing crisis from 2007, starting with the dangerous financial instruments that were one of the factors that enabled excessive risk-taking to take place out of sight. Failures in financial regulation and risk management also played a role and are the subject of the following chapter. After this, we bring together the main lessons from the book into a three-chapter discussion on the ongoing crisis, first the credit phase from 2007 until 2009, then how the crisis is shaping financial regulations, and finally sovereign debt crises, both generally and with specific reference to the ongoing European sovereign debt crisis. Because this crisis is ongoing, we maintain a final chapter online at www.GlobalFinancialSystems.org addressing day-to-day developments in the crisis. This chapter is updated regularly to reflect new information.

1 SYSTEMIC RISK

The world's economy was on the brink of collapse in the autumn of 2008. *Confidence*, the lifeblood of the financial system, was evaporating at an alarming rate, financial institutions refused to do business with each other, people took their money out of banks and it looked like the real economy might be heading for a second *Great Depression*. Then, just as suddenly as the crisis materialised, it seemed like it was over.

What we experienced was a near-miss *systemic crisis*, generally defined as the collapse of the entire financial system, followed by an economic depression. The full crisis was only averted thanks to the swift actions of the authorities.

Over the past half-century, until a few years ago, systemic risk had been the purview of a few academics and policy makers, very much a backwater discipline. The prevailing approach was to study the risk of the individual parts of the financial system separately, not in aggregate, since the objective of interest was the institution, not the system. An example is how the *Basel Accords* – the main body of international financial regulations – focus on individual prudential behaviour instead of the financial system in its entirety. The series of crises that started in 2007 demonstrated the folly of such thinking.

2007 was not the first time we faced systemic risk; it has been present ever since the first financial system was created, and is an inevitable part of any market-based economic system. It was a real and recognised danger during the era of the *first globalism* – 1873 to 1914. In the highly regulated financial world after the Second World War (WWII), systemic crises were a relatively remote eventuality, only to re-emerge with the collapse of the Bretton Woods system in the early 1970s.

Systemic risk is most damaging for advanced financial markets; after all, a country with a small and underdeveloped financial system is much more resilient to problems in the financial sector. The key question for policy makers in countries with advanced financial markets is how to limit the build-up of systemic risk and contain crisis events when they happen. To answer this we need to identify and understand the different aspects of systemic risk and the tools available to policy makers.

Links to other chapters

This chapter introduces the main concepts of financial stability and systemic risk, and many of these topics will be discussed in considerable detail in later chapters. For example, liquidity is discussed in Chapter 4, and the acceleration mechanisms for pro-cyclicality in Chapter 3. Ultimately, these concepts are applied to the various case studies of financial crises, most importantly the ongoing crisis, discussed in several chapters towards the end of this book.

Key concepts

- **Systemic risk**
- **Moral hazard**
- **Liquidity**
- **Bank runs**
- **Pro-cyclicality**
- **Firesale externality**

Readings for this chapter

Few academic studies of systemic risk are available in the existing literature, but this is now rapidly changing. Several authors have written about financial crisis from a historical point of view, for example, Ferguson (2008), Kindleberger (1996) and Reinhart and Rogoff (2009). On a more technical level, early analysis was provided by Minsky (1992), with Bandt and Hartmann (2000) discussing the latest work on the topic prior to the crises from 2007.

Notation specific to this chapter

γ **The money multiplier**
δ **Reserve requirement**

1.1 CASE STUDY: THE 1914 CRISIS

The biggest systemic event in recent history may have occurred in 1914. Brown (1940) and Ferguson (2008, p. 298) document the chain of events. The main crisis event was characterised by a rapid loss of confidence, with leverage, liquidity and interconnectedness all playing a major role.

In 1914, globalism amongst the world's industrial nations was perhaps as advanced as now, and maybe even more so. At the time, the major supplier of credit to the world was the *City of London* which had developed a highly sophisticated financial industry.

Unfortunately, that sophistication created particular vulnerabilities, such as *interconnectedness*, common to modern financial centres.

The crisis was triggered by an *exogenous shock*, the assassination of Archduke Franz Ferdinand of Austria on 28 June 1914. This led to posturing amongst the great powers of Europe and the build-up of the expectation of war. That expectation, in turn, created worries that financial institutions might experience difficulties in having cross-border loans repaid – after all, if two countries are at war, it is difficult to enforce contracts across borders. Surprisingly, even after the war started, remittance between the *Central Powers* and the *Allies* continued via neutral countries, especially Switzerland, helping to propel it into the ranks of major financial centres.

Cross-border creditors started to repatriate funds. The immediate financial consequence was that demand for sterling spiked, not least since London banks and finance houses called in their overseas balances. The pound appreciated from $4.89 to $6.35 in New York in July, but this soon reversed and the dollar became the world's dominant currency, a status it has enjoyed ever since.

However, not all loans are callable, and financial institutions heavily exposed to cross-border lending were vulnerable, as were those exposed to those exposed to cross-border lending, and so on. In effect, everybody was exposed, even those who only did domestic banking. This is an example of *network effects* in the financial system.

The supply of sterling dried up. The banks stopped loaning funds to the discount market, which was a sort of interbank market, as they needed to hold everything in cash in order to meet demand.

The collapse of the discount market, which was the single most important source of sterling funds, meant that London acceptance houses, already facing losses from clients unable to remit funds, were unable to take on more lending and, hence, stopped making acceptances on 27 July.

One example of this slowdown is seen in Figure 1.1 which shows the 1914 volume of new long-term foreign loans made in the City of London. In the second half of 1914 the volume collapsed, along with activity on the financial markets.

Foreign countries and domestic firms sought to convert their stock holdings into cash, but found no buyers on the London Stock Exchange. Finally, the stock exchange closed shortly after 10 a.m. on 31 July.

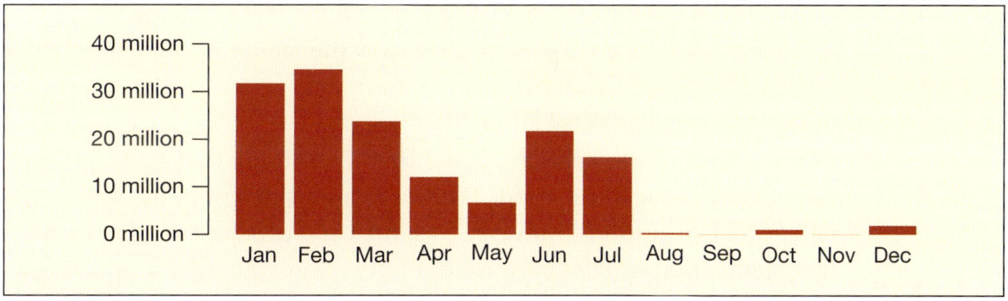

Figure 1.1 Amount of foreign loans made in the City of London in 1914 (in sterling)
Data source: Brown (1940)

A general moratorium was issued on banker acceptances, lasting for two months. The Bank of England (BoE) made further advances of £200 million to the money markets, and on 13 August obtained a government guarantee to discount bills in the market without recourse, whilst also allowing for delays in repayments. The London Stock Exchange was only reopened on 4 January 1915.

Analysis

It does not take all that much for a panic to happen when confidence evaporates. Even rumours that a large institution might fail can cause panic. In 1914, it was clear that some institutions were heavily exposed to cross-border lending and would fail in case of war. That was enough to trigger the crisis. We did not need the actual event of a war to make this happen; the expectation of a war was sufficient.

The authorities played a clear role, similar to what they did at the height of the crises from 2007 but on a much larger scale. The BoE resorted to what now would be called quantitative easing (QE), literally printing money. In the 10 days to 1 August, the Bank made securitised loans, worth £31,700,000, to discount houses and the Stock Exchange, most of which had to be paid back one year after the war. The bank rate jumped from 3% to 10% in three days in order to prevent the gold bleeding to France. On 1 August, the Peel Act was suspended and the Bank was allowed to issue notes in excess of its gold holdings.

The policy intervention was successful and the City of London did survive, even if not unscathed. A systemic crisis was averted. By comparison, events during the crises that started in 2007 are quite mild.

There are two main lessons to be taken from these events. First, in a crisis, the authorities have no choice but to take extreme measures if they want to save their economies. Secondly, because decisions have to be taken rapidly it is much better if the authorities are prepared. In 1914 the BoE did follow the established practice of lending of last resort (LOLR), developed half a century earlier.

1.2 THE CONCEPT OF SYSTEMIC RISK

The financial system is vulnerable to many different types of shocks, both coming from outside the financial system and generated by the financial system itself. Some shocks are *idiosyncratic*, affecting only a single institution or asset, whilst others are *systematic*, impacting on the entire financial system and the real economy.

An example of an idiosyncratic shock is the failure of a single small or medium-sized bank, perhaps due to internal fraud or mismanagement. Such failure is generally not a big public concern. Banks fail all the time and the authorities have robust resolution mechanisms in place for unwinding failed banks, ensuring that banking services are uninterrupted and contagion averted. The situation is different in the special case of 'too big to fail' (TBTF) institutions. However, in some circumstances an idiosyncratic shock can lead to systemic risk, usually because of in-built vulnerabilities amplifying a relatively small event into a full-blown systemic crisis.

We need to make a distinction between the term *systemic* and *systematic*. Systematic risk relates to non-diversifiable risk factors that affect everybody and is always present, perhaps the stock market, whilst systemic risk pertains to the danger of the entire financial system collapsing.

The consequences of a systemic crisis in the financial sector are more devastating compared to other economic sectors. Suppose a firm making chocolate goes bust: the shareholders and employees suffer, but competing chocolate firms will benefit. There is no significant damage to the economy, and such developments may even be positive, as argued by Joseph Schumpeter (1942) with his notion of creative destruction. By contrast, if a bank collapses, it may well lead to the seizure of the entire financial system, crippling the real economy.

1.2.1 Notions of systemic risk

Systemic risk is a term used frequently, both in popular media and by specialists. Unfortunately, most usage is imprecise and contradictory. Often one gets the impression that commentators are only talking about the last crisis event when they define systemic risk.

The global authorities, in the form of the International Monetary Fund (IMF), the Bank for International Settlements (BIS) and the Financial Stability Board (FSB) (2009), define a systemic event as:

> 'the disruption to the flow of financial services that is (i) caused by an impairment of all or parts of the financial system; and (ii) has the potential to have serious negative consequences for the real economy.'

A more comprehensive definition is:

Definition 1.1 Systemic risk The risk that the entire financial system may fail, causing a general economic collapse, as opposed to risk associated with an individual part of the system.

Systemic risk arises from the interlinkages present in the financial system, where the failure of an individual institution may cause spillovers and even cascading failures, amplified by the inherent pro-cyclicality of banking and regulations.

The conditions for systemic risk tend to be created when all outward signs point to stability and low risk.

There are few or no recorded instances of a systemic event according to this strict definition. We have seen events that got close in their severity, and other events that, if left to fruition, might have ended up as a systemic event.

It is important to recognise that there is no single generally accepted definition of systemic risk. Some commentators have a much looser definition than the one above, often considering a severe crisis, and even a routine crisis, to be a systemic event. However, the most common usage is similar to Definition 1.1.

1.2.2 Who is vulnerable?

A systemic event can be global in reach, or just affect a single country. Some countries are more vulnerable to systemic risk than others, especially those that have based their economies on finance and are exporters of financial services.

One way to identify who is susceptible is to consider the size of the banking system. Within the European Union (EU), the European Central Bank (ECB) publishes statistics on the size of the banking system, split into domestic and foreign parts. Figure 1.2 shows the relative size of the banking system in EU member states, measured using the ratio of total banking assets to GDP, both before the crisis in 2007 and also in June 2011.

The country with the smallest banking system, Romania, comes in at 64% whilst the largest banking counties are Luxembourg, Malta, Ireland and Cyprus. The latter two have been badly hit by the European sovereign debt crisis. This does not necessarily mean that these large banking countries are more vulnerable to systemic risk than the rest. It matters how much of the banking system is domestic owned and how much is foreign owned. The countries with the smallest and largest banking systems have predominantly

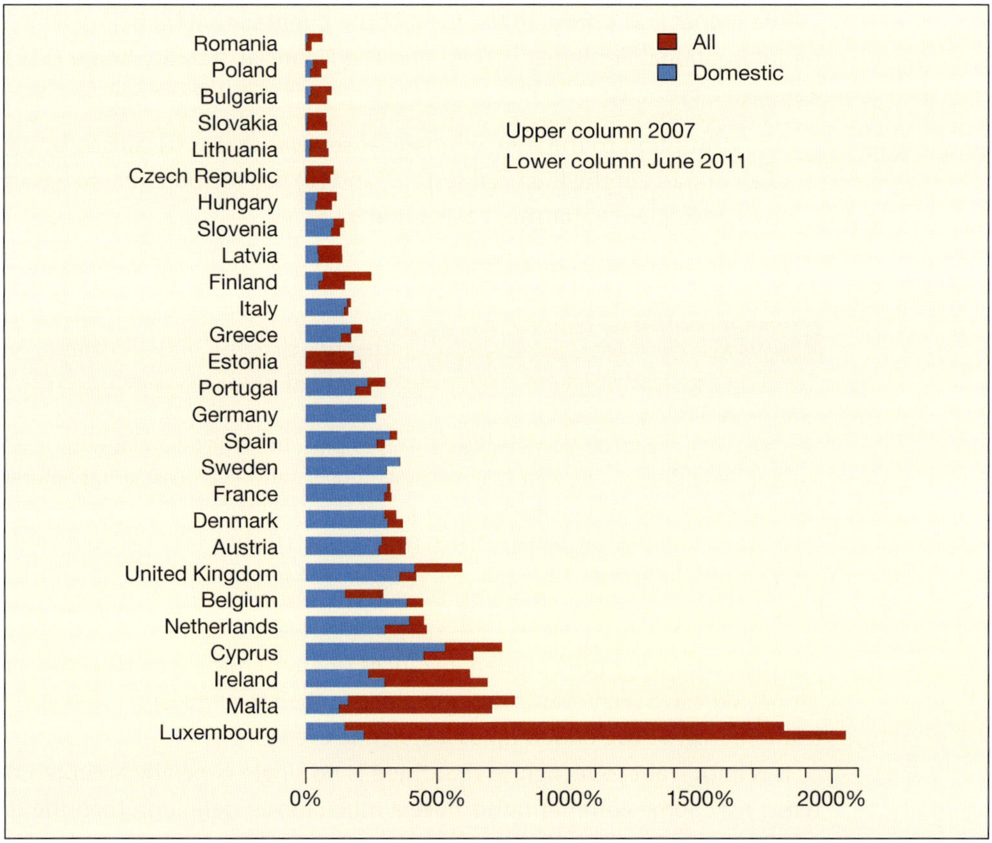

Figure 1.2 EU banking system, total assets/GDP ratio in 2007 and June 2011, ordered by size of banking system in 2007

Data source: ECB and Eurostat

foreign banking, albeit for different reasons. For the small banking countries regular banks are owned by foreigners, whilst for the large banking countries the foreign-owned banks mostly service foreign clients. These countries export banking services, produced by foreign-owned banks.

This reduces vulnerability. For example, even if the assets of the Luxembourg banks exceed its GDP 20 times, Luxembourg is relatively insulated because the failure of a bank would not directly involve taxpayers' money in most cases. Of course, if a number of the banks failed, the Luxembourg government might find itself short of funds from taxes, so it is directly connected to the banks. This threat is, however, less direct than if Luxembourg would be called on to bail out the banks. This suggests that in a country like Ireland or Cyprus, even if their banks are relatively smaller than the banks in Luxembourg, bank failures pose a much bigger danger.

The large banking countries are also at risk of Dutch disease,[1] where the banks become the dominating part of the economy, crowding out other economic activity.

The United Kingdom

Figure 1.2 shows that the United Kingdom (UK) had the seventh largest banking system in the EU in 2007, and the largest amongst the big economies. This means that banking is more important for the UK than for most other countries. The importance of banking can be seen in Figure 1.3, which shows the UK output index. Essentially, all economic growth has come from finance, highlighting the growing importance of the City of London.

This suggests that countries with large financial systems need to pay special attention to financial sector policies, such as financial regulations. The UK aims to be at the forefront of developing policies towards the financial system, developing the doctrine of the '*hands-off approach*' before 2007. This was widely admired at the time. The UK now demonstrates its frontier thinking by activities such as the *Independent Commission on Banking* and the activities of the government's *Foresight group*.

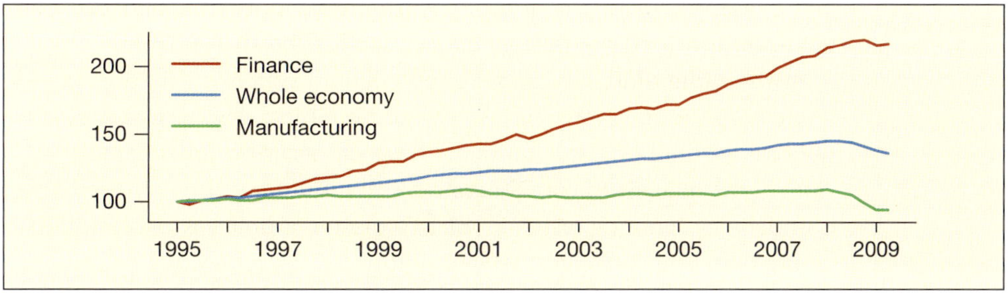

Figure 1.3 UK output index, 1995 Q1 = 100
Data source: Thomson Datastream

[1]Dutch disease arises when a new large profitable economic sector, traditionally exploiting natural resources, causes a decline in the manufacturing sector. This happens because the new revenue from natural resources strengthens the currency, making the manufacturing sector less competitive. It is used here in a more general sense where one sector crowds out other sectors.

Banks, bank size and politics

The contribution of the financial sector to systemic risk also depends on the structure of the financial sector. For example, suppose two countries have banking systems of the same magnitude. The first country has one bank while the second has 10 equally sized banks. In this case, the first country is much more vulnerable.

This happens for two main reasons. First, the country with the single bank is likely to suffer significantly if its single bank fails, whilst the country with 10 banks would find it easier to cope with the failure of several, but not all, of its banks. Second, the single large bank is likely to have more political power than the 10 smaller banks combined. The reason is that the single large bank is more important and therefore carries more political weight, whilst the 10 banks would be unlikely to speak with a single voice and maintain a uniform lobbying agenda, implying that the single big bank has more political power.

The stronger political power would probably mean that the bank creates more systemic risk because it could use its lobbying power to *push back* on regulations and could appeal to the politicians if the supervisor is giving it difficulty.

1.2.3 Should we eliminate systemic risk?

This leaves the question of whether it is a desirable policy objective to prevent financial crises altogether and reduce systemic risk to zero. While it is quite straightforward to do so, the cost may not be acceptable.

The answer depends on the definition of systemic risk. While it may not be desirable to prevent systemic risk altogether in its loosest definition, we are willing to do what it takes to prevent a general economic collapse according to the strict definition.

Systemic risk is created by risk taking and the complex interactions within the financial system, so all that is needed to prevent systemic crises is to drastically reduce the size of the financial system. Countries with small and unsophisticated financial systems are not very vulnerable to systemic risk. They may suffer, of course, if the outside world enters into a systemic crisis. The question is whether a modern society can exist and grow without a sophisticated risk-taking financial sector. The answer is no.

At the same time, we cannot simply ignore systemic risk; the consequences of a systemic crisis are so severe that we would do almost anything to prevent it. Indeed, as we see later in the book, governments have on occasion proclaimed they would not intervene in the markets to contain systemic risk, but have then reneged once a crisis episode is under way. Ignoring systemic risk as a matter of policy is not credible.

The correct balance lies between those two extremes. We need to encourage enough risk taking by the financial industry so that economic growth is not hampered, whilst at the same time have mechanisms in place that prevent risk taking from causing systemic crises. This is a classical risk–return trade-off but is not a trivial undertaking since regulations change the behaviour of economic agents and can by themselves lead to undesirable outcomes, like systemic risk. This means that one cannot look at individual policies in isolation; policymakers instead need to consider the impact of government regulations of the financial system in their entirety.

The current financial crisis gives us a good example of the challenge facing the authorities. The failure of individual institutions like Bear Stearns, Lehman Brothers and AIG caused serious disruptions. Deciding on whether these institutions should have been bailed out is a clear example of the risk–return trade-off we have discussed here.

That task is made easier by the observation that most crises are fundamentally similar, even if the details differ. For example, the 1914 crisis and the ongoing crisis have strong commonalities — financial institutions building up risk in good times, as if a crisis could never happen, only to see confidence and liquidity evaporate suddenly, causing cascading failures. The authorities reacted similarly by providing liquidity injections. This suggests that policymakers should be well prepared and know their history. Getting caught short in 2007 did not reflect well on many policymaking institutions.

1.3 WHO CREATES SYSTEMIC RISK?

While episodes of (near) systemic events seem to happen quite suddenly, in reality they take a long time to build up, as noted by the former head of the BIS, Andrew Crockett, in 2000:

> 'The received wisdom is that risk increases in recessions and falls in booms. In contrast, it may be more helpful to think of risk as increasing during upswings, as financial imbalances build up, and materialising in recessions.'

In other words, when looking for the origins of systemic risk one should not focus on current events; decisions made long ago are usually to blame.

This leaves open the question of who is responsible for a crisis episode. The public media and affiliated pundits delight in blaming the target of the day, whether the greedy bankers, incompetent politicians, pernicious academics or some other easy scapegoat. The reality is more nuanced. It is the interplay between the various parties that creates conditions for systemic risk, with no key players blameless. It is equally difficult to identify what is the real problem when confronted by the news of the day.

1.3.1 Role of financial institutions

Financial institutions are in active competition with each other; they are ranked by size, number of clients, profits, etc. Because of the relationship between risk and return, perhaps coupled with a short-term outlook, profit-maximising behaviour can cause financial institutions to take on considerable risk. We do not even need competition for this to happen; greed is sufficient.

Over time, risk taking of that nature can become destabilising, creating systemic risk. One problem is that during boom times the risk is often hidden, so financial institutions experience large profits at what seems like low risk. However, the risk builds up and can materialise quite suddenly. This is an example of the theories of Minsky (1992) who argued that economies have either stable or unstable financial regimes. Even if the economy starts out stable, continued prosperity paves the way for an unstable system. The essence of Minsky's financial instability hypothesis is that *stability is destabilising* because financial institutions have a tendency to extrapolate stability into infinity, investing in ever more risky debt structures that ultimately undermine stability. At some point, a disruptive event occurs, and markets go through an abrupt correction — the further along in the cycle, the more violent the repricing.

A clear example of such mechanisms occurred prior to 2007, when the financial industry, and almost everybody else, were blind to the hidden risk being created. The pre-crisis period was even labelled the '*great moderation*'.

This also demonstrates the double-edged nature of otherwise useful risk control methods such as mark-to-market accounting, which enable financial institutions to realise profits up-front. This makes the banks even more profitable when things are good, but at the expense of larger losses when the markets take a turn for the worse — a clear example of *pro-cyclicality*.

1.3.2 Role of the government

Financial institutions do not operate in a vacuum. Their behaviour is shaped by government policies and they also influence government decisions. Government policies can create conditions for low or high systemic risk, because after all, financial institutions react to the rules of the game. A direct example of this is *moral hazard*: if the governments bail out banks, the banks will take more risk.

Governments can also be direct sources of systemic risk, where the most extreme examples are wars. The main creator of systemic risk in the European sovereign debt crisis is European governments, with the financial system in a supporting secondary role. Of course, it didn't help that the banking system was already in a vulnerable state.

The impacts of government policies on systemic risk are often indirect and counter-intuitive. It may be desirable to implement policies to contain a particular type of 'high risk' behaviour by the industry; unfortunately, any policy carries with it unforeseen adverse consequences. For example, regulations preventing risk taking in a highly visible part of the financial system can simply shift risk-taking activities into more opaque corners of the system where the banks can continue as before, undetected, perhaps in *shadow banking*. That outcome increases systemic risk. Competition makes this near-certain. Consequently, it is necessary to consider the systemic impact of the entirety of government banking policies together.

It is useful to draw an analogy to a different sector of the economy, using an example provided by Kaufman (1996) who in discussing Merton (1995) points out that governments often provide flood insurance and information about water levels. The reason why the government provides flood insurance is that the private sector, knowing the risks, refuses to do so at a reasonable price. This means that homeowners have an incentive to build on floodplains in the knowledge that they would be bailed out by government flood insurance when the eventual flood comes. Flood insurance creates moral hazard that makes the eventual costs much higher than they otherwise would be.

As a consequence, some commentators have made robust remarks on the origins of systemic risk. Fisher Black (1995), of Black–Scholes fame, states:

'When you hear the government talking about systemic risk, hold on to your wallet! It means that they want you to pay more taxes for more regulations, which are likely to create systemic risk by interfering with private contracting . . . In sum, when you think about systemic risks, you'll be close to the truth if you think of the government as causing them rather than protecting us from them.'

1.4 FUNDAMENTAL ORIGINS OF SYSTEMIC RISK

Systemic risk arises because of inherent structural weaknesses in the financial system, for example *pro-cyclicality*, *information asymmetries*, *interdependence* and *perverse incentives*. These factors enable systemic risk to be created without much scrutiny, only to be realised when it is too late. Therefore, it is necessary to address the underlying causal factors in order to develop policies to mitigate systemic risk.

1.4.1 Fractional reserve banking and systemic risk

One avenue for systemic risk is the inherent vulnerabilities in the financial system because of fractional reserve banking and the nature of money.

It may seem surprising that such a fundamental economic concept as money does not have a clear and unambiguous real-world definition, but it does not. Anything that can be freely used to make purchases falls within most definitions of money, but what about highly liquid assets that can easily be converted into money, or even savings accounts that will become money at some stage in the future? Economic agents also consider such assets to be money.

Types of money

It is useful to classify money into several different categories, or *monetary aggregates* as they are technically known, as illustrated by Figure 1.4.

M0, also known as monetary base, or high-powered money, consists of paper money in circulation and reserves at the central bank. *M1* is known as narrow money, and consists

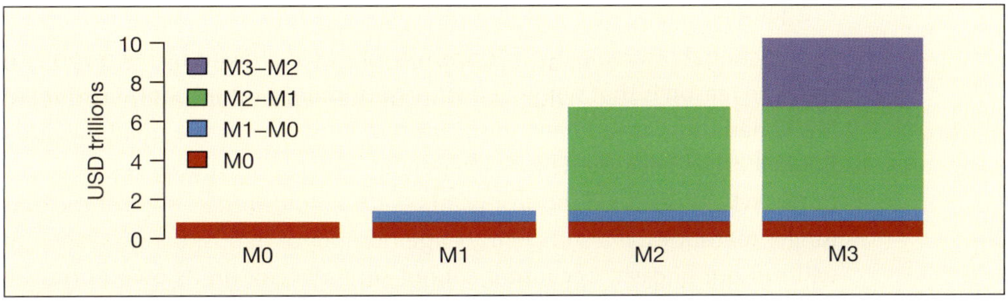

Figure 1.4 **United States (US) monetary aggregates at end of 2005. Identifies unique components of each aggregate, and labels the main component**

Data source: Federal Reserve Board. Data ends 2005 since that is the last full year when M3 was published

of M0 plus current (checkable) accounts, in essence funds that are readily accessible for spending – liquid funds. *M2* is M1 plus savings accounts and represents money and close substitutes for money. It is a key indicator for inflation forecasting. *M3* is the broadest measure of money, including M2 plus large time deposits, institutional money market funds, short-term repurchase and other larger liquid assets. The higher forms of money are created out of the lower forms, typically by means of *fractional reserve banking*.

Reserve requirements

Today, most banking systems use fractional reserve banking which is an arrangement whereby most of the money is created by the banks; subject to a particular limitation – the *reserve requirement*, δ – banks are required to hold a certain fraction of deposits on account with the central bank. Fractional reserve banking expands money supply beyond what it would otherwise be, as seen by the following example:

EXAMPLE 1.1 Fractional reserve banking

Person X deposits \$100 (M0) into bank A. δ is 10% so the bank lends \$90 to person Y who deposits \$90 at bank B which keeps fraction δ and lends out \$81 and so on. Hence, in the limit $M1 = 100 + 90 + 81 + \ldots = 1/\delta = 1000$. The relationship between $M1$ and the monetary base can be expressed as:

$$M1 = \gamma \times M0 = \frac{1}{\delta} \times M0$$

γ is the *money multiplier*, which tells us how much the money supply changes for a given change in the monetary base. If the reserve requirement is 10%, every dollar in the form of deposits uses up only 10 cents of high-powered money, or each dollar of high-powered money held as reserves can support \$10 of deposits. Hence, the higher the required reserve ratio, the lower the money multiplier. We see in Figure 1.5 how fractional reserve banking aids the expansion of credit.

Fragilities

The fractional reserve banking system is inherently fragile and hence is a cause of systemic risk. The reason is that when depositors put money into a bank, creating M1 from M0, the bank then turns around and lends most of it out, keeping a small fraction as reserves. The fragility arises because deposits generally are of short maturities, and some can be withdrawn whenever the depositor wants – *demand deposits* – whilst the loans tend to be of longer maturities. If a sufficiently large number of depositors want their money, the bank will run out of cash, because it cannot similarly call on its own borrowers to repay their loans. We call such an event a *bank run*. Bank runs are contagious and can spread quickly throughout the financial system. The reason is that the banking system is built on trust, so if depositors lose confidence in banks, they flock to withdraw their deposits as cash.

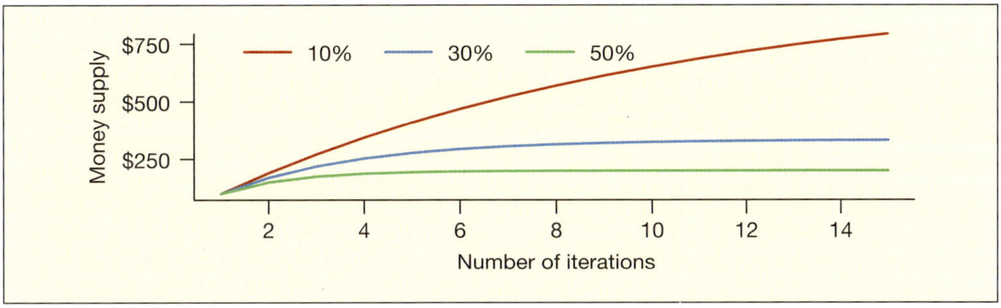

Figure 1.5 Credit expansion of $100 under fractional reserve banking and various reserve ratios

1.4.2 Pro-cyclicality

A process that is positively correlated with the economic cycle is described as pro-cyclical. Bank capital and leverage are two examples of pro-cyclical processes in which risks build up during stable periods. Banks tend to have surplus capital when the economy is booming, whilst capital levels drop during recessions. Likewise, economic agents have a tendency to borrow too much during good times, and borrow too little in downturns.

Pro-cyclicality is often created by the various amplification mechanisms built into the financial system, and is encouraged by risk-weighted capital, mark-to-market accounting and the fact that the strength of financial regulations tends to erode in boom times and come back with a vengeance during crises.

Amplification mechanisms

Financial crises often seem to be triggered by relatively small events. This is not dissimilar to what chaos theorists mean when they say that a butterfly in Hong Kong causes a hurricane in the Caribbean. Many such *butterfly effects* exist in the financial system.

The main enabling factor is leverage, whereby a bank borrows money to make investments. High degrees of leverage enable a bank to multiply profits when investments are successful. For this reason, banks remain highly leveraged. Unfortunately, rapid de-leveraging amplifies losses, perhaps resulting in bank failures and causing *firesale externalities*.

Firesale externalities

Definition 1.2 Externality Externality occurs where cost or benefit accrues to someone who was not involved in the decision-making process that led to the cost or benefit.

Firesale externalities (see, e.g., Kashyap *et al.*, 2008) arise when financial institutions need liquidity and aim to convert risky assets into cash. At that time, there are many sellers and few buyers of risky assets. That means prices collapse, making it even harder to raise cash and forcing institutions to sell even more risky assets, in what has become a vicious cycle (Figure 1.6). It is the individual self-preservation behaviour of each institution that causes negative externalities for the rest of the financial system. Such behaviour can cause a relatively innocuous shock to become a full-blown crisis.

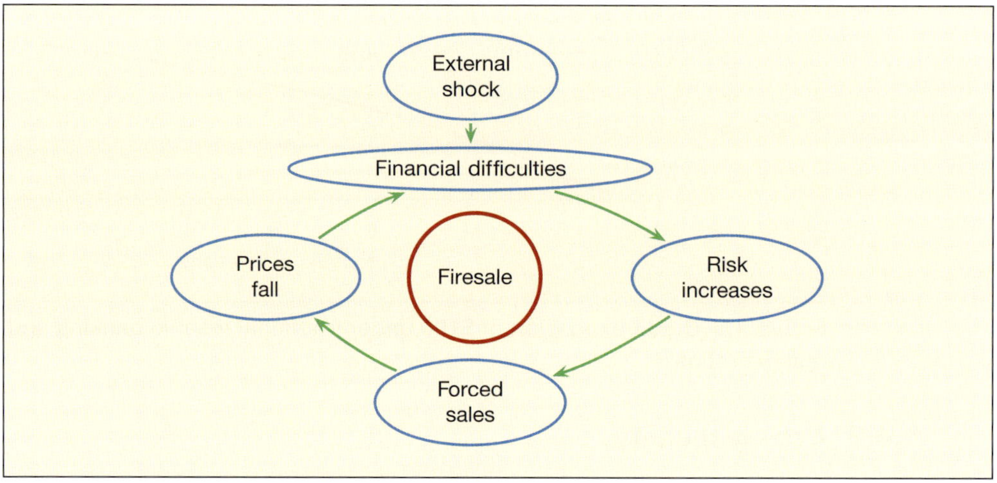

Figure 1.6 Firesales and acceleration effects

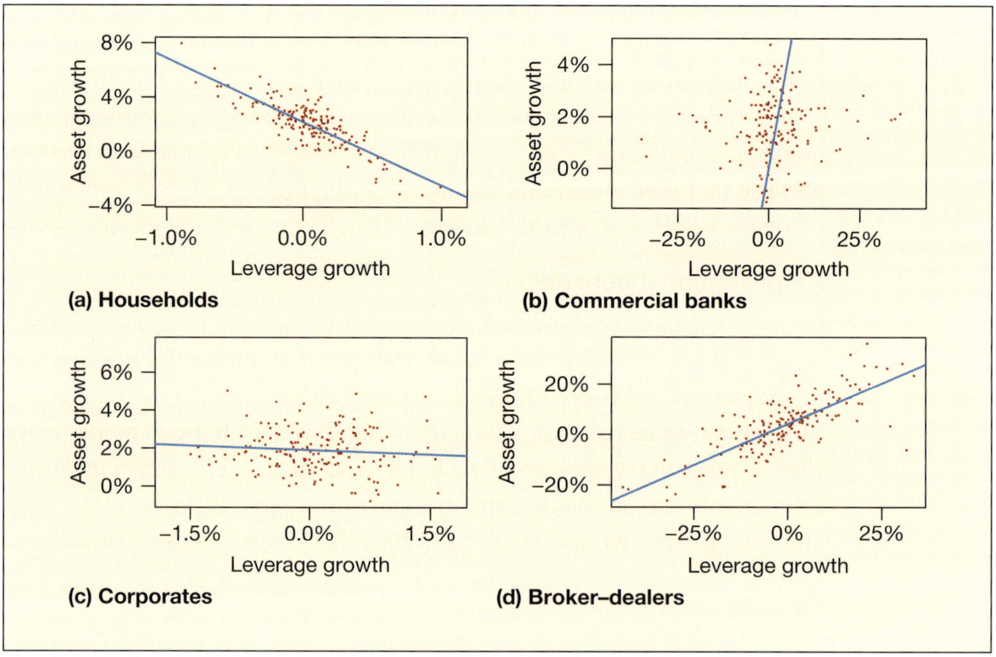

Figure 1.7 Asset growth and leverage growth, with a regression line

Data source: Adriam and Shin (2010)

Asset growth and leverage growth

Adrian and Shin (2010) document how the various categories of economic agents contribute to systemic risk, focusing on the relationship between asset growth and leverage growth. We use their data in Figure 1.7 which shows the relationship between asset growth and leverage growth for four categories of agents: households, commercial banks, corporates and broker–dealers. The last is a term used in the US for an institution trading securities for its own account or on behalf of its customers.

For households, the relationship is negative: the richer we become the less leverage we use. If a household owns a house financed by a mortgage, leverage falls when the house price increases, since the equity of the household is increasing at a much faster rate than assets. Similarly, most people pay back their mortgages over time, reducing leverage. For corporations and commercial banks there is little correlation, but for the broker–dealers it is highly positive.

For such firms, leverage is pro-cyclical, increasing when balance sheets are expanding and decreasing when balance sheets are shrinking. The slope is close to 1 for broker–dealers, suggesting that equity is increasing at a constant rate on average.

This result is counter-intuitive in light of standard theories in corporate finance, where it should not make a difference how a firm is financed. Here, the willingness to use borrowed funds to increase leverage is a key factor in firm growth.

From the point of view of systemic risk, this suggests that broker–dealer type institutions have a tendency to continually increasing leverage. The owners of these institutions might be rewarded by higher profits when things go well, but at the expense of increased systemic risk.

1.4.3 Information asymmetry

Banks rely on the confidence of their depositors and counterparties to operate. Depositors trust the bank to guard their money and counterparties need to be reassured that the bank will honour its obligations. A loss of confidence can lead to bank failure. It does not matter much whether the loss in confidence arises from unfounded rumours or from real negative information. This leads to what is known as an *agency problem* between counterparties and the bank, caused by *information asymmetry* — the bank knows more than the counterparties.

A confidence crisis at one bank can quickly spread if other institutions are perceived to share the same weakness. A loss in confidence may result in a *bank run* — depositors queuing up to withdraw their money. Depositors at other banks, observing problems at the first bank and lacking information about the soundness of their banks, may decide to pull out their deposits too, for fear of losing their deposits. If left unchecked, bank runs may swiftly spread to the entire system, causing significant economic damage.

Similarly, counterparties may refuse to enter into new transactions or renew existing ones if they suspect a bank is in trouble. For example, if bank A is allegedly holding toxic assets, then other banks may stop trading with it, and if bank B is thought to be active in that asset class then other banks may also stop trading with bank B. This can lead to markets collapsing.

In both these examples, the loss of confidence adversely affects liquidity. Financial institutions often operate under the general assumption that liquidity is infinite, and the evaporation of liquidity can cause acute distress for the financial system and, hence, is often the first sign of a pending crisis.

1.4.4 Interdependence

The financial system consists of a network of interwoven obligations that during normal times significantly increases the efficiency of financial markets. This means a financial institution can have an indirect exposure to another financial institution without any

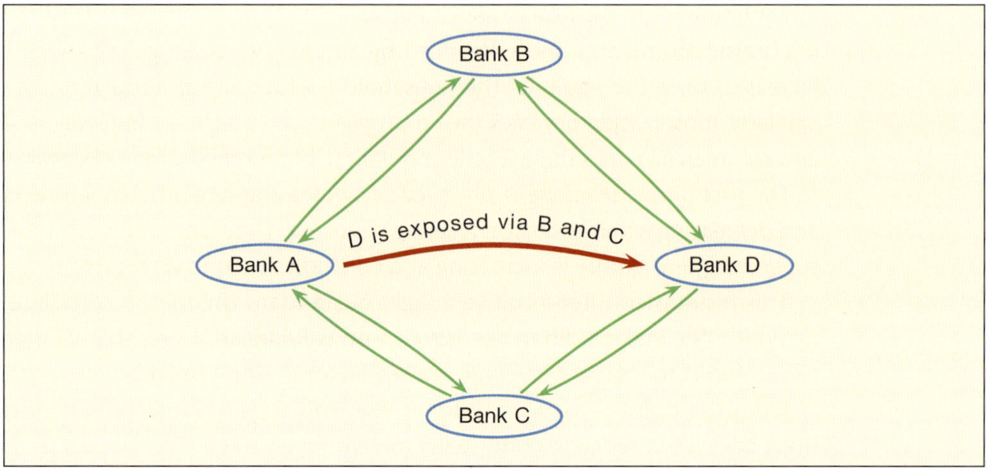

Figure 1.8 D is indirectly exposed to A via B and C

direct dealings with it. This can be quite dangerous during crises, most obviously because of interlocking exposures, which create the potential for one institution's failure to have 'knock-on' effects on the financial health of other institutions. At any given time, a financial institution simultaneously owes money to other institutions and is owed money often from the very same institutions. These linkages make the financial system fragile.

For example, consider the situation depicted in Figure 1.8, where we have four banks A, B, C and D. A borrows and lends from B and C, which also borrow and lend from D. Suppose A suffers a negative shock, and needing funds calls in a loan to B and C. They now need funds, and in turn may call in their loans to the hitherto healthy bank D. The difficulties facing A have now been transferred to D, even if A and D have no direct business relationships. This is exactly the situation in the 1914 example discussed above.

Because banks have only a limited amount of liquid funds, even a relatively small but immediate demand for cash, or an interruption in the flow of funds, can cause serious difficulties and even failure. This means that if financial institutions suspect others may be in difficulty, their natural instinct is to withdraw, spreading a crisis throughout the financial system.

We see a particularly damaging example of this in the interbank market during the crisis from 2007. The proliferation of derivatives, in particular structured credit products such as structured investment vehicles (SIVs), credit default swaps (CDSs) and collateralised debt obligations (CDOs), has been increasing the interdependence between financial institutions, in turn increasing the fragility of the financial system.

1.4.5 Perverse incentives

Because of the interconnectedness of the financial system and the very high cost of systemic crises, the government will have no choice but to do anything it can to prevent such an outcome. This often takes the form of bailouts of various types, creating moral hazard. A small, prudently run and non-systematically important institution is less likely to get support from the government than a very large, badly run, interconnected bank.

This can have the unfortunate outcome that a badly run bank actually has a lower cost of funding than a well-managed bank because only one of them would be bailed out. Ultimately, this means banks have incentives to become as big, interconnected and dangerous as possible in order to maximise the chance of a bailout. A particularly interesting example can be seen by the supposedly expressed desires by some hedge funds to become 'banks' in order to enjoy low-cost government guarantees of funding.

There are many other types of perverse incentives. For example, lenders who ultimately intend to securitise their loan books do not have proper incentives to monitor the quality of their loans. In addition, the presence of financial instruments, such as CDSs, may create incentives for some market participants to increase instability.

1.5 SUMMARY

Systemic risk has always been a part of the financial system, and many crisis events of the past are quite similar to modern crises, for example, that of 1914.

There are many definitions of systemic risk, but most emphasise the risk of widespread failures in the financial system, caused by the interlinkages between financial institutions, eventually resulting in a severe economic downturn.

Systemic risk is the inevitable result of having a market-based economy and is not easily eliminated or reduced significantly without unduly restricting risky activities, adversely affecting the real economy. This means that the authorities need to balance the various pros and cons in their approach to systemic risk policies, doing cost–benefit analysis. Stated differently, the authorities have to find the appropriate risk–return combination, similar to what investors do for their own portfolios.

Although any sector of the economy may be subject to systemic risk, it is especially relevant for the financial sector, because it is uniquely dependent on the interplay between confidence and network effects. The failure of a single institution quickly spreads to other banks, even if they have been prudently run. The damage caused by even relatively small events in the markets can be amplified into systemic proportions because of the inherent pro-cyclicality in the financial system, perhaps aided by the perverse incentives of market participants.

Questions for discussion

1. What is systemic risk?
2. How frequently can we expect systemic crises?
3. What does it mean when we say that systemic risk builds up out of sight, and what could that mean for the government's formulation of financial stability policies?
4. How does the European country with the largest banking system relative to GDP manage to be mostly unaffected by the banking crisis whilst other countries with relatively smaller banking system suffer serious banking crises?
5. Do you think it would be prudent for the British government to reduce the size of its banks in order to reduce systemic risk?

6 Can you think of some systemic events in the past, anywhere in the world, excluding what has been happening since 2007?

7 What is pro-cyclicality, how is it amplified, and how could it be mitigated?

8 Explain the concept of firesale externality.

9 Do you think Europe is at the risk of a systemic event at the moment?

10 What are the main origins of systemic risk?

References

Adrian, T. and Shin, H. S. (2010). Liquidity and leverage. *J. Finan. Intermed.*, 19: 418–37.

Bandt, D. and Hartmann, P. (2000). Systemic risk: a survey. Working paper no. 35, European Central Bank.

Black, F. (1995). Hedging, speculation, and systemic risk. *J. Derivatives*, 2: 6–8.

Brown, W. A. (1940). The international gold standard reinterpreted, 1914–1934. Technical report, National Bureau of Economic Research.

Crockett, A. (2000). Marrying the micro- and macro-prudential dimensions of financial stability. The General Manager of the Bank for International Settlements, www.bis.org/review/rr000921b.pdf.

Ferguson, N. (2008). *The Ascent of Money*. The Penguin Group.

International Monetary Fund, Bank for International Settlements, Financial Stability Board (2009). Report to G20 finance ministers and governors. Guidance to assess the systemic importance of financial institutions, markets and instruments: initial considerations. Technical report.

Kashyap, A. K., Rajan, R. G., and Stein, J. C. (2008). Rethinking capital regulation. http://online.wsj.com/public/resources/documents/ Fed-JacksonHole.pdf.

Kaufman, G. G. (1996). Bank failures, systemic risk, and bank regulation. *Cato J.*, 16(1): 17–46.

Kindleberger, C. P. (1996). *Manias, Panics, and Crashes: a History of Financial Crises*, 3rd edition. John Wiley & Sons.

Merton, R. (1995). A functional perspective of financial intermediation. *Financial Management*, 24: 23–41.

Minsky, H. (1992). The financial instability hypothesis. Working paper. Mimeo, Yale University.

Reinhart, C. M. and Rogoff, K. (2009). *This Time Is Different: Eight Centuries of Financial Folly*. Princeton University Press.

Schumpeter, J. (1942). *Capitalism, Socialism and Democracy*. Harper, New York.

2 THE GREAT DEPRESSION, 1929–1933

The *Great Depression*, 1929–1933, was the largest *worldwide* economic catastrophe the world has ever seen. A Wall Street crash in 1929 was followed by the collapse of financial institutions and an implosion of activity on financial markets, soon spilling over to Main Street. This happened because of vicious feedback loops between contracting economic activity, financial crises and government mistakes.

The Depression shaped economic policy long after it ended. While its impact had been diminishing, that all changed with the crises from 2007, and over the past few years, the lessons from the Depression have significantly impacted on policy. The reason why events in the fall of 2008 did not lead to another depression is because policymakers had learned the lesson of the Great Depression and acted correctly. The continuing influence of the Great Depression on government policy make it a worthwhile subject in studies of financial stability in the twenty-first century.

The Depression came after one of the longest expansion periods in history, the *roaring twenties*, with rapid economic growth and rampant stock market speculation, when many investors were highly leveraged, buying stocks *on the margin*. Underneath were significant frictions. The First World War (WWI) fundamentally affected the international order, and universal suffrage – for both women and the poor – altered political power structures as did the emergence of labour unions. Extreme political ideologies, communism and fascism, gained a significant foothold, not least as a result of the economic turmoil marking those years.

International trade patterns were altered considerably, as non-combatants profited and extended their global reach. Many countries attempted *export-led growth*, typically via agricultural products, leading to overproduction and price deflation. And

finally, disputes over war debt, and the determination in some countries to extract reparations from the losing *Central Powers*, poisoned international relations and acted to prevent effective crisis resolution once the Depression was underway.

The first sign of the problems leading to the Great Depression emerged in the agricultural sector and industries dependent on agriculture such as banks and insurance companies, spreading economic turmoil from the farm to the city. This was followed by widespread bank collapses, contraction in money supplies, with surpluses, liquidity crises, exchange rate depreciations and trade restrictions, all acting in a vicious feedback loop, compounding the problems.

Note that it can be difficult to assess the costs of the Great Depression because only limited data exists and it is often contradictory. This especially applies to national accounts, as global standards for the calculation of GDP were only determined in the late 1940s, so comparisons before that time are difficult.

Links to other chapters

Many of the concepts discussed in this chapter are addressed in much greater detail elsewhere in the book, for example, in Chapter 4 (liquidity), Chapter 5 (the central bank), Chapter 14 (bailouts), Chapter 8 (bank runs and deposit insurance) and Chapter 17 (the ongoing crisis: 2007–2009 phase).

Key concepts

- **Deflation**
- **Trade policy**
- **Monetary policy**
- **Bank runs**
- **International coordination**
- **Firesale externality**

Readings for this chapter

The seminal work on the Great Depression is Kindleberger (1986) and much of the material is drawn from him, as well as Eichengreen (1996), Friedman and Schwartz (1963) and Bernanke (1995). More recent books and articles, for example Ferguson (2008), Ahamed (2009) and Eichengreen and Irwin (2009), discuss the various aspects of the Depression in a more modern context.

2.1 BUILD-UP TO A DEPRESSION

Many factors contributed to the Great Depression and the underlying causes remain controversial to this day. The single most important causal event is WWI and the significant social and economic upheaval caused by the war. The countries that participated in the war were in a much weaker position than before; some even ceased to exist, with new countries formed. Those that stayed away from the war profited from selling to the combatants. This meant that after the war ended, the relative position of countries altered, for example, the United Kingdom (UK) was no longer the world's superpower, yielding to the United States (US).

Following the war, what would now be called significant *global imbalances* built up, with resentment and conflict resulting. Many countries accumulated large debts, with the largest creditor being the US.

GDP rankings in 1929

It is interesting to note the evolution of the various economies from the start of the Great Depression in 1929 until today. Figure 2.1 shows the GDP per capita of a selection of countries in 1929. The US was richest, followed by Switzerland, with the UK in fourth place. Argentina was in the 11th place, wealthier than Germany in 13th place, with Norway poorer than Venezuela, and Japan below average in 27th place.

Paying for the war

Perhaps the worst single source of tension was the question of *war reparations*. The countries on the losing side of WWI, the Central Powers (Germany, the Austro-Hungarian Empire, Turkey and Bulgaria), were blamed for causing the war, whilst the countries suffering most on the winning side (the Allies), especially Belgium and France, demanded compensation.

The question of war reparations remained a continuing source of friction in the international agenda throughout the 1920s. The US refused to accept reparations from Germany and only wanted to be repaid for war loans extended to the Allies. The UK was in favour of cancelling war debts but, given the US position, had no choice but to collect debts, at least up to the limit of the British debt to the US. France and Belgium, however, wanted to collect reparations from Germany and suggested that Germany borrow from the US in order to make reparations to them, so they could pay off their obligations to the US.

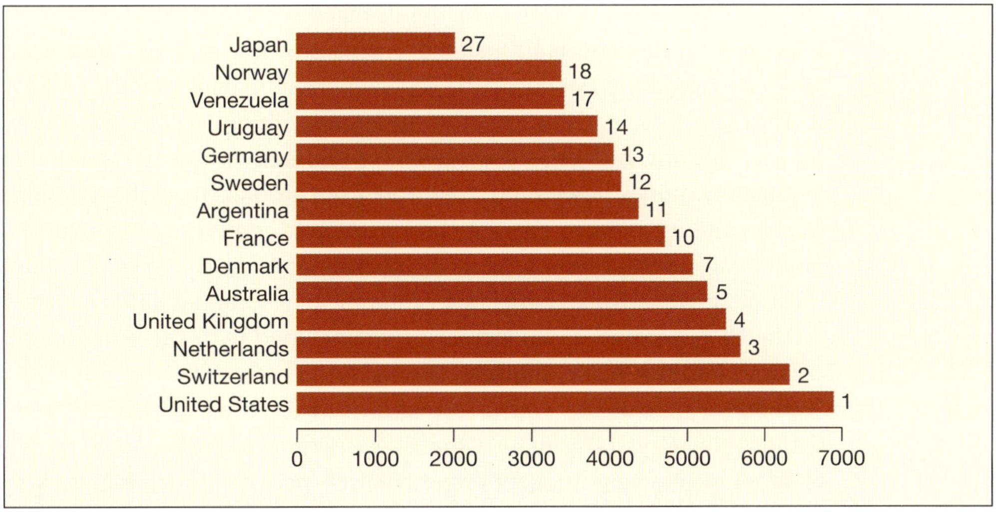

Figure 2.1 1929 GDP per capita in constant 1990 dollars and global rank out of 52 countries

Data source: www.ggdc.net/MADDISON/oriindex.htm

The policy of extracting very large reparations from the losers was quite popular right after the war, but opinion soon changed as it was recognised that the amounts demanded were simply too large. Some voices, most importantly Keynes (1920), warned against the consequences of treating the losers that way. In order to pay reparations, Germany began a credit-fuelled period of growth, ending in hyperinflation in 1923.

2.1.1 Bad monetary policy in the UK

The UK made one of its worst policy mistakes ever in 1925 when the Chancellor of the Exchequer, Winston Churchill, decided to put the UK back onto the gold standard at prewar parity. Churchill later admitted that going back on gold was one of his biggest mistakes. He was advised by the Bank of England (BoE) that it was the right decision, needed to restore the credibility of the UK. Keynes argued strongly against the decision, maintaining correctly that it would lead to deflation and general economic misery, having said the year before that 'In truth, the gold standard is already a barbarous relic' (Keynes, 1924).

As the UK had experienced significant inflation during the war, going back on gold at prewar parity meant that sterling was now significantly overvalued. Therefore, it had no choice but to implement what is now called an *internal devaluation*, lowering various factor costs. This led to significant economic upheaval, such as long-running strikes and the haemorrhaging of gold, not least to France. The UK remained on gold, and with an overvalued currency, for the next six years, in recession for the duration.

2.1.2 The United States

The war strengthened the competitive positions of American manufacturers and opened new markets for its exporters. As a consequence, the US enjoyed a trade surplus, building up significant capital reserves. After the war, the US maintained a relatively accommodating monetary policy with low interest rates that encouraged American gold to flow abroad. The monetary policy also acted as to stimulate the capital markets, in particular the *Wall Street bubble*.

The main danger arising from the stock market boom was not the immediate impact on prices or volume, but rather the interconnectedness with global credit markets. Significant amounts of money flowed into New York from around the globe, causing other countries to raise interest rates to prevent the loss of gold reserves to New York. This meant that money was diverted from productive investment to stock market speculation, both in the US and abroad, adversely affecting economic development and monetary policy.

The US government was increasingly concerned with the amount of resources being diverted into the equity markets. Federal Reserve System (Fed) officials concluded that Wall Street speculation was diverting funds from more productive uses, and began to tighten monetary policy. In turn, that adversely affected debtor nations, which were forced to adopt increasingly stringent monetary fiscal policies to maintain their exchange rate.

The New York Federal Reserve Bank (NYFed) raised its discount rate to 6% on 9 August 1929 in order to slow down the market, but to little effect. In September, the stock exchange added more seats, with the price of a seat at an all-time high. The higher interest rates in the US set off a round of interest rate increases in Europe.

These problems are not dissimilar to the problems currently affecting the euro zone and the European exchange rate mechanism (ERM) before that. A monetary policy appropriate for a leading country in a boom is likely to be too strict for other countries facing recessions. This leaves the weaker countries with only two options, either to implement an internal devaluation or to devalue their currency, with neither choice palatable.

2.1.3 Agricultural depression

Up until the middle of the nineteenth century, the harvest was the main measure of business conditions. A bumper crop lowered the price of bread and increased industrial output and farm income. Crop failures led to depression. At some point around the 1860s, business cycles in the industrialised countries became independent of agriculture but it remained a big part of the economy for countries outside western Europe. Farming accounted for a quarter of total employment in the US in 1929.

Major agricultural countries suffered significantly from overproduction in the 1920s, causing a fall in prices and income, as can be seen in Figure 2.2. There was an initial boom in prices right after the war, but from about 1926 prices were steadily falling, bottoming in the main crisis year of 1933.

The reaction of many governments to overproduction and falling prices was to protect their producers, subsidising exporters and accumulating stockpiles of agricultural products. In many countries, for example, the US and Canada, attempts were made to support the price of wheat (which fell by 50% between December 1929 and 1930). Many other countries had neither the necessary financial capacity nor the required storage facilities, feeling obliged to export wherever they could, forcing prices downwards.

2.1.4 Competitive devaluations and deflation

In order to help their exporters, some countries resorted to currency devaluations. From the point of view of an individual country this may seem a sensible policy. It should help exporters and reduce imports, strengthening the economy. However, such '*beggar-thy-neighbour*' policies encourage others to follow, leading to waves of competitive devaluations, making everybody worse off. The sentiments are captured by the comments of NYFed governor Benjamin Strong to the House Committee on Banking and

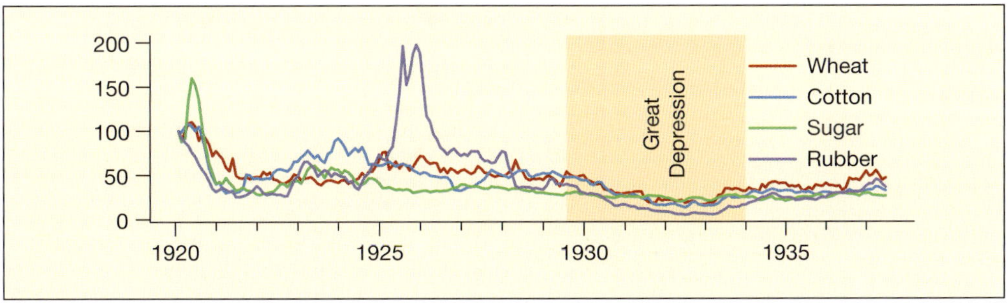

Figure 2.2 Commodity prices

Currency in 1926: 'It should not be overlooked that one of the greatest menaces to the trade of this country is depreciating foreign exchange.'

Effectiveness

Surprisingly, the devaluations were not all that effective in helping the producers. When a country devalues, two things happen: the local currency price of exports increases and the foreign currency price falls. Elasticities determine which effect ends up dominating. For a small country with no impact on world prices, local currency prices will increase. For a major exporter facing an inelastic demand, prices abroad will fall. For example, when Argentina devalued in the 1930s, local currency prices did not increase but foreign prices fell, exacerbating that country's difficulties. The experience of other major agricultural exporters, like Australia, was similar.

Deflation

The falling agricultural prices hit sectors that depended heavily on credit especially hard, because deflation erodes the price of commodities while increasing the real value of debt. Throughout the 1920s farm debt was increasing, in the US from \$3.3 billion in 1910 to \$9.4 billion in 1925.

One might expect the ever falling prices of commodities to stimulate global spending and prosperity. This did not happen because the response of countries facing the improved terms of trade (lower import prices) is slow, as it takes time to realise that real incomes increased, permitting an increase in spending. The adverse impact on producers is more immediate.

This is similar to how financial crises reallocate wealth: the losers scream immediately, but the winners are harder to identify and don't really notice for a while, and hence delay spending their newfound wealth.

The end result is a deflationary cycle, as seen in Figure 2.3: prices fall, causing difficulties for debtors, who in turn curtail consumption. Creditors realise they will get more for their money in the future and also delay spending. This causes demand to contract and prices to fall further.

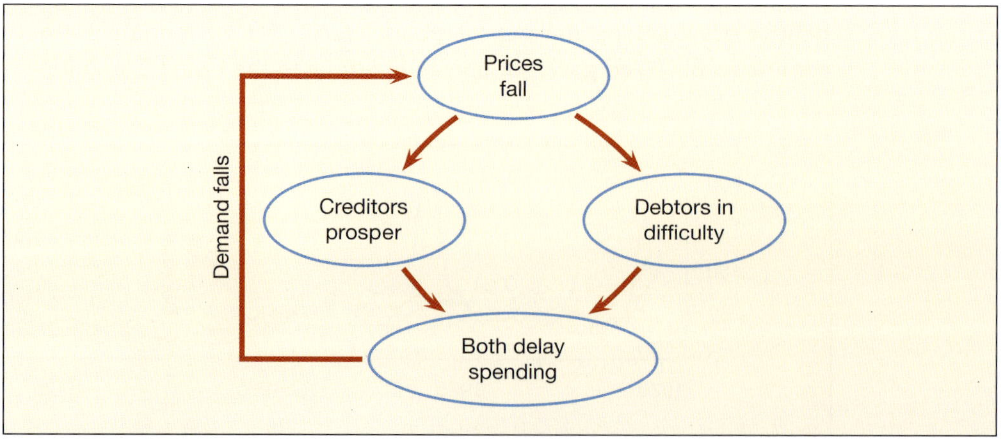

Figure 2.3 Deflationary cycle

2.2 THE GREAT DEPRESSION

While the Great Depression is often said to have started with the stock market collapse in Wall Street, most analysis indicates that a serious downturn commenced earlier. The economy started sliding from April 1929 in Germany, from July in the US and from August in the UK. Only in France was production rising. The conditions were the worst in Germany, with high levels of unemployment and business failures.

As the crisis picked up pace, a sharp deflationary cycle, like that in Figure 2.3, emerged. International lending and investment dropped off. Bankruptcy, default, currency depreciation and falling commodity and asset prices made many businesses and foreign countries unattractive risks for loans. Spreads between high-quality and low-quality bonds increased, reflecting a loss of confidence, apparent in the sharp decline of direct investment.

Impact on the US economy

As the crisis in the US started, real-estate prices crashed and industrial production collapsed. Figure 2.4(a) shows net investment from 1929 until 1939. In 1929 it was $10.5 billion, but it fell by $15 billion during the crisis. The impact on GDP was even more significant, as seen by Figure 2.4(b), whilst unemployment exceeded 25% at the height of the crisis. As the crisis continued, inventories were reduced and durable goods wore out. Eventually, this helped recovery by stimulating demand.

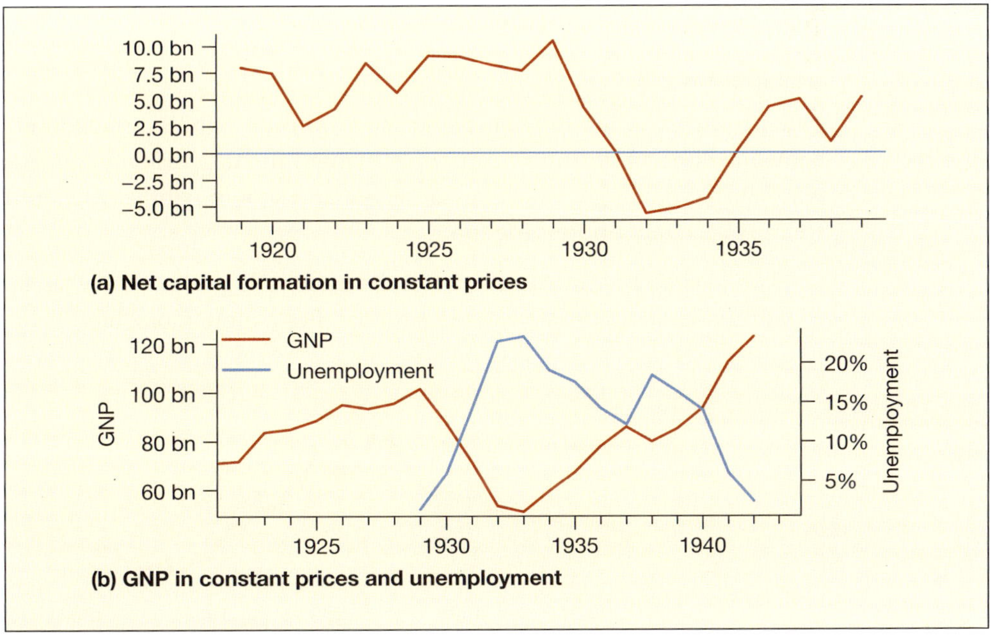

Figure 2.4 US macroeconomic data
Data source: NBER

2.2.1 Financial markets

Before the Great Depression, the stock markets, and especially the New York market, enjoyed spectacular price increases. The DJIA (Dow Jones Industrial Average) increased from 191 in early 1928 to a peak of 381 in September 1929, with both prices and volume doubling in two years.

Stock market crash

The initial outward sign of the Great Depression was seen in the financial markets. September 1929 marked the peak of the New York market. It started slipping on 3 October and declined throughout the week of 14 October. On 24 October, known as 'Black Thursday', panic ensued and a record number of 12.9 million shares were traded. On Monday 28 October, more investors exited the market, and the slide continued with a record loss in the Dow for the day at 13%. The next day, about 16 million shares were traded. This volume was a record not broken for nearly 40 years. The DJIA fell by another 12%. In total, the market lost $14 billion in value that day, bringing the loss for the week to $30 billion, 10 times more than the annual budget of the federal government and far more than the US had spent in all of WWI. The crash is shown graphically in Figure 2.5. The DJIA did not regain its 1929 peak until 1954.

Capital markets

The collapse of the stock market caused large losses to individual investors, and affected firms that relied on capital markets for liquidity, conspiring to create a liquidity crisis which soon spread to other sectors of the economy such as mortgages. At the time, mortgages were normally unamortised three-year obligations, rolled over every three years. Because of the liquidity crisis, homeowners were unable to refinance, leading to widespread foreclosures and a large drop in house prices. All these factors fed on themselves, in an example of an *endogenous risk* feedback loop.

Schadenfreude

Initially, the crash led to widespread *schadenfreude* – the satisfaction or pleasure felt at someone else's misfortune – as people blamed the depression on greedy speculators. It was felt that banks got what they deserved and should rightly suffer. In the words of the treasury secretary Andrew Mellon:

> 'It will purge the rottenness out of the system. High costs of living and high living will come down. People will work harder, live a more moral life.'

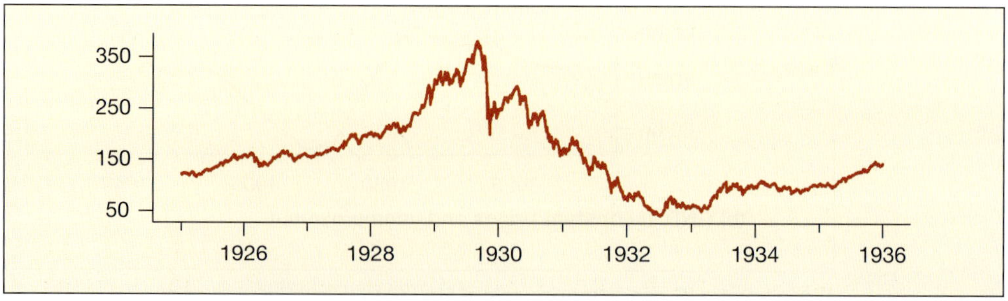

Figure 2.5 Stock market crash 1929 – DJIA

While such views were common, others, such as Keynes, worried about the adverse impact of falling markets, arguing that a more useful policy would be for the authorities to prevent the extreme price drops.

2.2.2 Financial crisis of 1931

Even though the crisis had started around 1929, initially it seemed like a financial markets crisis, with serious but not catastrophic real economy impacts. The consensus of most post-Depression studies indicates that the various authorities around the world could have prevented the recession from turning into the Great Depression, but failed to do so.

The financial crisis in 1931 became a turning point. As deflation continued, commodity prices fell, businesses lost money and the stock markets collapsed, adversely affecting banking. Eventually, this led to banking crises in several countries.

Austria

Austria was the first country to experience a general economic crisis. The balance sheet of its largest bank, Credit-Anstalt, equalled total government expenditure. In May 1931, bank officers informed the government that deteriorating loan performance had completely wiped out its capital. It was bankrupt. The authorities and some private financial institutions attempted to mount a rescue, but were unable to secure the necessary loans in time. In response to the crisis, Austria went off the gold standard and imposed capital controls.

Credit-Anstalt had a controlling interest in Budapest's largest bank, and as soon as the crisis erupted in Vienna, foreign investors withdrew their deposits from this and other Hungarian institutions. By 15 May, bank runs in Budapest were underway.

Germany

The crisis in Austria provoked immediate withdrawals in Berlin. There were worries that if Austria could freeze foreign deposits so could Germany. In July a fully-fledged banking panic erupted, starting with Danat Bank, the financier of a failed textile firm, Nordwolle.

As the German government was dependent on foreign creditors for its own financing, the crisis caused a sudden stop in lending, triggering a run on the mark. The German central bank, the Reichsbank, lost $250 million in gold and was forced to ration credit to the banking system.

US president Herbert Hoover announced the so-called *Hoover Moratorium* in June, which called for a one-year moratorium on debt arising from WWI. Whilst quite unpopular, especially in France, it got support from 15 major nations and Congress. The Hoover Moratorium was not effective in engineering an international support operation, and Germany was forced to abandon the gold standard.

The UK and the gold standard

The UK was already in serious economic difficulties as a result of its decision to go back on the gold standard in 1925, and suffered persistent capital account and budget deficits. The European banking crisis caused Austria, Hungary and Germany to freeze British deposits, whilst earnings from services declined and capital income from abroad collapsed. Unemployment exceeded 20% and foreign banks were unwilling to provide credit.

As the domestic currency denominated assets were converted into foreign exchange, the BoE, committed to pegging the exchange rate, was haemorrhaging gold. To defend the gold parity, the Bank raised interest rates and restricted credit, aggravating the banking crisis.

Eventually, this forced the BoE to abandon the gold standard in September 1931. In retrospect, this was the right decision as the British economy quickly recovered, and the impact of the Great Depression was not as big in the UK as in some other countries.

The decision to abandon the gold standard in 1931 resonates strongly in the ongoing crisis. Because it was key to economic recovery, it has been used to justify subsequent policies of devaluing sterling, in particular quantitative easing (QE). Similarly, many commentators maintain that the gold standard has strong parallels with the euro, and if only countries like Spain could devalue, their economies would recover.

2.2.3 The US crisis

More than one-third of all banks in the US failed in the Depression, but the government's reaction was for most parts inadequate in the early stages. A right move was made in December 1931, when the Reconstruction Finance Corporation (RFC) was set up to provide finance for banks and firms in need of liquidity. However, the Speaker of the House then insisted that the loans to banks were publicised. The immediate impact of implementing this requirement in January 1933 was that banks receiving RFC loans were hit by bank runs, and other banks in difficulty therefore became unwilling to seeking help from the RFC.

With the benefit of hindsight, it is now well understood that any liquidity assistance provided to banks needs to be done in secret. A modern equivalent is that the run on Northern Rock only started when the BoE announced it was providing liquidity assistance to it. Most liquidity support in the ongoing crisis has been secret, with some central banks going so far as to force all banks to borrow from the central bank, even the healthy ones, so as to hide the identity of those in difficulty.

While Federal Reserve (Fed) officials were fully aware of the pending banking crisis, the governors of the various Federal Reserve Banks refused to act. A large number of the banks in trouble were not members of the Federal Reserve system and as such the regional bank governors did not feel any responsibility for these non-member banks, despite their obvious impact on the nation's overall supply of credit. The feeling was that propping up failing banks would be throwing good money after bad and the regional governors made it a principle to let them fail.

New president – Roosevelt

The US voted in a new president in November 1932, Franklin Delano Roosevelt, who took office in March 1933. As one of his first acts, he declared a nationwide banking holiday, closing all banks for more than a week. Eventually, good banks were to be reopened and insolvent banks closed down, and those facing difficulties but not insolvent received government support to reopen. This was enough to restore confidence, and as the banks reopened, long lines of depositors formed outside the reopened banks, waiting to put their money back in. By the end of the week, a total of $1 billion had been redeposited in the banks.

Impact on financial regulation

The incoming administration saw excesses and abuses within the financial system as a major cause of the Depression. There was little to no oversight of financial institutions, individuals frequently used 10 times leverage when buying stocks on the margin, insider trading was rampant, and lack of deposit insurance directly contributed to the domino-style failures of the country's banks.

As a consequence, widespread regulations were introduced, such as the Glass–Steagall Act separating commercial and investment banking, the guaranteeing of bank deposits up to $2,500 and the establishment of the Securities and Exchange Commission (SEC). These regulations remained in place for decades, and many are still with us. Many commentators have blamed the loosening of the Great Depression regulations as a major factor in the crisis starting in 2007.

Double dip

While the worst of the Great Depression occurred at the beginning of 1933 and the US economy recovered significantly in the subsequent years, the crisis returned in 1937. There are several reasons why that happened. The surviving banks had massive amounts of cash on reserve with the Fed, both as insurance and also because of lack of demand. The Fed worried about inflation and tightened monetary policy. Inevitably, this led to a contraction in lending. At the same time, taxes were on the increase. All these factors left the economy fragile and susceptible to a *double dip* in 1937.

In retrospect, a looser fiscal and monetary policy in the years immediately after the main crisis year of 1933 might have prevented the double dip. That was of course not known to the policymakers at the time. Eventually, it was the rapidly increased government spending with the onset of the Second World War (WWII) that pulled the US out of the recession.

2.3 CAUSES OF THE GREAT DEPRESSION

The Great Depression has generated significant academic research. Whilst there are many explanations for the Depression, and the various factors are hotly debated to this day, most commentators attribute the main blame to trade policy and monetary policy. Other factors include the lack of global leadership and a narrow focus on national interests, exchange instability and allowing the banks to fail.

2.3.1 Trade and tariffs

Trade restrictions were a common tool in the 1920s and 1930s for stimulating domestic economies. This was especially common among agricultural exporters. Trade restrictions took various forms, ranging from import tariffs and outright restrictions on imports to export subsidies and the manipulation of exchange rates. Policymakers at the time were aware of pitfalls in using trade restrictions, and many attempts were made to discourage their use, for example in the World Economic Conference of 1927, but overall such attempts were not effective.

Trade restrictions were seen much more favourably than today, and both mainstream political parties and well-known economists like Keynes advocated their use. One reason is that governments were prevented from employing other measures to stimulate their economies because of the gold standard and the prevailing orthodoxy that government should run balanced budgets, even in downturns.

Smoot–Hawley Act

The most infamous example of trade restrictions is the *Smoot–Hawley Act* of 1930 that significantly raised US average tariffs. Even before the Act became law, France, Italy, India and Australia increased their tariffs in response. Once it became law, it let loose a wave of retaliation. Spain sharply increased its tariffs in July 1930, Switzerland boycotted US exports, Canada raised tariffs three times, and there were similar tariff increases in many other countries, such as Cuba, Mexico, France, New Zealand and Australia.

In his 1932 presidential campaign, Roosevelt attacked the Smoot–Hawley Act as a cause of the Depression. He claimed that when other countries ran out of gold, they paid their debts by sending more goods, which meant that tariffs had the effect of lowering prices rather than raising them.

Collapse in trade

As a consequence of the Smoot–Hawley Act, and the various other similar initiatives in other countries, global trade seized up, with countries experiencing serious difficulties because they could not export, and frequently defaulting. The severity of the collapse of trade during 1929–1933 can be seen in the list below and in Figure 2.6, the numbers being taken from Kindleberger (1986). Globally, trade was reduced by more than two-thirds. The impact on a sample of countries can be seen in the following list.

- Over 80%: Chile
- 70–80%: Cuba, China, Peru
- 60–70%: Netherlands, Greece, Brazil, Spain, Estonia
- 50–60%: Denmark, New Zealand, Finland, Columbia.

2.3.2 Role of monetary policy

One of the main causes of a recession in 1930 turning into the Great Depression in 1933 was the rapid contraction in money supply. This can be seen for the US in Figure 2.7. Note how M0 increases rapidly whilst M2 contracts even more sharply. This indicates that people were converting less liquid money to deposits. Running the calculation in Example 1.1 in reverse shows that money available for productive uses contracted sharply. This is a form of *deleveraging* and was a major contributor to the Great Depression, since when the money supply is reduced, individuals and firms do not have sufficient access to capital to invest and consume, which slows down the economy. This can become a form of vicious feedback

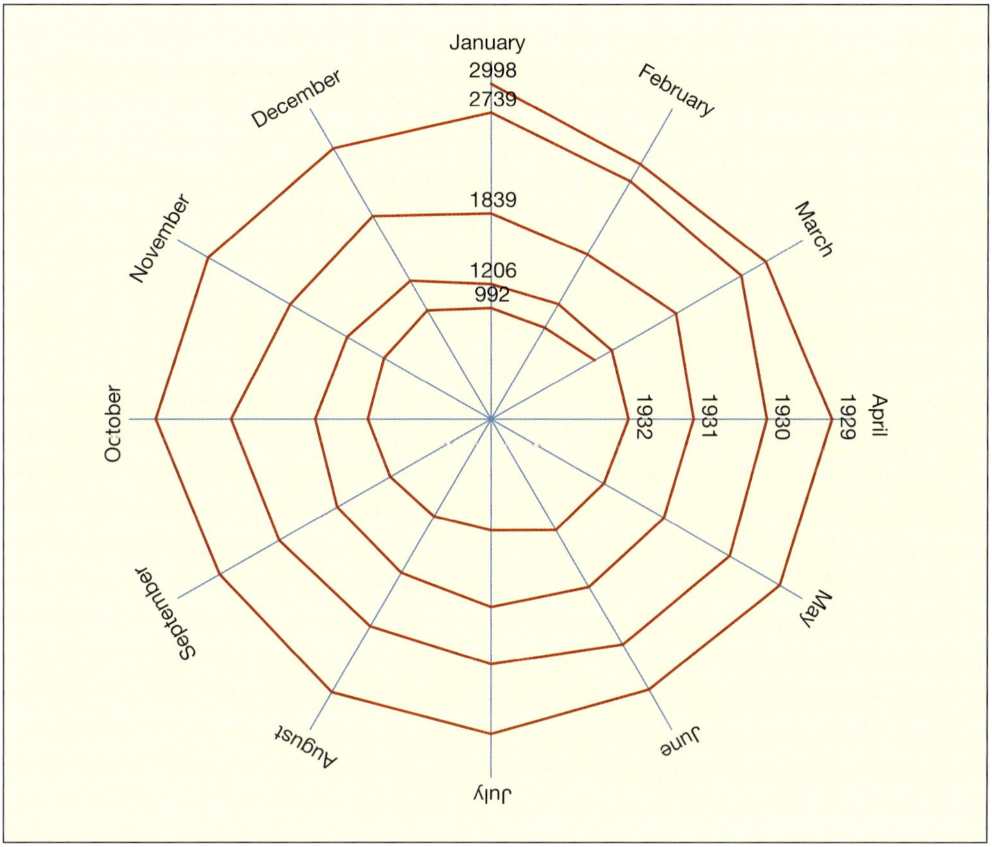

Figure 2.6 Reduction in trade 1929–1933

Source: adapted from Kindleberger (1986) with data from the League of Nations

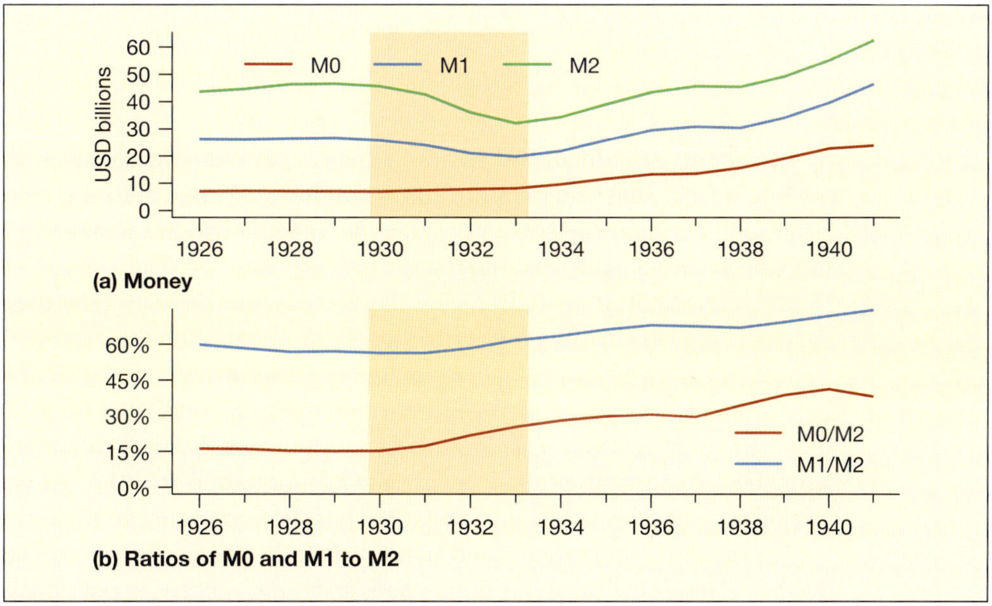

Figure 2.7 US money supply 1926–1941

cycle, with the reduction in money supply leading to deflation, further restricting the money supply and contributing to a liquidity trap.

Post-Depression analysis is mostly unanimous in identifying the contraction of the money supply in the US as a major cause of the Depression, in no little measure due to one of the most influential economic studies ever made, by Friedman and Schwartz (1963) in their book *A Monetary History of the United States: 1867–1960*, where they argued that it was the Fed that was primarily responsible for turning the crisis of 1929 into the Great Depression.

Friedman and Schwartz critique

The mistakes of the Fed, as discussed by Friedman and Schwartz, are summarised as follows:

1 The Fed did too little to counteract the credit contraction caused by failing banks. If banks fail, money supply (credit) contracts, therefore the Fed should have increased the money supply to counteract the reduction.

2 The Fed actually *reduced* credit between December 1930 and April 1931. This led to more and more banks being forced to sell assets at firesale prices, and to deteriorating liquidity conditions.

3 When the UK abandoned the gold standard in September 1931, the Fed raised discount rates in anticipation of a rush to convert dollars into gold. This did stop the drain of gold but drove yet more banks into insolvency. But the Fed was in no immediate danger of running out of gold, since it held 40% of global gold reserves and had more than enough to meet its legal requirements.

4 Only under enormous political pressure did the Fed start undertaking open market operations in April 1932. Unfortunately, this was too little, too late, and failed to prevent a wave of bank failures in the last quarter of 1932.

5 When rumours that the incoming Roosevelt administration would devalue the dollar led to a renewed flight from dollars into gold, the Fed once again raised the discount rate.

According to Friedman and Schwartz, the Fed should have aggressively injected liquidity into the banking system from 1929 onwards, using open market operations on a large scale, and encouraging lending through the discount window. Gold outflows should not have been such a priority consideration.

It is still a matter of debate why the Fed reacted the way they did. Friedman and Schwartz argued that it was the death in 1928 of Benjamin Strong, the Governor of the NYFed, which caused the deterioration in Fed performance.

An alternative explanation by Epstein and Ferguson (1984) and Anderson *et al.* (1988) maintains that this was a deliberate act by the Fed to protect the interests of member commercial banks rather than the general economy, and that the Fed was content with seeing non-member banks fail, so that the relative importance of the Fed would increase.

The conclusion of Friedman and Schwartz that the collapse in money supply was a major factor in causing the Great Depression has significantly influenced policymaking in the ongoing crisis, and is a key reason why central banks have provided significant amounts of QE.

The US goes off gold

The incoming president, Roosevelt, recognised that the Depression had been associated with a deflationary spiral, so recovery could only come about when prices began to increase again. The question vexing him and his advisers was how to get prices to increase without waiting for economic recovery. One of his economic advisers, George Warren, noticed that when large gold discoveries came onto the world market and the supply of gold outstripped demand, commodity prices tended to rise. Therefore, one way to raise prices would be to devalue the dollar by going off gold.

This proposal was met with outrage given the Fed's vast gold reserves, with pundits arguing that confidence in the US would be dented. Indeed, almost all of the president's economic advisers opposed going off gold. Roosevelt was in favour nonetheless, and slipped the necessary legislation into an agriculture bill so as to escape notice. On the evening of 18 April, he announced to his team: 'Congratulate me. We are off the gold standard.'

In the days after, as the dollar fell against gold, the stock market soared by 15%. Going off gold seemed to have reversed the psychology of deflation because of a renewed confidence in banks, an activist Fed, and a government commitment to drive up prices. In the following three months, wholesale prices increased by 45%, vehicle sales doubled, and overall industrial production went up by 50%. This was not the end of the matter, however; by October 1933, though the dollar had fallen by more than 30%, commodity prices began to sink again and it was time for a new initiative – buying gold in the open market.

In the following three months after October, every morning at 9 a.m., Roosevelt and his economic advisors would determine the price of gold for that day, in a completely random fashion – one day, Roosevelt priced an increase of 21 cents, and when asked why, replied that it was a lucky number! Keynes dismissed this exercise as 'the gold standard on the booze'. In January 1934, Roosevelt agreed to stabilise gold at $35 an ounce. In total, the dollar had been devalued by over 40%.

Impact of going off gold

The US was not alone in going off gold; every major country did the same during the Great Depression. Argentina was one of the first to leave in 1929 and Switzerland the last in 1936. We show GDP per capita and year of going off gold in Figure 2.8.

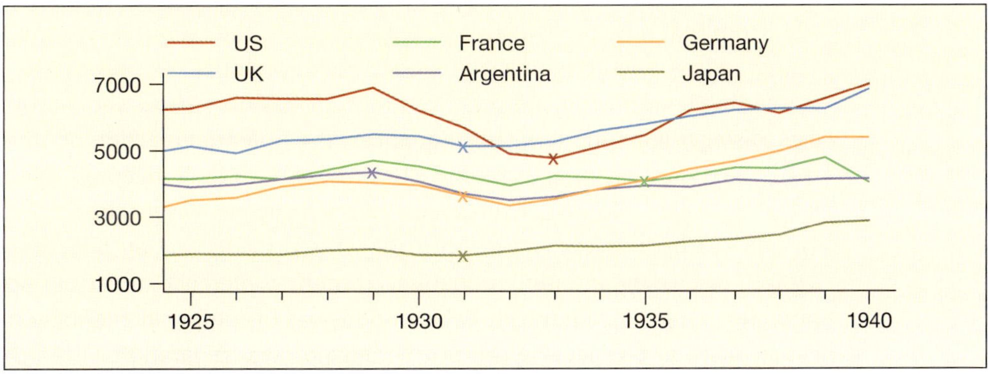

Figure 2.8 GDP per capita in constant 1990 dollars, and year of going off gold

Data source: www.ggdc.net/MADDISON/oriindex.htm

Abandoning the gold standard was successful. Once prices started rising, the real value of debt was reduced, making businesses more willing to borrow and consumers more ready to spend.

This happened after a long period of little or no investment and sharply reduced personal consumption, meaning there was significant pent-up demand for both industrial goods and consumer goods. Once consumers and companies realised that there was less benefit in holding onto savings because prices were rising sharply, they were encouraged to spend, thereby stimulating the economy. Note the difference between the global abandonment of the gold standard and the piecemeal approaches discussed in Section 2.1.4. There, an individual country in difficulty devalued whilst the major industrialised nations, and the main importers of agricultural goods, did not. In this case, it was the industrialised countries that allowed their money supply to expand, resulting in prices increasing across the board.

Implication for future policy

The post-Great Depression analysis has mostly concluded that going off gold was a turning point in fighting the Great Depression. The implications of this success had a significant impact on future policy. Governments following WWII started to employ very loose monetary policy as a routine technique to stimulate their economies, with the consequence that monetary policy lost its effectiveness and inflationary expectations got built in. Solving that problem was very costly in the 1980s.

2.3.3 Lack of global leadership and narrow focus on national interests

An important reason why the Great Depression happened was the lack of global leadership and international coordination. At the time, international organisations, like the League of Nations, were in their infancy and we did not know how to use them to exercise effective diplomacy. International coordination and policymaking were not seen as important. This meant that the leadership role of individual countries was more important than today.

In the second part of the nineteenth century, right up until WWI, the UK assumed the role of a leading nation, helping to quickly prevent pending crises from getting out of control. From that time the effective global leader was the US but it was not ready to assume that mandate when the time came to formulate a global crisis response.

Leading countries at the time tended to focus on narrow short-term national interests, disregarding long-term consequences, the potential reaction of other countries and the impact on the global economy. They had various long meetings, but strong disagreements prevailed and no conclusion on policy response was reached.

One example of the failure to respond is provided by an anecdote from Ahamed (2009), discussing an international government conference in Paris in April 1929. At the time, the danger facing the global economy was becoming increasingly clear. Regardless, France insisted on focusing the proceedings on war reparations, even though Germany had no ability to pay. In the words of the report of the observer from the Swiss National Bank (SNB), Felix Somary:

'Almost all the great powers have been negotiating for months about how many billions a year should be paid until 1966, and thereafter until 1988, by a country that is not even in a position to pay its own civil servants' salaries the next day.'

2.4 IMPLICATIONS FOR FUTURE POLICY

The Great Depression had a strong impact on policymaking and academic research. Economists were blamed for providing bad advice, before and during the Depression, and the field of macroeconomics was developed in response.

Since the Great Depression, the authorities have been well aware of which pitfalls to avoid if threatened by another crisis episode: avoid protectionism, employ fiscal and monetary stimulus, coordinate crisis response internationally, and do not let banks fail. Stimulus in one country benefits its neighbours as well, by encouraging international trade, leaving no reason to employ protectionist measures. This leaves a problem of free riding since stimulus packages create positive externalities. However, if countries focus on the common objective of preventing another Depression, free riding will not be a significant problem.

In the early 1940s, the Allied leaders, excluding the Soviet Union, discussed how the world economic order should be set up, and ended up establishing a new range of international government bodies and coordinating mechanisms. Of those, the most important was the establishment of the *Bretton Woods system*, especially the International Monetary Fund (IMF) and the World Bank. Policymakers also decided to implement specific mechanisms to prevent the use of trade restrictions. The most prominent example of this is the General Agreement on Tariffs and Trade (GATT) in 1947, eventually replaced by the World Trade Organisation (WTO) in 1995. While free trade has remained a controversial subject, and many countries employ trade restrictions in various forms, the scale of such restrictions is much lower than in the 1920s and 1930s. Finally, as a direct response to the Depression, many countries have set up formal mechanisms for safeguarding financial stability, such as rules for lending of last resort (LOLR), deposit insurance and bank regulations. Most of these arrangements are fundamentally with us to this day, even if the specific form has changed.

2.4.1 Parallels with the crisis of 2007–2009

In the decades after the Great Depression ended, financial and economic crises were common but were always confined to individual countries, or at worst a handful of countries. This finally changed in 2007 when a global financial and economic crisis started. Below, we directly draw parallels between the Great Depression and the crises from 2007.

The crisis response this time around is directly influenced by the Great Depression. It has often seemed as if authorities had made the list of Great Depression mistakes, with the intention of not repeating them. This policy was broadly successful for the first phase of the crisis from 2007 to 2009, but less so for the European sovereign debt phase.

Comparisons

Great Depression	Crisis from 2007
Roaring twenties	**Great moderation**
The 1920s enjoyed rapid economic growth, with new technology, silent films and the Model T Ford, and the beginnings of radio and commercial air services. Stock market speculation was rampant, leverage was high and capital flowed to Wall Street.	The boom prior to 2007 was based on new technology like the Internet, and the renewed prominence of financial markets. The financial system used high levels of leverage, with strong capital flows to financial markets.
Financial markets	
Rapid development of financial markets, with ordinary citizens for the first time having access to financial services such as mortgages and stock market investments bought on the margin. A stock market and real-estate boom ensued, creating the feeling that prices could rise indefinitely, leading to reckless risk taking.	Financial innovation, with new forms of real-estate financing, like subprime, emerged, and a rapid increase in homeownership and low-cost mortgages fuelled a real-estate boom. The market boom led to the belief that prices could rise indefinitely. New financial practices like structured credit and shadow banking enabled risk taking out of the view of supervisors and the market.
US bailouts	
RFC	**TARP**
In 1931, President Hoover set up the RFC, making loans to financial institutions of all types, with $500 million outright, and the possibility of issuing up to $1.5 billion in government debt (1% to 3% of GDP respectively). The RFC is seen as a failure, not least because the bailouts were public.	The main bailout programme was the Troubled Asset Relief Program (TARP), authorised at $700 billion, but total disbursements were only $431 billion, 4.8% and 3% of GDP respectively.
Short selling	
President Hoover compelled the New York Stock Exchange to curb short selling.	The Bush administration temporarily imposed restrictions on short selling of shares in some financial institutions.
LOLR	
The US did not do LOLR until Roosevelt took office in March 1933.	Various large-sized LOLR-type credit and liquidity facilities were provided.
Trade	
The Smoot–Hawley Act and various other trade restrictions reduced global trade by more than two-thirds.	No restrictions on trade have yet been imposed.
Money and liquidity	
The US authorities allowed the money supply to shrink and deflation to set in.	Significant QE was provided and deflation was prevented.

Lesson learned

Generally, it seems that the policy response in the fall of 2008 was the right one, and the authorities did not repeat the mistakes made in the Great Depression. Deflation was avoided, widespread bank failures were prevented, trade remained free and global authorities actively cooperated in their crisis response. These measures seemed successful in preventing the crisis from turning into another Great Depression.

2.4.2 European sovereign debt crisis

There are fewer parallels between the Great Depression and the European sovereign debt crisis. The latter is created by the unique circumstances of a common European currency without the necessary conditions being met, with no comparable problem in the Great Depression. There is one important commonality, the gold standard.

Impact of the gold standard

The presence of the gold standard meant that the money supply grew slower than the real economy, resulting in deflation. This was especially problematic in countries like the UK that opted to reenter the gold standard at an overvalued rate, as well as the various agricultural exporters exposed to the commodity price deflation. The only way for these countries to remain on the gold standard was by internal devaluation.

The gold standard frustrated efforts at containing the banking crises by limiting the scope for individual central banks to do LOLR. When the central banks provided liquidity to domestic banks, it signalled that the government attached a higher priority to the stability of the banking system than to the defence of the gold standard. Inevitably this encouraged depositors to get money out of the country in advance of the expected devaluation, in a self-fulfilling crisis scenario. Any liquidity injected into the banking system just leaked back out as the inevitable balance of payments crisis loomed.

Impact of the common currency

Similar forces are at work with the common European currency. For some countries, such as Germany, the Netherlands, Finland and Austria, European inflation rates and exchange rates have been appropriate, whilst for others the euro has been significantly overvalued, as is the case for Greece, Italy, Spain and Portugal. The latter countries, therefore, are in a similar situation as were the gold standard countries during the Great Depression, being forced by the constraints of the monetary system to make internal devaluations and impose extreme austerity, rather than simply allowing their currency to devalue.

2.5 SUMMARY

The biggest economic crisis the world has ever seen is the Great Depression. The causes of the Depression are varied and remain controversial, though they include war reparations, agricultural overproduction, inappropriate monetary policies (too loose and too strict), competitive devaluations and trade restrictions.

When the crisis was underway, the policy response could not have been worse; countries focused on narrow national interests, trade collapsed by more than two-thirds, liquidity (money supply) was allowed to contract and deflation to set in, and banking systems were allowed to fail in some countries.

The causes of the Great Depression, as well as the needed policy response, have been extensively studied. The world authorities facing a new global crisis in 2007 effectively prevented a new Great Depression from emerging by explicitly avoiding the mistakes made before and during the Great Depression.

The European authorities fighting the European sovereign debt crisis have not been as willing to take on board Great Depression lessons, especially problems arising from the gold standard.

Questions for discussion

1 The Great Depression is the most severe global economic crisis we have ever seen. In what way was it more damaging than the ongoing crisis in 2007?

2 Winston Churchill is said to have stated that going on gold in 1924 at prewar parity was his biggest mistake? What were the implications of this decision of his?

3 What was the impact of competitive devaluations in the 1920s, and how has the memory of those events shaped current policy debate?

4 What role did tariffs play in worsening the Great Depression, and how has the memory of those events shaped current policy debate?

5 Explain the role of monetary policy in the US as contributor to the Depression.

6 What are the main lessons of the Depression that policymakers seem to have learned when fighting the crisis in 2008?

7 What is the main lesson from the Great Depression that has not been applied in the European sovereign debt crisis? Why do you think that is the case?

References

Ahamed, L. (2009). *Lords of Finance, The Bankers Who Broke the World*. The Penguin Group.

Anderson, G. M., Shughart, W. F., II., and Tollison, R. D. (1988). A public choice theory of the great contraction. *Public Choice,* 59: 3–23.

Bernanke, B. (1995). The macroeconomics of the Great Depression: a comparative approach. *J. Money Credit and Banking,* 27(1): 1–28.

Eichengreen, B. (1996). *Golden Fetters: The Gold Standard and the Great Depression, 1919–1939.* Oxford University Press.

Eichengreen, B. and Irwin, D. (2009). The slide to protectionism in the Great Depression: who succumbed and why? NBER Working Paper 15142.

Epstein, G. and Ferguson, T. (1984). Monetary policy, loan liquidation, and industrial conflict: the Federal Reserve and open market operations of 1932. *J. Econ. Hist.,* 44: 957–83.

Ferguson, N. (2008). *The Ascent of Money*. The Penguin Group.

Friedman, M. and Schwartz, A. (1963). *A Monetary History of the United States: 1867–1960.* Princeton University. Press.

Keynes, J. M. (1920). *The Economic Consequences of the Peace*. Harcourt Brace, New York.

Keynes, J. M. (1924). *A Tract on Monetary Reform*. Macmillan.

Kindleberger, C. (1986). *The World in Depression, 1929–1939,* 2nd edition. University of California Press.

3 ENDOGENOUS RISK

The term endogenous describes an outcome or process having an internal cause or origin. In the context of financial markets, *endogenous risk* refers to the view that risk is created by the interplay between market participants, rather than the chance that a shock might arrive to the financial markets from the outside — *exogenous risk*. The classification of risk into endogenous and exogenous risk was first proposed by Danielsson and Shin (2003).

Endogenous risk arises when individual economic agents react to their environment and their actions in turn affect their environment to such a degree that an endogenous feedback cannot be ignored. Financial markets, where all market participants are constantly competing against each other, trying to gain advantage by anticipating each other's moves, are a clear example of an environment creating endogenous risk.

Endogenous feedback between the behaviour of market participants can suddenly create a vicious cycle, causing a crisis. This arises from the presence of mechanisms creating accelerator effects, whereby a relatively small event can trigger a large outcome. This is similar to the idea by chaos theorists of a butterfly in Hong Kong triggering a hurricane in the Caribbean. Many commentators, and the popular press, focus on the trigger event — the butterfly — while it is the mechanism that enables the butterfly to trigger the hurricane that really matters.

Endogenous risk tends to be low most of the time, because economic agents usually behave individually and have different objectives and information sets. This means that in aggregate their behaviour resembles noise when viewed from the outside. Under certain conditions, market participants start behaving much more harmoniously than usual, amplifying price movements that result in asset price *bubbles* and finally market crashes. This creates risk that is hidden until it is too late, providing a false sense of stability, while the market is really heading for the precipice.

Such spirals of coordinated selling need to be strong enough to overcome the usual stabilising forces in markets such as arbitrageurs, hedge funds, sovereign wealth funds and the like that could be expected to step in and buy the cheap assets, putting a floor under prices.

Financial markets are subject to both exogenous and endogenous risk, but it is the latter that is more damaging. It is behind some of the biggest financial crisis episodes in history, while being much harder to model than exogenous risk. For a single bank, most risk is exogenous. For the financial system, risk is almost entirely endogenous, even if not to a high degree most of the time. As an approximation, those concerned with financial risk might not be too far off by assuming risk is exogenous 99.9% of the time. It is, however, the other 0.1% when endogenous risk becomes a serious concern. That is when economic agents become harmonised in behaviour, and the conditions are ripe for a crisis to emerge.

Endogenous risk has direct implications for financial models, since most such models assume risk is exogenous. This suggests that the models may work well 99.9% of the time, but fail when needed the most — at times of extreme market turmoil. In turn, this leads to direct policy conclusions on financial stability, the use of risk models by bank supervisors and the wisdom of prudential regulations.

The concept of endogenous risk directly relates to other economic theories, such as the beauty contest in Keynes (1936). It also connects to Minsky (1992) who argued that economies have either stable or unstable financial regimes; even if the economy starts out stable, continued prosperity paves the way for an unstable system.

Similarly, endogenous risk impacts on policies towards financial stability. For example, prudential banking regulations aim at ensuring that each and every financial institution behaves properly, avoiding excessive risk. Endogenous risk analysis predicts that such prevention regulations are directly destabilising, because as banks act prudently in a crisis, their very acts of self-preservation cause them to dispose of the same risky assets and buy the same safe assets, amplifying price movements and distress. This suggests that any financial stability policies explicitly need to consider the potential for endogenous feedbacks.

Links to other chapters

This chapter focuses on the hidden mechanisms that create potential crashes. Many of the concepts mentioned in this chapter are discussed in much more detail later, for example in Chapter 4 (liquidity) and Chapter 9 (trading and speculation).

Key concepts

- Endogenous risk
- Firesale externality
- Trading strategies
- Actual and perceived risk
- Dual role of prices

Readings for this chapter

While the chapter is self-contained, the material is drawn from several of my papers, all of which are available on my website (www.RiskResearch.org). The notion of endogenous risk was first introduced by Danielsson and Shin (2003) and further developed by Shin (2010). Two recent papers discuss endogenous risk from a policy point of view, Danielsson *et al.* (2012a) and Danielsson *et al.* (2012b), with the former focused on systemic risk and financial regulations while the latter addresses extreme outcomes in financial markets. Finally, a more theoretical treatment is provided by Danielsson *et al.* (2012c).

Notation specific to this chapter

A	Value of assets
C	Cash
D	Debt
d	Change operator
E	Equity
f	Option price
L	Leverage
n	indicates iteration
P	Prices
Q	Quantity (units of assets held)
X	Strike price
Δ	Option delta from the Black–Scholes equation
ε	Random number
λ	Price impact factor
σ	Standard deviation

3.1 MILLENNIUM BRIDGE

Endogenous risk is not exclusively confined to financial markets, and we start with an illuminating example from engineering. The first new bridge to span the River Thames for 100 years was the pedestrian *Millennium Bridge*, opened by Queen Elizabeth on 10 June 2000. On the opening day, thousands of people used it to cross the river. This should not have been a problem, as the bridge was designed to cope easily with such large crowds.

Within moments of being opened to the public the bridge began to wobble violently, and was soon closed to the great embarrassment of the bridge's designers – Arup and Lord Foster – and the authorities. In the process, it earned the nickname the wobbly bridge.[1]

The wobble came as a surprise, as no such outcome had been predicted by the extensive computer modelling and human testing conducted by Arup. It is well known that soldiers marching across bridges can cause them to collapse, which is why they are asked

[1]See http://news.bbc.co.uk/hi/english/static/in_depth/uk/2000/millennium_bridge/default.stm and www.youtube.com/watch? v=eAXVaXWZ8.

to break step when crossing bridges. This happens because marching soldiers generate harmonised frequencies that can create a feedback between the internal frequency of a bridge and the soldiers' steps, leading to a collapse. However, the people crowded on the Millennium Bridge on the opening day were not soldiers, but people of all walks of life. The chance of them spontaneously marching was considered next to impossible.

Diagnosis

Every bridge is designed to move with the elements, and the Millennium Bridge was supposed to sway gently in response to the Thames breeze. A gust of wind – an exogenous shock – hit the bridge, causing it to move sideways and wobble. When this happens a natural reaction is to adjust one's stance to regain balance. By doing so, the bridge gets pushed back, making it sway even more, causing people to adjust their stance yet again – more and more at the same time – this time pushing the bridge in the opposite direction. As an ever increasing number of pedestrians started to adjust their stance simultaneously, the bridge moved more and soon almost all the pedestrians joined in. This created a mutually reinforcing feedback loop between the synchronised adjustments of the pedestrians' stance and the bridge's wobble,[2] shown in Figure 3.1.

We cannot identify the endogeneity of the Millennium Bridge by considering either the properties of the bridge or the crowd in isolation; they have to be studied jointly. This is what makes endogenous risk problems hard.

Wider lessons

The wobble of the bridge was created by people reacting to a gust of wind pushing the bridge. The wobble continued and intensified even though the initial gust of wind had long passed. This is a concise example of how a relatively small exogenous shock (the gust of wind) causes a large endogenous response. It is a clear example of endogenous risk in action, unlike, for example, an earthquake which is an exogenous shock. The ultimate lesson from the Millennium Bridge is that it is not the shock that matters but the feedback mechanism that allows a small shock to be amplified into a large event.

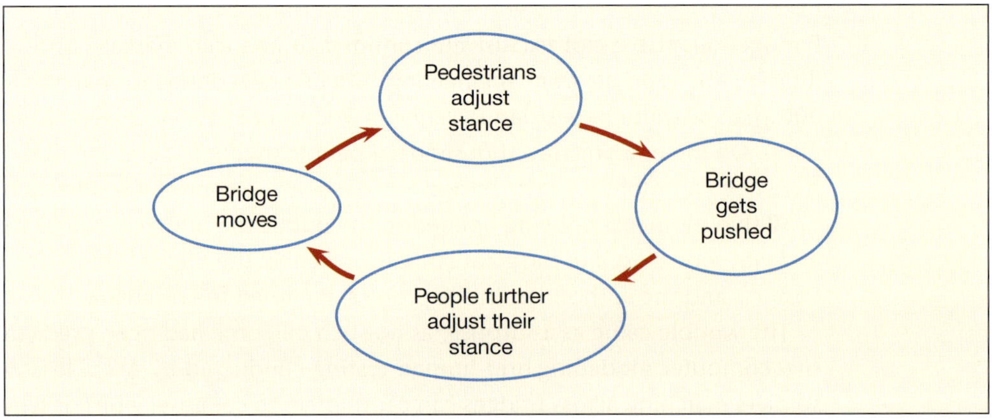

Figure 3.1 Feedback loop of the Millennium Bridge

[2]For more information, see www.arup.com/millenniumbridge/challenge/results.html.

The financial system is replete with analogous processes, whereby an innocuous shock has the potential to trigger a systemic crisis. Financial markets are examples of environments whereby individuals not only react to events around them, but also by their actions directly affect market outcomes, because of balance sheet adjustments. The pedestrians on the Millennium Bridge were like traders reacting to price changes, and the movement of the bridge was like price moves in markets. Consequently, the notion of endogenous risk provides a clear mechanism for analysing feedbacks in financial systems.

3.2 DUAL ROLE OF PRICES

Prices of financial assets play two important roles. The first is quite familiar.

Prices reflect the underlying fundamentals, and aggregate all available information into a single number, the price. For example, prices might be the present discounted value of dividends. This means that market prices provide the best indication of the current value of an asset. However, it does not mean that current prices provide a reliable guide to the future value or future risk of an asset, because prices also affect the future behaviour of market participants.

Prices are also an imperative to action, not least because of constraints on market participants, constraints above and beyond the basic objective of maximising profits. This can include accounting rules, legal obligations, disclosures, risk constraints or marking to market. A bank may not react to market outcomes in the way we expect, because the constraints dictate a certain type of behaviour. If the bank is large, it will significantly affect prices by its trading activities, which means that its constraints may directly affect the statistical properties of market prices. One could say that the presence of constraints undermines the integrity of the prices, taking them away from their fundamental values. In extreme cases, prices can become so distorted that they lead to undesirable extreme outcomes, like bubbles and crashes.

What this means is that while market prices are the best guide to the current valuation of an asset, they might not provide a good indication of the future valuation or future risk. The deterministic impact of constraints gets in the way. While this may result in prices being predictable, traders cannot exploit this because of the constraints they are under. This has particular implications for investment decisions and policy. In particular, the practice of treating prices as exogenously determined by an efficient market might be a poor policy guide in times of crisis.

3.2.1 Leverage constraints and upward-sloping demand

We illustrate the surprising impact of external constraints on trading decisions by a simple model of *leverage constraints*. Even in this basic example, a financial institution does behave unexpectedly, buying when prices increase and selling when prices fall.

Standard microeconomic theory predicts that demand functions are downward sloping. When the price of something falls we buy more, and when prices increase we buy less. The only exception is a strange asset called a *Giffen good*. The leverage constraint example below demonstrates that constraints can lead to upward-sloping demand functions for regular assets.

Setup

Suppose a bank's leverage (L) is restricted to 5. In other words, the ratio of assets (A) to equity (E) has to be 5:

$$L = \frac{A}{E} = 5$$

We set the initial price of the asset, P, to \$10, where the bank holds $Q = 100$ units of the asset, and has debt of $D = \$800$. This means that the value of its portfolio is $A = Q \times P = \$1000$, and its equity is $E = A - D = \$200$. The initial balance sheet is therefore:

Assets	Liabilities
$A = 1000$	$E = 200$ $D = 800$

and the bank meets its leverage constraint. Suppose the asset is hit by a negative exogenous shock, causing its price to fall to $P = \$9$. This price drop directly affects equity and the balance sheet becomes:

Assets	Liabilities
$A = 900$	$E = 100$ $D = 800$

Leverage is now $9 = 900/100$, and the bank needs to take action to meet the constraint. The most direct way is to reduce debt by selling assets.

Consider two different cases. In the first case, the bank is a price taker, meaning that no matter how much it buys or sells, prices remain unaffected. Prices are exogenous. In the second case the bank exerts a significant market power, so that its buying or selling decisions cause prices to move. Prices are endogenous. The former case corresponds to a small individual trader, whilst the latter case reflects a large bank or fund.

Prices are exogenous

Suppose the bank is a price taker and as a response to the price drop sells enough of the asset to keep leverage at 5. The change in debt, $D_1 - D_0$, will be the amount sold at current market prices P:

$$\begin{aligned} D_1 - D_0 &= P(Q_1 - Q_0) \\ D_1 &= D_0 + PQ_1 - PQ_0 \end{aligned} \tag{3.1}$$

The leverage constraint is then:

$$L = \frac{A_1}{E_1} = \frac{PQ_1}{PQ_1 - D_1}$$

Substitute D_1 by its value in (3.1):

$$L = \frac{PQ_1}{PQ_0 - D_0}$$

$$Q_1 = L\left(Q_0 - \frac{D_0}{P}\right) \tag{3.2}$$

In our example, the bank should now hold 500/9 units of the asset. By selling $100 - 500/9$ units, the target leverage ratio is reached and the bank needs to do nothing further. Its balance sheet becomes:

Assets	Liabilities
$A = 500$	$E = 100$ $D = 400$

This means that in order to meet the leverage constraint, the bank had to sell \$400 worth of the asset. This happened because prices dropped, so the demand function is upward sloping. If the price shock had been positive, the bank would have bought the asset. We show the demand function in Figure 3.2.

Prices are endogenous

Consider the case where the bank is a large market participant, and thus exerts a significant price impact. When it buys, prices increase, and when it sells, prices fall. We capture this phenomena by the so-called *price impact function*, showing how much prices change. Because there are several steps in the calculation, we use n to indicate the step. The change in price $P_n - P_{n-1}$ due to a transaction worth $P_{n-1}(Q_{n-1} - Q_{n-2})$ is

$$P_n - P_{n-1} = \lambda P_{n-1}(Q_{n-1} - Q_{n-2})$$

λ is known as the price impact factor, with $P_{n-1}(Q_{n-1} - Q_{n-2})$ the amount the bank wants to sell, in our case \$400.

Because prices fall in response to the sale, the bank will not be meeting the leverage constraint even after selling the same amount as in the exogenous case above. It will have to sell more assets. That in turn triggers a further price drop, and so forth, until we get convergence. The process to compute the variables is as follows:

1. $P_n = P_{n-1} + \lambda P_{n-1}(Q_{n-1} - Q_{n-2})$
2. $Q_n = L(Q_{n-1} - D_{n-1}/P_n)$
3. $A_n = P_n Q_n$
4. $E_n = A_n/L$
5. $D_n = A_n - E_n$

Let the price impact factor be $\lambda = 0.001$. We then repeatedly apply (3.2) until we get convergence, with the results of 10 rounds shown in Table 3.1.

Table 3.1 Ten selling iterations

Iteration	Q	P	A
1	100.000	10.000	1000.000
2	55.556	9.000	500.000
⋮	⋮	⋮	⋮
9	42.934	8.492	364.585
10	42.934	8.492	364.585

The initial sale was for 44.444 units of the asset, but as we keep on iterating we get further sales of 12.6 units, causing prices to drop further to $8.492.

Supply and demand functions

We can demonstrate this more generally by considering the bank's demand for various magnitudes of initial price shocks. This is shown in Figure 3.2 for both the exogenous and endogenous cases.

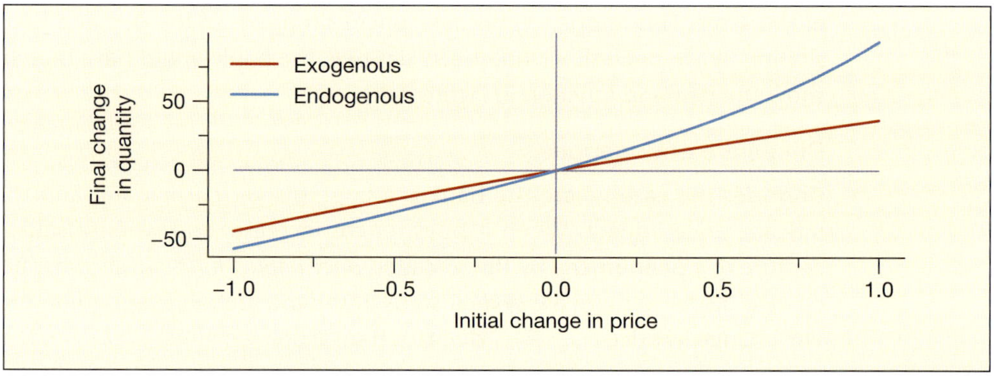

Figure 3.2 Demand functions

The x-axis shows the initial price change, with our $1 price drop from above on the extreme left. We then go all the way to a $1 price increase on the right. The y-axis shows the final change in the bank's holding of the asset. On the extreme left we get 55.55 for the exogenous case and 42.93 in the endogenous case. This demonstrates the upward-sloping demand functions and shows that when prices are endogenous, the impact is much stronger.

In this case, the price impact was quite small, 0.001, and we still manage to get a sizable endogenous change in prices and quantity. This succinctly demonstrates how a small exogenous shock can trigger a large outcome, where the constraints dictate a '*sell cheap*, *buy dear*' strategy that generates precisely the kind of vicious feedback loops that destabilise markets.

3.3 RISK

There is no single way to define risk. A basic textbook definition is the volatility of returns, but that is only a complete description if financial returns are normally distributed, with constant unchanging volatility. Neither assumption is true in reality. This means that any textbook way of making investment decisions, such as a mean–variance diagram or a capital asset pricing model – essential elements of modern portfolio theory (MPT) – will be approximate because the underlying assumptions are violated.

One could argue that even if the underlying assumptions are problematic, MPT provides reasonably good approximations to the real world. We can distinguish low risk from high risk, we can often assume markets are sufficiently liquid, and we can partly predict volatility. For this reason, many, even most, practitioners make some use of MPT, perhaps extending it to incorporate fat tails and volatility clustering. When considering longer horizons, especially for assets that are illiquid or have very fat tails, other alternatives may be preferred. In the words of Warren Buffett (2012):

> 'The riskiness of an investment is not measured by beta [a Wall Street term encompassing volatility and often used in measuring risk] but rather by the probability – the reasoned probability – of that investment causing its owner a loss of purchasing power over his contemplated holding period. Assets can fluctuate greatly in price and not be risky as long as they are reasonably certain to deliver increased purchasing power over their holding period. And as we will see, a nonfluctuating asset can be laden with risk.'

Financial regulations employ Value-at-Risk (VaR) (see the appendix to Chapter 13) as a preferred way to quantify market risk. This is based on the risk of daily outcomes (linearly scaled to 10 days) that happen with 1% probability, so once every five months. In most cases, the VaR is calculated by volatilities. It therefore falls under Buffett's criticism.

Risk-free

Some assets have such low risk that they are referred to as *risk-free*. This is typically a short-term obligation of sovereigns considered extremely unlikely to default, like the United States (US), United Kingdom (UK) and Switzerland. Even in that case, the investment is not totally risk-free because it involves putting money into a local currency which is at risk from inflation. Some governments offer inflation-linked bonds which come close to being risk-free.

Gold is, however, often considered a good hedge against inflation, and one might be tempted to invest in an asset like gold in order to avoid risk, but it is far from risk-free, as can be seen in Figure 3.3.

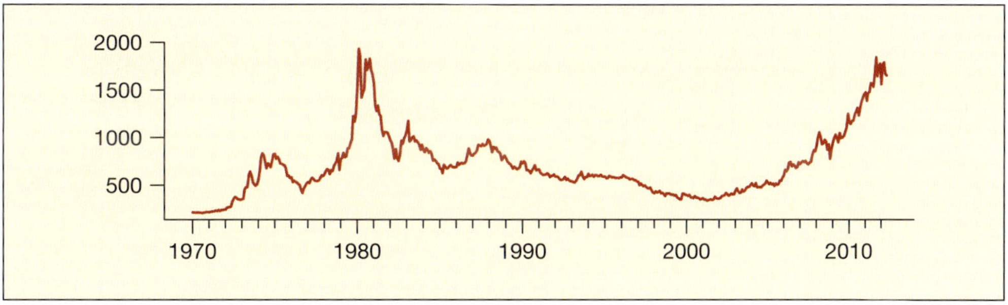

Figure 3.3 Real USD spot price of an ounce of gold
Data source: World Gold Council and US Department of Labor

3.3.1 Dependence

Correlations between asset returns are often higher when the markets are falling, even tending to 1 in a market crash. An increased level of correlations is often a sign of market turmoil. While the theoretical analysis above focused on the interaction between market and funding liquidity for a single security, it also has implications for how multiple asset prices move together in times of stress.

Definition 3.1 Non-linear dependence and correlations A common way to refer to how two random variables are related is by the concept of correlations. However, correlations only properly describe the interrelationship when it is linear, and often variables are related in a complicated non-linear way, not captured by correlations. Therefore, it is more accurate to use terms like dependence or non-linear dependence.

Danielsson *et al.* (2012b) demonstrate that a chain of events like that described in Figure 4.4 in Chapter 4 also affects the dependence between assets. In normal times, dependence between assets is generally based on the inherent properties of the assets themselves, with similar assets tending to move in similar ways.

In a crisis, the situation changes, and is much more affected by the liquidity positions of the banks that trigger the crisis. This can happen because if a bank suffers from a lack of funding liquidity, it may be forced to sell its assets across the board, adversely impacting on the price of each and every one. This is manifested in higher correlations.

Forced selling in a firesale externality scenario tends to create new forms of dependence between assets held by similar investors. This leads to the empirical prediction that correlations increase sharply in times of market turmoil, and especially in crises.

3.4 DYNAMIC TRADING STRATEGIES

While the leverage constraint example above is somewhat artificial, we have seen many concrete examples of endogenous risk causing extreme outcomes in financial markets. One of the clearest examples is the stock market crash of 19 October, 1987 when global stock markets fell by around 23%. We show the impact in Figure 3.4.

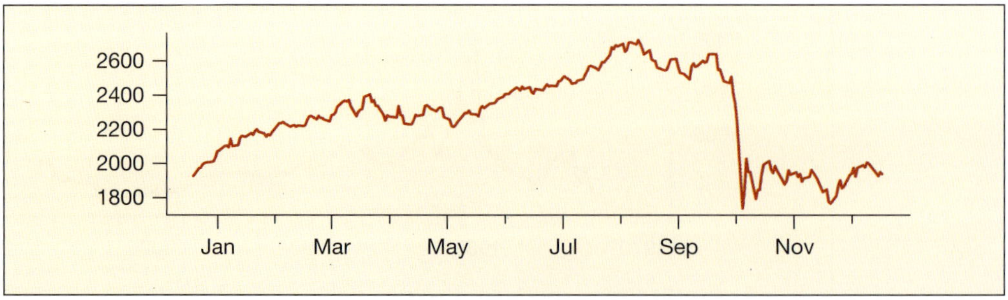

Figure 3.4 **1987 Dow Jones Industrial Averge index values**
Data source: finance.yahoo.com

The postmortem analysis by the US government, the Brady Commission (1988) report, found that the main underlying cause was the use of an automatic trading strategy called *portfolio insurance*.

Portfolio insurance

Portfolio insurance is a trading strategy whereby an investor wishes to hedge downside risk by *dynamically replicating* a put option. In principle, the investor could just buy the put option, but it may not be available for the particular asset, or be illiquid and/or too expensive. Under the assumptions of the option pricing model of Black and Scholes (1973b), there should be no difference between the price of an option bought outright and a dynamically replicated option.

Delta and dynamic replication

An option gives the holder the right but not the obligation to buy (call) and sell (put) an asset at a pre-agreed price (the strike price, X) at a fixed date in the future. While one can use the model of Black–Scholes to get the option price, we can also dynamically replicate the option by a combination of cash and the underlying asset.

The delta (Δ) of a put option is the rate of change of its price, denoted by f, with respect to the change in price of the underlying asset, P. We can obtain Δ from the derivative of the Black–Scholes equation with respect to prices.

$$\Delta = \frac{df}{dP}$$

The Δ of a put option is negative. Graphically, Δ is the slope of a curve representing the option price against the price of the underlying asset, as shown in Figure 3.5.

A put can be replicated by holding Δ units of the underlying asset, so a portfolio consisting of

$$\Delta \text{ of underlying asset} - 1 \text{ put}$$

is risk-free for small movements in the underlying price. When the price changes, the gain or loss from holding the underlying asset is matched by an exactly offsetting loss or gain from the change in the price of the put option.

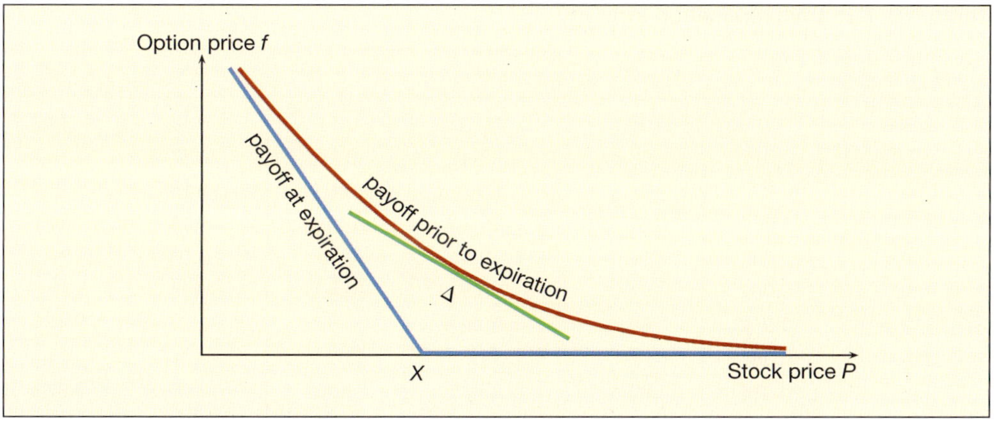

Figure 3.5 Put option and delta

3.4.1 Numerical example

Let us examine the impact of dynamic delta hedging by means of numerical simulations. This example is adopted from Shin (2010) where it is explained in more detail. We first decide on the magnitude of the inputs, and set the strike price at \$90, the risk-free rate at 0%, the annual volatility at 25% and the time to maturity to 9 weeks. The underlying stock is currently trading at \$100. If we plug these values into the Black–Scholes equation, we get the value of the put as \$0.8012. We simulate the market in one-week increments, and show the details of the simulation in Table 3.2.

We use a superscript * to denote the actual outcomes, so for example *P* refers to the theoretical price and *P** to the actual price. *C* refers to cash holdings.

Simulation

The realised return from day $t-1$ to day t is

$$1 + \varepsilon_t + (A_t - A_{t-1}) \tag{3.3}$$

where ε_t is the exogenous random return and $A_t - A_{t-1}$ the purchase (or sale) of the stock.

First week. The trader starts with no funds. The initial stock price is 100. The trader shorts the stock by Δ units, and from the Black–Scholes equation we find that $\Delta = -0.14$. This gives the trader 14.3 in cash. We assume this is the same in both the endogenous and exogenous price cases in order to start both off in the same place.

Exogenous prices

Second week. We start by drawing a random shock,

$$\epsilon \sim \mathcal{N}\left(0, \frac{0.25^2}{52}\right)$$

resulting in −0.016 in this particular case, so the price falls to 98.4, and Δ becomes −0.17. As a consequence, we sell more of the stock, increasing the cash balance to 16.8.

Table 3.2 Dynamic replication strategy

$T-t$	ε	P	P^*	Δ	Δ^*	C	C^*
9/10		100.0	100.0	−0.14	−0.14	14.3	14.3
8/10	−0.016	98.4	98.4	−0.17	−0.17	16.8	16.8
7/10	0.022	100.6	98.1	−0.10	−0.16	10.3	16.1
6/10	0.004	101.0	99.3	−0.08	−0.12	7.9	11.5
5/10	−0.040	97.0	99.9	−0.16	−0.08	15.5	8.4
4/10	−0.062	91.0	96.8	−0.42	−0.14	39.6	13.6
3/10	−0.014	89.7	90.2	−0.51	−0.47	47.1	43.6
2/10	−0.085	82.1	52.6	−0.97	−1.00	84.9	71.5
1/10	−0.018	80.6	23.8	−1.00	−1.00	87.5	71.5
0/10	0.045	84.2	24.8	−1.00	−1.00	87.6	71.5

We continue repeating this until at expiration, when $T - t = 0$, the price of the stock ends up in the money at 84.2, the price where we have to buy it back, while the final cash position is 87.6. This means that the final payoff is

$$87.6 - 84.2 = 3.4$$

If we had instead bought a put option at the Black–Scholes price of \$0.80, the payoff would have been

$$90 - 84.24 - 0.80 = 4.96$$

So why the discrepancy? If we had delta hedged continuously, as assumed by the Black–Scholes model, the outcomes would have been identical. However, with one week passing between re-hedging, the error becomes non-trivial.

Endogenous prices

Third week. We start by drawing a random shock,

$$\epsilon \sim \mathcal{N}\left(0, \frac{0.25^2}{52}\right)$$

resulting in 0.022. In the exogenous case this would make the price rise to 100.6; however, we sold at the end of the previous week and (3.3) indicates that the price falls further to 98.1.

This continues for a few weeks, but it is really by the eighth week that things heat up and the downward spiral begins to gather momentum.

Eighth week. The random shock is −0.085, coming after a price drop of 6.6 over the previous week, resulting in a large negative price movement, all the way to 52.6. Delta is on its way to become −1, which is obvious from Figure 3.5 since we are so deep in the money.

This continues on in the following week, slightly reversing in the last week. At that time, the actual price has fallen to 24.8 and the cash balance is 71.5. This means the profit from the strategy is

$$71.5 - 24.8 = 46.7$$

If we had instead purchased a put option, and the prices had followed the same pattern, the profit would have been

$$90 - 24.8 - 0.80 = 64.4$$

Here the difference between the dynamic trading strategy and an outright purchase of the option is much larger than in the exogenous case. This is not surprising, since it follows from Figure 3.5 that if prices move a lot, the delta approximation becomes less accurate. This is an illustration that the Black–Scholes formula is underpricing the put option when there is feedback.

Analysis

We summarise these results in Figure 3.6 which shows the two price columns from Table 3.2.

The dynamic strategy amplifies the price movements, both going up and going down. If the price shocks are small, it doesn't make much difference, but by the middle of the

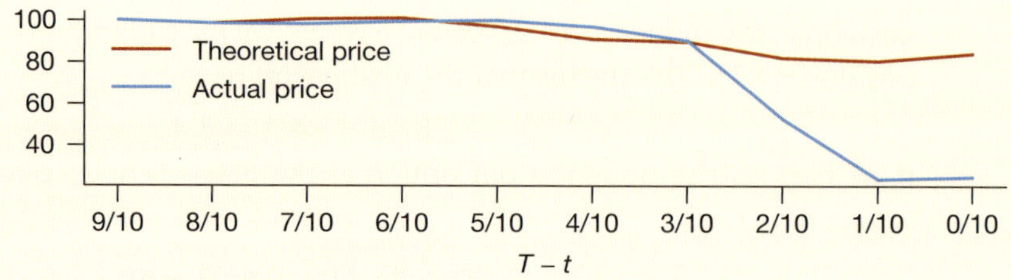

Figure 3.6 Dynamic replication strategy

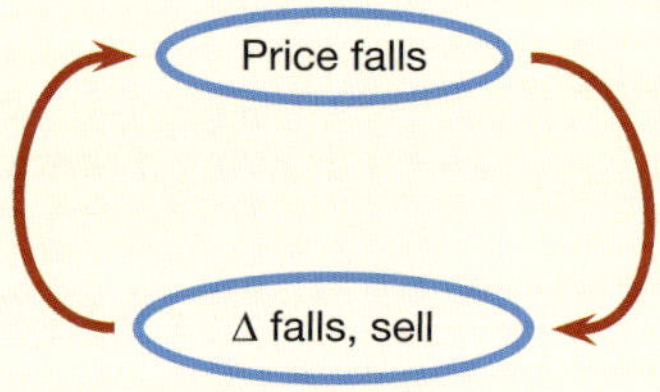

Figure 3.7 Endogenous dynamics of delta hedging

period we get a few small but negative price shocks in a row. Initially, it does not matter much, but all of a sudden the endogenous shock kicks in and prices fall sharply over the span of two weeks. This is captured in Figure 3.7. This is exactly how many market crashes happen, and demonstrates the importance of considering endogenous feedback.

3.4.2 Endogenous risk and the 1987 crash

Estimates in 1987 indicated that around $100 billion in funds were following formal portfolio insurance programmes, representing around 3% of the pre-crash market capitalisation. However, this is almost certainly an underestimate of total selling pressure arising from informal hedging techniques such as stop-loss orders.

In the period from Wednesday 14 October to Friday 16 October, the market declined by around 10%, with sales dictated by dynamic hedging models amounting to around $12 billion (in either cash or futures), but the actual sales were only around $4 billion. This means that by Monday morning, there was a substantial amount of pent-up selling pressure, causing the Dow Jones to fall by over 20% on Monday 19 October.

Trading rules

The stock market crash of 1987 is a classic example of the destabilising feedback effect on market dynamics of concerted selling pressure arising from certain mechanical *trading rules,* like the *sell-on-loss* considered here.

What is especially striking in this example is that the underlying destabilising behaviour is completely invisible so long as trading activity remains below some critical but unknown threshold. It is only when this threshold is exceeded that the endogenous risk becomes apparent, causing a market crash. This clearly demonstrates the difference between *perceived risk* and *actual risk*.

3.5 ACTUAL AND PERCEIVED RISK AND BUBBLES

Endogenous risk is relevant when individuals not only observe and learn what is happening in the environment around them but also react to what they observe, and thus affect their operating environment. By exerting a significant price impact, market participants change their environment. This means that the financial system is not invariant under observation.

By incorporating endogenous risk, we quickly arrive at situations whereby we cycle between virtuous and vicious feedbacks. When things are good, we are optimistic and buy, which endogenously increases prices, with a bubble feeding on itself. This eventually goes into reverse, and negative news feeds on falling prices, with the markets spiralling downwards.

This manifests itself in the difference between the risk reported by most risk forecast models – perceived risk – and the actual underlying risk that is hidden but ever present. As a bubble is building up, perceived risk is low and falling, whilst actual risk is increasing. After the bubble bursts, prices will not continue falling so actual risk falls, but because observed volatility increases, so does perceived risk. We illustrate this phenomenon in Figure 3.8.

Consider first the evolution of prices, shown by the blue line. They start low and increase at an ever more rapid rate, peaking around period 13, after which they collapse and remain thereafter constant. This is typical of a bubble, where we say the *prices go up by the escalator and down by the elevator (lift)*. We see many examples of such price patterns in this book, just one being the 1987 crisis shown in Figure 3.4.

Perceived risk

The two risk lines are even more interesting. The red line labelled perceived risk shows how market participants view risk when using typical risk forecast models used by the industry. As the prices increase, perceived risk falls.

When market participants observe increasing prices and falling risk they are encouraged to continue buying, an example of a *momentum strategy*. In the short run, this becomes a virtuous cycle of ever increasing prices and lower risk.

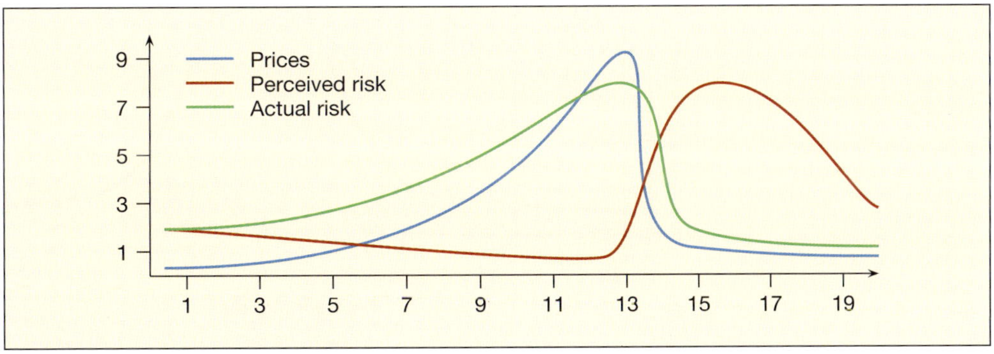

Figure 3.8 Endogenous bubble

Eventually, the bubble bursts. It is as if somebody yells 'the Emperor has no clothes' with traders realising there is nothing fundamental behind these high prices. This prompts them all to sell at the same time, causing prices to collapse. Because the fall in prices makes perceived volatility increase, risk forecast models will report sharply increasing risk.

Actual risk

What happens to the actual risk? We show that in the green line. Actual risk builds up before market prices shoot up, eventually indicating a constant high probability of a crash in the near future. Eventually, as the market collapses, so does actual risk.

This means that perceived risk sends the wrong signals in all states of the world. Before the crisis, it is biased downwards, giving a too optimistic view of the world, and after the main crisis event, it becomes too high, making us too pessimistic. This is one manifestation of pro-cyclicality.

This is one of the main explanations for the phenomenon observed by Andrew Crockett (2000), mentioned earlier:

> 'The received wisdom is that risk increases in recessions and falls in booms. In contrast, it may be more helpful to think of risk as increasing during upswings, as financial imbalances build up, and materialising in recessions.'

Active risk management and empirical predictions

These results have a direct impact on how risk management is generally practised in financial institutions. We can expect banks to become increasingly good at managing day-to-day risk, but at the expense of an increased probability of very large and uncommon outcomes. Borrowing language from the statistical literature on risk modelling, we can say that active risk management may cause *volatility to decrease and the tails to thicken*.

We see a depiction of this in Figure 3.9. The blue line shows what the distribution of market outcomes could be if financial institutions were not actively trying to manage

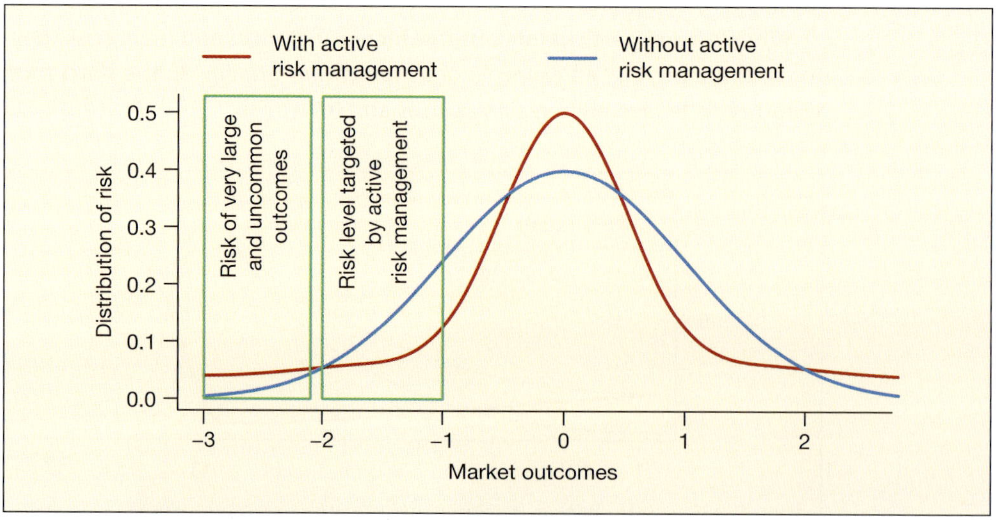

Figure 3.9 Impact of active risk management

day-to-day risk, whilst the red line shows what happens when they do. The impact is to reduce the probability of uncommon events, shown by the red line being below the blue line in the sides of the distribution, but at the expense of the red line being higher in the tails, signalling the higher probability of extreme outcomes. Keep in mind that the area under both functions must be 1 because these are probability distributions.

3.5.1 The crisis from 2007

The causes of the crisis that started in 2007 show many elements of the distinction between perceived and actual risk. The crisis was initially triggered by turmoil in the US subprime market, but quickly spilled over to most other markets, causing a massive wipe-out of wealth across the globe.

Up until 2007, US house prices had been rising relentlessly, as we can see in Figure 3.10, fuelled by low interest rates and an explosion of money coming in because of securitisation. The popularity of the various types of structured credit products ultimately led to a flood of cheap credit and allowed NINJA ('no income, no job, no assets') borrowers to become home owners.

The first sign of an impending problem was noted in February 2007. Moody's put 21 US subprime deals on 'downgrade review', indicating an imminent downgrade on these bonds. This led to a deterioration of prices of mortgage-related products.

As mortgage-related structured credit products fell in price, lenders to the purchasers of these products started to demand higher margins, causing difficulties for many highly leveraged traders, forcing many to sell. This spread, with forced sales depressing prices, leading to more margin calls, and so on. A vicious feedback loop was formed, causing the bubble to burst. Endogenous risk was doing the harm.

One of the implications of a highly leveraged market going into reverse is that a moderate fall in price is unlikely. Prices either remain unchanged or crash. This is because of the mutually reinforcing effects of selling into a falling market, causing a firesale externality.

Figure 3.10 also provides a real-world depiction of the phenomena shown in Figure 3.8, both for prices and especially for perceived risk. Perceived risk – delinquency rates – was very low between 2005 and 2007; meanwhile significant problems were building up in the real-estate market, clearly highlighting the distinction between perceived risk and actual risk.

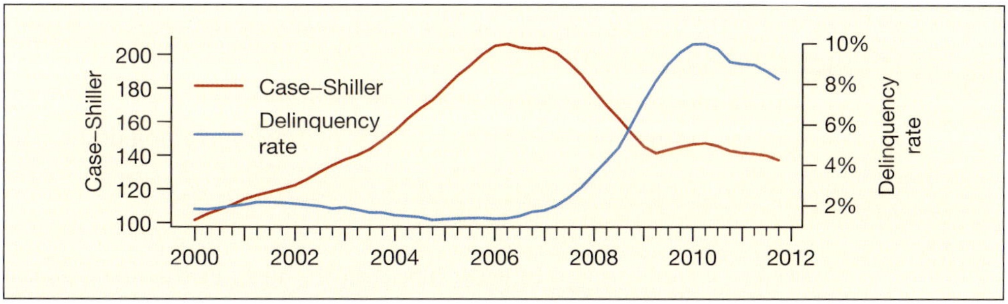

Figure 3.10 US real-estate prices (Case–Shiller index) and delinquency rates

Data source: Standard & Poor (S&P) and Board of Govermors of the Federal Reserve System

3.6 THE LTCM CRISIS OF 1998

One of the most turbulent times in financial markets prior to the recent crisis episodes was the summer of 1998.[3] For a lucid description of events see, for example, Lowenstein (2000).

Long term capital management (LTCM) was the most celebrated *hedge fund* of its time. It was founded in 1994 with illustrious partners such as Myron Scholes and Robert C. Merton of Black-Scholes fame, who shared the 1997 Nobel Memorial Prize in Economic Sciences.

LTCM started with over $1 billion in capital, and was very successful initially in spite of charging exceptionally high fees. A typical hedge fund charges 20% of profits earned plus 1% of an investor's assets as fees. LTCM charged 25% and 2% and investors were required to commit their funds for at least three years.

In the first two years investors received profits of 43% and 41% after fees. $10 million invested in 1994 was worth $40 million four years later. In September 1997, LTCM's net capital was $6.7 billion, leveraged to $126.4 billion. They returned $2.7 billion to investors in December 1997, to focus on investing their own money.

An impression was created that the firm would make extraordinary profits from technical expertise unavailable to anyone else. Myron Scholes summed up the strategy thus:

> 'LTCM would make money by being a vacuum sucking up nickels that no one else could see.'

LTCM operated with high leverage, at around 30. It drove very hard bargains on financing and was able to get low rates and special deals because its *prime brokers* did not want to get left out of LTCM business and were prepared to cut corners both on the rates charged and on the amount of collateral demanded.

Trading strategies

The mainstay of LTCM's trading strategies was convergence or relative value trades, in which a long position in one asset is hedged by a matching short position. The underlying principle is that two fundamentally identical assets should have identical prices, otherwise there is an arbitrage opportunity. Their VaR in 1998 indicated that it would take a 10σ event for it to lose all capital in a single year. Since it makes sense to analyse sigma events only under the normal distribution, this implies a probability of default of 7.6×10^{-23}. By comparison, the Earth is 4.5×10^{9} years old and the Universe is 1.3×10^{10} years old.

LTCM's very success attracted copycats. As more and more players with similar trading strategies crowded into the market, spreads narrowed, eroding profit margins.

---

[3]The events are well summarised in two official reports by the Bank for International Settlements (BIS) (Committee on the Global Financial System, 1999) and the International Monetary Fund (IMF) (1998). The first is at www.bis.org/publ/cgfs12.htm, and the second in Chapter III of www.imf.org/external/pubs/ft/weo1298/index.htm.

Central bank of volatility

By 1998, LTCM took large positions in areas such as merger arbitrage and short options on the S&P index. In other words, they were net short of the S&P volatility, that is the VIX index, seen in Figure 3.11.

The long-run average VIX until the middle of 1998 was 17%, and as we see in Figure 3.11(b), the VIX exceeded that level throughout 1998.

Note that the statistical properties of volatility are different from those of some other financial instruments, such as stock prices or exchange rates, because it is unlikely that volatility will become very low or very high, at least not for any appreciable amount of time. In other words, volatility is *mean reverting*.

With volatility much higher than the long-run mean, it was quite likely that one could make money by betting on mean reversion, exactly what LTCM intended, becoming a major supplier of S&P 500 vega.[4] In order to make significant profits, LTCM needed very high degrees of leverage.

A perfect storm

In May and June 1998 fund returns were −6.42% and −10.14% respectively, reducing LTCM's capital by $461 million. This was further aggravated by the Russian financial crises in August and September 1998, when the Russian government defaulted on their government bonds on 17 August. This triggered a panic: investors sold Japanese and European bonds to buy US

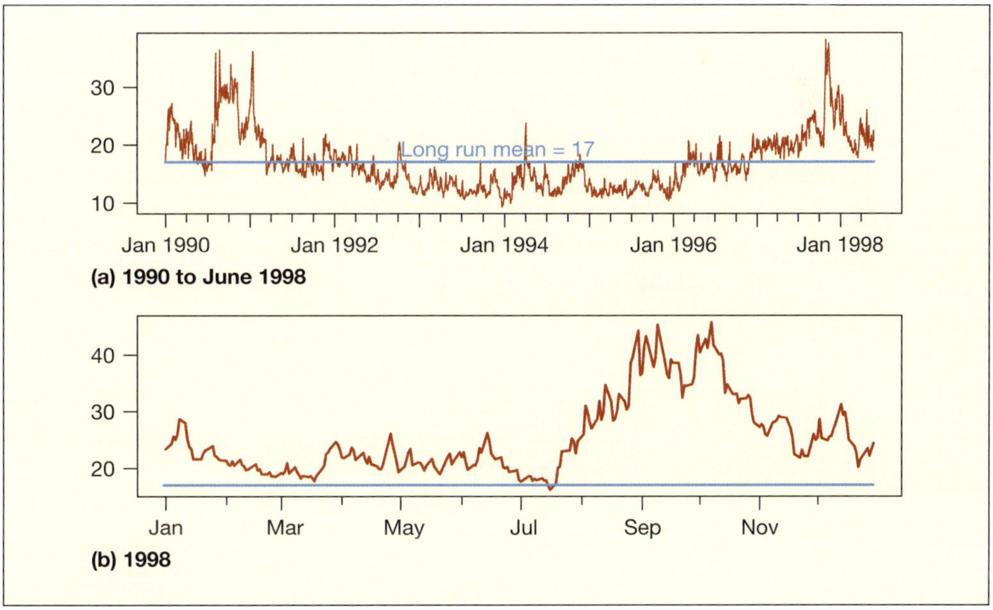

Figure 3.11 VIX

[4]Vega is the sensitivity of the Black–Scholes price of an option with respect to volatility, that is, the first derivative of the Black–Scholes equation with respect to volatility.

Treasury bonds (flight to quality), and hoped-for profits from convergence trades became large losses, as the value of the bonds diverged. Meanwhile, credit spreads widened, volatility shot up to 45%, and correlations went to 1, as usually happens in crises.

In the first three weeks of September, LTCM's equity tumbled from $2.3 billion to $600 million, leading to a sharp increase in its already high leverage, further increasing its fragility. Eventually, it had to unwind the convergence trades, sell the long positions, and buy back the short positions. This caused an adverse price shock for all other traders with similar positions and for some triggering margin calls. A vicious feedback loop was set in motion in which adverse price moves led to liquidations, which further fed adverse price moves. Schematically, this can be seen in Figure 3.12.

Realising the potentially disastrous consequences of letting LTCM fail, the New York Federal Reserve Bank (NYFed) organised a bailout of $3.625 billion by the major creditors of LTCM to avoid a wider collapse in the financial markets. In return, the participating banks got a 90% share in the fund and a promise that a supervisory board would be established. After the bailout, the panic abated, and the positions formerly held by LTCM were eventually liquidated at a small profit to the new owners.

Analysis

What befell LTCM was a classic example of endogenous risk. The owners of LTCM maintained that it was quite safe as perceived risk was low. Investors could expect losses in excess of 20% in one year out of 50.

One LTCM partner said that 'what happened to LTCM was a perfect storm – a 100-year flood'. But does that stand up to scrutiny? The endogenous risk analysis above suggests otherwise: the unprecedented price movements in the summer of 1998 were not the results of extremely bad luck, in the same way that the Millennium Bridge did not wobble because of bad luck. Instead, it was only a matter of time before a small exogenous shock would hit LTCM, triggering its failure. Once the bubble started collapsing, the internal dynamics of the feedback loop took hold with a vengeance. Under the right conditions, the crisis was a near certainty, with endogenous risk doing the harm, because of the endogenous feedback loops between margin calls and distress.

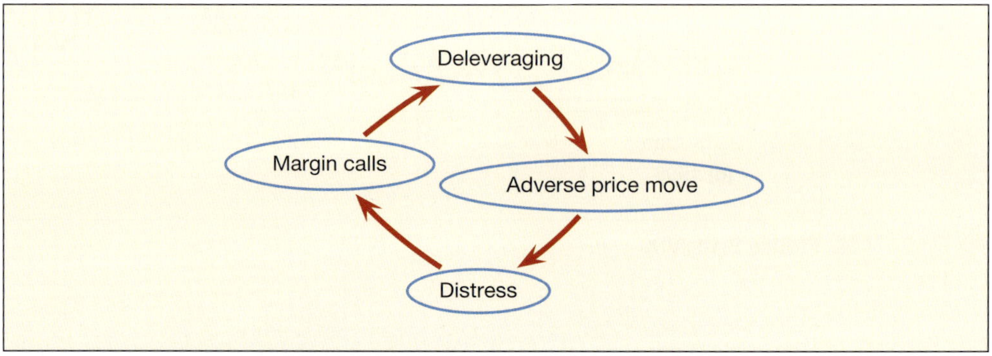

Figure 3.12 The vicious circle of deleveraging and margin calls

Irrationality of markets?

LTCM invested in a mean reverting asset whose value was far away from the long-run mean. We would expect that given time, the VIX would eventually fall, bringing significant profits to LTCM. Indeed, profits were made, but only by those who bailed LTCM out.

So why did LTCM not profit from this? The explanation is provided by an observation often attributed incorrectly to Keynes, who supposedly said 'The market can stay irrational longer than you can stay solvent.' The very high levels of VIX were explicitly caused by the uncertainty created by LTCM's existence. That meant that a necessary condition for the VIX to return to its long-run mean was the failure of LTCM.

3.7 CONCLUSION

Most risk models and pricing models used by the financial industry and financial supervisors assume risk to be exogenous, that is, risk arrives to the markets from outside but is not endogenously generated within the financial system. While this assumption is clearly incorrect, it is usually accepted as a necessary evil because modelling endogenous risk is very hard.

The concept of endogenous risk is not confined to finance. For example, the Millennium Bridge wobbled when it was opened in 2000 because of endogenous feedbacks.

One reason why endogenous feedbacks are so prevalent within the financial system is the constraints imposed on market participants, like leverage constraints. Endogenous risk is also created when a substantial number of market participants mechanistically follow the same trading rules, which is exactly what caused the biggest stock market crash in history in 1987.

The most infamous hedge fund failure in history, that of LTCM, happened because the managers of the fund did not understand the endogenous risk it created, and naively assumed that in essence it could not fail. That led them to take ever more risk, ensuring the fund's eventual failure.

Questions for discussion

1 Define the terms endogenous and exogenous risk, and provide examples of each.

2 The former general manager of the BIS, Andrew Crockett stated in 2000:

> 'The received wisdom is that risk increases in recessions and falls in booms. In contrast, it may be more helpful to think of risk as *increasing* during upswings, as financial imbalances build up, and *materialising* in recessions.'

How does his view on risk relate to endogenous risk, and what is the implication for governments' policies on financial stability?

3 It has been said that financial risk models are least reliable when needed the most. Do you agree?

4 Discuss financial bubbles, considering both prices and risk, from the point of view of endogenous and exogenous risk, using the terminology of actual and perceived risk.

5 To what extent can crisis events from 2007 be explained by the notion of endogenous risk?

6 To what extent is the sovereign debt crisis an endogenous risk story, and to what extent is it not?

7 Suppose a hedge fund operates with four times leverage (assets over equity), where its equity is worth $10 and the current price of the asset it holds is $5.
   (a) Suppose the fund is currently meeting its leverage constraint. How many units of the asset does it told?
   (b) Suppose the price of the asset increases to $6 and the fund is a price taker. How does it respond?
   (c) Suppose instead the fund exerts a price impact, whereby the price of the asset moves by 0.1% of the amount the fund trades. How does it react to the price increase?

References

Black, F. and Scholes, M. (1973b). The valuation of option contracts and a test of market efficiency. *J. Finance,* 27: 399–418.

Brady Commission (1988). Report of the presidential task force on market mechanisms. Technical report, Government Printing Office, Washington DC.

Buffett, W. (2012). Why stocks beat gold and bonds. *Fortune,* 27 February.

Committee on the Global Financial System (1999). A review of financial market events in autumn 1998. Technical report, Bank for International Settlements.

Crockett, A. (2000). Marrying the micro- and macro-prudential dimensions of financial stability. The General Manager of the Bank for International Settlements, www.bis.org/review/rr000921b.pdf.

Danielsson, J. and Shin, H. S. (2003). Endogenous risk. In *Modern Risk Management – a History*. Risk Books, London. www.riskresearch.org.

Danielsson, J., Shin, H. and Zigrand, J.-P. (2012a). Endogenous and systemic risk. In Haubrich, J. G. and Lo, A. W., editors, *Quantifying Systemic Risk*. University of Chicago Press for NBER; www.riskresearch.org.

Danielsson, J., Shin, H. and Zigrand, J.-P. (2012b). Endogenous extreme events and the dual role of prices. *Ann. Rev. Econ., 4*(1): 111–29; www.riskresearch.org.

Danielsson, J., Shin, H. and Zigrand, J.-P. (2012c). Procyclical leverage and endogenous risk. Mimeo, LSE, www.riskresearch.org.

International Monetary Fund (1998). World economic outlook and international capital markets: Interim assessment. Financial turbulence and the world economy. Technical report. www.imf.org/external/pubs/ft/ weo/weo1298/ index.htm.

Keynes, J. M. (1936). *The General Theory of Interest, Employment and Money*. Macmillan.

Lowenstein, R. (2000). *When Genius Failed – the Rise and Fall of Long-Term Capital Management*. Random House, New York.

Minsky, H. (1992). The financial instability hypothesis. Working paper. Mimeo, Yale University.

Shin, H. S. (2010). *Risk and Liquidity. Clarendon Lectures in Finance*. Oxford University Press.

4 LIQUIDITY

Liquidity is essential for the functioning of the economy. It increases the efficiency of markets, makes individual assets more attractive to investors, enables financial institutions to withstand maturity mismatches and gives central banks the ability to conduct monetary policy. Unfortunately, liquidity is transient and has a tendency to evaporate suddenly.

It is quite easy to miss the importance of liquidity. When it is ample, which is usually the case, markets function well. Herein lies a hidden danger. When market participants and governments take liquidity for granted, they assume more risk than is prudent. This means that over time hidden liquidity risk builds up. Eventually, the risk becomes so high that a crisis is inevitable. When it finally happens, liquidity becomes of paramount importance. Unfortunately, when liquidity hits the newspaper headlines it is too late: a crisis is already under way.

It is easier to talk informally about the importance of liquidity than to formally conceptualise it, making it hard to measure and manage. Many a disagreement has arisen because different problems are analysed under the mistaken assumption that they are the same. This is no wonder, since the notion of liquidity is elusive and poorly understood both in the economic literature and by practitioners.

Links to other chapters

Several other chapters expand on the various aspects of liquidity in much more detail, for example Chapter 3 (endogenous risk) and Chapter 14 (bailouts), whilst some chapters draw directly on concepts introduced here, especially the various crisis-focused chapters like Chapter 6 (the Asian crisis of 1997 and the IMF), Chapter 17 (the

ongoing crisis: 2007–2009 phase) and Chapter 19 (sovereign debt crises). Liquidity also impacts on the ongoing developments in financial regulation as described in Chapter 18.

Key concepts

- **Market liquidity and funding liquidity**
- **Limit order markets**
- **Feedback loops**
- **Cash-in-hand pricing**

Readings for this chapter

The most commonly used notions of liquidity are based on the Basel Committee on Banking Supervision (2006). Two early influential papers on liquidity are Allen and Gale (1994) and Kyle (1985), whilst recent analysis, taking into account the crisis from 2007 and endogenous risk, are Brunnermeier and Pedersen (2009) and Danielsson *et al.* (2012b).

Notation specific to this chapter

Q **Quantity (units of assets held)**

4.1 THE LIQUIDITY CRISIS OF 1998

By the mid-1990s the world's main financial markets had shown considerable stability for quite some time. There had been crises, but they mostly involved falling asset prices, such as in 1987 or happened in developing countries, for example, in Asia in 1997. Then the unthinkable happened in the autumn of 1998, when liquidity in the world's most mature markets suddenly collapsed. The then Chairman of the Federal Reserve System (Fed), Alan Greenspan, stated that 'we do not as yet fully understand the new system's dynamics'. We follow the story as told by Davis (1999).

Chain of events

From the mid-to late 1990s, the bond and equity markets of the United States (US) experienced a long bull run, growth was steady and inflation low. This was sometimes referred to as '*a new era of high productivity*', a phrase that was echoed a decade later in the '*great moderation*'. Spreads were falling, and the issuance of debt securities saw strong growth, reflecting a move away from more traditional bank lending.

The Asian crisis which started in July 1997 had initially little effect on OECD countries until it become apparent in July 1998 that recovery would take longer than expected. Banks with exposure to the Asian markets saw their share prices drop and corporate bond spreads widened in the first half of August 1998 on concerns about US growth, a sign of the impending flight to quality and liquidity.

The trigger for a major crisis was when Russia declared a moratorium on its sovereign debt and devalued the rouble on 17 August. This accelerated the repricing of emerging market risk and led to large-scale *deleveraging*. A flight to quality caused yields on

US government bonds to fall and spreads on less safe bonds to increase, reaching an eight-year peak. Figure 4.1 reveals how sudden these events were; issuance of new debt fell from $228 billion to negative $156 billion, signalling very severe and rapid deleveraging.

It was then that LTCM ran into trouble. The uncertainty created by its pending collapse, and the resulting impact on the markets, triggered a global collapse in liquidity which was the motivation for its bailout, organised by the New York Federal Reserve Bank (NYFed).

The stable pre-crisis environment resulted in low *margin requirements* and the increase of *leverage*. It was not surprising, therefore, that highly leveraged investors suffered heavy losses during the crisis. They had to meet margin calls, further aggravating the crisis, in an example of an *endogenous risk feedback loop*.

A clear example of the liquidity problems can be seen Figure 4.2 which shows the rapid increase in spreads as the crisis unfolded. This parallels the impact on volatility (VIX) we saw in Figure 3.11. The crisis spread to even supposedly safe assets, like US Treasuries, as investors cared only about investments that could be monetised quickly. This rejection of even the safest of assets is a typical characteristic of liquidity crises.

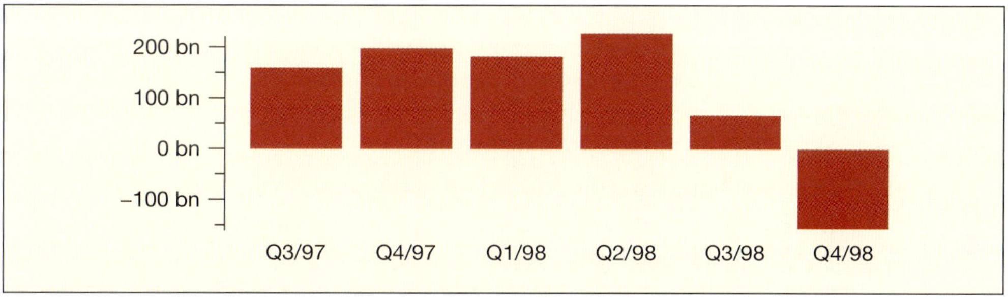

Figure 4.1 **Net funds raised in US capital markets, USD billions**
Data source: US Flow of Funds

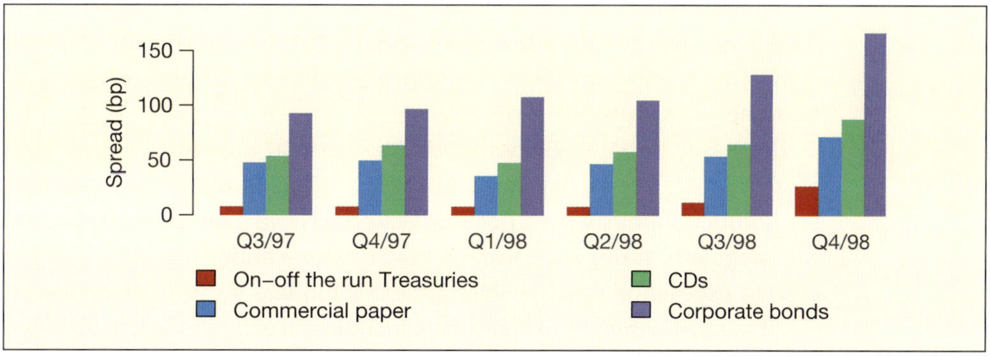

Figure 4.2 **Spreads of various debt instruments (b_p = basic point, one-hundredth of a percentage)**
Data source: Bank for International Settlements (BIS)

As the International Monetary Fund (IMF) (1998) noted, '... markets became one-sided until prices declined enough to bring buyers back ...'. The *Wall Street Journal* reported that market makers 'cut back on the size of the trades, quoted wider bid–offer spreads or did not quote at all' (as noted by Davis, 1999), further contributing to the general illiquidity.

The crisis finally ended when LTCM collapsed and the Fed, along with other major central banks, lowered interest rates, increasing liquidity. The pace of recovery did surprise many commentators at the time. However, for a pure liquidity crisis, where no productive resources are destroyed, that is to be expected.

Analysis

The 1998 liquidity crisis highlights the common features of all liquidity crises, and many a banking crisis. Securities markets usually help investors and borrowers to engage in maturity transformations and help in ensuring against idiosyncratic liquidity shocks. One criterion in investors' decisions is based on the convertibility of assets into cash, that is liquidity. The more liquid an asset, the less it yields, other things being equal. If investors fear a liquidity crisis, their rational response is to sell before anybody else. If everybody thinks the same, the result is a rush to sell, ending in a crisis.

Before a crisis, financial institutions often seem to assume that liquidity is infinite, that they can always execute their trading strategies and borrow what is needed. Unfortunately, these assumptions hold only when things are good, at the time when increasing prices create an illusion of credit-worthiness, resulting in seemingly infinite liquidity. However, during crises, such virtuous feedback loops suddenly turn vicious, causing distress.

Why did the safeguards not work?

The 1998 liquidity crisis was typical of liquidity crises, just like those of 1914 and 1863 and many others. These crises have the same underlying fundamental cause – liquidity – even if the details differ. After every crisis there is a clamour for safeguards preventing future crises, often ineffectively, as the next crisis takes new forms. This does not mean that the safeguards do not work: we do not see the successes, only the failures. After 1998 new extensive crisis prevention mechanisms were put in place, though it took only nine years for the next liquidity crisis to occur.

Fighting crises is like fighting bacteria. We are able to develop a medicine that fights the parasite in the short run, but eventually the bacteria evolve and the medicine becomes ineffective. It is the same with policy: we can prevent the old crises from recurring, but the next one will simply take a new form.

The reason is that regulations look backwards at the causes of previous crises, while the next invariably takes a new form. Market participants seek to take more risk than is considered prudent from society's point of view, and have a direct incentive to find loopholes in the safeguards, taking excessive risk exactly where nobody is looking. Often, it takes a fresh crisis to expose the risk, by which time it is too late to do anything about it. In a way, we could say that designers of financial regulations face the same problems as successful generals who only prepare to fight the last war, whilst the enemy changes the rules of the game.

In this, 1998 was no different. The previous crises facing Europe and the US had been the S&L banking crisis in the US in the 1980s, the 1987 crash and the Scandinavian banking crisis of the early 1990s. Regulators worked to prevent those from happening again, for example, by further developing *prudential regulations* and in the US *prompt corrective action*.

The 1998 crisis happened elsewhere. It was a conjunction of several events, most importantly the Asian crisis, the Russian crisis and LTCM. Therefore, it is not surprising that decision makers were caught off guard. Once the problem was identified, the NYFed acted decisively and correctly to address the problem.

This left us with the view that the next crisis would involve hedge funds. Many safeguards to prevent hedge fund crises were put into place, and the role of the *prime broker* (the hedge fund bankers) was beefed up. However, the crisis that started in 2007 happened elsewhere, in the most regulated part of the financial system, banking, which had been thought to be kept safe thanks to the Basel Accords.

4.2 WHAT IS LIQUIDITY?

There is no single answer to this question. Those concerned with liquidity often focus on one particular aspect of it, at the expense of the overall picture. This may happen because liquidity takes many different forms and different pundits may use very different language when talking about essentially the same concept, perhaps appearing to strongly disagree while fundamentally having the same view.

4.2.1 Funding liquidity and market liquidity

Currently, most discussion of liquidity follows the Basel Committee for Banking Supervision (BCBS) in 2006, which indirectly defined liquidity by means of liquidity risk, decomposed into two interrelated parts.

Definition 4.1 Funding liquidity and market liquidity ***Funding liquidity risk*** is the danger that a firm may be unable to obtain the cash it needs to maintain smooth operation of its business activities.

Market liquidity risk describes the possibility of being unable to reverse or eliminate a position in the securities markets without significantly and adversely affecting the price.

Funding liquidity refers to the ready availability of cash to finance day-to-day operations, and market liquidity to the ease of buying and selling securities at a fair price.

These two notions of liquidity are of course highly interdependent. When things are going well, cash is ample and trading is easy, whilst during market turmoil and especially crises, financial institutions simultaneously will find access to cash curtailed and trading difficult. Therefore, market liquidity and funding liquidity impact on each other, either virtuously or viciously.

Regardless, policy initiatives directed at liquidity often focus exclusively on funding liquidity, ignoring market liquidity. One reason is that risks associated with funding illiquidity have been acknowledged for several hundred years, but market liquidity is a newer topic and perhaps harder to understand.

4.2.2 Distinction between illiquidity and insolvency

In the analysis of liquidity, it is important to identify the distinction between *insolvency* and *illiquidity*. A firm that is insolvent is bankrupt. It owes more money than it has assets, assets minus liabilities are negative and all capital has been exhausted. Generally, banks are closed down long before this happens. If a bank gets close to hitting its regulatory 8% capital adequacy ratio (CAR), warning bells are likely to ring with the supervisor who then takes action.

Illiquidity is where assets minus liabilities are positive, but the bank does not have enough liquid assets on hand to pay off creditors. In the simple case of a bank collecting demand deposits and making long-term loans, if enough depositors demand their money at the same time and the bank is unable to monetise the assets quickly enough, the bank faces an illiquidity crisis, which could trigger its failure, even if it is not technically bankrupt. The reason is that if a firm fails to meet a single payment, all of its obligations might be considered in default, perhaps because of *pari passu* clauses.

Illiquidity means that banks cannot raise cash by selling assets, because they cannot get acceptable prices in the short run. In a clear liquidity case, it should be possible to set a timescale in weeks or months for the required sales to be implemented and the cash raised. In a clear insolvency case, the market value of a bank's aggregate asset holdings is below the cash it needs, even before sales are attempted. Naturally, many cases fall in between.

In practice, it can be difficult to distinguish between illiquidity and insolvency. Suppose a country is facing a financial crisis and one of its banks is in difficulty. Before the crisis, this bank was considered very solid, with no visible problems. However, it has the same fragility as all banks, such as significant maturity mismatches. During the crisis, it needs to meet demands for cash, but because of the crisis it finds it is much harder to monetise its assets, and the bank may only be able to get *firesale* prices for them. This could even apply to assets that are otherwise safe, like government bonds. Is this bank insolvent or only illiquid? It depends on whether the value of the assets is low because of special circumstances during the crisis or because they were just overvalued before and now are getting to more realistic valuations. It is often impossible for the authorities to make a distinction between insolvency and illiquidity in real time when fighting a crisis.

If the authorities believe that the only issue is one of liquidity, then supporting their banking system is a natural decision; support can be given on a temporary basis, and the money lent can be recouped later when pricing returns to normal. With insolvency, however, the costs will be greater because the difference between assets and liabilities will not be recoverable.

4.2.3 Funding liquidity

Of the two notions of liquidity, the more traditional and straightforward is funding liquidity. It relates to the availability of funds, both for individual financial institutions and also for the financial system as a whole.

Funding liquidity and crises

Funding liquidity risk often arises because of maturity mismatches, for example, when a bank borrows short term and lends long term. This could arise in traditional banking operations where banks collect demand deposits and make long-term loans, but could happen just as easily in most funding models.

An economy that suffers from a scarcity in funding liquidity is usually also experiencing a sharp reduction in money supply – reduction in liquidity – arising from fractional reserve banking and how M0 gets converted into M1 and M2. Because of the money multiplier, if the financial system is deleveraging – converting fewer liquid assets such as bonds into cash – the money supply contracts sharply, with adverse consequences for the real economy.

During such crisis episodes, there are often calls for liquidity injections by central banks, perhaps in the form of temporary increases in the money supply by means of open market operations, interest rate reductions, direct lending to financial institutions in the interbank market, lending of last resort (LOLR) or direct bailouts.

A similar problem arising from liquidity happened in the Asian crisis of 1997. Several countries of East Asia had resorted to short-term borrowing from international capital markets to finance longer-term domestic investment. Eventually, a lack of confidence caused the creditors to refuse to roll over loans, triggering a crisis.

4.2.4 Market liquidity

The second notion of liquidity, market liquidity, is less well understood and refers broadly to the ease of buying and selling financial instruments. If one is able to buy or sell infinite amounts of an asset in financial markets at the same price at any time, that asset can be said to be perfectly liquid. Of course, no such asset exists in the world, even though many come close, at least enough for the needs of all but the very largest entities.

Increasing importance of market liquidity

Market liquidity has gained more attention over time. Banks are increasingly active in securities markets, involved in not just underwriting and issuance, but also trading, market making and providing backup credit lines to clients. Therefore, if the market becomes illiquid, banks suffer losses on both their positions and market-making activities, and depositors may lose confidence and *run the bank*. The popularity of *securitisation* has also led to a greater dependence on liquidity. One example is the funding difficulties experienced by many banks in 2007. Non-financial companies may also depend on markets for funding, providing a direct channel from liquidity crises to the real economy.

Moreover, the rapid growth of the derivatives markets has also raised concerns because of its particular susceptibility to liquidity risk. Over-the-counter (OTC) derivatives are illiquid by definition, as they are bespoke instruments. More crucially, many banks use derivatives such as swaps and options for risk management and hedging. A lack of liquidity not only exposes banks to significant risk, but also increases the possibility of other counterparties refusing to trade, spreading the illiquidity further afield.

4.2.5 Limit order markets

A key ingredient in the concept of market liquidity is *price impact*. If we sell an asset, its price drops, and if we buy the asset, the price increases. This is clearly seen in markets using *limit order books*, which includes most actively traded assets. A limit order market is a computer system where traders can make two types of trades, *limit orders* and *market orders*.

Definition 4.2 Limit order A ***limit order*** is an order that specifies an offer to buy or to sell the security, the volume to be bought or sold and a price at which to execute a transaction.

Definition 4.3 Market order A ***market order*** specifies buying or selling immediately at the best price.

Market orders usually execute immediately upon entry, provided there are existing limit orders in the system. By contrast, limit orders are executed only if they are hit by a market order.

There is not a single price for a security in limit orders markets, but two: one price at which you can buy a security, called the *ask* or *offer*, and another, lower price at which you can sell the security, called the *bid*.

Almost all exchanges now use limit order books. This includes assets such as foreign exchange, equities and many of the more common forms of derivatives. A more traditional form of exchanges uses a market maker, but this is becoming less common over time.

It is perhaps best to explain the mechanics of limit order books by means of an example.

We see from the example that a sufficiently large market order will exhaust the supply of limit orders at that particular price, causing the price to move, an example of a *price impact*. As is apparent from Figure 4.3, the price impact for an order of a given volume

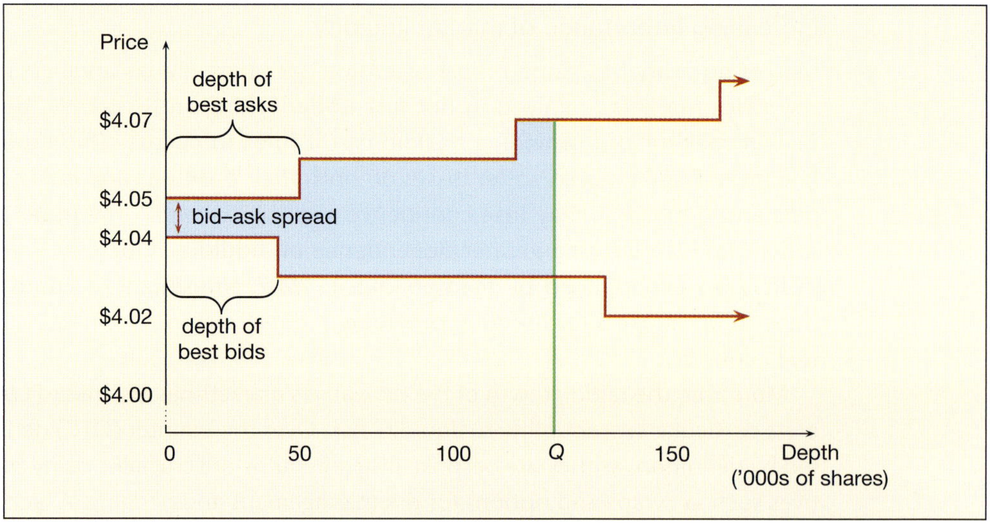

Figure 4.3 Market depth in a limit-order book. The figure depicts the depth of the top of the book for shares of Citigroup on the BATS Exchange, 08:10 EDT, 21 July 2010

EXAMPLE 4.1 Citigroup

Figure 4.3 shows the limit order book for Citigroup at one point in time in 2010. The available limit buy at the best bid totals 35,000 shares at \$4.04, whilst sell orders at best equal 41,800 shares at \$4.05. More shares are available at inferior prices.

The figure shows the amount of shares available at particular prices, and the figure can be interpreted as showing the excess supply and demand curves for Citigroup.

A market bid received should execute at \$4.04 and the next market ask received should have executed at \$4.05. We could write 'did' instead of 'should' if we knew that the next market ask was for a volume of 41,800 shares or fewer and the next market bid was for 35,000 or fewer shares, and additionally that the next market orders arrived before the composition of the book changed as traders cancelled their outstanding limit orders.

For example, a large market ask order for $Q = 120{,}000$ shares would execute against the best outstanding limit asks to a total of 120,000 shares. In the situation shown in Figure 4.3, where Q is marked with a vertical green line, this would be 41,800 shares at \$4.05, then 66,500 shares at \$4.06, and finally 11,700 shares at \$4.07. After the order executes, the best asks would be priced at \$4.07.

The best bids would be unaffected, so the spread would have widened from 1 cent to \$4.07 – \$4.04 = 3 cents. Similarly, a market bid order for $Q = 120{,}000$ shares would drop the best bid to \$4.03 and widen the spread to 2 cents.

is lower in markets with higher volumes of limit orders outstanding, and with larger volumes at and near the current best bids and asks – that is, price impact is smaller in deeper markets.

Market liquidity terminology

In order to better understand how liquidity relates to financial markets, many researchers have classified the categories of market liquidity in limit order markets. Of those, the best known are due to Kyle (1985) (first three in the following list) and Black (1971) (the last in the list):

- **Tightness** is the cost of turning around a trading position in a short period of time. Tighter markets mean lower trading costs.
- **Depth** refers to the size and continuity of the market, in terms of participants and volume of trading. Large orders can be absorbed by deep markets without affecting the price much.
- **Resiliency** refers to the speed with which the market price recovers after being driven away from its intrinsic value by uninformative shocks.
- **Immediacy** refers to the time it takes to find a counterparty, initiate, clear and settle a trade.

Taken together, these notions provide the formal way to understand the various facets of market liquidity in financial markets. For example, if applied to the *quant crisis of 2007*, both depth and tightness sharply fell, because of the large amount of orders on the same side of the market, usually sell, which were unusually large compared to the depth. Similarly, the *investor strike* that commenced in the fall of 2007 signified the near disappearance of depth in asset backed securities (ABS) markets.

4.3 LIQUIDITY MODELS

A number of important theoretical models of liquidity have been proposed, helping to clarify this elusive concept. Below, we discuss two of the most important liquidity models: the interaction between funding and market liquidity, and cash-in-the-market pricing.

4.3.1 Interdependencies between market and funding liquidity

If only a single financial institution is facing liquidity problems it is usually due to funding liquidity difficulties. The reason is that if the rest of the market is functioning as normal, the institution in difficulty would not face any special difficulties in trading, beyond its own idiosyncratic funding problems. This might be different if the institution was especially large or in a special situation like LTCM. However, when funding liquidity problems are widespread, they invariably imply shortages of market liquidity as well, and vice versa. Market and funding liquidity go hand-in-hand and cannot usually be separated.

Vicious feedback loops

There are several different ways one can capture this interplay between market liquidity and funding liquidity. Just one example comes from Brunnermeier and Pedersen (2009), and another from Danielsson *et al.* (2012b). In what follows, we draw on both strands of the literature.

Consider a leveraged trader subject to *margin requirements*, perhaps a hedge fund or a proprietary trading desk, making large bets on a stock. At the same time, many other traders are actively trading large positions in the same stock. Individually, these traders might not exert that much price impact, but in aggregate they do. In the terminology of endogenous risk, if something unifies their beliefs and constraints, their behaviour becomes harmonised, so in aggregate they will make similar decisions and hence exert a significant price impact.

So long as the market is doing well and prices are increasing, some of these traders will increase their positions whilst others decrease them, because of heterogeneous beliefs, objectives and constraints. Suppose, however, that the market is hit by an exogenous shock. Prices fall, the traders are hit by *margin calls*, and they need to obtain funds to pay the margin, where the only way to do that is by selling the stock. This happens exactly when the price is falling, further amplifying the price collapse.

In other words, the exogenous shock triggers a margin call – a funding liquidity problem. In order to meet the margin call the traders have to sell the stock into a falling market – a market liquidity problem. This in turn leads to more margin calls, triggering more selling, etc. A *vicious feedback loop* is formed between deleveraging and funding problems. These feedback loops are further amplified by client redemptions, as investors have a tendency to redeem from poorly performing funds. Such loops explain much of the quant event of 2007. Figure 4.4 illustrates these mechanisms.

A fundamental result, shown mathematically by Brunnermeier and Pedersen (2009), is that the cumulative effect of a margin spiral coupled with a loss spiral is greater than the sum of their separate effects. This can be seen mathematically by using simple convexity arguments, and intuitively from the flow diagram in Figure 4.4.

4.3.2 Liquidity and asset pricing

A different way to analyse how liquidity affects the price of assets is the mechanism of *cash-in-the-market pricing* proposed by Allen and Gale in a series of papers over the past couple of decades, for example, Allen and Gale (1994, 2005). In their models, markets are incomplete and financial institutions may be forced to sell assets to obtain liquidity. Because the supply of and demand for liquidity is likely to be inelastic in the short run, small aggregate uncertainties may result in large fluctuations in asset prices, which might become so severe that financial institutions are unable to meet their obligations, ending in a crisis.

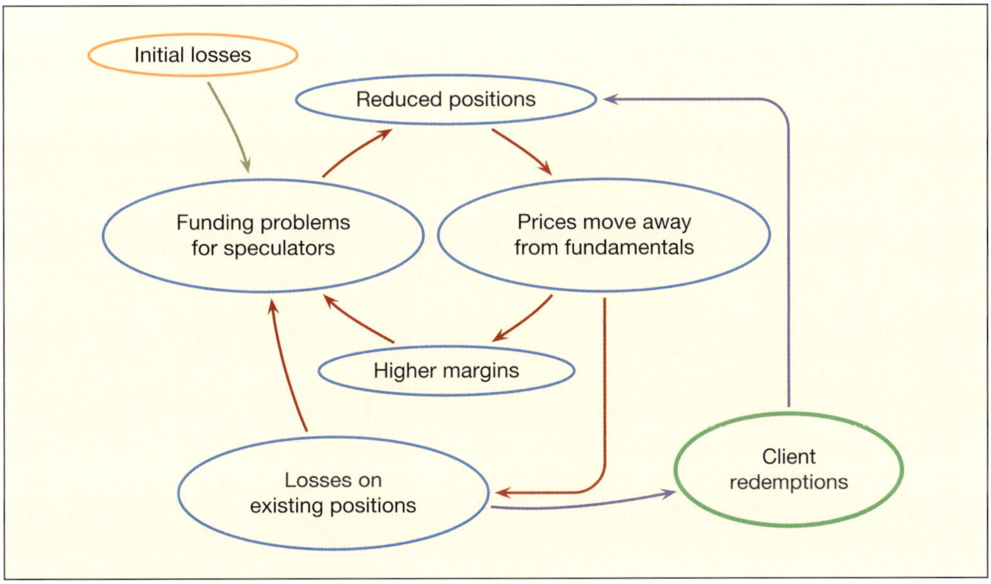

Figure 4.4 Vicious liquidity feedback loops

Source: based on Brunnermeier and Pederson (2009) and further modified

Allen and Gale refer to the relationship between liquidity and asset prices as cash-in-the-market pricing, whereby the price of a risky asset in equilibrium is equal to the lesser of the present discounted value of future dividends and the amount of cash available from buyers divided by the number of shares sold – the cash-in-the-market price. The latter case arises when there is a shortage of liquidity, resulting in assets being underpriced and returns therefore excessive.

If funding liquidity is scarce, the price of cash gets bid up and the price of the risky asset bid down. This could happen, for example, if banks hoard cash because of some precautionary principle. It may even happen with longer-dated government bonds of an AAA-rated government. We have seen this phenomenon in crises past, and it played a key role in the events in the fall of 2008, and with some banks in the European sovereign debt crisis.

One could say that the opportunity cost of holding cash goes down during such crisis episodes. Not only are there fewer investment opportunities, but financial institutions are under risk constraints and thus prevented from increasing their holdings of risky assets, or even longer maturities of safe assets. This creates an endogenous risk feedback loop between falling prices for illiquid assets, preference for cash and difficulties in holding illiquid assets, demonstrated in Figure 4.5.

Taken to the extreme, if everybody wants liquidity (cash), the price of risky assets falls to zero, which in turn creates incentives for some agents to buy those assets, which then puts upward pressures on prices. If the prices increase too much, everybody prefers the risky asset, but then no liquidity is provided, so its price gets bid up. Of course, rational economic agents realise this and, as a consequence, there must be an equilibrium price where the profit in the states of the world with high liquidity demand is sufficient to compensate for all the other states where no profits are made, so that the agents simply bear the opportunity cost of holding liquidity.

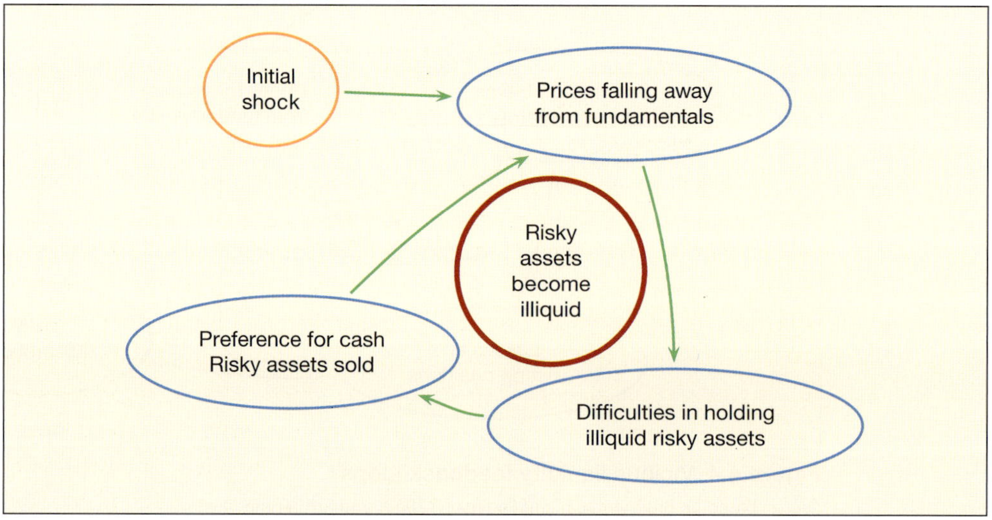

Figure 4.5 Cash-in-the-market pricing

In other words, asset prices are low in states where banks need more liquidity. But this is exactly the wrong time from an efficiency point of view for there to be a transfer from the banks needing liquidity to the providers of liquidity.

Liquidity premium

This suggests that assets should bear a liquidity premium, where liquidity, or the lack thereof, is priced in by the markets. Investors require compensation for taking on liquidity risk when they purchase securities that may later be difficult or expensive to sell. Thus, illiquid securities must offer higher returns than liquid assets.

Several empirical studies have shown that liquidity effects are indeed priced. For example, Acharya and Pedersen (2005) tested their liquidity adjusted CAPM model on portfolios of stocks varying by firm size and found that illiquid stocks – defined as stocks with high average transactions costs – are shown to have high liquidity risk. These results help to explain the higher than expected returns on small-cap stocks and other illiquid investments such as private equity.

4.4 POLICY IMPLICATIONS

Theoretical analysis of liquidity suggests that small changes in funding conditions, or liquidity demand, can lead to sharp reductions in liquidity, and even crisis. This has direct policy implications.

Central banks' liquidity injections

Central banks have a direct role in mitigating market liquidity problems by breaking the vicious feedback loop between market and funding liquidity, preventing a relatively small event from spiralling into a full-blown crisis. They can do that by boosting market participants' access to funds during a liquidity crisis, or by simply stating their intention to provide extra funding during times of crisis, which in turn loosens margin requirements and other constraints.

The liquidity provision needs to be substantial, because if the authorities can only credibly promise to provide some finite amount of liquidity, that might by itself provide enough comfort to market participants to ensure that they build up sufficiently large imbalances so as to exceed the amount of liquidity provided by the authorities. In other words, an insufficient liquidity guarantee may perversely create incentives for traders to worsen a crisis. This suggests that the guarantees may have to be infinite.

However, we do not know what that means. The most obvious way a government can provide infinite guarantees is by printing infinite amounts of money, leading to hyperinflation. Another way is to make the guarantee uncertain enough to prevent the changes in behaviour from causing a self-fulfilling crisis event – often referred to as *constructive ambiguity*. In other words, a policy that is too explicit might be counterproductive.

The insufficiency of the IMF facilities in the Asian crisis, and the ineffectiveness of the seemingly colossal funds promised in the European sovereign debt crisis' demonstrates the importance of magnitude and credibility of the liquidity provision.

Moral hazard problems

Central bank liquidity provisions have to be made reluctantly and be of very short term, otherwise market participants may take them for granted, creating *moral hazard* and making the central bank the *liquidity provider of first resort*. If the financial industry starts to rely on the central bank for day-to-day funding, it creates dependency problems that are very difficult to break. We see a clear example of this in the European sovereign debt crisis, when the European Central Bank (ECB) is increasingly the only liquidity provider to some banks and even entire national banking systems.

4.4.1 Liquidity and the crisis from 2007

Prior to 2007, financial regulation focused on credit risk and market risk, with liquidity risk taking a distant secondary role. The reason was that liquidity crises were considered infrequent and financial markets efficient providers of liquidity, whilst the nebulous nature of liquidity made it quite challenging to translate justifiably high-level concerns about liquidity into hands-on regulations. Since liquidity was not a priority and the problem was hard, it got neglected. After all, the architects of financial regulations are constantly being pulled into many directions by the various stakeholders, and liquidity seemed relatively unimportant.

With the crisis this view has changed significantly. Liquidity is of a first-order priority to policymakers, and researchers have made significant contributions in understanding the nature of liquidity.

Regulations

In the ongoing reform of financial regulations, especially Basel III, liquidity is for the first time an integral part of international regulation, in the form of the net stable funding ratio (NSFR) and the liquidity coverage ratio (LCR). These aim at bringing the funding needs of banks more in line with their outflows, both with maturity matching liabilities and assets and ensuring that banks have sufficient liquidity to withstand a short-term liquidity dry-up.

Macro-prudential policies

Liquidity is at the heart of what makes systemic crises different from more routine market turmoil. This arises when all financial market participants – not only the banks – withdraw all possible liquidity from the market. In today's highly integrated economy, that is extremely grave.

The challenges in mapping out the financial network mean that even though it is clearly necessary to consider network effects when formulating macro-prudential policy, it is less clear how the immense complexity of the interconnections can be handled in practice. The challenge for the supervisor is that in order to adequately address concerns about liquidity, not only do they have to collect more and better information about the amount of risk taken by financial institutions individually, but more importantly they need to consider the impact of aggregate positions across the financial system. They further have to take into account factors that may lead to heavy selling as a response to a small exogenous shock.

Many initiatives have been launched for the purpose of mapping out the network infrastructure of the financial system, with all major supervisory agencies, various partnerships between public and private entities, private institutions and academic researchers all working on this problem. This is not an easy task. Interbank exposures, followed by lender/borrower relationships, are probably clearest and easiest to map out, though true exposures are obscured by collateral and contingent liabilities. Supervisors are able to get access to every financial transaction made, including quantity and prices and names of counterparties, and some preliminary steps have been made in making use of this information in network analysis. It is, however, not sufficient to look at direct exposures, because market participants have to make decisions about the creditworthiness of other financial institutions, even those to which they have no direct link. These decisions may influence how reputation is perceived by third parties. This is the problem that was analysed in Figure 1.8.

4.5 SUMMARY

Liquidity is essential for the functioning of financial markets. Because the financial system works best when liquidity is ample, it is easy to take it for granted, only to miss it during crises. One reason is that liquidity is a complicated and multifaceted concept, with no single understanding of what it is.

The most common high-level notions of liquidity were provided by the BCBS, identifying two interrelated facets: funding liquidity and market liquidity. The former relates to the availability of cash to the markets and the second to the ability to trade. These are highly interrelated and their disappearance during crisis is often caused by feedback effects from one to the other. That gives rise to policy actions cutting the feedback loops. Liquidity directly affects the pricing of financial assets, which can be demonstrated by cash-in-the-market impacts.

Liquidity has a direct impact on government policy, for example, LOLR provision by central banks, but carries with it problems of moral hazard. Liquidity has become a priority since 2007, and many initiatives have been launched trying to understand it and incorporate it into macro-prudential policies.

Questions for discussion

1. Why is it so difficult to formally conceptualise the notion of liquidity?
2. Explain what it means when we say that 'liquidity is priced'.
3. Compare and contrast the two notions of liquidity proposed by the Basel committee.
4. What is a limit order book, and how can we think about liquidity from the point of view of limit order books?
5. Describe a mechanism whereby margins and fire selling viciously interact with each other, creating a crisis.
6. How can the supply and demand for an asset move its price away from the fundamental price?

References

Acharya, V. and Pedersen, L. H. (2005). Asset pricing with liquidity risk. *J. Finan. Econ.*, 77: 375–410.

Allen, F. and Gale, D. (1994). Limited market participation and volatility of asset prices. *Amer. Econ. Rev.*, 84: 933–55.

Allen, F. and Gale, D. (2005). From cash-in-the-market pricing to financial fragility. *J. Eur. Econ. Assoc.*, 3: 535–46.

Basel Committee on Banking Supervision (2006). The management of liquidity risk in financial groups. Technical report, pp. 1–25.

Black, F. (1971). Toward a fully automated exchange, part I. *Financial Analysts J.*, 27: 28–35.

Brunnermeier, M. and Pedersen, L. H. (2009). Market liquidity and funding liquidity. *Rev. Finan. Stud.*, 22(6): 2201–38.

Danielsson, J., Shin, H. and Zigrand, J.-P. (2012b). Endogenous extreme events and the dual role of prices. *Ann. Rev. Econ.*, 4(1): 111–29; download from www.riskresearch.org.

Davis, E. P. (1999). A reappraisal of market liquidity risk in the light of the Russian/LTCM global securities markets crisis. Bank of England.

International Monetary Fund (1998). World economic outlook and international capital markets: interim assessment. Financial turbulence and the world economy. Technical report. www.imf.org/external/pubs/ft/weo/weo1298/index.htm.

Kyle, A. (1985). Continuous auctions and insider trading. *Econometrica*, 53(6): 1315–36.

5 THE CENTRAL BANK

The most important single institution in the financial system is the *central bank*, also known as a *reserve bank*. Central banks have a monopoly on the creation of money and hence play a key role in ensuring price stability, as well as ensuring stable macroeconomic conditions and the soundness of the financial system. Even though these objectives are often in conflict with each other, they also lead to the same ultimate objective, succinctly expressed by William McChesney Martin Jr, former head of the United States (US) Federal Reserve System (Fed) who said that the Fed's most important job is 'to take away the punch bowl just as the party gets going'.

Central banks were initially created with a narrow purpose in mind, to help commerce or, as in the case of the United Kingdom (UK), to provide stable war funding. Over time, the roles of the central banks have expanded significantly, they acquired a monopoly on the printing of banknotes, and they have significant autonomy in the setting of interest rates. Most central banks started out as private institutions, but all are now directly controlled by the central government, and most are owned by it.

With the expansion of objectives and power of the central banks, they often find it difficult to reconcile the various tools and objectives. For example, the exercise of financial stability may require significant injections of liquidity into the economy, undermining price stability. Over time, as the nature of the challenges facing the economy has changed, their priorities have shifted. From the second part of the nineteenth century, until 1914, financial stability was the main objective of most central banks as monetary stability was taken care of by the gold standard. During the Bretton Woods era, and until the 1980s, these roles switched and inflation became the main problem facing central banks, with financial stability less important because heavy regulations limited the scope for financial crises.

Eventually, this led to the neglect of financial stability, contributing to the build-up of systemic risk, and the crisis starting in 2007. This, in turn, has made financial stability the main objective of central banks. However, massive injections of liquidity into the financial system in recent years are likely to make monetary policy yet again the main objective of central banks.

Links to other chapters

This chapter directly relates to Chapter 2 (the Great Depression, 1929–1933), Chapter 7 (banking crises) and Chapter 14 (bailouts).

Key concepts

- Quantitative easing
- Open market operations
- Central bank interest rate
- Objectives of central banks
- Independence of central banks

Readings for this chapter

For a good overview of monetary policy, see Lewis and Mizen (2000), and for banking supervision Goodhart and Schoenmaker (1995) and Goodhart (2002). For a discussion of central banks, see www.centralbanksguide.com.

Notation specific to this chapter

a_π, a_γ	Parameters
i_t	Target short-term nominal interest rate
r_t^*	Real interest rate
y_t	Logarithm of real GDP
$\bar{y}_t$	Logarithm of potential output
γ	Money multiplier
δ	Reserve requirement
π_t	Inflation rate (GDP deflator)
π_t^*	Desired rate of inflation

5.1 THE ORIGINS OF CENTRAL BANKS

The formal objective of the various central banks is specified in their governing law or internal regulations. The first central bank, the Swedish Riksbank established in 1668, engaged in collecting deposits, lending and facilitating trade. It pioneered the practice of *fractional reserve banking*, which meant it was susceptible to bank runs. Indeed, it was created out of Stockholms Banco which was the first European bank to print banknotes and collapsed because it printed banknotes on a seemingly unlimited scale.

The Bank of England

The second central bank was the Bank of England (BoE), created in 1694, sometimes referred to in Britain as *the Bank*. It was initially a private bank set up to assist the government with war finance and, in order to facilitate that function, it was endowed with certain privileges such as permission to issue banknotes.

The Bank obtained a monopoly on issuing banknotes in England and Wales in 1844 with the Peel Act, which fixed the amount of notes that could be issued for a given amount of gold, thus preventing an excessive expansion of the money supply. Existing provincial banks could still issue money, with the last bank in England doing so in 1921. This did not apply to banks in Scotland and Northern Ireland where private banks still issue money.

The government retained the power to suspend the Peel Act in case of a financial crisis, which happened a few times, including during the 1914 crisis and the 1866 Overend and Gurney (O&G) crisis. After the 1866 crisis, the Bank's role in lending of last resort (LOLR) was formalised. This can be considered the first modern statutory financial stability function of a central bank.

The BoE was nationalised in 1946 and it now has two main objectives – monetary stability and financial stability. The first entails meeting an inflation target set by the government. Subsidiary to that, the bank is to achieve 'high economic growth in a low-inflation environment'. The UK inflation target is 2% as measured by the consumer prices index (CPI), but has been significantly above the target in recent times.

The Federal Reserve System

Amongst the major economies, the US was unique in the nineteenth century for not having a central bank. While that may not have mattered much most of the time, it was increasingly felt that a central bank was needed during financial crises. Ultimately, it was a severe crisis episode in 1907 that convinced lawmakers of the necessity to establish a central bank. During that crisis, the private sector provided LOLR, in particular, J. P. Morgan. The authorities at the time felt that it would be better for a government agency to have that role rather than a private individual.

As a consequence, the United States established the Fed in 1913. It could not be called a central bank for political reasons. The system is made up of 12 federal reserve banks, with each responsible for member banks located in its area. The best known is the *New York Federal Reserve Bank (NYFed)*. Over time, the Fed's function has evolved and it is now directly under the control of the federal government whilst retaining significant autonomy. It is responsible for monetary policy and financial stability, and is the supervisor for some banks. The formal objective of the Fed is 'to promote effectively the goals of maximum employment, stable prices, and moderate long-term interest rates'.

The ownership structure of the Fed is somewhat convoluted. All nationally chartered banks hold stock in one of the federal reserve banks. These are not regular stocks, since they cannot be sold or traded nor used to exercise control, but provide a dividend of 6%. The remainder of the Fed's profits go to the government. In 2009 over 98% of the dividends went to the government.

5.2 BANKING SUPERVISION

Central banks are sometimes responsible for the supervision of financial institutions, that is the enforcement of financial regulations. Sometimes it is felt that supervision is an integral part of the central bank's core function; at other times it is thought that it should be left to a separate institution. The discussion below draws on Goodhart and Schoenmaker (1995) and Goodhart (2002).

Arguments for separation

The main argument for separating bank supervision from monetary policy is that the combination of the two functions may lead to a conflict of interest between the monetary authority and the supervisory authority. The central bank might desire higher interest rates to fight inflation, while the supervisor is worried about the adverse impact of high interest rates on solvency and the profitability of the financial sector. Similarly, a central bank may want to close a failing bank because of systemic stability concerns, while banking supervisors may want to rescue it to protect depositors. Clearly, the decision on how these conflicts should be reconciled is political and will depend on recent experience.

The cyclical effects of financial stability and monetary policy tend to be in conflict because monetary policy is usually countercyclical, while the effects of regulation and supervision tend to be procyclical.

If the central bank were the sole supervisor, it would need to be in charge of activities quite distinct from its core mission, such as consumer protection. Having the same government agency in charge of many different functions is not efficient and is likely to lead to some being favoured and others neglected. Central banks are already burdened by a multiplicity of conflicting objectives.

Finally, in the situation where a central bank is in charge of supervision, it will also be subject to *reputation risk*, since when banks fail, the supervisor takes the blame, and the credibility of the central bank is dented. This happened to the BoE following the failure of BCCI in 1991. Such reputation risk is inevitable for any supervisor, and since supervisors get blamed for failures but do not tend to get credit for crises prevented, it can make them excessively risk averse. For a central bank that depends on its reputation for competence when it comes to monetary policy, such reputation risk is something it may prefer to do without, and hence the central bank may want to keep supervision in a separate agency.

Maintaining central bank credibility might not be compatible with being in charge of supervision.

Arguments against separation

If the central bank is only concerned with monetary stability, there is no need for supervision to be part of the central bank. However, in reality, central banks will have to engage with financial stability, whether they want to or not, and may be called upon to provide liquidity support to banks.

In order for the central bank to be responsible for financial stability, it needs to have detailed knowledge of the financial institutions within its domain, exactly the type of information provided to supervisors. It might be more efficient, therefore, for the central bank to be in charge of supervision.

As universal banking becomes more common, the same bank may be engaged in very different activities and, therefore, fall under the supervision of several different regulatory agencies. Having a multiplicity of separate supervisors, all crawling over parts of the self same institution, is neither efficient nor cost effective.

EXAMPLE 5.1 The UK and the tripartite regulatory system

In 1998, the incoming government in the UK transferred responsibility for the prudential supervision of commercial banks from the BoE to the newly created Financial Services Authority (FSA). This meant that the UK had a '*tripartite*' regulatory system, which included the BoE, the FSA and the Treasury. However, when the crises started in 2007, the tripartite arrangement was found lacking. It failed to identify the build-up of problems in the financial system prior to the crisis and did not deal adequately with the early stages of the crisis.

A major reason for these failures was that the tripartite arrangement lacked a leadership structure. It gave the Treasury responsibility for maintaining the overall legal and institutional framework, with the Bank responsible for financial stability but without the tools and information needed to carry this out adequately; the tools lay instead with the FSA, which did not bear the responsibility. This meant that nobody was really in charge. The government partially rectified this in 2009, giving the Bank the statutory objective of contributing to the maintenance of financial stability. The Bank took over the FSA's macroprudential role in early 2013.

EXAMPLE 5.2 Supervision in Europe

The situation is more muddled in the euro zone where the European Central Bank (ECB) has responsibility for monetary policy but supervision is primarily under national control. Even though it is generally considered desirable for a central authority to be responsible for supervision within the European Union (EU), or at least the Euro zone, this is difficult given the current political structure of the Union.

The reason is that when a supervisory authority takes action, it often has substantial national implications, potentially reducing revenues (and tax income) or committing large amounts of taxpayers' money. The government agency in charge of the taxpayers' funds is the treasury or the ministry of finance. Under the current EU structure, each country is directly responsible for its own finances, and therefore supervision has to be the purview of the nation state.

This means that the ECB is in the rather curious situation of being in charge of monetary policy, as well as financial stability, but without any supervisory powers. The EU has attempted to partially solve this problem by hosting the new European Systemic Risk Board (ESRB) within the ECB, in principle, providing the necessary information for the ECB to efficiently exercise its financial stability function. However, with supervision in the hands of the nation states, its powers are necessarily more limited than those of other central banks.

The EU is currently aiming to set up a common supervisor in Europe, and eventually a banking union, starting with the single supervisory (SSM).

5.3 MONETARY POLICY

The main day-to-day function of central banks is monetary policy, the control of the supply of money. Monetary policy is either *expansionary*, where a central bank increases the total supply of money in the economy, *contractionary*, when it decreases the money supply, or neutral.

The most commonly used tool for monetary policy is interest rates, but central banks may also use *open-market operations*. A traditional method is *reserve requirements*, but this is now more common in emerging markets. A more recent tool is *quantitative easing (QE)*. Often described as unorthodox monetary policy, it was adopted by the Bank of Japan (BoJ) in response to their problem with deflation after the crisis in the early 1990s. Similar measures have since been adopted by many major banks in response to the crisis from 2007.

5.3.1 Central bank interest rate

The most visible demonstration of monetary policy is the setting of interest rates. A number of different terminologies are used when referring to central bank interest rates and often these can be confusing and even contradictory. Common names include the target rate, the short rate, the risk-free rate and the Fed funds rate. We discuss these in detail in the appendix to this chapter.

The central bank rates determine the overnight risk-free market rate, because it would not be profitable for banks to conduct business at other rates because of the presence of such a large counterparty. The central bank rates affect money supply directly. By increasing the interest rate, banks are more likely to deposit money with the central bank, taking money out of circulation, causing borrowing rates to increase throughout the financial system, and reducing demand and hence money creation.

Interest rates can be raised without limit and so provide an effective contractionary tool under inflationary conditions. The contrary is not true, because deflation would require negative interest rates, something not possible except in special circumstances. That means different tools are needed to combat deflation.

Central banks exercise only limited control over longer maturities, which are based on supply and demand in the bond markets, with inflationary expectations an important ingredient. The central banks' control of interest rates is sometimes compared to holding a string on one end. The central bank can control one endpoint, but the other end of the string does what it wants and intermediate maturities obey only a smoothness requirement.

Taylor rule

Having a monetary policy objective, perhaps a formal inflation target, does leave open the question of how the central bank should meet the objective. One approach is the *Taylor rule*, proposed by Taylor (1993), whereby the central bank sets the nominal interest rates based on changes in inflation, output and possibly other economic variables. Under the rule, the central bank should increase nominal interest rates by more than 1% in response to a 1% increase in inflation. By having a formal rule, a central bank may avoid inefficiencies induced by a discretionary policy. Mathematically, we can state the Taylor rule as:

$$i_t = \pi_t + r_t^* + a_\pi\left(\pi_t - \pi_t^*\right) + a_y\left(y_t - \bar{y}_t\right)$$

where i_t is the target short-term nominal interest rate, π_t is the inflation rate (the GDP deflator), π_t^* is the desired rate of inflation, r_t^* is the equilibrium real interest rate, y_t is an estimate of the logarithm of real GDP, and $\bar{y}_t$ is the logarithm of potential output, obtained by a linear trend. $y_t - \bar{y}_t$ is the *output gap*. The parameters are restricted to be positive, $a_\pi, a_y > 0$, and Taylor (1993) proposed setting them at 0.5.

In general terms, the Taylor rule seeks to apply negative feedback to the economy, increasing rates when either capacity is stretched or inflation is above target and reducing them when the opposite applies. This clearly matches central banks' objectives in qualitative terms, but an important practical problem is the dependence of the rule on quantities that can only be approximated. In particular, GDP is only known with a considerable lag, and is subject to frequent revisions. Even in the long run, GDP is only an approximate measure of the economy.

Many central banks, explicitly or otherwise, use a form of the Taylor rule to set interest rates. It is, however, most suited for very large currency areas, such as the US, because it disregards the impact of interest rates on exchange rates. For much smaller countries, higher interest rates may lead to inflows of *hot money* and *carry trading*.

5.3.2 Open-market operations

Central banks can directly control the supply of money by *open-market operations*. This entails buying or selling securities, normally the debt obligations of the central bank's own government, in the open market. Typically, the counterparties are major banks.

When a central bank buys securities, it pays by increasing the reserve account (a bank's account with the central bank) of the seller's bank. It is not a transfer into the account; rather the central bank simply increases the account balance by some number by *fiat*. Doing so increases the total volume of reserves (money) held collectively by the banking system. This is a modern version of printing money. Similarly, when the central bank sells securities, it deducts the proceeds from the reserve accounts of the buyers, which reduces the total volume of reserves, and hence money.

Expanding or shrinking the total volume of reserves in this way matters because banks can trade reserves among one another or exchange them for other assets. Because the central bank pays only a low rate of interest (often zero) on these balances, any bank that has more reserves than it needs typically will try to exchange them for some interest-bearing asset.

Expansionary open-market operations, when the central bank buys short-dated securities, create a downward pressure on short-term interest rates via two main routes. A direct impact arises because this removes an instrument from the market, increasing their prices and lowering yields. An indirect effect arises because the bank now has cash instead of a security, and hence has a greater capacity to lend, also lowering interest rates.

5.3.3 Reserve requirements

Reserve requirements give the central bank a degree of control over the money supply. Recall Example 1.1:

$$M1 = \gamma \times M0 = \frac{1}{\delta} M0$$

Changes in the reserve requirements, δ, lead to changes in the money multiplier, γ, and the volume of M1 given an amount of M0. Lowering the reserve requirement has a similar effect as an expansionary open-market operation, provided that banks are constrained by reserve requirements. Altering the reserve requirement used to be relatively common, but nowadays most central banks rely on other methods. The main exceptions are in less developed economies, for example Brazil, China, India, Russia and Uruguay. For an example of the Chinese use of reserve requirements, see Figure 5.1.

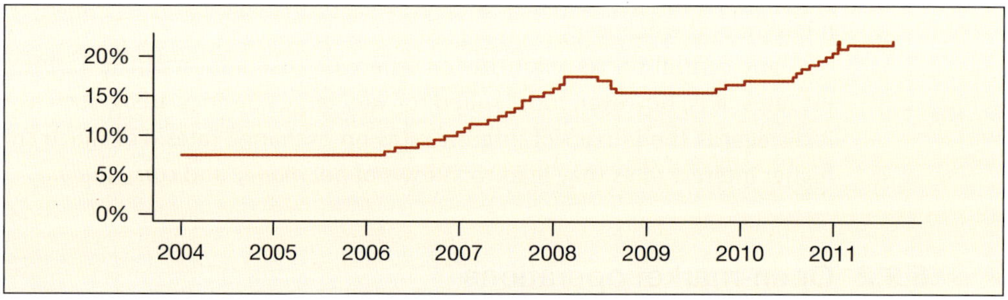

Figure 5.1 Chinese reserve requirments

Data source: The People's Bank of China

5.3.4 Quantitative easing

The monetary policy measures discussed above can be expected to be successful when an economy is not in a recession and inflation is comfortably above zero. If the economy is close to deflation, traditional monetary policy tools may not be effective, because the central bank interest rate cannot be negative, and deflation provides an incentive to banks to hold on to funds and not to lend them out, making open-market operations ineffective. This can be viewed as a form of *liquidity trap*, as illustrated in the following example.

EXAMPLE 5.3 Liquidity traps

John Maynard Keynes (1936) identified the pathological case of liquidity traps, illustrated in Figure 5.2. The supply of money intersects the demand for money (D) on the perfectly elastic part of the demand curve (the flat part to the right), and an increase in money supply from S^1 to S^2 does not therefore change the interest rate. That means a conventional monetary policy is unable to stimulate an economy.

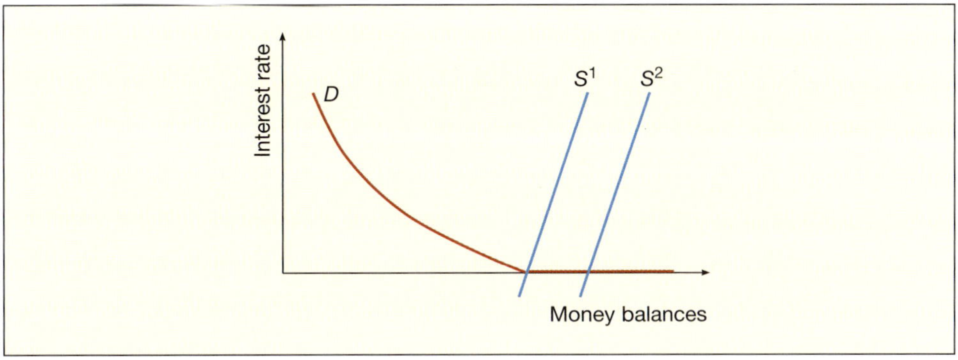

Figure 5.2 Liquidity trap

In order to prevent the economy from sliding into deflation and to provide an economic stimulus, some central banks have resorted to a more direct control of the quantity of money, called *quantitative easing* (QE), to be used when other measures are not successful. Conceptually, open-market operations and QE may seem to be the same, because in both cases the central bank is purchasing assets from banks using money (M0 or M1) it has created *ex nihilo* (out of nothing). In practice, the difference between these two operations is significant, in scale, frequency, asset composition, maturities and motivation. We might say that while open-market operations are a scalpel, QE is more like a sledgehammer.

In QE, the central bank may buy exactly the same assets as in open-market operations, typically short-dated government bonds, but under QE a much broader range of assets may be purchased, including longer-dated securities and even non-government assets, such as corporate bonds. Open-market operations tend to be more frequent and to involve much smaller amounts and shorter maturity assets than QE.

The motivation is also different for open-market operations and for QE. In the former, the explicit objective is to fine-tune the quantity of money, while QE is also presented as a way to stimulate the economy and a means for the central bank to directly support the government financially. The stimulus happens for several reasons, for example, because the increased money supply encourages demand whilst putting downward pressure on exchange rates, helping exporters and the trade balance. The direct support of governments happens because the central banks have become significant purchasers of government bonds in some countries, helping to keep yields and government debt down. Even though central bank holdings of government debt count as much as any other holding of government debt, because the central bank is owned by the government, on a net basis government debt falls when the central bank buys it.

EXAMPLE 5.4 Friedman's helicopter

Milton Friedman proposed an innovative solution to the problem of liquidity traps whereby the central bank bypasses banks and gives money directly to consumers and businesses.

> 'Let us suppose now that one day a helicopter flies over this community and drops an additional $1000 in bills from the sky, . . . Let us suppose further that everyone is convinced that this is a unique event which will never be repeated . . .'
>
> Milton Friedman (1969)
>
> The BoE's QE operations amount to £325 billion at the time of writing, or £5,242 for each of the 62 million people that live in the UK. Instead of buying government bonds, the Bank's QE operations would probably have been much more effective if it had simply sent an envelope with £5,242 in notes to each person in the UK.

5.4 FINANCIAL STABILITY

One of the key functions of central banks is financial stability, even if it is not usually one of their statutory obligations. One reason is that while financial stability has been an integral part of central banking from the beginning, it played a secondary role during the highly regulated Bretton Woods era. It is only with the crises from 2007 that financial stability has again become a core function of central banks. The term itself is not of a recent vintage, originating from the convention establishing the OECD in 1960.

Definition 5.1 Financial stability Financial stability refers to policies aiming to moderate the extremes of financial volatility, prevent crises, contain systemic risk, keep financial markets functioning efficiently and resolve financial crises.

Financial stability ends up being a responsibility of central banks in part by default. Governments need to implement financial stability policies and the only government organisation capable of doing so is the central bank because it is the only entity capable of printing money at will. This also means it is often difficult to separate out the monetary policy and financial stability functions of the central banks. In particular, they often use monetary instruments to implement financial stability and in some cases the particular implementation may be in conflict between either the financial stability or the monetary policy objective.

Implementing financial stability

While the concept of financial stability is broad and touches on many different aspects of policymaking, we can delineate it into three different components: *passive prevention*, *active prevention* and *resolution*.

Passive prevention refers to the prevention of adverse outcomes *ex ante*, by setting up the rules of the game in a way intended to enhance financial stability. This can take many different forms: just to name a few, loan to value ratios, central counterparties (CCPs) and limits on how much a bank can lend to a single counterparty. Some of the clearest examples of passive prevention policies were implemented in the US following the Great Depression and include regulations on buying equities on the margin, the Glass–Steagall

Act keeping the commercial banking separate from investment banking, and rules aiming at minimising liquidity risk in mortgages.

Active prevention relates to policies designed to smooth outcomes in financial markets *in real time*, making sure that regular activity does not get out of hand. Active prevention is intended to be reactive to the situation at hand rather than being an essentially static framework like passive prevention. Examples include rules specifying minimum bank capital and reserves, amount of liquidity or maximum leverage. These are generally based on a dynamic assessment of bank activities, and nowadays may involve sophisticated financial models.

Finally, **resolution** refers to dealing with a crisis already underway – *ex post*. Such policies were first formalised after the O&G failure in 1866 which led to the establishment of LOLR, aiming to provide liquidity to solvent but illiquid banks. Resolution also relates to having a *special resolution regime* for failed banks, such as *prompt corrective action* in the US. Policies like *living wills* and *bail-ins* also fall under this category.

Resolution and passive prevention share in the advantage that the key decisions are made during previous crises, with policies less exposed to shifting priorities than in active prevention.

The introduction of new financial stability tools often follows when the authorities do a postmortem analysis on a crisis. Besides the examples mentioned above, a prominent case is establishment of the Bretton Woods system, especially the World Bank and the International Monetary Fund (IMF).

5.5 BAILING OUT GOVERNMENTS

One of the core functions of central banks is printing money and it is not surprising that governments, upon finding themselves in a spot of financial trouble, resort to money printing as a revenue source – the *central banks bail out the government*.

The obvious way to do this is for the central bank to print money and purchase government bonds. As an emergency device, this is a core function of central banks, but if abused, it leads to inflation and economic difficulties.

A second way for central banks to bail out governments is by creating unexpected inflation and reducing the real value of past borrowing. Of course, for this to be fully effective, the central banks must first invest many years of effort in establishing the strength of their commitment to fighting inflation.

While any government with its own central bank enjoys the benefits of *seigniorage* – revenue from printing money – explicitly using the central bank to finance the government has long been considered a taboo amongst developed economies, that is until the recent crises when several governments, such as those of the US and the UK, have resorted to extensive QE to prop up their economies.

Figure 5.3 shows relative holdings of the Fed and the BoE of government bonds. The ECB has engaged in similar activities but on a much smaller scale, around 2% of GDP. However, it has lent massively to the banking sector and, hence, indirectly to governments.

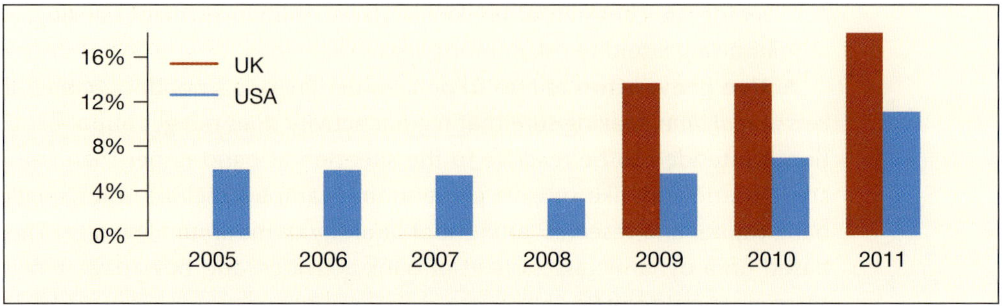

Figure 5.3 Central bank holdings of government bonds relative to GDP, end of year
Data source: Federal Reserve Board, UK Debt Management Office and the World Bank

Pros and cons

Printing money to finance a government is not recommended except in exceptional circumstances. When done as a routine response to an economic downturn, it locks in inflationary expectations and increases government financing costs, ending in instability. When inflation eventually becomes a priority for the central bank, it will find it very costly to fight.

There are special cases, however, where a central bank bailout of governments is justified. If inflation is low during deep recessions and the economy is way below its output potential, printing money to finance the government carries with it two significant benefits: first, it relieves the pressure on the government's budget, and secondly it reverses a contracting money supply.

This should only be done when the economy is below its output potential, because newly minted money will increase demand; if the economy is close to its output potential, the demand will pass directly through to increased prices, whilst if the economy is operating below its output potential, such price increases are much less likely.

5.5.1 The European Central Bank

Bailout of member governments

Printing money is in effect a tax on assets denominated in that currency because of inflation. The assets lose purchasing power and a smaller amount of wealth is transferred to the central bank, the rest being made up of *deadweight loss*. Since the majority of assets are held by domestic agents, printing money can be seen as just a tax like any other, with its particular distributional effects, but where most of the impact is confined to the country. When a central bank buys the debt of its own government with freshly printed money, we can therefore view that in the same light as any other tax.

The situation is more complex in the euro zone because the ECB is the central bank for the 17 countries that are members of the zone. If the ECB only buys the debt of some member countries, it is indirectly subsidising those at the expense of the others. By doing so, the EU takes an important step towards becoming a *transfer union*. That is a major political decision that the Union has been unwilling to make.

That means the ECB has limited legitimacy in its efforts to to fulfil one of the fundamental objectives of a central bank – bailing out its government in times of crisis. This is the reason why the ECB's purchases of European government bonds have been so limited compared to the purchases of the BoE and Fed. Instead, the ECB tries to do its job indirectly, by supplying liquidity to financial institutions, in the hope that it will relieve the pressure on the sovereign. This is not as efficient as using the central bank to bail out the sovereign directly. The ECB signalled change in policy in September 2012, announcing its intention to buy the bonds of distressed European sovereigns. This has run into significant opposition, not least from Germany, and at the time of writing it is unclear what the outcome will be.

Private sector bailouts

If a national central bank bails out financial institutions in its home country, it is understood that this is directly paid for by the people of that country, via either taxes or currency debasement. It is up to the authorities of the country to weigh the pros and cons of such operations.

The situation is different if the central bank is owned by many countries. Bank bailouts by the ECB imply that taxpayers of one country have to support a financial institution in another country. If you feel your banks are sound and well supervised, you might feel aggravated if your money is being used to bail out banks in countries with unsound banks because they are imprudently run and supervised. This means that bailouts by the ECB cannot have as much political support as bailouts by the national central banks. Furthermore, this leaves open the question of who bears the cost. In the extreme case of a central bank going bust because of ill-advised bailouts, who bails the central bank out? In the eurozone the cost would likely be split amongst member governments.

Ownership and operational independence

A national central bank has direct connections to the national government. The governor and board members are generally residents of that country and are appointed by the government. This ties the national central bank close into the power structure of the country. The ties between a multinational central bank and the political superstructure are not as strong. This means the ECB is weaker than national central banks, which can make it easier for the political leaders to use, or abuse, an international central bank to provide bailouts. While this can be prevented by strict rules, it reduces the flexibility of the central bank.

This means that a mutually owned central bank like the ECB might be less effective in its role as a guarantor of financial stability than a national central bank. However, the lack of accountability and independence of the ECB might actually make it more active than a national central bank. With national banks there is always a threat of the government taking control, while with the ECB this is one step removed because treaties make fundamental change a matter of international unanimity, not national vote. This can then make the ECB become a law unto itself. However, it might also make it highly rule and bureaucracy driven, and the same requirement for unanimity restricts and limits its scope for action.

5.6 CHALLENGES FOR CENTRAL BANKING

Central banks often find it difficult to reconcile the various conflicting objectives they have to meet. Traditionally, the main disputes have involved those in charge of the macroeconomic objectives and monetary policy. The former demanded low interest rates to stimulate the economy and the latter high interest rates to prevent inflation. During the 1980s, when the defeat of inflation was a key goal, the debate was settled in favour of monetary policy, which central banks made independent to prevent political interference. More recently, financial stability has become a priority, threatening not only the primacy of monetary policy but also the independence of central banks.

5.6.1 Conflict between financial stability and monetary policy

In the early years of central banking, during the gold standard, monetary policy mostly took care of itself, leaving financial stability as the most important function of central banks. By contrast, in the decades after the second World War (WWII), the financial system was heavily regulated, limiting systemic risk and hence the importance of the financial stability function. Many governments came to rely on a rather unfortunate interpretation of the theories of Keynes, whereby they used monetary policy to stimulate the economy on a more or less permanent basis. The eventual outcome was persistently high inflation and economic stagnation, termed *stagflation*. Conquering the inflation in the 1980s was very painful, leading to the establishment of policies aimed at preventing the re-emergence of inflation. A key element was the doctrine of central bank independence, preventing politicians from manipulating interest rates for election purposes.

This meant that in the 1980s and 1990s monetary policy became the main, and some would say the only, objective of central banks, which generally were in the comfortable position of being able to ignore issues of financial stability. The central banks were content to be in that situation because financial stability operations often require the injection of liquidity or the lowering of interest rates, upsetting the monetary policy objective.

Of course, these objectives may coincide. Economic agents may deleverage during a crisis, converting illiquid funds into liquid cash, resulting in a sharp reduction in the money supply, the end result being deflation. In this case, an increase in liquidity is needed for both the monetary policy objective of meeting a target inflation rate and the financial stability objective of providing liquidity to an economy in distress.

Generally, however, the financial stability objective and the monetary policy objective are quite different. Central bank employees are likely to be specialised in one field or the other, but not both, leading to the danger of silos within central banks, one with the monetary policy staff and the other with the financial stability employees, who may not talk much to each other even if both functions reside within the same institution.

One reason is that we are trying to do two different things with one tool – interest rates. With interest rates fundamental to monetary policy, it would be better for the financial stability policymakers to have access to independent tools, if these can be developed, in order to make it more practicable to pursue both sets of objectives at the same time.

One of the clearest manifestations of how the emphasis is shifted from monetary policy to financial stability and macroeconomic objectives is UK inflation, which has frequently exceeded its annual target rate since the crises from 2007. The risk is the creation of inflationary expectations, which would be costly to eventually fight. It is far from obvious that interest rates could currently be raised without a recurrence of the crisis. With this key lever unavailable it is not clear that a contractionary monetary policy could be effective.

5.6.2 Central bank independence

The financial stability objective of central banks conflicts with the monetary policy objective when it comes to central bank independence. Politicians take great interest in the setting of rates. Low rates stimulate the economy in the short run, and therefore help the prospects of unpopular governments facing election. For this reason, central banks are often under considerable pressure to keep interest rates low. While tempting politically, this is bad economic policy, except in special cases, since any temporary well-being is outweighed by the costs of long-term inflation. This might be prevented by central bank independence, and most countries have made significant steps in that direction over the past decades.

It is not as obvious that central banks should be independently in charge of financial stability. When the authorities are called upon to fight financial crises, this necessitates deep involvement in the structure of the financial system and the use of public money to bail out private sector institutions. The central banks should not have the authority to implement such policies on their own. The ultimate guardian of the public purse is the treasury, or the ministry of finance, which should assume the pivotal role when it comes to using significant amounts of public money to fight a financial crisis. This places the treasury directly above the central bank, which then cannot be considered independent. The supervisor, the central bank and the treasury all need to cooperate in implementing financial stability, and the treasury has to have the ultimate power. This does not mean the treasury is better at exercising financial stability than the central bank. The opposite is more likely to be true. The central bank is more likely to have the necessary expertise and be less sensitive to cronyism and corruption.

This is a recipe for conflict. It is essential for central banks to be independent to effectively implement monetary policy, but they cannot be fully independent when it comes to implementing financial stability. Some compromise is called for, perhaps leaving the central banks in charge most of the time but yielding to the treasury when needed. This seems to be the direction taken by the governments of the UK and US and arguably Europe.

5.6.3 Losing control of money

Many governments have used massive amounts of money creation as part of the resolution of the 2007 crisis, obeying the imperative need to prevent a systemic collapse, stimulate their economies, and pay for the large amounts of debt assumed by the government. In the short run, printing money has been a success and has prevented the financial system from collapsing, the economy from sliding into a full-blown depression, and governments from defaulting.

In the longer term, there is a price to pay. Until the crises from 2007, such policies were generate generally dismissed out of hand, because of their inevitable inflationary effects and the cost imposed on the economy because of increased uncertainty. The only legitimate use of monetary policy was to maintain low and stable inflation, a point made explicit in many central bank charters.

Many of the governments now enthusiastically embracing money creation have in the past condemned others for responding to domestic crises in exactly the same way. For the next decade or two this will make it very hard for them to credibly forswear the further use of monetary policy for such purposes: financial entities will simply assume that if the need is sufficient, governments will do what it takes.

This has serious implications. At present, contractionary influences remain strong and there is little evidence that inflationary expectations are building up, but the threat and the associated costs are clear. It took many years to defeat the 1970s inflation, with central bank independence and credibility playing a vital role in that fight. These have now been impaired, suggesting that the coming battle against inflation will be similarly long and painful.

Hyperinflation

Governments sometimes completely lose control of money. The reason might be that as inflation increases, government revenue decreases, so the government needs to print money to finance itself. That, however, leads to more inflation, and a vicious cycle is formed. This process was modelled by Cagan (1956) who showed that it is necessary to increase the money supply at a double exponential rate for the government's revenue to keep up. The empirical evidence is consistent with his model, as seen in Figure 5.4 which shows the growth of money supply during the hyperinflation in Germany and Zimbabwe.

Even though the *y*-axis in the figure is on a logarithmic scale, the growth is exponential, so inflation is growing at a double exponential rate. Besides Zimbabwe and Germany, many countries have experienced hyperinflation, as seen in Table 5.1.

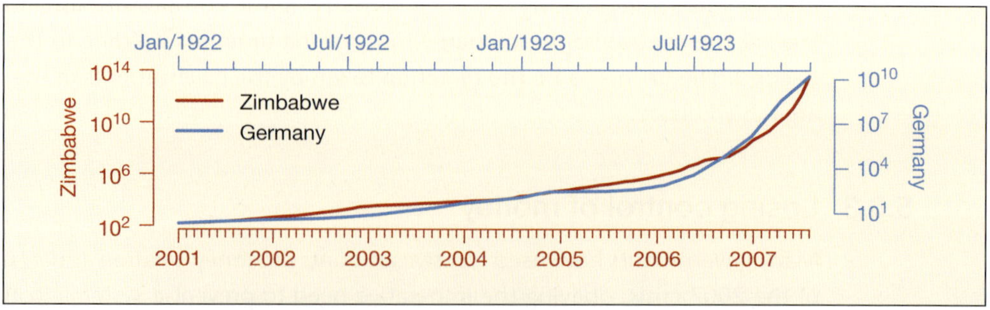

Figure 5.4 Hyperinflation in Germany and Zimbabwe

Table 5.1 Highest monthly inflation rates in history

Country	Month with highest inflation rate	Highest monthly inflation rate	Equivalent daily inflation rate	Time required for prices to double
Hungary	July 1946	4.19×10^{16}%	207%	15.0 hours
Zimbabwe	November 2008	7.96×10^{10}%	98.00%	24.7 hours
Yugoslavia	January 1994	3.13×10^{8}%	64.60%	1.4 days
Germany	October 1923	29,500%	20.90%	3.7 days
Greece	October 1944	13,800%	17.90%	4.3 days
China	May 1949	2,178%	11.00%	6.7 days

Notes. The Reserve Bank of Zimbabwe reported inflation rates for March 2007–July 2008. The authors (Hanke and Kwok, 2009, Table 2) calculated rates for August 2008–14 November 2008

Source: On the measurement of Zimbabwe's hyperinflation, *Cato Journal*, Vol. 29, No. 2, 356 (Hanke, S. H. and Kwok, A. K. F. Spring/Summer 2009).

The general reason why a country ends up with hyperinflation is that the government surrenders control of money creation because it is under some imperative to raise revenue at all costs. In the end, hyperinflation is extremely costly. As Vladimir Lenin said: 'The best way to destroy the capitalist system is to debauch the currency', as quoted by Keynes (1920).

5.7 SUMMARY

The central bank is the most important institution in the financial system because it has a monopoly on creating money. It generally has five objectives: price stability, macroeconomic performance, financial stability, banking supervision and bailing out its government. There are differences between countries. The first two objectives are likely to be legal objectives, but financial stability has risen in prominence during the ongoing crisis. The supervisory function remains controversial with good arguments for and against the central bank taking on the responsibility. The bailout function is more like a dirty secret, not something the central banks or governments want anyone to notice.

Central banks control the supply of money either directly or indirectly to achieve price stability. Central banks have resorted to unconventional methods, such as QE, since 2007 to stimulate the economy and finance the government. Their long-term impacts are unclear but include some risk of inflation.

The priorities of the central bank objectives have changed over time, from financial stability to price stability and back to financial stability. These objectives are quite different and often in conflict with each other. For example, financial stability may require money creation, undermining price stability, whilst prudential banking supervision could lead to the creation of hidden risks. Another contentious issue is central bank independence, considered desirable for monetary policy but not entirely compatible with financial stability. In a worst case scenario, the central banks may lose control of money, resulting in hyperinflation.

APPENDIX: CENTRAL BANK INTEREST RATE

The most visible demonstration of monetary policy is the setting of interest rates. Several different terminologies are used when referring to central bank interest rates and these can often be confusing and even contradictory. Common names are the target rate, the short rate, the risk-free rate and in the US the Fed funds rate.

The interest rate set by a central bank is typically a short-term rate, usually overnight rates for secured or unsecured large institutional borrowers and depositors with the central bank. It is often called the target rate because it is the interest target for the central bank, the short rate because it refers to short maturities, the risk-free rate because the government is risk-free, the discount rate for historical reasons, and the Fed funds rate in the US because the Fed stands for the federal reserve which sets the rates.

Confusingly, the short rate could also refer to the interest rate on short maturities bonds issued by commercial entities, while the risk-free rate could also refer to the interest rate paid by the government on any of its borrowings, regardless of maturity.

The term discount rate has multiple meanings. It originates from an old type of loan where a borrower would sell an obligation at a discount, promising to buy it at the full price in the future, which might be called a repo today. The effective interest rate is the discount rate. This term is most commonly used nowadays for short-term borrowing from the discount window of the Fed. However, it could just as easily be used for the interest rate used in regular present value calculations.

The term prime rate also has multiple meanings. Traditionally it referred to the interest rate charged by banks to their best clients, hence the word prime. It now means generally interest rates paid by somebody who is very low risk, but we could easily see interest rates below the prime rate. Furthermore, in different countries it can refer to particular institutional setups. The US prime rate is not a single standardised rate. Each bank has its own prime rate, and the one that is quoted most frequently comes from the *Wall Street Journal*, which polls the 30 largest banks in the country.

Benchmark interest rates

We outline the terminologies of the three major central banks here. The Fed sets a *target* federal funds rate. This is the unsecured rate that banks charge each other in the interbank market for borrowing reserves held at the Fed (known as federal funds), usually overnight. The federal funds rate is determined in the market, but the Fed can influence this rate through open-market operations, reserve requirements and the discount rate. The discount rate is the interest rate charged to banks when they borrow overnight directly from the Fed, through the Fed's discount window.

The main interest rate for the ECB is known as the main refinancing operations fixed rate. This is essentially a one-week repo rate where banks put up acceptable collateral with the ECB and get a loan in return. Refinancing operations are conducted via auctions, where the ECB specifies the rate at which it is willing to lend money and the amount of liquidity available, and the banks then express their interest. The ECB also sets the 'marginal lending facility', which is a secured overnight rate. Banks can use this facility to borrow overnight from their national central banks after providing acceptable collateral. This rate provides a ceiling for the overnight market interest rate, and is similar in nature to the discount rate used by the Fed. There is also a deposit facility where banks can make overnight deposits with their national central banks. The interest rate on this facility similarly provides a floor for the overnight market interest rate.

The benchmark interest rate for the BoE is known as the BoE base rate, which is the rate that the BoE charges banks for secured overnight borrowing. It is usually transacted as an overnight repo against high-quality collateral. This is more comparable to the Fed's discount rate rather than to the federal funds rate.

Questions for discussion

1 What are the main functions of a central bank?

2 What is more important as a central bank function: financial stability or monetary policy?

3 How have the common views of the relative importance of financial stability versus monetary policy changed over time?

4 What is the danger of deflation, and what policy remedies for it do you recommend?

5 Should the central bank be in charge of supervision?

6 What is quantitative easing, and how does it compare to more conventional monetary policy operations?

7 Why is quantitative easing discussed more widely today than in the past?

8 What is the long-term danger of quantitative easing?

9 Who are the main losers from quantitative easing?

10 What are some of the unique challenges facing the ECB?

11 How can a central bank bail out its government? Why is it harder for the ECB to fulfil this function than central banks in other countries?

12 What are the main arguments for central bank independence?

13 What are the main arguments against central bank independence?

References

Cagan, P. (1956). The monetary dynamics of hyperinflation. In Friedman, M., editor, *Studies in the Quantity Theory of Money*. University of Chicago Press.

Friedman, M. (1969). The optimum quantity of money. In Friedman, M., editor, *The Optimum Quantity of Money and Other Essays*, chapter 1, pp. 1–50. Adline Publishing Company, Chicago.

Goodhart, C. (2002). The organizational structure of banking supervision. *Economic Notes*, 31(1): 1–32.

Goodhart, C. and Schoenmaker, D. (1995). Should the functions of monetary policy and banking supervision be separated? *Oxford Economic Papers*, 47: 539–60.

Hanke, S. H. and Kwok, A. K. F. (2009). On the measurement of Zimbabwe's hyperinflation. *Cato.*, 29(2): 353–64.

Keynes, J. M. (1920). *The Economic Consequences of the Peace*. Harcourt Brace, New York.

Keynes, J. M. (1936). *The General Theory of Interest, Employment and Money*. Macmillan.

Lewis, M. K. and Mizen, P. D. (2000). *Monetary Economics*. Oxford University Press.

Taylor, J. B. (1993). Discretion versus policy rules in practice. *Carnegie-Rochester Conference Series on Public Policy*, 39: 195–214.

6 THE ASIAN CRISIS OF 1997 AND THE IMF

In 1997, several countries in East Asia experienced one of the most severe currency and financial crises since the Great Depression. Exchange rates, asset prices and economic activity collapsed with financial and corporate insolvency widespread.

The crisis caught everybody by surprise. The East Asian countries seemed to have done everything right, avoiding mistakes causing crises elsewhere, for example, in Latin America and Europe. The macroeconomics appeared sound, and the countries had balanced budgets and tight monetary policy.

Instead, the underlying weaknesses were in the private sector, with excessive foreign currency borrowing that led to bad investment decisions. This was fuelled by the apparent belief that the governments would ensure stable exchange rates, and even bail out borrowers. The macroeconomic fundamentals were sound, the financial fundamentals not.

There is not complete unanimity on which countries were affected. Four are always included: Indonesia, South Korea, Malaysia and Thailand, as all experienced spectacular growth in the 1990s, followed by the 1997 crash and respectable recovery. All but Malaysia were forced to call in the International Monetary Fund (IMF), so we mostly omit Malaysia from the analysis. Other Asian countries affected include Hong Kong, Singapore and Taiwan, but these avoided the worst, so we also exclude them here.

Detailed analysis of the Asian crisis, *with the benefit of hindsight*, indicates that foreign currency speculation and a sudden stop in foreign lending were a significant immediate cause of the crisis, fuelled by weak fundamentals. Given the weaknesses in the financial fundamentals, a crisis in all of the countries was probably inevitable; if it had not happened in 1997, it would have occurred within a few years.

The main policy conclusion drawn by the crisis countries themselves was that they could only rely on themselves for liquidity support and, in response, have built up vast currency reserves.

These reserves did not protect them from significant exchange rate fluctuations once the global crisis was underway in 2007, and South Korea had to enter into currency swap contracts with the Federal Reserve System (Fed), helping to stabilise its exchange rate. This clearly demonstrates the limited protection afforded by vast reserves, and it is quite possible that the reserves only serve to prevent small crises, making the eventual one large. In particular, large reserves do not imply that a country should avoid addressing underlying structural weaknesses.

The IMF, or the Fund as it is sometimes referred to, played an important and controversial role in the crisis. It is a part of the United Nations and was originally set up as a part of the Bretton Woods system, to manage the fixed exchange rate regime at the time. Over time, the role of the Fund has shifted; for the past few decades it has been the main international mechanism for responding to financial and economic crises, as well as the enforcer of foreign claims on governments. It can provide significant amounts of money as emergency assistance – a *package* – but does in return demand what is known in the Fund's jargon as *structural adjustments*. This includes macroeconomic policies like fiscal and monetary tightening and improving the capital accounts, but also some microeconomic adjustments, for example, labour market reform, cuts in subsidies and more recently anti-corruption measures. These policies are a part of the *Washington consensus.*

At its core, the Asian crisis was not very different from many other crises throughout history, a clear example of the observation that all crises are fundamentally the same, only the details differ. It has clear parallels with the ongoing global crisis; many of the underlying fundamental weaknesses are the same, and some policymakers involved in the European sovereign debt crisis have drawn direct lessons from the Asian crisis. Perhaps the most interesting parallel between the Asian crisis and the crisis from 2007 is how different policies are when they have to be implemented domestically or abroad.

Links to other chapters

This chapter draws on the theoretical concepts discussed in Chapter 4 (liquidity) and Chapter 14 (bailouts), and relates to the policy analysis in Chapter 11 (currency markets) and Chapter 19 (sovereign debt crises).

Key concepts

- East Asia crisis of 1997
- IMF
- Maturity and currency mismatches
- Challenges in fighting crises
- Washington consensus
- Structural adjustment

Readings for this chapter

A large number of studies have been produced on the Asian crisis. We drew on the early works of Goldstein (1998), Radelet and Sachs (2000) and Alba *et al.* (1998). We also used two more recent papers: Weisbrot (2007) focusing on the role of the IMF, and Ito (2007) providing a summary of recent analysis.

6.1 BUILDING UP TO A CRISIS

Large capital flows have long been an integral part of the global economy. In the era of the *first globalism*, 1873–1914, much of the world's infrastructure was financed by London. Capital flows were lower between the two world wars and during the Bretton Woods era, but took off significantly in the early 1970s, with newly wealthy investors in the Middle East and liberalised financial institutions working together to build up global capital markets.

Investors and borrowers alike often prefer short-term loans, those with maturity of less than one year. Investors want to minimise risk, whilst borrowers prefer the lower cost of the short-term loans. Therefore, maturities on foreign loans to developing countries are often quite short. The ultimate use of the funds is generally longer-term, perhaps the construction of a factory that will only start production in a few years. Therefore, international capital flows often result in significant *maturity mismatches*.

In the 1970s, the preferred destination for excess capital was the Latin America, but it soon became apparent that the continent made poor use of the money and a series of sovereign debt crises ensued, followed by difficulties for many of the lenders. Consequently, lenders were looking for new borrowers.

Lending to East Asia

In the 1990s, capital flowed to East Asian countries, helped by their adherence to the Washington consensus, which is a term used to capture the common view of the major economies, the World Bank and the IMF, and the European Union (EU) that emphasises free capital mobility.

Definition 6.1 Washington consensus

1. Fiscal discipline (eliminate deficits)
2. Broaden the tax base, keep taxes low
3. Market interest rates
4. Raise spending on health and education
5. Secure property rights
6. Privatisation
7. Deregulation
8. Free trade
9. Competitive/sensible exchange rates
10. Free capital flows (remove barriers to foreign direct investment).

The East Asian countries opened up their *capital accounts* and liberalised the financial sector, all while maintaining sound macroeconomics. Sovereign debt was low and falling: see Figure 6.1. GDP growth was quite spectacular, ranging from 7.9% to 9.5% across the region, as can be seen in Table 6.1. Other standard indicators, like inflation and unemployment, all pointed to macroeconomic stability.

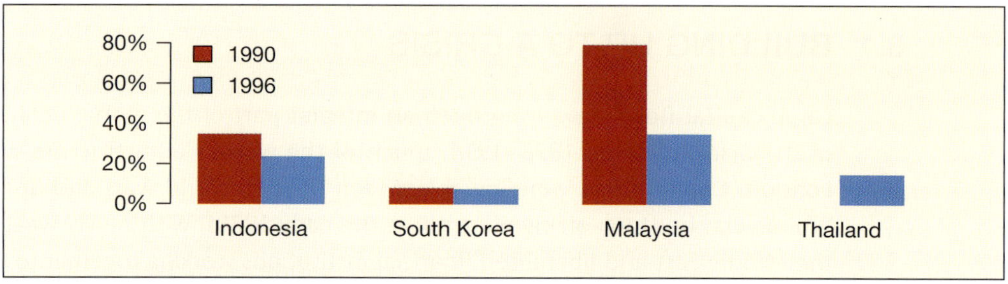

Figure 6.1 Debt to GDP ratio 1990–1996

Data source: World Bank and IMF. Indonesian starts 1991. No data for Thailand 1990

Table 6.1 Average GDP per capita growth

Annual average	Indonesia	South Korea	Malaysia	Thailand
1990–1996	6.3%	6.8%	6.7%	7.5%
1997	−14.3%	−7.5%	−9.6%	−11.6%
1999–2007	3.8%	4.7%	3.4%	4.0%

Data source: World Bank, http://data.worldbank.org.

Money and investment

Respectable macroeconomic performance does not mean much if based on transient factors. The success of the East Asian countries was founded on extraordinarily high investment rates, as can be seen in Figure 6.2, ranging from 28% to 40% of GDP. By comparison, investment rates are around 18% in Europe.

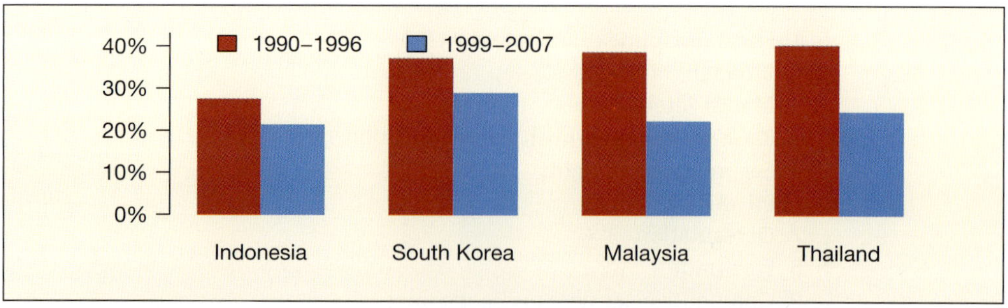

Figure 6.2 Investment rates (gross fixed capital formation, % of GDP)

Data source: World Bank

If investment is based on domestic savings, and especially if loans are maturity matched to the ultimate investments, high investment rates are not a big concern for financial stability, even if one might question whether the funds can be sensibly invested. If, however, the origin of the funds is short-term foreign currency borrowing from international capital markets, the picture is different.

Initially, this was not the case for the East Asian countries; financing from international markets was less than 1% of GDP in 1990. International borrowing was growing rapidly, however, reaching 4% to 6% in 1996, as seen in Figure 6.3. Because these funds were predominantly short-term, this rapidly growing exposure to international capital markets signalled the building up of vulnerabilities to liquidity crises.

The high economic growth was partially reflected in the stock market (Figure 6.4). The best year was 1993, caused by foreign inflows, both from direct purchases of equities by foreigners and also from the indirect effect of domestic companies borrowing from abroad. From 1994, the stock markets were doing poorly.

Perhaps the stock market anticipated the pending crisis better than foreign creditors, the government or the IMF. After all, many investors in the stock market are well-connected and well-informed local investors who would know of the build-up of vulnerabilities better than most. Alternatively, those relatively poor returns may represent divestment by foreigners, belatedly realising that with poor minority protection they had very limited real ownership. The lenders felt themselves safe from the corporate governance problems, protected by convertibility, short duration, government guarantees and good macroeconomic policies, and so continued to lend.

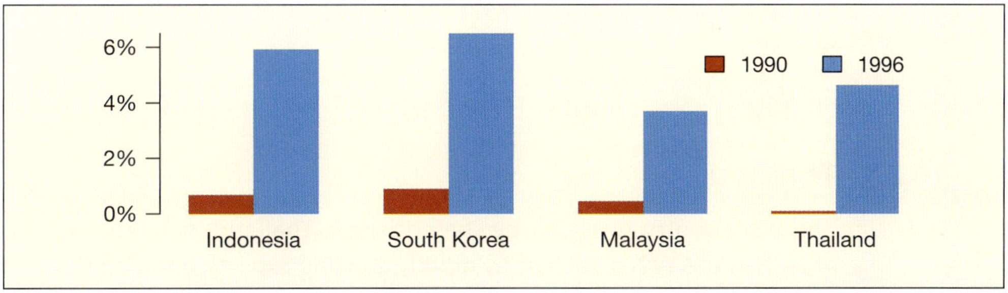

Figure 6.3 Financing via international capital markets (gross inflows, % of GDP)
Data source: World Bank and IMF

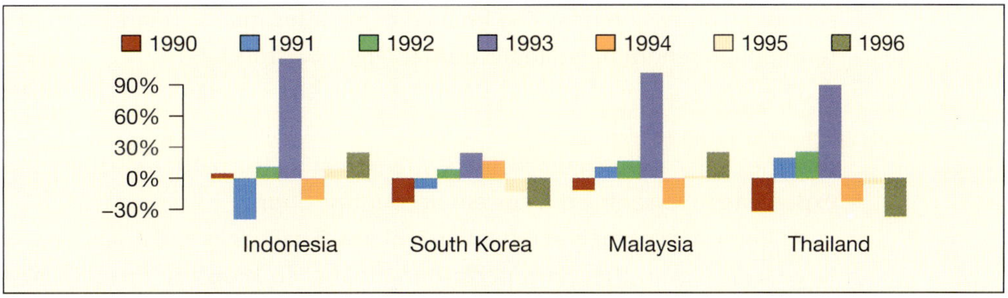

Figure 6.4 Annual stock market performance 1990–1996
Data source: Global Financial Data

6.2 THE CRISIS IN INDIVIDUAL COUNTRIES

The main crisis event started with a speculative attack on the Thai baht in 1997, and soon spread throughout the region. Within weeks practically every currency in East Asia came under pressure, and subsequently the currencies of South Korea, Indonesia, Malaysia, Taiwan and the Philippines were devalued. Singapore and Hong Kong managed to maintain their exchange rates.

As investors pulled out of the region, asset prices plunged and GDP growth turned sharply negative. The crisis severely undermined public finances in a number of countries and the IMF was called in to help.

We see the impact on the stock market and exchange rates for the second part of 1997 in Figure 6.5. The markets collapsed, with the stock market in Malaysia and the foreign exchange market in Indonesia worst affected.

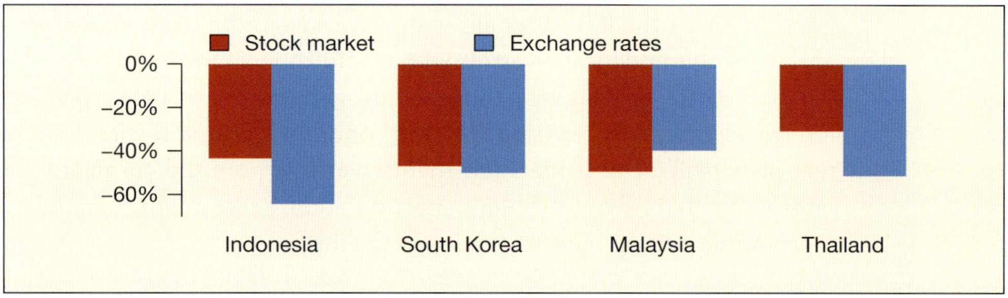

Figure 6.5 Drop in stock markets (local currency) and exchange rates in the second part of 1997

Data source: Global Financial Data

6.2.1 Thailand

The first country to be hit by the crisis was Thailand. It had experienced spectacular growth in the 1990s, fuelled by rapidly growing exports, and had maintained a relatively fixed exchange rate of roughly 25 baht per USD since 1984.

A particular feature of the economy of Thailand was the prominence of special finance companies, which were similar to banks and provided about 20% of all the credit in the economy, on easy terms. The finance companies mainly financed themselves by short-term dollar denominated loans from foreign investors.

The Thai economy started to run into difficulties towards the end of 1996, when interest rates rose, and the economy slowed down due to sagging exports. One reason was that the dollar appreciated in 1995, strengthening the baht, reducing the attractiveness of exports and worsening the current account position.

As domestic companies ran into problems, Thai banks and finance companies reported large increases in their non-performing loans. To keep the financial system stable, the Central Bank of Thailand secretly lent about $20 billion to finance companies and weaker banks at below market interest rates. These loans do not seem to have been a part of a lending of last resort (LOLR) operation, but direct bailouts. Ultimately, this meant that the Central Bank had lower reserves than expected, reducing confidence when that became known.

The currency came under pressure towards the end of 1996, with the Central Bank intervening in the currency market, building up increasingly large forward positions, further reducing the effective amounts of reserves. Finally, a massive speculative attack took place on 14 and 15 May 1997. Figure 6.6 shows the evolution of the currency. The Central Bank of Thailand lost $10 billion defending the baht without success. On 15 May, the Central Bank ordered all local and foreign banks to stop lending baht to anyone outside the country, which eased the selling pressure for about a month.

Fresh concerns about the Thai economy surfaced on 19 June, prompting Thai banks and corporations to sell baht in large numbers. The foreign creditors, which used to roll over short-term debts, were suddenly demanding immediate repayment as their loans matured. Few Thai borrowers had hedged against the possibility of a collapse of the baht, and it would have been silly to do so, since the borrowing costs when the frictional costs are included are higher than just borrowing in baht. On 2 July, the authorities concluded that the fixed rate system could not survive and let the baht float.

This turned out to be the trigger for a fully fledged crisis in East Asia. The baht devalued swiftly and lost more than half of its value, reaching its lowest point of 56 bahts to the USD in January 1998. The Thai stock market dropped by 75% in baht terms and Finance One, the largest Thai finance company at that time, collapsed.

Thailand got an IMF programme on 20 August 1997, with a package of $17.2 billion. The markets were not impressed by the size of the package, nor the disclosure of $23.4 billion in forward commitments by the Central Bank of Thailand, especially considering that short-term private sector debts exceeded $30 billion. The baht continued falling.

The IMF recommended the closure of weaker financial institutions, but problems in distinguishing between liquidity problems and solvency problems frustrated this process, partly because financial institutions would rationally pay almost limitless bribes to be placed on the list of liquid institutions. The Fund attached further conditions to its aid, requiring fiscal and monetary tightening, the raising of taxes and reduction in expenditures. This is a recipe it continued to follow in the other crisis countries.

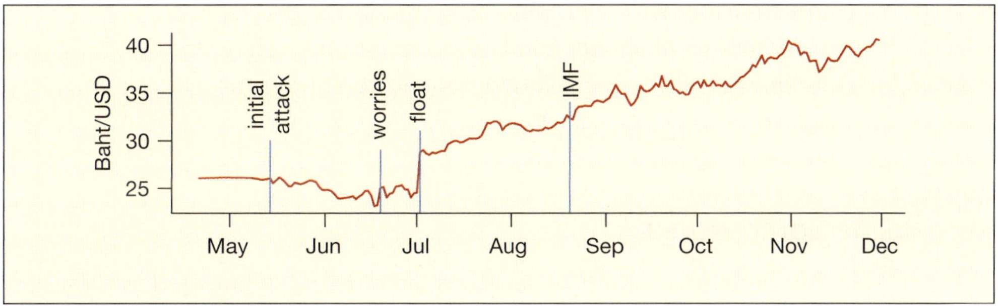

Figure 6.6 Thai baht in 1997

Data source: Global Financial Data

6.2.2 Indonesia

Indonesia under President Suharto embarked on an economic reform agenda in the early 1980s, restraining government spending, opening the economy to foreign investments and easing regulations. The economy grew rapidly, whilst enjoying a current account surplus, with foreign exchange reserves substantially increasing.

Similar to Thailand, Indonesian corporations were increasingly using short-term dollar denominated debt to finance themselves. This worked well when the currency appreciated during the 1980s and early 1990s, setting up a virtuous feedback loop between currency inflows, reduced cost of debt service and currency appreciation.

Behind it all was a strong culture of what was called 'KKN': corruption, collusion and nepotism. Any foreign firm investing in an Indonesian company had to hand over partnership rights to a presidential relative to ensure smooth approval. Individuals with personal relationships to the Suharto regime made some of the largest fortunes in Indonesia.

Throughout the 1990s, difficulties were building up in the banking system whilst the number of banks grew rapidly. The government heavily influenced lending decisions so it could channel funds to favoured businesses, with banks made to lend to borrowers who already had stopped servicing old loans – that is, in default. By the mid-1990s, non-performing loans exceeded 25% of total loans made. The Indonesian currency came under increasing pressure after the baht floated in July 1997, adversely affecting corporations with unhedged dollar liabilities.

Indonesia asked for IMF assistance in October. The IMF General Manager, Michel Camdessus, responded by saying that 'The IMF strongly supports the approach that has been followed by Indonesia, which sees this as an occasion to strengthen its economic policies even if fundamentals are basically sound' (IMF, 1997). This statement sounds naive: a country with 'basically sound' fundamentals should not suffer a crisis. In its analysis, the Fund seems to have focused on macroeconomic fundamentals and neglected the financial fundamentals.

The IMF provided a package of $40 billion, attaching conditions to its programme, most controversially that 16 banks be closed immediately, with limited protection to depositors. The particular 16 banks seemed to have been chosen quite arbitrarily, and it was unclear whether other banks would also be closed. Not surprisingly, the end result was a run on the banking system and the country. While closing the 16 banks might have been designed to demonstrate strength, within a few weeks a son of the president reopened his bank under a different name, demonstrating a lack of commitment by the Indonesian government, thus undermining the programme.

Similar to Thailand, the Fund required monetary and fiscal tightening, which the Indonesian government found difficult to implement. For example, riots ensued when subsidies were reduced. Eventually, the policies were adjusted and the Indonesian government agreed on another letter of intent with the Fund in January 1998.

6.2.3 South Korea

The situation in South Korea was quite different. It emerged as one of the poorest countries in the world from its civil war in the 1950s, and was governed by a series of military regimes that dictated financial system lending decisions. South Korea pursued an industrial policy to build up world-leading corporations called *Chaebol*. The Chaebol responded by investing rapidly, with investments rising by nearly 40% a year in the early 1990s, and by then South Korea had become the second most industrialised economy in Asia after Japan.

The Chaebol were financed with extremely high levels of debt, exceeding 400% of shareholder equity in some cases. The largest became in effect too big to fail (TBTF), as their default would threaten systemic crisis. Very high domestic savings rates were not sufficient to meet industry demand for funding, and liberalised South Korean banks increasingly resorted to borrowing dollars short-term internationally and lending long-term to the Chaebol. Behind it all was an understanding that the government would bail out any Chaebol that got into trouble.

Not all Chaebol used the seemingly unlimited amount of funds wisely and by early 1997 some were unable to meet their obligations, straining the banking system. The government decided to bankrupt the Daewoo Group and the Hanbo Group in mid-1997, and prosecuted their owners.

The currency depreciated in the beginning of 1997, and after holding steady for a few months, the depreciation accelerated in August. This further increased the difficulties for the corporate sector, with its large dollar denominated liabilities, and put a strain on the foreign currency reserves of the Central Bank.

There was little immediate fear about the solvency of the South Korean state – recall that its debt was quite low – or the bulk of its financial and non-financial corporations. However, if the Central Bank ran out of its limited foreign currency reserves, a crisis would likely ensue.

South Korea's foreign currency reserves started to fall at an accelerated rate from October, and by November a rumour that usable reserves were far smaller than the official statistics spooked the market. The Central Bank started to intervene in the currency market, further depleting its reserves. According to official statistics, foreign reserves declined from \$30 billion at the end of October to \$24 billion at the end of November, and to \$20 billion at the end of December. However, usable foreign reserves were exhausted by November. Realising this, foreign investors stopped rolling over South Korean loans by November. A self-fulfilling crisis was created: a vicious feedback between solvency problems, falling exchange rates and the depletion of currency reserves.

Faced with massive defaults in the financial sector, the government requested IMF assistance, getting a package of \$57 billion. The IMF demanded significant conditions, including its customary fiscal and monetary tightening, along with trade and capital account liberalisation, and labour market and financial sector reforms.

The package was not effective, and the currency continued falling. There are several reasons for this, not least that the IMF had lost credibility by this time as neither the Thai nor the Indonesian packages had proven effective, whilst the South Korean package was considered insufficient. As a response, the IMF accelerated the payout of funds and along with the G7 applied what was known as '*jawboning*', strongly leaning on creditor banks to roll over South Korean exposures. This succeeded in halting the currency decline and prevented more corporate defaults.

6.3 REASONS FOR THE CRISIS

One of the most striking features of the Asian crisis was how surprising it was. Strong growth rates concealed many of the weaknesses building up. Over time, we have gone through several waves of explanations of the crisis. Initially, it was explained by weak fundamentals and moral hazard, but as the crisis developed, such explanations were found lacking. Eventually, after the crisis countries recovered sharply, most commentators found that liquidity and sudden stop had been a central element.

6.3.1 Weak fundamentals and moral hazard

Initial explanations for the crisis focused on rampant moral hazard problems and weakening macroeconomic conditions. Politics and corruption were key ingredients in the allocation of capital and guaranteeing of loans, with Indonesia the worst offender. The end result was not surprising: substantial over-investment in risky and poorly performing projects and asset price bubbles.

When the crisis erupted, most outsiders, in particular the IMF, focused on weak fundamentals and moral hazard. In that case, the optimal policy response is to directly address the problem of corruption and moral hazard and to improve macroeconomic fundamentals. This view is reflected in the IMF conditions.

Subsequent analysis has played down the pivotal importance of those two factors. Many other countries that are not afflicted by crises have similar problems, and other countries with better macroeconomic fundamentals and less moral hazard get hit by crises.

6.3.2 Panic and contagion

Another category of explanations emphasises *panic* in financial markets that leads to contagion, whereby the initial devaluation of the Thai baht caused a panic, which spread to other countries in the region. Many statistical studies have focused on such explanations, and it is quite straightforward to document the presence of interconnectedness and causality amongst the affected economies. The problem is that any such analysis is conditional on an actual crisis happening and simply provides a statistical description of how a crisis moves from one country to the next.

A panic does not happen by itself; there must be an underlying reason. Sophisticated investors providing short-term funds to the East Asian countries were interested in profit maximisation and panicking is not compatible with that objective. Deeper reasons are needed to understand their motives.

Statistical descriptions focusing on panic and contagion may help in mapping how a crisis evolves, but do not help very much in understanding the underlying causes nor more importantly in formulating future policy.

6.3.3 Market factors

A different class of explanations focuses more directly on financial markets. All the countries liberalised their financial markets quite rapidly but had little experience in supervising sophisticated open financial markets. Related to this was the problem of *maturity and currency mismatches.* Much funding was short-term foreign currency while lending or investments were long-term in domestic currency. This creates a classical mismatch problem for borrowers. What was special, but not unique, in the Asian crisis was how prevalent such mismatches were.

The capital markets in East Asia were relatively underdeveloped, so that most financial intermediation occurred through the banking system. If a country does not have sufficient reserves to cover a sudden stop in the rollover of loans, it is vulnerable to a liquidity crisis. Ito (2007) reports that the ratio of short-term bank borrowing to foreign reserves at the end of June 1997 was 2.1 for South Korea, 1.6 for Indonesia and 1.4 for Thailand, signalling significant fragility. In later analysis, the so-called *Guidotti–Greenspan rule* argues that the ratio should not exceed 1.

A major ingredient was overconfidence. A history of currency stability encouraged foreign banks to lend, for the simple reason that their whole experience had always been profitable. Central banks tolerated this for the same reason. Faith in convertibility and the IMF made lenders comfortable, which is a necessary condition for future crises to develop.

6.3.4 Performance before and after the crisis

With the benefit of hindsight, we can use post-crisis data to analyse what sort of a crisis hit the East Asian countries. The latest year is 2007 in order to avoid being affected by the ongoing crisis since then.

If the crisis had been driven by fundamental weaknesses, recovery would have taken many years, with a successful implementation of the reform programmes demanded by the IMF a necessary condition for sustainable recovery. This is not what happened. Instead, the main crisis period was quite brief, and partial recovery swift, as seen in Figure 6.7.

Such crises are often called 'V-shaped' because they happen quickly and are over quickly. Economic growth has been lower post-crisis than before, but is more sustainable and based on a more sensible model of investment. Evidence of a V-shape is not as clear if we look at the exchange rates, as seen by Figure 6.8. All four countries suffered a significant fall in the exchange rates in the crisis, and the recovery was only partial. This applies especially to Indonesia which suffered worst from the crisis and had very high inflation rates in 1997 and 1998.

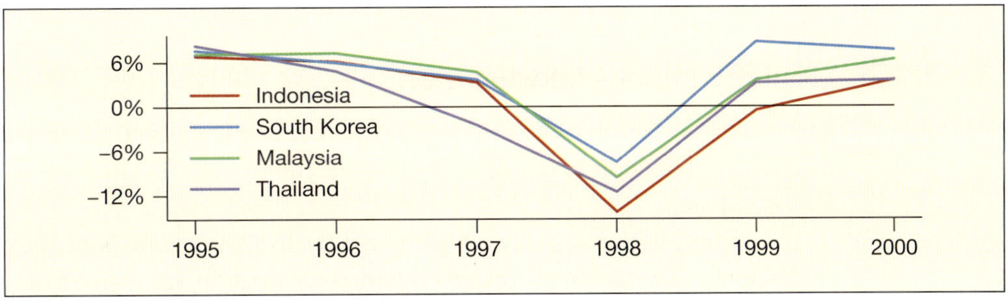

Figure 6.7 GDP per capita growth

Data source: World Bank

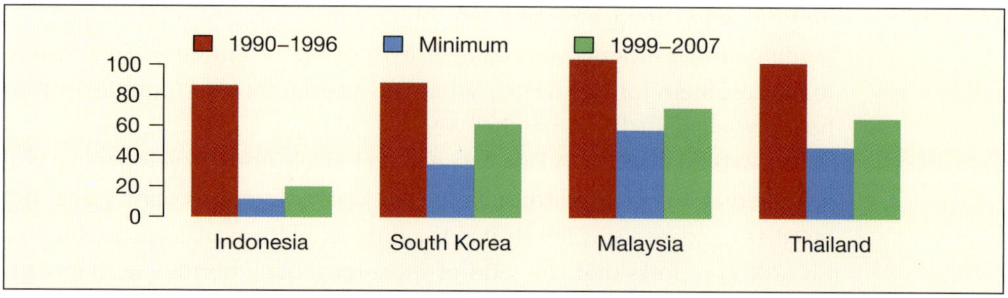

Figure 6.8 Average and minimum (in crisis) exchange rates. USD/local currency, 1990 = 100

Data source: Global Financial Data

Table 6.2 Relative GDP per capita ranking in percentiles

Year	Indonesia	South Korea	Malaysia	Thailand
1960	88%	36%	48%	71%
1990	74%	26%	44%	58%
1996	66%	23%	37%	47%
1999	70%	23%	39%	51%
2007	72%	20%	39%	49%

Data source: World Bank, http://data.worldbank.org.

Instead, a V-shaped crisis is more indicative of a liquidity crisis, where a sudden stop causes significant temporary difficulties. This causes the currency to collapse, making local corporations more competitive than before, often with much lower debt, creating conditions for rapid export-led growth. This is exactly what happened in the East Asian crisis.

These effects were most pronounced in South Korea, which has performed best since the crisis. Table 6.2 shows the relative per capita GDP ranking of the four countries at key points, expressed in percentiles. Notably, Indonesia was essentially in the same place in 1990 and 2007, consistent with other empirical results presented. Malaysia has shown a small improvement, but Thailand has made the largest move in the ranking, but is still below its 1996 place.

6.3.5 Liquidity crisis – sudden stop

Recent analysis emphasises the role of liquidity in the crisis. Liquidity is a multifaceted concept, and difficult to define concisely, but the use of the term here is more related to *funding liquidity*.

The importance of liquidity is highlighted by Ito (2007), who finds the crisis to a significant extent to be caused by foreign exchange speculation, rather than fundamental weaknesses, moral hazard or market panic. In other words, the crisis was caused by a *sudden stop*, and reversal of capital flows. Net inflows were $93 billion in 1996 and net outflows

$12 billion in 1997. The observation that the crisis was broadly V-shaped does support the view that it was more the sudden stop, rather than structural weaknesses, that caused the crisis.

Of the four countries, South Korea exhibited the strongest signs of a pure liquidity crisis. Events in the autumn of 1997 indicate that the possibility of the Central Bank running out of reserves scared off investors and encouraged holders of the South Korean currency to exchange it for dollars. This in turn become a self-fulfilling chain of events, only ending after domestic assets became very cheap for holders of foreign currency, and the IMF helped to provide liquidity. The fact that South Korea has the smallest difference between pre- and post-crisis GDP further supports this observation. For the other three countries, the picture is more muddled. There was a clear liquidity crisis but the relatively large shortfall in growth indicates that the very high pre-crisis growth was caused as much by inflows of money as by the build-up of economic strength.

Why did the sudden stop happen? If there had been no worries about the soundness of the economies, there would have been no reasons for creditors to deny credit all of a sudden. Furthermore, the fact that the economies performed well after the crisis does not by itself justify the conclusion that everything was fine: after all, the affected economies underwent significant structural changes as a consequence of the crisis. This means that a sudden stop or liquidity explanations for the crisis are inadequate and only a manifestation of more fundamental problems.

6.4 POLICY OPTIONS FOR THE CRISIS COUNTRIES

The affected countries themselves have come to the conclusion that the crisis was caused by a sudden stop, and hence was a liquidity crisis. This view leads to particular policy conclusions.

6.4.1 Fighting a crisis

Consider the problem of policy response from the point of view of one of the Asian countries under attack. The attackers are motivated by the belief that if they go short on local currency and long on dollars they will later be able to cover their short at a rate that pays for the interest rate differential.

A first response might be to say that the country will never devalue. The speculators will not believe that.

Next, the country can raise interest rates, pushing up the cost of maintaining the attack for those short local rates; with luck the attackers will give up and close their position, and the problem is over. This works provided the high local rates are not damaging the economy, but if speculators perceive that the government is not prepared to take the pain for as long as they are, they will wait the government out. If this does not work, the country is in deep trouble. It can buy some time by closing off speculators' access to currency, but eventually the speculators will do a deal with a local entity that will do the transaction on their behalf. There is a myriad of ways to implement a speculative attack, and the only way to plug all the holes would be to implement such draconian measures that all foreign trade grinds to a halt.

The next step is to approach the IMF for a loan. The benefits come in two parts:

- **Soft.** A humiliating set of anti-corruption and austerity measures should ratchet up credibility with lenders by a notch or two and lend weight to statements about not devaluing. Certainly such measures are likely to be popular with lenders, and other things being equal should reduce local currency borrowing rates by reducing credit risk and inflation expectations. Provided all goes well, this approach should be less damaging to the economy than the rise in nominal rates rejected earlier.

  Unfortunately, this optimistic outlook relies critically on the steps being credible. Even if the government is entirely behind the process, there is plenty of potential for disputes, ranging from votes of no confidence to mass riots. If these suggest that the government cannot take the pain for long, then the overall effect may well be negative.
- **Hard.** The country takes delivery of a large loan in dollars that has to be repaid in dollars, with interest. This signals strong commitment because if the country devalues it loses money on the deal. This is still problematic because if the excess foreign borrowings were part of the problem to begin with, that problem just became worse, and might offset all other benefits.

6.4.2 Long-term policy response

The affected countries drew the conclusion that a sovereign state, ultimately, can only depend on itself if it is facing a liquidity crisis. While the IMF might be willing to help, its aid may not prove particularly effective, it comes at an unpalatable political cost, and it benefits mainly pre-existing lenders rather than the borrowing country, so a country might prefer to rely on itself. According to this view, it is only prudent to take steps to prevent such a crisis from happening in the first place. There are two alternatives.

First, a country can avoid having significant currency and maturity mismatches. This may mean depending on local savings, matching the maturity of foreign loans to the maturity of the ultimate investments and encouraging foreigners to make direct investments rather than just lending funds. The country may want to take steps to minimise carry trading, and have an independent and credible central bank and a credible commitment to convertibility. Of course, these may conflict.

Alternatively, a country might want to keep reserves higher than needed in any plausible crisis. So long as it has more reserves than it has short-term foreign currency borrowings, a liquidity crisis of the type discussed here should be forestalled. This is exactly what the four crisis countries have done since the crisis. Before 1997, their reserves were quite small but they have been building up rapidly since, as can be seen in Figure 6.9.

However, reserves that are never meant to be used are useless, and having outsized reserves might result in crises being less frequent than otherwise but being larger when they do happen. Large reserves also come with a significant cost. A developing country

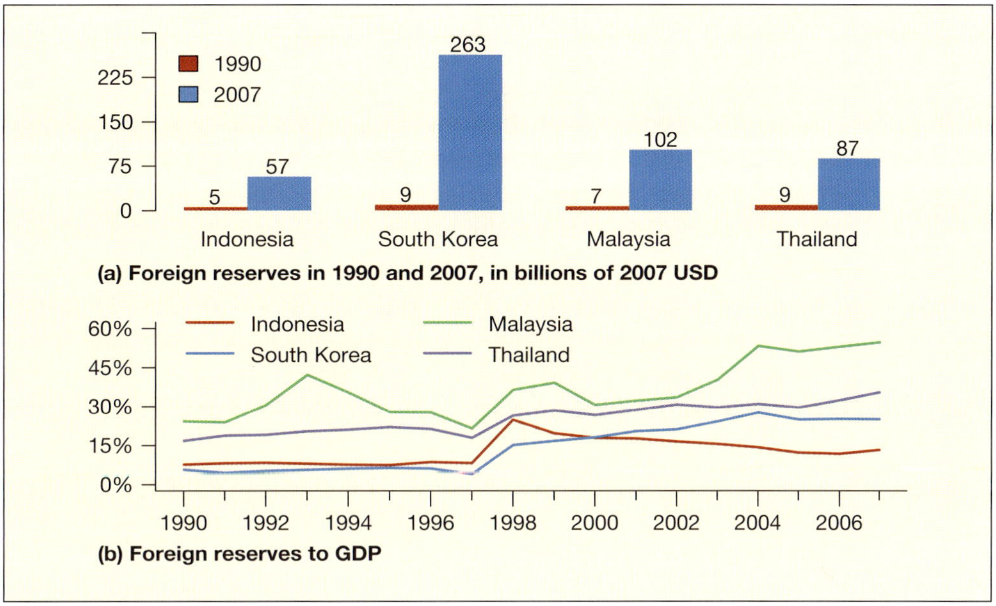

Figure 6.9 Foreign reserves

Data source: World Bank

with rapid growth provides much better investment opportunities than a wealthy developed country. It would seem more natural for a wealthy country to export its capital to a developing country rather than the other way around. Indeed, that had been the norm until recently; during the first globalism, between 1873 and 1914, the United Kingdom (UK) was the greatest exporter of capital, and since then the United States (US), until recently. The lesson drawn by the Asian Tigers, however, is that while the benefits are shared, the risks of this arrangement fall almost entirely on the borrower.

By accumulating foreign currency reserves, the crisis countries, in effect, are subsidising the wealthiest countries, in particular, the US as the owner of the world's reserve currency. This keeps interest rates in the US low and its currency relatively strong. This adversely affects the exports of the high-reserve countries.

The policy adopted after the crisis was the sacrificing of wealth for greater financial security and policy independence. It is an open question whether that is an advisable policy. While this does subsidise US consumers, it also encourages them to buy the very products exported by these countries, helping domestic industry.

There are also very conflicting opinions on the sensibility of maintaining substantial holdings of US government bonds. Some might say that by becoming a large creditor, it gives these countries power. Others highlight the potential for the US to effectively 'tax' the capital exporting countries simply by debasing its currency, perhaps by quantitative easing (QE).

Some other developing countries have emulated the foreign exchange (FX) and reserve policy of the East Asian countries. While that does not indicate the policies are sensible, it does signal they have widespread support.

6.5 ROLE OF THE IMF

The IMF was severely criticised for its performance in the Asian crisis, condemned by almost all commentators. Amongst the many critics are Ito (2007) and even more scathingly Weisbrot (2007), who, with the benefit of hindsight, point out that the IMF misjudged the nature of the crisis throughout. However, such criticisms might be founded on the view that the Fund has to fix crises at any cost. That is not true: the Fund has many other priorities, including protecting lenders. Furthermore, the Fund's reaction to the Asian crisis, however misguided in subsequent analysis, needs to be considered in the context of the time of the decision.

The previous round of crises was in Latin America a decade earlier, where the underlying factors were weak fundamentals. This suggests that the Fund's approach to the Asian crisis was based on recent experience, with the Fund a victim of the successful general's problem: fighting the last war.

In its defence, the Fund's performance also reflected the many limitations of the environment it operated in, the inability to do LOLR and the need to seek widespread consensus along with slow decision making.

The Fund can be partly blamed for the build-up of the maturity and foreign exchange mismatches. The rapid opening of capital accounts and liberalisation of financial markets prior to the crisis were a part of the Washington consensus and of the IMF's favoured policy prescriptions.

Initial focus on moral hazard

The earliest reports of the emerging crisis focused on moral hazard and corruption as a significant, and even the only, causing factor. The IMF embraced this view. The financial systems certainly could do with more discipline, but should that be pursued to the middle of a crisis, when it is hard to separate insolvency from liquidity problems? Demanding more capital and seemingly arbitrarily closing down financial institutions just deepens the crisis, but the problem for the Fund is that if it does not pursue reform policies when it has the lever, it will never achieve them.

For example, there is no reason to believe that President Suharto of Indonesia had any intention of asking the IMF for advice on how to clean up. The Fund's sole opportunity was when he wanted help, to which it could attach strings.

The worst example seems to have been the closure of the 16 financial institutions in Indonesia. Not only did those 16 seem to be chosen arbitrarily, but the closure signalled that anybody having dealings with the financial sector in Indonesia might be facing losses because of policy decisions. Not surprisingly, runs on the banking sector and the country followed, causing significant damage. This could have been prevented by a more nuanced policy response.

Initial focus on structural adjustments

The second plank of the IMF programme was structural adjustment. This included macroeconomic policies such as fiscal and monetary tightening and improving capital accounts, but also microeconomic adjustments like labour market reform, cuts in subsidies and anti-corruption policies.

The fiscal and monetary tightening was questionable. None of the countries had demonstrated a lack of discipline on that front prior to the crisis, and a sensible crisis response was loosening, not tightening. The policies demanded by the Fund also were out of touch with the underlying realities; for example, it set an inflation target for South Korea of 5.2% for 1998, an impossible task given the sharp currency depreciation.

To achieve this, interest rates in South Korea were pushed above 20%, hitting the industrial base, already reeling from the crisis, and further deepening the recession. The demand for high interest rates disregarded the accumulated experience of fighting crises over the preceding century or more, and is contrary to the policies used subsequently, for example in the ongoing crisis. The Fund has demanded very high interest rates in some countries to which it has provided assistance in the ongoing crisis, suggesting a deep-seated attachment to what most analysts consider an inappropriate policy response.

Other reforms, such as cuts to subsidies and labour market reforms, might have been laudable long-term goals but are hard to implement in the middle of a crisis. In Indonesia, the resulting cuts in food and energy subsidies led to riots, and the end result in South Korea was mass layoffs, leading to strikes and riots.

The problem is that the IMF can only exert influence when a country wants a cheque. While riots are not palatable, avoiding them does not guarantee good policy. The IMF's policy was unpopular and disruptive, but one could argue that its structural adjustment programmes laid the groundwork for the strong sustainable post-crisis growth.

Heavy-handedness

The IMF was seen as acting heavy-handedly by the crisis countries, with the signature manifestation of this being the signing ceremony of the agreement with Indonesia in 2008. In order to demonstrate commitment, both President Suharto and Managing Director Michel Camdessus attended the ceremony. The photo taken at the occasion – see Figure 6.10 – became the visible face of the IMF's power. Of course, the photo says nothing about the actual relationship between the IMF and Indonesia, but it did resonate with popular perceptions of events.

Strong resentment against the Fund lingered, and the countries did their best to repay their loans ahead of schedule: South Korea in 2001, Thailand in 2003 and Indonesia in October 2006. The resentment was fuelled by politicians deflecting blame from themselves, by the real economic disruption in the crisis and by the dislike anybody feels when beholden. Of course, the ability to repay early can also be seen as a testament to the easy terms of the loans and the effectiveness of the Fund's policy demands.

6.5.1 IMF as a lender of last resort

If the crisis was essentially a liquidity crisis, the optimal real-time response was a sufficiently large provision of liquidity – LOLR.

The IMF, however, is not a suitable LOLR. LOLR operations can be quite large and any LOLR needs to have ready large amounts of liquid money. Similarly, any provider of LOLR

Figure 6.10 IMF Managing Director, Michel Camdessus and President Suharto, in 1998
Source: Agus Lolong/Getty Images

needs to be able to act decisively, providing funds in a very short amount of time. That is exactly the advantage the central banks have in the provision of liquidity during crises.

As an international lender of last resort (ILOLR), the IMF does not have the ability to print money on demand, and needs a significant amount of time to get support for lending operations. Therefore, the Fund is not in a position to be a LOLR, except perhaps in special cases. It is consequently unable to deal directly with an international liquidity crisis. If it is not the IMF in such circumstances, it is nobody.

Furthermore, the loans from the IMF are in dollars. If the dollars are spent defending the local currency, which then devalues, the government's local currency liability is increased and this will worsen whatever the market is worried about – unsustainability of finances, excess foreign borrowings, etc. Hence, the dollar loans would do little to change market perception. To be effective, the loans would have to be fully in local currency and the IMF would need to put its money where its mouth is, as one expects of a LOLR.

This means that comparing the scale of the IMF loans to the scale of changes in reserves is not correct. IMF loans enable countries to take bigger bets, but the loans do not remove the risk, and the country is presumably under attack because the risks were already perceived as excessive.

That said, the IMF does represent member governments and hence has considerable powers of persuasion beyond simply providing funds. In January 1998, it helped by jawboning, backed up by realistic carrots and sticks. Still, the IMF packages were in hindsight clearly insufficient, even though that was not clear at the time.

What the IMF could have done

What was primarily needed in the summer of 1997 were not structural reforms nor hectoring over moral hazard but LOLR at the onset of the crisis. If foreign investors had not feared significant losses if they rolled over loans, the sudden stop would not have happened, the speculative attacks would not have occurred and most of the crisis would have been averted. The countries would then have had time to improve their capital accounts and address the most direct vulnerabilities. It is an open question whether the countries would have taken advantage of this breathing space.

The IMF did not see things this way in 1997, and even successfully prevented other efforts to provide emergency liquidity assistance, most importantly a Japanese-led initiative in September 1997 for an 'Asian Monetary Fund', amounting to $100 billion, to provide rapid liquidity assistance without many conditions. Besides Japan, several countries including China, Taiwan, Hong Kong and Singapore signed up. This met strong opposition from the US Treasury and the IMF, indicating that the Fund does not want competition.

Eventually, the Fund adjusted its position, moving away from immediate structural reforms and especially fiscal macroeconomic tightening, towards helping the countries cope with the liquidity crisis.

6.6 WIDER LESSONS

The Asian crisis was a typical crisis, and any student of financial crises from the nineteenth century would have recognised events and mistakes made both by the countries themselves and by the international community.

The underlying causes of the crisis were familiar. The East Asian countries had a desire for rapid economic growth, and therefore needed high investment rates. Since domestic savings were not enough, they had to resort to international capital markets. Being overconfident of their ability to repay, they were prepared to accept terms that exposed them to risks that proved to be excessive. Similar mechanisms have been at the heart of many previous crises.

The authorities could have attempted to minimise the risk by keeping mismatches low, but instead the balance was swung towards excessive risk by the opening of the capital account and financial liberalisation, without appropriate safeguards. Left to their own devices, the overconfident tend to go for the shortest-term funding because that is the cheapest.

There is nothing unique about the Asian crises and, perhaps with benefit of hindsight, observers should have seen the vulnerabilities build up. The fact that nobody was concerned at the time is a cause for worry. Perhaps one reason is that crisis watchers were focusing on the last round of crises, in Latin America. It is a reminder of how much easier it is to diagnose problems with hindsight than when they are building up.

We should continue to question the extent to which the lessons that have been learned from the last crisis will be relevant to the next. In the Asian crisis, as is so often the case, the most damaging decisions were not those made before the crisis, but those during the crisis. A longer-term view, focusing beyond the immediate newspaper headlines, might have demonstrated that the crisis was as much about liquidity as structural deficiencies. Provision of liquidity, backed up by a credible reform programme, would have prevented the worst.

Thinking back, it now seems that the countries' governments have not sufficiently taken on board the necessary lessons, perhaps with the exception of South Korea. The objective of the structural adjustment programmes was to help the affected countries, and their failure to grow sufficiently, demonstrated by their failure to improve their global ranking post-crisis, suggests that the programmes did not take hold.

This is partly because the issues were misdiagnosed at the time, but also because many of the regimes reverted to type as soon as the pressure came off. A thorough implementation of many of the Fund's programmes would probably have helped the countries perform better. For example, corruption remains a serious problem in all of the countries, except perhaps South Korea, and the IMF's anti-corruption stance is laudable.

The crisis marks the beginning of a reduction in GDP per capita growth, but correlation does not imply causation. The very high pre-crisis growth was in part based on unsustainable policies, such as the dependence on short-term foreign capital. Therefore, it is just as likely that the post-crisis slower growth is more sustainable and less prone to crises, and therefore to be preferred.

Ultimately, this means that Asian crisis countries remain vulnerable. Their large currency reserves might provide protection, but in the absence of sensible reforms, helping to move them up the relative wealth ladder, a future crisis remains a likely eventuality.

6.6.1 Relation to the ongoing crisis

The Asian crisis has many connections with the ongoing crisis. It is a direct causal factor, because the crisis response at the time – the low exchange rates, accumulation of foreign reserves and export-led growth – all contributed to low interest rates and low inflation in developed countries. This fuelled the growth and excessive optimism, leading to the 2007 crisis.

There are also direct parallels between the Asian crisis and the ongoing crisis. The authorities in the US and Europe were quick to identify liquidity as a main cause, providing vast amounts of funds to the financial system. In spite of considerable evidence that risk taking had been excessive prior to the crisis, concerns about moral hazard and reduction in risk, with the sole exception of the decision to allow the collapse of Lehman, have very much taken the backstage in the crisis-fighting efforts.

Furthermore, there has been little serious discussion of structural reforms in the main industrialised countries suffering from the crisis; reform is focused on those receiving bailouts.

The current phase of the global crisis has perhaps more parallels with the Asian crisis. Here, the main crisis countries – Ireland, Greece, Spain, Portugal and Cyprus – play the role of the Asian countries, and Germany and other northern European countries act as the international creditors, with the IMF in a similar role.

Before the European crisis countries get assistance, they have to implement extreme austerity programmes and structural reforms, just like the East Asian countries had to do in 1997. Also, while some liquidity assistance is provided, it is far from enough to assure the markets. Meanwhile, no end to the European sovereign debt crisis is in sight.

6.7 SUMMARY

Some countries in East Asia suffered a severe financial and economic crisis in 2007, in particular South Korea, Malaysia, Indonesia and Thailand. Of these, all but Malaysia requested assistance from the IMF.

Prior to the crisis, the fundamentals appeared sound, and the crisis came as a surprise, but underneath were significant private sector problems, in particular, extensive short-term foreign currency borrowing.

Initial explanations for the crisis focused on weak fundamentals and moral hazard, with subsequent analysis highlighting the importance of liquidity.

The IMF came under strong criticism for its performance in the crisis, but it was hampered by institutional difficulties beyond its control. Many of the mistakes made by the Fund are visible only with the benefit of hindsight.

Some of the lessons from the Asian crisis have been taken on board in the current crisis, especially the early stages. Unfortunately, similar mistakes now appear to be repeated in Europe.

Questions for discussion

1. How does the Asian crisis differ from the previous major regional crisis, in Latin America?
2. What does it mean when we say that the economic fundamentals were sound but not the financial fundamentals?
3. Compare and contrast the causes of the crisis, the resolution of the crisis and the post-crisis reactions across the three countries.
4. Some commentators have argued that panic and contagion played an important role in the crisis. What is your view on this analysis?
5. Initial explanations for the crisis focused on moral hazard and related issues. These were eventually dismissed as a main cause. Why?
6. Later analysis, especially in the countries affected, focuses on liquidity. Explain the basis of the argument; discuss why it might be correct and what might be missing.
7. What was the role of the IMF? Did it give necessary help and support to the countries concerned or did it make matters worse?
8. Is the IMF a suitable provider of liquidity, or even a LOLR?
9. Are there parallels between the Asian crisis and the crisis dating from 2007?

References

Alba, P., Bhattacharya, A., Claessens, S., Ghosh, S. and Hernandez, L. (1998). Volatility and contagion in a financially integrated world: lessons from East Asia's recent experience. Paper presented at the PAFTAD 24 Conference, 'Asia Pacific Financial Liberalization and Reform', 1998.

Goldstein, M. (1998). *The Asian Financial Crisis: Causes, Cures, and Systemic Implications*. Institute for International Economics, Washington DC.

International Monetary Fund (1997). Camdessus announces IMF support for Indonesia's economic program. News brief no. 97/19, 8, October 1997, www.imf.org/external/np/sec/nb/1997/nb9719.htm.

Ito, T. (2007). Asian currency crisis and the International Monetary Fund, 10 years later: Overview. *Asian Econ. Policy Rev.,* 2: 16–49.

Radelet, S. and Sachs, J. (2000). The onset of the East Asian financial crisis. In Krugman, P., editor, *Currency Crises*. University of Chicago Press. www.nber–org/chapters/c8691.

Weisbrot, M. (2007). Ten years after: the lasting impact of the Asian financial crisis. Technical report. www.cepr.net/documents/publications/asia_crisis_2007_08.pdf.

7 BANKING CRISES

Policymakers formulating banking policy and fighting banking crises need to consider several conflicting objectives. We want banks to actively finance economic activity and hence take on risk, but at the same time we want to curtail excessive risk-taking. Once a crisis is under way, we need to balance *moral hazard* considerations against the benefit of robust recapitalisations of banks, all whilst trying to minimise the costs to the taxpayers.

Banking crises cannot easily be avoided, as they are an inevitable consequence of having a vibrant banking system and economy. The only way to completely prevent banking crises is to restrict the banking system so severely that banks are unable to fulfil their socially useful role of financing risky activities, seriously holding back economic growth. What we can do is to reduce the incidence of banking crises and to minimise the costs of fighting them once they are underway.

Banking crises tend to have the same underlying causes. When times are good, banks enjoy access to significant amounts of credit. The banks, flush with money, look for borrowers, but traditional companies can only absorb so much money, not enough for all the liquid funds available. Therefore, as the banks search for borrowers, those they find are increasingly of low quality, often involved in real-estate speculation. Initially, the resulting weaknesses in the banks' loan books are not very visible since the price of real estate and equities increases sharply, creating a virtuous cycle between bank lending and prices. High prices create the illusion of a good collateral which further stimulates lending.

Eventually, valuations of assets are increasingly out of tune with the underlying economic fundamentals, and as in the tale by Hans Christian Andersen, it is as if somebody cries out 'the Emperor has no clothes' and everything reverses at warp speed, prices collapse and credit is withdrawn. This is typical of *endogenous risk*.

The reason why such booms and busts in asset prices cause banking crises is the inherent *fragility of banks* that comes from *fractional reserve banking*. Under this arrangement, when depositors put their money into a bank, the bank then turns around and lends most of it out, keeping a small fraction as reserves. The fragility arises because deposits generally are of short maturity, and some can be withdrawn whenever the depositor wants – *demand deposits* – whilst the loans tend to be of longer maturity. If a sufficiently large number of depositors want their money, the bank will run out of cash, because it cannot similarly call on its own borrowers to repay their loans. We call such an event a *bank run*. Bank runs are contagious, and can spread quickly throughout the financial system. The reason is that the banking system is built on trust, so if depositors lose confidence in banks they flee to cash.

Bank failures matter because they create *negative externalities*, adversely impacting on the economy. Banks provide essential services, and without banks companies cannot do business, nor can individuals go about their lives in their usual way. The failure of an individual bank might not be that costly because the authorities have in place robust mechanisms for preventing collateral damage from bank failures, but if we experience a wave of bank failures – a banking crisis – the impact on society will be serious.

The incidence and seriousness of banking crises in the developed world has fallen significantly since the Great Depression because the authorities in most countries have in place effective regulations preventing bank failures and robust mechanisms for coping with the failure of individual banks, preventing failures from spreading to the entire banking system.

Historically, this was not the case, and bank crises have caused significant economic damage. For example, Kupiec and Ramirez (2009) studied the United States (US) from 1900 until 1930 and found that bank failures significantly reduced economic growth. A one-standard-deviation shock to the share of liabilities in failed banks was found to cause a 17% decline in industrial production and a 4% decline in GDP.

Links to other chapters

This chapter draws on theoretical concepts discussed in Chapter 1 (systemic risk), Chapter 3 (endogenous risk), Chapter 4 (liquidity), Chapter 8 (bank runs and deposit insurance), Chapter 14 (bailouts) and Chapter 13 (financial regulations).

Key concepts

- Banking crises
- Moral hazard
- Good bank – bad bank
- Causes of banking crises
- Why it is so hard to prevent banking crises

Readings for this chapter

No specific readings are required for this chapter as the material is self-contained, but for a good survey see Kaminsky and Reinhart (1999), Banking Committee on Banking Supervision (2004), Caprio and Honohan (2009) and Reinhart and Rogoff (2009). For

a good account of early banking history and further discussions on fractional reserve banking, de Soto (2009) is an excellent book. Ferguson (2008) documents the history of money and Graeber (2011) provides a comprehensive survey of the history of money and credit.

7.1 MONEY AND EARLY BANKING

Money is defined by its function as a means of payment in exchange: in a monetary economy, goods and services are bought and sold in exchange for money. Historically, various goods have served as money, anything from seashells to copper. For example, the Swedish government established a copper standard in 1625, which turned out to be an effective way to prevent theft, but transaction costs were somewhat high.

Over time, the basic unit of money has converged to precious metals, a portable commodity which derives its value from its scarcity, with silver and gold most common. By the early nineteenth century, the world was divided into three metallic blocs: *gold*, silver and both (bimetal). Over time gold became dominant, lasting until 1914, due to the political and military dominance of the gold bloc. Various forms of the gold standard played an important role in the various monetary arrangements between the two world wars, and gold was the cornerstone of the Bretton Woods system. Since the US left the Bretton Woods system, and hence the gold standard, in 1971, almost all countries have used *fiat money*, which is money that has value because of government regulation or law but is without intrinsic value. Consequently, fiat money necessarily has to be legal tender. Fiat money is not a new invention; an early example is its introduction in the twelfth century in China as documented by Selgin (2003), leading to the first recorded nationwide inflation. The first European bank to print banknotes (fiat money) was Stockholms Banco in 1656. It eventually printed too much money and went bust.

A major problem with most forms of money is the temptation of governments to debase it. There are examples going back to the Roman Empire of governments reissuing coins in the same denomination, but increasing the relative content of cheap metals at the expense of gold and silver – the original form of *debasement*. The more recent practice of printing too much money and creating inflation is simply a modern form of currency debasement.

Early banking

It is unclear who was first engaged in fractional reserve banking. Initially, such banking was illegal, not least because of the Catholic Church's ban on the charging of interest – *usury*. Fractional reserve banking began to gain legal recognition as governments realised they could also benefit by borrowing large sums of money from banks, often to finance wars. Inevitably, banks often failed because of sovereign defaults.

Below we discuss two examples of early banks, the famous Medici bank of Florence, which functioned as a fractional reserve bank, and the Amsterdamsche Wisselbank in the Netherlands, which operated as a full reserve bank for most of its existence. We will see how they innovated and made their money, what risks they faced and how they eventually failed.

Medici bank (1397–1494)

The *Medici bank*, 1397–1494, was the largest and most respected bank in Europe during the fifteenth century, making the Medici family perhaps the wealthiest family in Europe. The Medici bank was highly diversified, being involved in silk and cloth manufacturing as well as facilitating trade, for example, by lending to English sheep farmers and wool merchants in return for buying their goods for low prices, thus bypassing usury laws.

The Medici bank made most of its money by selling bills of exchange, which were invented to circumvent usury laws. When a depositor paid money into a branch of a Medici bank, the general manager of the branch issued a bill of exchange to the depositor, instructing another Medici branch in a different country to pay the money back in local currency upon the depositor presenting the bill, but at a pre-agreed exchange rate. Thus, the interest rate charge could be hidden in the exchange rate.

The way the bank facilitated trade can be seen in Figure 7.1. If a merchant was travelling from Florence to London, he could buy a bill of exchange for 15 florins from the Florence branch, agreeing at the time of purchase that the London branch would cash the bill at an exchange rate of 3 florins per pound. Three months later when the merchant arrived in London, if the florin had appreciated against the pound, the merchant would suffer a loss. This instrument meant that the Medici bank faced a significant exchange rate risk, and the heads of different Medici branches often wrote to each other to obtain information and forecast the direction of exchange rates. This risk could be hedged by offsetting trades, for example, facilitating the business of a London-based merchant travelling to Florence.

Bills of exchange were freely traded, and were effective in acting as a medium of exchange. The Medici bank has also been credited with the invention of double entry accounting; all in all, it was a hugely profitable business, making around a 32% annual return on equity from 1397 to 1420.

The Medici bank eventually failed for a variety of reasons, one of them too much lending to high-risk borrowers, like sovereigns. Just one example is the failure of the London branch which lent too much to the English King Edward IV who could not repay due to

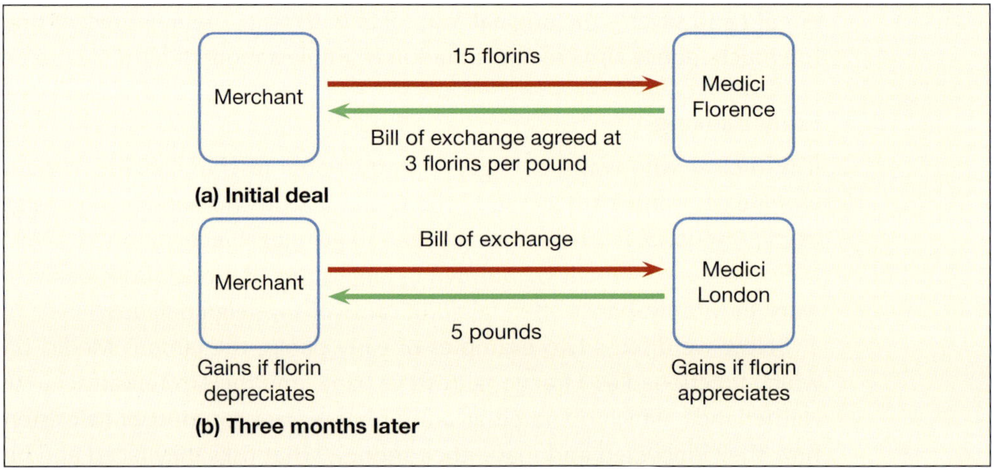

Figure 7.1 An example of a bill of exchange transaction

a civil war. Failure of the Bruges branch followed, due to poor management, fraud and, again, excessive lending.

Amsterdamsche Wisselbank (1609–1795)

In the late 1500s, Amsterdam was the up and coming financial centre. Its merchants pioneered new methods and the city's wealth multiplied. The growth in its prosperity was held back by the large number of foreign coins in circulation. The burghers of Amsterdam solved that problem by creating a new form of bank, in a way an early form of a central bank, called the *Amsterdamsche Wisselbank*, backed by the city of Amsterdam.

It was fundamentally based on a type of money, new to Europe but used earlier in the middle east, known as *bank money*. The bank received foreign and local coins at their intrinsic value, deducted a management fee, and then credited the client's account with bank money for the remainder value. The bank was helped by a law stating that all bills drawn in Amsterdam and worth more than 600 guilders had to be paid in this bank money, in effect, granting the bank a monopoly on the issue of currency. By allowing merchants to set up accounts, the bank pioneered the system of cheques and debits. Bank money was secure from accidents and theft, and essentially free from debasement worries. Often bank money was worth more than its nominal value.

Most of the banks' capital was composed of gold and silver bullion deposits, which clients deposited for safekeeping. The client would receive a *receipt* for an amount that was 5% less than the mint price, and could withdraw their bullion upon presenting the receipt. Like the bills of exchange, receipts were freely traded; if a merchant was in need of coins, he could sell his receipt, and if he wanted bullion, he would purchase a receipt. The bank allowed no withdrawal of bullion except by means of receipt, and it maintained that it did not lend out the deposited bullion.

This meant that the amount of deposits was almost the same as the money supply and there was no credit expansion. In other words, Amsterdamsche Wisselbank practised *full-reserve banking*. It is a practice in which the full amounts of each depositor's funds are available in reserve, as cash or other highly liquid assets. This made the bank very secure but not very profitable. The bank made most of its profits from various fees. The bank survived for almost 200 years, and its eventual demise began when the city's government ordered it to hand over its deposits to finance the Anglo-Dutch war; the bank also lent out funds secretly to other provincial states of the Netherlands and the East India Company. Its reserve ratio declined from 100% to 25% and it stopped exchanging receipts for bullion when a liquidity crisis hit in 1790–1791, destroying its reputation.

7.2 MORAL HAZARD

Moral hazard is fundamental to any study of financial crises.

Definition 7.1 Moral hazard Moral hazard is what happens when those taking risk do not have to face the full consequences of failure but get to enjoy all the benefits of success. The consequence of moral hazard is that those fortunate enough to be in that situation are encouraged to take on more risk than they otherwise would do.

Moral hazard is pervasive throughout the economy, such as in standard insurance contracts. Moral hazard is not something that should be eliminated, since that would sharply curtail socially optimal risk taking. For example, an important development in modern economies was the creation of limited liability corporations, firms where the owners do not face the full consequences of failure but get all the benefits. Even though limited liability corporations create moral hazard, few would argue they should be banned or that the underlying moral hazard should be substantially reduced, since the benefits outweigh the costs.

Moral hazard is usually not much of a problem when those subject to moral hazard get compensated for doing so. That compensation is why insurance companies are content to write insurance contracts in the full knowledge that such contracts induce the insured to take more risk. To contain such risk taking, insurance companies write into the contracts clauses designed to prevent excessively risky behaviour, and try to price risk properly.

Unfortunately, this is often not the case in the financial system. Banks receive explicit or implicit guarantees from the government but such insurance is almost never priced. Governments can try to prevent excessive risk taking, but this is also frequently ineffective. Addressing this problem is a main motivation for financial regulations. The problem arises because the externalities from the failure of an important financial institution can outweigh any possible moral hazard considerations. This leaves the authorities with a typical risk–return trade-off between the benefits of preventing panic now against the costs of inducing riskier activity later.

Financial institutions, of course, know this and are incentivised to take on too much risk when things are good in the full expectation of a bailout when things are bad. The bigger, the more dangerous, the worse-run and more interconnected a financial institution is, the more likely it is to be bailed out.

Taken together, the moral hazard problem in the financial industry is particularly hard, with no obvious solution. In order to contain the problem, governments regulate the financial industry, but it can be difficult to the point of impossible to effectively contain excessive risk taking. The powerful tools at the government's disposal tend to be very blunt and could easily curtail risk taking excessively, whilst the more surgical tools may not be effective.

7.3 COSTS OF BANKING CRISES

The World Bank and the International Monetary Fund (IMF) have developed and made public a very comprehensive database on financial crises. We made use of the 2008 version of the data, due to Laeven and Valencia (2008), although they are only the most recent maintainers of the database and many others have preceded them. All data mentioned in this section are from this database unless otherwise mentioned. The latest version of the data can be downloaded.[1]

Before the crises from 2007, the frequency of banking crises had been slowing down, as indicated by Figure 7.2, with the worst year being 1995 when 13 countries suffered

[1]www.imf.org/external/pubs/cat/longres.aspx?sk=26015.0.

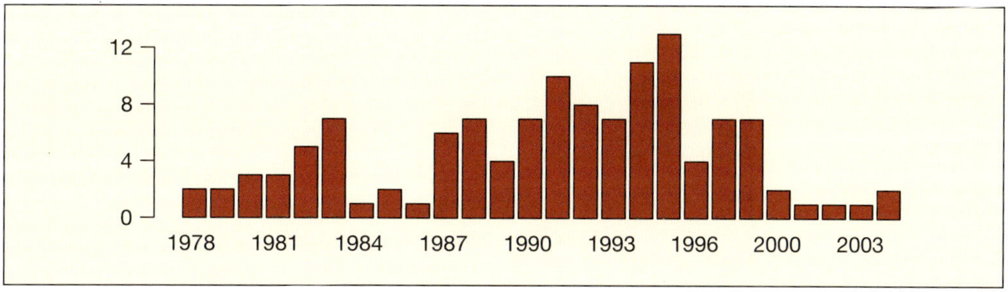

Figure 7.2 Frequency of banking crises

Data source: Laeven and Valencia (2008)

banking crises. The relative calm before the 2007 crisis led to the misleading conclusion that the world was becoming safer; instead, this period was more like the calm before the storm.

It is remarkably hard to make sustained changes in levels of risk, because improvements addressing existing fears have the side-effect of improving confidence, leading to greater risk taking.

Costs

Banking crises impose costs on the economy in two main ways. The first is from the direct fiscal costs of resolving a crisis, like the provision of deposit insurance, liquidity support, recapitalisation and the like. This cost can be more or less accurately measured.

The second cost is the indirect effect on the economy, for example, the impact on asset markets, reduced consumption and investment, the impaired channelling of funds from savers to ultimate users, the contraction of government revenues, sharply expanding fiscal expenditures and the shortfall in economic growth. This is much harder to measure, and the available studies inevitably have to rely on fairly crude methods to do this. Consequently, we do need to take such measurements with reservation. Laeven and Valencia (2008) estimate output losses by extrapolating from the trend of real GDP prior to a crisis, and calculating the aggregate difference between the trend prediction and actual outcomes during and after a crisis. There are many other ways of doing this analysis.

This calculation will often overstate the output losses. For example, suppose a country is on an unsustainable growth path fuelled by inflows of foreign money. In this case, the GDP growth in the years before the crisis will be artificially high, and the output loss, therefore, will be overstated. Since most of the necessary macroeconomic data are in publicly available databases, it would be straightforward to use alternative methodologies to calculate the costs of crises, and many authors have done so.

A small sample of the results is shown in Table 7.1. We see that Argentina in its 1980 crisis used more than half of its GDP to resolve the crisis, but the impact on GDP was relatively small at 11%. This calculation is of course complicated by the fact that Argentina experienced hyperinflation at the time.

The Scandinavian crisis of the early 1990s imposed significant direct fiscal costs on Finland, but less so on Sweden. However, the output shortfall is significant. Note that it is likely to be overstated because the GDP was artificially high at the top of the boom, and

Table 7.1 Country systemic banking crises. Fiscal cost and output loss are represented as percentages of GDP

		Fiscal cost	Output loss
Argentina	1980	55.1%	10.8%
Finland	1991	12.8%	59.1%
Indonesia	1997	56.8%	67.9%
South Korea	1997	31.2%	50.1%
Mexico	1994	19.3%	4.2%
Sweden	1991	3.6%	30.6%
Turkey	2000	32%	5.4%
United States	1988	3.7%	4.1%
Venezuela	1994	15%	9.6%

Source: Systemic Banking Crises: a New Database, IMF Working Paper, pp. 34–51 (Laeven, L. and Valencia, F. 2008), International Monetary Fund

these numbers do not quite correspond with those in Section 7.5.3 below, produced by one of the central banks involved.

The size of the country matters: while the cost of the S&L crisis in 1988 in the US was quite significant in monetary terms, relative to GDP the cost was not very high, in part because only a small part of the financial sector was directly affected.

Costs of resolution

The IMF database was originally developed by the World Bank and some of the developers of the database published an interesting paper (Honohan and Klingebiel, 2003) focusing on the fiscal costs of banking crises and how the various government responses contribute to this cost. They found that if countries do not extend some policies of unlimited deposit guarantees, open-ended liquidity support, repeated recapitalisations, debtor bailouts and regulatory forbearance, the fiscal costs of resolution will be around 1% of GDP on average, one-tenth of the actual costs. If, however, governments employ all of the approaches above, the fiscal costs will be six times larger than in actuality.

It is important to note, however, that quantifying the costs of crisis and government action, or inaction, is quite challenging. There are strong causal effects, where a bad crisis might lead to bad outcomes, so that some of the policy measures taken might be associated with the severity of the outcomes.

It is also hard to estimate the cost of inaction. For example, the decision to allow Lehman to fail was followed by a reversal of policy and effectively unlimited support to many other institutions. Many commentators argue that the cost of continued inaction would have been much higher than the cost of this support, but this remains controversial.

7.4 CAUSES OF BANKING CRISES

The causes of banking crises are usually fundamentally the same: financial institutions over-expand during good times, artificially inflating asset prices, creating positive feedback loops between bank lending, market prices and firm profitability. This is often coupled with inflows of hot money from abroad, and/or an accommodating fiscal and monetary policy.

However, such booms are artificially created by money, not fundamentals, and eventually prices become so misaligned with the underlying economy that a small shock can trigger a rapid reversal. This means that banking crises are often directly linked with macroeconomic crises.

There are often country-specific differences. A report from the Basel Committee for Banking Supervision (BCBS) in 2004 discusses the origins of banking crises in G10 countries and identifies several common factors – the regional economy, asset prices, financial liberalisation and poor regulation in addition to bank specifics. We report a subset of these results in Table 7.2. What is interesting is that bank-specific factors are least common and financial liberalisation is always present.

Financial liberalisation

Many governments faced with a heavily regulated financial sector and anaemic growth opt for financial liberalisation in the belief that it may promote growth. If a government opts for this policy, the execution does have to be right. A common mistake is to reduce oversight and activity restrictions but maintain implicit or explicit government guarantees such as deposit insurance. This creates a nasty moral hazard problem because it can enable financial institutions to borrow cheaply and use the money for high-risk activities.

Deregulation has been at the core of many banking crises, such as the S&L crisis in the US in the 1980s and the Scandinavian crisis in the late 1980s and early 1990s.

Corruption

A frequent cause of individual bank failures is corruption and mismanagement. We discuss one example in detail below, that of BCCI. Caprio and Honohan (2009) describe two examples of what they call bad banking and bad policies in Latin American countries, in Venezuela in 1994 and the Dominican Republic in 2003. In both cases, it involved banks that were so large as to be systematically important. The banks did not seem to

Table 7.2 Banking crises in G10 economies

Shock	Macroeconomic factors		Banking system		Bank-specific factors
	Real economy	Asset prices	Financial liberalisation	Poor regulation	
Switzerland (1991–1996)	✓	✓	✓	×	×
Spain (1978–1983)	✓	✓	✓	✓	×
UK (1991)	✓	×	✓	×	✓
Norway (1988–1993)	✓	✓	✓	✓	×
Sweden (1991–1994)	✓	✓	✓	✓	×
Japan (1994–2002)	✓	✓	✓	✓	×
US (1982–1995)	✓	✓	✓	✓	✓

Source: Table 6 in BCBS Bank Failures in Mature Economies, Basel Committee, Working Paper 13, p. 67 (Ms Natalja v. Westernhagen et al. 2004), Bank for International Settlements

record deposits as liabilities, enabling their insiders to loot the banks' assets from inside, that is, steal the banks' assets. Because of the banks' systematic importance, the central bank of each country felt it necessary to make depositors whole, destabilising the macroeconomy. Furthermore, the rogue bank in Venezuela paid high deposit rates, forcing other competing banks to do the same.

Zombie banks

If financial institutions, in effect, are insolvent but able to continue operating because of government support, they are often referred to as *zombie banks*. The term was first used by Kane (1989) when referring to the S&L crisis, but it became especially common when referring to the Japanese banking sector following that country's crisis in the early 1990s. See BCBS (2004) for more details on the Japanese crisis. In the 1980s, Japanese banks made large loans that eventually turned out to be bad, with many involving real estate. Instead of resolving the bank failures, closing down the failed banks or recapitalising them, the government opted to keep them on life support, often using a process called *evergreening*, whereby a bank is allowed to keep a non-performing loan on its books as if it were performing. That often involved lending money to failed borrowers, just so that they could repay old loans, steadily increasing loan losses to the bank.

Eventually, this meant that a large proportion of the Japanese banking system consisted of zombie banks, significantly associated with the Japanese financial and economic malaise. While the zombies were not the cause of the crisis, their presence adversely affected recovery.

The Japanese lesson is that policymakers should prevent the emergence of zombie banks at all costs, and hence aim to resolve, restructure or shut down failed banks as quickly as possible. That was the approach taken by the Scandinavian governments in resolving their banking crisis in the early 1990s. In the ongoing crisis, the governments of the US, Switzerland and the UK have actively tried to prevent the emergence of zombie banks. However, this has not been the case in many of the European countries affected by the European sovereign debt crisis, and there are significant fears that zombie banks may be emerging in Europe. The fact that the European Central Bank (ECB) has become the sole provider of liquidity for certain banks, and even entire national banking systems, whilst losses have not been properly recognised, supports the view that some European governments prefer to let their banks turn into zombies to make the necessary effort to resolve their banking crises.

7.5 BANK AND BANKING SYSTEM FAILURES

7.5.1 Individual bank failures

Among the many individual bank failures throughout history, several had an especially important impact on future policy and financial regulations. We discuss three of the most important cases below.

Herstatt

Herstatt was a large German bank that was forced into liquidation by the German authorities on 26 June 1974. On that day a number of banks had released payments of German marks to Herstatt in Frankfurt in exchange for USD that were to be delivered in New York. Because of time-zone differences, Herstatt ceased operations between the times of the respective payments. Herstatt had taken receipt of payment from European banks (in marks) but not yet made the corresponding dollar payments. Consequently, mostly US creditors were left holding unsecured claims. This is an example of *settlement risk*. The failure of Bank Herstatt was one factor that led to the creation of the *continuous linked settlement platform*, which was launched almost 30 years later in 2002. For more details on the Herstatt case, see BCBS (2004).

Banco Ambrosiano

Banco Ambrosiano was an Italian bank which collapsed in 1982 with important consequences for future regulations. See, for example, Stoler and Kalb (1982) for a description of events, and Herring and Litan (1995) for the regulatory implications. It was the largest private banking group in Italy in its time, with operations in 15 countries. At the centre of the bank's failure was its chairman, Roberto Calvi, called by the Italian press 'God's Banker' due to his close association with the Holy See.

Calvi was determined to transform his bank into a major international financial institution from a relatively small regional bank with strong religious overtones. One of his initial steps was to form a Luxembourg holding company not subject to Italy's banking regulations.

Calvi's problems began in 1978, when the Bank of Italy conducted an extensive audit of his financial empire, noting unorthodox operations involving $1.2 billion in unsecured USD borrowings. Calvi was buying up Ambrosiano stock, using money borrowed on international financial markets. The bank collapsed because the Italian lira fell relative to the dollar.

Calvi was sentenced to four years in jail, but released pending appeal. He fled Italy but was found hanged under Blackfriars Bridge in London in 1982. The failure of Ambrosiano left more than 200 international financial institutions with large losses, threatening the stability of the entire international banking system. Ultimately, this brought changes in the way the world's major banks do business. The BCBS responded to the Banco Ambrosiano collapse in 1983 with the first major revision of the *Concordat*.

BCCI

BCCI was a bank registered in Luxembourg with head offices in Karachi and London. In July 1991, BCCI, one of the 300 or so branches and subsidiaries of foreign banks operating in London, failed because of widespread fraud. BCCI's complex structure consisted of a holding company, incorporated in Luxembourg, and two main subsidiaries incorporated in the Cayman Islands and Luxembourg. See Truell and Gurwin (1992) for more information. BCCI had branches in over 70 countries with the UK offices being branches of the Luxembourg subsidiary. Its principal shareholders were in Abu Dhabi.

It is now believed that BCCI's financial statements had been falsified from its establishment in 1972. A scheme of deception was developed to support BCCI's rapid growth and to conceal lending losses. To achieve this, BCCI failed to record deposit liabilities and created fictitious loans that generated substantial profits. Fraud also took place within BCCI's treasury operations. BCCI used depositors' money to fund their own proprietary trading activities, and covered up the resulting losses with more fictitious loans.

Prior to these problems surfacing in 1990, supervisors and commercial bankers were wary of BCCI because of its rapid growth and opaque corporate structure. However, while BCCI was sometimes mentioned in the press 'chiefly for the mystery that surrounded it', financial market participants generally saw BCCI as a bank that made losses through incompetence rather than fraud.

From the spring of 1990, concerns about the evidence of fraud within BCCI led to ongoing discussions between BCCI's auditors (Price Waterhouse), banking supervisors and BCCI's shareholders. In 1991, Price Waterhouse became increasingly convinced that the fraud within BCCI was endemic, with published financial statements grossly inaccurate, and informed the Bank of England (BoE) of its findings.

The liquidators, Deloitte & Touche, filed a lawsuit against the bank's auditors, Price Waterhouse and Ernst & Young. This was settled for $175 million in 1998. BCCI creditors also attempted to sue the BoE as BCCI's regulators. This case demonstrated the reputational risk for central banks that also oversaw banking supervision, and was one motivation for the separation of banking supervision from the BoE in 1997.

7.5.2 Savings and loans in the US in the 1980s

The US suffered a banking crisis in the 1980s in its S&L (savings and loans) sector. S&Ls used to be a fairly quiet part of the US financial landscape, a category of financial institutions common in many countries, often under the name of savings banks or something similar.

The S&L industry suffered from the high interest rates and inflation of the late 1970s, and as a consequence the authorities deregulated the industry with the view that the S&Ls could grow their way out of trouble. At the time, deregulation took place in many parts of the US economy and the S&L deregulation was a part of that process. The intention was to allow the S&L sector to expand into more parts of banking services previously closed to them, because the objective of the S&Ls had been to promote housing and homeownership. Other changes in oversight included authorising the use of more lenient accounting rules to report their financial conditions, and the elimination of restrictions on the minimum numbers of S&L stockholders. Such policies, combined with an overall decline in regulatory oversight, contributed to the risk-taking in the sector.

The US has a fragmented regulatory structure and had a specific regulator for the S&L, the Federal Home Loan Bank System. The government continued to provide deposit insurance but did not increase oversight of the industry. There were clear signs of *regulatory capture*, whereby the regulated have undue influence on the supervisor. This is a classical problem in deregulation. The final cost of resolving failed S&Ls is estimated at just over $160 billion, including $132 billion from federal taxpayers.

Lessons from the S&L disaster

The S&L crisis has particular lessons for the resolution of banking crises, as identified by Moysich (2000):

- First and foremost the need for strong and effective supervision of insured depository institutions, particularly if they are given new or expanded powers or are experiencing rapid growth.
- Second, this can be accomplished only if the industry does not have too much influence over its regulators and if the regulators have the ability to hire, train and retain qualified staff. In this regard, the bank regulatory agencies need to remain politically independent. The S&L supervisor was too close to the industry it regulated during the early years of the crisis, and its policies significantly contributed to the problem.
- Third, the supervisors need adequate financial resources. The S&L supervisor was given insufficient resources for the supervision of the newly deregulated industry, with many new activities.
- Fourth, the S&L crisis highlights the importance of promptly closing insolvent, insured financial institutions in order to minimise potential losses to the deposit insurance fund and to ensure a more efficient financial marketplace. The failure to promptly close failing institutions creates uncertainty, adversely affecting both the financial system and the economy at large.
- Finally, resolution of failing financial institutions requires that the deposit insurance fund be strongly capitalised with real reserves, not just government guarantees. The reason is that a deposit insurance fund is allocated to its intended purpose, ensuring efficiency and rapid disbursement. It takes much longer to raise funds from the government, because a political decision is needed.

The S&L crisis, and other bank failures in the US at the same time, had a significant impact on how the US authorities have approached financial regulation. In response, they have significantly improved the quality of supervision, absorbing the lessons of the S&L crisis, for example, by developing one of the best resolution regimes in the world, *prompt corrective action*.

7.5.3 The Scandinavian crisis in the 1990s

Three Scandinavian countries, Sweden, Norway and Finland, suffered a severe banking crisis in the early 1990s caused by a huge lending boom in the late 1980s followed by severe deleveraging in the 1990s. Finland was especially badly affected because it had the extra factor of its important trading partner, the Soviet Union, collapsing. The crisis has been documented in BCBS (2004).

The governments of these countries liberalised their financial markets and implemented pro-cyclical macroeconomic policies in the late 1980s. This included removing caps on lending and interest rates and encouraging more competition within the banking sectors, whilst reducing the level of oversight.

The banks were not used to operating in such a free environment and neither were the supervisors. The banks did not develop the necessary risk management systems, so at the time when risk-taking was on the increase by inexperienced banks, government oversight was decreasing. This is typical of the problems of deregulation as discussed above.

This led to a rapid increase in the balance sheets of the banks, as well as asset prices generally, with increased leverage the main cause. For example, nominal non-financial private sector debt increased by 52% in Norway and by 87% in Sweden, causing asset price bubbles. Housing prices in the five years before the peak increased in real terms by 80% in Finland, 44% in Sweden and 38% in Norway. Similarly, equity prices tripled in nominal terms in Sweden and Finland and doubled in Norway.

Moe *et al.* (2004) argue that the fiscal cost of the banking recapitalisation was 8.9% of GDP in Finland, 3.9% in Sweden, and 2% in Norway. Table 7.2 gives 12.8% for Finland, highlighting the challenge of estimating the cost of banking crises.

7.5.4 Bad bank – good bank

A common way for governments to resolve a banking crisis is the method of *good banks – bad banks*. This was the method used to good effect by the Scandinavian governments in resolving their crises. This has now become the 'gold standard' in banking crisis management, and is the model many look to for resolving the European sovereign debt crisis.

The government splits up a failing bank, hiving the dodgy assets into one institution – the bad bank – whilst keeping most of the bank's operations and solid assets in the good bank. In effect, the bad bank becomes an asset management firm. Over time, the government aims to sell the good bank but will often hold onto the bad assets, like corporate loans, until they expire or can be sold individually.

If the assets are valued at firesale prices at the time of doing this, the government has the potential to make significant profits, an argument often used to justify this approach to taxpayers. However, if the original bank was insolvent and the good bank is solvent, then the bad bank must, by definition, have a negative value, so a profit for the government is not the expected outcome.

Realistically, taxpayers should expect to lose money, but hopefully the efficiency gains from having a well-functioning bank replacing a failing bank outweigh the expected loss.

7.5.5 Iceland, 2008

Iceland was the first country to be severely affected by the crises from 2007. The narration in this chapter follows Benediktsdottir *et al.* (2011), and all the statistical data (except where otherwise indicated) come from the parliamentary Special Investigation Commission (SIC) whose report was published in 2009. One of the authors of Benediktsdottir *et al.* (2011) sat on the commission.

The crisis started when the banking system of Iceland, mostly composed of three banks, failed in early October 2008. A decade earlier, all three either had been in government hands or were highly regulated. The government banks were sold to politically connected buyers for what was considered below fair market prices. The banks enjoyed an enviable asset growth of 54% a year, and in the end, their asset size exceeded 800% of GDP, placing Iceland close to the top among European banking nations, if compared to the countries presented in Figure 1.2.

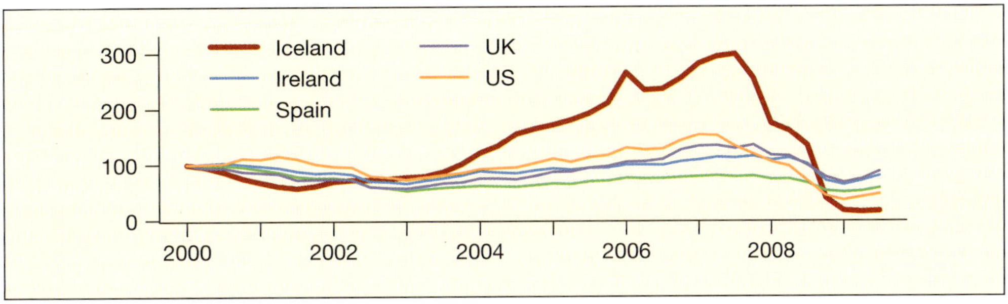

Figure 7.3 Stock market prices, 2000 = 100

A distinguishing feature of the Icelandic crisis was that the real-estate bubble was smaller than in other bubble economies, with the bubble manifesting itself more clearly in the stock market, as seen in Figure 7.3. While there are several reasons for this, the most important is that the stock market was more easily manipulated and more useful in providing collateral in the alleged fraud committed.

Although the banks were highly risky, this was not evident from publicly available numbers, as they were amongst the most highly capitalised banks in Europe according to the Basel capital regulations – see Figure 16.4. One reason is that the bank capital numbers were illusory, since the banks funded purchases of their own equity issues. After that was prevented by the supervisor, banks simply funded equity issues in other Icelandic banks, hedging the exposure by using a contract for difference. This served the dual purpose of increasing tier 1 capital, without the dilution causing prices to fall. All of this helped to create the appearance of high demand for the stocks, fuelling stock-price increases early in the bubble, and preventing prices from falling late in the bubble, after the professional investors caught on to what was happening and started to sell the stocks.

Another way to inflate bank stock prices was by goodwill which was continually increasing, sanctioned by the banks' accountants, the main international accounting firms, without much apparent concern as to value. This contributed to the accounts overstating the value of assets.

Taken together, the causes of the banking crisis were over-ambitious goals without the competence to pull it through, supported by aggressive accounting treatment and permitted by poor regulatory oversight. As the banks expanded, this developed into corruption, incompetence and looting the banks from inside. The privatisation of the banking system delivered the banks in the hands of politically connected groups, who continued enjoying strong connections to the political classes. When the banks started to expand, the government did not correspondingly expand the supervisory structure, so over time the supervisors became less and less effective. The supervisor took an excessively legalistic approach, making it easy for the banks to find loopholes in the regulations. In other words, the enforcement of the regulations targeted the letter of the law, not the spirit of the law, and lost touch with the objectives for which the rules were created.

The banks enjoyed seemingly unlimited access to funds until late in the bubble, and used some of those funds to manipulate their own capital and share prices, all in a positive feedback loop. Analysis by financial professionals did not seem to provide much

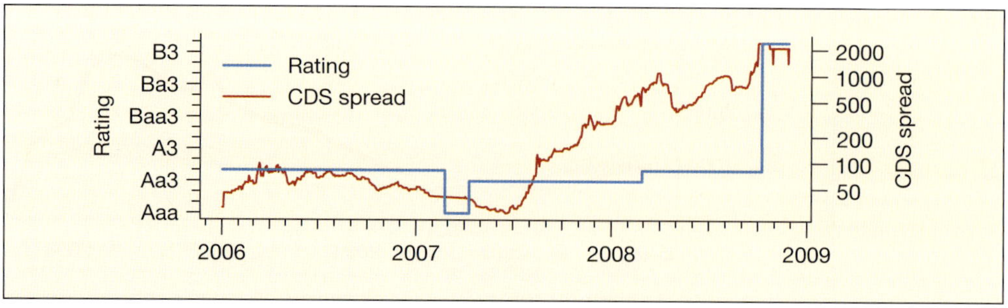

Figure 7.4 Moody's credit ratings for Kaupthing and CDS spreads
Data source: Moody's, Markit and Bloomberg

discipline. We can see this from Figure 7.4, showing the credit ratings and credit default swap (CDS) spreads for the largest bank, Kaupthing. The ratings, in particular, were surprisingly good right up until the collapse, whilst the CDS spreads were steadily increasing from the middle of 2007 when the global crisis started.

Lessons

Countries with large financial systems have spent many decades or centuries developing banking structures and the related supervisory structures. Creating such a setup from scratch in the span of a few years is quite challenging and needs significant political commitment. This demonstrates the importance of institutions in ensuring that markets function efficiently.

This relates to peculiarities caused by operating within Europe.[2] Because of the common European market, European banks were able to operate across the EU, with minimal scrutiny from the host country, since supervision was mostly in the hands of the home supervisor. The absence of pan-European supervision was exploited by the Icelandic banks, enabling their rapid expansion.

7.6 SUMMARY

Banking crises are an unfortunate consequence of modern economies, and while we can significantly mitigate their incidence and consequences, they cannot be prevented altogether in a cost-effective way. The main culprit is the inherent vulnerabilities in banking, such as the fractional reserve system. Another factor is the importance of trust and interdependence in banking, and the overconfidence and tendency to conceal weakness that result.

Banking crises, while well understood, are still quite frequent, because it can be difficult to identify the underlying problems until it is too late, and banks have incentives to ignore and hide the problems.

The authorities are in a difficult position when it comes to resolving banking crises, having to balance a robust response against moral hazard considerations.

[2]Iceland is not a member of the European Union (EU) but is a member of the European Economic Area (EEA), giving it full access to European markets.

Several bank crises have had a profound impact on financial regulations, such as those of Herstatt, Ambrosiano and BCCI. Doubtless the current crisis will also be influential. We discussed three banking crises in some detail: the S&L in the US in the 1980s, the Scandinavian crisis of the early 1990s and the recent Icelandic crisis.

Questions for discussion

1 What are the main causes of banking crises?

2 Banking crisis are frequent and well understood. We know why they happen, the best way to deal with them and we have a good understanding of how to prevent them. Why then are they so frequent?

3 Do you think financial liberalisation is a recommended course of action for a country aiming to stimulate economic growth?

4 What are the ingredients that enable some countries to remain financial centres for centuries, while other countries do not seem to manage it?

5 What are the main lessons from the the savings and loan crisis?

6 The Swedish resolution of its banking crisis in the early 1990s is usually considered the 'gold standard' in crisis resolution. Why might that be the case?

7 What is the good bank – bad bank model?

References

Basel Committee on Banking Supervision (2004). Bank failures in mature economies. Working paper no. 13, Bank of International Settlements.

Benediktsdottir, S., Danielsson, J. and Zoega, G. (2011). Lessons from a collapse of a financial system. *Economic Policy,* 26: 183–231.

Caprio, G. and Honohan, P. (2009). Banking crises. In Berger, A., Molyneux, P. and Wilson, J., editors, *The Oxford Handbook of Banking*. Oxford University Press.

de Soto, J. H. (2009). *Money, Bank Credit, and Economic Cycles*. Ludwig von Mises Institute, Auburn, AL.

Ferguson, N. (2008). *The Ascent of Money*. The Penguin Group.

Graeber, D. (2011). *Debt: The First 5,000 Years*. Melville House Publishing, New York.

Herring, R. J. and Litan, R. E. (1995). *Financial Regulation in the Global Economy*. The Brookings Institution, Washington DC.

Honohan, P. and Klingebiel, D. (2003). The fiscal cost implications of an accommodating approach to banking crises. *J. Banking Finance,* 27(8): 1539–60.

Kaminsky, G. L. and Reinhart, C. M. (1999). The twin crises: the causes of banking and balance-of-payments problems. *Amer. Econ. Rev.,* 89: 473–500.

Kane, E. J. (1989). The S&L insurance mess: how did it happen? Technical report, Urban Institute Press.

Kupiec, P. H. and Ramirez, C. D. (2009). Bank failures and the cost of systemic risk: evidence from 1900–1930. Technical report, FDIC.

Laeven, L. and Valencia, F. (2008). Systemic banking crises: a new database. Technical report, IMF. IMF Working Paper.

Moe, T. G., Solheim, J. A. and Vale, B. (2004). The Norwegian banking crisis. Technical report, Norges Bank. Occasional Paper no. 33.

Moysich, A. (2000). The savings and loan crisis and its relationship to banking. In Federal Deposit Insurance Corporation, *History of the 80s — Lessons for the Future. Volume I: an Examination of the Banking Crises of the 1980s and Early 1990s,* Chapter 4. FDIC, Washington DC.

Reinhart, C. M. and Rogoff, K. (2009). *This Time Is Different: Eight Centuries of Financial Folly*. Princeton University Press.

Selgin, G. (2003). Adaptive learning and the transition to fiat money. *Econ. J.,* 113(484): 147–65.

Stoler, P. and Kalb, J. B. (1982). The great Vatican bank mystery. http://time.com/time/magazine/article/0,9171,951806,00.html.

Truell, P. and Gurwin, L. (1992). *False Profits: the Inside Story of BCCI, the World's Most Corrupt Financial Empire*. Houghton Mifflin, Boston, MA.

8 BANK RUNS AND DEPOSIT INSURANCE

During the Great Depression of 1929 to 1933, the United States (US) lost over one-third of its banks to bankruptcies and people preferred to store their money under their mattresses to keeping it in banks. At the same time, a loss of confidence in Austria led to a run on its banks and government, spilling over to Hungary and Germany. These bank failures were a major contributor to the Depression.

While the Great Depression is the worst example of contagious bank runs in history, waves of bank runs were quite common in the nineteenth and early twentieth centuries. Since then, they have been much less common, especially in developed economies, not least because policymakers have much clearer understanding of the damage caused by bank runs and have developed much better tools for preventing them. The run on Northern Rock in 2007 is unique. This does not mean we have become successful in preventing bank runs, rather they have changed form and are more likely to happen in the wholesale markets.

Bank runs happen because of a fundamental weakness in *fractional reserve banking systems*. A basic model of a bank is an institution that collects demand deposits and makes long-term loans. If a sufficient number of depositors want to get their money back, the bank fails because most of its assets are tied up in long-term loans. For this reason, if depositors are worried that a bank's loans are of a low quality they will demand their deposits back, and cause a *bank run*. A bank run can happen even if there is nothing wrong with the bank; all we need is for depositors to get worried, and then a bank run becomes a *self-fulfilling prophecy*. A bank run can lead to cascading failures within the banking system because depositors might view the failure of a single bank as a symptom of system-wide difficulties. Depositors have limited information about the quality of banks' assets and may feel that if hidden problems have been allowed to develop in one bank, the same may have happened in other banks. Another explanation for cascading failures is through cross-held assets, a failure in one bank directly impacting on other linked banks, and on banks exposed to those banks, etc. This was a key reason behind the 1914 crisis.

Deposit insurance is often successful in preventing bank runs. Such schemes became common after the Great Depression, and are now used in some form by most major economies. The fundamental problem solved by deposit insurance was eloquently modelled by Diamond and Dybvig (1983). The fundamental conclusion of their model is that so long as depositors believe they will be protected, they will not run the bank and, in consequence, a deposit insurance scheme will never be used.

Links to other chapters

This chapter directly relates to Chapter 2 (the Great Depression, 1929–1933), Chapter 4 (liquidity), Chapter 7 (banking crises) and Chapter 13 (financial regulations).

Key concepts

- Bank runs
- Deposit insurance
- Retail and wholesale funding
- Moral hazard
- Diamond and Dybvig model

Readings for this chapter

The main theoretical analysis in this chapter comes from the model of Diamond and Dybvig (1983), but more broadly it fits in with the more general analysis of prudential banking regulation such as Dewatripont and Tirole (1994).

More specific analysis is provided by Santos (2000). Miller (1996) studied the Argentinian experiment of abolishing deposit insurance in the early 1990s, whilst Shin (2008) is concerned with the run on Northern Rock. Finally, Borio (2009) focuses on the intersection between more general liquidity provision and wholesale markets with deposit insurance for retail depositors.

Notation specific to this chapter

c_1, c_2	Consumption at $t = 1, 2$
N	Number of depositors
R	Gross return on deposits if withdrawn at $t = 2$
$t = 0, 1, 2$	A particular observation, e.g. a day
$U(\cdot)$	Utility function
λ	Fraction (probability) of early consumers
π	Transfer from late to early agents

8.1 BANK RUNS AND CRISES

8.1.1 The United States in the Great Depression

The nineteenth-century economy of the US was characterised by frequent bank panics, with corresponding economic downturns and unemployment. After a particularly severe panic of 1893, legislators sought to arrange better security for bank deposits.

The resulting combined state–federal system failed to prevent bank panics during the Great Depression which saw 4,004 banks close (see Figure 8.1). The panic suffered by the US banking system in 1931 originated with the Bank of United States in New York, which made a big bet on the value of New York real estate. In early 1931, as rumours that the Bank of United States might be in trouble circulated, the New York Federal Reserve Bank (NYFed) tried to engineer a merger and arrange a rescue package. But the Bank of United States was clearly insolvent and in the end was allowed to fail.

Its failure marked a profound change in public sentiment towards banks. A real-estate bubble in Chicago collapsed soon after in May 1931, and 30 Chicago banks defaulted. Depositors, who were unable to tell whether a bank was good or not, began pulling their cash indiscriminately out of all banks, good and bad, triggering multiple bank runs. Such withdrawals had a negative multiplier effect on the supply of money, since in order to maintain their own liquidity, banks had to call in three or four dollars of loans for each dollar in cash withdrawn and to liquidate assets in a falling market at firesale prices. In a fractional reserve system, this leads to a drastic fall in the supply of money. Moreover, as their loans were called, borrowers in turn withdrew their deposits from other banks, further fuelling the contagion.

In this climate, all banks felt the need to protect themselves, with bank failures snowballing as desperate bankers called in loans which the borrowers did not have time or money to repay. With future profits looking poor, capital investment and construction slowed or completely ceased. In the face of bad loans and worsening future prospects, the surviving banks became even more conservative in their lending. The effect was to speed up the scramble for liquidity right across the system. Banks built up their cash reserves and made fewer loans, which intensified deflationary pressures. Servicing debts became harder, because prices and incomes fell significantly but the debts remained at the same dollar amount.

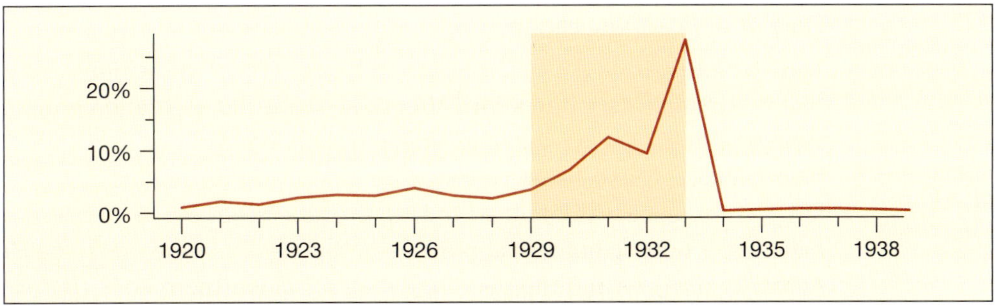

Figure 8.1 Bank failure rate 1920–1939 in the US. Main years of Great Depression highlighted

The government reaction to the bank failures was inadequate. A potentially useful move was made in December 1931, when the Reconstruction Finance Corporation (RFC) was founded to provide finance for banks and firms in need of liquidity. However, then the Speaker of the House insisted that RFC loans to banks be publicised and once this requirement was enacted, in January 1933, banks in trouble stopped seeking RFC aid because to be seen receiving RFC loans simply triggered runs.

The Federal Reserve System (Fed) was not prepared to sign off on a federal guarantee for bank deposits in March 1933, nor did it feel there were any additional measures it should recommend. Finally on 4 March, President Roosevelt closed all the banks in the country for more than a week – *bank holiday* – and under the federal government's supervision, weaker banks were merged into stronger banks. Depositors received compensation for roughly 85% of their former deposits.

In response to this crisis, the Glass–Steagall Deposit Insurance Act was passed in June 1933 establishing deposit insurance coverage in the amount of $2,500, and the Federal Deposit Insurance Corporation (FDIC) as the authority to regulate and supervise state non-member banks. We can see from Figure 8.1 that these measures were successful in stopping the cascading failures, since the US experienced virtually no bank failures for the remainder of the decade, even if the Great Depression had a double dip in 1936.

8.1.2 Northern Rock

The first bank run in the United Kingdom (UK) since Overend & Gurney in 1866 was the run on Northern Rock on 14 September 2007 (see Figure 8.2). For detailed analysis, see Borio (2009) and Shin (2008). The immediate bank run seemed to have been triggered by an announcement by the Bank of England (BoE) that it was providing emergency liquidity support for Northern Rock.

The underlying cause of its demise was its funding structure: borrowing on the asset backed securities (ABS) markets to fund mortgages which then would be securitised and sold off on the markets, with the proceedings used to pay back the ABSs. When that market froze in the summer of 2007, the fate of Northern Rock was sealed. This meant that the bank run shown on TV screens in September 2007 was only the endgame in a bank run that started a month earlier.

Role of deposit insurance

The UK had a partial deposit insurance scheme in place at the time, and one might argue that it was an invitation to a run. After the first £2,000, legislation protected only 90% of savings up to £33,000 – guaranteeing a maximum payout of £31,700 – in the event of a bank collapse, the so-called co-insurance. It took several months to get the insurance payout. Co-insurance was intended to help provide incentives for depositors to monitor the banks, thus putting prudential pressure on the banks. In the event, the Financial Services Authority (FSA) missed the pending problems at Northern Rock, and it would be quite surprising if ordinary depositors with less information could do better. The only sensible strategy for depositors was to run the bank. As Sir Callum McCarthy, the former chairman

Figure 8.2 Northern Rock run

Source: Cate Gillon/Getty Images

of the FSA, said, the UK could have avoided the run on deposits at Northern Rock had there been a depositor protection scheme such as exists in the US.

Role of wholesale markets

Northern Rock was vulnerable because of its unusually heavy reliance on wholesale, that is non-retail, borrowings for 77% of its funding. This made it uniquely vulnerable when the asset backed commercial paper (ABCP) market collapsed in early August 2007, in the opening shots of the global crisis. Northern Rock informed the FSA and the BoE of its funding problems by the middle of August, after which the authorities tried to resolve the crisis behind the scenes. The wholesale depositors' run on Northern Rock demonstrated that the financial markets had a much better understanding of the bank's problems than the supervisor or the general public.

Summary

Until its failure, the funding model of Northern Rock was considered sound by the bank itself, its supervisors and the capital markets. With the benefit of hindsight, we recognise that all of these parties were misguided. Northern Rock remained solvent only so long as liquidity was in effect infinite. Because liquidity was thought infinite, Northern Rock and most other banks in the world behaved in a way that ensured liquidity would dry up. Therefore, the failure of Northern Rock was almost certain, given time.

If the deposit insurance scheme of the UK had been effective, the actual run on Northern Rock probably would have been prevented, sparing the authorities the embarrassment of seeing it play out on the TV screens. Deposit insurance would not have prevented the failure of the bank, considering that only 23% of its funding came from deposits.

As a response to the Northern Rock failure, the authorities were forced to announce unlimited deposit insurance in order to reassure bank clients and prevent contagious runs across the UK banking sector. This demonstrates the problem created when the authorities have inadequate policies in place and then are confronted by a crisis. The authorities are forced to overreact in order to prevent more damage. In other words, the UK went from having a deposit insurance scheme that was too weak to one that was too strong.

8.2 MODELLING DEPOSIT INSURANCE

One of the most influential models in economics is the deposit insurance model proposed by Diamond and Dybvig (1983). The model captures the fundamental uncertainty leading to bank runs and answers how deposit insurance can prevent bank runs.

In their model, banks are viewed as pools of liquidity providing consumers with insurance against their own idiosyncratic shocks. The banks transform illiquid assets into liquid liabilities, and because the idiosyncratic shocks are not highly correlated, banks need to hold only a small fraction of their total assets in liquid form. This is the basis of the fractional reserve banking system.

The paper by Diamond and Dybvig demonstrates three important points. First, banks providing demand deposits can improve on a competitive market by providing better risk-sharing among people who need to consume at different random times. Second, a demand deposit contract can prevent an undesirable equilibrium (a bank run). Finally, deposit insurance provided by governments can prevent bank runs.

Background

In the simple version of the Diamond–Dybvig model presented here, the banking system is illiquid, meaning that not all banking system obligations can be met if all holders of those obligations simultaneously claim what they have been promised.

There are two main ingredients in the model:

1. Depositors are initially individually uncertain about their profile of consumption, that is whether they prefer to consume *early* or *late*.
2. The banking system deals with depositors on a first-come, first-served basis.

Setup

The economy has three periods, $t = 0$, 1 and 2, the economy starts at date 0 and all agents have an endowment of \$1. There is an intertemporal technology (reflecting the illiquidity of assets) which can be represented by the following:

$t = 0$	$t = 1$	$t = 2$
-1	1	R

So \$1 deposited at $t = 0$ will yield \$1 if withdrawn at $t = 1$ and $R > 1$ if withdrawn at $t = 2$. This captures the cost of early liquidation of assets.

Each agent can be either early or late. Early agents only care about consumption at $t = 1$, with utility $U(c_1)$, where $U(\cdot)$ is their utility function, and late agents only care about consumption at $t = 2$, with utility $U(c_2)$, where we implicitly assume the discount factor is 1, without loss of generality. The agent does not know if she is early or late at $t = 0$ but learns it at $t = 1$. Realisations are independent across agents. Prior to learning their type, all agents have identical preferences. A fraction (probability) λ of agents are early, taken to be constant.

Autarky

Autarky is the condition of economic self-sufficiency, without trade. Under autarky, there are no means to shift consumption and agents solve the optimisation problem individually. *Ex-ante* ($t = 0$), all agents are identical. The expected utility for each agent is given by

$$\begin{aligned} \mathrm{E}(U) &= \lambda U(c_1) + (1 - \lambda)U(c_2) \\ &= \lambda U(1) + (1 - \lambda)U(R) \end{aligned}$$

Assuming the utility function is increasing and concave – standard form with non-satiation and risk aversion – the late agent will have higher eventual utility than the early agent.

Utility under autarky

Given the presence of risk aversion, there is an optimal social insurance contract that would allow agents to insure against the unlucky outcome of being early. This assumes that types of agents are *publicly observable* as of period 1 (Figure 8.3(a)).

Suppose there are two agents; one is late, the other is early, so $\lambda = 0.5$. They make the following contract at $t = 0$: at $t = 1$ the late agent will pay the early agent some amount

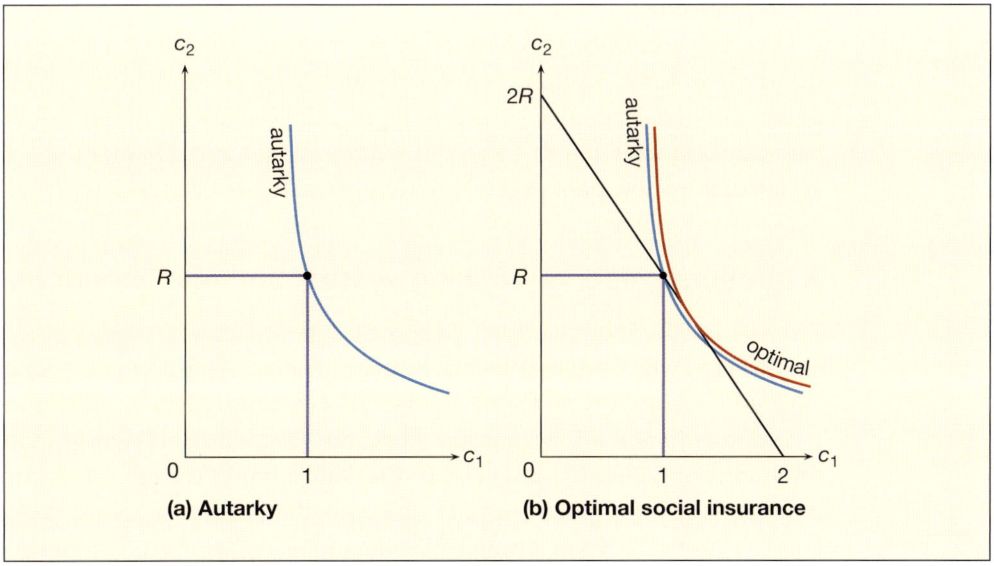

(a) Autarky **(b) Optimal social insurance**

Figure 8.3 Autarky and optimal social insurance

π, thus the early will have consumption $\tilde{c}_1 = 1 + \pi$ and the late $\tilde{c}_2 = R(1 - \pi)$. If π is chosen correctly, there will be improvement on the autarkic outcome of $c_1 = 1$ and $c_2 = R$.

The intertemporal budget constraint is

$$\tilde{c}_2 = R(2 - \tilde{c}_1)$$

The economic problem is then

$$\begin{aligned}\max_{\tilde{c}_1} \mathrm{E}(U) &= U(\tilde{c}_1) + U(\tilde{c}_2) \\ &= U(\tilde{c}_1) + U(R(2 - \tilde{c}_1))\end{aligned}$$

Optimisation, differentiating with respect to $\tilde{c}_1$, and setting the result to zero, gives the standard result (assuming an interior solution) that the *marginal rate of substitution* equals the *marginal rate of transformation*:

$$\frac{U'(\tilde{c}_1)}{U'(\tilde{c}_2)} = R \qquad (8.1)$$

The optimal consumption allocation satisfies the first-order condition and the budget constraint. At the optimum, we do not want to give consumption to those who do not value it, therefore, early agents' date – 2 consumption is equal to late agents' date – 1 consumption, which is zero.

Utility under optimal social insurance

Since by assumption, $R > 1$, it follows that optimal consumption levels satisfy $\tilde{c}_1 > 1$ and $\tilde{c}_2 < R$. The optimal *indifference curve* is higher than the indifference curve under autarky (Figure 8.3(b)), so there are *gains from trade*. The optimal outcome devotes more resources on average to date – 1 consumption and less to date – 2 consumption than the autarky outcome.

Diamond and Dybvig show that under certain circumstances it is possible to achieve the above optimal insurance contract given there is a bank in the economy. Banks can underwrite this insurance by providing liquidity (allow for better risk sharing), guaranteeing a reasonable return when the investor cashes in before maturity. This provides an explanation of how banks subject to runs can still attract deposits.

8.2.1 A fractional reserve banking system and equilibrium decisions

The optimal allocation characterised above can be implemented by a fractional reserve banking system in which banks collect consumers' endowments and invest a fraction of them in long-term investments while offering depositors the possibility of withdrawal on demand.

Suppose there is a large number of agents. Diamond and Dybvig show that the same solution is obtained if a financial institution (a bank) creates a bank account or a traditional demand deposit contract that pays the optimal amounts $1 + \pi$ in $t = 1$ and $R(1 - \pi)$ in $t = 2$. Then it is an *equilibrium* for early agents to withdraw at $t = 1$ and for late agents to wait.

This *good equilibrium* achieves *optimal risk sharing* and demonstrates the role of *financial intermediation* in increasing welfare. A crucial question regarding this fractional reserve system is whether the bank will be able to fulfil its contractual obligations. This depends on investors' anticipation about the safety of the bank.

Consider first the case that a late investor anticipates that the bank will be able to fulfil its obligations. If late investors trust their bank, they will prefer to withdraw at $t = 2$, thus the proportion of time $t = 1$ withdrawals will be λ. So in order to avoid premature liquidation, the bank should have a liquid reserve of at least λc_1^*.

Multiple equilibria

There is a potential for multiple equilibria in this model: a good equilibrium of no run described above and a *bad equilibrium* where a bank run takes place. The good equilibrium is better than the bad in the sense of *Pareto efficiency*. In the bank run equilibrium, everyone prefers to receive a risky return with a mean of 1 even if holding the endowment until $t = 2$ provides a return exceeding 1 if there is no run.

Bank runs are a type of *self-fulfilling prophecy*, caused by a shift in expectations. This shift could happen for almost any reason. Each depositor's incentive to withdraw her funds depends on what she expects other depositors to do. If enough depositors anticipate that other depositors will withdraw their funds, they all have an incentive to rush to be the first in line to withdraw their funds, since the face value of deposits is larger than the liquidation value of the bank's assets.

Bank runs

To illustrate a bank run, suppose there are N depositors, each endowed with \$1, so the amount the bank has on hand at $t = 1$ is $\$N$. Given the optimal contract, the total value of deposits is $\$N(1 + \pi)$, hence, the bank does not have enough cash to pay off all depositors at $t = 1$.

The first person to demand her money at $t = 1$ will get the full amount $1 + \pi$ and this applies to all the agents in the queue up to the fraction $1/(1 + \pi)$ when the bank runs out of assets. The bank's payoff to any agent depends only on the agent's place in line and not on future information about agents behind her in the queue. Therefore, the last $N(1 - 1/(1 + \pi))$ get nothing, and all agents will want to be the first in the queue.

Note that for runs to be an equilibrium, demand deposits must yield more than 1 if withdrawn at $t = 1$. If deposits yield 1 when withdrawn at $t = 1$, the outcome is not an improvement on the autarkic outcome, with the bank simply mimicking each agent holding their endowment, but then this shows that a demand deposit which is not subject to runs provides no liquidity services. It is precisely the transformation of illiquid assets into liquid assets that is responsible both for the liquidity service provided by banks and for their susceptibility to runs.

Decisions and utility

The inferiority of bank runs seems to rule out runs, since no one would deposit in the bank if they anticipate a run. However, all agents will choose to deposit at least some of their wealth in the bank even if they anticipate a positive probability of a run, provided that the probability is small enough, as the good equilibrium dominates autarky. Since in a run, the fraction $1/(1+\pi)$ get $\tilde{c}_1$ at $t = 1$, while the rest get nothing, the expected utility is

$$E(U) = \frac{U(\tilde{c}_1)}{1+\pi}$$

We therefore get that the run utility is inferior:

$$\text{No run} = E(U) = \lambda U(\tilde{c}_1) + (1-\lambda)U(\tilde{c}_2)$$

$$\text{Run } E(U) = \frac{U(\tilde{c}_1)}{1+\pi} < \lambda U(\tilde{c}_1) + (1-\lambda)U(\tilde{c}_2)$$

Analysis

The instability of fractional reserve banking systems comes mainly from the coordination failure among investors. Once they have made their deposits, anything that causes them to anticipate a run will lead to a run. In this framework, banks with pure demand deposits will be very concerned about maintaining confidence because they realise that the good equilibrium is very fragile.

8.2.2 Regulatory response: deposit insurance

Deposit insurance provided by the government can result in an allocation that dominates the best that can be offered without insurance and never do any worse, resulting in a *dominant strategies equilibrium*. The government makes the first agents pay a tax of π, which is enough to compensate the unlucky ones late to the queue. The important feature here is that the government imposes the tax on the agent after she withdraws the money, an option not open to the bank.

The effect of this policy is to *guarantee* that every agent can get \$1 at $t = 1$. So regardless of whether there is a run or not, agents know they will get their initial deposits back. As long as the probability of a run is not 100%, late agents are better off not running, since they get $\tilde{c}_2 > 1$ at $t = 2$.

Deposit insurance prevents bank runs because, for all possible anticipated withdrawal policies of other agents, it never pays to participate in a bank run. As a result, no strategic issues of confidence arise. This in turn makes the good equilibrium unique, so there will be no run. Without runs, the insurance is never claimed, and hence is costless in equilibrium.

The presence of deposit insurance increases the efficiency of the banking sector, because the bank does not have to worry about the potential for runs and, therefore, can follow an optimal asset allocation policy. Otherwise, the bank might have to allocate resources to reassure depositors, reducing its efficiency.

Analysis

Within the stylistic framework of the model, a government deposit insurance scheme has a natural advantage over a privately funded scheme. The reason is that the government has the power to tax depositors to finance insurance, therefore effectively preventing a run. A private scheme cannot rely on such powers, and instead would need to have sufficient reserves to make the insurance credible. Since holding such reserves would be costly, a government provision of deposit insurance is more efficient than private provision.

In the real world, this is not as clear-cut. For example, it would be politically very difficult to actually tax those withdrawing early, and as a consequence the government might have to maintain a funded deposit insurance fund, or provide guarantees. This might remove the efficiency advantages of the government.

One example of difficulties in taxing agents withdrawing early can be seen from the process of resolving the failure of Bernie Madoff. The authorities are trying to claw back funds from those who successfully took the money out of the fund, but this has turned out to be a very long and very expensive process, with uncertain outcomes.

8.3 PROS AND CONS OF DEPOSIT INSURANCE

In the simple Diamond–Dybvig model above, deposit insurance is effective in ensuring socially optimal outcomes. However, in the real world more issues are at work, and deposit insurance has often been controversial. The opposition to deposit insurance was succinctly stated by Kovacevich (1996), President and CEO of Wells Fargo:

> 'The deposit insurance system is indeed a monster and it is a monster that threatens to devour the very system it is intended to protect.'

Deposit insurance is often criticised for creating moral hazard and incentives for excessive risk-taking by banks. By guaranteeing deposits, market incentives to monitor banks and to demand an interest payment commensurate with the risk of the bank are diminished.

Moral hazard

Moreover, it can be difficult for insurance premiums to properly internalise the cost of risk, because of problems of asymmetric information. The bank knows more about its operations than outsiders, which therefore gives the bank incentives to take more hidden risk – moral hazard. Furthermore, risk-sensitive deposit insurance gives rise to problems of pro-cyclicality.

The depositors themselves also contribute to moral hazard. If they know they are protected regardless of what the bank does, their incentive is to put their money into the bank with the highest interest rates. This is very similar to the problem analysed in the Krugman model of governments guaranteeing borrowers, and the problem in the S&L crisis. In addition, it creates competitive problems for banks that are prudently run, because they cannot attract deposits. This was the case in the Venezuelan banking crisis.

Impact of wholesale markets

The discussion so far has focused on bank runs by retail banking clients, the traditional source of funding for banks. In recent years, banks have increasingly been relying on the wholesale markets for funds. Borio (2009) argues that in this case, bank runs come in two waves, first from sophisticated institutional investors and then by unsophisticated retail depositors. Provided the institutional investors run the bank, deposit insurance is not sufficient to prevent the retail depositors from running the bank. This was the case with Northern Rock.

This picture is somewhat muddled by the fact that post-Lehman, it is often assumed that governments insure all providers of liquidity to the banks, both institutional and retail. This is supported by the fact that in the crisis from 2007, credit losses have been very small. For example, by the middle of 2012 only two European countries had imposed losses on bank creditors, the UK and Denmark, a minuscule amount in the former case and small in the latter. In spite of the massive amounts of public money provided to the banks, the authorities have not wanted to hit private creditors.

More generally, changes in the structure and functioning of financial markets have been reducing the significance of deposit insurance schemes as devices to deal with systemic risks of runs. This reflects the greater importance of wholesale financial markets and funding in the system, as well as the increasing systemic relevance of institutions that either do not have deposit insurance protection, such as money market mutual funds and hedge funds, or are perceived as too big to fail (TBTF).

8.3.1 Argentina, 1991–1994

The case of Argentina's short-lived effort to repeal its programme of deposit insurance is instructive, and we follow this story as presented by Miller (1996). Before 1991, the Argentine banking system operated under a regime of optional, explicit deposit insurance, coupled with an extensive implicit deposit insurance in the form of central bank assistance to failing banks. In 1991 and 1992, Argentina reversed this policy by repealing the country's deposit insurance programme, intending to convince financial markets that it would not under any circumstances rescue a failing bank.

The government decision to forswear providing deposit insurance had several reasons. One was the product of the unusual political and economic circumstances of 1989–1991. Plagued by the disaster of hyperinflation and exhausted by years of political instability, the Argentine public reached a consensus that fundamental reforms were necessary, with the population willing to engage in a radical experiment to rectify a deteriorating situation. The decision to abolish deposit insurance did not appear to impose extreme risks, compared to the dangers and costs of rampant hyperinflation. The government utilised a variety of pre-commitment devices to assure the markets that it would not bail out depositors. These included the newly established independence of the central bank, statutory prohibitions on deposit insurance and stringent limitations on the central bank's ability to loan money to governments or to shaky banks.

Some private market mechanisms did also develop to respond to the withdrawal of the government safety net. Although these private responses did not turn out to be adequate to cope with the systemic crisis induced by the Mexican devaluation, they showed signs of promise before being overwhelmed by events.

In 1995, in the face of a forthcoming election and a severe economic crisis sparked by the Mexican peso devaluation of December 1994, the Argentine government reinstituted a form of deposit insurance in an effort to stave off an all-out bank panic.

The financial crisis happened at a time of maximum political pressure, in the months before elections. This forced the government to reinstitute deposit insurance for its banks, even if the government and the central bank president had said strongly and often that they would never do so. Even though the authorities at the time held the view that deposit insurance creates moral hazard and free-rider problems, and therefore should be limited, this view proved unsustainable.

This experience suggests that deposit insurance is a practical necessity for any industrialised nation, and that governments cannot credibly commit to not providing deposit insurance, because the political and economic pressures to do so in times of crisis become overwhelming. Consequently, governments are better off recognising the eventuality and maintaining a deposit insurance scheme.

8.4 SUMMARY

The fractional reserve banking system is inherently fragile and subject to bank runs. The experience from the Great Depression demonstrated how devastating contagious bank runs can be, and how effective deposit insurance is in preventing bank runs. This is not as clear-cut with modern banks depending significantly on wholesale funding.

The fragility of banks and the importance of deposit insurance are succinctly modelled by Diamond and Dybvig who clearly demonstrate the positive contribution of financial intermediation and simultaneously how it can increase the fragility of the financial system. This fragility can be addressed by the government by providing deposit insurance, perhaps by taxing those who aim to run banks and by compensating those who are at the end of the queue and otherwise would not get their funds back. Within the simple confines of the model, this is sufficient to ensure bank runs will not happen.

At the same time, full deposit insurance does lead to moral hazard. If depositors do not care what a bank does with its money, a badly run or even fraudulent bank will simply offer more interest than its competitors, expand rapidly, and make dodgy loans.

The alternative of having no deposit insurance scheme is not politically credible, as the example of Argentina demonstrated. In case of a bank run, depositors will exert enormous political pressure to fix the problem and make them whole. A bank run is a highly visible event, demonstrating that the authorities have failed to adequately supervise the financial system. This is highly embarrassing, as we saw in the case of Northern Rock. The authorities are left to scramble to implement deposit insurance, and since the worst time to make policy decisions is usually during a crisis, it is much better to be prepared and have a well thought-out deposit insurance scheme in place.

Questions for discussion

1 The Northern Rock bank run embarrassed the British authorities in 2007. The previous British bank run was in 1866, and the general view was that bank runs just did not happen in advanced economies anymore.

(a) What were the underlying risk factors that ultimately caused the the failure of Northern Rock?

(b) How did the reaction of the British authorities to the crisis at Northern Rock directly contribute to the bank run?

(c) Compare and contrast bank runs in wholesale markets and retail markets from the point of view of Northern Rock.

2 Recall the model of Diamond and Dybvig (1983).

The model has three periods, $t = 0$, 1 and 2, with 1\$ deposited in $t = 0$, yielding 1 if withdrawn at $t = 1$ and yielding $r > 1$ if withdrawn at $t = 2$. Agents are identical and have a wealth of \$1 in $t = 0$. There are 2 types of agents:

Early Prefer to consume c_1 in $t = 1$, getting $U(c_1)$

Late Prefer to consume c_2 in $t = 2$, getting $U(c_2)$

An agent does not know if she is early or late at $t = 0$, but learns it at $t = 1$. Fraction λ are early, and $1 - \lambda$ late.

(a) Suppose the utility function takes the form

$$U(c) = 1 - 1/C$$

Derive the utility levels of both early and late agents under autarchy.

(b) Design an optimal insurance contract for the two agents.

3 Before the crisis from 2007, the general trend was for deposit insurance being reduced or even abolished. Very quickly, this sentiment changed, for example, in the case of Northern Rock. Why was that, and do you think extensive deposit insurance is here to stay?

References

Borio, C. (2009). Ten propositions about liquidity crisis. Working paper no. 293, Bank of International Settlements.

Dewatripont, M. and Tirole, J. (1994). *The Prudential Regulation of Banks*. MIT Press.

Diamond, D. and Dybvig, P. (1983). Bank runs, deposit insurance, and liquidity. *J. Polit. Econ.*, 91: 401–19.

Kovacevich, R. M. (1996). Deposit insurance: It's time to cage the monster. www.minneapolisfed.org/publications_papers/pub_display.cfm? id=2682.

Miller, G. P. (1996). Is deposit insurance inevitable? Lessons from Argentina. *Int. Rev. Law Econ.*, 16: 211–232.

Santos, J. A. C. (2000). Bank capital regulation in contemporary banking theory: a review of the literature. Technical Report 90, Bank for International Settlements. www.bis.org/publ/work90.pdf?noframes¯1.

Shin, H. S. (2008). Reflections on modern bank runs: a case study of Northern Rock. Mimeo, Princeton University.

9 TRADING AND SPECULATION

Trading is an essential part of economic life, facilitating the needs of economic agents to acquire or dispose of tradable assets. For example, the main transaction for most people involves real estate, and that is trading. Intimately connected to trading is speculation. Few economic terms evoke such strong and different reactions as speculation. For some, speculation is the root of instability, undermining sensible government policy, while for others it brings rationality to a world where governments constantly manipulate the economy for political reasons.

The term speculation has multiple meanings in common parlance. In a classic text, *Security Analysis*, by Graham and Dodd (1934), speculation is the opposite of investment, borrowing money to buy assets without proper fundamental research. A more common usage suggests that speculation is the making of risky investments for the purpose of short-term profit. Most people tend to distinguish between speculation and investing based on the amount of risk. A trader in a bank using 1 million to buy an asset with a 50% chance of delivering nothing and a 50% probability of doubling the money might be said to be speculating, whilst allocating the funds to a long-term position in an AA corporate bond is investment.

There is a fine line between what might be considered legitimate and illegitimate speculative activity. Speculators play a useful role in society, providing useful risk-sharing and hedge facilitation, since for anybody wishing to hedge away risk, someone needs to be willing to take on that risk – to be the *counterparty* to the trade. That counterparty is often a speculator.

For example, farmers need to make decisions about their crops early in the year, but can sell them only much later, when they harvest. If crop prices collapse on the market, the farmer may be wiped out. It is not surprising that the first hedging markets in the world developed in agriculture. Aristotle describes the use of a futures contract for olive oil, but the first documented futures exchange is the Dōjima rice exchange in Japan in the 1730s, set up to help the Samurai, who were paid in rice, needing to get stable conversion to coin. The first exchange-traded commodities futures contracts were listed on the Chicago Board of Trade in 1864, a model soon replicated around the world, for example in India in 1875, covering cotton futures.

Other speculative activity is less salubrious and it might be tempting to impose rules to prevent such behaviour. Large financial institutions are able to make such large speculative bets that they not only risk bankruptcy but also threaten financial stability, causing systemic risk. One of the most infamous examples is the failure of LTCM in 1998. Unfortunately, it is not easy to effectively regulate speculation, because it can be quite difficult to distinguish between illegitimate and legitimate speculative activities, and if one is concerned about speculation, it may be better to target the tools employed by speculators, rather than the motives of those trading.

Links to other chapters

This chapter directly relates to Chapter 1 (systemic risk), Chapter 3 (endogenous risk), Chapter 13 (financial regulations) and Chapter 18 (ongoing developments in financial regulation).

Key concepts

- Speculation
- Moral hazard
- Proprietary trading
- Financial transaction tax
- Trading strategies

Readings for this chapter

There are many books that address the topics in this chapter, and we have found the following to be especially useful: Kohn (2003), Madura (2010), Mishkin and Eakins (2011) and Hull (2011).

9.1 TRADING SCANDALS AND ABUSE

Illegal activities of various types are quite common in the financial system. In simple cases an individual may be stealing from his or her employer or clients, and in sophisticated cases a large financial institution may be subtly manipulating the system in an illegal way for profit. Below, we discuss some well-known scandals.

EXAMPLE 9.1 JP Morgan Chase and the 'London whale'

One of the largest banks in the world, JP Morgan Chase, disclosed in May 2012 that it had lost over $5.8 billion from proprietary trading in a bank unit called the chief investment office (CIO), as reported in the *Financial Times* (2012a, 2012b). The losses arose from the activities of Bruno Iksil, a well-known player in the credit default swap (CDS) market, who accumulated such large positions that he got nicknamed the '*London whale*', supposedly moving prices with his trading.

It seems that the bank had little understanding of what he was up to, finding his strategy 'flawed, complex, poorly reviewed, poorly executed, and poorly monitored. The portfolio has proven to be riskier, more volatile and less effective as a hedge than we thought', according to senior bank management. The trading scandal will not much affect the financial fortunes of JP Morgan Chase; its first-quarter profits in 2012 dropped to $4.9 billion, from $5.6 billion a year earlier. The scandal may, however, have a significant indirect impact on the bank because of how it affects the debate on the regulation of financial institutions and whether banks should be allowed to engage in proprietary trading under the Volcker rule.

While the 'London whale' reflected the activities of few individuals over a relatively short period of time, a much larger scandal involving LIBOR price-fixing was first reported by the *Wall Street Journal* in 2008, with Barclays Bank fined for its participation in the scandal in 2012.

EXAMPLE 9.2 LIBOR-fixing scandal

In June 2012, it emerged that Barclays Bank was fined £290 million for its part in a LIBOR price-fixing scandal: see BBC (2012b) for a timeline of events. According to the Financial Services Authority (2012), derivatives traders at Barclays made 257 requests to fix LIBOR and EURIBOR rates between 2005 and 2009, conspiring with other banks.

There are several reasons why the bank might want to do this. If derivative traders are able to manipulate LIBOR, they profit because they know its value before it is made public. Even more importantly, the banks might have been short LIBOR so low values fed directly into profits; after all, LIBOR is the rate 'at which London banks can borrow'. Similarly, at the height of the crisis in 2008, Barclays seemed to have had higher funding costs than comparable institutions, signalling vulnerability, which it could hide by reporting artificially low funding costs.

The manipulation of LIBOR significantly affects other market participants: many mortgages are linked to LIBOR, and it is used to set rates in $800 trillion worth of derivatives and borrowings.

Barclays cooperated with a number of other banks in fixing LIBOR; at the time of writing, the Royal Bank of Scotland group and UBS have also been fined for this.

The LIBOR price-fixing scandal is quite serious, as it undermines the integrity of a key interest rate and the banking system as a whole. The scandal will embolden efforts to strictly regulate the financial system.

Ponzi schemes

A classical, and common, fraudulent investment operation is a *Ponzi scheme*. A fund pays investors profit from their own money, or money paid in by new investors, rather than profits made by investments. Operators of Ponzi schemes entice unsuspecting investors by promises of large profits. However, the scheme can go on only so long as new money comes in, at ever increasing rates. Eventually, all such schemes are doomed to failure. Ponzi schemes are well known in history, but are named after Charles Ponzi who created a large scheme in 1920, taking money from all over the United States.

The best-known recent Ponzi scheme was run by Bernie Madoff, who might have caused paper losses to investors of perhaps $18 billion and consequently was sentenced to prison for 150 years. The scheme is notable because he was a well-known establishment figure, well connected on Wall Street and highly respected, attracting supposedly sophisticated investors.

Rogue traders

Employees of banks are not always willing to accept the restrictions imposed by risk policies, giving rise to the phenomenon of *rogue trader*. A recent example is Jérôme Kerviel's liberal interpretation of 'low-risk arbitrage' causing a €4.91 billion loss to his employer, Société Générale, possibly costing him three years in prison. This may be the largest loss attributed to a rogue trader.

EXAMPLE 9.3 Nick Leeson and Barings

Perhaps the most infamous rogue trader is Nick Leeson, whose unchecked risk-taking and manipulation of his risk controls caused the collapse of Barings Bank in 1995, landing him 6.5 years in a Singapore prison. We follow events as described by himself in Leeson (1999).

Leeson started working for Barings Bank in 1989, and three years later became the general manager of its futures market operation in Singapore. His trading activity caused significant losses for the bank, but he hid those losses by manipulating the accounts, putting losses into a special account numbered 88888, the number 8 being considered lucky in Chinese numerology. Eventually, the losses reached £827 million, bankrupting Barings. Leeson fled from Singapore but was captured in Germany and sent to prison. Since then, he has gained celebrity status, helped by his book and a popular film about his activities.

9.2 TRADING AND RISK

The most publicly visible part of the financial market is the equity market, often in the form of a *stock market index* like the FT100 index in the United Kingdom, S&P-500 in the US and DAX in Germany. The fixed income markets are even larger in volume, and a number of other types of assets are traded, including foreign exchange and commodities, as well as many types of derivative assets. We present the basic terminology and institutions relating to trading in the appendix to this chapter, and will refer to those terms throughout the book.

9.2.1 Market participants

Within the financial system, a number of different types of financial institutions are engaged in trading, and we use the term *market participants* as a catch-all term to refer to them. Most trading takes place in banks, which dominate the debt markets and are actively involved in the market for most other financial assets. Banks are engaged in trading on behalf of their clients, but also often trade on their own account, termed *proprietary trading*, or *prop trading* in short. This is done with the explicit purpose of making profit by taking on risk – that is, speculating.

While some market participants are engaged in proprietary trading, most act instead on behalf of investors like pension funds, insurance companies, mutual funds and sovereign wealth funds. Investors often choose to subcontract investment decisions to those market participants, not exerting direct control over investment decisions but usually monitoring investment performance by various means, such as comparison with a *benchmark*, which might be a stock market index. This is often referred to as the '*institutionalisation*' of the market. A large number of different investment schemes are on offer, and relatively unsophisticated investors can find it rather hard to evaluate the different options. This means there is an obvious risk of fraud or misrepresentation, or even *Ponzi schemes*. As a result, mutual funds are highly regulated in most jurisdictions.

Hedge funds

An important category of financial institution is *hedge funds* which exist in some markets influenced by a relatively liberal US approach to financial services. Hedge funds are less regulated than other financial institutions, provided they sell their services only to relatively sophisticated and wealthy investors, often called *accredited investors*.

It is sometimes said that hedge funds are unregulated, but that is not strictly true. They are subject to securities law, their manager is typically regulated, and all their counterparties such as brokers and lenders will also be regulated, so they are at least indirectly subject to regulation.

Beyond their regulatory status and types of clients, it is very difficult to classify hedge funds. They are extremely diverse, engaging in a large number of different trading activities, often using very complicated trading strategies. Because of the lack of regulation, hedge funds are able to take on risk and investment strategies not open to other market participants, perhaps their defining characteristic. Hedge funds are designed to provide good performance to investors, where performance fees supposedly improve the alignment of interests between clients and manager, though how much of this gain is captured by clients is less clear.

Before 2007, most commentators on financial stability thought the next crisis would originate in the hedge fund sector, due to the impact of the failure of LTCM in 1998. However, the crises from 2007 instead took place in the most regulated part of the financial system, and as a consequence, concerns about hedge funds do not attract a high priority from policymakers, except in Europe where there has recently been a wave of regulatory initiatives aimed at the sector.

9.2.2 Financial innovation

Market participants have always had the tendency to create new and different types of financial instruments, a practice falling under the general heading of *financial innovation*. The question of whether financial innovation is positive for society remains controversial. Before the crisis, it was generally viewed favourably, perhaps because only the advocates understood the nature of the newly created instruments and the adverse effects had not materialised. However, as it turned out, many of the new financial instruments proved to be quite damaging, enabling financial institutions to amass significant amounts of hidden risk.

As a consequence, some commentators have argued that financial innovation provides no value to society whilst destabilising the financial system. Perhaps most succinctly, this is stated as: 'the most important financial innovation that I have seen in the past 20 years is the automatic teller machine' (Paul Volcker in the *Wall Street Journal,* 2009b). Volcker further notes that financial innovation 'moves around the rents in the financial system', benefiting the inventor, not the clients.

9.3 TRADING ACTIVITIES

Trading and speculation typically involve the use of specialist trading activities, which is how traders go about implementing their price forecasts. This may imply buying or selling stocks or bonds, trading derivatives or any number of different activities. Several of these have come under particular scrutiny by politicians and the popular press, in particular short selling and carry trading.

Traders of financial assets use what is called a *trading strategy* to make decisions, which can be considered as a set of rules that the trader follows when deciding what to buy and sell. The extent to which trading rules are formalised varies greatly. At one extreme, some investors employ largely automated strategies with formal rules. Perhaps more frequent are less formal systems, for example, the common investor preference for 'low risk' or 'safe' investments, with the exact nature of safety left undefined. Rules may even be unconscious; for example, if an investor prefers to repeat investments that have been successful in the recent past, they may unconsciously engage in trend following.

Whether conscious or not, investor behaviour can be analysed in terms of trading strategies, and because asset prices are determined by these strategies, their analysis is as important as the types of instruments employed.

Value investing

A classical approach to investing is *value investing*, a strategy proposed by Graham and Dodd (1934). This involves finding companies that are trading below their inherent worth, by finding stocks with strong fundamentals, like earnings, dividends, book value and cash flow. The most successful investor of all times, Warren Buffett, follows value investing.

Value is an example of a mean reversion trade, where assets are bought when prices have fallen and sold when prices have risen. As such, under normal conditions, when prices move within their typical ranges, value investing has a stabilising effect on prices, increasing demand when they are low and reducing it when high. In extreme conditions, however, this may not be the case, because value investors are likely to take severe losses and may be forced to liquidate portfolios, in a firesale. Value investors stabilise prices only when they are making money.

Seeking yield is maximising risk

Warren Buffett has argued that if one is seeking yield, one is maximising risk. It is important to keep in mind that this risk is usually obscure, because management or supervisors spot the obvious risk. This suggests that traders are actively seeking to take risk in an area that is subject to the least amount of scrutiny. We will see many examples later in the book of how this might done in practice and the consequences it has had.

9.3.1 Carry trades

A trading activity that has come under considerable criticism is *carry trading*, a form of value investing in bonds or currencies based on exploiting yield differences. A higher-yield asset is bought and a lower-yield asset sold, with the hope of profiting from the spread in yields. This will be successful provided that capital losses are not taken on the higher-yield asset.

The most controversial form of carry trading is the foreign exchange carry, borrowing money in a country with low interest rates, exchanging the money for the currency of a country with high interest rates and lending it out at the higher rate. This creates profits from both the interest rate differential and also the price impact on the exchange rates.

EXAMPLE 9.4 Yen–dollar, 1998

Over two memorable days in October 1998, the 7th and 8th, the dollar fell from 131 yen to 112 yen by lunchtime in London on Thursday the 8th, bouncing back sharply by the end of New York trading to 119 yen. The precipitous drop is shown in Figure 9.1.

The fall in the dollar was unexpected given its strength throughout the spring and summer of 1998, reaching a high of 147.26 yen on 11 August. The US enjoyed strong growth during the period, Japan was suffering from a long recession and the conventional wisdom was that the yen was set to continue its fall, with only the speed and the magnitude uncertain.

The combination of an appreciating dollar and the large interest rate differential, 4.9% between Japan and the US, gave rise to the singularly profitable trading opportunity of borrowing yen, buying dollar assets, and gaining on both the appreciation of the dollar and the interest rate differential. This carry trade was widespread among hedge funds, prop desks and Japanese commercial banks.

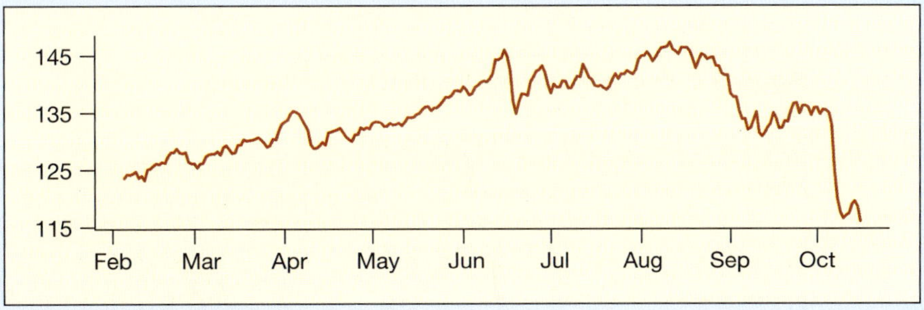

Figure 9.1 Yen/USD in 1998

Feedback effects

When carry traders are borrowing the low interest rate currency and buying the high interest rate currency, it is likely to lead to the appreciation of the latter. Initially the effects may not be particularly apparent, as positions are likely to increase gradually, but the price impact becomes stronger with time.

However, it is quite likely at some point that traders will realise the currency has appreciated too much, causing them to rapidly unwind their positions. The rapidity is self-generating because unwinding increases losses, leading to a currency crash. This results in a weakening of the high-interest currency, which in itself is an incentive for other traders to unwind their positions. If everyone tries to unwind at the same time, the high-interest currency is sold into a falling market, creating an adverse endogenous risk feedback loop, shown in Figure 9.2. It is sometimes said that the *prices go up by the escalator and down by the elevator (lift)*.

These effects were formally modelled by Morris and Shin (1998, 1999) in their global games model, showing that speculators have incentives to wait until the last minute to exit the trade, but no longer. If a trader exits too early, she will lose money, and also if she exits too late. This leads to herd behaviour among speculators, caused by strategic complementarities. We present their model in detail in Chapter 12, Section 12.5.

Carry trades as a source of contagion

Carry trades can be a source of contagion. Suppose a hedge fund is engaged in carry trades with multiple countries, using a high degree of leverage. If a crisis hits one of the countries, the hedge fund will face margin calls and will have to liquidate some of its positions to meet those margins. It is likely that it will unwind some trades with countries not in crisis, putting downward pressure on the exchange rate of those countries, causing them to fall, and thus transmitting the crisis. See Figure 9.3 for a graphical description of this.

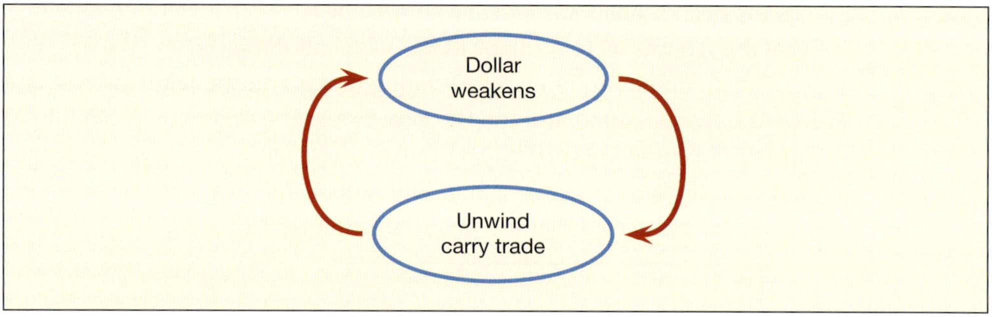

Figure 9.2 Endogenous risk feedback in unwinding

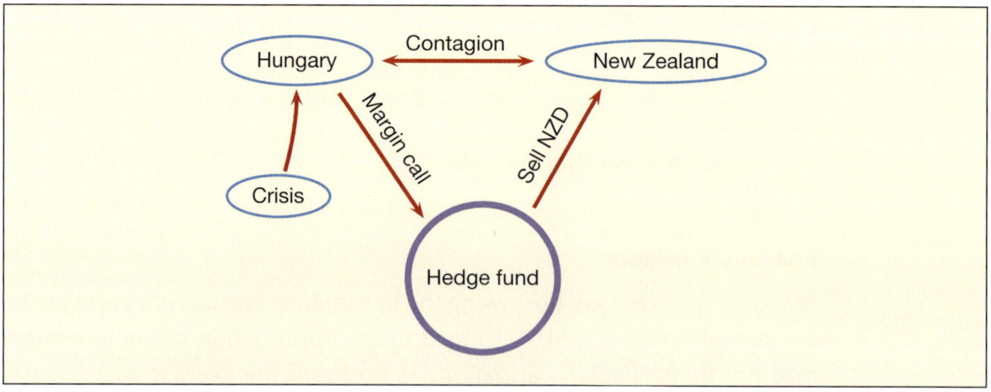

Figure 9.3 Carry trades as a source of contagion

This has happened several times, for example, in February 2006 when a mini-crisis in Iceland adversely affected the exchange rates of several countries such as Hungary, New Zealand and South Africa.

9.3.2 Technical trading

Technical trading is a broad category where a trader attempts to forecast future prices based on statistical analysis of historical data, combining behavioural finance and quantitative methods. These methods remain quite controversial and it is hard to verify whether they are successful or not, because those developing successful technical trading rules keep them strictly proprietary.

At high and very high observation frequencies, technical trading takes the form of *statistical arbitrage* and *HFT*, where it can be highly successful, as information in prices arrives at a much greater rate than that from any other sources. However, on human decision-making timescales of hours or days the effectiveness of technical trading is very much in doubt.

There is a long list of studies proclaiming that it is possible to forecast prices with statistical methods, and it is not hard to apply common methods to historical data and find significant forecasting ability in-sample. However, as argued by Sullivan *et al.* (1999), such statistical relationships tend to be spurious. If we test 20 variables to see if they help forecast prices, one of them can be expected to be statistically significant at the 5% level, even if none is related to prices. If we correctly take into account the impact of searching in the calculation of statistical significance, common technical trading rules become statistically insignificant.

Momentum – following trend

A common technical trading strategy is *momentum trading*, buying assets that have seen recent price increases and selling those that have fallen in price. If a sufficient number of traders follow the momentum, their trading activities will directly impact on prices, in the short run reinforcing the profitability of the trading strategy. Over long time periods, momentum trading may cause asset price bubbles, followed by market crashes.

Momentum may be followed as a conscious trading strategy, but there are many ways in which institutional decision-making can subconsciously lead to momentum trading. For example, if investors prefer not to repeat losing decisions, or are prepared to take more risk on positions that have in the past been successful, their trading will have a momentum component. Similarly, it is widely surmised that investors who subcontract management to external managers tend to award contracts to recently successful managers, and cancel contracts with unsuccessful managers, leading to buying assets that have risen and selling those that have fallen. This suggests that a large proportion of momentum trading is unconscious, perhaps taking the form of not repeating losing decisions rather than actively seeking to repeat winning decisions.

9.3.3 High-frequency trading

Market participants have always employed various techniques to speed up their access to information in order to gain an advantage on their competitors. Nathan Rothschild set up a network of pigeons in Europe so he could send information between his operations faster than anybody else. As legend has it, he was able to profit from the defeat of Napoleon at Waterloo in 1815 because his pigeons brought the first news of the defeat to the City. Other technologies, such as post riders, semaphore and the telegraph, have served the same purpose.

Since the 1970s, high-speed computers, data networks and algorithmic trading have become the main tools for gaining trading advantages. Today, computer algorithms directly interface with trading platforms and place orders without immediate human intervention, and are now the biggest generator of trading volume. As a consequence, policymakers have become quite worried about the potential for systemic risk arising from computer-based trading (CBT), especially after the *Flash Crash* of 2010.

EXAMPLE 9.5 Flash Crash, 6 May 2010

The US stock market experienced a very sudden crash on 6 May 2010 when the market went down by almost 10% in a span of a few minutes and recovered just as quickly. This has been called the *Flash Crash*. Figure 9.4 shows the impact on the DJIA whilst Figure 9.5 demonstrates the impact on two stocks, Accenture and Sotheby's. The former saw its stock price drop from \$40 to one penny at 14:48, whilst the latter jumped from about \$42 to \$100,000 nine minutes later, when the market was already recovering. This happened because the limit order books had been exhausted, and those desiring to buy or sell found no counterparties.

> 'These trades occurred as a result of so-called stub quotes, which are quotes generated by market makers . . . at levels far away from the current market in order to fulfil continuous two-sided quoting obligations even when a market maker has withdrawn from active trading.'
>
> (Securities and Exchange Commission (SEC) and Commodity Futures Trading Commission (CFTC) report)

The causes of the flash crash remain controversial. A joint report by the SEC and the CFTC in September 2010 blames a fragmented and fragile market, where a single institution selling a large number of so-called E-Mini S&Ps, that is a stock market index futures contract on the S&P-500 index, exhausted available buyers.

> 'Still lacking sufficient demand from fundamental buyers or cross-market arbitrageurs, HFTs began to quickly buy and then resell contracts to each other – generating a "hot-potato" volume effect as the same positions were rapidly passed back and forth. Between 2:45:13 and 2:45:27, HFTs traded over 27,000 contracts, which accounted for about 49 percent of the total trading volume, while buying only about 200 additional contracts net. At this time, buy-side market depth in the E-Mini fell to about \$58 million, less than 1% of its depth from that morning's level. As liquidity vanished, the price of the E-Mini dropped by an additional 1.7% in just these 15 seconds.'
>
> (SEC and CFTC report)

The crisis quickly spilled over from the futures markets into equities markets. As trading systems detected the large volumes and price drops, many HFTs then exited

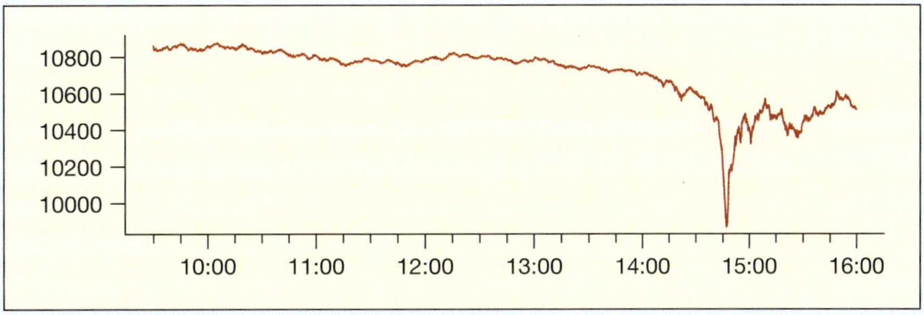

Figure 9.4 Flash Crash, 6 May 2010, DJIA

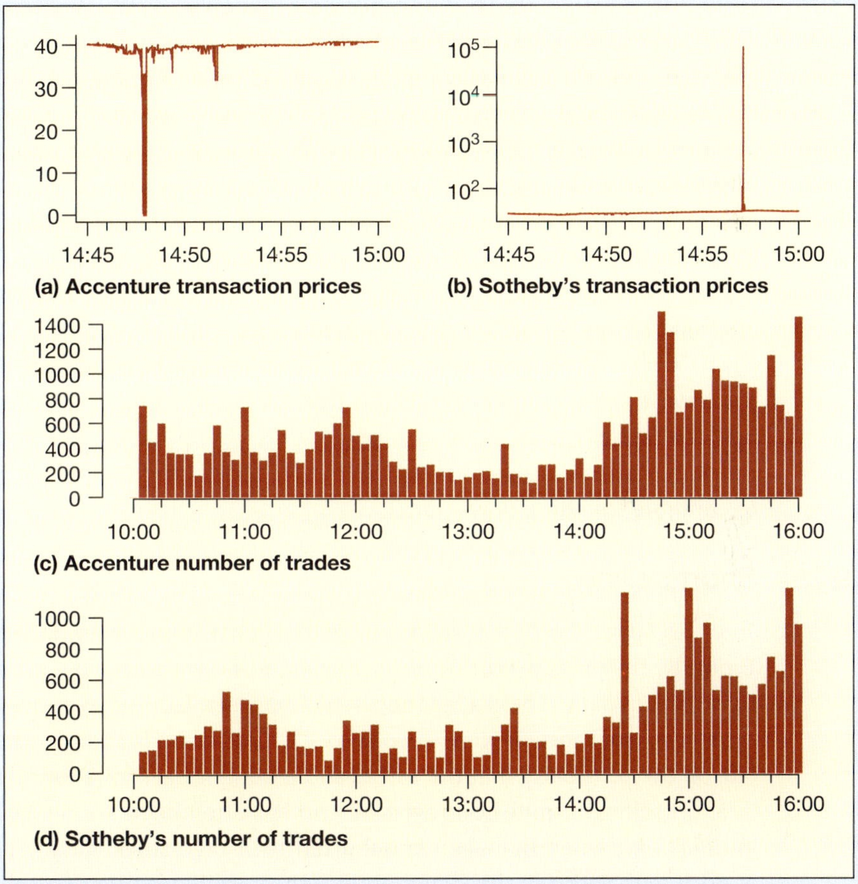

Figure 9.5 Flash Crash, 6 May 2010, individual stocks

Data source: NYSE, TAQ and Tick Data

from the market. The official report finds that the crash eventually stopped when the Chicago Mercantile Exchange implemented automatic stabilisers, pausing trading. That enabled market participants to react, verify prices and the system, leading the market to recover quickly. This chain of events is typical of endogenous risk.

The official conclusion remains controversial, and many commentators have disagreed with both the assumptions and the conclusions.

Analysis

The speed of trading may make it easier for anomalous outcomes and asynchronicities between different markets to self-correct, compared to human-only trading. Therefore, events like the 1987 crash might have been less severe if trading had been faster. The fact that the Flash Crash played out within a single day, and high-frequency extreme outcomes do not generally result in extreme daily outcomes, indicates that problems in high-frequency trading (HFT) self-heal. In other words, HFT might reduce the incidence of market crashes. However, this issue has not been well studied, and it is not obvious whether the effects will always be benign.

The critical difference between human and automated trading systems is common sense. Faced with a new and unexpected situation we know that traders make some decisions that look strange with hindsight, but their decisions will be expressed in shades of grey and have some guiding principles behind them. By contrast, fully automatic systems may fail catastrophically, and because of this will often shut down entirely when market parameters exceed those of normal conditions. The price for liquidity always increases under extreme circumstances, but where systems are highly automated and much of the liquidity depends on them, this tendency becomes much stronger and the price may approach infinity for short periods, as illustrated by Figure 9.4.

In the event, the Flash Crash did not cause much damage, because the markets recovered quite quickly and the crash happened early in the trading session. If, however, the Flash Crash had happened at the end of the trading day, and the markets closed around the lowest point, the damage could have been substantial. It would have affected anybody using daily marking, and many traders would have been hit by margin calls. It is possible that an endogenous risk vicious feedback loop could have set in, causing prices to continue spiralling downwards.

9.3.4 Short selling

Short selling, or *shorting*, is selling by market participants who do not own the asset sold. Typically, they might borrow a stock or bond from somebody, promising to return it at some future date. The trader then sells the asset. Until they repurchase and return the asset, they are short. Typical reasons to short are to hedge some other position, or speculate on the possibility that the asset can be bought back for a lower price in the future.

Short selling is quite controversial, and has often been a source of abuse, for example, in times past when management shorted their own stock, clearly putting their interests at odds with those of the shareholders. Short selling is often perceived as profiting from the misfortunes of others and contributing to price drops and even crises. As a result, it is quite often banned in times of crisis.

Shorting has many legitimate uses, for example, in hedging where somebody making a loan to a risky counterparty can hedge that risk by selling short the stock of the counterparty. More generally, short selling increases liquidity, helps in preventing overvaluation and provides incentives to produce negative research.

The problem with short selling is separating out economic from political or moral arguments. While a short seller might be seen as attempting to benefit from the misfortunes of others, in terms of market impact there is no difference between a short sale and a regular sale from an asset. Both cause prices to fall. There is no reason to assign a pernicious motive for short selling, any more than it is malicious to profit from prices increasing.

Naked short selling

Usually, most criticism is directed at *naked short selling*, which refers to two different practices, either a short speculative position rather than a hedge against another security, or more recently the practice of short-selling an asset without first borrowing the asset.

It is often claimed that naked short selling in a crisis makes the crisis worse, and is hence morally wrong. However, it is not clear why short sales are any worse than sales by long holders or hedging with derivatives, with the latter practices more voluminous and hence affecting markets much more than shorting.

Restrictions and bans

Short selling remains banned in many jurisdictions, and because of its connections to profiting from and exacerbating crises, has often been temporarily banned once a crisis is underway. For example, after the Great Depression started in 1929, one of the first steps taken by President Hoover to regulate the activity of the markets was to compel the New York Stock Exchange to curb short selling. Similarly, the SEC temporarily banned in 2008 what it called 'abusive naked short selling' in major banks in order to prevent their share prices falling more than they were already. In 2011, France, Italy, Spain, Greece and Belgium banned short selling of the shares of banks and other financial companies.

The available empirical evidence is unclear on whether such bans achieve their intended purpose. They may even be counterproductive, as some studies suggest greater falls for shares covered by a short selling ban, perhaps because this provides a powerful signal that others would sell if permitted. Banning short selling signals panic on behalf of the authorities which equally contributes to a crisis.

9.4 POLICY ISSUES

Before 2007, the prevailing view amongst policymakers was that most concerns about trading and speculation were best left to the market. That did not mean that these activities were unregulated, far from it, and the world's securities regulators, such as the SEC in the US, have imposed a number of controls and checks on the trading process. These, however, were more focused on improving the efficiency of markets and preventing fraud and abuse, rather than improving financial stability.

There are many exceptions to this. Many of these policies date back to the Great Depression. Just one example is US regulations on margins and counterparties. These are explicitly aimed at addressing systemic risk concerns arising from the Depression. The problem with these rules was that they were only partially effective when needed and did not adequately address new areas of risk.

There was a general consensus that lightly regulated private enterprises lead to greater efficiency than state enterprises in the provision of services ranging from telecommunications to finance, and that the state's role should be peripheral – essentially to provide a level playing field and restrict monopolies.

The financial crises starting in 2007 demonstrated the complacency of such attitudes. Certain trading activities directly contributed to the crises, and policymakers ever since have sought to develop rules that would regulate trading in a way that increases financial stability.

9.4.1 CCPs and financial stability

One problem that quickly became apparent when the crisis was underway was the myriad of over-the-counter (OTC) derivative instruments. In the boom times before the crisis, this did not seem such a big problem because the main risk factors, asymmetric information, complexity and counterparty credit risk, were not apparent.

The problem of asymmetric information is demonstrated in Figure 9.6. In Figure 9.6(a) we have four banks, representing the banking system, where all have exposures to each other. The exposures are net zero, that is, if we add them all up, and hence net out all the positions, the end result is zero. This is not how the individual bank sees it. For example, bank A owes money to B, C and D, and is owed money by the same. If it worries about the solvency of, say, B, it also fears not being able to make payments to C and D. At the same time, it also expects C and D to be exposed to B. This means that if it becomes worried about the stability of the system, a prudent course of action would be to reduce its exposures to everybody, even to the extent of causing a run on B.

This is what happened with Bear Stearns and Lehman in 2008. We call this problem *information asymmetry*, since each participant does not know the full picture. If there was a way to net out the positions across the system, the problem of information asymmetry

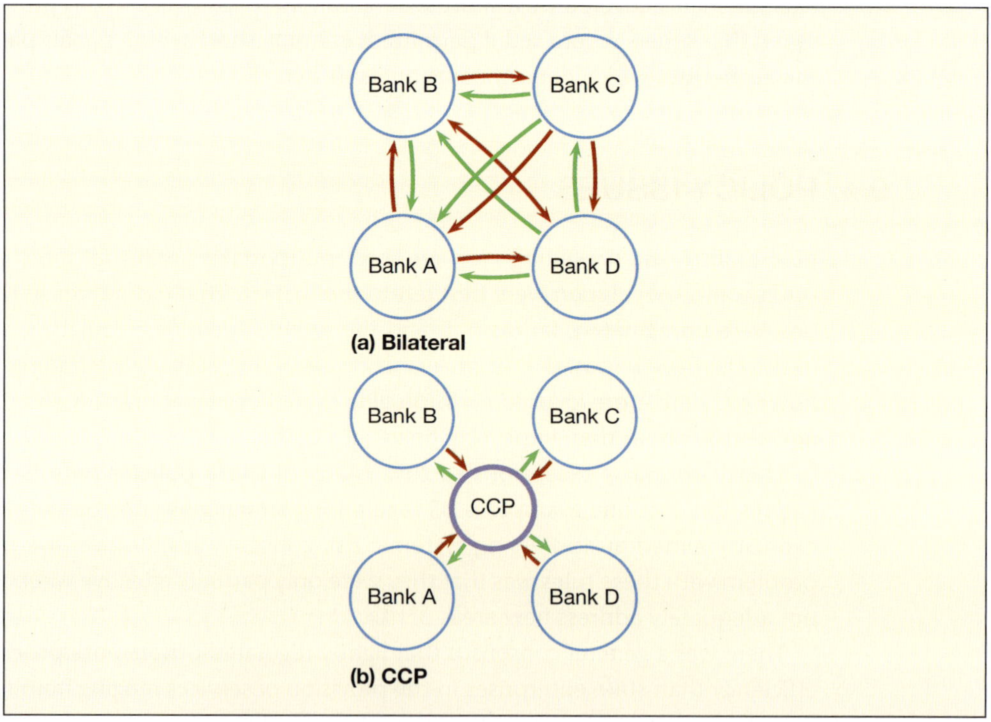

Figure 9.6 Role of CCPs

would be reduced. This is exactly what a central counterparty (CCP) does, because it acts as a counterparty to each and every trade, and therefore knows all the exposures and can net them out, as seen in Figure 9.6(b). This also solves the problem of counterparty credit risk, provided there are no worries about the solvency of the CCP. As a side benefit, it reduces complexity in the financial system because the CCP will prefer only a relatively small number of standardised instruments.

Contrast the situation in which most contracts are bilateral. In this case the contracts are likely to be customised, making it difficult to calculate aggregate positions for the banks involved. For a third party such as a regulator it would be impossible.

How many CCPs?

Ideally, there should be only one CCP in the world, so that we could net all exposures globally. That is impossible politically because major countries would want the CCP to be within their own jurisdiction. At the very least, we would see one CCP in the US, another in Europe and the third in Asia, and quite possibly more. Within the European Union (EU), there are strong disagreements among member states as to who should host the CCP, and similar debates rage in Asia.

If it is not possible to have a single global CCP, a particular problem is created as noted by Duffie and Zhu (2011). If an institution has to use more than one CCP, its net position across all CCPs might be zero, but this may not be visible to each CCP individually, which sees only its own positions. The problem may be partially solved by different CCPs having cross-margin arrangements and information sharing. This would somewhat reduce the benefits of the CCP, particularly if CCPs do not standardise contracts between themselves. However, so long as the number of CCPs is much smaller than the number of market participants, significant benefits still accrue.

Safety of CCPs

CCPs eliminate most, but not all, counterparty credit risk, because market participants are still exposed to the credit risk of the CCP itself. The failure of a CCP would significantly contribute to systemic risk, since a substantial part of the financial system will be directly exposed to it. For these reasons, the CCPs need to be safest of institutions, and they usually do enjoy explicit or implicit government guarantees. CCPs have been bailed out in the past, for example, in Hong Kong in 1987. This, however, means that the CCP is an institution that is too big to fail (TBTF), with its own attendant problems.

The need for CCP safety creates another problem, as noted by Zigrand (2010). During a crisis, the CCP might feel compelled to sharply increase margins, in order to protect itself, thereby transmitting problems to members. Of course, the same might happen regardless because any counterparty in bilateral transactions might behave in the same way. Counting the arrows in Figure 9.6, it is clear that a CCP market with N participants has $2N$ margined relationships, while without a CCP there are $N(N-1)$ relationships. Assuming perfect netting between partners, exactly half of these will require margin.

In the special case where position sizes are the same in each market, and if we make the assumption that the CCP would respond to the crisis by increasing margins by an amount similar to that of any other participant, the total increase in required margins will be roughly $2/N$ of the size. Even if there are multiple CCPs, the pro-cyclical effect of margin increases could be reduced by the presence of CCPs. In practice, gains will be more modest, because in the CCP market the individual positions will typically be larger, and the institution might have offsetting positions, recognised in the bilateral market but not the CCP market, but the benefits of netting can still be significant.

Conclusion

The move towards CCPs is broadly positive, and to the extent that the various political difficulties can be overcome, would lead to a more stable financial system. However, CCPs contribute to the commoditisation of the finance industry and will reduce profits; consequently, industry opposition will be entrenched. Within the US most trading will move to CCPs because of the Dodd–Frank Act.

Clearing houses follow recommendations made by the Bank for International Settlements (BIS) in 2004, and the ongoing crisis has triggered a review of those standards. It is likely that CCPs will be required to further boost their financial safeguards, especially given their renewed importance.

9.4.2 Bonuses

A particular issue that has become quite controversial recently is *bank bonuses*. Bank employees are amongst the most highly compensated individuals in the world, enjoying bonuses that in theory are connected to their individual profitability, their division or bank.

In most cases, those engaged in trading for somebody else are incentivised by performance bonuses, so that when they achieve high returns they share in the profits, but if profits are low, or losses incurred, the trader receives only regular income. While this does incentivise good performance and risk-taking, it does create certain problems, related to the issue of incentives of guaranteed intermediaries discussed later in Section 14.7, as both payoff structures have a similar option-like structure.

Perhaps the main problem is that the trader shares in the profits but not the losses. In other words, the risk-return profile is asymmetric. This means that an individual trader might be quite content taking significant amounts of risk; if the bet turns out well, she will get large bonuses, but otherwise her employer fails. While that might not be the type of risk profile her superiors, shareholders, supervisors and other stakeholders desire, she is the one making the trading decisions. See Macrae and Watkins (1998) for more on these issues.

Various stakeholders might want to prevent such excessive risk-taking, employing many layers of controls intended to restrain risk. Management typically restricts traders in the types of securities they may trade, the level of risk anticipated, and the amount of capital employed. Senior management will impose similar restrictions on divisions, and regulators on banks. Despite all these many-layered restrictions, in practice, it can be difficult to contain risk-taking. Trading strategies are often very complicated and it may be impossible for any outsider to make sense of what is happening. In addition, the trader has an incentive to make the trading activities as complicated as possible, to prevent outside scrutiny, and to take risk in areas that receive the least amount of scrutiny.

Does limiting bonuses reduce systemic risk?

Arguments against high bank bonuses often cloak unhappiness with high compensation levels with arguments that bonuses increase risk. However, little evidence exists either way, despite the strong *a priori* argument that incentives *should* influence behaviour, and one can treat arguments on either side only as assertions rather than as evidence-based conclusions. These issues are discussed by Danielsson and Keating (2009), for example.

Looking at crises past, there seems to be a recurring thread of overconfidence and herding. This may happen because competitive pressures cause market participants to emulate the successful initiatives of their competitors, even if it may look imprudent to outside observers. Such pressures would be present regardless of any bonuses paid.

What is clear is that historically we have seen excessive risk playing a central role in financial crises without a bonus in sight. Perhaps the best example is the Japanese excesses and subsequent crisis in the 1980s and early 1990s. Similarly, the largest loss to a rogue trader in history, that of Jérôme Kerviel, was caused by an individual paid mainly via a fixed salary, with no prospects of receiving a bonus commensurate with his vast positions.

Similarly, strict punishments for failure have not prevented banks from collapsing. The largest nineteenth-century bank that failed, Overend & Gurney, was a partnership, so that its failure presumably meant poverty for the partners. Still, it did not dissuade them from plunging headlong into the junk bond market at the time. Similarly, Francesch Castello knew the punishment for bank failure was execution, and still took too much risk, failed and was executed.

However, the presence of asymmetric risk-return profiles can only increase risk, and the payment of large bonuses for successful risk-taking will therefore encourage socially undesirable levels of risk-taking and the manipulation of the financial system. For example, the LIBOR price-fixing would have been less likely if derivatives traders in Barclays did not directly gain from fixing prices.

How easy is it to limit bonuses?

Policymakers have recently become concerned about bonuses, as expressed by the Financial Services Authority (2009a), and several initiatives aiming at regulating compensation have been launched. Even if the case for limiting bonuses seems fairly clear-cut, it is not obvious how that could be done in practice, at least in a manner that clearly improves financial stability.

If financial institutions attempt unilaterally not to pay bonuses, they are at the risk of star employees – sometimes called *rainmakers* – leaving the firm. The banks maintain that they cannot cut bonuses unilaterally for competitive reasons, but such arguments are of course self-serving and not much support exists for or against that assertion. National regulators face similar threats from their banks if they aim to regulate compensation. Head offices are mobile, a point made clear in negotiations with regulators.

For this reason, it is sometimes argued that the only way to prevent excessive bonuses is for governments to coordinate in regulating compensation. Within the EU, bankers' bonuses are to be limited by law. A new rule, from the European Parliament, applies to senior employees of EU-based banks anywhere in the world as well as to EU-based staff of non-European banks. This covers all forms of bonuses, where the ratio of bonuses to salary will be limited to 1:1. This would have several different implications: we could expect base salaries to increase, non-European banks to move trading activities away from the Union, and traders to resign from European banks and move out of the Union.

If we could assume that funding for their activities (and hence the risk) would actually move with them, it could then make banking safer within the EU, provided that all core banking activities actually remained onshore and European governments did not simply find themselves obliged to bail out foreign banks. The extensive support provided by the Federal Reserve System (Fed) to foreign banks, like Royal Bank of Scotland (RBS) and HSBC, discussed later in Section 14.5.1 is an interesting precedent.

Such initiatives also raise employees' incentives to gain and retain a bank job, while reducing the optionality that incentivises risk-taking. However, other distortions are introduced. For example, there are indications that basic salaries in banking are sharply increasing from their already high levels. This improves the industry's position in the competition for new graduates, to the detriment of other employers like regulators and the non-financial industry.

9.4.3 Universal and narrow banking

Many observers have become worried about the fact that the same commercial banks that are essential for the functioning of the economy are also engaged in significant risky investments and speculation, where large losses might cause an otherwise solvent commercial bank to fail, seriously disrupting economic activity.

For this reason, following the Great Depression, the US passed the Glass–Steagall Act, which sought to separate risky investment banking from presumably safer commercial banking. Over time, the Glass–Steagall Act became progressively watered down, and was eventually repealed in 1999. It is ironic that by the end of 2008, all of the remaining investment banks in the US became commercial banks as a result of Fed efforts to prop up the financial system. This was, in effect, a recognition of the Lehman lesson that the investment banks were systemically vital and that, as with commercial banks, regulators could not, in practice, stand back and allow them to fail.

The end of the Glass–Steagall Act, and the lack of a similar law in Europe, is frequently blamed for contributing to the excessive risk-taking in the banking system and, hence, the ongoing crisis.

Initiatives

It is therefore not surprising that several initiatives aiming at preventing excessive risk-taking in banks have been launched by various policymakers. For example, the US, as a part of the Dodd–Frank Act, has proposed the so-called *Volcker Rule*, named after a former governor of the Fed, Paul Volcker, aimed at restricting commercial banks from engaging in proprietary trading.

A similar proposal was made by the UK Independent Commission on Banking[1] in 2011, in the Vickers report, named after the chairman of the commission. It states that British banks must separate out high street banking activities from investment banking operations. This means ring-fencing all retail and small business deposits, with investment banking activities, such as derivatives, debt and equity underwriting, and investing in proprietary trading, falling outside. This protects the retail and payments operations of banks so that a bank failure would not result in failure of the more economically important divisions of the bank.

The effectiveness of these proposals is untested, and it is also unclear whether they will in fact be adopted. One of the largest banks in the UK, HSBC, has warned that it may move its headquarters if the government were to break up big banking groups (*Financial Times*, 2010b). As well as the predictable opposition from UK banks, the measures also face hostility from other European countries, which would prefer all European banks to be regulated on an equal basis, in this case a less stringent one.

After the US and UK initiatives, the EU commissioned a study from Erkki Liikanen, governor of Finland's central bank (Liikanen, 2012), to look into possible reforms of the European banking sector. The Liikanen report reaches similar conclusions in some aspects as the other two reports, addressing ring-fencing and trading restrictions. It also aims to limit bonuses and reduce risk in real estate. It remains unclear whether the EU will adopt the report's conclusions.

9.4.4 Financial transaction tax

One of the oldest types of tax is a financial transaction tax (FTT), often referred to as a stamp duty or something similar. This does not tax profits or income but rather specific transactions. It is common in real-estate transactions, and many countries apply it to routine financial transactions. For example, the UK imposes a 0.5% tax on share transactions.

While FTT was used historically to raise revenue for the government, Keynes in 1936 proposed a different objective, that is to curb speculation. This works because FTT is by its nature proportional to turnover, and so creates a disincentive for rapid trading, thus reducing speculation.

Tobin tax

A specific example of an anti-speculative FTT is the *Tobin tax*, as proposed by the economist James Tobin in 1972, which is a uniform worldwide tax on spot currency transactions. He argued that, designed correctly, the tax would cushion exchange rate fluctuations by penalising short-term financial capital flows and 'throw some sand in the wheels of super-efficient financial markets and create room for differences in domestic interest rates, thus enabling national monetary policy to respond to domestic macroeconomic needs' (Tobin, 1996). He further claimed that such a tax could strengthen the weight of fundamentals on exchange rates, diminish excess volatility and expand the autonomy of national monetary policies.

[1]bankingcommission.independent.gov.uk.

Given the large trading volumes in foreign exchange markets, estimated by the BIS to be $4 trillion per day in April 2010, even a very small tax rate might be expected to bring in significant revenue. That is not true, however, because trading volumes would probably collapse as a consequence of the tax.

The main argument against the Tobin tax is that for it to be effective, it needs to be introduced in every financial centre, otherwise foreign exchange trading would move to the areas where the tax has not been implemented. It is hard to know how serious this problem would be, because there are significant costs in relocating and such offshore activities would still need to interact with the taxed onshore sector.

It might be harder to prevent the migration of trading to derivative contracts, beyond the control of the authorities. For example, if a bank sells beef for pounds and buys a matching quantity of beef for dollars, it has entered into two livestock contracts, not foreign exchange (FX) contracts, yet has still contrived to exchange dollars for pounds. There are myriad similar ways to mask the true nature of financial transactions.

The FTT debate

While some proponents of the FTT argue that it would bring in substantial tax revenue, the main arguments in favour of the tax focus on financial stability, like the fact that an FTT would be an excellent anti-complexity device. Each time a financial asset is traded, yet another link is created between financial institutions, whilst the distance between the owner of the asset and the originator becomes longer. Because an FTT will reduce the number of transactions, complexity is automatically reduced as a consequence. More generally, as argued by Tobin, according to the general principle of control theory, the introduction of friction into systems tends to increase stability.

The opponents of FTT, many from the finance industry, argue that the tax revenues are overestimated, that it would not be effective in increasing financial stability, that domestic banks would lose ground relative to foreign banks and hence jobs would be lost, that trading would migrate to offshore locations or derivative contracts, and finally that this is the wrong time to increase taxes on the financial sector, in the middle of a crisis, especially as the sector is already receiving significant public assistance.

While there are arguments on both sides of the discussion, little evidence exists either way, and the debate is more often than not based on general attitudes to finance and speculation, rather than the underlying facts. The question of FTT is under considerable scrutiny by researchers but no clear answer has yet emerged.

FTT in Europe

As a part of its post-crisis regulatory reform agenda, the EU proposed a FTT in 2011 to take effect in 2014. This would affect financial transactions between financial institutions, taxed at 0.1% for shares and bonds and 0.01% for derivative contracts. The FTT has met significant opposition, especially by the UK, the Netherlands and Sweden, and there have been proposals to apply it only to the euro zone. At the time of writing, it is unclear what the final outcome will be. Some states, including Germany and especially France, are implementing a unilateral FTT regime, which will provide interesting experimental data.

9.5 SUMMARY

Speculation and trading is an essential part of the financial system. They provide key services to economic agents, but also have the potential for destabilising financial markets and even causing crises.

Trading scandals of various types are common, such as the case of JP Morgan Chase and the London whale, the LIBOR price-fixing scandal, Ponzi schemes like the Madoff scandal, and rogue traders.

There are many categories of market participants, for example proprietary traders who aim to generate trading profits for their employer. Most market participants act on behalf of investors, a part of the institutionalisation of dishonesty markets. Perhaps the most controversial market participants are hedge funds.

Financial institutions have been very active in financial innovation, the creation of various types of new financial instruments, but this remains quite contentious, and some respected commentators claim that financial innovation benefits only the inventors.

Trading involves various types of activities like value investing, technical trading and momentum trading, but also carry trading which has frequently been blamed for undermining government policy. Perhaps the most controversial trading strategy is short selling.

Following the crisis from 2007, there have been various initiatives aiming at curbing perceived abuses in the financial system. These include protecting us from casino banking, limiting bonuses and taxing trading.

APPENDIX: BASIC TERMINOLOGY OF TRADING

We refer to each trading entity as a *party*, and when referring to the other party we use the term *counterparty*. The trading process has three distinct stages.

1. In the first, traders submit *orders* to buy or sell a security. Buy orders are matched with sell orders in the marketplace, often an exchange, and the parties trading are notified of a match and a successful trade.
2. This is followed by a process called *clearing* that involves the exchange of information, regulatory reporting and various other activities that must take place before a transaction can be completed.
3. The last stage, the actual exchange of money, securities or goods, is called *settlement*.

Definition 9.1 Exchange An exchange is an organised venue for trading financial assets, usually nowadays a computer system.

While some trading takes place in a formal venue called an exchange, most trading bypasses exchanges, and takes place over-the-counter in a bilateral deal between counterparties.

Definition 9.2 Market maker A market maker is a financial institution or an individual that quotes both a buy and sell price of a financial instrument, hoping to profit from the spread between the buying and selling prices.

Definition 9.3 Broker A broker is an individual or institution that arranges transactions between buyers and sellers, charging a commission when a deal is executed.

For example, on organised exchanges, market makers are often permitted to acquire stock for the purpose of later selling it to meet anticipated customer demand.

Clearing and settlement involve procedures meant to reduce the risk to each party that the other party will fail to complete the transaction as agreed, that is *counterparty risk*. These activities are often concentrated in an institution called a *clearing house*.

Definition 9.4 Clearing house A clearing house is a firm that sits in between buyers and sellers, acting as a counterparty for each, and also clearing trades, that is taking care of the movements of assets and money. They net trades among their members, manage collateral before facilitating payment and delivery at the settlement date, and take care of the various accounting details. See Figure 9.7 for the various steps.

Definition 9.5 Netting Netting means that we consider the net amounts owed by two counterparties, not the gross amounts. For example, if party A owes B $10 million, and B owes A $11 million, the gross amount is $21 and the net amount $1 million.

Definition 9.6 Central counterparty (CCP) A CCP is the legal counterparty on each side of every trade in the market, with the result that all market participants have contractual relationships only with the CCP rather than each other.

A clearing house may act as a CCP in a particular market. In order to be included in a CCP, it is necessary for a security to be standardised.

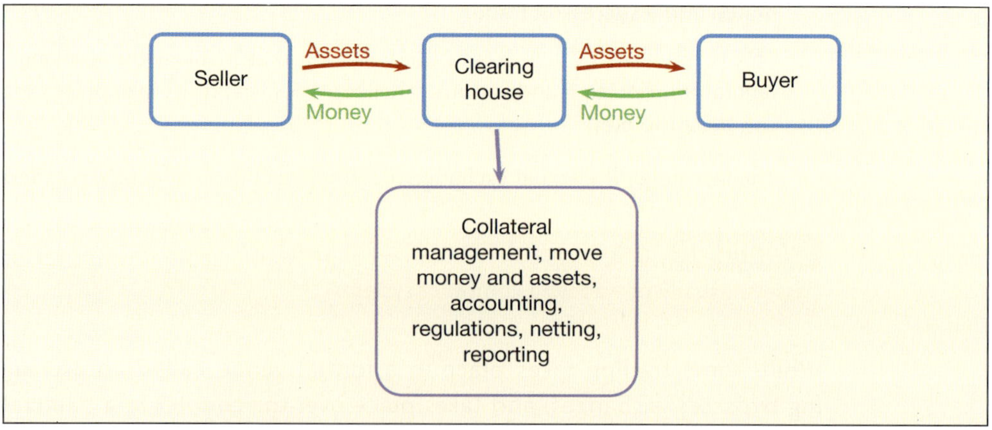

Figure 9.7 Clearing house

Questions for discussion

1 Do you think scandals like the JP Morgan 'whale' indicate that something is fundamentally wrong in the financial system?

2 What is the real damage caused by the LIBOR scandal?

3 Is Nick Leeson a hero, villain or neither?

4 Carry trades

(a) What are carry trades?

(b) Are speculative activities such as carry trades beneficial or not to the economy?

(c) How can carry trades be vehicles for contagion?

5 Is financial innovation a force for good or evil?

6 What are the main arguments in favour and against curbing high-frequency trading?

7 What is the main contribution of CCPs, and how could they increase financial instability?

8 Is naked short selling bad?

9 Is narrow banking a good idea?

10 Is the EU right in its pursuit of a financial transaction tax?

References

BBC (2012b). Barclays' widening Libor-fixing scandal. www.bbc.co.uk/news/business-18671255.

Danielsson, J. and Keating, C. (2009). Bonus incensed. *Vox EU,* 25 May. http://voxeu.org/index.php?q=node/3602.

Duffie, D. and Zhu, H. (2011). Does a central clearing counterparty reduce counterparty risk? Stanford University Working Paper.

Financial Services Authority (2009a). Reforming remuneration practices in financial services. Technical report.

Financial Services Authority (2012). Final notice. Technical report www.fsa.gov.uk/static/pubs/final/barclays-jun12.pdf.

Financial Times (2010b). HSBC in clearest warning over relocation. *Financial Times,* 3 September. www.ft.com/cms/s/0/5e0ba186-b6bd-11df-b3dd-00144feabdc0.html#axzz1zsblzMf.

Financial Times (2012a). DoJ probes $2bn JPMorgan trading loss. *Financial Times,* 15 May. www.ft.com/cms/s/0/39133792-9e9f-11e1-9cc8-00144feabdc0.html#axzz1x8DGs4zP.

Financial Times (2012b). JPMorgan whale harpooned. *Financial Times,* 11 May. ftalphaville.ft.com/blog/2012/ 05/10/995211/jpmorgan-whale-harpooned/.

Graham, B. and Dodd, D. (1934). *Security Analysis*. Whittlesey House (McGraw-Hill).

Hull, J. C. (2011). *Options, Futures, and Other Derivatives,* 8th edition. Prentice Hall.

Kohn, M. (2003). *Financial Institutions and Markets,* 2nd edition. Oxford University Press.

Leeson, N. (1999). *Rogue Trader*. Sphere, London.

Liikanen, E. (2012). High-level expert group on reforming the structure of the EU banking sector. Technical report, European Union.

Macrae, R. and Watkins, C. (1998). A disaster waiting to happen. Mimeo, www.cs.rhul.ac.uk/home/chrisw/Disaster.pdf.

Madura, J. (2010). *Financial Institutions and Markets,* 9th edition. South Western College, Cincinnati, OH.

Mishkin, F. S. and Eakins, S. (2011). *Financial Markets and Institutions,* 6th edition. Pearson.

Morris, S. and Shin, H. S. (1998). Unique equilibrium in a model of self-fulfilling currency attacks. *Amer. Econ. Rev.,* 88: 587–97.

Morris, S. and Shin, H. S. (1999). Risk management with interdependent choice. *Oxford Review of Economic Policy,* 15: 52–62, reprinted in *Bank of England Financial Stability Review,* 7, 141–50, www.bankofengland.co.uk/fsr/fsr07art5.pdf.

SEC and CFTC (2010). Findings regarding the market events of May 6, 2010. Technical report.

Sullivan, R., Timmermann, A. and White, H. (1999). Dangers of data mining: the case of calendar effects in stock returns. *J. Econometrics,* 105(1): 249–86.

Tobin, J. (1996). A currency transactions tax, why and how? *Open Economies Review,* 7: 493–9.

Wall Street Journal (2009b). Paul Volcker: think more boldly. *Wall Street Journal,* 14 December. online.wsj.com/article/SB100014 24052748704825504574586330960597134.html.

Zigrand, J.-P. (2010). What do network theory and endogenous risk theory have to say about the effects of CCPs on systemic stability? *Financial Stability Review,* 14, Banque de France.

10 CREDIT MARKETS

The most important financial products are *fixed income* assets, composed of various credit instruments, like bonds, structured credit products and credit derivatives. The reason is that credit is an absolute necessity for the modern economy, allowing people to save for retirement and get mortgages, governments to finance their operations and stimulate the economy in recessions, and private companies to finance operations and expansions.

Of the fixed income assets, the most important are *bonds*. Financial institutions, corporations and governments depend on bonds for financing, and any problems in accessing the bond markets can quickly cause significant difficulties. That means the bond markets exert significant power over borrowers. Perhaps the best expression of their power was by a Bill Clinton strategist, James Carville, who said that he wanted to be reborn as the bond market because it is the most powerful force in the universe. Currently, some European governments are facing the wrath of the bond markets.

Investors in fixed income markets are often faced with borrowers of an unknown quality and need some mechanisms to ascertain the credit quality, and monitor borrower performance. The most common way to achieve this is by using *credit ratings* issued by *credit rating agencies (CRAs)*. These are private companies whose business it is to report on credit quality.

Trying to forecast credit risk is difficult in the best of times and the CRAs have been under almost constant criticism for the quality of ratings and the impact downgrades have on borrowers. As a result, there are frequent calls for reforms of the credit rating business, but it is not obvious how that could be accomplished.

We can also use various types of mathematical credit models to forecast credit risk. Of these credit models, the so-called reduced form models are particularly useful when it comes to mapping between the probability of default and credit spreads.

Links to other chapters

This chapter directly relates to Chapter 9 (trading and speculation) and Chapter 15 (dangerous financial instruments).

Key concepts

- Fixed income
- Margins and haircuts
- Credit rating
- Reduced form credit models
- Spreads
- Securitisation

Readings for this chapter

There are many books covering the topics discussed in this chapter. Besides the specific references in the text, we have drawn on books such as those by Hull (2011, 2012). A comprehensive discussion of bond markets is in Fabozzi (2009). Murphy (2009) discusses many of these issues in context of the crises from 2007.

Notation specific to this chapter

c	Coupon payment
P	Price
p_d	Probability of default
r	Risky interest rate
r_f	Risk-free rate
s	Spread, perhaps $r - r_f$
T	Maturity (years)
z	Recovery rate

10.1 MARKET FOR CREDIT

The financial market that gets most attention in public discourse is the equity market, but in importance and size it is dwarfed by the bond market.[1] In 2010, the size of the bond market was $95 trillion whilst the global equity market reached only $55 trillion.

This counts only regular bonds, sometimes referred to as *plain vanilla* bonds. If we include other credit instruments up to and including bank loans, the amount of overall credit is much larger.

[1]See www.imf.org/external/data.htm, www.bis.org/statistics/secstats.htm, www.sifma.org/research/statistics.aspx and www.world-exchanges.org/statistics.

Fixed income assets

Fixed income assets are assets providing payments on fixed schedules. They are debt instruments with an issuer (borrower) and an investor (lender). The markets for fixed income assets range from simple instruments such as zero coupon bonds to the magical world of credit derivatives.

Firms and governments issue debt in the *primary market*, generally by engaging an investment bank to act as an underwriter or primary dealer via auctions. Subsequent trading takes place in the *secondary market*, which could be an organised exchange or a more informal over-the-counter (OTC) market. Secondary markets provide two important functions: they give the original purchasers of securities the ability to resell, thus creating liquidity, and they provide a near-continuous reassessment of securities' prices. Bonds are typically traded in OTC markets rather than on formal exchanges.

10.1.1 Bond markets

The Bank for International Settlements (BIS) publishes detailed statistics on global bond markets, segmenting debt securities into *domestic* and *foreign*. The former are generally issued by domestic residents in domestic currencies, sold to resident investors, whilst international securities are global issues, mostly sold to and bought by international residents and issued in foreign currency. Of course, it is often difficult to precisely delineate between the two, especially with regard to the buyers. The BIS distinguishes between three categories of issuers: governments, financial institutions and corporations.

We show the development of the bond market in Figure 10.1. Both the domestic and international markets have grown rapidly, but the international much more so. Most of the growth is derived from financial institutions. In the domestic market, the persistently

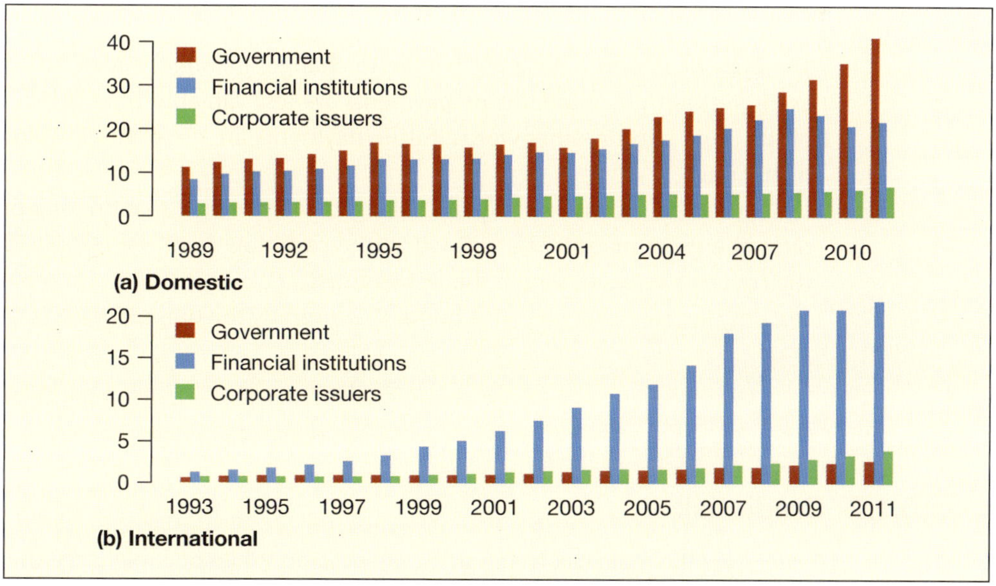

Figure 10.1 Outstanding bond volumes, 2011 prices, USD trillions
Data source: BIS and World Bank

Table 10.1 Outstanding bond volumes, June 2011, USD trillions

	Domestic			International		
	Gov.	FI	Corp.	Gov.	FI	Corp.
US	11.61	10.94	2.93	0.01	5.48	1.84
Japan	12.09	1.18	0.90	0.00	0.36	0.05
France	1.94	1.32	0.31	0.07	1.74	0.46
Italy	2.17	0.78	0.38	0.27	1.12	0.11
China	1.49	1.05	0.60	0.00	0.09	0.02
Germany	1.92	0.52	0.41	0.34	2.47	0.15
UK	1.38	0.31	0.02	0.12	2.83	0.32
Rest	8.46	5.72	1.48	1.86	7.88	1.02

Notes. Gov. is government, FI financial institutions and Corp. corporate issuers
Data source: Bank for International Settlements, http://www.bis.org

largest issuer is governments, followed by financial institutions and then corporations. This market has also grown rapidly: it is more than three times larger, in real terms, than it was 23 years ago, growing by more than 6% a year. The international market has grown by more than 13% a year.

Table 10.1 constitutes a snapshot of the the global bond market in June 2011, showing the seven countries with the largest domestic bond market. The world's largest economy, the United States (US), is the biggest issuer, followed by Japan, which has the highest government debt in the world. China is number five, driven mostly by government bonds. The United Kingdom (UK) is seventh, but in the market for paper issued by financial institutions it is the second, not surprising given the importance of City, the UK financial sector.

EXAMPLE 10.1 **Bond pricing**

The price of a bond is inversely related to changes in interest rates. The reason is that as interest rates increase, future payments are less valuable than before, so the price of the bond falls. In other words, future payments are discounted to the present at a higher rate.

This can be shown formally by looking at the pricing equation for a bond. Interest rates at a given maturity t are r_t, whilst the cash flow from the bond is $\{c_t\}_{t=1}^{T}$, that is the *coupon payments*, where the last payment, c_T, also includes the principal and T is maturity in years. The price of a bond, P, is given by the present value of the cash flow:

$$P = \sum_{t=1}^{T} \frac{c_t}{(1 + r_t)^t}$$

10.1.2 Credit risk

Credit risk is the main risk factor facing an investor. While one might see the term credit risk being used only for probabilities of default, most commentators use it in a broader sense as referring to the overall risk of losing money from fixed income instruments. This might happen because of a downgrade causing bond prices to fall in price, the failure of a borrower to make payments, changes in the probability that payments will not be made or will be delayed, changes in interest rates, or the amount of money recovered in case of default.

Default and recovery

Probability of default refers to the risk of borrowers failing to repay their debts as agreed, or otherwise failing to meet their contractual obligations by, for example, missing scheduled payments. The common *pari passu* clause in bond covenants means that debtors are considered in default on all their debt obligations as soon as they default on any particular one.

Loss given default quantifies how much a creditor can expect to get back after a default. It often takes many years, and even decades, to get recovery. In addition, there are significant national differences, so the failure of an otherwise identical company in two different countries might result in widely different recovery rates.

10.2 CREDIT RATING AGENCIES

The creditworthiness of borrowers is of key interest to anybody buying fixed income assets. While the buyers may want to estimate the creditworthiness by themselves, it can be a time-consuming and difficult task, especially for small and unsophisticated investors. As a consequence, they often outsource the analysis of creditworthiness to specialised companies called *credit rating agencies (CRAs)*. The two largest are Standard & Poor (S&P) and Moody's, with Fitch not far behind.

The CRAs do not provide investment advice or analysis of how much money an investor might lose; instead, in the words of S&P:

> 'A credit rating is S&P's opinion of the general creditworthiness of an obligor, or the creditworthiness of an obligor with respect to a particular debt security or other financial obligation, based on relevant risk factors.'

The two key terms to note are *opinion* and *creditworthiness*. CRAs do not provide advice, only opinion. There is an important legal difference between those terms, because advice implies an obligation to be right, while opinion does not. It is therefore easier to challenge advice in a court of law than it is to challenge opinion.

The CRAs are generally considered to have considerable expertise in credit risk and are regarded by many as unbiased evaluators of such risk. As a consequence, their ratings are widely accepted by both market participants and government agencies, and many investors are restricted to hold only rated instruments.

Ratings

Ratings take the form of a letter grade, as shown in Table 10.2 where we show ratings from both S&P and Moody's. For S&P the highest rating is AAA, followed by AAA–, AA+ all the way down to default. Moody's has a similar arrangement, but note that ratings from two different agencies are not directly comparable, even if we broadly expect them to provide similar information.

Table 10.2 Ratings

S&P	Moody's	Quality
AAA	Aaa	Prime
AA +	Aa1	High grade
AA	Aa2	
AA −	Aa3	
A +	A1	Medium grade
A	A2	
A −	A3	
BBB +	Baa1	
BBB	Baa2	
BBB −	Baa3	
BB+	Ba1	Non-investment grade, 'junk'
BB	Ba2	
BB −	Ba3	
B +	B1	Highly speculative
B	B2	
B −	B3	
CCC +	Caa1	
CCC	Caa2	
CCC −	Caa3	Near default, limited recovery
CC	Ca	
C		
	C	In default
D		

Ratings can apply to either an issuer, such as a corporation or sovereign, or to a specific debt issue. The rating process includes quantitative, qualitative and legal analysis. The quantitative analysis is mainly financial analysis based on a firm's financial reports like the balance sheet, cash flow statement and profit and loss account. The qualitative analysis is concerned with the quality of management, a firm's competitiveness and the expected growth of the industry it operates in, as well as its vulnerability to technological, regulatory and labour changes. The nature of this assessment is, of course, subjective. Ratings are usually reviewed once a year.

Spreads

The *yield curve* is a curve showing several yields or interest rates across different maturities, that is, the time at which the payment is due. Each debt issue has its own yield curve, determined by its credit rating. The difference in the yields for different ratings is called a *spread*. The lower the credit rating, the higher the yield. We show in Figure 10.2 a typical term structure for bonds of different rating categories.

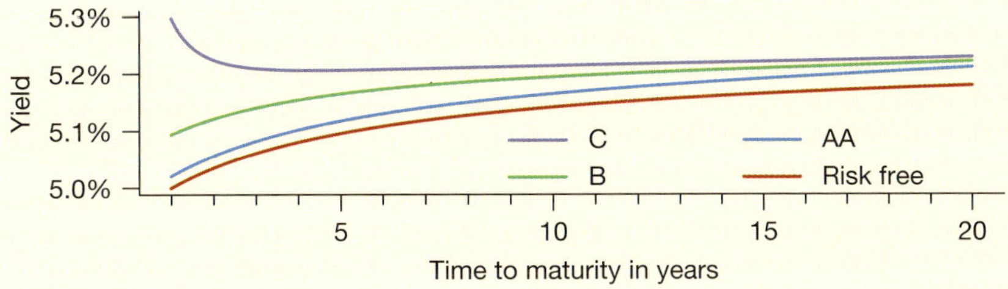

Figure 10.2 Yields, maturity, and credit spreads

10.2.1 Issues with rating agencies

Because of the fundamental role played by the CRAs, it is not surprising that they are under constant criticism. Ratings are an inexact field and involve forecasting future company performance and implicitly the economy generally, inevitably meaning that ratings are inaccurate. Ratings are used in the regulatory process, and therefore both are especially important and attract special scrutiny.

Critics have been quick to jump on mistakes, attacking ratings for missing individual defaults, such as those of Enron, WorldCom and Parmalat, and country problems as in the Asian crisis of 1997 and more recently problems in European sovereigns. The CRAs have also come under criticism for their aggressive approach to collecting fees. This was documented by the *Washington Post* (2004) and we discuss one case from that article, that of Hannover Re and Moody's.

EXAMPLE 10.2 Hannover Re and Moody's

When the CRAs made a big push into Europe, they allegedly used aggressive tactics to collect fees. According to the Washington Post (2004), Moody's informed the German insurance company Hannover Re in the mid-1990s that it had decided to rate the company at no charge, but was looking forward to the day Hannover Re was willing to pay for the ratings. Hannover Re refused, and never paid Moody's. Moody's rated Hannover Re anyway, starting with Aa2 in 1998 and downgrading three times, eventually to Baa1 (near junk) in 2003; while S&P, which did get paid by Hannover Re, has rated it *AA*– from 2003 until 2012. Moody's stopped rating Hannover Re in 2008.

Conflict of interest

Ratings are generally solicited and paid for by the issuer of debt and not the investor. Good ratings enhance the marketability of debt issues, enabling issuers to place debt more easily at lower interest rates. The prospect of bad ratings may cause an issuer not to go ahead, thus depriving CRAs of substantial fees. This leads to the perception that the

CRAs are too willing to provide good ratings in order to generate fee income. The agencies strongly reject the possibility of any conflict of interest.

However, in a world where issuers can go *ratings shopping*, that is, talk to several CRAs before picking one to rate an issue, worries about conflict of interest are unlikely to disappear. These problems have become especially pertinent following the crises from 2007 because of how banks were able to use the ratings models to structure credit products. We discuss that topic in detail later in the book.

Evaluating ratings quality

The term ratings quality refers to how accurate a rating is in predicting future performance of a debt issue. The CRAs publish historical records on ratings and defaults, enabling researchers to ascertain the long-run quality of ratings. This is especially relevant in the case of US corporate ratings since the CRAs have operated there since the 1920s, resulting in almost a century's worth of data. It is hard to access the ratings quality of sovereigns as well as non-US corporations because the historical record is limited.

It is perhaps most difficult to determine and evaluate the highest ratings because the failure rates are so low that adequate data may not be available. This means that the potential for model risk is especially important for AAA ratings.

European sovereign debt crisis

The CRAs have been severely criticised for their performance in the European sovereign debt crisis, both missing the pending problems in Cyprus, Portugal, Italy, Ireland, Greece and Spain, and then exacerbating their problems with downgrades.

A typical example was the reaction of European leaders to the downgrades of Portugal, in the summer of 2011. Viviane Reding, the European Union (EU) justice commissioner, said: 'We can't have a situation where a cartel of three US enterprises decides the fates of entire national economies and their citizens.' Either their 'cartel' should be smashed or 'independent' European and Asian ratings agencies set up, she said. The implication of this remark is that EU commissioners seem to believe that the reason for the sovereign debt crisis is downgrades by the CRAs, and not the mismanagement of public finances by some European states. If the EU were to set up its own 'independent' European CRA, it is unlikely that the ratings would be taken seriously. The EU announced in 2012 that the Union was to set technical standards and regulate CRAs under the auspices of the European Securities and Markets Authority (ESMA).

The oligopoly of ratings agencies

In the early 1970s, the US securities regulator, the Securities and Exchange Commission (SEC), started to mandate that certain investors could only buy debt instruments rated by a recognised CRA. That amounted to the creation of an *oligopoly* of recognised ratings agencies, and over time the requirements that issues be rated before purchase became more common. The oligopoly of the CRAs was enhanced by their central role in the Basel regulations. Throughout this time, the authorities had no objections to the merger of CRAs, and by the start of the crisis in 2007, following a wave of mergers, two agencies had 80% of the market.

More recently, the US and European authorities have been encouraging the creation of new CRAs, and we can expect new CRAs in the future, including some that charge buyers, not issuers.

Legal protection

Given the importance of CRAs, it is no surprise that they are frequently sued by aggravated investors. However, in the US, they have consistently maintained that they are no different from financial journalists offering opinions, thus getting protection from the First Amendment to the US constitution – free speech. This would make them different from consultants and auditors who have a contractual obligation to provide a correct opinion, given the facts available to them at the time.

The CRAs have until now prevailed in US courts, but changes in law may alter that. Furthermore, no such protection of free speech exists in Europe so they need different legal protection there.

This leaves the question of whether the CRAs should be held legally accountable for inaccurate ratings. While it might seem just that investors be able to sue them for damages, the end result would only be that the expected cost of damages be built into their fee structure. Since any damages would probably be substantial, the cost of ratings would increase significantly. It is not clear if that would be of benefit to investors.

Furthermore, in a world where two agencies have 80% of the market it would be difficult to punish either severely, because that might force it to leave the business, leaving only one major CRA. The case where the accounting firm Arthur Andersen had to close down following its mistakes with Enron serves as a cautionary tale.

Solution

While it is not feasible to do away with the ratings agencies altogether, nor would it be sensible to substantially restructure the existing ones, there are several steps that could be taken to minimise the problems created by ratings agencies. It would be of significant benefit to encourage competition in the ratings business, to try to move away from a model whereby the issuer pays for the ratings, and finally to reduce the impact of CRAs in financial regulations. Some steps have been taken in these directions, but it remains to be seen how effective they will be.

10.3 CREDIT MODELS

There are several alternatives to using ratings for assessing credit risk, and sophisticated investors may prefer more formal theoretical or statistical modelling of credit risk. There are two main alternative approaches, *structural models* and *reduced form models*. The latter is particularly useful in providing a mapping between spreads and probability of default.

The structural models derive from option pricing theory, such as the Black–Scholes–Merton (Black and Scholes, 1973a; Merton, 1974) option pricing model, and consider risky debt as a combination of safe debt and a short put option on a firm, struck at the face value of a firm's debt. Under this approach, a firm's liabilities are considered to be contingent claims against the firm's assets, where a default occurs whenever the firm's asset value falls below the debt value. A key advantage of this approach is that the probability of default and recovery rates is directly related to firm-specific characteristics. However, a disadvantage is that asset values are not directly observable and may be difficult to estimate.

10.3.1 From credit spreads to probability of default

Credit spreads indicate what the market thinks about the credit quality of a particular bond compared to a benchmark, typically the bond of a *risk-free* government. This means that if we know the credit spread, it is possible to infer the implied probability of default.

The spread, s, is the difference between the yield on risky bond r and the yield of a risk-free but otherwise identical bond, r_f. While differences between risky and risk-free rates can arise from many factors, such as convexity, tax and liquidity, the main reason is due to the probability of default. In what follows we assume that the probability of default is the sole determinant of the credit spread.

Supposing the yield is continuously compounded and quoted on an annual basis. The realised returns on a risky and risk-free bond are e^{rT} and e^{r_fT} respectively, where T is the maturity of the bond measured in years. If an investor is *risk neutral*, she will be indifferent between owning the risk-free bond and the risky bond, weighted by the risk-neutral probability of default, p_d adjusting for the recovery rate, z:

$$(1 - p_d)e^{rT} + p_d z e^{rT} = e^{r_fT}$$

We therefore get:

$$e^{rT}(1 - p_d + p_d z) = e^{r_fT}$$

Note here that the p_d is the *cumulative* risk-neutral probability of default: if $T = 2$, then p_d gives the probability of default in two years, not the conditional probability of default, which is the probability of default occurring in year 2 given no default in year 1. Since the credit spread is defined as $s = r - r_f$, we can substitute to get:

$$1 - p_d + p_d z = e^{-sT}$$

Therefore

$$p_d = \frac{1 - e^{-sT}}{1 - z}$$

EXAMPLE 10.3 EU defaults

Consider the yields on European sovereign bonds in December 2011, where German bonds are risk-free whilst Italian bonds are risky. If we assume a recovery rate of 40%, the table below shows the implied probabilities of default for Italy. The markets find that Italy has an almost 10% probability of default every year.

	Yield		Probability of default	
Maturity	German	Italian	Cumulative	Annual
1	0.079%	5.753%	9.19 %	9.19%
2	0.320%	5.956%	17.77%	8.57%
3	0.493%	6.254%	26.45%	8.69%
4	0.751%	6.436%	33.90%	7.45%
5	1.030%	6.665%	40.92%	7.02%

10.4 MARGINS, HAIRCUTS AND MARK-TO-MARKET

The two entities on either side of a fixed income transaction are known as *counterparties*, and generally one of the two owes money to the other. The risk of one counterparty not getting paid is called *counterparty credit risk*. In some cases, it is always the same party owing money to the other, such as the seller of a bond, but in other cases it could be either, like in a swap contract. Several mechanisms have been developed to address this counterparty credit risk, for example *margins*, *haircuts*, and *mark-to-market*.

10.4.1 Margins, haircuts and leverage

Margins

Market participants are very often required to post a type of collateral called the *initial margin*, and maintain a portion of that, called the *maintenance margin*, in case the market goes against them. We sometimes use the terminology to be *in red* when we owe money and to be *in black* when we are owed money. If the posted margin is not sufficient, the party in red may receive a *margin call*, requiring funds within a short period of time, perhaps the end of the business day. Unless the trader provides the funds, the underlying position might be closed out and the trader declared bankrupt.

Margins do provide significant protection, both as a buffer against possible losses and also because they incentivise those in red not to default on their positions. Margins are, however, a double-edged sword. Consider a trader whose position is in red and facing a margin call. They will have to come up with the funds almost immediately, which may require them to liquidate some of their positions at short notice, perhaps at firesale prices, suffering significant losses and perhaps transmitting a crisis across markets.

If only one trader is in difficulty, this is not a serious problem. If, however, the problems are widespread, such forced sales and difficulties in meeting margins may lead to a vicious spiral between selling, prices falling and more margin calls, perhaps giving rise to a *firesale externality*. Such endogenous risk feedback loops are at the heart of many crisis episodes.

Haircuts

Haircuts are intimately related to initial margins. When securities are pledged as collateral for a transaction, only a portion of the current market value counts as a pledge, with the rest termed a haircut. Used this way, the haircut serves the same function as initial margins.

The term haircut has other related meanings, such as indicating losses to bondholders in credit restructuring. For example, when discussing the losses facing the owners of Greek sovereign debt, the term used is a haircut.

Leverage

Haircuts and margins are directly related to leverage. In particular, the inverse of the haircut or initial margin shows implied leverage. Suppose a trader enters into a financial transaction, buying a security for $100 million, posting a 25% initial margin and borrowing the rest from her broker. Therefore, the trader uses $25 million of her own money and $75 million borrowed from her broker. The trader has therefore leveraged her $25 million three times.

10.4.2 The case of haircuts in the 2007–2008 crisis

We show typical haircuts on a range of fixed income assets in Table 10.3, along with approximate implied leverage, inverse haircut, over two sample periods, right before and at the height of the 2008 crisis. The table shows directly how the riskiness of the underlying security is reflected in the haircut. Risk-free US government bonds or investment-grade bonds have a haircut of almost zero, allowing almost infinite leverage, while high-risk bonds and risky tranches of CDOs attract a much higher haircut. What is perhaps most interesting is how rapidly the haircuts increase for the fixed income assets but not for the equities. The biggest change is observed for the safest assets, the government bonds and investment-grade bonds.

All classes of securities see a significant increase in haircuts, with haircuts on even supposedly safe US government bonds increasing from 0.25% to 3%, with the various collateralised debt obligation (CDO) tranches losing their collateral value.

Table 10.3 Typical haircut or initial margin for selected securities

	Haircut (%)		Leverage	
	Jan–May	April	Jan–May	April
Securities held as collateral	2007	2008	2007	2008
US government bonds	0.25	3	399	32
Investment-grade bonds	0–3	8–12	∞–32	12–7
High-yield bonds	10–15	25–40	9–6	3–2
Equities	15	20	6	4
Investment-grade CDS	1	5	99	19
Asset-backed CDOs rated:				
AAA	2–4	15	49–24	6
AA	4–7	20	24–13	4
A	8–15	30–50	12–6	2–1
BBB	10–20	40–70	9–4	2–0
Mezzanine	50	100	1	0

Data source: Financial Stress and Deleveraging Macrofinancial Implications and Policy, Global Financial Stability Report, p. 42 (Citigroup and IMF staff estimates 2008), International Monetary Fund

10.4.3 Mark-to-market, model or magic

A traditional approach in accounting is based on historical values and cash flows. Cash flow *in* is profit and cash flow *out* is loss. While this may be an appropriate approach in many situations, for many financial assets, whose value changes continually in financial markets with maturities that span multiple years, the historical value approach may lead to valuations that are very far away from the most likely eventual profit or loss. For this reason, accountants have developed the concept of *marking-to-market*, using current prices to account for the value of assets or liabilities on a firm's book. This means that values on balance sheets change along with market conditions, unlike historical cost accounting which uses the original value. Note that while the initial margin functions like a haircut, the maintenance margin is more akin to marking-to-market.

Mark-to-model or magic

A requirement for marking-to-market can cause particular problems when assets are illiquid because in that case there may not be a proper market price or, even if a market price were available, it would change if the firm bought the asset. In these conditions, firms may have to resort to *marking-to-model*, by using an internal pricing model to get valuations. This became common practice in the crises from 2007 for many structured credit products. The obvious problem is that no model is correct, and some are particularly bad. As a result, it is sometimes said that marking-to-market really means *marking-to-magic* because the dependence on untestable assumptions is so strong.

10.4.4 Marking and financial stability

While margins and haircuts generally provide useful protection to counterparties, they do carry with them a danger to financial stability if used improperly. In practice, they tend to be pro-cyclical, meaning that if the markets are booming, margins and haircuts are low, encouraging further borrowing which further inflates asset prices; and if the markets are heading for a crisis, margins and haircuts may increase, causing difficulty for market participants who may be already in trouble. This can lead to a vicious feedback loop between increasing margins and market distress. One manifestation of this was seen during the crises from 2007, as seen in Table 10.3.

It is important to recognise how the problem created by marking-to-market arises. Any investor would prefer to know the mark-to-market values and more transparency about asset values is generally of a positive benefit. Lack of transparency might be helpful in hiding risk or even mistakes, but in a crisis investors tend to assume the worst, so a lack of transparency directly leads to the worst possible expectations. The financial stability problem created by marking-to-market arises because of how marking is misused by rule-based systems, whereby more certainty can lead to undesirable results. In other words, the problem created by marking-to-market is not the fact that we report assets at their market values, but rather that the reporting of market values mechanically affects other rules and requirements, for example, forcing banks to cut positions or raise capital in a pro-cyclical way.

10.5 SECURITISATION

New fixed income assets are often created out of other fixed income assets in a financial practice called *securitisation*. Securitisation has long been a common practice in financial markets, often resulting in useful products, and is not itself problematic. Such views have changed following the crisis of 2007 because of the role played by securitisation in the *shadow banking system*, which undermined financial regulations prior to the crisis.

Some of the clearest examples of this are the failure of Northern Rock in the UK in 2007 and the subprime mortgage crisis in the US.

Securitisation is where various types of credit assets are pooled together and sold in various forms to creditors. Common examples of credit assets include credit card debt, car loans and mortgages. Securitisation is often related to what is known as the *originate and distribute* model of banking, whereby a bank specialises in lending and then sells off a portfolio of loans on the secondary market.

Securitisation has long been a feature of financial markets and throughout history various forms of securitisation have been used. For example, a particular securitisation instrument called a *covered bond*, or *Pfandbriefe* in German, was first created in nineteenth-century Germany and has been in use ever since. A more recent example is the US government creating a government-sponsored entity called Fannie Mae whose purpose is to create a liquid secondary market for mortgages.

EXAMPLE 10.4 Bowie Bonds

Bowie Bonds are bonds backed by the revenues from David Bowie's 25 albums recorded before 1990. (Bowie was a 1960s and 1970s rock star.) They were issued in 1997 with a face value of $55 million, paid an interest rate of 7.9% and had an average life of 10 years.

Mechanics of securitisation

While there are many different ways to design structured products, a common way is to pool assets that pay cash regularly in a reasonably predictable manner, put them into a special purpose vehicle (SPV) and sell rights to the cash flow.

Definition 10.1 Special purpose vehicle A special purpose vehicle (SPV), also known as a special purpose entity, is a legal entity, usually a limited company or limited partnership, set up for specific, narrow and often temporary purposes. They might, for example, be used to isolate a firm from risk or to hide ownership. SPVs can be very useful, but can also be used for more nefarious reasons, such as Enron's use of them to commit fraud.

Definition 10.2 Sponsor The financial institution that sets up the SPV is known as a sponsor. It chooses the assets and engages a manager, and may provides guarantees to it. It is the owner of the SPV and often retains an equity position.

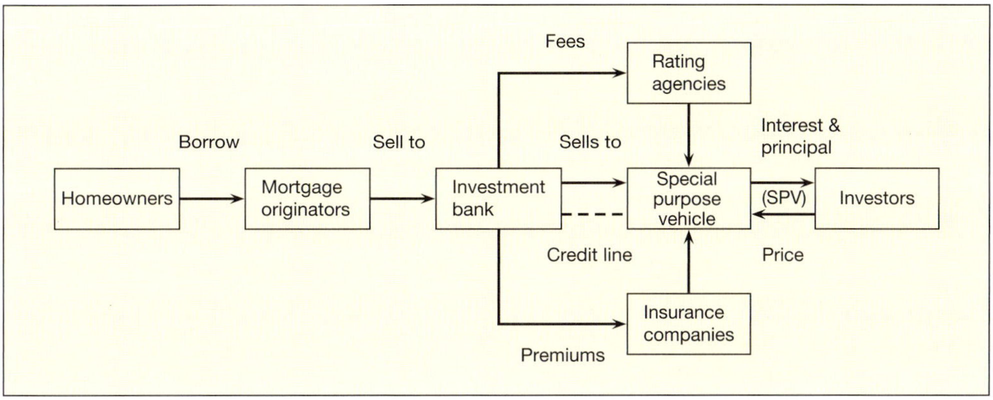

Figure 10.3 Securitisation chain

In securitisation, the sponsor sets up an SPV which often buys assets already held by the sponsor, perhaps financing the purchase by issuing bonds to outside investors. Typically, the value of the bonds is lower than the value of the assets, with the difference being equity contributed by the sponsor. The bonds are known as asset backed securities (ABSs) since the bonds are backed by the underlying assets. Additional protection may be provided by equity and junior tranches.

Figure 10.3 shows a typical securitisation process, the players involved and the flow of funds. The process starts by a homeowner borrowing from a *mortgage originator*. After the mortgage originator has accumulated enough mortgages, it sells them to an *investment bank* that intends to package them into a structured credit product.

The investment bank creates an SPV out of the mortgages it bought, and sells the rights to the payment flow to investors. The bank then pays fees to CRAs to obtain ratings to reassure the investors, and may pay premiums to insurance companies to protect some parts of the SPV.

10.5.1 Advantages and disadvantages

Advantages

The main advantage of securitisation is that by setting up a separate company, the originator does not have to count the SPV's debt amongst its liabilities, nor does it have to count the SPV's assets as its assets. If the originator is regulated it may not have to keep capital against the assets, depending on regulations.

Securitisation allows the originating bank to remove business loans, credit card loans, mortgages and other assets from its balance sheet, whilst retaining control of the assets. It also allows for the transformation of illiquid assets into liquid securities. Rather than holding the asset on a balance sheet financed with liquid deposits, securitisation transforms the asset itself from an illiquid one (perhaps a pool of loans) into liquid securities issued by the SPV. Furthermore, by creating a separate SPV, the firm isolates the cash flow generating assets and collateral so that securities issued by the SPV are not a general claim against the company, just against those assets.

The obvious reason to securitise assets is to transfer risk. In the originate and distribute model of banking, securitisation frees up capital and funding, allowing the firm to lend again. Securitisation allows banks to provide more and cheaper credit than they otherwise could, lowering the total cost of financing loans.

Investors also benefit in that securitisation allows them to invest in otherwise inaccessible assets, which is desirable for diversification purposes. For example, if you want to have some exposure to Japanese retail credit risk, without securitisation you would need a presence in Japan, advertising, regulatory approvals and so on. But if a Japanese bank securitises its credit card portfolio, then a Western investor can get access to this class of investment without the costs associated with opening a credit company in Japan.

Securitisation also allows for increasing specialisation in the financial system. One can separate what used to be one process in traditional banking into multiple different steps. For example, the origination of loans might be done by those specialising in local markets but not rich in capital. Borrowers get better terms and access to lending than they would get otherwise.

These loans are then sold on to investment banks with specialised skills in packaging loans and the necessary capital to buy them off the originators. Finally, the packaged loans can be split up into different risk categories, so that the risk can be precisely targeted at those who most desire it and will pay the most to get it.

Drawbacks

While the seller of portfolios of mortgages or credit card receivables might benefit from getting rid of the risk, the buyers of the loans face a 'lemons' problem[2] because the originators are likely to be better informed about the loans than the sellers and, therefore, may be tempted to securitise the lowest-quality loans and hold on to the better loans.

This directly relates to moral hazard because if a seller is not intending to hold the loan for more than a few months, it may care less about credit quality than if it held the loan until maturity. This was exactly the key problem in the market for subprime mortgages prior to the crises from 2007: the lenders did not care much about mortgage quality, as noted for example by Bitner (2008).

Securitisation also carries with it risk for the sellers. In the case of Northern Rock, the bank was dependent on securitisation, and when it encountered difficulties in placing its mortgage portfolios on the secondary markets, it collapsed.

[2]The term lemon problem relates to a famous paper by Akerlof (1970) on asymmetric information. In American English a lemon is a dodgy used car.

10.6 SUMMARY

The credit markets are fundamental to the functioning of modern economies, channelling savings to productive investments. In order to lend money, investors like to know the credit risk of their counterparties. The most common way to do that is by using ratings from CRAs. These are controversial, with many critics claiming that ratings quality is low.

An alternative way to access credit quality is by using mathematical models, such as structural models and reduced form models. The latter are especially useful in allowing for a conversion from spreads to probabilities of default.

Fixed income assets are often used as inputs into new assets, generally called structured credit. This is a long-established practice in financial markets, providing useful benefits to market participants, but can also be abused. Such products were at the heart of the crisis from 2007.

Margins and haircuts provide useful information to investors, but can increase financial instability when used in a mechanistic fashion.

Securitisation, whereby different fixed income instruments are packaged together and sold as one, is an old financial technique, dating back to the nineteenth century. When used properly, it can increase the efficiency of financial markets, but when misused may cause moral hazard and even crises.

Questions for discussion

1. What are OTC assets and markets?
2. Why are interest rates and bond prices inversely related?
3. What are the main components of credit risk?
4. What is a rating agency?
5. What are the main limitations of ratings?
6. Why is the EU so cross with the rating agencies? Is this warranted?
7. Suppose the markets view a one-year bond issued by the US government at 1% to be risk-free. If Argentina issues a one-year USD bond at 10%, what is the implied probability of default?
8. Explain the relationship between initial margins/haircuts and leverage.
9. What does it mean when we say mark to magic?
10. What is the reason why margins may increase financial instability?

References

Akerlof, G. (1970). The market for 'lemons': quality uncertainty and the market mechanism. *Quart. J. Econ.*, 84(3): 488–500.

Bitner, R. (2008). *Confessions of a Subprime Lender: An Insider's Tale of Greed, Fraud, and Ignorance*. John Wiley & Sons.

Black, F. and Scholes, M. (1973a). The pricing of options and corporate liabilities. *J. Polit. Econ.*, 81(3): 637–54.

Fabozzi, F. J. (2009). *Bond Markets, Analysis, and Strategies*, 7th edition. Pearson.

Hull, J. C. (2011). *Options, Futures, and other Derivatives*, 8th edition. Prentice Hall.

Hull, J. C. (2012). *Risk Management and Financial Institutions*, 3rd edition. Prentice Hall.

International Monetary Fund (2008). Global financial stability report: containing systemic risks and restoring financial soundness. April 2008, pp. 1–211.

Merton, R. C. (1974). On the pricing of corporate debt: the risk structure of interest rates. *J. Finance*, 29: 449–70.

Murphy, D. (2009). *Unravelling the Credit Crunch*. CRC Press.

Washington Post (2004). Credit raters' power leads to abuses, some borrowers say. *Washington Post*, 24 November. www.washingtonpost.com/wp-dyn/articles/A8032-2004Nov23.html.

11 CURRENCY MARKETS

No financial market sees more government intervention than the foreign exchange (FX) market. After all, every economy is sensitive to the exchange rate and policymakers often want exchange rates to reflect the underlying economic fundamentals, because misalignments and excessive exchange rate volatilities imply significant economic costs.

Every government needs to decide on what type of exchange rate regime it wants, ranging from letting its currency float freely, to various ways it can tie the currency to that of another country, all the way to joining a currency union. However, determining an exchange rate regime is not a trivial proposition. Leave it to the market, and the result may be FX volatility. Leave it to the government, and the outcome may be misalignment and currency crisis. Choosing a sensible exchange rate regime is hard, and governments are sometimes guided by wishful thinking and blind pursuit of outdated goals, perhaps only wanting to replace the existing arrangement.

A key reason why governments find it so hard to manage their exchange rates is because of the size of the FX market, as it has more trading volume than any other financial market – see Figure 11.1.

Volume in the FX market has increased rapidly, from $1.5 trillion per day in 1998 to $4 trillion in 2010, or around one quadrillion dollars per year. The most actively traded currency is USD, involved in 42% of all trades. This is not surprising given the reserve currency status of the dollar. Because the dollar is so liquid, most currency pairs do not trade bilaterally; for example, going from the Malaysian ringgit to the Hungarian forint would probably involve a detour to the dollar. The dollar is followed by the euro, the yen and sterling. Surprisingly, even though China is the second largest economic area in the world, its currency constitutes only 0.15% of trading. This is

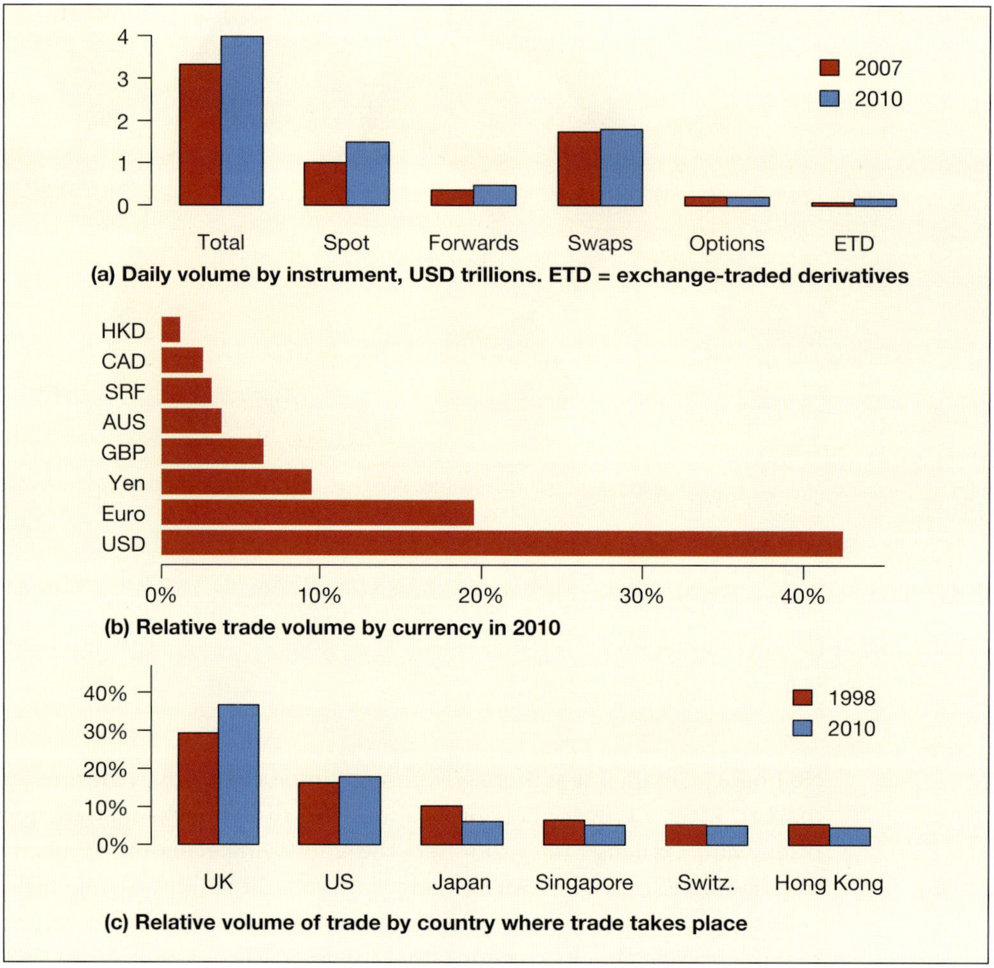

Figure 11.1 Bank for International Settlements (BIS) survey of the FX market

Data source: BIS triannual survey of the FX market: www.bis.org/publ/rpfx10.htm

because the Chinese government actively discourages currency trading and employs capital controls.

At least 92% of FX trading involves the currencies of large developed economies,[1] with the rest mostly smaller developed economies or larger stable developing economies.

The FX market has no single physical location, and instead takes place on computer systems. However, the individual traders and banks do have a physical location and the main geographic centre of FX trading is London, making up 37% of the global total trading volume, a number that has been steadily increasing; in 1995 it was 29%. This is not that surprising, since trading is concentrated in the largest financial centres and large volumes in one geographical area attract traders, further increasing volume. There are many reasons for this, for example, the supply of specialised human resources and technical support.

[1]In the order of volume: USD, euro, Japanese yen, pound sterling, Australian dollar, Swiss franc, Canadian dollar, Hong Kong dollar, Swedish krona, New Zealand dollar, Norwegian krone and Danish krone.

The daily FX turnover dwarfs the underlying economic activities. The International Monetary Fund (IMF) found the world's GDP in 2010 to be \$63 trillion and the World Trade Organization (WTO) global trade to be \$18.5 trillion. In other words, the global trade in goods and services is only around 1.85% of the global trade in FX. It follows that the bulk of the activity in FX markets is due to speculation, the buying or selling of currencies solely to profit from anticipated changes in exchange rates, by means of high frequency trading (HFT), exploiting arbitrage between currencies (triangular arbitrage) and prices on different trading platforms.

Links to other chapters

This chapter directly relates to Chapter 2 (the Great Depression, 1929–1933), Chapter 9 (trading and speculation) and Chapter 12 (currency crisis models).

Key concepts

- Currency regimes
- Capital controls
- Bretton Woods
- Gold standard
- Reserve currency
- Sterilisation

Readings for this chapter

There are many excellent texts on currency markets, and in writing this chapter we have drawn on McCallum (1996), Sarno and Taylor (2003), Krugman and Obstfeld (2006) and Marsh (2010). Eichengreen (1996), Ferguson (2008) and Ahamed (2009) contain some of the historical discussion.

Notation specific to this chapter

B	Net domestic currency bonds
$\mathrm{E}_{t-1}\Delta e_t$	Expectation of change in exchange rate from period to $t-1$ to t
e_t	Nominal exchange rate at time t
i_t	Interest rate at time t
M	Domestic nominal money supply
P	Price level
Q	Index of the real value of expenditures
R	Government foreign exchange reserves
V	Velocity of money
*	A star indicates a foreign variable

11.1 FIXED OR FLOATING

One of the most important decisions made by governments is what sort of currency regime it chooses to have. On one extreme, it could fix the exchange rate to the currency of another country or, alternatively, it could let it float freely on the open market.

Arguments in favour of fixed rates and interventions

Many governments opt to fix the exchange rate at a value the central bank finds best. This is based on what is known as the '*wrong-rate argument*'. There is a '*correct*' exchange rate, fully reflecting the economic fundamentals. The market, however, does not arrive at it.

The reason floating exchange rates are the 'wrong rates' is that the market is inefficient: it does not make use of available information and it is prone to destabilising speculation. Markets may attach too high a probability on a devaluation or appreciation, not usually justified by economic fundamentals. In some cases, speculators may deliberately manipulate the exchange rate away from the fundamentals, perhaps so they can profit from the resulting exchange rate volatility.

One of the best manifestations of the inefficiency of market-determined exchange rates is very high exchange rate volatility, inconsistent with slow-moving economic fundamentals. Many of the most important fundamentals are measured quite infrequently, for example, GDP is known only quarterly, hence, there should be no reason for exchange rates to fluctuate as much as they do.

Such FX volatility might happen because speculation is subject to a bandwagon effect: it feeds on itself rather than fundamentals, perhaps because traders use simple forecasting methods, like momentum trading, or other simple extrapolative techniques or subjective pattern recognition.

Since there are several reasons why the actual exchange rate may be driven away from the rate implied by fundamentals, official intervention may be a useful instrument to stabilise the exchange rate at or close to a 'correct' rate.

Countries with fixed exchange rates expect significant benefits because transaction costs and risk are minimised, encouraging trade and investment. However, in order to obtain those benefits, the exchange rate needs to be sensible and backed up by a credible monetary policy. If a government chooses the exchange rate incorrectly, or undermines it by unwise monetary policy, the end result would be a costly realignment. Fundamentally, a fixed exchange rate regime depends on the ability of the experts who set it, and their independence from political interference.

Arguments in favour of floating rates

Opponents of official interventions in FX markets might argue that it is far from clear that the authorities are capable of identifying the correct exchange rate in practice. Even if they do have the ability, when trying to do so, they might arrive at the wrong exchange rates for political reasons, perhaps preferring an overvalued currency to make voters feel artificially wealthy, or an undervalued currency to help industry.

The costs of an incorrect exchange rate might be significant, with interventions to maintain the official exchange rate distortionary. The exchange rate is likely to affect the expectations of speculators, who may then trade in a way that undermines the interventions so that the government might only be able to maintain the official rate at very high costs.

If the exchange rates deviate from the presumed fundamental rate, it can be hard to identify whether this is a permanent or temporary phenomenon; consequently, it is difficult for the authorities to identify when an intervention is justified.

Furthermore, floating exchange rates might not be any more unstable than fixed exchange rates; one is more likely to see more gradual adjustment in floating rate regimes rather than the sudden and sharp jumps resulting from devaluations in fixed regimes. Floating regimes might have higher volatility but fixed regimes bigger jumps.

Perhaps the main argument in favour of a flexible exchange rate is that it allows for an independent monetary policy, enabling the government to respond to economic concerns more easily. As a consequence, floating rate regimes might be less crisis prone than fixed rate regimes. Furthermore, since differences in national inflation rates and price levels are more likely to be directly reflected in the exchange rate, floating rate countries are less likely to have an under- or overvalued currency for longer periods.

Conclusion

Both sets of arguments have compelling elements. Over time, countries have alternated from one arrangement to another, usually not satisfied with their choice. The ultimate conclusion seems to be that no exchange rate regime is perfect; governments are quite willing to experiment with a new arrangement, as the large number of regimes discussed in the appendix bear witness to.

Most, if not all, governments, however, take the view that at least some interventions in the FX market are necessary. Whilst academic economists are often vocal in their opposition to FX interventions, those actually in charge disagree.

11.2 FOREIGN EXCHANGE INTERVENTIONS

Governments intervene more in the market for FX than in that of any other market, and every country has to implement some FX policy. When a central bank decides to fix its exchange rate, it has two choices: either it must implement capital controls or it must always be willing and able to trade with market participants at the target rate.

Mechanics of interventions

Denote the exchange rate by e, which is the amount of domestic currency per unit of foreign currency, and the interest rate by i. Denote foreign variables by *. It is common to assume the foreign country is the United States, since it has the *reserve currency*. Suppose a central bank decides to fix its exchange rate (*peg*) at level $\bar{e}$. The FX market is in equilibrium when the *uncovered interest rate parity (UIP)* condition holds, meaning that the domestic interest rate equals the foreign interest rate plus the expected movement in the exchange rate:

$$i_t = i_t^* + \mathrm{E}_{t-1}\Delta e_t$$

where $\Delta e_t = e_t - e_{t-1}$ and E_{t-1} refers to expectation at time $t - 1$. When the exchange rate is fixed at $\bar{e}$ and market participants expect it to remain fixed, then

$$\mathrm{E}_{t-1}\Delta e_t = 0$$

Given that investors are not expecting any changes in the exchange rate because of the peg, they are only willing to hold the foreign and domestic currency if they offer the same interest rate. To ensure equilibrium in the FX market, the central bank must set $i_t = i_t^*$.

That imposes a particular restriction on the central bank. When it intervenes by printing money, it would normally affect interest rates, but they must not change. Hence, the bank needs to adjust the money supply in order to keep the interest rates constant. In other words, it *sterilises* the intervention. This eliminates any independence or discretion that the central bank has over the money supply and therefore over monetary policy, leading to the 'impossible trinity' discussed in Section 11.4.3.

11.2.1 Sterilisation

When a central bank intervenes in the currency markets to prevent an *appreciation* of the currency, the money supply usually increases; after all, the central bank is buying foreign currency with freshly printed domestic money. This is, of course, inflationary, and since the central bank may prefer to prevent the inflation, it often couples interventions with *sterilisation*. Sterilisation means that the domestic money supply is held fixed, while an unsterilised intervention is where the central bank intervenes without offsetting the domestic money supply.

Mechanics of sterilisation

Consider the balance sheet of the central bank in Table 11.1, where it purchases \$10 billion.

Step 1. The central bank purchases USD 10 billion and invests that amount in US Treasuries, so $B^* = \$10$ billion.

Step 2. Its liabilities (monetary base) increase by the same amount: $M\uparrow$ by $e \times \$10$ billion.

Step 3. The central bank now sells domestic bonds by the same amount and, therefore, takes money out of circulation: $M\downarrow e \times \$10$ billion and $B\uparrow e \times \$10$ billion.

Step 4. After the intervention the net assets of the bank have not changed, but:

- Its holdings of foreign currency bonds have increased by $e \times \$10$ billion.
- Its holdings of domestic bonds have decreased by the same amount.
- Overall the monetary base has not changed.

The changes in the holdings of foreign assets are offset one-for-one by the changes in domestic asset holdings, and the purchase of foreign assets has no effect on the domestic money supply. However, the exchange rate would probably fall because of the purchase of foreign currency.

Table 11.1 Central bank balance sheet

Assets	Liabilities
Net foreign currency bonds (B_t^*)	Monetary base (M_t)
Net domestic currency bonds (B_t)	Net worth

Sterilisation in developed markets

Sterilisation might not be a very effective tool in advanced countries where assets are almost perfectly substitutable. The reason is that a sterilised intervention might lead to an increase in the interest rate because it implies the selling of domestic bonds. In turn, that might make domestic assets more attractive to outside investors, causing an inflow of currency and appreciation of the exchange rate. Ultimately, this would undermine the sterilisation.

The developed economy that has been the most active user of interventions and sterilisations – Japan – has faced exactly this problem. Currency interventions might lead to a temporary fall in the exchange rate but the yen soon appreciates again. As a consequence, Japan has very sizable holdings of US government bonds, $956.8 billion in September 2011, according to the US Treasury.

Sterilisation in emerging markets

The situation is different in emerging markets, whose assets are not as substitutable for foreign assets. The reason may be that the government employs capital controls, or the markets lack transparency and liquidity, deterring foreign investors. In this case, a non-sterilised intervention would lead to an increase in the monetary base, resulting in inflationary pressures and even asset price bubbles. As a consequence, sterilisation is likely to be more effective in preventing inflation than in developed economies.

Uses of sterilisation

The use of intervention to keep exchange rates low has become increasingly common in recent years. Lavigne (2008) estimates that from the $1.3 trillion in accumulated reserves between 2000 and 2006 in emerging markets in Asia, 75% have been sterilised. He further finds that China has been the biggest user of sterilisation, sterilising 80% of its intervention. This is in addition to using extensive capital controls, administrative controls and regulations, and state ownership of large parts of the banking system as means to manage the exchange rate.

Limitations

In principle, a government can intervene indefinitely to prevent appreciations; however, its ability to sterilise the interventions depends on the central bank's holdings of government bonds. This is not a major problem because the government, as the owner of the central bank, of course, can just issue new debt. This does not mean that sterilisation is always a recommended policy when intervening.

Sterilisation is costly because the central bank acquires foreign bonds and sells domestic bonds. Since the yield on foreign bonds is likely to be much lower than the yield on domestic bonds, the difference is a cost to the central bank.

Sterilisation involves encouraging banks to accumulate government bonds and so might be considered as a tax on banks. The banks are holding government bonds instead of lending to private investors, potentially holding back economic growth. Finally, as the central bank continues to intervene and sterilise, sovereign debt keeps on accumulating, affecting the solvency of the state.

11.3 CAPITAL CONTROLS

Governments wishing to control the flow of foreign currency may resort to *capital controls*. This can take the form of taxes on transactions or outright restrictions on the buying/selling of a foreign currency in order to maintain fixed exchange rates. We term the latter case *strict* or *traditional capital controls*, and the former *capital controls 2.0*.

11.3.1 Traditional capital controls

Traditional capital controls (1.0) relate to policies aimed at controlling inflows and outflows of currencies for the purpose of maintaining fixed exchange rates or the balance of payments. While these controls vary in severity, they often involve a licensing regime.

EXAMPLE 11.1 United States

During the 1950s, the US was battling a balance of payments deficit. As a response, the government imposed a surcharge on the purchase of foreign stocks and bonds, excluding Canada and the developing world.

Investors were able to evade the tax by trading via Canada and using bank loans instead of securities. The government moved to close the loopholes, but eventually faced the controls out after leaving the Bretton Woods system.

Developed countries' move away from capital controls

While capital controls were widespread in the early years of the Bretton Woods system, they were always controversial and became to be seen as increasingly damaging. They were always quite leaky and encouraged corruption. As a consequence, most developed countries abolished them early, see Table 11.2.

The move away from capital controls was connected to the trend towards free global flows of capital. Amongst the developed economies, Germany was the biggest historical

Table 11.2 Abolition of capital controls in OECD countries

Country	Year	Country	Year	Country	Year
Australia	1978	Greece	1980	Portugal	1992
Austria	1980	Iceland	1993	Spain	1985
Belgium		Italy	1984	Sweden	1986
Canada		Japan	1979	Switzerland	1979
Denmark	1983	Luxembourg		Turkey	1985
Finland	1991	Netherlands		United Kingdom	1971
France	1986	New Zealand		United States	1974
Germany	1980	Norway	1989		

Note. Belgium, Canada, Luxembourg, the Netherlands and New Zealand did not have capital controls in the OECD's time

Source: OECD (2002), Forty Years' Experience with the OECD Code of Liberalisation of Capital Movements, OECD Publishing. http://dx.doi.org/10.1787/9789264176188-en

proponent of free capital flows, with most major economies, such as that of the US, opposed. Abdelal (2007) argues that Germany was in favour of free capital flows not least because they saw it as a fundamental component in the establishment of a common European currency. When the French governments of the 1980s came to the German view, support for free capital flows globally was pushed to the forefront of the Washington consensus agenda.

Capital controls in developing countries

Developing countries have been frequent users of capital controls, either as a part of their permanent arrangement for managing currencies or as a temporary reaction to a crisis. In recent times, one of the best examples of the latter is Malaysia during the Asian crisis.

EXAMPLE 11.2 Malaysia

With the onset of the Asian crisis in 1997, in order to protect its currency and to avoid asking the IMF for help, Malaysia banned transfers between domestic and foreign accounts and between foreign accounts, eliminated credit facilities to offshore parties and prevented repatriation of investment until September 1999, whilst fixing the exchange rate to the dollar. Foreign exchange transactions were allowed only at authorised institutions. In February 1999, a system of taxes replaced prohibition on repatriation of capital. The net effect was to discourage short-term capital flows but permit longer-term transactions. The aim of this policy was to enable the government to lower interest rates without fearing devaluation.

While many developing countries have permanent capital controls in place, the best known and most controversial use of capital controls is in China.

EXAMPLE 11.3 China

China tightly controls its exchange rates by means of capital controls. The capital account is closed for inflows and outflows, except for foreign direct investment. External debt is strictly controlled. However, more recently, China has been relaxing the controls. Portfolio investment has been slowly liberalised, with foreign investors allowed to invest in special categories of shares and bonds.

Re-emergence of strict controls

With the crisis starting in 2007, traditional capital controls have re-emerged as a crisis-fighting tool amongst developed economies. The most prominent example of this is Iceland: see Arnason and Danielsson (2011) for more details.

EXAMPLE 11.4 Iceland and the IMF

The Icelandic capital controls were imposed following the collapse of the country's economy in 2008. The IMF made capital controls a requirement for providing aid.

This was a U-turn in Fund policy, because up until that point the IMF had been opposed to capital controls, at least from the 1970s. This is also the first case of a country subject to European Union (EU) rules resorting to capital controls. While Iceland is not an EU member, it is in the European Economic Area (EEA). In order to comply with both EEA and IMF requirements, Iceland had to impose traditional strict capital controls, requiring Central Bank authorisation for all purchases of foreign currency, and in practice preventing foreign direct investment.

11.3.2 'Hot money' and capital controls 2.0

A different reason for capital controls is the danger posed by '*hot money*'. While the term was first used by President Roosevelt in 1936, it has become more relevant in recent times with free global capital flows. *Hot money* refers to the type of flows that come quickly into a country, often as part of carry trades, and can leave just as quickly. It is not foreign direct investment but rather portfolio investment.

Such money flows are controversial because speculators can move significant amounts of funds into a small country, causing the exchange rate to appreciate sharply, resulting in significant difficulties for exporters. At the first whiff of problems, the money then leaves, causing what is called a *sudden stop*, and the exchange rate collapses, perhaps ending in a crisis.

To prevent this problem, some authorities have resorted to a special type of capital controls designed to discourage hot money. They can take the form of a special tax on inflows that leave within a certain amount of time, or even on particular types of investments. Since controls on hot money are quite different from the traditional controls discussed above, we might label them *capital controls 2.0*.

EXAMPLE 11.5 Chile

Chile experienced heavy capital inflows in the 1990s, causing both a build-up of short-term debt and fears of a real currency appreciation. The government announced in 1991 that direct investment was to become subject to a three-year stay, which was reduced to one year in 1993. Portfolio flows were restricted to mandatory non-interest paying deposits at the Central Bank with early withdrawal penalties. The effect was to reduce the return to the investor and, hence, discourage inflows.

The effectiveness of the controls was controversial. Some commentators argued that they prevented a real appreciation of the peso and changed the composition of the inflows but not the magnitude of the flows. Others found that they did change the magnitude of the inflows, and had real adverse impacts.

Since the crisis starting in 2007, several countries have employed various forms of 2.0 capital controls. For example, Brazil introduced a tax on financial transactions in October 2010. It is a tax of 6% on non-resident equity and debt inflows and also requires a 6% margin payment to trade derivatives. Thailand also imposed controls in October 2010, in the form of a withholding tax on non-resident interest income and capital gains from state bonds. South Korea has restricted the size of the FX derivative books of its banks as a macro-prudential measure, and imposed a 14% withholding tax and a 20% capital gains tax on foreign purchases of government bonds.

11.3.3 Pros and cons of capital controls

Capital controls are quite controversial and have been rejected by policymakers in developed countries. The abolition of capital controls is central to the *Washington consensus*: see Definition 6.1 in Chapter 6.

Arguments against capital controls

The main argument against capital controls is that they prevent investments and savings from being used in the most productive manner. Economic agents will attempt to evade the controls, finding loopholes, with a cat-and-mouse game ensuing between the authorities and market participants, with ever tightening of the controls leading to yet more evasion. Keeping capital controls watertight is an impossible task. This often leads to corruption whereby exports are under-invoiced and imports over-invoiced, enabling funds to remain abroad. Licensing regimes create the potential for corruption of government officials. Authorities might have to choose between either making them much stricter or abolishing them altogether.

Arguments in favour of capital controls

Those in favour of capital controls point out that they can reduce the risk of crisis and the associated costs. As a consequence, they are a useful *macro-prudential tool*. Reinhart and Rogoff (2009) suggest that they were to thank for the low incidence of banking crises during the Bretton Woods era. Uncontrolled inflows of hot money followed by a sudden stop are quite damaging to countries, first creating a boom whilst undermining exporters and then terminating in a crash. As a consequence, countries often prefer to restrict flows of hot money.

Targeted 2.0 capital controls can be successful in preventing excessive capital inflows, at small cost. They are designed to be genuinely countercyclical, aimed at preventing excesses when times are good.

A rethink on capital controls

Capital controls have had a bad reputation for a few decades, with the opposition to them led by the IMF and some European countries. Those introducing capital controls in recent decades, such as Malaysia, came under strong criticism.

This has now changed. The IMF has in recent years expressed support for capital controls. They were an enthusiastic supporter of the Icelandic capital controls from November 2008, and have continued to support their use. The current support for capital controls usually refers to the 2.0 variety, aiming to use them as a macro-prudential tool to prevent hot money flows, rather than a means to maintain an unsustainable exchange rate.

11.4 EXCHANGE RATE REGIMES

A number of exchange rate regimes have been proposed and implemented. Generally, the choices are between either fixing the exchange rate to some value or letting it float freely. Alternatively, countries can adopt the currency of another country or even join a currency union. In between those choices are the various alternatives discussed in the appendix at the end of this chapter.

11.4.1 The gold standard

The gold standard is the most important historical example of a fixed exchange rate regime. Countries fixed the value of their currency to the price of gold and committed to its free convertibility to and from gold. The gold standard developed gradually, with more and more countries adopting it in the nineteenth century, led by the world's most important economy at the time, that of the United Kingdom.

Under the gold standard, gold is money, so the supply of gold restricts the growth in the money supply, thus preventing inflation and ensuring long-run price stability, unless there are massive gold discoveries. The result was long-term stability and predictability in the international monetary system never before or since accomplished, with a positive effect on trade and economic development.

The mechanics of the gold standard

The mechanics of the gold standard were described by David Hume (1752), who may have created the first monetary model in economics. In his basic model, only gold coins circulate and no banks exist, prices are flexible and the supply of gold is fixed. This gives the *quantity theory of money*:

$$M \times V = P \times Q$$

where M is the total amount of money in circulation, V the velocity of money, P the price level and Q an index of the real value of expenditures. Whenever goods are exported, payment is received in gold, which can be converted into domestic currency. To pay for imports, the importer exchanges domestic currency for gold. If a country has a trade deficit, it is losing gold and, hence, prices must fall, assuming V and Q are constant. This encourages exports and discourages imports, helping to eliminate the trade deficit. The system self-corrects and *speculation is stabilising*. See Figure 11.2 for how this works.

Why the gold standard survived

The absolute credibility of the commitment of the central bank to maintain gold convertibility was the main reason why the gold standard system was stable and flourishing between 1870 and 1914. But the system also benefited from other unique factors. The UK's leading economic position allowed sterling to anchor the international system. The openness of markets and surge in trade supported the operation of the gold standard adjustment mechanisms. On the political side, the monetary authorities enjoyed an extraordinary political insulation, partly because of the lack of universal suffrage, allowing them to commit themselves to the maintenance of an unquestionable gold convertibility.

Problem of deflation

The main downside of the gold standard is deflation. The world money supply of gold is tied to the production of gold, and when gold discoveries are rare, the normal situation, the world supply of gold will not increase as fast as global production and real world income, especially

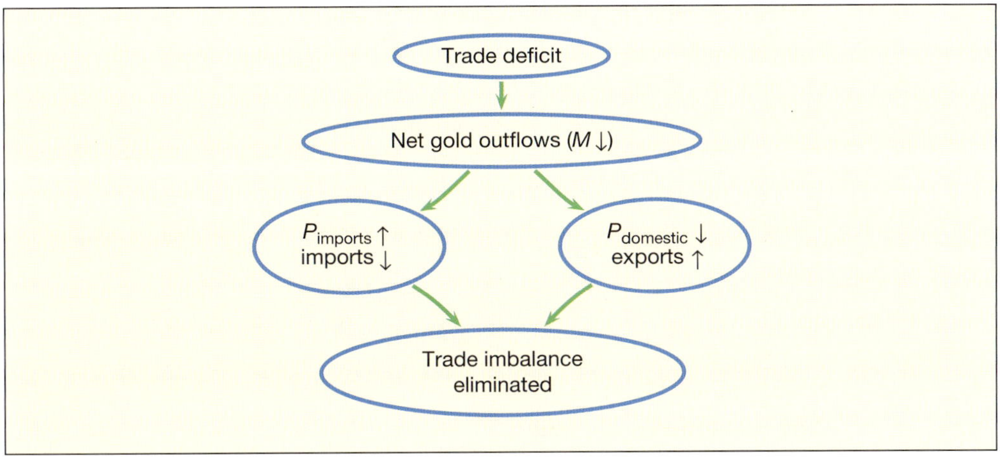

Figure 11.2 Gold standard adjustment mechanism

in times of a booming world economy, having a strong deflationary effect. Accordingly, British price levels fell by 18% between 1873 and 1879 and by a further 19% by 1896.

Deflation is more costly than inflation for several reasons, the most important of which is that since interest rates cannot fall below zero, those owning money benefit from delaying purchases because they know their money will be more valuable in the future.

Deflation affects agricultural producers badly. For example, a farmer with a fixed mortgage receives less and less money for his products and has to pay more interest in real terms. The main agricultural exporters, like the US, Australia, Canada and Argentina, all suffered from deflation, and were quite crisis prone as a consequence. By contrast, capital exporters like the UK did well out of the deflation and the stability of the gold standard.

The benefits for the capital exporters were not uniformly distributed. The landed classes who supplied the capital profited, but those working, and especially the working class, lost out. Voting rights were restricted to property owners, so governments remained firmly in favour of the gold standard.

Several factors contributed to the increasing instability of this system and led to its breakdown after its reintroduction following the first World War (WWI). The introduction of universal suffrage and the emergence of political parties representing the working class made domestic considerations more important than maintaining convertibility.

11.4.2 Bretton Woods

The time period between the two world wars was marked by extreme uncertainty in the world's financial markets, culminating in the Great Depression. As a consequence, the Allied leaders in the early 1940s decided to create a new world financial order, more stable and less prone to destabilising activities by the markets.

These efforts led to what is known as the *Bretton Woods system*, named after the hotel in New Hampshire in the US where the final agreement was signed in 1944. The participants wanted stable exchange rates but realised they could not go back on the gold standard. Instead they replaced it with the US dollar, which became the *reserve currency*.

Member countries were to adopt an adjustable peg system, with capital controls, fixing their currencies to the dollar. The dollar, in turn, was pegged to gold at a value of $35 per ounce. Par values could be changed to correct a '*fundamental equilibrium*', which was to be decided by the newly created International Monetary Fund (IMF), which was also responsible for monitoring national economic policies and could extend balance of payment financing to countries facing problems.

The capital controls were somewhat effective, especially early on, but required extensive regulation. When current account convertibility was reintroduced in 1959 it became easy to avoid the capital controls.[2] The adjustable peg meant, in theory, that trade deficits could be eliminated without experiencing painful deflations. In reality, parity changes were rare as they eroded the credibility of a central bank, and were often accompanied by a political crisis.

Why Bretton Woods failed

There are three main reasons why the Bretton Woods system failed:

1 Domestic priorities had become increasingly important and led to policies that were inconsistent with the exchange rate system.

2 The main mechanisms were not really working. Capital controls were envisaged to allow governments to follow their own monetary policies but were difficult to enforce since it was easy to over-invoice and under-invoice trade.

3 The final problem area was the so-called *Triffin dilemma*, named after the economist Robert Triffin, who observed that the tendency for the Bretton Woods system to meet excess demand for reserves through the growth of foreign dollar balances made it *dynamically unstable*. Accumulating dollars as reserves was attractive only as long as there was no question about their convertibility into gold. As foreign dollar balances grew relatively large compared to the gold reserves of the US, doubts started to grow about its commitment to convertibility. If all countries sought to convert their reserves into gold, the US would be forced to abandon the dollar peg to gold.

   This happened in the end, with a run on the dollar, because of inadequate monetary and fiscal discipline in the US. Faced with high expenditure for the war in Vietnam and an expansion of welfare programmes, the US increased spending, disregarding the consequences on the Bretton Woods system. In the spring of 1971, flows from the dollar to the German mark surged and Germany finally allowed the mark to float upwards. Other countries followed. As the flight from the dollar grew stronger, the Nixon administration finally suspended convertibility, bringing about the end of the Bretton Woods system.

Should we adopt Bretton Woods now?

The ongoing crisis has prompted some commentators to argue that the more ordered Bretton Woods financial system would be preferable to the current arrangement. The reason is that excessive activity in financial markets, speculation and hot money flows

---

[2]Current and capital account convertibility refers to the freedom to convert the local assets into foreign assets and vice versa at an exchange rate determined by the market.

are all destabilising, and direct government intervention is needed to bring the system under control.

Such views often seem to be based on a reinterpretation of what Bretton Woods was rather than a call for the adoption of the particular arrangement. The Bretton Woods system failed for particular reasons. It is not possible to maintain a fixed exchange rate regime in a world where countries have widely differing prospects and economic policies. Even in the relatively small world of Europe, it is proving to be quite challenging. It would be necessary to reimpose strict capital controls, and even in that case, countries would be subject to damaging periodic realignments.

Consequently, returning to a Bretton Woods-type arrangement for the world's financial system would not be a sensible response to the ongoing crisis.

11.4.3 Impossible trinity

The choice of currency regimes directly affects a government's ability to pursue other policies. This is expressed by the *impossible trinity*, which states that it is impossible for a country to pursue the following three goals simultaneously:

1 Fixed exchange rate
2 Free capital movements
3 Independent monetary policy.

At best, a country can achieve two out of the three. Suppose we start with a country in equilibrium and with fixed exchange rates. If the country then embarks on an expansionary monetary policy, or simply loses control of inflation, the money supply is increasing. In this case, speculators can borrow the country's currency and exchange it for foreign money. Such a trade is likely to attract a large number of market participants. In order for the government to maintain the exchange rate, it can either continue selling its foreign currency reserves until they run out, at which time the exchange rate peg will collapse, or impose capital controls.

We have seen many combinations of these policies over time as shown in Table 11.3.

During the time of the gold standard, member countries gave up independent monetary policy in order to get fixed exchange rates and free capital mobility. This was the single longest period of a stable international currency regime ever recorded. The Bretton Woods system opted for capital controls, as did China.

Table 11.3 The impossible trinity

	Fixed exchange rates	International capital mobility	Independent monetary policy
Gold standard	✓	✓	×
Bretton Woods	✓	×	✓
China today	✓	×	✓
EU/US today	×	✓	✓

11.5 PERILS OF OVERVALUATION

Countries rarely set out to have an overvalued currency. Instead, they usually tend to end up with an overvalued currency as a result of a losing fight with inflation, or the tail-end of a prolonged crisis when they can finance themselves only by printing money, as Germany did in the early 1920s.

In some cases, an overvalued currency may be forced on a country from the outside. The best-known recent example of this is the *Plaza Accord* in 1985, which was an agreement between France, Germany, Japan, the US and the UK to depreciate the USD relative to the Japanese yen and the German mark.

In the short run, an overvalued currency is often quite popular with voters because it makes imported goods artificially cheap. However, in the longer run it hurts exporters who are no longer competitive, and often ends in a currency crisis.

In order to maintain the exchange rate, the central bank has to stand ready to sell foreign currency to all-comers at the artificially cheap rate, which it can do only as long as it has reserves to sell. Speculators, who are usually well-connected local companies and political families, observe this and seek to export the domestic currency – in effect, speculating against the currency regime. The end result is a *speculative attack*.

The government may give in or resort to desperate measures like capital controls or multiple exchange rates, which in turn are often a recipe for corruption. All of this suggests that it is difficult to the point of impossible for a government to maintain an artificially strong exchange rate for long without resorting to very costly measures.

11.5.1 Currency crises

We use the same IMF database as in Section 7.3 to identify the frequency of currency crises, seen in Figure 11.3.

The frequency of currency crises seems to be holding steady over time, with the worst year being 1994.

The medium- and long-term effects of currency crises have been studied by Bussiere *et al.* (2010) who found that three years after a currency crisis the level of GDP is between 2% and 6% lower than in the absence of a crisis.

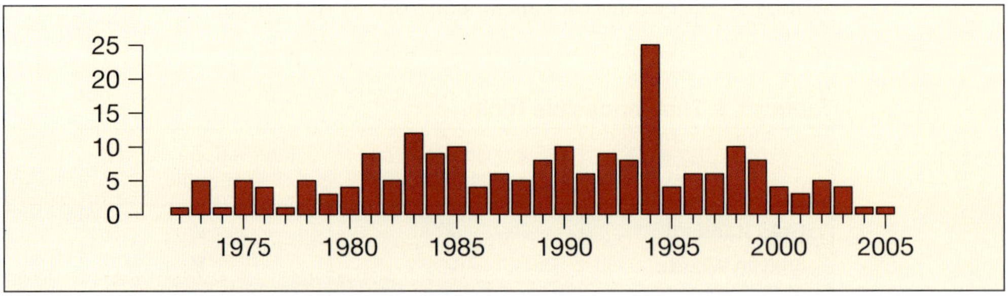

Figure 11.3 Frequency of currency crises

Source: Laeven and Valencia (2008)

The interesting part is that these losses tend to materialise mainly *before* the currency collapses. The authors conclude that the economic costs of a currency collapse do not appear to arise from the collapse of the currency itself but reflect other factors.

They find that the collapse seems to actually have *positive* effects on output. Output growth tends to slow down prior to a currency crisis, with positive growth rates the norm post-crisis.

11.6 UNDERVALUATION AND 'CURRENCY WARS'

Deliberate policies of manipulating exchange rates downwards to increase domestic competitiveness have recently been given the name '*currency wars*', but in years past have been called *competitive devaluations* and *beggar-thy-neighbour* policies.

Countries often deliberately undervalue their currencies in order to increase their competitiveness. Unlike overvaluation, in principle, a country could maintain an undervalued currency indefinitely, printing money as needed to sell in the currency markets.

The effect of undervaluing a currency in the short run is to make imports more expensive and exports cheaper. It is a subsidy given to exporters paid for by domestic consumers and foreign companies and their workers because their profitability is eroded.

This does not mean that undervaluing a currency is an easy way to encourage export industries. On the contrary, the costs can easily become quite significant. First, it will not make other countries very happy. After all, the country is deliberately manipulating its exchange rate to favour its industries at the expense of other countries. For very small countries this may not be a problem, but it usually creates a lot of friction.

In the worst case, it can lead to competitive devaluations, where countries compete to devalue their currencies. The end result is likely to be high inflation and a huge disruption to domestic industries. This can also lead to restrictions on trade. Because the country is trying to gain what is painted as an 'unfair advantage', other countries may impose trade restrictions as a consequence. This can then spiral out of control in the same way as competitive devaluations can. Finally, such a policy can create hidden inflation that makes later realignment a necessity.

11.6.1 The UK and France

The cases of Britain and France in the interwar years provide an illustrative example of the effects of a currency misalignment. In 1925, Britain decided to go back on the gold standard at the same rate of convertibility as before WWI, overvaluing sterling by perhaps 40%. France, on the other hand, having experienced high volatility and depreciation of its currency in the afterwar years, restored convertibility in 1926 at a devalued rate of around 15–20%. The French policy was analysed by Sicsic (1992).

The results of the different types of misalignments were quite predictable. Gold flowed from the country where it had less value (the UK), due to an overvaluation of the currency, to where it had more value (France). Britain, with the overvalued pound and thus a competitive disadvantage in exports, experienced a persistent balance of payments deficit, draining its gold and FX reserves. In order to deal with the overvaluation, the UK had to lower domestic costs, by doing what is now called an *internal devaluation*. This led to significant social disruption and strikes. As a consequence of the overvaluation, Britain was more or less in continuous recession for six years.

The effects of the undervaluation of the French franc were as expected. The undervaluation meant a highly competitive export industry leading to an export-led boom with large accompanying inflows of gold reserves. The central bank of France sterilised the inflows to mitigate the inflationary effects of the gold inflows.

This led to considerable friction between France and the UK, as well as many other countries. Eventually, other countries devalued their currencies, for example the UK left the gold standard in 1931, after which Britain became quite competitive. This, however, meant that France became increasingly uncompetitive because its economy had adjusted to the weak currency regime and found it difficult to cope when the currency appreciated, leading to significant economic and political instability in the years after.

11.6.2 China and the US

The largest country deliberately maintaining an undervalued currency now is China, and we can find many parallels between the problems of Britain and France in the interwar years and the conflict between China and the US today. Just like France, China maintains a deliberately undervalued currency, accumulating vast amounts of reserves, in the case of France gold and for China mostly USD, now exceeding $3 trillion. The undervalued currency has been a key contributor to the economic performance of China and has led to the aura of invincibility and the feeling that it is on track to become the world's biggest economy.

It is, however, difficult to gauge exact performance in China. According to official statistics, inflation is next to zero, but anecdotal evidence indicates it is much higher. That might suggest that the country's stellar economic performance might be lower if adjusted for higher inflation.

As a consequence of its FX policy, China has increasingly strained relationships with the outside world, especially the US.

In the case of France, the end-game proved quite costly. The question remains whether China will be more fortunate.

11.7 RESERVE CURRENCY

Definition 11.1 Reserve currency Reserve currency is the currency most governments hold as reserves and the currency in which most international trade is priced.

Historically, one currency, or asset, tends to assume the role of a *reserve currency*. In the nineteenth century it was gold and the pound sterling, but over time, the US dollar has taken over that function.

There are significant advantages in owning a reserve currency, most importantly that foreign countries hold it as reserves. That means foreigners have exchanged real goods for paper, a deal which is quite good for the country with the reserve currency.

It is often argued that the fact that major products are priced in a reserve currency conveys some benefits to the owner of the reserve currency, perhaps because it eliminates currency risk. That is not true. Prices are set in a competitive international market, and if the reserve currency weakens, the price of commodities will increase by an offsetting amount, other things being equal. The risk does not go away; it just moves from FX to prices.

Reserve currencies tend to make other countries unhappy. When reserves are building up there is a transfer of real goods in return for a nominal asset. Furthermore, if that country decides to misbehave, creating inflation or doing quantitative easing (QE), it is taxing reserves held by other countries.

Having a reserve currency can create particular problems when a country is declining in power and wealth. Even though the USD had long overtaken sterling as a reserve currency, some countries with particularly close relationships to the UK, like Canada, Hong Kong and Kuwait, continued keeping reserves in sterling until the early 1970s. This meant that when the UK was forced to devalue the pound, it adversely affected their closest allies. To keep these allies happy, the UK was forced to make side payments to them, further increasing the British difficulties.

11.7.1 Threats to the US dollar reserve status

When a country enjoys the world's largest economy, has solid economic growth, low inflation and a strong military to back it up, the reserve status of its currency is undisputed. This was the situation for the US until the 1960s. Today, interest rates in the US are close to zero, and government debt is close to historically high levels. Its economic growth is anaemic, and still it is running a trade deficit. If the US did not have a reserve currency, it would probably have experienced a sharp depreciation, stimulating exporters and correcting the trade balance.

Because of the reserve status of the dollar, it remains artificially strong, as foreign countries directly intervene in the currency markets. As a consequence, global imbalances build up.

There is a way out for the US, by creating inflation. That will achieve two goals simultaneously, depreciating the currency and reducing the real value of its debt, an increasingly significant proportion of which is held by foreigners.

This is partly the path the US has taken. Its debt has been increasing sharply, and also it has been monetising part of the debt by means of QE so that the Federal Reserve System (Fed) has become a significant purchaser of government debt. We show some of the debt numbers in Figure 11.4.

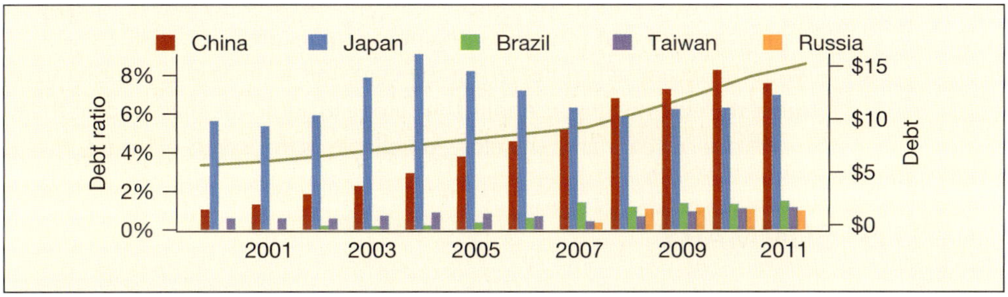

Figure 11.4 Fraction of US government debt held by major creditor countries, and total debt, USD trillions

Data source: US Treasury

By December 2011, US government debt was $15 trillion, having tripled since 2000. The largest owner of US debt is the Social Security Trust Fund with 19%, followed by the Fed at 11.3%, leaving China in third place at 8%. Overall, 33% of the debt is held by foreign entities, not necessarily governments. Traditionally, Japan has been the largest holder but it is now in second place, followed by Brazil, Taiwan and Russia. The US itself does not feel the need to hold large foreign reserves, which by the end of 2011 amounted to $147 billion.

11.7.2 The Chinese renminbi

Many countries resent the reserve status of the dollar, and if the US continues to rapidly increase its debt whilst suffering from poor economic growth, some observers have been trying to identify what the next reserve currency might be.

The most obvious candidate is the Chinese renminbi, as China is the second largest economy in the world, and if its current growth trend holds, is on track to surpass the US by the end of this decade. China has been the most vocal complainer about the dollar being reserve currency, promoting alternatives, such as the SDR. But what about its own currency?

Several factors prevent the renminbi from becoming the reserve currency. So long as China maintains strict capital controls, that is not possible, because a reserve currency needs to be freely traded abroad. Foreigners need to be able to hold it without any worries about converting it into their own currencies at a later date. Related to this is the fact that the Chinese government maintains a closer control of its economy than any of the other candidates for reserve status, with widespread fears that the economic statistics it puts out are not reliable. This means that in the current environment, foreigners would not trust China with a reserve currency. Finally, at the moment China does not seem to want to have a reserve currency.

If we look towards the future, and China continues to grow, with its economy becoming more transparent, whilst the US declines, it is possible, if not likely, that China might regain reserve status over the next few decades.

11.7.3 The euro

Until its recent problems, the euro was touted as the next reserve currency. It is the currency of the largest economic area in the world, the euro zone, is freely traded and transparent. Until recently, many countries were increasingly using the euro for foreign currency reserves and trade was beginning to become priced in euros.

With the recent difficulties facing the euro, this is unlikely to happen soon. Not only is the future of the euro no longer certain, the European authorities have shown themselves to be poor stewards of a currency and, therefore, unreliable as the issuers of the future reserve currency.

11.8 SUMMARY

The largest financial market by volume is the market for foreign exchange. Since the level of exchange rates is vitally important for most countries, it is not surprising that few, if any, markets see more government intervention than the FX market. Every government needs to have a currency regime in place, ranging from being fully tied to other currencies to freely floating.

Governments have various mechanisms for intervening in the FX market. If the exchange rate is overvalued, it can only continue intervening until it runs out of foreign reserves, but it can intervene indefinitely to maintain an undervalued currency. Governments often couple such interventions with sterilisation, a simultaneous reduction in the money supply.

Because of the 'impossible trinity', governments do not have full choice in the policy measures they can implement, and often resort to capital controls. While the traditional sort of capital controls was aimed at tightly controlling the flow of foreign currency in and out, 'capital controls 2.0' target hot money.

If a country undervalues its currency, this often leads to significant friction with its trading partners, sometimes called 'currency wars'.

One country in the world has the reserve currency. Historically, that was sterling, but over the past century or so the US dollar has been the reserve currency. Its status is under threat, and other currencies such as the renminbi or the euro may take over.

APPENDIX: EXCHANGE RATE REGIMES

The following is a presentation of the varieties of exchange rate regimes based on Frankel (1999) and Gosh *et al.* (2002).

Currency or monetary union

A group of countries agree to use a common currency issued by a central monetary authority. The member countries give up an independent monetary and exchange rate policy to the central monetary authority. This is a multilateral arrangement whilst most others are unilateral.

The prime example of a currency union is the euro zone of 17 countries that have adopted a common currency as their sole legal tender. Even a currency union can be reversed, for example, the Czech Republic and Slovakia gave up the koruna when the countries split up, but it is the firmest possible commitment to a fixed exchange rate.

Currency board

A country pegs its exchange rate to a foreign currency, setting the exchange rate regime and the actual exchange rate into law. A key example is Argentina up until late 2001, which had the peso linked to the dollar.

Single currency peg

A country's currency is pegged at a fixed rate to the currency of another country. The rate is generally adjustable and the credibility of the peg is related to the level of FX reserves. Examples are the East Asian countries linking their currencies to the dollar in the 1990s, and francophone West African countries that pegged to the French franc. The costs of readjusting or giving up the peg altogether are lower than in the case of a currency union or currency board.

Adjustable peg

The adjustable peg is similar to a single currency peg but with less commitment and more open and frequent adjustments. In practice, it is rather difficult because adjustments put a strain on central bank credibility. The Bretton Woods system was based on an adjustable peg setup.

Basket peg

The currency is not pegged to a specific currency but is fixed to a weighted basket of two or more currencies. This is a useful approach for countries with geographically diversified trade patterns. The basket can be designed according to country-specific criteria or to a composite currency (SDR, for example). Theoretically a basket peg can be as rigid as a single currency peg. In practice, however, countries that use a basket peg frequently keep the weights secret and can thus adjust the weights or the exchange rate level at their own discretion.

Crawling peg

The exchange rate is set in a rule-based manner and can be regularly reset in a series of mini-devaluations, which can occur as often as weekly, usually based on a predetermined rate or a function of inflation-rate differentials. High-inflation countries frequently opt for a crawling peg, since the exchange rate can be readjusted to allow for inflation differentials without giving up the benefits of a deterministic exchange rate.

Target zones or bands

A target zone establishes fixed exchange rate margins but allows the exchange rate to fluctuate within those margins. The monetary authorities intervene when the exchange rate hits the pre-announced margins on either side of the central parity. The European exchange rate mechanism (ERM) was an example of a target zone.

Managed float or dirty float

The monetary authority allows the exchange rate to move freely in the market, but has a general view on the broad level and path of the exchange rate, standing ready to intervene. The government does not defend any particular parity or follow any intervention rule.

Free float

The exchange rate is determined by demand and supply in the FX market without any or with just minor official intervention. This option requires little or no official reserves but also mostly prevents the accumulation of reserves. There are no truly freely floating currencies today.

Dollarisation (or euroisation)

This is a special case of currency arrangement, where a country uses a foreign currency as legal tender in addition to or instead of a domestic currency. Typically, the foreign currency is the dollar or the euro.

Dollarisation can be bilateral or unilateral. Examples of the former are Panama and Kosovo, and of the latter Ecuador and Montenegro. Bilateral dollarisation means that the central bank of the country is the central bank of the main country, like the Fed or the ECB, which makes the arrangement firm and provides for lending at last resort. Unilateral dollarisation is more unstable, since the country needs to have enough foreign currency reserves to meet all possible demands for foreign currency, extending to all types of money including M0, M1, M2 and M3, otherwise the setup is subject to runs.

Questions for discussion

1. Why is the volume of currency transactions so much higher than the volume of trade?
2. Do you prefer fixed or floating rates?
3. Why do governments sterilise FX interventions, and mechanically how do they go about doing it?
4. What are traditional capital controls and capital controls 2.0?
5. What is a speculative attack? Do they force the government to abandon a sensible policy, or make the government see reality?
6. What is the 'impossible trinity'?
7. What was the Bretton Woods system, and would you want to see it adopted now?
8. What is a currency war, and why is it damaging?
9. Can a country maintain an overvalued exchange rate indefinitely?
10. Can a country maintain an undervalued exchange rate indefinitely?
11. Is China's foreign exchange policy sensible?
12. What is a reserve currency?
13. Is it likely that the euro will become the next reserve currency?
14. Is it likely that China will have the next reserve currency?

References

Abdelal, R. (2007). *Capital Rules: the Construction of Global Finance*. Harvard University Press.

Ahamed, L. (2009). *Lords of Finance, the Bankers Who Broke the World*. The Penguin Group.

Arnason, R. and Danielsson, J. (2011). Capital controls are exactly wrong for Iceland. *Vox EU*, 14 November. www.voxeu.org/article/iceland-and-imf-why-capital-controls-are-entirely-wrong.

Bussiere, M., Saxena, S. C. and Tovar, C. E. (2010). Chronicle of currency collapses re-examining the effects on output. Technical report, ECB. Working paper series no. 1226, July.

Eichengreen, B. (1996). *Golden Fetters: the Gold Standard and the Great Depression, 1919–1939*. Oxford University Press.

Ferguson, N. (2008). *The Ascent of Money*. The Penguin Group.

Frankel, J. A. (1999). No single currency regime is right for all countries at all times. Working paper 7338, National Bureau of Economic Research.

Gosh, A. R., Gulde, A.-M. and Wolf, H. C. (2002). *Exchange Rate Regime: Choices and Consequences*. MIT Press.

Hume, D. (1752). On the balance of trade. In *Essays, Moral, Political and Literary*. Edinburgh and London.

Krugman, P. R. and Obstfeld, M. (2006). *International Economics: Theory and Policy,* 7th edition. Pearson.

Laeven, L. and Valencia, F. (2008). Systemic banking crises: a new database. Technical report, IMF. IMF Working Paper.

Lavigne, R. (2008). Sterilized intervention in emerging-market economies: trends, costs and risks. Discussion paper 2008-4, Bank of Canada.

Marsh, D. (2010). *The Euro: the Politics of the New Global Currency*. Yale University Press.

McCallum, B. T. (1996). *International Monetary Economics*. Oxford University Press.

OECD (2002). Forty years' experience with the OECD code of liberalisation of capital movements. Technical report.

Reinhart, C. M. and Rogoff, K. (2009). *This Time Is Different: Eight Centuries of Financial Folly*. Princeton University Press.

Sarno, L. and Taylor, M. P. (2003). *The Economics of Exchange Rates*. Cambridge University Press.

Sicsic, P. (1992). Was the Franc Poincaré deliberately undervalued? *Explorations in Economic History,* 29: 69–92.

12 CURRENCY CRISIS MODELS

Countries that peg their exchange rates are susceptible to currency crises if the exchange rate is out of alignment with the underlying economic fundamentals, especially if the exchange rate is overvalued, the case considered in this chapter. This often leads to *speculative attacks*, where speculators aim to force a devaluation by a massive sale of the currency on the open market. If speculators believe that the exchange rate is sustainable, and the government is determined to keep the peg, they will act in a way that supports the currency regime. If, however, they lose that belief, the speculators may force a realignment.

Mechanically, a speculative attack can be implemented by borrowing large amounts of domestic currency and immediately selling it for a foreign currency, or alternatively by entering into forward foreign exchange contracts. Once the peg is abandoned, the speculator can realise her profits by converting foreign currency to domestic currency at the more advantageous rate and repay the loan, or buy the foreign currency at the now cheap rate.

A key factor in whether an exchange rate regime is sustainable is the strength of the underlying economic *fundamentals*, referring to variables like inflation, the balance of payments, unemployment, economic growth and the budget deficit. A country with strong fundamentals is better able to maintain its exchange rate policies and repel speculative attacks, which in turn makes it less likely that an attack will be launched in the first place.

Links to other chapters

This chapter relates directly to Chapter 11 (currency markets).

Key concepts

- Speculative attacks
- First-generation currency crisis models
- Second-generation currency crisis moments
- Global games models
- Argentina
- ERM crisis

Readings for this chapter

The specific readings in this chapter relate to the 1G, the 2G and the global games models. Background reading for 1G models is provided in Obstfeld and Rogoff (1996), pp. 559–566, and the original paper we studied is Flood and Garber (1984). Our discussion of the 2G models is based on Copeland (2000), with Obstfeld (1996) providing more detailed mathematical treatments. The global games discussion follows Morris and Shin (1998, 1999).

Notation specific to this chapter

The lower-case variables *d, m, p* and *r* are expressed as logarithms. Variables with an asterisk, e.g. p^*, are from the foreign country.

c	Cost to speculators
d	Log of domestic credit
e	Spot exchange rate (domestic/foreign)
$\bar{e}$	Fixed exchange rate
$\tilde{e}$	Shadow exchange rate
$\hat{e}$	Desired exchange rate
i, i^*	Domestic and foreign interest
$\bar{k}$	Threshold level of reserves
ℓ	Proportion of speculators who attack
$\mathcal{L}$	Loss function of the government
m	Log of domestic nominal money supply
p	Log of price level in the domestic country
Q	Cost of abandoning the peg
r	Log of government foreign exchange reserves
T	Timing of attack
v	Payoff from attacking
x	Noisy signal of fundamentals
$\text{Cost}(\Delta e)$	Indicator function of cost of abandoning the peg
α	Elasticity of agents' demand for money
θ	Fundamentals
μ	Growth rate in domestic credit
ψ, η	Parameters

12.1 FIRST-GENERATION MODELS

The first modern currency crisis model is the first-generation currency crisis model (1G model), dealing with speculative attacks. The model is quite simple, assuming the government pegs the currency whilst running an unsustainable monetary policy. When the government runs out of foreign currency reserves, the currency devalues. Speculators know this, and attack the currency before the government runs out of foreign currency. This was first modelled by Krugman (1979), though the specific model we discuss was designed by Flood and Garber (1984) and we follow the presentation in Obstfeld and Rogoff (1996), pp. 559–566.

The model assumes continuous time in a small open economy characterised by purchasing power parity (PPP), uncovered interest rate parity (UIP) and agents that possess perfect foresight. There are no private banks, hence the money supply equals the sum of the domestic credit provided by the central bank, plus the value in domestic currency of foreign exchange reserves, which by assumption do not produce any interest.

Setup

The assets available to domestic residents are domestic money, domestic bonds, foreign money and foreign bonds. The domestic government uses the stock of foreign currency it holds to fix the exchange rate. The model is built around five equations:

$$\text{log money market equilibrium: } m_t - p_t = -\alpha i_t \tag{12.1}$$

$$\text{log nominal money supply: } m_t = d_t + k_t \tag{12.2}$$

$$\text{log domestic credit expansion: } d_t - d_{t-1} = \mu \tag{12.3}$$

$$\text{log PPP: } p_t = p_t^* + \log e_t \tag{12.4}$$

$$\text{log UIP: } i_t = i_t^* + \mathrm{E}_{t-1}\Delta e_t \tag{12.5}$$

The money supply, m, and prices, p, are in logs, as well as the growth in domestic money, μ. i is the interest rate and e is the nominal exchange rate, neither in logs. Equation (12.1) describes the equilibrium condition in the money market. The elasticity α is positive, so the real demand for money is a decreasing function of the domestic interest rate. Equation (12.2) shows that the nominal money supply equals the sum of domestic credit and the foreign exchange reserves. Equation (12.3) is the first derivative of domestic credit in relation to time and shows that domestic credit is increasing at the positive, constant, rate of μ.

The government runs *persistent deficits* that are financed by money creation at rate μ. Equations (12.4) and (12.5) respectively indicate that the price level follows the PPP rule and the interest rate obeys the UIP condition.

The model

Under an assumption of perfect foresight, and assuming the exchange rate is fixed and equal to $\log \bar{e}$, it follows that:

$$\mathrm{E}_{t-1}\Delta e_t = 0$$

$$i_t = i_t^*$$

Substituting (12.2) for the nominal money supply in m in (12.1), (12.4) for the domestic price level p_t in (12.1), and (12.5) for the domestic interest rate i_t in (12.1) leads to:

$$k_t + d_t - p_t^* - \log \bar{e} = -\alpha\left(i_t^* + \mathrm{E}_{t-1}\Delta e_t\right) \quad (12.6)$$

By assumption, the foreign price level p_t^* and the foreign interest rate i^* are constant, as is $\bar{e}$. According to (12.6), the depletion rate of foreign exchange reserves is $-\mu$, so it follows that:

$$k_t = k_0 - \mu t \quad (12.7)$$

Equivalently:

$$d_t = d_0 + \mu t \quad (12.8)$$

k_0 and d_0 are the initial levels of reserves and credit, respectively, at time $t = 0$. Equation (12.7) shows that the foreign exchange reserves decrease proportionally to the growth in domestic credit in order to keep the nominal money supply and thus the exchange rate fixed.

Unsustainability

To keep the foreign exchange rate fixed, the central bank uses its foreign currency reserves to absorb any currency the public does not want to hold at the fixed rate $\bar{e}$. Therefore the foreign reserves decrease at the same speed as the increase in the central bank holdings of domestic government debt.

This is obviously not sustainable as the central bank will eventually run out of foreign exchange reserves, supposing it has no means to increase them. At that time, the fixed exchange rate regime will have to be abandoned. We assume that the government will support the fixed rate as long as its net reserves remain positive. After the fixed rate regime collapses, the exchange rate floats freely for ever.

Timing of the attack

The 1G model predicts that the fixed exchange rate regime will be abandoned *before* the central bank has completely exhausted its reserves. To solve for the timing of the attack, we introduce the concept of a *shadow exchange rate*. The shadow exchange rate, denoted $\log \tilde{e}$, is the exchange rate that would prevail if the currency was allowed to float. If the currency was not pegged and the government continued with the domestic credit expansion at rate μ every period, the currency would depreciate by μ every period. This means that in the absence of a pegged exchange rate, the rate of depreciation would equal the rate of money growth.

Under perfect foresight, agents expect that the exchange rate moves in line with the money growth rate:

$$\mathrm{E}_{t-1}\Delta e_t = \log \mu$$

Employing the shadow exchange rate, the money market equilibrium in (12.6) becomes:

$$d_t - \log \tilde{e}_t = -\alpha(\mathrm{E}_{t-1}\Delta e_t)$$

Solving for the shadow exchange rate $\log \tilde{e}$:

$$\log \tilde{e}_t = \alpha\mu + d_t$$

Time of attack, *T*

First, suppose the attack happens *late* when $\log \tilde{e} > \log \bar{e}$, after which the peg is abandoned. In that case we would see a perfectly anticipated discrete rise in the exchange rate equal to $\log \tilde{e} - \log \bar{e}$ and the speculators would reap an instantaneously infinite rate of profit. This represents an arbitrage opportunity giving speculators the incentive to attack earlier and pre-empt their competitors, which will lead to an attack happening before $\log \tilde{e} > \log e$.

If, on the other hand, speculators attacked *early*, when $\log \tilde{e} < \log \bar{e}$, they would suffer a loss since the currency would actually appreciate following the attack. Therefore, there is no incentive to attack and the fixed exchange rate regime will survive.

Therefore, the attack must happen when $\log \tilde{e} = \log \bar{e}$, that is when the shadow exchange rate equals the fixed exchange rate. Let T denote the time of attack. Substitute (12.8) for d_t and knowing that at T the shadow exchange rate is equal to the peg, we get:

$$\log \bar{e} = \alpha\mu + d_0 + \mu T$$

Solving for T:

$$T = \frac{\log \bar{e} - d_0 - \alpha\mu}{\mu}$$

Prior to the crisis, the quantity of money remains constant but its composition varies: domestic credit grows at rate μ while reserves decrease at the same rate. After the crisis, the government has lost all its foreign reserves and the money stock equals domestic credit and thus grows at the same rate μ. The solution can be seen graphically in Figures 12.1 and 12.2.

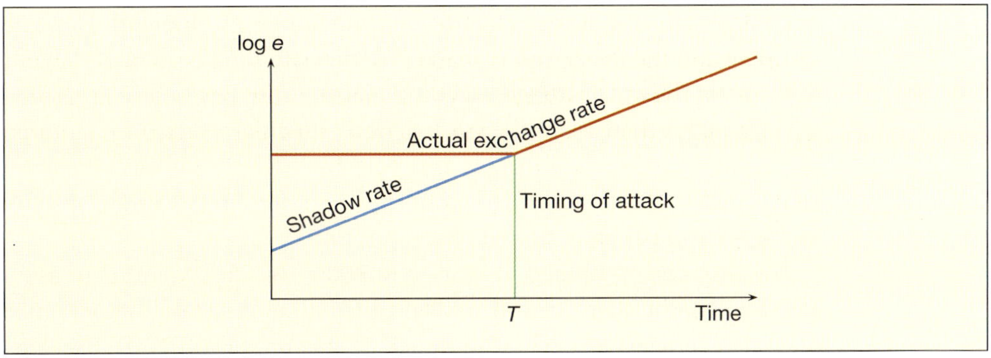

Figure 12.1 Shadow exchange rate

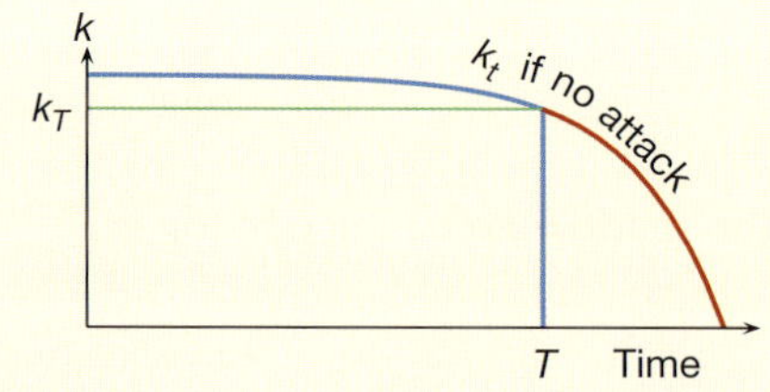

Figure 12.2 Foreign reserves

Analysis

The 1G model suggests that currency crises originate from an expansionary monetary policy incompatible with a fixed exchange rate regime. Speculators rationally anticipate that the fixed exchange rate regime cannot be indefinitely maintained and launch an attack before the foreign exchange reserves are exhausted. The model relies on strong assumptions such as perfect foresight, UIP and PPP.

In this model, all agents are completely rational except the government itself, since its policy of ongoing monetary expansion eventually destroys the fixed exchange rate regime. The underlying message of the model, however, is not that speculative attacks can be foreseen perfectly, but rather that it illustrates how private agents respond to inconsistent economic policies. The 1G model shows that a large asset market event, for instance an attack, does not necessarily need to be associated with a large shock but can build up gradually.

12.2 THE ARGENTINIAN CRISIS

Argentina has long suffered high inflation, at times bordering on hyperinflation. In order to find stability, the Argentinian government in 1989 embarked on a strong programme of market-oriented structural reforms.

Part of the agenda was the introduction of a currency board, whereby the exchange rate was fixed at one-to-one with the US dollar. Initially, this was quite successful: inflation fell to single digits as seen in Figure 12.3, the exchange rate was stable as seen in Figure 12.4, and economic growth was high in the early years of the programme.

Underneath this success significant vulnerabilities emerged. Not only did countries competing in the same export markets depreciate their currencies, Argentina was unable to maintain the fiscal strength necessary for the currency board. Persistent budget deficits led to a steady increase in the stock of debt, much of which was denominated in dollars, of increasingly short maturities, and held by foreign investors. The government, facing an election in 1999, responded by pursuing an *expansionary fiscal policy* with dire consequences for the already strained fiscal position.

The situation continued to worsen in 2000, leading Argentina to ask the IMF for help at the end of the year. The IMF did lend $17 billion but stabilisation remained elusive and Argentina suffered a speculative attack on its currency in 2001. Spreads on Argentinian bonds rose sharply in the course of 2001, shutting it out of international capital markets

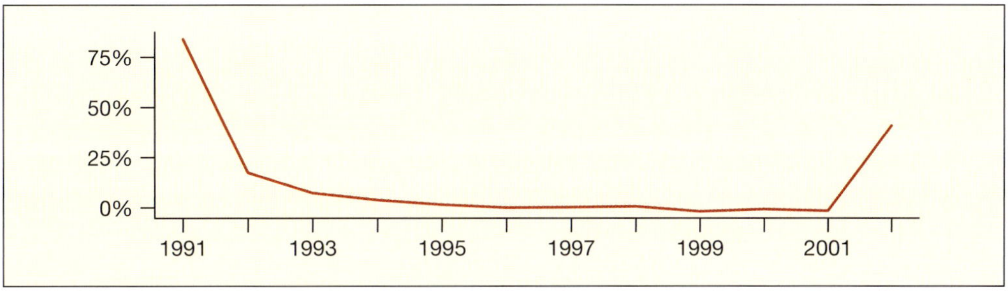

Figure 12.3 **Year-on-year inflation, Argentina 1991–2002**
Data source: International Monetary Fund (IMF)

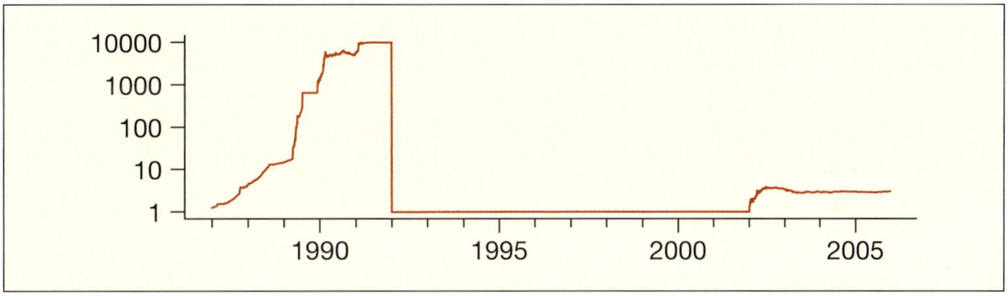

Figure 12.4 **Argentinean peso/USD, 1987–2004**
Data source: www.globalfinancialdata.com

and making Argentina dependent on IMF financing. The beginning of the end was when the IMF, dissatisfied with the Argentinian government for not complying with fiscal targets, held back on more loans.

Argentina partially defaulted on its international obligations in December 2001 and abandoned the currency board a few weeks later. As a consequence, Argentina went into a deep crisis, experiencing a GDP decline of 15% in 2002, with unemployment rising to over 20%. Since then, Argentina has been mostly shunned by the capital markets, and is still in negotiations with creditors over the sovereign default of 2002.

While Argentina has reached settlement with many of its creditors, it is being pursued by so-called '*vulture funds*' who buy distressed sovereign obligations and pursue the debtors in international courts. One example of this was the seizure of an Argentine naval ship in Ghana in October 2012, at the request of a subsidiary of the American hedge fund Elliot Capital Management: see BBC (2012a). This is the same fund as in Section 19.3, where we discuss the enforcement of sovereign debt claims.

Analysis

At the heart of the problem was a fiscal policy inconsistent with the currency board. The dollar peg eliminated monetary policy as a policy tool and put strong restrictions on fiscal policy to keep debt sufficiently low to avoid an overvaluation of the peso. Fiscal prudence was also needed to maintain the credibility of the guarantee to convert pesos to dollars at parity, which was needed to attract capital inflows, and to support the ability of the government to act as a lender of last resort (LOLR).

This issue was especially delicate in Argentina with its history of irresponsible fiscal policy. The fiscal policy was the result of institutional weaknesses, which persistently pushed the government to commit more fiscal resources than it was capable of mobilising. A key reason was fiscal federalism, whereby regional governments could raise debt with limited central government oversight. The IMF was an enthusiastic supporter of the currency board, but after the crisis the chief economist of the IMF, Michael Mussa (2002), recognised the mistakes:

> 'In these kinds of conditions, the choice of the currency board, though effective in the short-term as a tool to stabilize the economy and the price level, was risky over the medium- to long-term. The currency board eliminated an expansionary monetary policy and money creation as a mean to raise revenues, while it required long-term fiscal discipline at the same time. If fiscal discipline was not adhered to, the medium-term dangers were strongly increased. Adding to these dangers was the fact that in Argentina only a limited market for long-term debt issued in pesos existed, forcing the government to finance its deficit by external borrowing in dollars, raising the costs of a devaluation even further.'

The Argentinian crisis is consistent with the 1G model. The government ran an unsustainable monetary and fiscal policy, exhausting all foreign currency resources before abandoning the currency board. Towards the end, it was subject to a speculative attack.

While it employed extensive capital controls, they were always quite leaky, for example, one could buy stocks in Argentinian companies, exchange them for American depositary receipts (ADRs) in New York, sell them there and receive dollars. Interestingly, the ADRs traded at a 40% discount, which was the amount of the eventual depreciation.

12.3 SECOND-GENERATION MODELS

The 1990s saw a number of currency crises that were inconsistent with the 1G models, and as a response a new class of models, the 2G models, were developed. Below we present one of the simpler 2G models, that of Copeland (2000), capturing the essential intuition whilst leaving out some of the richer features of these types of models.

The underlying premise is that a government pursues a fixed exchange rate, $\bar{e}$, but would prefer a floating regime to achieve its domestic policies. The model focuses on the government's continuous comparison of the net benefits from staying in the fixed regime versus floating the exchange rate.

The government faces three types of concerns:

1 First, it would like to run the economy with a higher level of aggregate demand, requiring a currency devaluation. We can summarise these wishes into a variable denoted $\hat{e}$, which we call the *desired exchange rate*, that is, the exchange rate the government would choose if it had not made a commitment to the fixed rate.

2 Second, there is a cost if the fixed rate peg is to be abandoned. This could be interpreted as political pain or loss of credibility of the monetary institutions. We

summarise this by the cost of exchange rate change, Cost(Δe). For simplicity we assume that the function Cost (Δe) can take only two possible values:

$$\text{Cost}(\Delta e) = \begin{cases} 0 \text{ for } \Delta e = 0 \\ Q \text{ for } \Delta e > 0 \end{cases}$$

3 Finally, the peg will be more costly to defend when a devaluation is expected than when it is not. By the UIP condition, an expected devaluation means that the domestic interest rate will have to rise to defend the peg and this is likely to hurt the economy.

Decisions

We capture these three concerns in the following loss function that the government faces:

$$\mathcal{L} = \{\psi(\hat{e} - \bar{e}) + \eta \text{E}(\Delta e)\}^2 + \text{Cost}(\Delta e) \quad \psi, \eta > 0, \hat{e} > \bar{e}$$

The term $\eta\text{E}(\Delta e)$ reflects the expected economic pain associated with defending the peg with increasing interest rates. η is a parameter that shows the strength of this loss.

We assume that the desired exchange rate of the government, $\hat{e}$, is always higher (weaker) than the fixed exchange rate, $\bar{e}$, which means that the government is bothered only by an overvaluation of the currency but not by an undervaluation. The term $(\hat{e} - \bar{e})$ is then the extent to which the currency is overvalued relative to the level which the government would like. ψ is a parameter of the magnitude of the loss associated with the overvaluation.

We assume that if the government chooses to devalue, it will have no further reason to change the exchange rate further, so from then on, the expected depreciation would be zero. Hence, the cost of devaluation is simply Q. Figure 12.5 is a graphical description of this situation, highlighting the multiple equilibria. Two cases can be distinguished, each with two subcases.

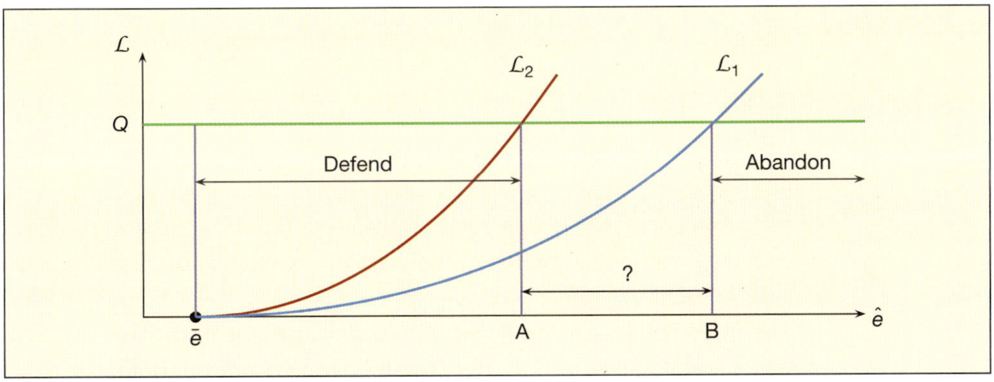

Figure 12.5 Multiple equilibria

Case 1: Market participants expect the government to resist the pressure to devalue, therefore, $E(\Delta e) = 0$.

The government now has two options. It can either stick to the peg or it can devalue. If it decides to keep the peg, the cost of abandoning the peg is equal to zero, $\text{Cost}(\Delta e) = 0$, and the government faces the following loss function:

$$\mathcal{L}_1 = \{\psi(\hat{e} - \bar{e})\}^2$$

If, however, the government decides to devalue, it bears the costs of the abandonment and its total loss becomes:

$$\mathcal{L} = \text{Cost}(\Delta e) = Q$$

Facing these options, the government will defend if the loss associated with keeping the peg is lower than the abandonment cost:

$$\mathcal{L}_1 < Q$$

This condition is satisfied for all values of $\hat{e}$ between $\bar{e}$ and B in Figure 12.5. If $\hat{e}$ surpasses point B, the loss function passes the abandonment cost of Q and it becomes more costly to defend the peg than to devalue.

Case 2: Market participants expect the government to surrender to market pressure and allow the currency to depreciate, which means that $E(\Delta e) > 0$. The government again has two options. Either it can decide to defend the peg, leading to the following loss function:

$$\begin{aligned}\mathcal{L}_2 &= \{\psi(\hat{e} - \bar{e}) + \eta(\hat{e} - \bar{e})\}^2 \\ &= \{(\psi + \eta)(\hat{e} - \bar{e})\}^2\end{aligned}$$

Alternatively, it can decide to give up the peg, suffering the loss of the abandonment cost function:

$$\text{Cost}(\Delta e) = Q$$

In this case the government will defend the peg if

$$\mathcal{L}_2 < Q$$

The government will now defend its exchange rate for all $\hat{e}$ between $\bar{e}$ and A in Figure 12.5.

Analysis

Figure 12.5 shows that for levels of $\hat{e}$ just slightly higher than $\bar{e}$, it is optimal for the government to defend the peg, no matter what market participants expect. For very high values of $\hat{e}$ the exact opposite is true and it is always optimal for the government to devalue. This causes trigger effects, whereby a very small change in fundamentals can cause a large change in exchange rates.

The interesting case occurs when the government finds itself in a situation between points A and B in Figure 12.5. Here the following condition holds:

$$\mathcal{L}_1 < Q < \mathcal{L}_2$$

In this intermediate situation, the government will find it optimal to validate the market's expectations. If the market expects the government to defend, the government faces $\mathcal{L}_1$ and will find it optimal not to devalue. If market participants expect the government to abandon the peg, the government is confronted with $\mathcal{L}_2$ and will find it optimal to abandon. In this region there are *multiple equilibria* and the government will follow market participants' expectations, which are, therefore, *self-fulfilling*. A speculative attack would then succeed simply because it was expected to succeed.

A country whose desired exchange rate, $\hat{e}$, falls between A and B could find it easy or completely impossible to defend a fixed exchange rate regime, depending on whether the market *expects* it to devalue or not.

Role of fundamentals

The state of the fundamentals is reflected in the difference between the desired exchange rate, $\hat{e}$, and the current peg, $\bar{e}$. If fundamentals are strong, there is no need to stimulate the economy by devaluing. On the other hand, a country with weak fundamentals may wish to depreciate so it can improve its economic situation. Figure 12.5 shows that the smaller the gap between the desired exchange rate and the fixed parity, the easier it will be to defend.

The state of fundamentals is also expressed through the slope of the loss functions of the government, which are determined by the level of $\hat{e}$. The higher the value of Q (a country with a sizable political investment in the peg), the easier the government will find it to defend, *ceteris paribus*.

The main points of the 2G model are the following:

1 There are self-fulfilling crises in a model with rational investors.
2 Events completely disconnected from the economy may change expectations and trigger a currency crisis.
3 Fixed exchange rate regimes that work well in the absence of speculative attacks may fail without major fundamental imbalances.
4 Crises are not fully predictable.

These are summarised in Figure 12.6.

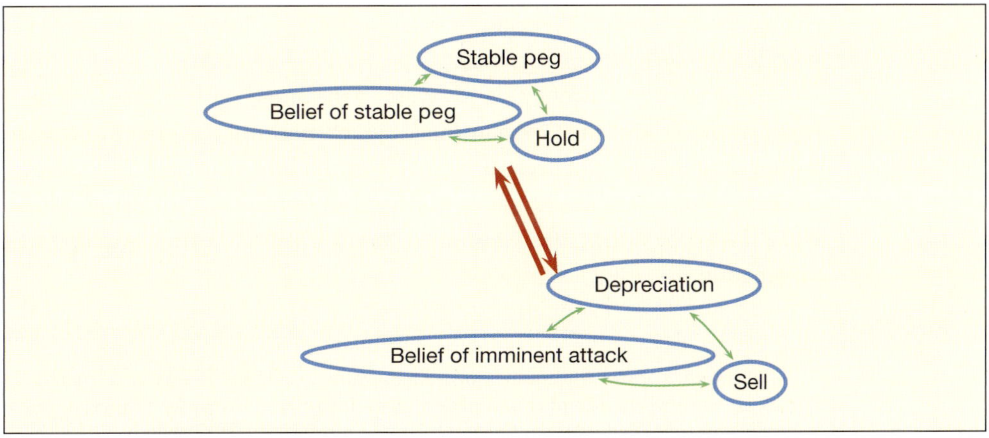

Figure 12.6 Multiple equilibria

Criticism of multiple equilibria

The relevance of second generation models has been disputed as far as they rely on the existence of multiple equilibria. Both theoretical and empirical criticisms are levelled against multiple equilibria.

The main criticism of the 2G models is the notion of multiple equilibria: how can a model place the economy in two different states at the same time? However, this is not strictly a multiple equilibria solution, because which equilibrium is chosen depends on the expectations of the speculators, so conditional on those there is a single solution. This makes the multiple equilibrium models a useful device to capture the role of expectations in determining government behaviour and economic outcomes.

More modern versions of speculative attack models are able to dispense with the multiple equilibria solution by explicitly modelling information available to speculators. We present one such model later in the chapter.

12.4 THE EUROPEAN CRISIS, 1992–1993

One of the largest currency crises to hit European countries happened in 1992. This came after the member countries of the European Union (EU) had been experimenting with ways to reduce foreign exchange (FX) instability in Europe following the collapse of the Bretton Woods system. From 1979 to the 1990s, EU countries formed a joint system for coordination of monetary and exchange rate policies consisting of two major components: the creation of an artificial unit of account named the European currency unit (ECU)[1] and an exchange rate regime, known as the European exchange rate mechanism (ERM). The ERM was set up to reduce exchange rate volatility and achieve monetary stability in Europe and to pave the way for a single currency in the future.

The ERM was a *target zone* exchange rate regime. A grid of bilateral exchange rates to the ECU was calculated for each country, where currency fluctuations had to be contained within a margin of 2.25% on either side of the rate. The Spanish peseta, Portuguese escudo and Italian lira had wider bands of 6%. Member countries had to intervene to ensure their currencies stayed within the prescribed band. In a crisis, the country with strong currency – read Germany – was supposed to lend its currency to countries needing help to strengthen their currency.

In practice, the currency bands were maintained with respect to the most stable currency of the group, the German mark, which became the effective *reserve currency* in the ERM, giving Germany a pivotal role. This arrangement meant that Germany was the only country able to set its monetary policy independently. All other countries in the ERM were forced to adopt the German monetary policy if they wanted to stay within the target zone.

[1]This was only a unit of account, not a medium of exchange. It was constructed as a fixed basket of European currencies. Member countries were Belgium, Denmark, France, Germany, Ireland, Italy, Luxembourg, The Netherlands, Portugal, Spain and the United Kingdom.

If, for example, Italy decided to use its own discretion over monetary policy and expand its money supply, this would result in higher inflation in Italy, weakening the lira. This gave Italy two choices: either the Italian Central Bank intervened to buy lire on the open market or it devalued the lira, choosing a new central parity for the lira to fluctuate around. Neither choice was attractive, intervening was costly and may not have been effective, and devaluing was also costly, causing the Central Bank to lose credibility, setting in inflation and making speculative attacks more likely. Therefore, the best choice for Italy was to adopt the German monetary policy to ensure the strength of the lira.

The country with the strongest currency did not face these problems, especially if it chose to contract its money supply. Therefore, the country with the strongest currency has freedom of action, and the others have to follow.

Start of the crisis – German reunification

The starting point of the ERM crisis was the German reunification. The German government embarked on a massive fiscal expansion to transfer resources to the former East Germany, increasing the government budget deficit from 5% of GDP to 13.2%, whilst East German marks could be converted to West German marks at a highly favourable rate of 1.8:1, massively increasing the money supply. The German Central Bank became worried about inflation because the economy was overheating, and opted to raise interest rates by more than 3%.

Other countries

The German decision to raise interest rates strengthened the mark, putting pressure on other members of the ERM who felt they had no choice but to also raise their interest rates, in effect importing the German monetary policy. However, the German decision was based on the special considerations of the reunification, and other members of the ERM were in a different situation, with many in a recession. This meant that the optimal monetary policy for them was an interest rate reduction, not an increase, and the need to follow Germany meant their economic situations further deteriorated.

The situation could have been alleviated if Germany had lowered its interest rates, but it refused to do so, recommending realignment instead. Other member countries of the ERM rejected realignment, increasingly advocating abandoning the ERM altogether.

Speculative attack – Black Wednesday

The tensions between the ERM member states did not escape unnoticed, and speculators recognised that a realignment was increasingly likely. In the context of the 2G models, some member states had neither the strength of the fundamentals nor the desire to resist a speculative attack. That made an attack inevitable, and by the beginning of September 1992 a massive speculative attack against the lira was underway, with the lira finally devalued by 7% against the mark.

Just a few days later, on 16 September 1992, on what has been termed '*Black Wednesday*', speculators turned their attention to the pound. The Bank of England (BoE) raised the minimum lending rate from 10% to 12%, promising to raise it to 15%. This did not deter the speculators, and at the end of the day the pound closed below its ERM floor, prompting the Bank to announce a 'temporary' withdrawal from the ERM, made permanent on 19 September. The cost of defending the pound was estimated by the UK Treasury to be £3.3 billion, around £800 million being due to direct trading losses, with the rest lost profit from foreign reserves, sold before the pound depreciated.

Italy followed the UK out of the ERM, while Spain, although staying in the ERM, devalued the peseta by 5%. The attacks continued well into 1993, with the franc, peseta, krone and escudo under pressure. On 30 July 1993, all the ERM currencies except the Dutch guilder and Irish punt were quoted at the bottom of their bands against the mark. A thorough revamping of the ERM was announced on 1 August, with the size of the bands widened from ±2.25% around par to ±15%, which finally managed to ease speculative pressures.

1G analysis

The ERM crisis is not easily explained by the 1G model. The member countries devaluated long before they ran out of reserves, but perhaps most importantly, the currencies of many of the countries recovered over the next 18 months, suggesting that the initial weakness of the exchange rates was not due to long-run increases in the money supply and high inflation. Instead, the countries might just have had an overvalued exchange rate, with a small devaluation necessary for them to become competitive again. In other words, the devaluation was useful for the affected countries. While this is contrary to the workings of the 1G model, it does point to the positive benefits that speculation can bring about in forcing governments to abandon inappropriate economic policies.

2G analysis

The 2G models were directly motivated by the ERM crisis and consequently describe the crisis much better than the 1G models. The link between fundamentals and the attack was weak in the crisis, with the timing random. At this time, the fundamentals were in an indeterminate state in the language of the 2G models. The only thing that determines whether an attack takes place is the speculators' self-fulfilling expectations, and a small change in expectations can then trigger a crisis.

Choices

Member countries were left with a difficult choice. They could match the German interest rates, but that might not even be sufficient, because if the speculators perceived the government as being unable to withstand the pressure, the interest rate increase had to be very high. However, since that would have adversely affected the real economy, the governments were unwilling to maintain very high interest rates, except perhaps in the very short run. The speculators realised this, making the attack inevitable. The only way to prevent the attack was either to maintain a credible monetary policy, matching Germany, or to have sufficient reserves to repel any attack. With the benefit of hindsight, an attack on the ERM was inevitable.

The level of fundamentals played an important but indirect role. Countries with weak fundamentals, like high unemployment, low growth, weak banking systems or high short-term debt, were the first to be attacked. In the context of the Copeland model in

Figure 12.5, this means that those countries had a higher slope of the loss functions and, hence, a smaller defend area $\bar{e} - A$ and also a smaller indeterminate area A – B.

12.4.1 Implications for the euro

The problems of the ERM are eerily familiar in the current euro crisis. Then as now, the key problem was that different countries need different monetary policies. Germany, the Netherlands and other strong economies perform well, needing a strict monetary policy to keep inflationary expectations in check. Other countries, such as Portugal, Italy, Greece and Spain, face economic difficulties, their currency is overvalued and they need an accommodating monetary policy and a devaluation. The same problem applied then as now, with many of the same countries in the same roles.

There is one crucial difference between the ERM crisis and the ongoing euro crisis. In 1992, the countries with overvalued currencies could revalue or exit. They had an escape hatch. There is no such possibility now, and their difficulties therefore threaten the monetary arrangement and even a systemic crisis.

12.5 GLOBAL GAMES CURRENCY CRISIS MODEL

One of the main problems with the 2G models is the multiple equilibrium result, which comes from the assumption of common information among the speculators. Morris and Shin (1998, 1999) propose a different model for the same problem, called a *global games* model, resulting in a unique equilibrium.

The main innovation of their model is that speculators have only imperfect information about the state of the fundamentals. This means that the speculators are trying to guess what other speculators know, and want to attack the currency if and only if all other speculators also attack.

Setup

The government maintains a peg and gets net benefits from holding the peg:

$$f\left(\overset{+}{\theta}, \overset{-}{\ell}\right) = \theta - \ell$$

where θ, uniformly distributed, is the underlying strength of the economy – the *fundamentals*. There is a continuum of speculators, where only some number may choose to attack the currency. Denote $\ell \in [0, 1]$ as the proportion of speculators who attack.

The peg fails regardless of what the speculators do when $\theta \leq 0$, and always survives when $\theta \geq 1$. When $0 < \theta < 1$, the peg is 'ripe for attack', and is abandoned if and only if $\theta < \ell$, that is, if and only if a sufficiently large speculative attack is launched.

In the context of the Copeland model in Figure 12.5, $\theta < 1$ corresponds to the area $\bar{e} - A$, $\theta < 0$ to the area beyond B to the right, and the intermediate $0 < \theta < 1$ corresponds to A – B. Unlike the Copeland model, the decision to attack in the immediate area is explicitly linked to how many speculators attack, which is what provides a unique equilibrium solution.

Decision problem for speculators

The speculators can do one of two things: *attack* the currency or *refrain* from doing so. The payoff from refrain is zero and the cost of attack is c, whilst the profit from the peg collapsing is 1. The payoff from attacking, v, therefore depends on the state θ and the proportion ℓ who attack:

$$v(\theta, \ell) = \begin{cases} 1 - c & \text{if} \quad \ell > \theta \\ -c & \text{if} \quad \ell \leq \theta \end{cases}$$

The speculators face a coordination problem when $\theta \in (0,1)$. If one speculator attacks and nobody else does, the attack fails and she loses money. If, however, everybody attacks except the one speculator, she also loses money. The speculators, therefore, want to attack only when everybody else attacks.

The speculators have imperfect information and receive a noisy signal about the fundamentals:

$$x_i = \theta + s_i$$

where s_i is uniformly distributed over $[-\varepsilon, \varepsilon]$. The distribution over θ conditional on x_i is uniform over

$$[x_i - \varepsilon, x_i + \varepsilon]$$

The speculator makes a decision based on what she thinks everybody else will do. This means there is a unique equilibrium in switching strategies, that is switching from refraining to attacking. Denote the switching point as x^*.

Solution

The level of fundamentals where the peg will fail, θ^*, depends on the switching point x^*, which in turn depends on the failure point θ^*, solving $\theta = \ell$.

If all follow x^* – switching, ℓ is the proportion whose signal is below x^* when the true state is θ^*:

$$\ell = \frac{x^* - (\theta^* - \varepsilon)}{2\varepsilon}$$

So, $\theta^* = \ell$ if and only if

$$\theta^* = \frac{x^* - (\theta^* - \varepsilon)}{2\varepsilon}$$

At the switching point x^*, the speculator is indifferent between attacking and refraining:

$$\begin{aligned} & \Pr(\text{peg fails} \mid x^*)(1 - c) + \Pr(\text{peg stays} \mid x^*)(-c) \\ = \; & \Pr(\text{peg fails} \mid x^*) - c \\ = \; & 0 \end{aligned}$$

The peg fails if and only if $\theta < \theta^*$. So

$$\Pr(\theta < \theta^* | x^*) = c$$
$$\frac{\theta^* - (x^* - \varepsilon)}{2\varepsilon} = c$$

These are two equations in two unknowns – θ^* and x^*. Solving,

$$\theta^* = 1 - c$$
$$x^* = 1 - c - \varepsilon(2c - 1) \tag{12.9}$$

As $\varepsilon \to 0$, $x^* \to \theta^*$.

Verification of solution

We can verify that when $x_i < x^*$, the speculator wants to attack, and when $x_i > x^*$, she wants to refrain. Suppose $x_i < x^*$:

$$\begin{aligned}\Pr(\text{peg fails} \,|\, x_i) &= \frac{\theta^* - (x_i - \varepsilon)}{2\varepsilon} \\ &> \frac{\theta^* - (x^* - \varepsilon)}{2\varepsilon} \\ &= \Pr(\text{peg fails} \,|\, x^*)\end{aligned}$$

and conversely for when $x_i > x^*$. Switching strategy around x^* is equilibrium. In fact, it is the unique equilibrium.

Strategic and fundamental uncertainty

There is a distinction between *fundamental uncertainty* and *strategic uncertainty* that arises from the solution in (12.9). Fundamental uncertainty disappears as $\varepsilon \to 0$. However, there is still uniqueness of equilibrium (the difference between $\varepsilon = 0$ and the limit as $\varepsilon \to 0$).

This leaves the question of what happens to the strategic uncertainty as $\varepsilon \to 0$?. Suppose the signal is exactly x^*. What is the probability that proportion ℓ or less of the speculators attack the currency?

The answer to this question is important, since the fact that a speculator is indifferent between attacking and not attacking happens due to the uncertainty about the incidence of attack. The reasoning must take account of the uncertainty over the true state θ and the uncertainty over the incidence of attack.

There are two steps to answer the question. First, if the true state θ is higher than some benchmark level $\hat{\theta}$, then the proportion of speculators receiving a signal lower than x^* is ℓ or less. This benchmark state $\hat{\theta}$ satisfies:

$$\frac{x^* - (\theta - \varepsilon)}{2\varepsilon} = \ell$$

or

$$\hat{\theta} = x^* + \varepsilon - 2\varepsilon\ell$$

Second, the answer is given by the probability that the true state is higher than $\hat{\theta}$, conditional on signal x^*. This is

$$\begin{aligned}\frac{(x^* + \varepsilon) - \hat{\theta}}{2\varepsilon} \\ &= \frac{(x^* + \varepsilon) - (x^* + \varepsilon - 2\varepsilon\ell)}{2\varepsilon} \\ &= \ell\end{aligned}$$

Call the proportion of speculators who attack the *incidence of attack*. The cumulative distribution function over the incidence of attack is the identity function. Therefore, the density function over the incidence of attack is *uniform* over [0, 1].

How is this answer affected by the size of the noise ε? Not at all! As $\varepsilon \rightarrow 0$, the uncertainty concerning θ dissipates, but the strategic uncertainty is as severe as ever.

Analysis

A key difference between the global games model and the 2G model is that in the former there is only one equilibrium. Speculators have imperfect information about the state of the fundamentals, leading them to guess what other speculators would do, and launching a speculative attack if and only if they think other speculators will join them – strategic complementarity.

This means that the markets react suddenly, one moment supporting the peg, with an attack the next moment, causing the peg to fail. This means that a very small change in the speculators' beliefs can lead to a very large outcome.

At the same time, the likelihood of an attack is directly correlated with the state of the fundamentals. This leads to interesting results on the impact of transparency and disclosure.

When fundamentals are weak, greater public disclosure of the state of the fundamentals increases the probability of attack, since the strategic uncertainty dissipates, making coordinated attack easier. Fundamental uncertainty also dissipates, increasing the incentive for attack. This provides support for a policy of *constructive ambiguity*.

When fundamentals are strong, greater public disclosure of fundamentals decreases the probability of attack. Strategic uncertainty dissipates, causing a coordinated pull back from attack. Fundamental uncertainty also dissipates, further increasing incentives to refrain from attack.

There is an important difference between *ex ante* decisions on disclosures and opportunistic disclosures. In the former case, the authorities are providing regular updates on the economy outside a crisis state, while in the latter they are disclosing information opportunistically, with the explicit purpose of affecting the behaviour of speculators. This, of course, is noted and can backfire on the authorities.

12.6 SUMMARY

The focus in this chapter has been on formal models of currency crises. We started out with the earliest crisis model, the 1G model, where the authorities run an unsustainable monetary policy, using reserves to intervene to maintain a peg. Speculators know this, and launch an attack on the currency before the authorities run out of reserves. This model is quite simplistic and is not directly consistent with most crises, except that of Argentina.

In response, the 2G models were developed, where a key ingredient is the expectation of speculators of the intentions of the authorities. A main result is that we can get self-fulfilling crises. If speculators believe the authorities will maintain the peg they will not attack, but if they believe the authorities will not, an attack is forthcoming. Therefore, the speculators will be seen as correct, regardless of what they do.

These models can be used to analyse the ERM crisis of the early 1990s, where speculators attacked the British pound when they realised that the UK would not stay within the ERM target zone.

An important problem with the 2G is the presence of multiple equilibria. This is solved by the global games models, where speculators have imperfect information about the fundamentals and need to coordinate to launch an attack. Here, the markets can very suddenly transit from stability to crisis as a tiny bit of extra information affects expectations.

Questions for discussion

1 Consider the 1G model presented in the lecture notes. Recall the system of equations on which the model is built:

log money market equilibrium	$m_t - p_t = -\alpha i_t;$	(1)
log nominal money supply	$m_t = d_t + k_t;$	(2)
log domestic credit expansion	$d_t - d_{t-1} = \mu;$	(3)
log PPP	$p_t = p_t^* + \log e_t;$	(4)
log UIP	$i_t = i_t^* + E_{t-1}\Delta e_t.$	(5)

Now suppose the government imposes permanent capital controls, we can capture this by replacing (12.5) by:

$$i_t = (1 - \theta)(i_t^* + E_{t-1}\Delta e_t)$$

where θ is the tax rate on profits.

(a) Following the same steps as in the chapter, derive the timing of the speculative attack T

(b) How does your answer differ from the standard case in the chapter? Explain.

2 Was the currency board a mistake for Argentina?

3 Do you think the first-generation models accurately capture speculative attacks?

4 Recall the 2G model by Copeland. At the centre of the model is the loss function of the government

$$\mathcal{L} = \{\psi(\hat{e} - \bar{e}) + \eta E(\Delta e)\}^2 + C(\Delta e) \quad \psi, \eta > 0, \hat{e} > \bar{e} \qquad (6)$$

where $C(\Delta e)$ is an indicator function that can take only one of two values:

$$C(\Delta e) = \begin{cases} 0 & \text{for } \Delta e = 0 \\ Q & \text{for } \Delta e > 0 \end{cases}$$

For simplicity assume throughout this question that the fixed exchange rate is set at $\bar{e} = 0$, and that if the government devalues, it will directly move to the desired exchange rate, so that $E(\Delta e) = (\hat{e} - \bar{e})$.

(a) Assuming that the government has a reputation of defending the exchange rate, and speculators expect that it will stick to that policy in the future, what level of the desired exchange rate, $\hat{e}$, would induce the government to give up the peg and devalue? Derive your results analytically and mathematically and show them in a graph.

(b) Now the government appoints a new president of the central bank who has a reputation of being 'soft' on the exchange rate commitment. Now speculators expect that a devaluation is probable. What level of the desired exchange rate, $\hat{e}$, would induce the government now to give up the peg? Again, derive your results analytically and mathematically and plot them.

(c) Assuming now that speculators have not finally decided whether the appointment of the new central bank president weakens the exchange rate commitment,
   (i) For what levels of $\hat{e}$ does the government definitely devalue?
   (ii) For what levels of $\hat{e}$ does the government definitely defend?
   (iii) What happens in between?
   (iv) What role do fundamentals play?

(d) You can now assume that $\psi = 2$, $\eta = 3$ and $Q = 64$
   (i) For what levels of $\hat{e}$ does the government definitely devalue?
   (ii) For what levels of $\hat{e}$ does the government definitely defend?
   (iii) Show how good fundamentals give the government more leverage in defending the exchange rate.

5 Was the speculative attack on some European currencies in the early 1990s positive or negative for the economies of the affected countries?

6 Why does the global games model only have one equilibrium while the 2G model has two?

7 Explain the role of strategic complementarities in how speculators all agree on whether to attack or refrain.

References

BBC (2012a). Argentina ship in Ghana seized over loans default. www.bbc.co.uk/news/world-africa-19827562.

Copeland, L. (2000). *Exchange Rates and International Finance*. Prentice Hall.

Flood, R. P. and Garber, P. M. (1984). Collapsing exchange rate regimes: some linear examples. *J. Int. Econ.*, 17: 223–34.

Krugman, P. (1979). A model of balance-of-payments crises. *J. Money Credit Banking*, 11(3): 311–25.

Morris, S. and Shin, H. S. (1998). Unique equilibrium in a model of self-fulfilling currency attacks. *Amer. Econ. Rev.*, 88: 587–97.

Morris, S. and Shin, H. S. (1999). Risk management with interdependent choice. *Oxford Review of Economic Policy*, 15: 52–62, reprinted in *Bank of England Financial Stability Review*, 7, 141–50. www.bankofengland.co.uk/fsr/fsr07art5.pdf.

Mussa, M. (2002). *Argentina and the Fund: from Triumph to Tragedy*. Institute for International Economics, Washington DC.

Obstfeld, M. (1996). Models of currency crises with self-fulfilling features. *Eur. Econ. Rev.*, 40(3–5): 1037–1047.

Obstfeld, M. and Rogoff, K. (1996). *Foundations of International Macroeconomics*. MIT Press.

13 FINANCIAL REGULATIONS

Compared to other segments of the economy, financial institutions are special. Suppose a firm making chocolate goes bust: the shareholders and employees suffer, but competing chocolate firms will benefit. There is no significant damage to the economy, and such developments may even be positive, such as argued by Joseph Schumpeter in his 1942 notion of creative destruction.

Financial institutions are different. The failure of a single bank can have catastrophic consequences as it may induce domino-style defaults, culminating in a systemic failure. These *negative externalities* justify financial regulations aiming at reducing the incidence of banking crises and the damage caused by crises.

Financial institutions view this differently. They tend to find regulations to be a costly nuisance. This does not mean they oppose regulation. On the contrary, they directly benefit from regulations, not least because they act as a barrier to entry, reducing competition and increasing rent. Regulations also act as a barrier to exit, because financial institutions subject to regulations are likely to be seen as less risky than otherwise, and when in difficulty may receive bailouts.

While regulations do mitigate the worst impacts of the externalities arising from financial sector risk-taking, they can also impose significant costs on society, especially when poorly conceived. These costs could easily exceed the immediate benefits from the reduction of the externalities. This might happen when banks have to excessively curtail risk-taking, adversely affecting the sensitive small and medium-sized enterprise (SME) sector. Because SMEs are often the main creator of new jobs, it is important they receive funding, but as they are risky, financial institutions need to be able to take risk in order to fund the SMEs. This causes a conflict for supervisors because they cannot simultaneously curtail risky banking activities and want banks to participate in economic recovery.

Financial regulations may also have other less visible costs. They may just encourage financial institutions to continue the same risky activities out of sight – perhaps creating a *shadow banking system* – making it even harder for the authorities to understand and regulate banking activities. Regulations may also encourage financial institutions to move activities to other jurisdictions, depriving the domestic economy from some of the benefits banks bring.

Designing and implementing financial regulations is difficult. They are essential for the protection of society, but all too frequently fail, not providing protection, and even perversely increasing systemic risk.

Definition 13.1 Regulation and supervision The term regulation encompasses two different terms in common parlance: the laws passed by the nation's parliament, and the specific implementations of those laws, regulations, designed by a regulatory agency.

The term supervision refers to the enforcement of regulations. The term supervisor refers either to an individual working in banking supervision, or more generally to the supervisory agency.

The supervisory agency and the regulatory agency can be the same or distinct.

Links to other chapters

This chapter directly relates to Chapter 3 (endogenous risk) and Chapter 7 (banking crises). We discuss the failure of regulations prior to the crises from 2007, and the post-crisis reforms in Chapter 16 (failures in risk management and regulations) and Chapter 18 (ongoing developments in financial regulation).

Key concepts

- Motivation for financial regulations
- Macro-prudential and micro-prudential policies
- Bank capital and capital ratios
- Unintended consequences of regulations
- Basel Committee for Banking Supervision (BCBS)
- Basel I and Basel II

Readings for this chapter

While a number of books address banking regulation, Dewatripont and Tirole (1994) stands out. Most banking regulations derive from the activities of the BCBS, whose history was written by Goodhart (2011). Most information about current financial regulations is provided on the web pages of the regulatory authorities, for the BCBS www.bis.org/bcbs, and for the FSA in the UK www.fsa.gov.uk. For an early criticism of the Basel Accords, see Danielsson *et al.* (2001).

Notation specific to this chapter

A	Assets
C	Capital
p	Probability
T_1, T_2	Tier 1 and Tier 2
w	Risk weight
α	Minimum regulatory capital ratio

13.1 BANKING REGULATIONS

Banking has traditionally been the most regulated segment of the economy. The history of the great financial centres in Europe in the thirteenth and fourteenth centuries as told by Kohn (1999) provides some guidance. At the time, the places to be if one wanted to do finance were Genoa, Florence, Venice, Bruges and Barcelona. Of those, one of the most innovative was Barcelona, establishing the principle that banks had to have substantial capital, and had to pay cash within 24 hours of demand. If banks failed, their owners got into serious trouble, both with the Almighty and with city authorities. The punishments could be severe. The banker Francesch Castello was beheaded in front of his bank in 1360, and a failed banker was permanently prohibited from opening another bank.

Reasons for regulating banks

There are several reasons why it is considered necessary to regulate banks. Left to their own devices, banks have a tendency to over-extend themselves, take too much risk and fail. Because efficient and uninterrupted banking services are essential for any economy, bank failures can impose costs on society far exceeding the private costs of the banks' owners, employees and counterparties.

This means that banking entails significant *externalities* where the private incentives of bankers are not aligned with that of society. For bank employees, working with other people's money, there is little *downside*, at worst dismissal, but they can enjoy a significant *upside* in terms of high salaries and bonuses. This means that banks have an incentive to take more risks than are desired by either their clients, their shareholders or society at large. It is this externality that has often been the main motivation for regulating banks.

Banks also have a significant advantage over their clients, especially retail clients. Banks sell sophisticated financial products to clients who have a very rudimentary knowledge of finance, perhaps not even understanding basic percentages or present-value calculations. It is quite easy for a bank to take advantage of clients and it is felt that this merits regulation. The frequent mis-selling scandals in the United Kingdom (UK), most recently with payment protection, indicate that such concerns are justified.

This advantage of sophistication can also extend to otherwise sophisticated corporate and public sector clients. History is replete with examples of large entities suffering large losses from buying complex financial products they did not understand. For example, the recent bankruptcy of the city of Birmingham in the United States (US) is directly attributed to its purchase of risky financial products the city's managers did not seem to understand.

Because of the complexity of bank products, and the high costs of monitoring bank performance, it is beyond anybody, except experts, to understand the underlying risks. Certainly, for retail clients this is quite infeasible. It is more efficient for a dedicated government agency to monitor financial institutions on the behalf of bank clients.

Laissez-faire

A frequently expressed view on banking regulation is *laissez-faire*. A bank should be left alone to prosper and fail like any other private enterprise; the government should exercise minimum regulations and certainly not protect banks in times of failure.

This has been the prevailing official policy at many times in history, for example, in the nineteenth and early twentieth centuries. Some forms of this view also affected banking policy prior to the crisis starting in 2007. However, such a *laissez-faire* approach to banking is not credible.

The reason is the externalities arising from bank failures. When the authorities are faced with large losses being imposed on society as a result of a banking crisis, they have no choice but to act because the political pressure on the government becomes unbearable. If it refuses to act, the government faces punishment by the voters. Just three examples discussed elsewhere in this book are the crises of 1866 in the UK, of 1907 in the US, and of Argentina in the early 1990s. Deciding not to regulate the financial sector is not a credible option for the authorities. Being forced to intervene in times of crisis without adequate preparation is a worst-case outcome. It is better for the authorities to regulate the financial sector and be prepared for the eventual crisis.

Macro- and micro-prudential regulations

The objectives and scope of financial regulations range from preventing or coping with a systemic crisis to protecting small retail clients – the widows and orphans, as they often called. It is now common to refer to those two separately as *macro-prudential* and *micro-prudential* regulations, in the terminology of Andrew Crockett in 2000, then the General Manager of the Bank for International Settlements (BIS).

Macro-prudential refers to regulations and policies designed to protect the financial system in its entirety. This may mean something as extreme as coping with a systemic crisis or more commonly the setting of minimum bank capital.

By contrast, micro-prudential regulations are concerned with protecting the individual small clients of financial institutions. This may include fraud prevention, rules on what information to provide to savers or the design of mortgage contracts.

Micro- and macro-prudential regulations are quite different from each other, in both motivation and implementation. The supervisors working on either objective often work in distinct parts of the same agency or might even belong to different organisations. This means that the intersection between macro- and micro-prudential supervisors is often limited.

In some cases the objectives of both coincide, but direct conflict is not uncommon. For example, a micro-prudential regulator may prefer to prevent an individual financial institution from failing in order to protect its clients, whilst the macro-prudential regulator would want to see it fail so that moral hazard is minimised.

Therefore, it is an open question whether macro-prudential and micro-prudential regulators should work for the same agency. The most recent approach in the UK is to hive the macro-prudential off to the BoE, leaving the micro-prudential with the Financial Services Authority (FSA). In the European Union (EU), micro-prudential regulations are by and large national concerns, while macro-prudential regulations are increasingly the domain of the EU. In the US, most micro-prudential regulations are in the hands of the individual states, while macro-prudential regulations are mostly in federal hands.

Implementing macro-prudential regulations

There are various different ways the authorities can implement macro-prudential regulations. They may restrict or prevent certain activities, control day-to-day risk-taking or resolve a crisis once it is underway.

Activity restrictions is where the authorities limit what financial institutions can do. A well-known example is the *Glass–Steagall* Act in the US in 1933 where banks were split into investment banks and commercial banks. More generally, banks are often restricted by how much they can lend to any individual borrower, perhaps 10% of the bank's overall assets.

Some regulations aim to control *day-to-day risk* in financial institutions. The Basel Accords discussed below are a typical example of this. Here the objective is to ensure that a financial institution does not behave in an excessively risky way.

Finally, macro-prudential activities also relate to the *resolution of crises*. This may take the form of LOLR, direct bailouts or even the taking over of financial institutions by the government. The authorities therefore need to be prepared, have a detailed understanding of the financial system and its risks and even require *living wills*.

13.1.1 Challenges in banking regulations

The financial system is very complex, and authorities face many challenges in regulating and supervising finance. Poor regulations can impose unnecessary costs, create perverse incentives, reduce transparency and even increase risk.

Endogenous risk

Some prudential regulations, especially those addressing risk-taking, can directly increase *endogenous risk*. This happens exactly because the regulations aim at preventing excessive risk-taking by banks, thereby preventing large losses or even bankruptcies. This is sometimes referred to as *smoothing the road*. Reducing excessive risk is a laudable goal but can be difficult to implement in practice, and regulations aiming at containing risk taking may have the perverse consequence of actually increasing risk. There are several reasons why this may happen.

Risk is very hard to measure. From a statistical point of view, it involves volatility clusters, fat tails and non-linear dependence, which means that the basic statistical problem of risk forecasting is quite hard. Often, these risk forecasts are then input into complicated models, where, because of non-linearities, risk can be amplified in a way that is hard to detect. In addition, banks have an incentive to under-report risk, and even worse, some employees of banks – the traders – have even stronger incentives to under-report risk.

If the road is smooth, and risk is perceived as low, it creates incentives to take more risk. Because after all, if everything is safe, what is wrong with a little bit more risk? The problem is that such risk-taking is not immediately visible but is seen only much later. For example, it was decisions taken in the supposedly low-risk environment between 2003 and 2007 that created the conditions for the subsequent crisis. From a statistical point of view, it is impossible to detect such hidden build-up of risk.

Smoothing the road is pro-cyclical, encouraging banks to take too much risk when things are good and too little risk when things are bad.

Incentives of supervisors

A particular problem arises because of the incentives of banking supervisors. When the banking system is functioning well without headline failures, the supervisors are unlikely to get much credit whilst bankers and even politicians complain about excessive regulatory burdens on this profitable economic activity. If then a big failure occurs, the head of the supervisory agency may face acrimonious hearings in the country's parliament and be pilloried in the press. After all, the supervisor had all the information about the bank but did not act on it to prevent failure.

There is a danger that the incentives of supervisors are to prevent failure at all costs and, hence, for the supervisor to become too risk-averse. This means that the incentive problem of the supervisor is inverse to that of the banker.

It is therefore necessary to have some mechanisms in place to prevent excessive supervisory risk aversion. One way to do so is by performing cost–benefit analysis on regulations. Unfortunately, that is quite difficult to do in practice.

This problem leads to a particular form of pro-cyclicality. During upswings, regulations become increasingly lax, amplifying the boom, and after a crisis they become excessively strict, magnifying the downturn. There are clear signs of this in the current cycle.

'Tick-the-box' and legal approaches

After the Icelandic banking system collapsed in October 2008, the head of that country's banking supervisor was asked in a TV interview what was the purpose of the supervisor. He replied 'to ensure the banks don't break the law'. This answer is problematic, because it is important to make a distinction between the spirit and the letter of the law. The objective of banking regulations is not to ensure banks do not break the law, rather that they do not behave in a way that harms society, and help in economic development.

This means that there is a danger of an excessively legalistic or formulaic approach to banking regulations, often referred to as *tick-the-box regulations*. In the case of the Icelandic crisis, as documented by its parliamentary Special Investigation Commission (SIC) report, when some banks wanted to increase their equity, bank A would sell new equity to bank B, and then do a *contract for difference*, that is hedge the exposure of bank B. Then, bank B would do exactly the same transaction with bank A. From a strict tick-the-box legal point of view, it looked as if both banks had significantly increased their equity, with the end result that the banks' capital ratios looked strong. However, in practice, this bank capital was purely illusionary, and while legal, did not afford any protection. Even worse, it gave the appearance of protection, encouraging market participants to engage with these banks *as if* they were safe. We see one manifestation of this problem in Figure 16.4 in Chapter 16.

This is an example of the conflict between principle-based regulations and tick-the-box-based regulations. The latter are much easier to implement and often end up being the default approach. Different agencies often have very differing views on this topic. For example, in the US, the Securities and Exchange Commission (SEC) takes a legal approach to regulation, whilst the Federal Reserve System (Fed) prefers a more principle-based approach. In the ongoing crisis, the SEC has seen responsibilities transferred to the Fed, because the latter has been seen as a more effective agency.

Transfer of responsibility to government

Any regulation of banks transfers responsibility for the banking system to the authorities. The supervisors get confidential information about bank activities and powers to prevent illegitimate activities. This implies that if banks fail, the authorities are partly to blame, which may mean that the authorities are compelled to use taxpayers' money to sort out the crisis.

The banks, of course, fully know this and, therefore, are incentivised to behave in a way that internalises the possibility of sharing the burden with the government. In other words, because banks are supervised, they have an incentive to take on more risk than otherwise.

This means that it is important to consider the secondary impact of regulations. It is not enough to identify a particular problem and remedy that with regulations. Rather, all the secondary consequences, such as how the proposed regulations change bank behaviour and the impact on the relationship between the government and the banking system, need to be considered.

Perverse consequences of regulation

Financial regulations change the behaviour of banks, usually in a positive way; risk is reduced and the system becomes more stable. In some perverse cases, the outcome can be the opposite. This may happen because regulations drive risky activities under the radar. The banks continue as before, but with less oversight. An example of this is *shadow banking*.

Often, the banks' avoidance behaviour takes the form of *financial innovation*, where new and more complex financial instruments are created in response to regulation. Such instruments may be beneficial but just as easily could increase complexity without any discernible benefit, creating a form of *dead weight loss*. A clear example of this is capital structure optimisation. This may in turn lead to additional regulations, causing a ratcheting effect between regulation and bank activity, as seen in Figure 13.1.

Finally, regulations may move profitable and risky activities to other jurisdictions, leaving the country implementing the regulations worse off.

Two early examples of the unintended consequences of financial regulations is regulation Q in the US and the eurodollar market. A more recent case is the emergence of *shadow banking*.

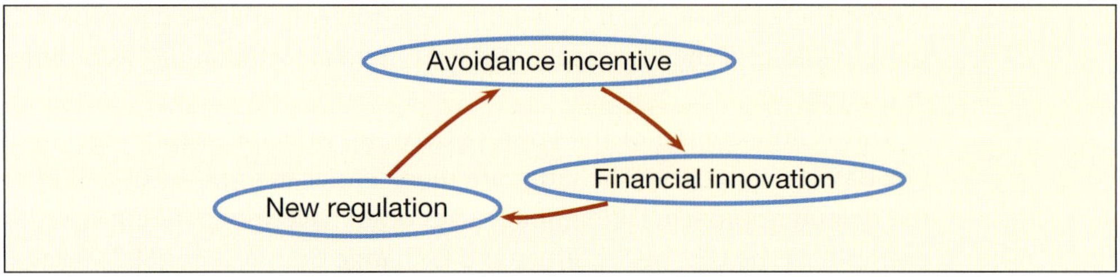

Figure 13.1 The circle of financial innovation and regulation

EXAMPLE 13.1 Regulation Q

Regulation Q was a US regulation limiting the interest rates that banks could pay on deposits. This created incentives to create a parallel banking system, money market mutual accounts, where market interest rates could be paid.

EXAMPLE 13.2 Eurodollar market

The Eurodollar market first came into being in the 1950s when the Soviet Union's oil revenue – all in US dollars – was being deposited outside the US in fear of being frozen by US regulators. This resulted in a vast offshore pool of dollars outside the control of US authorities, primarily held in Europe, hence, the term Eurodollar. This was a major contribution to London becoming a world-leading financial centre.

Regulatory capture

In an ideal world, the supervisors are concerned only with the safety and soundness of the banking system. In practice, there are often many other reasons why the government chooses to regulate the banking system. It may have altruistic ulterior motives, such as requiring banks to provide unprofitable banking services to disadvantaged sectors of society, or the government may want to have national champions. Bank lobbying is also quite strong and aims at creating banking regulations that favour the incumbents, discouraging entry into the banking system and providing protection for banks' profits and even the odd bailout.

In this case, banking supervisors may end up being *captured* by banks. This means that the supervisory agency no longer works for society; instead, in effect, it works in the interest of the banks. Such regulatory capture can happen for many reasons, for example, when banks recruit staff out of supervisory agencies at vastly higher salaries, which might give the staff an incentive to behave in a way that encourages private-sector recruitment. In other cases, the banks may bypass the supervisor by going directly to the politicians, who after all are in charge of the supervisor. Supervisory agencies are often accused of regulatory capture, but this can be hard to verify. For example, it is often claimed the SEC has been captured, but that case demonstrates the difficulty in distinguishing between deliberate laxness in enforcement, incompetence or regulatory capture. A better example was the supervisor for the S&Ls, as we discussed in Section 7.5.2.

Resource problems

Supervisory agencies have a serious resource problem compared to the banks they are supervising. The government is likely to pay much less than the banks and have fewer staff members, meaning the authorities can be seriously outgunned when dealing with the banks. Any well-performing supervisor is subject to poaching from the private sector, and the authorities often have real difficulty holding onto staff.

Summary

The challenges in banking supervision are indicative of how hard the problem is. It is not, and will not be, possible to create anything resembling a perfect regulatory structure; instead, we have to do our best and have multiple safeguards in place so we can simultaneously protect society and avoid excessive risk aversion.

Because each bit of regulation changes behaviour, we may need further regulation to address the newly created problem, and so forth. While such cycles are inevitable, they are also a sign of poor regulatory design. Regulations often have unforeseen consequences, and we should consider the regulation of the financial system holistically, taking into account the entire body of regulations and the financial system and not looking at individual components in isolation. That is not easy. Regulators are under constant demand from lobbyists, assorted pundits and politicians, generally demanding action on the specific point, disregarding the need for an integrated approach to regulations.

13.2 BANK CAPITAL

A direct way to improve the resilience of the banking system is bank *capital*, consisting of certain financial instruments, most importantly equity but also other instruments considered to be like equity. Bank capital has two main purposes:

1. To protect a bank against *unexpected* losses. After all, if the losses are expected, the bank should just provide for them or write the losses down. The higher the capital, the more protection the bank has and the less likely it is that the bank fails.
2. To restrict how much risk a bank can take by limiting leverage. Higher capital relative to assets lowers leverage and risk.

Equity

Consider a simplified balance sheet of a bank.

Assets	Liabilities
Assets (loans)	Liabilities (deposits) Equity

The bank has assets (loans), as well as liabilities (deposits). The difference between these two is net worth or *equity*:

$$\text{equity} = \text{assets} - \text{liabilities} \tag{13.1}$$

Equity is the amount of money the owners have invested in the bank, and has no direct connection with the market value of a bank.

We illustrate the calculation of bank equity by Example 13.3.

EXAMPLE 13.3 Equity

A bank started five years ago. Assuming the original stock price was 1000, and there are no dividends or taxes, profits in years 1, 2, 3 and 5 were 100 in each year, while the loss in year 4 was 250. In this case the shareholders' equity is

$$1000 + 100 + 100 + 100 + 100 - 250$$

There are several different types of equity, for example tangible equity which is cash raised from shareholders or retained through earnings. Those different types of equity are a function of the underlying accounting rules, local traditions and national law.

Capital

The concept of capital is broader than that of equity and includes a range of instruments, so that some of a bank's liabilities may be a part of its capital:

$$\text{capital} \geq \text{assets} - \text{liabilities}$$

It is useful to start with a simple balance sheet of a bank. Suppose we have two categories of assets, a riskless asset, perhaps a government bond, denoted by A_1 and risky corporate loans denoted by A_2. Then the total assets of the bank are $A = A_1 + A_2$. Capital is denoted by C.

The ratio of capital to assets is called the capital adequacy ratio (CAR).

Assets	Liabilities
Low-risk assets (A_1) High-risk assets (A_2)	Capital (C) Non-capital liabilities

Definition 13.2 Capital adequacy ratio

$$\text{CAR} = \frac{C}{A} \geq \alpha$$

where α is the minimum CAR specified in banking regulations.

In many cases, the capital ratio is risk-sensitive, so that low-risk assets contribute less to the denominator than high-risk assets. In this case, the CAR might become

$$\text{CAR} = \frac{C}{w_1 A_1 + w_2 A_2} \geq \alpha, \quad w_1 < w_2 \tag{13.2}$$

where w_1 and w_2 are risk weights.

Capital instruments

The most basic form of capital is (common) equity, but certain liabilities, known as *capital instruments*, can also be a part of capital. These include preference shares, subordinated debt, long-term bonds and *hybrid instruments* which are bonds that can be converted into equity.

Criteria for capital

Not all capital instruments are created equal, and the more equity-like an instrument is, the better protection it provides. Capital instruments are judged by four different criteria. First, they need to absorb losses on a going-concern basis, allowing an issuer to avoid liquidation in times of stress. Second, they need to be relatively permanent so that they provide a buffer against losses for an extended period of time. Third, they have to allow for sufficient freedom of action, or discretion over the amount and timing of payments made on the instrument, and there should be few, if any, covenants restricting the issuer's freedom of action. Finally, the instruments need to afford protection to general creditors in case a bank defaults.

13.2.1 Pro-cyclicality

An important problem with banking and capital is *pro-cyclicality*.

Definition 13.3 Pro-cyclicality A term that refers to how some economic quantity relates positively to economic fluctuations. It is the opposite of countercyclicality. See Figure 13.2 below for an example.

When the economy is doing well, banks have ample funds which they seek to lend out, but often find that high-quality borrowers have all the credit they need. Banks therefore start lending to increasingly low-quality borrowers, often in the real-estate sector, creating a real-estate bubble. When eventually the bubble bursts and the economy takes a turn for the worse, banks find themselves faced with large amounts of defaults and sharply curtail lending, often referred to as a *credit crunch*. This makes asset prices drop even further. This means that bank lending amplifies the business cycle and is hence pro-cyclical.

Pro-cyclicality and capital regulations

The presence of bank capital regulations amplifies this inherent pro-cyclicality in banking. When times are good, asset values are high, the CAR is high and the bank seems to employ a low degree of leverage.

EXAMPLE 13.4 Worked example

Start with the definition of equity from Equation (13.1) and assume equity = \$12 and assets = \$100. Suppose the authorities impose a minimum CAR of $\alpha = 8\%$. The CAR is then

$$\frac{\$12}{\$100} = 12\% > \alpha \qquad (13.3)$$

In this case, the bank is comfortably exceeding the regulatory CAR and employing leverage of

$$\frac{\$100}{\$12} = 8.3$$

If the economy takes a turn for the worse and the bank suffers losses of 3% of its assets, that is \$3, the CAR becomes

$$\frac{\$12 - \$3}{\$100 - \$3} = 9.3\% > \alpha \tag{13.4}$$

and the bank is closer to violating its regulatory constraint. Now the leverage has increased to 10.7.

Since the bank prefers to maintain a buffer above the minimum 8%, it will do what it can to increase its CAR, and the most obvious way to do so is to reduce leverage and sell off some of its more risky assets.

This means that capital constraints increase the pro-cyclicality of bank capital and bank leverage. For example, before 2007 banks were excessively free with their lending, but after the crises started, they sharply curtailed lending, especially to the politically sensitive SME sector.

Risk sensitivity

The problem of pro-cyclicality is made worse if the capital ratio is risk sensitive because the same asset would have lower weights at the top of the cycle than at the bottom of the cycle, amplifying the amplitude. This can be seen in Figure 13.2.

This can be seen clearly from the CAR in (13.2) and Example 13.4. Suppose A_2 represents high-risk real-estate lending. At the top of the cycle most signs point to the risk in real estate being low, and hence w_2 will be low, keeping the CAR high. If the bubble then bursts, real estate becomes more risky and w_2 increases sharply, causing the CAR to fall. The impact can be seen Example 13.5.

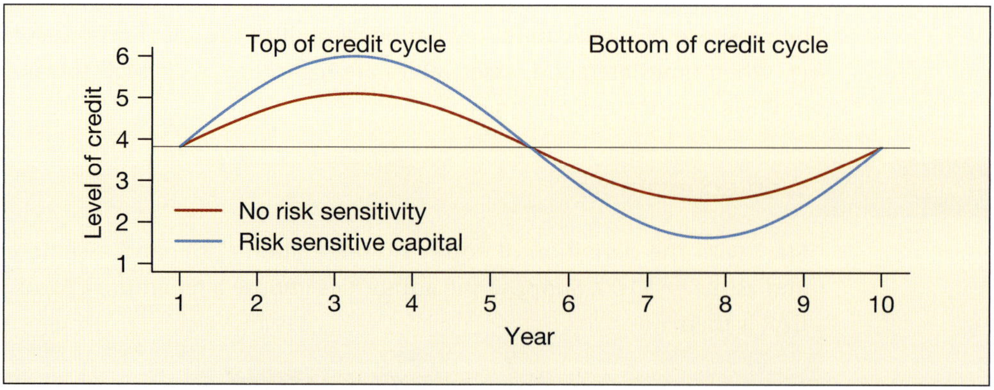

Figure 13.2 Credit cycle

EXAMPLE 13.5 Continuing from Example 13.4

Suppose before the shock the risk weight is 1, so $w = 1$. (13.3) therefore becomes

$$\frac{\$12}{w \times \$100} = \frac{\$12}{\$100} = 12\% > \alpha$$

Because of the shock, the risk weight increases to $w = 1.5$, and (13.4) becomes

$$\frac{\$12 - \$3}{w(\$100 - \$3)} = \frac{\$12 - \$3}{1.5(\$100 - \$3)} = 6.1\% < \alpha$$

Because of the risk sensitivity, the CAR fell further, and the bank is no longer meeting its regulatory constraint, causing it either to be shut down by the authorities or to receive a bailout.

13.2.2 Issues with capital

Traditionally, capital levels were quite high, often around 40% in the nineteenth century, if measured by shareholders' equity. Over time, this number has fallen dramatically as shown in Figure 13.3, using data from Alessandri and Haldane (2009), which shows the capital ratios of banks in the UK and the US from 1880 until recently.

Cliff effects

The presence of a rigid capital ratio may have unexpected adverse consequences. If a bank's capital ratio falls below the minimum specified by banking regulators, currently 8%, the bank most likely would be shut down, and as it gets closer to the 8% it draws increasing unwanted scrutiny from the authorities. For this reason banks prefer to keep a significant buffer above the minimum, generally around 12–13% before the crises from 2007.

Suppose a bank finds its capital ratio falling, needing to improve its CAR. The bank can increase capital by selling equity or other capital instruments on the financial markets. Because the bank is likely to be in this situation only in times of difficulty, this option is likely to be quite costly, and if it coincides with a financial crisis, it may be impossible.

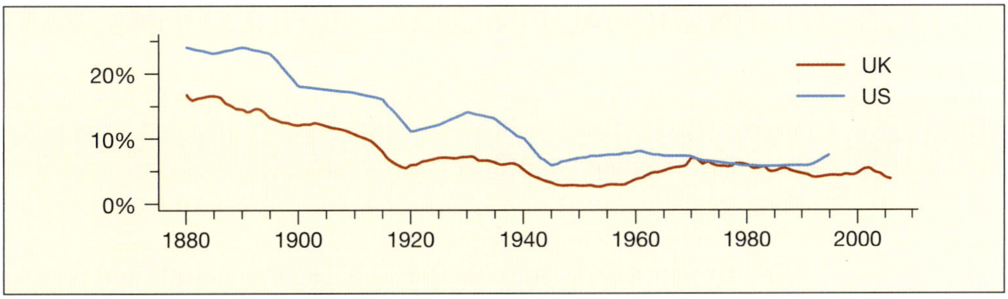

Figure 13.3 Core bank capital ratios in the US and UK

Data source: Chart 2 in Alessandri and Haldane (2009)

The bank can also reduce the amount of assets held or the riskiness of its portfolio by selling risky assets and refusing to provide new loans. This process is termed *deleveraging*. If only one bank is in difficulty, with the financial system generally in good shape, such deleveraging is not all that problematic. However, if it happens during crises the situation is rather different.

In this case, a general sell-off of risky assets throughout the financial system is likely to be taking place. This means that the price of risky assets is likely to fall precipitously, significantly below their fundamental values, and the bank may get only firesale prices. The bank may also refuse to provide new loans and to roll over existing loans, perhaps leading to a credit crunch. Those borrowers most likely to be affected are SMEs. This will lead to further economic slowdown.

Both actions exacerbate the crisis, and cause an endogenous risk of vicious feedback between worsening economic conditions and bank difficulties. This shows how fixed capital ratios can by themselves increase systemic risk.

How capital is used

In designing capital regulations, the authorities are left with the difficult question of whether a minimum CAR has to be maintained at all times, or can be reduced in times of difficulty. If capital cannot be allowed to fall below the minimum in any circumstances, it does not afford protection.

This has been aptly demonstrated by Goodhart's metaphor (Goodhart, 2009, chapter 8) of a weary traveller arriving by train to an unknown town late at night. Seeing one taxi outside the train station, the traveller asks the driver to take her to her hotel. The driver responds that he cannot do so, and points to a sign on the wall saying 'local regulations require that at least one taxi be outside the station at all times'.

The issue of drawing down protective buffers comes up in every crisis. For example, in their book on the 1907 crisis, Bruner and Carr (2007) relate the following anecdote. A banker complained to John Pierpont Morgan, of the eponymous bank, about his reserves falling to 20%. Morgan replied 'you ought to be ashamed of yourself. Your reserve ought to be down to 18% or 20%. What is a reserve for if not to be used in times like these?'

As we see below, the existing capital standards do not allow for relaxation of the CAR, whilst the proposals for the next version allow for more flexible capital buffers.

13.3 INTERNATIONAL FINANCIAL REGULATIONS: BASEL

Historically, banks have operated mostly within a single nation state, with multinational banks few and far between. This was enshrined in the Bretton Woods era when banks were heavily regulated and their international activities discouraged. This meant that banking regulations were mostly domestic, with little need for international coordination in either regulation or supervision.

Over the past few decades, this has changed significantly and banking is now a truly international business. When the financial system started opening up, the deficiencies of a purely domestic approach to financial regulation became apparent, and two bank failures in particular, those of Bankhaus Herstatt in 1974 and Banco Ambrosiano in 1982, served as a wake-up call to the authorities, making it clear that if we want to have regulations in the first place, they need to be international. This means that the *home regulator*, where the bank has its headquarters, needs to have oversight of its banks' activities everywhere in the world, and the *host regulators*, countries where the bank operates, need to cooperate actively with the home regulator and other host regulators.

Supervise everywhere

There are two main reasons why regulation needs to be international. First, there have been well-documented cases where a financial institution was regulated in one country but misbehaved in another. This happened because the home supervisor was responsible only for activities at home, while the host supervisors assumed the home supervisor was in charge, and at the same time the different national supervisors did not communicate. This suggests that it is necessary to have international regulations to ensure banks are regulated wherever they operate, with supervisors cooperating on enforcement.

Regulatory arbitrage

The second problem arises if financial regulations and supervision are not harmonised across jurisdictions, and financial institutions can shop for the jurisdictions with the most lax regulations or supervision, a process called *regulatory arbitrage*. In the best case, this leads to the most lax environment to be used, but in a worst case, countries may compete by relaxing financial regulations in order to attract multinational banks.

13.3.1 The Basel Committee

As policymakers came to recognise the challenges arising from international banking, the governments of the G-10 countries in the late 1960s and early 1970s[1] set up the *Basel Committee on Banking Supervision (BCBS)* as a new international organisation tasked with designing international banking regulations. It is hosted at the Bank for International Settlement (BIS), whose head office is in Basel, Switzerland, hence the name. More recently membership has been extended.[2] For an in-depth study of the BCBS see Goodhart (2011).

Countries are represented by their central bank and also by the authority with formal responsibility for the prudential supervision of banking businesses. Luxembourg has only one member.

The Committee does not possess any formal supranational supervisory authority. Rather, it formulates broad supervisory standards and guidelines and recommends statements of best practice in the expectation that individual authorities will take steps to implement them through detailed arrangements.

[1]Belgium, Canada, France, Italy, Japan, Germany, Sweden, the Netherlands, the UK and the US, as well as Luxembourg. Spain later became a member.

[2]To include Argentina, Australia, Brazil, China, Hong Kong SAR, India, Indonesia, South Korea, Mexico, Russia, Saudi Arabia, Singapore, South Africa, Sweden, Switzerland and Turkey.

At times, the Committee uses this common understanding to develop guidelines and supervisory standards in areas where they are considered desirable. In this regard, the Committee is best known for the *Concordat* and the *Basel Accords*.

One important objective of the Committee's work has been to close gaps in international supervisory coverage in pursuit of two basic principles: that no foreign banking establishment should escape supervision; and that supervision should be adequate. The Concordat, originally published in 1975 (in response to the Bankhaus Herstatt crisis), set down the principles for sharing supervisory responsibility for banks' foreign branches, subsidiaries and joint ventures between host and home supervisory authorities. A major review was made in 1983 following the failure of Banco Ambrosiano.

The most important part of the Committee's work is the Basel capital accords, a set of internationally harmonised rules for determining the adequacy of the capital of internationally active banks. The first Basel Accords, now referred to as Basel I, were proposed in 1988 and implemented in 1992, while their successor, Basel II, was proposed in the late 1990s and at least partially implemented from 2008. The Committee has already proposed the next iteration, Basel III.

13.3.2 Basel I

A key motivation for Basel I was events in the early 1980s when banks competed vigorously in making corporate loans. At the time, bank capital ratios of major banks in Europe and the US were perhaps 8–10%, while Japanese banks operated with lower bank capital and saw major gains in market share. This led to competitive pressures to lower bank capital in Europe and the US. Regulators became alarmed and proposed Basel I with the primary aim of specifying minimum capital for banks operating in the world's major financial centres.

Basel I was broadly successful in achieving its designated purposes, raising capital levels at a time when they were low and trending down.

Issues with Basel I

Basel I focused primarily on *credit risk*, employing crude discrete predetermined risk weights. For example, while corporations may get a 100% risk weight, OECD governments get zero risk weight. This means that a cash-rich corporation like Microsoft with its AAA rating might be weighted at 100% and OECD governments like Turkey, South Korea, Mexico and Greece with their substantially lower credit ratings get a 0% risk weight. This lack of risk sensitivity distorts economic decision-making by creating an incentive for banks to undertake transactions whose sole purpose is to reduce capital requirements with no commensurate reduction in actual risk-taking. The lack of risk sensitivity also impedes effective supervision, as regulators, rating agencies and market participants tend to focus on the capital ratios, which limit their information about a bank's overall risk and capital adequacy.

A different problem emerged because loans with maturity of less than one year did not attract a capital charge. This meant that loans with a maturity of 364 days were cheaper to make than loans with a maturity of 365 days. This is an example of *cliff effects* in financial regulation that can often lead to surprising outcomes. In this case, 364-day loans have become quite popular, replacing much longer-maturity loans, often with the tacit understanding that they will be rolled over after 364 days. They do create, however, unnecessary liquidity risk and therefore make the financial system more fragile and even increase systemic risk.

The 1996 Amendment

The BCBS introduced market risk into the Basel I accord with the 1996 Amendment. This introduced a Value-at-Risk (VaR) approach for the measurement of market risks, requiring banks to report daily 99% probability 10-day VaR using their internal risk models audited and permitted by the regulators: see the appendix for more details.

Minimum market risk capital is then the current VaR or the 60-day average VaR, whichever is the greater, times a multiplicative factor, plus an add-on. Banks are allowed to violate their VaR 2.5 times a year, that is, their trading losses can exceed the VaR 2.5 times a year.

The impact of the market risk amendment was quite small because for most banks market risk is an order of magnitude smaller than credit risk and, therefore, only marginally affects the banks' capital.

13.3.3 Basel II

The BCBS embarked on a revision of Basel I in the mid-1990s, which came to be called Basel II and was introduced to the world around the turn of the century. Since then, extensive lobbying has taken place, delaying its implementation to 2008 in most relevant jurisdictions. This means that Basel II reflects concerns and regulatory thinking from the mid-1990s, so it was already out of date by the time of its implementation.

Basel II improves on the capital regulations in several ways. It substantially improves the risk sensitivity of the minimum capital requirements. While market risk regulations remain unchanged, an internal rating based (IRB) approach is introduced for the calculation of credit risk. Basel II also introduces operation risk.

In the IRB approaches, banks' internal assessments of key risk drivers serve as primary inputs to the capital calculation. Because the approach is based on banks' internal assessments, the potential for more risk-sensitive capital requirements is substantial.

Menu of approaches

While Basel I took a one-size-fits-all approach to capital calculations, Basel II more explicitly recognises that banks are different. One reason is that Basel I applied mostly to large international active banks, while the EU intended Basel II to apply to essentially all banks in its member states, requiring a more nuanced approach for calculating capital, taking into account that some banks are sophisticated and run their own models whilst others engage in very basic activities, outsourcing the few needed calculations. Banks can choose between three different approaches for calculating capital, ranging from simple ratios to sophisticated internal modelling. The menu of approaches is demonstrated in Figure 13.4.

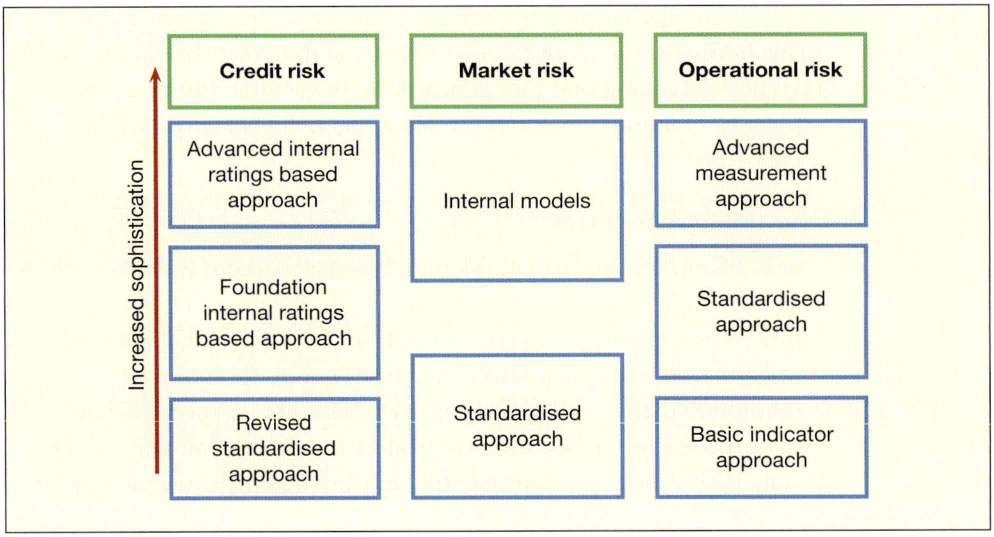

Figure 13.4 Menu of approaches for risk calculations in Basel II

The three pillars of Basel II

Basel II recognises that capital calculations are just one part of the regulatory process and identifies two other areas of concerns, making up the three pillars of Basel II.

Definition 13.4 The three pillars of Basel II

- **Pillar I. Minimum capital requirement** is based on the notion that a bank is able to communicate its overall risk level via one number to the supervisors.
- **Pillar II. Supervisory review process** is designed to ensure that this risk number is generated in a satisfactory manner.
- **Pillar III. Market discipline** depends on the communication of key statistics to the community at large.

While the main focus of Basel II is still on refining the minimum capital requirements, the attention has gradually shifted towards the pillars II and III as the current crisis calls for a more stabilising regulatory regime.

Pillar II forms an integral part of the proposal. It obliges regulators to assess the quality of the risk models of individual banks, allowing the models to be more flexible with respect to banks' particular circumstances whilst encouraging closer cooperation between the supervisor and the bank.

However, allowing regulators such flexibility raises the need for a mechanism ensuring that pillar II is implemented uniformly across countries and that quality assessments undertaken under its auspices are consistent across regulators.

Pillar III reflects the conventional wisdom that sufficient transparency in the market is helpful in increasing stability. This, however, has been somewhat disappointing and has not proven effective.

There are two main factors at work. First, the counterparties who are supposed to do the monitoring share in the same hubris as the banks that are being monitored. We see clear examples in a later chapter when we discuss the problem of toxic capital and assets. Second, it is very hard to make sense of the information being put out. Aggregate summary numbers can hide a myriad of problems, especially in complex asset classes, while the understanding of fine-grained disclosures depends on intimate knowledge of a bank's operations.

13.3.4 Criticism of Basel II

Basel II has come under considerable criticism, both during the early design stages and subsequently for its inadequacy exposed during the crises starting in 2007. Danielsson *et al.* (2001) submitted a paper to the Basel Committee in response to a call for comments on the initial Basel II proposals. The main parts of their arguments were summarised as:

> 'The proposed regulations fail to consider the fact that risk is endogenous. Value-at-Risk can destabilise and induce crashes when they would not otherwise occur.
>
> Heavy reliance on credit rating agencies for the standard approach to credit risk is misguided as they have been shown to provide conflicting and inconsistent forecasts of individual clients' creditworthiness. They are unregulated and the quality of their risk estimates is largely unobservable.
>
> Financial regulation is inherent procyclical. Our view is that this set of proposals will, overall, exacerbate this tendency significantly. In so far as the purpose of financial regulation is to reduce the likelihood of systemic crisis, these proposals will actually tend to negate, not promote this useful purpose.'

Sovereign debt

It is quite common for countries to consider their own domestic currency sovereign debt as riskless, often writing it into law. Even though very few countries are considered risk-free, traditionally this may not have been that big a problem because governments in difficulty with domestic debt payments simply resorted to inflating the debt away rather than directly defaulting.

The Basel I accord follows in this tradition, considering the debt of OECD member countries to be riskless, for the purpose of capital calculations. This means that any bank holding OECD government debt did not have to hold capital against it. This was, of course, a subsidy to the government, paid for by a tax on regular borrowers.

This practice is not that problematic so long as countries issue debt in their own currency, but with the establishment of the euro a new problem has emerged. Member countries of the euro zone issue debt in euros. This means that they cannot resort to inflating away their debt as they used to before the euro, a common practice in many countries such as Greece and Italy. While Basel II does not necessarily consider sovereign debt risk-free, the EU does in the case of 'exposures to Member States central government . . . denominated and funded in the domestic currency of that central government'.[3] This means all member governments of the euro zone issue risk-free debt, at least for the purpose of bank capital calculations. Note that this does not mean the governments can borrow at risk-free rates, but rather that loans to governments do not attract a capital charge.

This has caused particular problems in the euro zone since it sent the signal that government debt was risk-free and in turn meant that banks did not consider the acquisition of sovereign debt as speculative investments, but rather the byproduct of prudent treasury operations.

13.3.5 Basel capital ratios

Under both the Basel I and the Basel II Accords, the CAR has to exceed 8%. The Accords define two categories of capital, tier 1 and tier 2.

Tier 1 capital

The most important part of tier 1 capital is common equity. Depending on the jurisdiction, there are two other types of tier 1 capital, disclosed reserves and preferred stock. These instruments differ depending on each national regulator, but are always close in nature to common equity, usually referred to as *upper tier 1 capital*. In the US, regulators prefer tangible equity, as it provides the most protection. This is disliked by European banks.

Tier 2 capital

Tier 2 capital contains a much broader range of instruments, and is the lesser of the two ratios. Note that just like in tier 1, there may be important differences between jurisdictions as to what is allowed as a part of tier 2.

A relatively unimportant part of tier 2 capital is undisclosed reserves, revaluation reserves and general provisions. The key instruments are *subordinated debt* and hybrid instruments. The former has a flaw in that it provides protection only in case of default and not prior to bankruptcy, when it is most needed. The second instrument had an important deficiency that manifested itself during the crises from 2007, where the protection thought to be afforded by the hybrid capital instruments turned out to be illusionary.

Capital adequacy ratio

The Basel capital ratio is the ratio of capital to *risk-weighted assets* (Definition 13.5).

Definition 13.5 Basel capital ratio

$$\text{CAR} = \frac{C = T_1 + T_2}{\sum_{i=1}^{N} w_i A_i} \geq 8\%$$

where T_1 and T_2 denote tier 1 and tier 2 capital, respectively, $w_1 = 0$ is the risk weight on the safe asset A_1 and $w_{i,i>1}$ are the risk weights on the risky assets. N is the number of assets.

---

[3]Article 89(1)(d) of the EU capital requirements directives (CRDs) (amended by Directive 2009/111/EC or 'CRD II'), and Annex VI Part 1 paragraph 4.

For larger banks, the risk weights are calculated by using internal models, whereby the bank uses historical data and statistical models to forecast the risk of its assets. These models need to be approved by the supervisor.

Capital calculations

Recall the discussion from Section 13.2 above. We replicate it here in the table below, having added in tier 1 and tier 2.

Assets	Liabilities
Riskless assets (A_1) Risky loans (A_2)	Capital ($C = T_1 + T_2$) Non-capital liabilities

EXAMPLE 13.6 Capital ratio calculation

Suppose a bank holds \$1 billion in sovereign debt and \$2 billion in corporate loans, whilst it has tier 1 capital of \$50 million and tier 2 capital of \$200 million. Its capital ratio is then:

$$\frac{50 + 200}{0 \times 1000 + 1 \times 2000} = 12\%$$

13.4 SUMMARY

The focus of this chapter has been on banking regulations. Banking has always been one of the most regulated parts of the economy because of the externalities induced by banking, whereby the downside from failure can seriously affect society while the bankers enjoy the upside.

However, financial regulations carry with them serious side-effects. They can result in the hiding of risk-taking, prevent socially desirable activities or spur undesirable financial innovation.

One of the most common ways to regulate banks is by capital requirements, and under current regulations banks are required to have capital to risk-weighted assets of at least 8%.

Traditionally, financial regulations were the purview of the nation state, but following the post-Bretton Woods deregulation of the global economy, banking is increasingly global, and banking regulations have followed with first the Basel I and then the Basel II accords.

APPENDIX: VALUE-AT-RISK

The Basel committee introduced an amendment to Basel I in 1996, stipulating that a new category of capital requirements was to be created, those arising from market risk. Fundamental to the amendment is the concept of VaR defined as a loss threshold: for a given probability, p,

$$\Pr[-\text{ losses} \geq \text{VaR}] = -p$$

For more details see, for example, Danielsson (2011). The probability specified by the Committee is 99% and the holding period is 10 days. Capital arising from trading activities is defined as

$$\text{Capital} = 3\ \text{VaR}^{99\%}_{10\text{-day}} + \text{constant}$$

Because it is hard to obtain a proper 10-day VaR, the Committee allows banks to use the *square-root-of-time* rule and do the calculation as

$$\text{Capital} = 3\sqrt{10}\ \text{VaR}^{99\%}_{\text{daily}} + \text{constant}$$

This means that the bank capital for trading activities is based on a multiple of the risk of an event that happens 2.5 times a year on average, the $\text{VaR}^{99\%}_{\text{daily}}$.

Questions for discussion

1 What is the difference between regulation and supervision?

2 What are micro-prudential regulations and macro-prudential regulations? When might the objectives of these two types of regulations coincide and when might they conflict?

3 What are the main challenges in banking regulations?

4 What is the difference between bank capital and bank equity?

5 What are the main two purposes of bank capital?

6 What is pro-cyclicality, and to what extent are regular banking activities pro-cyclical?

7 Outline the specific mechanism by which bank capital and capital regulations are pro-cyclical

8 Can bank capital that cannot be drawn down in times of need still fulfil a useful function?

9 What are the main objectives and achievements of the Basel Committee?

10 What is your view on risk weighing assets for CAR purposes?

11 What you think about the assumption in Basel that sovereigns are risk free?

12 Consider a bank that has \$100 in cash, no other assets, and no liabilities. The bank operates in a country with a 8% minimum CAR requirement

(a) Suppose the bank raises \$900 in deposits and invests all of its cash on hand in risk free government bonds. What will its CAR be?

(b) Suppose instead the bank invests \$800 in a AA rated bond that attracts a risk weight of 1, with the rest in the government bond. Is the bank meeting its CAR requirement?

(c) If the bank instead allocates \$500 to a BB rated bond with a risk weight of 2, \$300 to the AA bond, with rest to the government bond. Is the bank meeting its CAR requirement?

(d) The bank invests \$800 in a AA rated bond that attracts a risk weight of 1, with the rest in the government bond. Suppose the markets fear inflation and interest rise by 4% and as a consequence the market value of all bonds drops by 4%. Is the bank meeting its CAR requirement?

(e) Comment on the last answer from the point of view of the impact of leverage on the bank's capital structure.

References

Alessandri, P. and Haldane, A. G. (2009). Banking on the state. Mimeo, Bank of England.

Basel Committee on Banking Supervision (1996). *Amendment to the Capital Accord to Incorporate Market Risks*. www.bis.org/publ/bcbs24.pdf.

Bruner, R. F. and Carr, S. D. (2007). *The Panic of 1907: Lessons Learned from the Market's Perfect Storm*. John Wiley & Sons.

Crockett, A. (2000). Marrying the micro- and macro-prudential dimensions of financial stability. The General Manager of the Bank for International Settlements, www.bis.org/review/rr000921b.pdf.

Danielsson, J. (2011). *Financial Risk Forecasting*. John Wiley & Sons.

Danielsson, J., Embrechts, P., Goodhart, C., Keating, C., Muennich, F., Renault, O. and Shin, H. S. (2001). An academic response to Basel II. www.bis.org/bcbs/ca/fmg.pdf.

Dewatripont, M. and Tirole, J. (1994). *The Prudential Regulation of Banks*. MIT Press.

Goodhart, C. (2009). *The Regulatory Response to the Financial Crisis*. Edward Elgar, Cheltenham, UK.

Goodhart, C. (2011). *The Basel Committee on Banking Supervision: a History of the Early Years 1974–1997*. Cambridge University Press.

Kohn, M. (1999). Early deposit banking. Mimeo, Dartmouth College, Hanover, NH.

Schumpeter, J. (1942). *Capitalism, Socialism and Democracy*. Harper, New York.

14 BAILOUTS

We could define a financial crisis as an event where the public is called on to bail out privately owned financial institutions. The bankers may tell the government that if a bailout is not forthcoming immediately, the country's financial system will collapse. This leaves the political leaders in a difficult situation. Should they take the gamble that the bankers are exaggerating? Should they believe the bankers and bail them out?

Bailouts create *moral hazard*, as defined in Section 7.2. This arises when the government is unable to properly price the bailout, something it usually cannot do. If policymakers appear to be willing to bail out the banks, the banks are encouraged to take on more risk in the future. If creditors believe that a financial institution will be bailed out, they will factor that in when pricing credit extended to the institution. In other words, if a bank can be expected to be bailed out, it can borrow more cheaply than if bailing out is unlikely. This also reduces the incentives of creditors to monitor and discipline the bank. This means that bailouts provide perverse incentives and increase financial fragility.

However, if the authorities do not bail out the banks, the country risks a *systemic crisis*. The total breakdown of payments systems and the inability of individuals and firms to receive funds and make purchases is not pleasant to contemplate. During the Great Depression, the last time we faced a global financial crisis, it may have been possible for the economy to function without a banking system. People had access to basic necessities such as food without banks. In the modern, highly linked world, financial services are much more interwoven into the economy, and very few people or companies could survive long without banking services. This means that the authorities have no choice but to do whatever they can to prevent a widespread banking collapse.

Although it is hard to justify using taxpayers' funds to support some of the wealthiest segments of society, bailouts have been the usual response in crises past, and are increasingly likely in the future. Of course, policymakers do not like being put in this position. They may proclaim before a crisis happens that they will never do bailouts, which if credible would constrain risk-taking. However, this threat is not particularly credible. Therefore, it is better for the authorities to be prepared for crises, recognise their likelihood, and have the necessary financial and legal structures in place. If well prepared, they could aim to impose stringent conditions on the banks, protecting taxpayers and minimising moral hazard.

Much of the damage caused by the crisis starting in 2007, and many a previous crisis, is due to the authorities being woefully unprepared, because of the complacency created by years of apparently benign economic conditions.

This suggests that when it comes to regulating the financial industry and providing bailouts, the interests of the taxpayers are at a serious disadvantage. Not only can the banks exert targeted lobbying at the government to water down any regulations, but the technical ability of the government to respond effectively is limited. Senior government ministers and their advisers are unlikely to understand the underlying problem in detail. How is the government to know whether a banker is bluffing when saying 'if you do not bail me out this afternoon the financial system will collapse'?

Links to other chapters

This chapter directly relates to Chapter 5 (the central bank) and Chapter 7 (banking crises). It also connects to the crisis discussion in Chapter 17 (the ongoing crisis: 2007–2009 phase) and Chapter 18 (ongoing developments in financial regulation).

Key concepts

- Bailouts
- Liquidity support
- Lending of last resort
- Moral hazard
- Guarantees and bubbles
- Bailouts in the crisis from 2007
- The ECB and European banking problems

Readings for this chapter

There are few texts addressing bailouts in a comprehensive way. The first influential analysis of how the government should deal with financial crisis was made by Bagehot (1873), and his proposals continue to shape policy response to this day. More recently, Goodhart (1999) and Capie and Wood (2006) studied lending of last resort (LOLR) in a more modern context. Little work exists on systematically analysing bailouts, and this chapter therefore contains more primary analysis than many other chapters in this book.

Notation specific to this chapter

K	Capital
N	Number of institutions
r	Returns
α, β	Parameters
ε	Random variable

14.1 SUCCESSFUL AND UNSUCCESSFUL BAILOUTS

Two bailouts in recent history, illustrated in Figure 14.1, stand out as examples of how to do them right and how to do them wrong.

Sweden, 1992

Perhaps the most highly regarded example of a government bailout of the financial industry is from Sweden in 1992. Sweden employed the approach of *good bank – bad bank*, with the government taking over dodgy bank assets in return for significant shareholdings. Since the government held on to the bad assets, some of which turned out to be more valuable than envisioned, the eventual cost to the Swedish government was found by Moe *et al.* (2004) to be 3.9% of GDP, significantly below the initial cost of the bailout. Government debt increased sharply following the crisis, as seen in Figure 14.1, reaching 73%, but falling steadily to 38% in 2011.

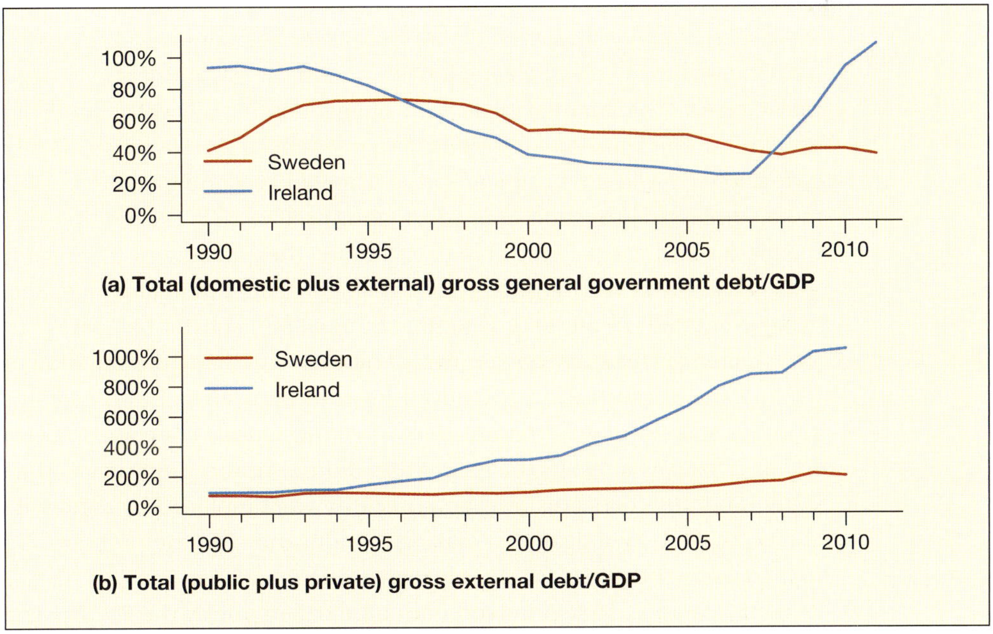

Figure 14.1 Irish and Swedish debt

Data source: Eurostat and www.reinhartandrogoff.com/data/browse-by-topic/topics/9/

Two things from this episode stand out. First, the bailout never threatened the solvency of the Swedish state; Standard & Poor's rating on foreign debt dropped from AAA to AA+, recovering quickly back to AAA. Second, shareholders lost out since there was no bailout of bank owners.

Ireland, 2008

The global crisis that started in 2007 was especially damaging to those countries that had rapidly growing banking systems, like Ireland, paid for by foreign borrowing. The amounts involved were significant, and growing rapidly as seen in Figure 14.1, where total (public plus private) gross external debt/GDP has grown by over 12% a year over the past two decades to over 10 times GDP. This is how Ireland got the funds to grow its banking system to become the third largest in the European Union (EU) relative to GDP by 2007, as indicated by Figure 1.2.

During the bubble years, this created a virtuous cycle between borrowing abroad, lending the money out domestically and increasing valuations of domestic assets. Because the valuations were based on demand fuelled by foreign money, once the money stopped flowing, prices collapsed, causing a banking and economic crisis.

By 2008, the Irish banks were facing significant difficulties, and unable to roll over loans. After Lehman collapsed, all funding dried up. The government at the time faced two choices: it could let the banks default, seriously disrupting the domestic economy but letting the bulk of the losses fall on foreign creditors; or it could provide guarantees for bank obligations in the hope that this would reassure foreign creditors so that they would continue providing funding, thus preventing a banking collapse. The government was pressured to adopt the second option by major creditor countries, such as France, Germany and the United Kingdom (UK), that wanted to shield their banks from the Irish problems.

The correct decision depended on the nature of the problem. If the problem was a short-term liquidity crisis, with the Irish economy basically sound and asset valuations realistic, the right choice was clearly a bailout, and the government proceeded on this basis, providing a state guarantee for all bank obligations, initially without taking over shareholders' equity. This transferred the private bank debt to the sovereign. The government may have analysed it in a way similar to the Copeland second generation (2G) currency crisis model discussed in Section 12.3, considering itself to be in the multiple equilibria region of the model, and hence being able to determine the outcome by a firm commitment.

Because of the very large scale of banking activities in Ireland, and the inability of the Irish government to print euros to finance a bailout, substantial losses on the guaranteed loans called into question government finances. This made the situation much more complex. The debt assumed by the government has proved to be so large that it dominated all other sources of government debt, creating serious concerns over the government's ability to pay. As a result, the guarantees did not restore confidence in the Irish financial system, because concerns over bank security were replaced by concerns over the state's ability to meet its obligations, making it endogenous to the problem. Figure 14.1 shows that government debt/GDP sharply increased from 25% in 2007 to 109% in 2011, beyond its debt tolerance, so that Ireland had to be bailed out by the EU. The Irish taxpayers will have to pay for the bank bailout for a long time to come, suffering a serious contraction in economic performance and austerity as a consequence.

With the benefit of hindsight, the decision to bail out the banks in the way it was done appears to have been a mistake. If the government was under so much pressure from the EU that it had no choice but to do the bailout, presumably it could have demanded concessions from the EU, sharing the burden. Although such a confrontational approach would have been unpopular with other European countries, it appears that the government's negotiating position was quite strong. If the government had refused to bail out the banks, they would have defaulted, but most of the losses would have fallen on foreign creditor banks. The government could then have implemented a much cheaper bad bank – good bank model, focusing on continuing to provide uninterrupted banking services but not providing a blanket guarantee. It may well be that the Irish bailout will be considered as a textbook illustration of a cardinal rule: do not attempt bailouts you cannot afford.

14.2 THE HISTORICAL ORIGINS OF LENDING OF LAST RESORT (LOLR)

A common theme runs through the past two centuries of financial crises. Before a crisis the authorities proclaim they will not bail out private institutions, but once a crisis is underway one of two things happens. Either the government gives in immediately, or it resists, leading to a big economic crisis, with the government subsequently vowing to provide liquidity in future crises. A transformative event for how the government engages with financial crises happened in London in 1866.

14.2.1 The Overend and Gurney crisis of 1866

One of the most respected financial institutions in London in the early 1860s was Overend and Gurney (O&G), called the 'greatest instrument of credit in the Kingdom' on 30 September 1866, the day after its collapse. It was the largest domestic bank in the UK and the world in its day. Our discussion of the downfall of O&G follows Elliot (2006).

Its business was based on commercial lending, taking the form of discounting, where a firm would sell at a discount a note promising to pay a certain amount in the future. The difference between the two is an interest rate. Modern repos work in a similar way. This was the major form of lending at the time.

The development of a market for such notes was a major reason why the UK became the first industrialised country in the world, because budding British capitalists found it easier to raise money than their counterparts anywhere else in the world. This market might be called venture capitalism today. At the time, one of the riskiest and most profitable types of ventures was shipping, and the development of new ships and shipping lines was the high-tech industry of the mid-nineteenth century. For most of its existence, O&G did not participate in such high-risk lending.

Financial institutions of the nineteenth century were principally partnerships, with the notable exception of the Bank of England (BoE). This meant that the partners were liable for all losses – at least in theory. O&G was founded by Quakers who, over time, wanted even more profits than the immense profits already made and ventured into what now would be called junk bonds – very high-risk lending. Soon some of the underlying ventures failed, but O&G did not recognise the losses on its books, instead carrying on as if it had no hidden losses. When its situation became serious, it sold shares to the general public proclaiming that the bank was safe and had no bad assets. At the time, this was legal and there was no obligation for any firm to publish accounts or reveal its true financial situation.

In 1866, O&G collapsed in spectacular fashion. Walter Bagehot, then editor of *The Economist*, wrote that the partners of the firm ran their business 'in a manner so reckless and foolish that one would think a child who had lent money in the City of London would have lent it better'.

In this case, the partners of O&G believed there would be a bailout by the BoE. A delegation of three bankers walked from the Bank to O&G, where a brief look at the ledgers told them all they needed to know. O&G was broke. The Bank faced a delicate decision. If O&G failed, there would be panic. If it was saved, the many other firms in the 'finance' game would also expect to be rescued. The Bank chose the former.

Because the Bank did not bail out O&G, nor provide liquidity support to other banks, even refusing to grant loans against government securities, panic spread through the banking system, and liquidity vanished. The market for otherwise safe assets like UK treasuries dried up as well.

It is not clear why the Bank took that view. Moral hazard was clearly a significant concern, but other factors weighed on it. The BoE was a private institution competing with the likes of O&G, and its future profits were likely to be enhanced by seeing important competitors fail.

The O&G partners were supposed to lose all of the assets in a bankruptcy. However, this was not the case. One of the senior partners, and a member of the family, was a Barclay who a few years later started a bank with the eponymous name. The last Overend became the largest shareholder in that bank.

The partners of O&G eventually faced private prosecution because the government did not feel they had done anything wrong; financial regulations and rules of conduct were unknown at the time. The only crime they could be charged with was theft, which was a narrowly defined concept. In the prosecution the O&G partners hired the UK government's senior lawyer to defend them, so that the same lawyer was representing both the accused and the government who would judge them. They were acquitted.

14.2.2 Bagehot and the crisis of 1866

At the time, there were no established procedures for dealing with the failure of a big bank. However, the disruption of this event turned out to be so costly that it was felt that some steps would be needed to address the externalities associated with the failure of a big institution.

In reaction to the O&G crisis, the BoE studied how it should respond to future crises, and the editor of *The Economist* and future Bank employee, Walter Bagehot, published a White Paper in 1873 on the topic, establishing the three principles of lending of last resort (LOLR):

1 The central bank should lend freely
2 At a penal rate of interest
3 On good banking securities.

Under the gold standard, the monetary arrangement in 1866, liquidity was gold bars. A country had a limited supply of gold bars, so if a central bank provided liquidity to one bank, it might not be able to provide it to another. Thus the central bank had to find a way to ensure that only the banks that really needed liquidity got it. The penalty rate was just a price to ration scarce liquidity so that it flowed towards the highest-value demanders. The Bank Charter Act of 1844, also known as Peel's Act, restricted the amount of paper money that could be created (paper backed by gold), but it could be suspended in an emergency, which happened in 1847 and 1857.

The BoE successfully dealt with the banking panics of 1878 and 1890 by following Bagehot's rules, while the panics of 1847, 1857 and 1866 led to acute financial crises because the BoE hesitated to engage in LOLR. Bagehot's analysis of the 1866 crisis, and his recommendations for how the government should resolve crises and provide LOLR, was the first modern analysis of financial stability and policy remedies. It has been hugely influential and has shaped policy throughout the world ever since.

It established the doctrine of LOLR, enabling the UK to successfully deal with the crises that came after O&G's. The inability to provide the necessary liquidity support in the 1907 crisis in the United States led that country to finally establish a central bank explicitly to provide LOLR. The failure to follow Bagehot's rules was a significant contributor to the Great Depression.

14.3 WHAT ARE BAILOUTS?

In a bailout, some entity, be it an individual, a country or a firm, is provided with funds in order to prevent its bankruptcy, where the money could come from anybody interested in preventing failure. In this chapter we are concerned with the special case of bailouts where the recipient of the funds is a privately owned bank and the provider is the government.

Bank bailouts, in principle, can be made at any time when a financial institution is facing difficulty, but generally happen only when the failure of an institution threatens the financial system. The reason is that ordinarily, the government has special resolution mechanisms for dealing with failing institutions that do not involve bailouts.

We classify the main categories of bailouts in Figure 14.2.

14.3.1 Direct bailouts

In a direct bailout, the government provides money to a financial institution facing difficulty. Such funds generally are provided by the treasury, and involve the direct use of taxpayers' money to prevent the failure of a private institution. The bailout usually takes the form of one of five options: the government buying equity or preference shares, making soft loans, guaranteeing the bank's obligations, or taking over the bank's problem assets.

Equity injections

The most obvious way to provide the bailout is by a *capital injection* by the government, whereby the bank issues new shares that are bought by the government. This is the best outcome for taxpayers because it is the only one that allows them to participate in the upside if the bank performs well after the bailout.

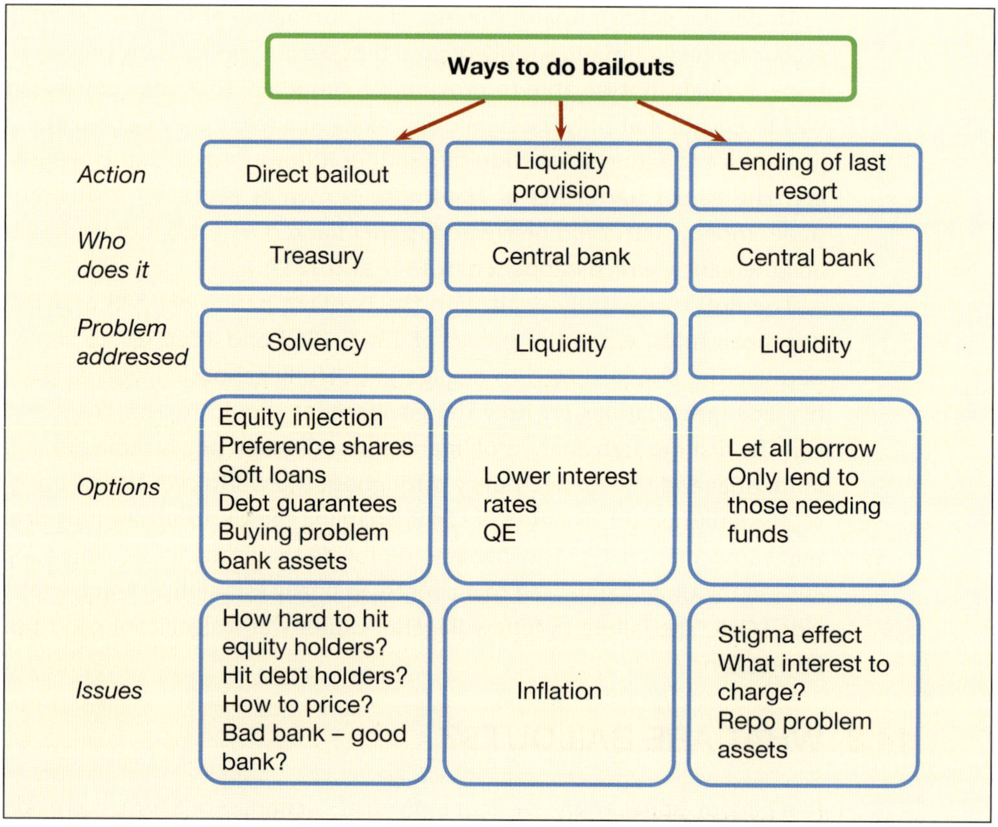

Figure 14.2 Bailout options

The main worry about equity injections is that they represent the partial nationalisation of the bank, with the government having the same rights as other shareholders. The government might be tempted to use its rights for political purposes, thus distracting the bank from its normal mission.

Preference shares

An alternative to a direct capital injection is *preference shares*. These are special types of shares that do not come with voting rights, but provide a special type of fixed dividends with priority over regular dividends. They do not have a maturity date, and the company can skip a payment without being declared bankrupt. We can think of preference shares as a hybrid between debt and equity. In a bankruptcy, preference shares are prioritised above common shares.

Loans

The third alternative is for the government to lend funds to the bank directly, replacing funds not provided by the market. This is related to preference shares, except that the loan will have a fixed term and will place the government higher in the repayment queue if the institution fails.

Loan guarantees

The government can also guarantee that banks' creditors get repaid, so that if the bank fails, the government picks up the tab. If the government has a sufficiently high credit rating, it lowers the cost of funding of the bank, making it equal to that of the government. The advantage to the government over directly lending to the bank is that the government does not have to come up with funds immediately.

Buying or guaranteeing banks' problem assets

The final alternative is to take over or guarantee some of the bank's problem assets. While this is an efficient way to provide support to a bank, it is troublesome for several reasons. It is a direct transfer to the banks' shareholders, and thus carries with it significant moral hazard problems, more than for any other option. Guarantees also cause problems of *adverse selection* whereby the government is at the risk of overpaying for the banks' worst assets. This might happen because the government is likely to be in a hurry and needs to provide large amounts of funds to many banks, not having time to do proper due diligence.

A prominent and controversial example of guarantees is the Troubled Asset Relief Program (TARP) in the US. President Obama called TARP 'a win–win–win proposal'. Joseph Stiglitz (2009), in an article for the *New York Times*, called it a 'win–win–lose proposal: the banks win, investors win, and taxpayers lose.' He argued that the government's plans in effect insured almost all the losses suffered by large financial institutions and spared private investors' losses. In effect both had been given a free put option by the government.

The problem arises because the banks get to choose the loans and securities that they want to sell to the government – the worst assets and especially the assets that they think the market overvalues. In principle, the government might participate in the choice of assets, but in practice it is a complicated task and beyond the technical means of the government, at least if it is to be done quickly enough. The market is likely to recognise this, driving up the price banks can demand.

Preferences

Of these options, the bank prefers them in reverse order, with the guarantee and buying problem assets the most desirable and the equity positions the most unpalatable. The reason is that when the government provides equity the owner's share is diluted. The taxpayers have the opposite ordering of preferences. They get most for their money by direct equity stake and least with the guarantee.

14.3.2 Liquidity provision

Another form of bailout is where the central bank directly increases the money supply in response to some crisis event, either by lowering its interest rates or more likely by open-market operations or quantitative easing (QE). Liquidity provisions have been frequently used by the Federal Reserve System (Fed) in recent years, for example, in reaction to the LTCM crisis and 9/11. Such liquidity injections even got the moniker '*Greenspan put*' after the then chairman of the Fed, because the Fed was seen as supporting the financial system when faced with shocks by providing large amounts of liquidity. This could be seen as a put option, insuring against bad outcomes.

The provision of liquidity is a standard central bank tool, to be used either as a part of regular monetary policy operations or to increase liquidity in times of stress. It does, however, have two side effects.

1 It involves an increase in the supply of money and, therefore, is inflationary, especially if the output gap is not large.
2 As with any support operation, it creates moral hazard. If market participants have reason to believe that their losses will be covered by the state, they will pay higher prices for risky assets than would otherwise be the case, so liquidity support can lead to bubbles.

14.3.3 Lending of last resort

Lending of last resort (LOLR) is where the central bank lends money to a financial institution facing illiquidity. As pointed out in Goodhart (1999), it is a bilateral loan between the central bank and an individual institution, for the purpose of assisting that institution, as opposed to an arms-length liquidity provision by the central bank.

The motivation for doing LOLR is that an illiquid financial institution may face the immediate failure to meet its own funding requirements unless it can monetise its supposedly safe assets. This is especially relevant when the failure threatens to become a full-blown financial crisis. In practice, the distinction between LOLR and direct bailouts might not be very sharp. As a general guide, LOLR relates to the central bank assisting financial institutions to rapidly monetise their illiquid but otherwise safe assets, while direct bailouts involve the treasury (and not the central bank) directly funding an institution in difficulty.

Because of their indirect nature, the authorities are often able to do LOLR without anybody knowing, while a direct bailout is highly visible. For example, both the UK and US governments provided significant liquidity support to some of their best-known institutions in the second part of 2008, which only became public much later.

LOLR is generally seen as the central bank lending to a financial institution facing liquidity difficulties, not problems of solvency, but it can be difficult to make a distinction. The central bank may be expected to err on the side of caution and be willing to lend even if it suspects insolvency. If the objective is a direct bailout of an insolvent bank, the treasury is a more appropriate institution to do the support.

Terms of lending

This leaves open the question of the terms on which the central bank should lend. On the one hand, it is preventing the failure of a financial institution and not only should it be rewarded for doing so, but the financial institution in question should be reprimanded. This calls for high interest rates.

However, high interest rates can have adverse consequences in that they can induce financial institutions to take on more risk than they otherwise would do. In addition, the institution is by definition vulnerable and higher interest rates may increase that fragility, both by increasing its cost and also because of signalling.

Asset choice

Another question facing the central bank is what assets to accept as collateral for the loans it is making to the bank. Ideally, it provides loans only against very high-quality assets such as government bonds. However, in a crisis the market is unwilling to accept assets that normally would be easy to pledge in the markets. This means that if a central bank insists on accepting only high-quality assets, it would be prevented from performing its LOLR role, because the banks in need of lending are in this position precisely because they have insufficient high-quality assets. Indeed, a common pattern in a crisis is that the central bank starts with stringent requirements on asset quality and then slowly relaxes them over time, perhaps accepting junk in the end.

An early example is from the 1825 crisis. This is a quote from a former director of the BoE, Jeremiah Harman, from 1825, commenting on that year's crisis, from Bagehot (1873):

> 'We lent by every possible means and in modes we have never adopted before; we took in stock on security, we purchased Exchequer bills, we made advances on Exchequer bills, we not only discounted outright, but we made advances on the deposit of bills of exchange to an immense amount, in short, by every possible means consistent with the safety of the Bank. Seeing the dreadful state in which the public were, we rendered every assistance in our power.'
>
> Jeremiah Harman, 1825

The stigma effect

Financial institutions are usually reluctant to avail themselves of central bank funding because of *reputation risk* (see Goodhart, 1999). If a bank requires assistance from the central bank, it signals that its liquidity needs cannot be satisfied on the wholesale interbank markets. This causes the *stigma effect*, whereby a financial institution in difficulty is shunned by the rest of the market, which then is sufficient to cause it to fail.

An example of this was discussed in Chapter 2 on the Great Depression where the US set up the Reconstruction Finance Corporation (RFC) to help banks, but then insisted that the loans to banks were publicised. The immediate impact of implementing this requirement in January 1933 was that banks receiving RFC loans were hit by bank runs, and other banks in difficulty therefore were unwilling to seek help from the RFC.

One way to overcome the stigma effect is to keep a LOLR operation secret, but that can be difficult to do in practice because banks do have a good idea of the liquidity needs of their competitors. This problem can be bypassed by forcing all banks to borrow from the central bank, regardless of whether they need it or not. This device was used by the BoE in the crisis from 2007.

The ECB

The European Central Bank (ECB) has made significant longer-term assistance to banks, as seen later in Figure 14.7. The scope, and especially the long duration, of this programme start to blur the distinction between a direct bailout and LOLR. A bank that needs support for many years is no longer facing liquidity problems, rather it is more likely to be insolvent. This signals that the European authorities are unable to recognise the difficulties in their banking system and instead of properly resolving the crisis are using the ECB to create 'zombie banks'. If the authorities want to help the banks, it would be better to recognise the problems and use taxpayers' money directly to recapitalise them. Using the ECB in this manner is not appropriate.

14.4 ALTERNATIVES TO BAILOUTS

While bailouts are based on using public money to aid banks, there are several other methods the authorities can use to provide help to banks in difficulty, or to mitigate the impact of the failure. Of those, perhaps the most important are '*bail-ins*' and *regulatory forbearance*.

14.4.1 Bail-ins

Bail-ins were proposed by Calello and Ervin (2010) at Credit Suisse who argue that the best way to handle a crisis at a large, systemically important bank is to force creditors, rather than taxpayers, to assume losses if the bank gets into difficulty. This would happen at a time when the bank is still operating as a going concern, thus preventing its failure. The bail-ins are overseen by the regulators rather than bankruptcy courts.

There are no automatic triggers for the bail-in; instead, regulators decide when to implement them, presumably right before collapse – *one minute to midnight*. That prevents banks from gaming the triggers, and investors from speculating on their activation. The idea of bail-ins is controversial, particularly with banks, which naturally expect the possibility of their adoption to push up their funding costs.

Bail-ins do have several benefits. They prevent bankruptcies and thus circumvent both the bankruptcy courts and more importantly cross-border issues in resolution. Furthermore, they shield taxpayers from having to bail out banks.

Bail-ins are designed for the failure of a single bank, where the creditors are sufficiently robust to take the hit. In a more systemic event, it is unlikely that the creditors would effectively be able to do so, and if forced, might simply spread the systemic event to other creditor banks and the wider economy via non-bank creditors. This means that a bail-in is not a general substitute for a bailout, but can lower the costs associated with bank failures.

14.4.2 Forbearance

Definition 14.1 Regulatory forbearance Regulatory forbearance is where the regulators refrain from using their full powers to intervene, for example to close an insolvent bank.

A different way to provide assistance to banks is to use *forbearance* and allow *evergreening*, also known as 'extend and pretend' or 'delay and pray'. Generally, this refers to the practice of not recognising losses on a loan and instead rolling it over when payments come due. The idea is that a bank can run down bad loans slowly and earn its way out of difficulty. While this can stave off the closure of the bank, it does not come without cost.

Evergreening makes banks' balance sheets look arbitrarily healthy, thereby deceiving shareholders and counterparties. Since the bank is using its limited funds to refinance bad loans instead of using those funds to make good new ones, it reduces the overall credit in the economy, holding back economic growth.

Evergreening is of course not a bailout, but contravenes accounting rules and prevailing laws, and normally would be discouraged by banking supervisors. If the authorities instead actively encourage evergreening, they are imposing a cost on the rest of the economy to support the banks. Furthermore, evergreening can easily lead to zombie banking, as in Japan from 1990. Of course, with near-zero interest rates the practice becomes much easier.

14.5 BAILOUTS IN THE CRISIS STARTING IN 2007

The largest international financial crisis since the Great Depression started in 2007. One of the first manifestations of the brewing crisis was the freeze-up of the interbank market in early August 2007, and central banks soon had no choice but to inject funds into the interbank market. The early interventions were not sufficient to get the interbank market functioning again, and after the failure of Lehman in September 2008, difficult financing conditions degenerated into a total freeze as all banks attempted to hoard cash and the authorities felt they had no choice but to provide much more widespread support to the financial sector.

14.5.1 The United States

While bailouts in various forms happened in many countries, perhaps the most visible and best documented type of bailouts happened in the US, primarily with TARP and the Fed credit and liquidity facilities.

Troubled Asset Relief Program (TARP)

The US government signed the TARP into law in early October 2008, primarily to address consequences of the subprime mortgage crisis. TARP originally authorised expenditures of $700 billion, but the eventual amount disbursed was $432 billion. Estimates in mid 2012 indicate that the cost to taxpayers may be $19 billion, a significant proportion of TARP loans have already been repaid with interest, and the government expects most of the rest to be repaid as well. The main outstanding amount is from AIG, as shown in Figure 14.3. The fact that the eventual loss was so small suggests that the crisis in the US was about liquidity, not solvency.

Credit and liquidity facilities

TARP was highly visible, with financial institutions not surprisingly reluctant to make use of it. This was not the case for the secret, and much larger, credit and liquidity facility programme of the Fed. The programme was initially meant to be secret, and the Fed maintained that the recipients should not be publicly disclosed, because of stigma effects,

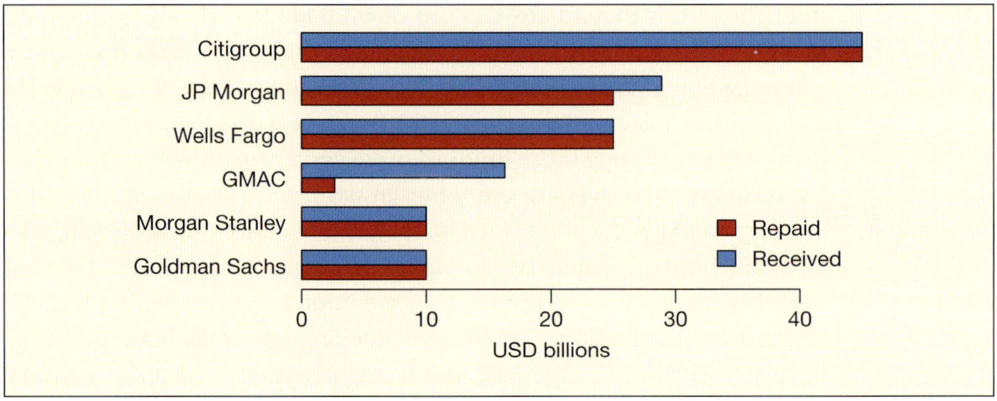

Figure 14.3 Largest TARP bailout recipients in the private financial sector, USD billions
Data source: propublica.org, as of 19 March 2012

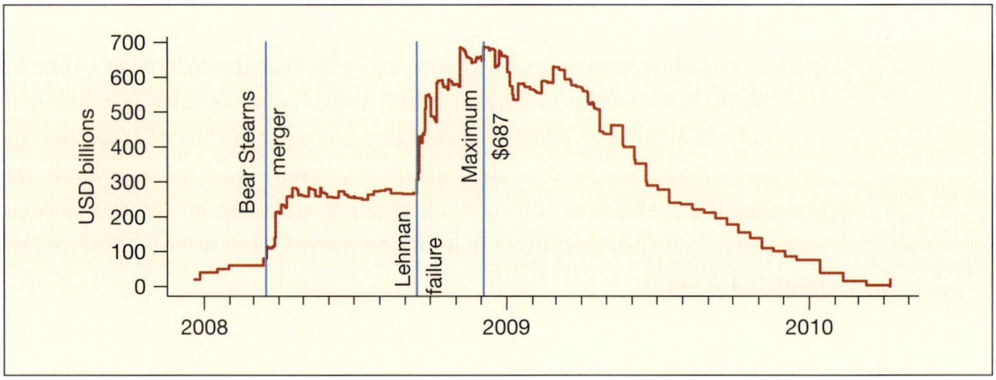

Figure 14.4 Fed emergency lending, USD billions
Data source: The Board of Governors of the Federal Reserve System

no doubt considering RFC. However, the Fed was forced to do so under the Freedom of Information Act, after a lawsuit brought by Bloomberg.

This programme, in its various forms, was much more comprehensive than TARP.[1] Below, we present information from three of the largest facilities,[2] with Figure 14.4 showing the aggregated amounts.

The programme started at the end of 2007, and peaked at the end of 2008, the worst time of the global crisis. At that time, the Fed had around $700 billion outstanding, but starting from early 2009 the numbers tapered off, and by the second quarter of 2010 all loans had been paid off.

The largest amounts outstanding were on 4 December 2008. Figure 14.5 shows the largest borrowers at that time. Citigroup was not surprisingly the largest, with $61 billion,

[1]See www.federalreserve.gov/newsevents/reform_transaction.htm for more information.

[2]Term Auction Facility, Primary Dealer Credit Facility, and Term Securities Lending Facility.

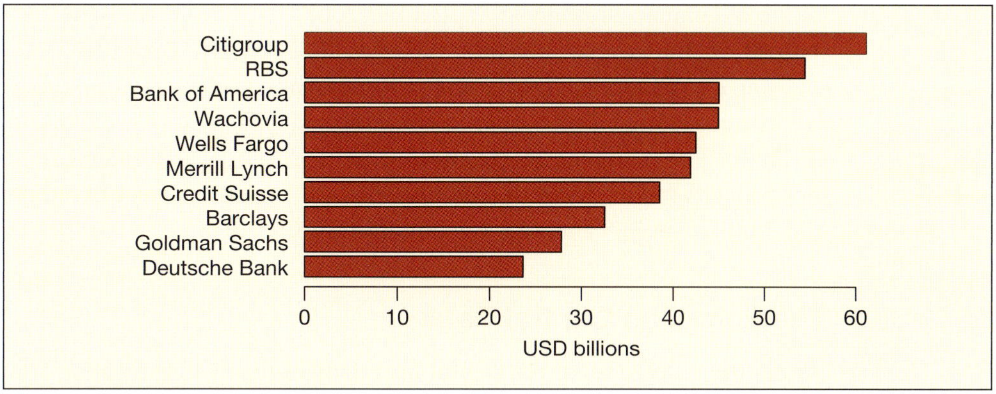

Figure 14.5 Largest borrowers from Fed emergency lending, outstanding loans on 4 December 2008, USD billions

Data source: The Board of Governors of the Federal Reserve System

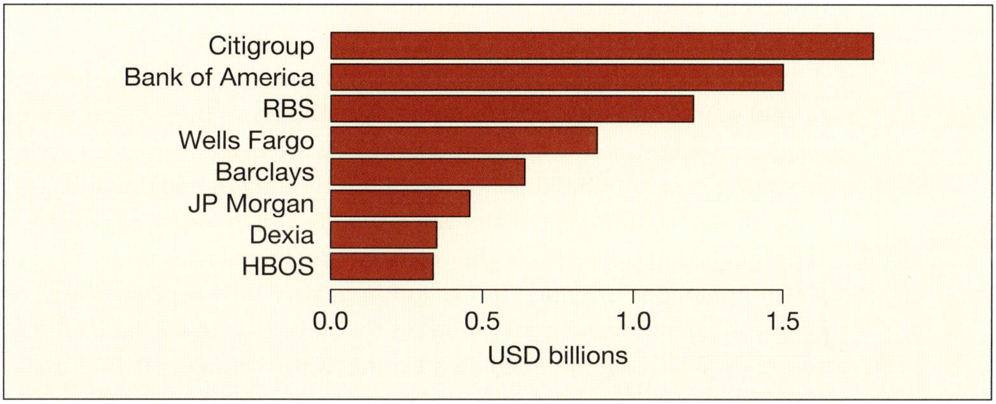

Figure 14.6 Profit of largest recipients from Fed emergency lending, USD billions

Data source: Bloomberg (2011)

but more surprisingly was followed by a foreign bank, the Royal Bank of Scotland (RBS). Below that, well-known American and European institutions were significant borrowers, for example Goldman Sachs at $28 billion and Deutsche Bank at $24 billion.

The interest rate on the loans was generally below market rates, in some cases only 0.01%, so the banks were able to make significant profits. Bloomberg (2011) has calculated those profits, and we report their numbers in Figure 14.6. Citigroup comes in largest at $1.8 billion, but many others made large profits. This constituted a direct subsidy of financial institutions at the expense of taxpayers.

14.5.2 The United Kingdom

The UK has a relatively large financial system, as can be seen in Figure 1.2, and is a significant exporter of financial services. It is therefore not surprising that it faced one of the earliest financial institution failures with Northern Rock in 2007. It was, however, with the failure of Lehman Brothers in September 2008 that the British banks faced their largest difficulties. The government took stakes in RBS, Lloyds TSB and HBOS in October 2008, injecting £37 billion of capital into the three banks, leaving it with more than a 50% stake in RBS and 43% of the combined HBOS and Lloyds TSB, after facilitating their merger. The government subsequently allocated an additional £19 billion of capital into RBS, increasing its stake to 84%. In addition, the BoE provided covert liquidity to some banks: £36.6 billion for RBS and £25.4 billion for HBOS.[3]

14.5.3 The European Central Bank

Within the euro zone, direct capital injections were left to the nation states, but the ECB also played a significant role. It started providing liquidity support to banks in 2007, and since then has been a significant provider of liquidity in the euro zone. In some cases it has been just about the only wholesale provider of liquidity to entire countries.

This can be seen from Figure 14.7 which shows total assets held by the ECB, as well as lending to euro area credit institutions. From before the crisis in January 2007 until mid-2012, both variables have seen a growth of about 160%.

What is interesting is that while the US was able to stop lending to financial institutions by mid-year 2010 (see Figure 14.4), and the largest amount of lending took place at the height of the crisis in the fall of 2008, the ECB has been both accelerating its lending and increasing the maturities of funds lent, most recently to three years.

Such long maturities go along way beyond what is commonly understood as liquidity support. This in part reflects the trajectory of the balance sheets of commercial banks, which in Europe continued to expand long after the US peak. It also reflects the huge geographical imbalance between savers (notably in Germany) and borrowers, in the crisis countries, which are intermediated via the ECB. This suggests that banks need not only current liquidity but also a commitment to future liquidity over the coming years.

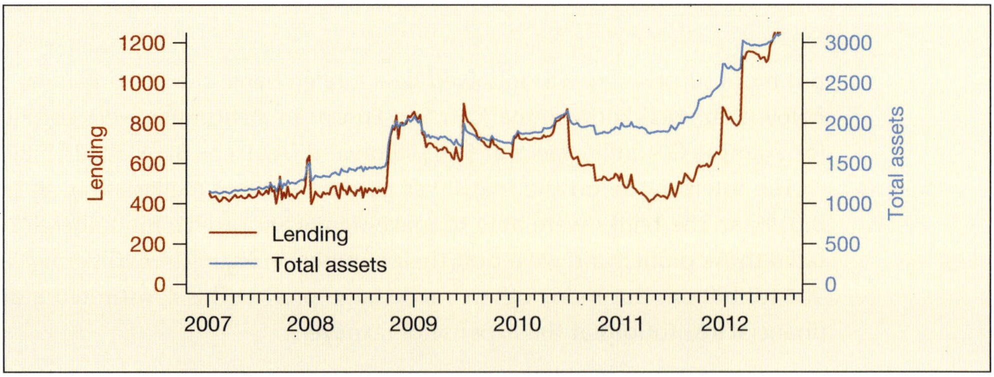

Figure 14.7 ECB lending to banks and total assets, billion euros
Data source: ECB

[3] www.publications.parliament.uk/pa/cm200910/cmhansrd/cm091125/debtext/91125-0004.htm#09112522000002.

14.5.4 Analysis

When the crisis started in 2007, the major central banks and financial institutions were not prepared for a liquidity crisis. After all, such a global event had not happened in developed economies for almost a century. The financial markets reacted in a way typical of crises past, and liquidity disappeared. The central banks eventually reacted by providing liquidity, at first quite reluctantly but eventually supplying seemingly infinite amounts of funds to financial institutions.

The defining event was the bailout of AIG and the failure of Lehman Brothers in September 2008. The latter was transformational and signalled the start of the most severe phase of the crisis, when central bank lending increased sharply. At the height of the crisis, bank lending by both the Fed and the ECB exceeded 5% of GDP, and direct bailouts in various forms were quite substantial.

Asian crisis analogies

The previous international liquidity crisis was in Asia in 1997. In that crisis, the diagnosis came too late, and initial policy responses focused on moral hazard and weak fundamentals. If more liquidity had been forthcoming, the severity of the Asian crisis would have been limited. However, the countries affected were unable to provide the necessary liquidity support because it had to take the form of US dollars, not domestic currency. Since there was no effective international lender of last resort (ILOLR), and the international community, led by the International Monetary Fund (IMF), reacted slowly and provided insufficient liquidity, the optimal crisis response was not forthcoming.

The US and European policymakers did not repeat that mistake. Their task was simpler because the liquidity support was in domestic currency, directly within their control.

Downsides

The authorities sent inconsistent signals, first bailing out Bear Stearns, creating the impression that any similar bank failure would be treated in the same way. When AIG failed, they had no choice but to bail it out, but the failure of Lehman demonstrates the main problem. While the question of whether Lehman should have been bailed out is debatable, and something we discuss later, it did establish the principle that the failure of a sufficiently large bank, one that is too big to fail (TBTF), will result in a bailout.

The fact that the liquidity support was highly profitable to the receiving banks is quite worrying, because it amplifies the moral hazard problems created by the bailout.

The efforts to draw a line under support and curtail moral hazard were unsuccessful, instead underlining the fact that the authorities could not in practice deny support. This weakened their bargaining position, and the generous terms of post-Lehman bailouts are a direct result of this miscalculation.

14.5.5 Europe and the ongoing ECB liquidity support

The amount of liquidity support provided by the ECB dwarfs that of the Fed, and is still increasing in size whilst the US was able to fully wind down its liquidity support by early 2010. The US is, of course, still providing liquidity support by maintaining near-zero interest rates. While the US problem was more liquidity based, the amount of support in Europe implies that the problem is deep-seated solvency difficulties amongst euro zone banks.

However, the European authorities are still addressing the problem as if it were a liquidity crisis and seem very reluctant to face up to the real difficulties. The historical experience of banking crises suggests that decisive action is necessary to minimise the costs, and by using the ECB to delay the inevitable, Europe is sharply increasing the eventual costs of this banking crisis. Apparently, large parts of the European banking system would not survive without ECB funding, meaning that these banks are, in effect, zombie banks.

There are several reasons why this might be the case. A single nation state, with its own central bank, can act much more decisively and quickly than a group of countries with divergent interests. This is why the US, the UK and Switzerland have addressed the problems of their banking systems much more robustly than the EU. While the EU squabbles over which measures to take, the banking crisis continually deepens, creating a solvency crisis out of a liquidity crisis.

If this crisis becomes another Great Depression, the inability of the EU to address its banking and sovereign debt problems will be the main reason. The EU has the resources to solve the problem, but what is lacking is the political will to implement the necessary programmes.

14.6 BAILOUTS, MORAL HAZARD AND POLITICS

An important ingredient in maintaining unsustainable credit expansion, or a bubble, is the unwillingness of everybody involved to stop what seems to be a mutually beneficial situation. Such sentiments are succinctly summarised by the former Citigroup chief executive officer (CEO) Charles Prince's infamous comment before the US housing crisis: 'As long as the music is playing, you've got to get up and dance.'

The general public sees the benefits brought by a bubble and does not generally have the expertise or the inclination to note it is unsustainable. Politicians follow. Most of the bankers enjoy the short-term benefits, and even if they should know better, are more likely to follow Charles Prince.

Those who understand the dangers are more likely to be technocrats within the banks, government agencies or academia, and not those in power. By sounding a warning, they risk being denounced as spoilsports, possibly jeopardising their livelihoods, and may even be threatened prosecution as has happened in both South Korea and Greece.

This may even apply to top policymakers. Alan Greenspan made his famous '*irrational exuberance*' comment in 1996, warning about a build-up of risk, which in retrospect seems very well judged. However, he did not act on it in a way that reflected a belief in his analysis. Perhaps, if he had done so, he would now be remembered as inflicting totally unnecessary damage on the economy rather than having presided over a golden era.

14.6.1 Morality of bailing out bankers

When a financial institution is bailed out, it involves a transfer from the relatively poor to the very rich. Bloomberg (2011) reports that those working for the six largest banks in the US earn twice as much as the average worker in the US, with a salary increase of 20%

between 2005 and 2010, while the salary of the average worker has increased by only 15%. Average bank pay was the same in 2010 as it was before the crisis in 2007.

While it might be surprising that the bankers earn the same before and after the crisis, it is not that unexpected when one considers how aggressive they can be in getting paid. For example, after AIG failed, the very employees in the credit default swap (CDS) division that brought down AIG and almost the world's financial system demanded, and got, bonuses in the millions of dollars if they were to continue solving the mess they created. Some got the retention bonuses and promptly left. The division's chief executive told the *Wall Street Journal* (2009a) that the ensuing public outcry 'stunned people [working for him] such that our wind-down has slowed down'.

Similarly, at the height of the European sovereign debt crisis, the BBC[4] interviewed a trader who said that:

> 'he had been looking forward to a recession in order to profit from it. "I dream of another moment like this", adding: "Anybody can actually make money. It's an opportunity."'

Politicians, therefore, need to consider the moral dimension in providing bailouts in addition to what they consider rational economic arguments.

14.6.2 Challenges

The government's problem in understanding the complexity of the financial system is made worse by the fact that its task is more difficult than that of the banks. A bank has only to worry about its own risk, while the government has to worry about the risk of each and every bank, individually and in aggregate. The reason is that the *endogenous risk* created by the banking system can be identified only if the financial system in its entirety is studied. The only body with the power to do that is the supervisor.

The government's task of effectively providing bailouts is complicated by the close connections between government and industry. The financial system in many countries is in effect an oligopoly of very large, powerful and well-connected financial institutions. Indeed, one could say the more banks a country has, the less political power they have. The opposite is now happening: the number of banks is falling while their size is increasing, making this problem worse. The revolving door between the industry and government in some countries can exacerbate this problem. Eventually, these problems may lead to *regulatory capture*.

14.7 MODEL OF ASSET BUBBLES

Government guarantees may cause bubbles as in the simple model of Krugman (1998), aiming to explain the underlying workings of the Asian crisis. We adapt it here to the more general context of asset bubbles. The main intuition of the model helps to explain many of the crises discussed in this book.

[4] www.bbc.co.uk/news/magazine-15095191.

Model

Suppose banks are perceived to operate under an implicit government guarantee but are otherwise unregulated entities and therefore subject to severe moral hazard.

The government guarantees lead to excessive lending, creating an asset price bubble, in a self-reinforcing process of more lending and further-rising asset prices. This will make the financial conditions of the banks seem sounder than they actually are. At some point the bubble bursts and asset prices plunge, making the problems facing the banks visible and forcing them to stop operating, causing a further fall in asset prices.

Model setup

The production function – a function that provides the output of a firm, an industry, or an entire economy for inputs under consideration – has the following quadratic form:

$$f(K) = (\alpha + \epsilon)K - \beta K^2 \tag{14.1}$$

where ϵ is a random variable and α and β are parameters. The economy is able to borrow at a fixed world interest rate, which we can, without loss of generality, set to 0. Capital will earn its *marginal product*, so the first derivative of (14.1) with respect to capital, the rental per unit of capital, will be

$$\frac{\mathrm{d}f(K)}{\mathrm{d}K} = \alpha + \epsilon - 2\beta K$$

We assume investors are risk neutral. In the absence of any distortions, capital will be invested up to the point where the expected return, r, equals the cost of funds, the world interest rate we set to 0. Therefore:

$$\left(\alpha + \mathrm{E}[\epsilon]\right) - 2\beta K = r = 0$$

Solving for K:

$$K = \frac{\left(\alpha + \mathrm{E}[\epsilon]\right)}{2\beta}$$

Moral hazard

At this point a large number of guaranteed financial intermediaries enter the picture. Their liabilities are guaranteed by the government and their owners do not need to put up any capital of their own and can simply walk away if their institutions fail.

The earnings of the financial intermediaries depend on ε, with a profit for any realisation of ϵ leading to $r > 0$. The intermediaries need not consider any negative outcome because the guarantee ensures their returns cannot be negative. Since any economic profit will necessarily be competed away among the intermediaries, two conclusions follow:

1 All available capital K will be purchased by guaranteed intermediaries in the end and all other agents will be driven out. This captures the extreme level of leverage of the guaranteed intermediaries.

2 Investment is pushed up to the point where $r = 0$ for the *highest possible value* of ϵ. This captures the over-optimistic investment behaviour of the intermediaries.

Moral hazard decisively influences the behaviour of financial intermediaries in such a setting. In normal economic conditions, investors are responding to the expected value of a certain investment. Guaranteed intermediaries, however, will focus not on the expected value of an investment but on what Krugman terms the *Pangloss value* – referring to a character from Voltaire's *Candide* – which is the return that would be achieved in the most favourable case.

EXAMPLE 14.1 Pangloss value

Suppose that $\alpha = 1$, $\beta = 0.25$ and ϵ is either 0 or 1 with both values occurring with equal probability so that the expected value of ϵ is $E[\epsilon] = 0.5$. The undistorted level of investment is

$$K = \frac{1 + 0.5}{2(0.25)} = 3$$

But guaranteed intermediaries will base their investment decision not on the expected value of $\epsilon = 0.5$ but on the Pangloss value and therefore assume that $\epsilon = 1$. The level of investment will be pushed up to

$$K = \frac{1 + 1}{2(0.25)} = 4$$

The result is over-investment which lowers expected welfare because the increased loss in the bad state will not be offset by increased gain in the good state.

Impact of perfectly inelastic assets like land

Up until now, we have assumed that the supply of capital goods is perfectly elastic, meaning that any increase in the demand for capital goods will be satisfied.

If we now assume that capital assets are perfectly inelastic, which would be the case for land, the increase in demand that accompanies the presence of guaranteed intermediaries will have an impact not on the quantity of capital but on its price.

Consider a three-period economy. In the first period, $t = 0$, investors bid for land; in the second and third periods they receive returns. In each period the return on one unit of land can be either 100 with a probability of $1/3$ or 25 with a probability of $2/3$. Table 14.1 shows the returns and probabilities for each period.

Table 14.1 Investment decisions

	$t = 1$		$t = 2$	
	p	Outcome	p	Outcome
Good state	$1/3$	100	$1/3$	100
Bad state	$2/3$	25	$2/3$	25

In an undistorted economy we can solve backwards for the price that risk-neutral investors are willing to pay. The expected return in the last period is 50, which is consequently the price of land purchased at the end of $t = 1$. At $t = 0$, therefore, the expected return on land purchased is the expected return at $t = 1$ of 50 plus the expected selling price at the end of $t = 1$, which is also 50, for an expected value at $t = 0$ of 100, the total expected return over the periods.

Guaranteed intermediaries will base their investment decision not on the expected value but on the Pangloss value – the best-outcome value independent of probabilities. Again, working backwards, at the end of $t = 1$, the intermediaries are willing to pay the Pangloss value of the third period return, which is 100. At $t = 0$ they will therefore be willing to pay the most they could hope to realise in both subsequent periods, which is the Pangloss return at $t = 1$ plus the Pangloss resale value at the end of $t = 1$, which is 100. Guaranteed intermediaries will therefore pay 200 for one unit of land, so that in the end they will have driven out all other investors and raised the price to double what it would have been in an undistorted economy. Figure 14.8 shows the Pangloss values for the three periods.

Implications for banking crises

In this example the probability of the guarantee being exercised is $^8/_9$, (1 minus the probability of the two good states, $^1/_3 \times {}^1/_3$) and if additional periods are added the likelihood rapidly approaches certainty because the guarantee is required on the first failure.

This remains the case even if we modify the odds of the two outcomes so that the poor outcome is unlikely. The asset will be priced ignoring the poor outcome, so if the number of periods is a sufficient multiple of the probability of a bad outcome, the guarantee is almost certain to be required.

This underlines the almost unavoidable nature of banking crises. We cannot exclude the possibility of a damaging mistake. This is clear when we consider that a large fraction of the US banking industry was until 2007 prepared to use models that assumed that US house prices could not fall, yet a small possibility is all that is required to guarantee that a crisis will eventually occur. Viewed from this perspective, the recurrence of crises at roughly 79-year intervals (2007 − 1929) could be seen as implying a roughly 1.3% chance on average that investors are unaware of some adverse possible outcome to their decisions.

Analysis

The central message of this simple model is the adverse impact caused by government guarantees of banks. Because creditors assume they will be bailed out, they are willing

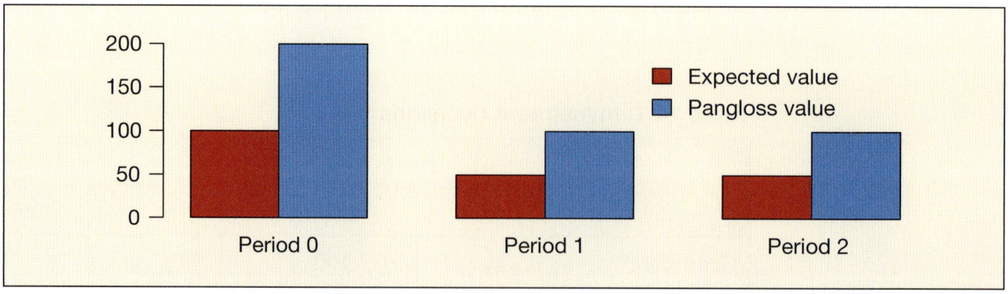

Figure 14.8 Pangloss values

to lend to banks at low interest rates even though they think the banks' investments are bad.

In addition, these guarantees give banks an incentive to price risky investments with over-optimistic assumptions. Any kind of activity involving uncertain but diminishing returns to capital – almost all activities – will as a consequence see higher levels of investment than would be made by equity investors focusing on expected returns. Nor do the banks' creditors have any incentive to withdraw funding.

This has two adverse impacts for society. First, it encourages excessive risk-taking at the expense of the taxpayer, a classic form of moral hazard. Second, it leads to asset price bubbles that are destined to burst, destabilising financial markets on the way up and causing a crisis on the way down.

14.8 SUMMARY

Governments often find it necessary to bail out private financial institutions in order to prevent an individual failure becoming a full-blown financial crisis. There is a right way and a wrong way to implement bailouts, with the Swedish government's actions in 1992 a model of a successful bailout, and the Irish bailout of 2008 less successful.

The main issue in bailouts is moral hazard where the expectation of government support induces financial institutions to take more risk.

The first formal government bailout policy was LOLR, formulated after the 1866 crisis. Bailouts have been used frequently, both before and after that date, for example, during the crisis from 2007 where central banks in effect replaced the interbank markets and large financial institutions received bailouts, most significantly AIG.

Bailouts can take many forms, in particular direct bailouts, LOLR and liquidity provision. The damage from bank failures can be mitigated by bail-ins and banks can be helped by regulatory forbearance. In implementing bailouts, it is important to distinguish between illiquidity and insolvency, even though conceptually their boundary is a broad grey area and identifiable only in extreme cases.

We demonstrated a simple model of how government guarantees can lead to asset price bubbles, which contributed to the 2007 crisis and is of continuing concern given the apparent determination of governments to prevent private sector bank losses.

Questions for discussion

1 Comment on the relationship between the size and credibility of a bailout package to its effectiveness.

2 Why did the Irish bailout of the banks end up causing the bailout of the Irish government itself?

3 What are the main ways a government can do a direct bailout? Which way is preferred by taxpayers and which by the banks?

4 Why should the treasury and not the central bank do a direct bailout?

5 Why does the central bank and not the treasury do liquidity injections and LOLR?

6 Should the central bank charge a penalty rate when doing LOLR?

7 Does the existence of LOLR encourage excessive risk taking?

8 How could the problem of moral hazard associated with bailouts be reduced?

9 Should the bailout be based on banks' size or interconnectedness? Offer one example for each form of bailout.

10 How can we justify using taxpayers' money to bail out those who own and run banks, especially when the bank owners and managers represent one of the richest segments of the population, who then receive a transfer from their poorer countrymen?

11 What are the main arguments for keeping bailouts secret and the main arguments for making them public?

12 If a central bank provides liquidity assistance to banks, what should the time span for the assistance be?

13 What is your view on the ECB liquidity programmes?

14 What is a Pangloss value?

15 How can the concept of Pangloss value be used to explain the behaviour of investors? Is it rational?

(a) Consider a two-period model with an initial investment at $t = 0$ and returns in periods $t = 1$ and $t = 2$. With probability p the returns will be y, otherwise the returns will be x. The following holds: $x > y$ and $0.5 > p > 1$. What is the value of the return that investors can expect? What is the Pangloss value?

(b) The government explicitly guarantees all investments, so that investors at $t = 0$ bid up the price to the Pangloss value. Now the government announces that it will bail out investors only once and will then withdraw all guarantees. Show that this leads to a situation of multiple equilibria.

(c) Prove that the government guarantee at $t = 0$ makes losses worse if things turn out to be bad in $t = 1$ than they would have been without any explicit or implicit guarantees.

References

Bagehot, W. (1873). *Lombard Street: a Description of the Money Market*. H.S. King, London.

Bloomberg (2011). Secret Fed loans undisclosed to Congress gave banks $13 billion in income. www.bloomberg.com/news/2011-11-28/secret-fed-loans-undisclosed-to-congress-gave-banks-13-billion-in-income.html.

Calello, P. and Ervin, W. (2010). From bail-out to bail-in. *The Economist*, 28 January.

Capie, F. and Wood, G. E. (2006). *The Lender of Last Resort*. Routledge.

Elliot, G. (2006). *Overend & Gurney, a Financial Scandal in Victorian London*. Methuen.

Goodhart, C. (1999). Myths about the lender of last resort. Technical report FMG SP 120, London School of Economics. http://fmg.lse.ac.uk/pdfs/sp120.pdf.

Krugman, P. (1998). What happened to Asia? Mimeo, MIT.

Moe, T. G., Solheim, J. A. and Vale, B. (2004). The Norwegian banking crisis. Technical report, Norges Bank. Occasional Paper no. 33.

Stiglitz, J. (2009). Obama's ersatz capitalism. www.nytimes.com/2009/04/01/opinion/01stiglitz.html?_r=1&scp=2&sq=stiglitz&st=cse.

Wall Street Journal (2009a). Action on AIG unit may cost taxpayers. *Wall Street Journal*, 13 April. online.wsj.com/article/ SB123957925343711995.html.

15 DANGEROUS FINANCIAL INSTRUMENTS

Financial institutions are continually creating ever more complex financial instruments, motivated by potential profits from new types of trading strategies, the ability to market new instruments to their clients, to move risk off their balance sheets, or to hide the risk-taking activity from other parts of the institution, supervisors and clients. While the new instruments may be highly profitable during boom times, they also act as enablers for excessive risk-taking and as accelerators for small events to spill out of control. They can contribute directly to financial crises, just one example being their role in the crisis from 2007 which included new instruments like CDOs, CDSs, SIVs and conduits. This is why we might term them *dangerous financial instruments*.

These dangerous instruments undermined the extensive monitoring process we had implemented to prevent the excessive build-up of systemic risk-taking. They did that by enabling banks to spin off a part of their balance sheet, helping banks to do more business and take on more risk with the same amount of capital, and even replacing bank supervisors with more emollient rating agencies.

The main problem arises because of the complexity of the financial instruments. Not only is it hard for non-experts to understand the inherent riskiness, but the financial instruments often depend on a number of assumptions about the stochastic behaviour of market variables and the estimation of complicated statistical models. In this process there are many things that can go wrong. The designer of the product may not understand all the issues, the underlying assumptions are likely to be inadequate, and the statistical models will be estimated with significant degrees of uncertainty. In short, these instruments are priced and their risk is assessed with complex statistical models, and since every statistical model is wrong by definition, prices and risk will similarly be incorrectly imputed.

The underlying modelling weaknesses are masked by high profits during boom times. A large adverse shock may be required to lay bare the mistaken model assumptions. The main problem is that this is most likely to happen when the financial system is already heading into a crisis, so that a reassessment of the riskiness of these instruments becomes part of a vicious endogenous risk feedback loop between reassessment, institutional difficulty and prices.

Fundamentally, the main problem of the dangerous financial instruments is that they ignore the likelihood of systemic losses.

Links to other chapters

This chapter relates directly to Chapter 10 (credit markets), Chapter 9 (trading and speculation) and Chapter 17 (the ongoing crisis: 2007–2009 phase).

Key concepts

- Complexity
- Derivatives
- Credit default swaps
- Collateralised debt obligations
- Special investment vehicles
- Conduits
- Rating agencies

Readings for this chapter

The underlying mathematics of complex credit instruments are discussed in detail in several good texts. We made use of Crouhy *et al.* (2000), Duffie and Singleton (2003) and Hull (2011, 2012). Murphy (2009) provides a good discussion of the role played by credit instruments in the crises, whilst the Board of Governors of the Federal Reserve System (2009) has a good overview of the various credit facilities and their role in the crisis.

Notation specific to this chapter

F, f	Factors
K, k	Number of defaults
N	Number of assets
X, x	Random outcomes
p_d	Probability of default
ϵ	Idiosyncratic shock
ρ	Default correlation
Σ	Covariance matrix
$\Phi(\cdot)$	Standard normal distribution
$\phi(\cdot)$	Standard normal density
α	$\sqrt{\rho}$

15.1 COMPLEXITY KILLS

Before the ongoing crisis that began in 2007, sophisticated financial models and intricate assets structures enabled many banks to reap significant profits. Complexity is profitable because complex products offer more scope for differentiation and profit than commoditised ones. Financial institutions have an incentive to maximise the complexity of their products and operations, and even in special cases may have as one of their objectives the minimisation of the quality of assets.

There is a clear advantage for financial institutions to move towards complexity. It makes it harder for others to see what they are up to, be they competitors, clients or the authorities, while at the same time complex structures help in exploiting arbitrage opportunities. Even better, as the more complex and less transparent an instrument becomes, the bigger the potential for high fees. The greatest profit opportunities often lie at the edge of chaos. Unfortunately, at that point it takes little to end up over the edge.

While lack of knowledge makes it hard to know how safe you are, it takes something else (perhaps greed and/or competition) to force you to the edge, which happens because of the over-reliance on a mathematical description of history. Complexity became a virtue, but not without costs. The banks often did not have a clear view of their risk exposures.

The impact of complexity is even worse, as it creates incentives to maximise low-quality investments and exploit model uncertainty. When financial institutions set up structured credit products, certain tranches were more profitable than others. The highest profits could be found where banks used assets with high loss given default and higher correlations than assumed in the models, assets often colloquially referred to as 'garbage'. It was the demand for garbage assets that was behind the demand for subprime assets. The enabling factor was complexity.

In such complex financial models, mathematics often assumes far greater importance than an accurate depiction of reality. The models generally ignored important risk factors, like *liquidity* and *non-linear dependence*, even disregarding the possibility of economic downturns.

Consequently, the valuations and risk assessments of complex products became increasingly out of sync with the economic fundamentals and underlying assets. Unfortunately, few mechanisms exist for identifying the looming problems. If the models indicate that everything is fine, backed up by mark-to-market accounting practices, it is not surprising that the market for structured products becomes over-inflated.

When the credit markets collapsed and liquidity disappeared in 2007, complexity became a vice. In a crisis, banks gain access to liquidity by being able to demonstrate solvency. If assets are so complicated that nobody – not the regulators, not the clients and not even the banks – is able to get any realistic assessment of valuations and risk, of course, investors will refuse to supply liquidity. Seen with a newly sceptical eye and a radical change in assumptions, it became clear that banks had simply become too sophisticated for their own good.

15.2 DERIVATIVES

> 'Derivatives are financial weapons of mass destruction, carrying dangers that, while now latent, are potentially lethal.'
>
> Warren Buffett (2003)

Derivatives are securities that derive their value from something else, called the *underlying asset*. The underlying asset is commonly another security, perhaps shares in IBM, a physical asset like bushels of wheat or a non-traded financial asset such as a bundle of mortgage loans. The underlying asset can also be something abstract, like the occurrence of an event or the prevalence of a special state of the world. For example, there are weather derivatives whose value depends on the temperature or rainfall in some place over a particular period, and credit derivatives whose value hinges on whether a firm files for bankruptcy in a set timeframe. Fixed-income instruments are one type of derivatives, their underlying asset being the interest rate.

Different sorts of derivatives are designed for different purposes. Many derivatives contracts were originally designed to bring together parties exposed to offsetting risks so that they could net them out, a practice called *hedging*. Others provide *optionality*, build in leverage, or create exposures to risks otherwise not tradable in financial markets.

Derivatives carry with them significant hidden dangers. Not only do they allow highly leveraged bets on financial markets, but also the risk is often deeply hidden.

Volume

The volume of trading in derivatives markets has grown significantly over the past few years. The Bank for International Settlements (BIS) collects data on the volume of derivatives trading, shown in Figure 15.1. Figure 15.1(a) shows the total notional amounts, or the face amounts, used to calculate payments. This amount does not change hands.

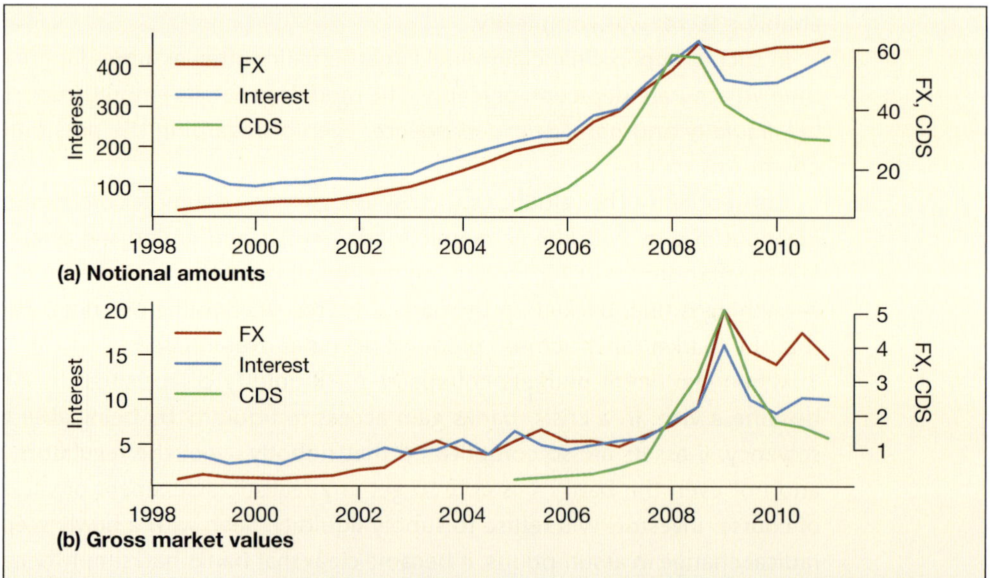

Figure 15.1 Amounts outstanding of over-the-counter (OTC) derivatives, USD trillions
Data source: BIS

By contrast, Figure 15.1 (b) shows the gross amount, which is the sum of the value of contracts owned by a financial institution, without taking *netting* into account. Therefore, it shows the worst-case situation of what happens when counterparties default and loss is 100%.

The amounts are shown in trillions of dollars, and we see that the notional amounts significantly exceed the global GDP of about $60 trillion. The more important gross amounts are slightly less than half the global GDP. The rapid growth over just a few years is a significant concern, and the lack of concern by the world's policymakers prior to the crisis starting in 2007 is itself a cause for concern.

15.3 CREDIT DEFAULT SWAPS

The derivative that saw the most rapid increase in volume in Figure 15.1 is the credit default swap (CDS). It is one of the two derivatives most closely associated with the crisis that began in 2007, not least because it was directly responsible for the largest ever single financial institution failure, that of AIG. It also more indirectly contributed to the failure of Bear Stearns and Lehman Brothers.

As a consequence, it is not surprising that CDSs have come under considerable criticism. Eric Dinallo, the insurance superintendent of New York state, who supervised AIG, called the CDS a

> 'catastrophic enabler of the dark forces that have swept through financial markets'.

The Economist observed on 6 November 2008:

> 'They are, says a former securities regulator, a "Ponzi Scheme" that no self-respecting firm should touch. [. . .] Alan Greenspan, who used to be a cheerleader, has disowned them in "shocked disbelief". They have even been ridiculed on "Saturday Night Live", an American TV show.'

Much of the criticism relates to the fact that the CDS market had blossomed without much oversight, allowing the sellers of CDSs to amass excessive amounts of risk. At the same time, the fact that CDSs are OTC instruments implies that the market for them is fairly non-transparent, so it is difficult to identify net exposure.

What is a CDS?

A CDS is an instrument providing insurance that protects the buyer of the CDS against the default of some third party called the *reference entity*. Suppose a bank owns a high-risk bond and wishes to hedge that risk. The bank, known as the *protection buyer*, would enter into a contract with another institution, the *protection seller*. The protection buyer pays a regular fee to the protection seller until the CDS expires, unless a *credit event* happens, which could be a default but might also include other occurrences. In this case, the protection seller would buy the risky bond at par value from the protection seller and no more payments take place. This is described in Figure 15.2. For detailed information on how CDSs are created, see Appendix A. In some cases, when the reference entity is high risk, all the fees may be up front. This, for example, has been the case for some Greek CDSs.

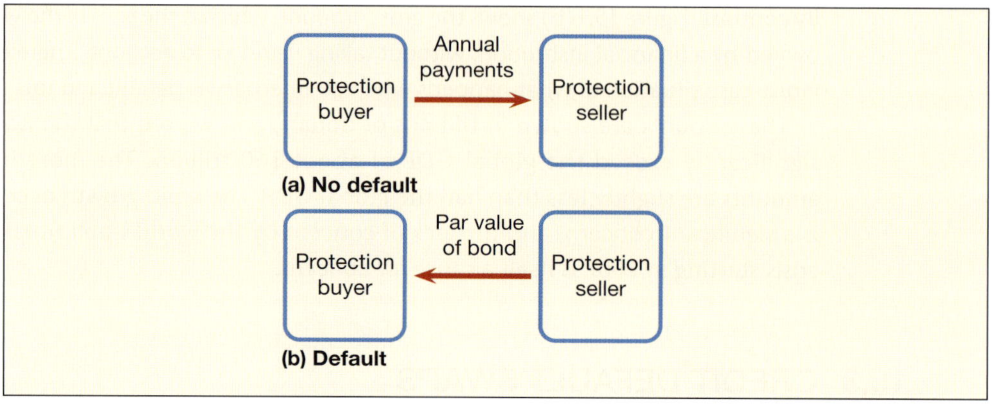

Figure 15.2 Simple CDS payment flow

Benefits of CDSs

In principle, CDSs are quite useful instruments, allowing users to trade and manage credit risk separately from other risks and cash flows. They provide an efficient way to hedge credit risk, spreading risk to those best able to assume that risk, and allowing users to efficiently diversify and tailor risk-taking. CDSs also enable speculation, in principle, increasing the efficiency of financial markets.

15.3.1 The problem with CDSs

Individual risks created by CDSs

One of the two major risk factors for those buying CDSs is counterparty risk, arising because they do not settle on a *clearinghouse*, or a central counterparty (CCP), but are instead traded and settled OTC. Since CDSs are often sold by major financial institutions, such counterparty risk directly relates to the institutions' failure probabilities. For example, if one had purchased a CDS protection from Lehman Brothers in January 2008, that protection would have lost effectiveness in September 2008 with Lehman's bankruptcy.

CDSs and network vulnerabilities

CDSs create their own types of risk. We illustrate this in Figures 15.3 and 15.4 and outline the key steps below. The arrows indicate exposure.

Step 1 Bank A makes a loan to a creditor and consequently is exposed to risk of default.

Step 2 To hedge the probability of default, bank A buys a CDS from bank B. The initial credit risk is now transferred to B, whilst A and B are exposed to each other; however, the degrees of exposure of A and B are not symmetrical, as it is much easier to make a stream of small payments in good times than a large payment in bad times.

Step 3 The creditor pays back the loan early to bank A, which is left with paying fees to bank B. To minimise costs, it sells a CDS to bank C. Now A and C are also exposed to each other.

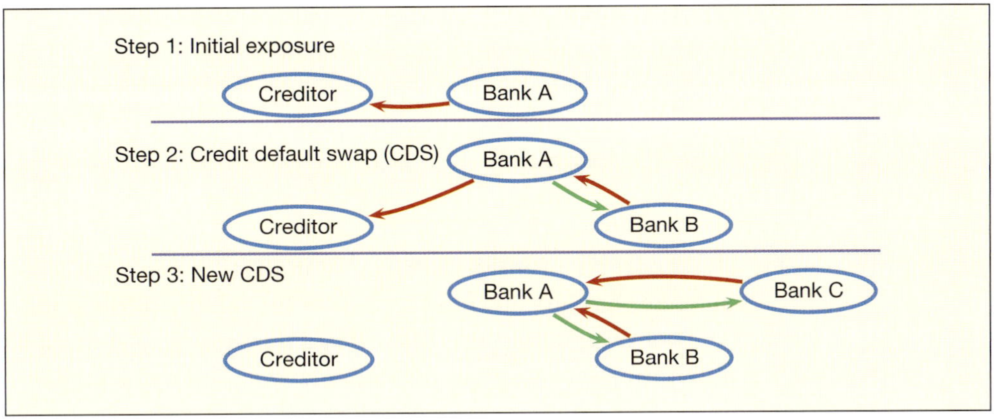

Figure 15.3 CDS network risk creation

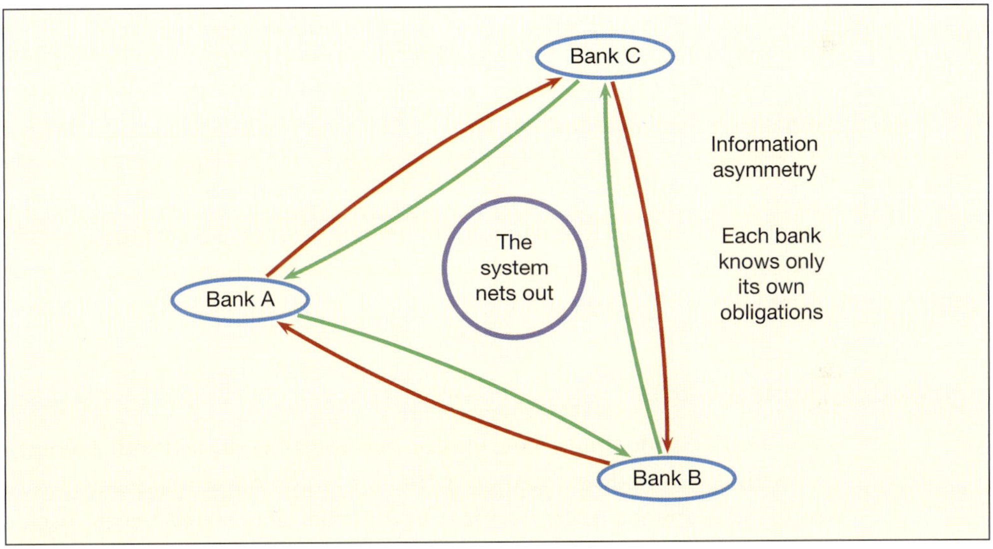

Figure 15.4 Netting out

Step 4 To hedge its exposure, bank B buys a CDS from bank C. Now A, B and C are all exposed to each other. This is shown in Figure 15.4.

Throughout this process, the gross amount increases with each step, but the net amount remains the original exposure to the creditor, who after all has paid back the loan so the net exposure in the system is zero. This problem is shown in Figure 15.4, showing the gross exposures and the zero net. This creates a chain of vulnerabilities, contributing to the problem of interconnectedness in the financial system, creating systemic risk.

Consequently, the failure of a major dealer would have major repercussions for the rest of the market participants, exactly the problem created by AIG and Lehman. Furthermore, because CDS contracts are not cleared on a clearinghouse, they are not government regulated, nor standardised, making it very difficult to calculate net obligations. There are no public records showing whether sellers have the assets to pay out if a bond defaults.

It is difficult to develop a clear picture of which institutions are the ultimate holders of some of the credit risk transferred. It can even be difficult to quantify the amount of risk that has been transferred. This is the main systemic risk posed by CDSs.

Related to this is the problem that the protection seller might need to come up with significant funds during a crisis episode, when it and the financial system are under stress.

Perverse incentives

A CDS affects normal incentives in financial markets. It can create moral hazard since the initial lender has less incentive to ensure the quality of the underlying loans and monitor the borrower if the risk is sold off to a third party, who probably has less information about the borrower than the initial lender. This can lead to a lower quality of loans.

CDSs also provide perverse incentives for creditors. Pragmatic lenders who hedge their economic exposure through CDSs can often make higher returns from CDS payouts than from out-of-court restructuring plans. Bankruptcy codes assume that creditors always attempt to keep solvent firms out of bankruptcy; however, if a creditor holds a CDS it may be more profitable to trigger a bankruptcy even if that significantly reduces the amount of money received by bondholders.

This may have been behind the bankruptcy of Six Flags, a failed American theme-park operator, as noted by *The Economist* (2009) where the Fidelity mutual fund turned down an offer that would have granted unsecured creditors an 85% equity stake, and as a consequence uninsured bondholders will receive less than 10% of the equity now that Six Flags has filed for protection.

15.3.2 Naked CDSs

Trading CDSs for purely speculative reasons as easily without owning the underlying assets is called trading *naked CDSs*. The buyer could just make a deal with the protection seller, whereby the buyer pays fees to the seller until a credit event occurs, at which time the seller pays a certain amount to the buyer. *Insurable interest* is missing for naked CDSs, so they are different from typical insurance contracts. A comparison is sometimes made with what might happen if a person could buy fire insurance on their neighbour's house. There is no insurable interest and the person would have a motive to burn the neighbour's house down to trigger an insurance payout.

Naked CDSs have become quite controversial, especially in Europe, as some European leaders have blamed speculators using them for undermining certain European economies.

> 'I think that derivative products [such as] the CDS on sovereign debt have to be at least very, very regulated, rigorously regulated, limited or banned [. . .]'
>
> Christine Lagarde, former French minister and now managing director of the International Monetary Fund (IMF), quoted in the *Financial Times* (2010a)

The EU has decided to impose a permanent ban on naked CDSs, strongly supported by Germany and opposed by the UK.

> 'These balanced measures will ensure that sovereign CDS are used for the purpose for which they were designed, hedging against the risk of sovereign default, without putting at risk the proper functioning of sovereign debt markets [. . .] Short selling did not cause the crisis, but can aggravate price declines in distressed markets.'
>
> Michel Barnier (2011), commissioner for the single market

Naked CDSs, however, are not the evil instrument the politicians sometimes make them out to be. A European Commission report concluded that CDSs had no adverse impact on bond markets, where the prices of CDSs and sovereign debt largely moved in tandem. These issues are discussed by Duffie (2010).

Banning naked CDSs could also deepen a crisis. Market participants might have an indirect exposure to a counterparty. Furthermore, by banning naked CDSs, market participants might attempt to reconstruct the hedge by other means, perhaps by shortening government bonds or bank equities or otherwise reducing their exposure. Because such activities would be less visible, it would be typical of regulations driving risk-taking underground, reducing transparency and financial stability.

15.4 COLLATERALISED DEBT OBLIGATIONS

A collateralised debt obligation (CDO) is a debt structure holding, whereby a portfolio of fixed-income assets is held in a special purpose vehicle (SPV). Investors buy rights to the payment flow from the underlying assets in the SPV. The sole purpose of the SPV is to collect collateral cash flows and pass them to CDO investors. CDOs typically allocate interest income and principal repayments from the underlying assets into what is known as *tranches*.

Definition 15.1 Tranche A tranche, French for slice, is a particular slice of the risk, and hence payments flow from a CDO. Tranches often get the same credit rating as regular bonds. The main tranches are:

- Super senior (AAA)
- Senior notes (AA)
- Mezzanine (A to BB)
- Equity (unrated), a.k.a. toxic waste.

Higher-rated (senior) tranches get paid before lower-ranked mezzanine tranches, with any residual cash flow paid to an equity tranche.

Tranches are usually sold separately. The CDO structure allows the senior tranches to obtain credit ratings in excess of the average rating on the collateral pool as a whole, because of an assumption of diversification within the pool of assets.

Maximising the size of desirable tranches is a key objective of the designers of CDOs. Often, the mezzanine tranches are the easiest to sell, with the sponsoring bank left holding the super senior and equity tranches. This depends on buyer preference, however, and in many cases the AAA and AA tranches are easiest to place because buyers simply count the As (see safety) while mezzanine investors do more modelling. By retaining AAA tranches, the sponsoring bank might obscure its profits on the structure, by selling it later and booking it as separate profit.

15.4.1 Example CDO

A bank creates a SPV which buys 10 bonds. Each bond has a maturity of 1 year and a total face value of $10 million, so the total face value of the assets held by the SPV is $100 million. The bonds have a 12% annual interest rate, while the probability of default over the next year is 25%. In default there is no recovery.

Suppose an AAA corporate bond has a probability of default $p_d = 0.3\%$ and an interest rate of 6% whilst a BBB bond has $p_d = 7\%$ and an interest rate of 8%. It is then straightforward to create three tranches (see Appendix B for details), assuming defaults are uncorrelated. We show the size of the various tranches in Table 15.1, with the CDO structure summarised in Figure 15.5.

In this sample CDO, the sponsor has been able to create $30 million worth of AAA-rated securities out of $100 million worth of high-risk instruments. This is achieved by

Table 15.1 Tranching

Rating	Interest rate	Number of bonds	Value of bonds	Interest payment
AAA	6%	3	$30 million	$1.8 million
BBB	8%	2	$20 million	$1.6 million
Equity	17.2%	5	$50 million	$8.6 million
Total	12%	10	$100 million	$12 million

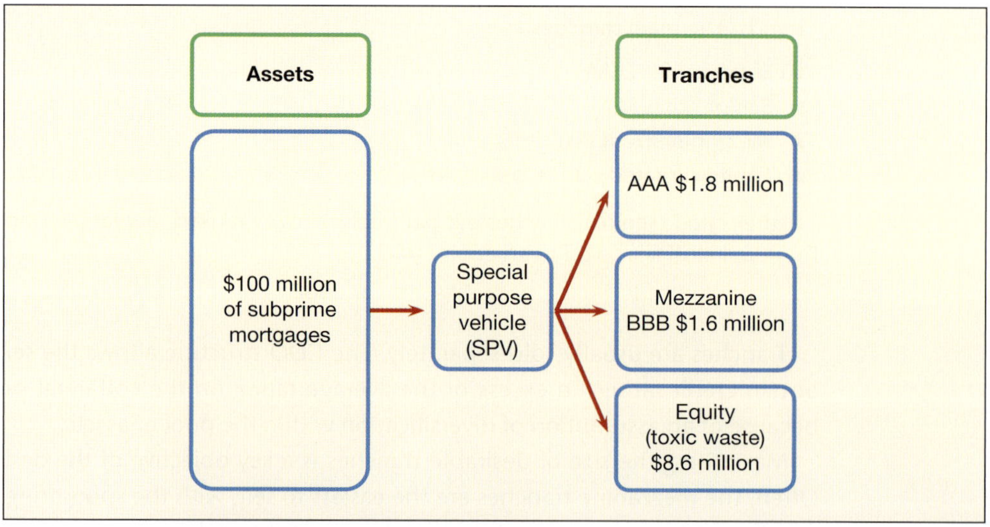

Figure 15.5 Payments from the CDO structure

concentrating the probability of default in the equity tranche, composed of $50 million. Provided the underlying mathematical assumptions are correct, in particular the probability of default is actually 25% and the bonds are uncorrelated, the tranching is correct.

Sensitivity to probability of default

CDO tranching is quite sensitive to the underlying probabilities of default. We show the tranche sizes for the example CDO, as we vary the probability of default, in Figure 15.6. As the probability goes from 0 to 50%, the AAA tranche is reduced from all 10 bonds to none, and by $p_d = 80\%$ the BBB tranche has essentially disappeared as well. Because of the binary nature of the CDO, even a small change in the probability of default can trigger large changes in the tranche sizes.

15.4.2 Correlated defaults

If defaults are independent events, that is, one bond defaulting has no bearing on the probability of other bonds defaulting, we can calculate each tranche's probability of default using the binomial distribution as in the simple example in Section B.1 of Appendix B.

But it is usually the case that defaults across bonds are correlated. Firms default more when there is an economic downturn or there is a shock affecting a whole sector. It is quite straightforward to incorporate correlated defaults into the calculation, perhaps by using the *Gaussian copula* approach, made (in)famous by Li (2000) whose contribution enabled the pricing of structured credit products (like subprime CDOs) that subsequently got blamed in the crisis that began in 2007. We present one approach to incorporating the Gaussian copula in Section B.3 of Appendix B.

Note the crucial impact that different assumptions about correlations have on the probability of default of each tranche. As correlations increase, the probability that all bonds will default increases, and the same applies to other tranches too. Increasing correlations increase the risk of all tranches.

Figure 15.7(a) shows the impact of changing default correlations for the example CDO. As the correlations increase from 0% to 100%, the probability that all 10 bonds will default rises from zero to 25%. Figure 15.7(b) zooms in on the bottom part from Figure 15.7(a), enabling us to see in detail the impact on tranches.

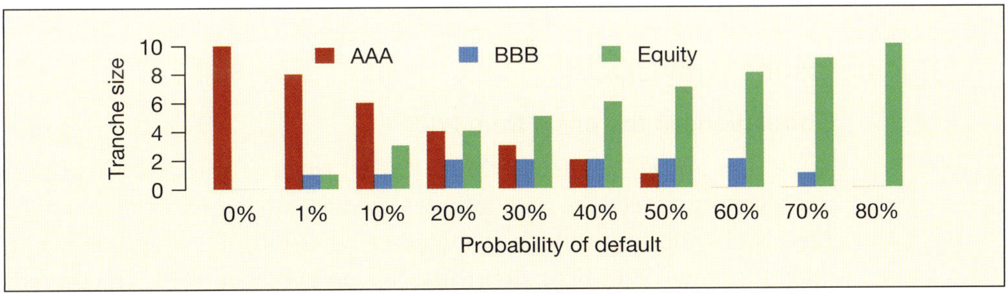

Figure 15.6 Effect of probability of default on tranche size

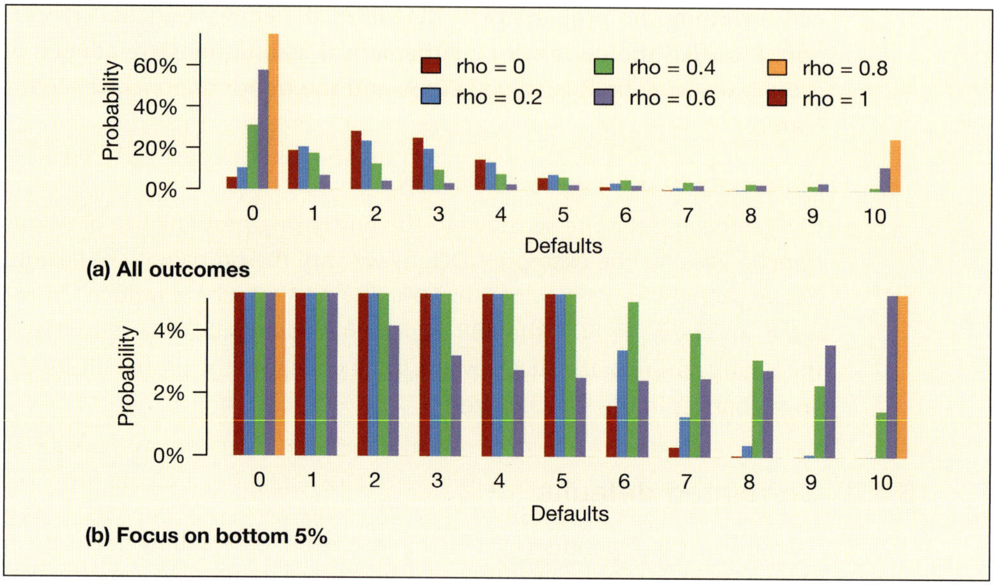

Figure 15.7 Effect of correlations on the probability of default

Table 15.2 Correlations and default probabilities

ρ	Probability of defaults	
	8 – 10	6 – 7
0%	0.04%	1.93%
20%	1.46%	6.84%
40%	4.77%	8.83%
60%	9.15%	8.59%
80%	14.47%	6.70%
100%	25.00%	0.00%

Table 15.2 presents the same information in a different way, focusing on what happens to the sizes for the AAA and mezzanine tranches when the correlations increase, compared to the benchmark case where the correlations equal 0.

15.4.3 Issues with CDOs

Correlations in the crisis from 2007

As we saw above, single-tranche CDOs are quite sensitive to small changes in correlations. Unfortunately, the data samples used to rate the CDOs containing subprime mortgages were not long enough to include a recession; the subprime market started taking off in the early 1990s right after the recession ending in 1991. The United States (US) was then recession-free until 2007, except for a few months in 2001, according to the NBER which keeps track of US recessions. The biggest boom years in the subprime market were entirely recession-free. Since mortgage defaults are highly dependent on the state of the economy, the estimation of default correlations would have been skewed towards zero. Even if the sample contained a downturn, it would be difficult to estimate the correlations because, as noted by Duffie (2007), there is a serious shortage of good models for estimating default correlations.

The problem of correlated defaults is worse than this, because even if accurate correlation estimates had been available, so long as the industry used Gaussian copula methods the dependence in mortgage defaults would still have been underestimated. The reason is that the Gaussian copula assumes constant correlations regardless of the state of the economy, while in actuality the correlations are much higher in downturns. The technical name for this is non-linear dependence (discussed in Section 3.3.1) and an asymmetric copula, properly taking this into account, is much more accurate. Unfortunately, it is very challenging to use such asymmetric copulae, not least because it is difficult to identify the best copula to use unless very large amounts of data are used, much more than are available.

CDOs as catastrophe bonds

A related problem is noted by Coval *et al.* (2008a, 2008b) who point out that some CDOs, such as those containing subprimes, can be considered a form of *catastrophe bonds*.

A traditional catastrophe bond is a security whose default probability is constant and independent of the economic state. Catastrophe bonds are typically used by insurers, and deliver their promised payoff unless there is a natural disaster, such as a hurricane or earthquake, in which case bond payments are no longer made. Investors are willing to pay a relatively high price for catastrophe bonds because their risks are uncorrelated with other economic indicators and, therefore, can be reduced through diversification.

Similar factors were at work with structured credit products containing subprime mortgages. In boom times, mortgage defaults tend to be idiosyncratic events, caused by a personal tragedy leading to a default. This means that if an individual defaults, it says little about the probability of anybody else defaulting.

In a recession it is different. Then an individual default may be caused by factories closing, causing widespread distress in a community, where an individual default is the harbinger of multiple defaults. The practice of geographically concentrating mortgages structured into CDOs amplified this effect.

For this reason, one can consider structured credit products containing subprime mortgages as a type of catastrophe bonds. In other words, the securitisation process substituted risks that are largely diversifiable for risks that are highly systematic. Structured finance products have far less chance of surviving a severe economic downturn than traditional corporate securities of equal rating.

Optimisation

Certain tranches of CDOs are more valuable than others. This means that banks might want to maximise the size of these tranches at the expense of the rest. This is known as *optimising the CDO structure*. In order to facilitate this process, the rating agencies supplied the banks with computer software enabling them to optimise the CDOs in-house before they were submitted to the rating agency.

This undermines the integrity of the whole process. The assignment of probabilities to the various tranches using the mathematical approach discussed above is correct conditional on the assets put into it. If the assets are preselected to maximise certain tranches, the probability assignments are biased. This is a variant of data mining as studied in econometrics.

A related and perhaps even more important problem is that the optimisation of the structure also minimises the quality of the asset pool. In other words, if the sponsor wants to optimise ratings, the cheapest way is to use assets with high loss given default and assets that have higher default correlations than are assumed in the modelling. This in turn affects the true value of all the tranches.

The end result is that before 2007, sponsors demanded assets that were high risk, with low expected recovery rates and high default correlations and probability of default, in other words, garbage assets. If one of the criteria for high profits is maximising the use of garbage assets, it should not come as a surprise that this all ends in tears.

Synthetic CDOs and CDOs squared

Before the crisis, the demand for CDO tranches significantly outstripped the supply, which led to frantic efforts to provide assets into those structures. This was a key reason for the boom in subprime lending in the US. Another manifestation of this demand was the creation of instruments that provide CDO-type risk by using *financial engineering* to create a synthetic CDO. When the supply of assets into CDOs was not sufficient, some financial institutions resorted to a concept called *CDO squared* (and cubed, etc.), CDO^2, CDO^3 or CDO^4. The input into a CDO^2 is not subprime mortgages or other bonds; instead it is tranches from other CDOs.

The logic behind this is to enable financial institutions to create yet more instruments and more finely tune the structures. However, such instruments amplify the errors in calculations. After all, if the initial CDO is subject to significant model risk, any structure using the equity tranches of the CDO will just magnify the model risk.

EXAMPLE 15.1 CDOs and fractional reserve banking

A CDO has many parallels with fractional reserve banking, and one could easily view a CDO as a type of bank. For example, both are subject to the same fundamental fragility in an economic downturn. A bank is vulnerable to a run and a CDO is sensitive to downgrades on the ratings of the tranches and funding problems as the probability of default or the correlations increase. This applies especially to conduits and SIVs (see below).

Both fractional reserve banks and CDOs substitute idiosyncratic risk with systemic risk. The reason is that both are vulnerable to idiosyncratic risk factors, perhaps problems facing an individual bank or bad CDO modelling. This may enable a relatively small idiosyncratic problem to undermine confidence in the banking system, spreading and amplifying idiosyncratic risk to systemic proportions.

Rating agencies

The rating agencies are private firms whose job it is to provide investors with information about the credit quality of financial instruments being offered.

For corporate bonds, especially in the US, investors can rely on over 80 years of ratings history to assess the quality of ratings, and thereafter make an independent determination of ratings quality. For bonds in other countries, both corporate and sovereign, the ratings history is much shorter, usually much less than two decades, making it much harder to ascertain ratings quality.

It is, however, with the various credit instruments where the ratings have been most severely criticised. The ratings on the many CDO-type instruments were significantly lacking in quality, ignoring the impact of correlations and how such instruments concentrate catastrophe risk. The market for dangerous credit instruments was fuelled by over-optimistic ratings, and the ratings agencies failed in their mission of providing independent quality advice to investors.

There is evidence that rating agencies made significant mistakes. For example, in May 2008, Moody's acknowledged that it had given AAA ratings to billions of dollars of structured finance products due to a bug in one of its rating models. In March 2007, First Pacific Advisors discovered that Fitch used a model assuming home prices could only increase.

15.4.4 Conduits and SIVs

While the misuse of CDOs was an important contributor to the crisis dating from 2007, two CDO-type structures were especially damaging, conduits and SIVs.

Conduits

A *conduit* is a simple structure involving a bank that sells some assets to a SPV, for example credit card receivables, loans or mortgages, in other words, various asset backed securities (ABSs). The conduit issues an asset-backed commercial paper (ABCP) to fund perhaps 90% or more of the purchases, the rest coming from its equity. The payments from the assets first go to pay interest on the ABCP; any excess belongs to the equity holder. The ABCP pays interest based on short-term rates, whereas the return from the assets is based on longer-term rates. The conduit's net interest income is comprised of a term structure component (long rates – short rates) and a credit spread component. The ABCP is usually AAA-rated due to over-collateralisation, so the cost of funding is low.

The sponsor guarantees funding for the SPV, so if it is unable to borrow sufficient amounts of money at reasonable terms, the sponsor steps in and funds the SPV. These liquidity guarantees provide a steady profit to the sponsor when times are good, but subject it to significant liquidity risk, realised at the worst time when the markets are already in turmoil.

EXAMPLE 15.2 A conduit as a bank

We can compare traditional banking with conduit banking, by considering the main balance sheet items:

	Old-style bank	Conduit
Equity capital	Provided by shareholders	Provided by sponsor
Debt	Short-term deposits	Short-term ABCP
Assets	Long-term loans	Various long-term loans

The conduit bank has direct parallels with a traditional bank, and is subject to the same main risk factors: default risk, bank runs (liquidity risk) and maturity mismatches. The problem is that the vulnerabilities of the conduit bank are less visible and understood than the vulnerabilities of the traditional bank, and the regulatory ways to address them less developed.

In good times, structures like conduits allow banks to enhance their earnings by benefiting from the return of the conduit's assets without having to hold the asset themselves. This means that banks can avoid regulatory capital requirements on those assets.

If the bank retains the equity portion, it retains most of the risk, both from losses on the assets and also from the liquidity guarantees. However, the exposure to the conduit was not covered by bank regulations before 2007, Basel I. This enabled the bank to take more leverage and more risk than regulations would otherwise allow.

SIVs

A structured investment vehicle (SIV) is similar to a conduit, but rather than just having equity and ABCP in its capital structure, it also has a mezzanine level, so that senior debt can be highly rated despite there being only a small amount of equity. This allows greater *leverage*. The mezzanine notes are typically of longer duration. They provide higher-yielding and longer-term instruments for investors seeking something riskier than ABCP.

Liquidity risks

Perhaps the main danger in these structures from a financial stability point of view is the hidden liquidity risk. The sponsoring banks generally provide *backup liquidity lines*, guaranteeing funds to the structure if it is unable to raise money elsewhere at reasonable rates. This has two purposes: first, it increases the security and attractiveness of the structure, and secondly it provides fees to the sponsor for providing the backup line. Even though the backup lines were quite risky to provide, they did not attract regulatory capital. This meant that these structures had a direct advantage over other forms of risk-taking, which generally require capital.

SIVs and conduits face serious funding liquidity risks. Their funding is short term, being rolled over frequently, often every three months. They are also highly sensitive to lenders' confidence in their structure, as the ability to borrow depends on the credit quality, since ABCP investors want to be convinced that the vehicle's assets are worth significantly more than the ABCP. If asset values dip even a little, it may suddenly be impossible to roll funding over. An ABCP buyer's strike is therefore the equivalent of a bank run. In this case, the vehicles may be forced to draw upon the backup liquidity line provided by the sponsoring bank.

In the end, it was the need to fund the structures at a time when the crisis had already started and funding was scarce, that caused significant problems in 2007, for example triggering the failure of IKB.

EXAMPLE 15.3 IKB

While the crisis started in the US, it quickly crossed the Atlantic, and seemed to affect medium-sized European banks especially badly. IKB, a small, partly state-owned German bank, was the first European victim of the subprime crisis. It had created a conduit some years earlier, and at the start of the crisis the assets held by the conduit suffered losses. Consequently, the conduit was unable to roll over its loans and had to draw on its credit line from IKB. The amount of money required was beyond the ability of IKB to provide, and it eventually received a bailout from private entities and the government amounting to €5 billion.

15.5 SUMMARY

Complexity in financial instruments can be quite profitable when things are good, but make financial institutions much more vulnerable both to an individual shock and especially to a systemwide shock.

The growth in volume of the various complex instruments has been exponential in recent years, especially that of CDSs. This is an instrument that significantly contributed to the crisis beginning in 2007, not least because of its OTC nature and general lack of transparency.

Another complex instrument that has proven to be quite dangerous is the CDO. The reason is that CDOs often contained a significant number of subprime mortgages, and mistakes in modelling created the illusion that high-risk assets could be repackaged into safe assets.

Two financial instruments caused significant problems in the early days of the crisis, SIVs and conduits, not least because of the embedded but hidden liquidity guarantees.

The rating agencies rated the tranches of the structured credit products with the same rating categories as corporate bonds, but it turned out that the risk characteristics of these two asset types were fundamentally different.

APPENDIX A: MECHANICS OF CDSS

A plain vanilla CDS is an OTC bilateral contract where in exchange for the payment of premium, the *protection seller* (the one writing the CDS) agrees that if any one of a number of credit events occurs on a reference instrument, they will compensate the *protection buyer* (the one buying the CDS) for the difference between the value of the reference instrument after the credit event (recovery value) and par (face value).

Terms and definitions

Reference entity The legal entity which borrows money; this may be a sovereign, financial institution, corporation or another specified entity.

Reference obligation Any holding, obligation, debt, or other credit instrument that is 'referenced' in the transaction.

Notional principal The hypothetical underlying quantity upon which interest or other payment obligations are computed.

Trade date The date on which the parties agree to the terms of a contract.

Effective date The date on which the parties begin calculating accrued obligations.

Termination date The date on which the CDS expires.

Credit event Any event that happens in respect of the reference entity that triggers payment under the CDS.

Settlement method The way in which the protection buyer is compensated after the occurrence of a credit event.

Typically, the reference instrument will be a debt security or a loan, where the allowed credit events include default, so the protection seller will compensate the protection buyer if the reference entity defaults. After a credit event, the holder of the reference instrument will get the recovery value, so the protection seller will suffer a loss of par minus recovery. Unlike a typical option, the premium on a CDS is usually paid periodically and this payment terminates in the event of a default.

The range of credit events on a CDS is usually chosen from bankruptcy, obligation default, violation of covenant, repudiation/moratorium, restructuring, reduction in interest or principal, or the lowering of seniority.

Terminology

'Buy' means buying protection:

- Pay premium
- Receive default payment if credit event occurs
- Sells/hedges credit risk
- Equivalent to selling a bond.

'Sell' means selling protection:

- Receive premium
- Pay default payment if credit event occurs
- Buys/takes on credit risk
- Equivalent to buying a bond.

An example

Suppose that two parties enter into a five-year credit default swap on 1 September 2012. Assume that the notional principal is $100 million and the buyer agrees to pay 90 basis points $\left({}^{90}\!/_{100} \text{ of } 1\%\right)$ annually for protection against default by the reference entity. The CDS is shown in Figure 15.8.

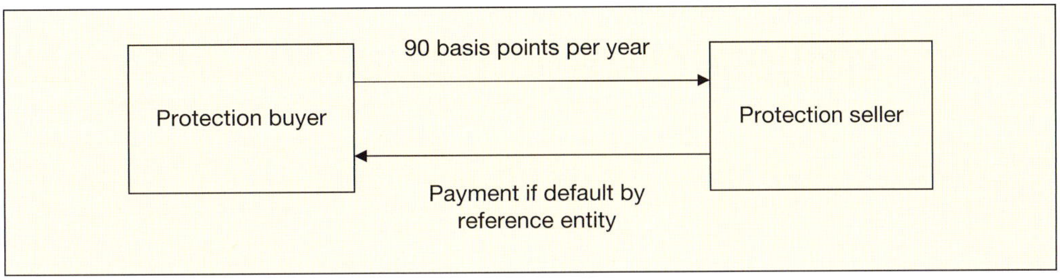

Figure 15.8 Credit default swap

If there is no credit event, the buyer receives zero payoff and pays \$900,000 (\$100,000,000 × 0.009) on 1 September in each of the years 2013, 2014, 2015, 2016 and 2017. If there is a credit event, a substantial payoff is likely. Suppose the buyer notifies the seller of a credit event on 1 April 2014. If the contract specifies physical settlement, and the reference entity is a bond, the buyer has the right to sell bonds to the writer issued by the reference entity at the full face value of \$100 million.

If the contract specifies cash settlement, an independent calculation agent will poll dealers to determine the mid-market value of the cheapest deliverable bond a predesignated number of days after the credit event. Suppose this bond is worth \$35 per \$100 of face value, then the cash payoff would be \$65 million (\$100 million − \$35 million). The total amount paid per year, as a percentage of the notional principal, to buy protection is known as the CDS spread. We can calculate the implied probability of default from the CDS spreads.

APPENDIX B: CDO CALCULATIONS

B.1 Simple example

Consider three bonds, *A*, *B* and *C*, each with a default probability $p_d = 0.1$, where defaults are independent. What is the chance that exactly two bonds will default? The possible outcomes with two defaults are *A*, *B* or *A*, *C* or *B*, *C*. We can calculate the number of combinations by using the binomial coefficient:

$$\binom{n}{k} = \frac{n!}{k!(n-k)!}, \binom{3}{2} = 3$$

where n is the total number of elements and k the desired number of elements we want in a combination, K is the random variable, and k the outcome.

But how to get the probabilities? The outcomes are binomially distributed. The probability of exactly k outcomes in a sample of size n with independent probabilities p_d is

$$g(k|n, p_d) = \Pr(K = k) = \binom{n}{k} p_d^k (1 - p_d)^{n-k} \tag{15.1}$$

Table 15.3 Probability of defaults

Number of defaults	Probability of defaults	Cumulative probability
0	0.729	0.729
1	0.243	0.972
2	0.027	0.999
3	0.001	1.000

where $g()$ denotes the binomial density. This gives 2.7% in our example. In our case, we are more interested in at least k defaults in a sample of n, that is, the binomial distribution, $G()$, with the outcomes shown in Table 15.3:

$$G\left(k \middle| n, p_d\right) = \Pr(K \leq k) = \sum_{i=0}^{k} \binom{n}{i} p_d^i \left(1 - p_d\right)^{n-i}$$

B.2 Worked example from Section 15.4.1

We show the probabilities and cumulative probabilities in Table 15.4 and use the default probabilities of benchmark corporate bonds':

- AAA has $p_d = 0.3\%$, interest $= 6\%$
- BBB has $p_d = 7\%$, interest $= 8\%$.

For simplicity, assume that if the benchmark corporate bond defaults, there is no recovery, so for a \$1 million AAA bond:

$$\text{payment} = \begin{cases} \$60{,}000 + \text{principal } (\$1 \text{ million}) & \text{with probability } 99.7\% \\ 0 & \text{with probability } 0.3\% \end{cases}$$

Table 15.4 Defaults and probabilities

Number of defaults	Probability of defaults	Cumulative probability	Cumulative probability from largest to smallest
0	0.05631	0.05631	1.00000
1	0.18771	0.24403	0.94369
2	0.28157	0.52559	0.75597
3	0.25028	0.77588	0.47441
4	0.14600	0.92187	0.22412
5	0.05840	0.98027	0.07813
6	0.01622	0.99649	0.01973
7	0.00309	0.99958	0.00351
8	0.00039	0.99997	0.00042
9	0.00002861	0.99999905	0.00002956
10	0.00000095	1.00000000	0.00000095

The SPV has a net inflow of \$12 million ($10 \times$ \$10 million $\times$ 0.12) if all goes well, but there is considerable risk that some of the loans will default so that it is very unlikely that all the money will come in.

From Table 15.4, the probability of all 10 bonds defaulting is 9.54×10^{-7}. The probability of 9 *or* 10 bonds defaulting is $9.54 \times 10^{-7} + 2.86 \times 10^{-5}$. This number is recorded in the last column of Table 15.4. Going up the table, the probability of 8 to 10 bonds defaulting is $4.158 \times 10^{-4} < 0.003$, while the probability of 7 to 10 bonds defaulting is $0.00351 > 0.003$. To summarise:

$$\Pr[8 \text{ to } 10 \text{ defaults}] < \Pr[\text{AAA defaulting}] < \Pr[7 \text{ to } 10 \text{ defaults}]$$

This means that the probability of getting \$3.6 million ($3 \times$ \$10 million $\times$ 0.12) in interest payments from the SPV, 99.958%, is higher than the probability of getting paid from the AAA bond, 99.3%, while the probability of getting \$4.8 million ($4 \times$ \$10 million $\times$ 0.12) in interest payments from the SPV, 99.65%, is lower than the AAA default probability. We conclude that the payment flow from the first three bonds gets an AAA rating. Similarly for the BBB:

$$\Pr[6 \text{ to } 10 \text{ defaults}] < \Pr[\text{BBB defaulting}] < \Pr[5 \text{ to } 10 \text{ defaults}]$$

Of the flow from the first five bonds that is less risky than the corresponding BBB, three are AAA, so the flow from the next two bonds gets BBB.

Tranching

We can tranche the payments in the following way. The SPV has a net inflow of \$12 million from interest payments ($10 \times$ \$10 million $\times$ 0.12), plus principal, if all goes well. Flow from the first three bonds, \$3.6 million ($3 \times$ \$10 million $\times$ 0.12) + principal, is safer than AAA, so that it gets AAA rating. An investor will get the AAA interest rate, or 6% plus the principal back (\$30 million).

Flow from the next two bonds, \$2.4 million ($2 \times$ \$10 million $\times$ 0.12) + principal, gets a BBB rating. An investor will get the BBB interest rate, or 8% plus the principal back (\$20 million).

The rest of the flow, \$12 − \$1.8 − \$1.6 = \$8.6 million + principal, goes to the equity investor. As she has rights to the last \$50 million, her interest rate is 17.2%.

B.3 Correlated defaults

The probability of default can be captured by a random variable whereby if the outcome of that random variable is below a certain threshold, a default occurs. For example, suppose the random variable X is standard normally distributed:

$$X \sim \mathcal{N}(0, 1)$$

Suppose the probability of default is p_d. We can then say that default happens if the outcome of the random variable is below the inverse normal distribution at the probability p_d;

$$\begin{array}{ll} \text{if } X \leq \Phi^{-1}(p_d) & \text{default} \\ \text{if } X > \Phi^{-1}(p_d) & \text{no default} \end{array}$$

where Φ is the normal distribution (CDF). Therefore, we have a simple way to deal with the probability of defaults mathematically, most importantly since this framework enables us to incorporate correlated defaults, via the Gaussian copula, quite easily. In this case, we need to make the random variable X correlated across multiple assets. This means that if we observe a low value of X for one asset, and hence observe a default, we are more likely to see the same for different assets (if the correlations are positive).

Generally speaking, suppose we have N assets, then we would say that the random variable X is an $N \times 1$ vector, with each element corresponding to an asset. Therefore, X has the distribution

$$X \sim \mathcal{N}(0, \Sigma)$$

where Σ is the covariance matrix. However, we want to consider a simpler case, where the correlations are all constant, denoted by ρ. We then have in the three-asset case:

$$\Sigma = \begin{Bmatrix} \sigma_1^2 & \rho\sigma_1\sigma_2 & \rho\sigma_1\sigma_3 \\ \rho\sigma_2\sigma_1 & \sigma_2^2 & \rho\sigma_2\sigma_3 \\ \rho\sigma_3\sigma_1 & \rho\sigma_3\sigma_2 & \sigma_3^2 \end{Bmatrix}$$

This means it is relatively straightforward to set up the problem using common factors, where the outcome for each asset has two components: the first is the common factor and the second is idiosyncratic. In our setup, we have constant correlations, so we get:

$$\begin{aligned} &a = \sqrt{\rho} \\ &x_i = af + \sqrt{1 - a^2}\epsilon_i && \text{outcome for bond} \\ &F \sim \mathcal{N}(0, 1) && \text{common factor} \\ &Z_i \sim \mathcal{N}(0, 1) && \text{idiosyncratic shock} \end{aligned} \tag{15.2}$$

where the factor is F, with common outcome f, whilst the idiosyncratic shock is ε_i. We then have that the probability of default conditional on the factor f is

$$\Pr\left(x_i < \Phi^{-1}(p_d) \,|\, f\right)$$

From (15.2) we have that the probability of default, conditional on the factor f, is

$$\begin{aligned} \Pr\left(x_i < \Phi^{-1}(p_d) \,|\, f\right) &= \Phi\left(\frac{\Phi^{-1}(p_d) - af}{\sqrt{1 - a^2}}\right) \\ &= p_d|f \end{aligned}$$

We are still left with the factor. Conditional on f we can get the expected cashflow from the portfolio (and indeed the entire distribution, perhaps for risk analysis). Suppose we want the probability of k defaults. From (15.1) we get:

$$g\left(k|n, p_d, f\right) = \binom{n}{k}\left(p_d|f\right)^k\left(1 - p_d|f\right)^{n-k}$$

This is the distribution of outcomes conditional on the factor. Of course, we do not see the factor and we eliminate it from the equation by integrating it out over its density:

$$\int_{-\infty}^{\infty} g\left(k \mid n, p_d, f\right)\phi(f)\mathrm{d}f$$

Questions for discussion

1 Who are the main beneficiaries from the complexity of financial products, and who are the losers?

2 Is the rapid growth of derivatives over the past few decades a cause for concern?

3 There are some proposals for using structured credit products to solve the EU sovereign debt problem. What sort of product could they be, why are they proposed, and would they work?

4 Do you think CDSs should be banned or heavily restricted?

5 The EU has effectively prohibited CDSs on European sovereign debt. It argues that the CDS market contributes to the crisis. Do you agree?

6 What are naked CDSs?

7 How can we use CDOs to turn high-risk assets into safe assets?

8 What is the role of correlations in the creation of CDOs?

9 Some commentators have said that CDOs, especially those containing subprime assets, are the equivalent of catastrophe insurance, in particular, the highest rated tranches. Identify the arguments in favour of the statement.

10 Spreads on AAA bonds have traditionally narrowed in times of financial uncertainty, and when the economy is in a deep recession yield on AAA tend to be very close to yields on government bonds. Has this been the case for AAA rated tranches of structured credit products?

11 What is your view on CDO^2 and CDO^3?

12 When the crisis started in 2007 it was often blamed on US structured credit products that crossed the Atlantic and adversely affected some European banks. What were those products, and why were some banks so badly affected?

13 We have three subprime mortgage backed securities, $S1$, $S2$, $S3$, each with a par value of 1 million dollars. Each of these securities has a 20% default probability, where the defaults are independent across securities.

Suppose an AAA bond has a 1% probability of default, an A bond 5% and a BB bond 8%.

(a) Calculate the probability and cumulative probability of 0, 1, 2 and 3 defaults.

(b) Suppose you package the securities into a collateralised debt obligation (CDO). How big would you make the AAA tranche?

References

Barnier, M. (2011) quoted in Barker, A., EU ban on 'naked' CDS to become permanent. *Financial Times*, 19 October, www.ft.com/cms/s/0/cc9c5050-f96f-lle0-bf8f-00144feab49a.html.

Board of Governors of the Federal Reserve System (2009). Revenge of the steamroller: ABCP as a window on risk choices. Unpublished paper, Division of International Finance.

Buffett, W. (2003). Avoiding a mega-catastrophe. *Fortune*, 24 March.

Coval, J., Jurek, J. and Stafford, E. (2008a). The economics of structured finance. Harvard Business School Working Paper 09-060.

Coval, J. D., Jurek, J. W. and Stafford, E. (2008b). Economic catastrophe bonds. Mimeo, Harvard University.

Crouhy, M., Galai, D. and Mark, R. (2000). *Risk Management*. McGraw-Hill.

Duffie, D. (2007). Innovations in credit risk transfer: implications for financial stability. Mimeo, Stanford University.

Duffie, D. (2010). Is there a case for banning short speculation in sovereign bond markets? *Financial Stability Review*, 14, Banque de France.

Duffie, D. and Singleton, K. (2003). *Credit Risk*. Princeton University Press.

Financial Times (2010a). The benefits of naked CDS. *Financial Times*, 2 March.

Hull, J. C. (2011). *Options, Futures, and Other Derivatives*, 8th edition. Prentice Hall.

Hull, J. C. (2012). *Risk Management and Financial Institutions*, 3rd edition. Prentice Hall.

Li, D. X. (2000). On default correlation: a copula function approach. *J. Fixed Income*, 9: 43–54.

Murphy, D. (2009). *Unravelling the Credit Crunch*. CRC Press.

The Economist (2009). No empty threat. Credit-default swaps are pitting firms against their own creditors. *The Economist* (US), 18 June.

16 FAILURES IN RISK MANAGEMENT AND REGULATIONS BEFORE THE CRISIS

The most damaging global financial crisis since the Great Depression started in 2007. While the underlying causes are varied, failures in financial regulations and financial risk management played a key role.

By 2007, the prevailing view by market participants and banking supervisors was that the problem of financial risk had been reduced to an engineering-type exercise. So long as risk was measured correctly and the appropriate correction mechanisms were employed, either imposed by banking supervisors or built into internal risk management, the financial system would remain in an almost permanent state of safety.

This was incorrect. The nature of financial risk was misunderstood because the risk controls not only failed to protect but also created conditions for excessive risk-taking, because economic agents have strong incentives to find areas of weakness and exploit those to make profit.

This happens clandestinely, outside the scrutiny of banking supervisors or even senior bank management and internal risk control. We learn about excessive risk-taking only when it is too late and things blow up. To the outside world, the system looks stable and the general perception of stability creates incentives to take on more risk, because, after all, 'what could possibly go wrong?' In the words of Hyman Minsky, *stability breeds instability*.

Links to other chapters

This chapter relates directly to Chapter 10 (credit markets), Chapter 9 (trading and speculation) and Chapter 17 (the ongoing crisis: 2007–2009 phase).

It also draws heavily on previous chapters in this book, such as Chapter 1 (systemic risk), Chapter 3 (endogenous risk), Chapter 13 (financial regulations) and Chapter 15 (dangerous financial instruments). It also connects to Chapter 18 (ongoing developments in financial regulation).

Key concepts

- **Why the safeguards failed**
- **Complexity and financial engineering**
- **Prudential versus system regulations**
- **Toxic assets and capital fragility**

Readings for this chapter

A large number of studies have been made of regulation and risk management failures leading to the crisis, with just about every relevant government body and private institution publishing a contribution. Of those, two are particularly important, the Larosiere (2009) EU report and the the Turner Review by the Financial Services Authority (2009b). Goodhart (2009) has a good analysis of the regulatory failures. Since the crisis is not over, no authoritative study has yet been published, and this chapter is mostly based on the author's own analysis.

Notation specific to this chapter

A	**Assets**
C	**Capital**
T_1, T_2	**Tier 1 and Tier 2**
w	**Risk weight**

16.1 REGULATORY FAILURES

In 2007, most financial institutions were highly regulated and practised sophisticated risk management. It was felt by both the authorities and the industry that this was sufficient to prevent bank failures and protect the real economy. After all, we had not seen a global financial crisis since the 1930s, and subsequent crisis episodes had a well-understood cause and effect. It might not be an exaggeration to say that both banking supervisors and risk managers thought they had regulations and risk management down to science, some tinkering needed on the margins, but generally the system was thought in good shape. We had seen some crises, for example in Asia in 1997, and LTCM in 1998, but those were either in developing countries, caused by imbalances thought not to affect more developed countries, or arising from specific deficiencies quickly identified and fixed.

Events since have demonstrated the folly of such views; the banks and supervisors were complacent, excessively trusting in quantitative approaches to regulation and risk management, and blind to the build-up of risk.

16.1.1 Was there excessive deregulation?

One view that is often expressed is that a key cause of the crisis was excessive deregulation. That is not strictly true, and in many aspects the financial system had never been more regulated than in 2007. During the Bretton Woods era, many governments exercised strong controls over their banking systems, but this was often more in the area of certain activities, especially capital flows. The most visible part of the post-Bretton Woods deregulation was global capital flows, liberalised from the 1950s, and essentially completely free since the 1980s. Over time, regulations have taken new forms, and sweeping restrictions on general activities have been replaced by a much more intrusive micro-approach, where even minute bank activities are liable to be closely supervised and controlled.

Until the 1980s, national regulations were a patchwork of conflicting and often ineffective rules, allowing regulatory arbitrage and casting a blind eye on dodgy practices taking place in other jurisdictions. Since then, regulations have been generally tightening, most directly due to the various activities of the Basel Committee for Banking Supervision (BCBS). While the capital accords are the best known of its activities, the Committee has also been effective in establishing common international standards for banking supervision, the Concordat. These have been implemented by member countries, as well as the European Union (EU) and a number of other countries.

The crisis from 2007 did not happen because of a lack of regulations or deregulation; it is rather that the regulations were not effective.

16.1.2 The focus of risk management and regulations

If we have to pick a single newspaper headline cause for the ongoing crisis it would be excessive risk-taking. If the banks had not taken on too much risk, the crisis would not have happened. While this is of course true, the relevant question is different: why wasn't this excessive risk-taking detected and prevented?

Based on the prevailing approaches of risk managers and banking supervisors at the time, risk-taking was not excessive. How did the excessive pre-crisis risk-taking pass undetected? There are two fundamental reasons. First, both regulations and risk management systems targeted day-to-day risk and not extreme risk. Perhaps the main reason for this is that it is much harder to model and manage extreme risk than day-to-day risk. The second reason is endogenous risk. Most risk models are based on forecasting risk based on historical samples, which explicitly excludes risk that is not visible in observed data. Both reasons suggest that risk controls focused on what was easy rather than what was relevant. This applies equally to the industry and to supervisors.

Risk target levels

Financial regulations, and especially the Basel Accords, have a close connection with how financial institutions internally manage risk. The 1996 amendment to Basel I and especially Basel II generally require banks to accurately forecast and manage risk with internal models, and create dual-use risk systems, whereby models are to be used both for internal risk control and for regulatory purposes such as reporting and capital calculations. The target risk levels were not very extreme, and ignored tail risk.

This can be seen in the calculation of market risk, specified in the 1996 amendment to Basel I as a multiple of value-at-risk (VaR). Bank capital for trading activities is based on a multiple of the risk of an event that happens 2.5 times a year on average, $\text{VaR}^{99\%}_{\text{daily}}$. Such events do not seem very systemic or a threat to financial stability.

Day-to-day risk and extreme risk

Definition 16.1 Tail risk or extreme risk We refer to the risk of very large and very frequent adverse outcomes in financial markets as extreme risk. Another name for it is 'tail risk' because extreme outcomes happen in the far left tail of return distributions. While there is no consensus as to what constitutes extreme risk, a useful definition is an event that happens no more than once every five years on average. We might observe two five-year events close to each other and none for 10 years. There is no specific time period over which the adverse event happens. It could play out in 10 minutes as in a flash crash type of event, in one day as in the 1987 crash, or even over several months as in 2008.

This regulatory and internal risk management focus on particular aspects of risk explains why the financial industry was able to take on excessive levels of risk undetected. Financial risk models have become quite successful at forecasting day-to-day risk and banks in turn have become very good at managing such risk. This success was noted by the supervisors. Unfortunately, it is much harder to model and understand *extreme risk*.

This focus on day-to-day risk levels impacted on the distribution of financial returns in a particular way. Borrowing language from the statistical literature on risk modelling, we can say that active risk management may cause the volatility to decrease and the tails to thicken. We see a depiction of this in Figure 16.1 (repeated from Figure 3.9). The blue line shows what the distribution of market outcomes could be if financial institutions were not actively trying to manage day-to-day risk, whilst the red line shows what happens when they do. The impact of active risk management is to reduce the probability of uncommon

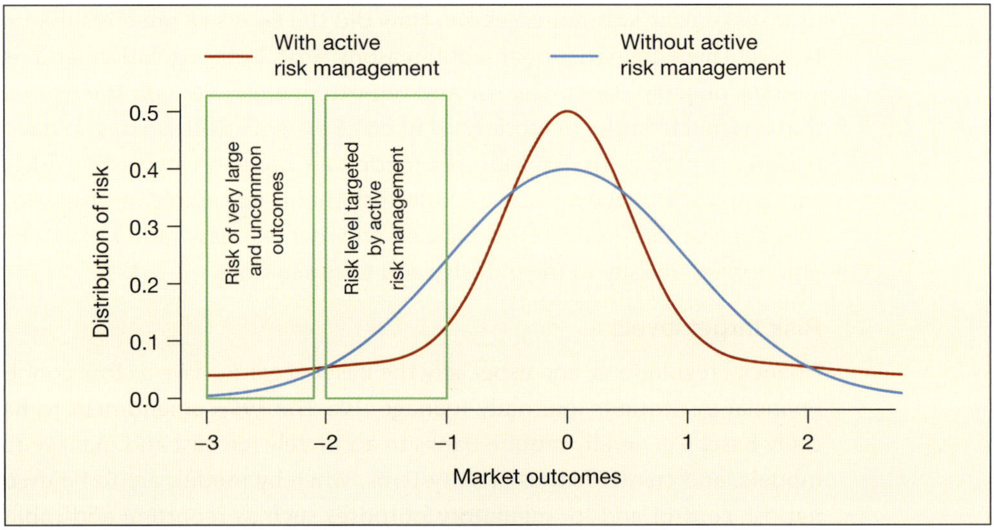

Figure 16.1 Impact of active risk management

events, shown by the red line being below the blue line in the sides of the distribution, but at the expense of the red line being higher in the tails, signalling a high probability of extreme outcomes.

This approach to risk management led to an attitude well described by an old joke. A policeman sees a drunk man crawling on the ground at night and asks him what he is up to. The drunk responds that he is looking for his keys. The policeman says why are you looking there? The drunk says that is where the light is. The lesson from this story is that financial institutions and banking supervisors became blinded by their success in finding risk where it is visible and neglected to search for risk elsewhere.

Unfortunately, those who really want to maximise risk, like bank traders, were actively searching for the dark areas, so almost by definition, if the supervisors or the bank risk managers were looking in one area, excessive risk-taking took place elsewhere.

This meant that prior to 2007, the financial system had all the outward signs of low risk, and the era became known as '*the great moderation*'. Alas, that very perception created conditions for excessive risk-taking and the subsequent crisis.

16.1.3 Normality and non-linear dependence

Financial returns are often assumed to be normally distributed. Empirically, that is not true; instead they adhere to three stylised facts, as discussed in Danielsson (2011). They have fat tails, volatility clusters and non-linear dependence. The first refers to the observation that outcomes in financial markets are more extreme than is consistent with the normal distribution, and the second that volatilities cluster and go through time periods with high volatility followed by periods of low volatility. Finally, non-linear dependence (see Definition 3.1) refers to the fact that correlations are inadequate in describing how financial returns behave, especially in times of stress.

Fat tails

Since many methods in portfolio theory and derivative pricing assume that returns are normally distributed, they break down in the presence of fat tails. It is, however, in the field of financial regulations and risk management where the lack of normality is crucially important. An inappropriate assumption of normality leads to the gross underestimation of risk:

> '[. . .] as you well know, the biggest problems we now have with the whole evolution of risk is the fat-tail problem, which is really creating very large conceptual difficulties. Because as we all know, the assumption of normality enables us to drop off the huge amount of complexity in our equations [. . .] Because once you start putting in non-normality assumptions, which is unfortunately what characterizes the real world, then these issues become extremely difficult.'
>
> Alan Greenspan (1997)

The summer of 2007

The apparent sudden emergence of fat tails and non-linear dependence caused difficulties for many financial institutions in the crisis from 2007. One of the first manifestations of the crisis was the quant event of 2007, causing some banks to lose large sums of money on quantitative trading. The markets began to move in a way that was inconsistent with the computer models used by banks. This triggered selling, resulting in price drops, further creating difficulties typical of the feedback loops associated with problems of endogenous risk. Goldman Sachs's flagship Global Alpha fund, which used quantitative strategies across a range of asset classes, had lost 27%:

> '"We were seeing things that were 25-standard deviation moves, several days in a row", said David Viniar, Goldman's chief financial officer. "There have been issues in some of the other quantitative spaces. But nothing like what we saw last week."'
>
> *Financial Times* (2007)

Lehman also had problems:

> '"Wednesday is the type of day people will remember in quant-land for a very long time", said Mr Rothman, a University of Chicago Ph. D. who ran a quantitative fund before joining Lehman Brothers. "Events that models only predicted would happen once in 10,000 years happened every day for three days."'
>
> *Wall Street Journal* (2007)

Volatility and fat tails

A common measure of financial risk is volatility or the standard deviation of financial returns. This is correct if and only if returns are normally distributed. If they are fat, volatility significantly under-represents risk. If we consider the 25-standard deviation moves that Goldman suffered a few days in a row, the only appropriate distributional assumption, in the absence of other information, is normality. A 25-standard deviation loss under the normal distribution has a probability of 3×10^{-138}. By contrast, the age of the universe is estimated to be 5×10^{12} days whilst the earth is only 1.6×10^{12} days old. This indicates that Goldman only expected to suffer a one-day loss of this magnitude fewer than one every 1.5×10^{125} universes.

The explanation is probably that Goldman's models never considered such extreme losses and, therefore, were unable to properly quantify the probability. This does point to the challenges presented by fat tails in risk modelling.

Value-at-risk

Perhaps the most common measure of financial risk is VaR. While it has been widely criticised, most of the commentators do not seem to properly understand the nature of the measure, in particular those claiming it is dependent on normality. That is not true, even if actual implementations frequently do so. The fault there lies with the modellers, not the concept.

VaR does, however, have several flaws, making it inappropriate in most cases for applications in financial stability.

- First, it is not sub-additive, meaning it is not relevant for assets that most of the time deliver steady returns but very rarely suffer large losses. An example of such assets is high-risk bonds. A misuse of VaR in this context has been at the heart of many losses, for instance, those suffered by UBS in 2007, as noted by UBS (2008).

- Second, VaR typically applies only to a single-day loss, independent of other days. This means that a series of small losses individually might not seem too worrying if judged by VaR, even if the accumulated losses might be so large as to cause a bank to fail.
- Third, VaR is only as good as the underlying statistical model, most of which are rather poor. In particular, attempting to model extreme outcomes or multi-day losses with VaR is generally impossible if an accurate risk assessment is desired.
- Finally, VaR can capture only *perceived risk*, not *actual risk*, because it depends on using historical data for the risk forecast.

We saw one example of this in the discussion of the JP Morgan Chase 'whale' in Example 9.1. The risk does not seem to have been picked up by the bank's internal models: the average VaR for the first three months of 2012 for chief investment office (CIO) activities was $129 million, compared to $60 million the year before. In other words, the perceived risk was only a small fraction of the actual risk, a clear example of how risk builds up out of sight. This also demonstrates the problems of relying on risk measures like VaR, because it is conceivable that JP Morgan Chase had many days with large losses but never violating its VaR limit on a single day.

16.1.4 Prudential versus systemic regulations

While the problem of non-extreme risk levels and endogenous risk comes from how risk modelling is practised, a bigger failure arises from the prevailing approach to financial regulations. Neither the financial industry nor the authorities seemed very bothered by systemic risk prior to the crisis. Financial regulations were almost exclusively prudential in nature. That meant banking supervisors were primarily concerned with the risk of each bank individually, rather than how the risk of all banks could aggregate up to systemic risk. They disregarded the potential for the prudential approach to banking supervision leading to the creation of hidden endogenous risk.

Systemic risk was ignored

If the interconnectedness between financial institutions is limited, the safety of the system can be ensured by each bank being prudentially run. However, in a world where financial institutions are highly interconnected and interdependent, such an institutional focus can lead to a situation where each and every institution is perceived as safe, and perversely because of that prudence, the system becomes unstable.

This can be explained by a simple stylised scenario. Perhaps some asset values fall for exogenous reasons. The self-preservation principle fundamental to any prudentially run institution will make it want to sell high-risk assets. But exactly because of that behaviour, prices fall further, causing further distress. In other words, because of the exogenous shock, risk is no longer exogenous and becomes highly endogenous. This is manifested by the *firesale effect*, seen in Figure 16.2 (repeated from Figure 1.6).

It is the self-preservation behaviour that is destabilising the system. The only way to properly prevent excessively large crisis events is to understand the interconnectedness between financial institutions and design mechanisms to mitigate the implied danger. Such views, however, ran contrary to the prevailing views of both financial institutions

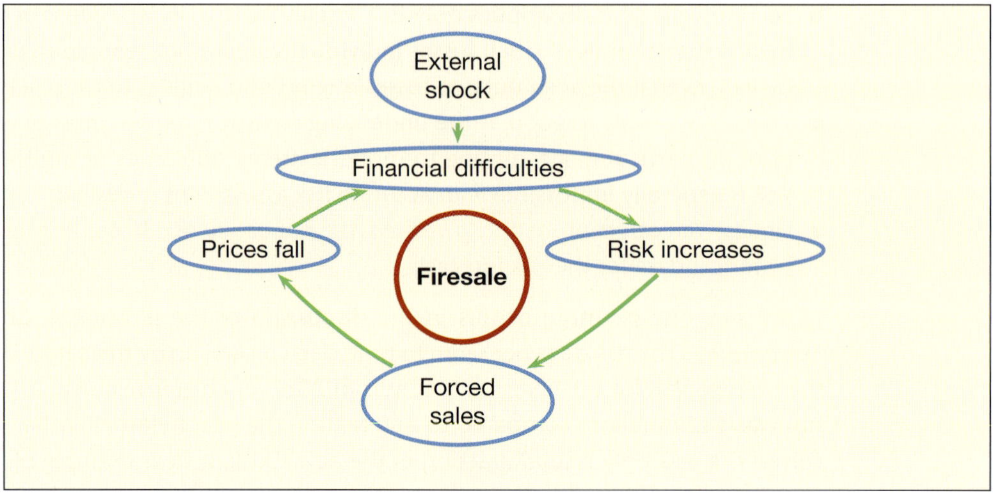

Figure 16.2 Firesales and acceleration effects

and banking supervisors. The banks wanted to focus on their own activities, and for the supervisors it was hard enough to ensure that each institution was prudently run without having to consider the more complicated issues of interconnectedness and its contribution to systemic risk.

Liquidity and asymmetric information

The first sign of the crisis starting in 2007 was the drying up of liquidity. When investors went on strike and the interbank market effectively ceased, financial institutions throughout the world, which had been accustomed to effectively infinite amounts of liquidity, found themselves in serious difficulties. Eventually, the central banks had to step in as liquidity providers. This liquidity crisis caught the supervisors and the banks unawares.

The focus on prudential regulations also meant that the authorities had ignored liquidity. The world had not seen a global liquidity crisis since the 1930s and the last regional liquidity crisis was in Asia in 1997, with liquidity also playing a big role in the LTCM crisis in 1998. One example of how liquidity was ignored was that some banks were able to create products like conduits and charge fees for liquidity guarantees for those products, disregarding the fact that any drying up of liquidity would probably cause the failure of the sponsoring bank.

A related problem arose because of interlocking exposures in over-the-counter (OTC) derivative contracts like credit default swaps (CDSs) and collateralised debt obligations (CDOs). The perception at the time was that banks were able to use high-quality internal models to both price and risk-assess these derivative instruments, and were always able to hedge or monetise them, that is, liquidity was thought infinite. As it turned out, liquidity was far from infinite and a key reason was asymmetric information: market participants stopped trusting valuations and risk assessments made by other institutions.

Liquidity is a system-wide phenomenon, and is therefore easy to miss when regulations focus on individual banks rather than on the system. Liquidity has been absent in the Basel regulations and while some countries did impose liquidity constraints, such as the United Kingdom (UK), other main financial centres took a more ambivalent attitude.

16.1.5 Complexity, incentives and resources

The complexity of the banking system directly contributed to the failure of financial regulations before 2007. The reason is that complexity makes it hard for the authorities to have an overview of risks being created, both within banks and system-wide. While this complexity arises naturally in finance, the problem is made worse because banks have a direct incentive to maximise complexity.

Complexity is attractive to banks for several reasons. It reduces transparency, making it harder to scrutinise their activities and replicate successful trading strategies, whilst increasing fees. It can create an aura of sophistication, helping in marketing. Furthermore, complexity directly contributes to financial institutions becoming too big to fail (TBTF), and hence increasing the probability of bailouts and lowering funding costs.

The complexity of the financial industry leaves banking supervisors at a distinct disadvantage. Banks throw a significant amount of resources at creating complex financial products and trading activities, effectively maximising complexity. The supervisors charged with monitoring bank activities do not have access to the same resources even though their problem is much harder than that of the banks, because the supervisors have to understand the aggregated risk across the financial system, which includes the complexity of one institution interacting with another.

The supervisory approach to complexity was inadequate. Instead of addressing individual practices and their inherent complexity, the supervisors opted to focus on the end result, either prices or risk forecasts. This misses the big picture because the problems are in the calculation of the risk forecasts and prices, so the only way to understand the danger being built up is to study the individual products and model assumptions, and then aggregate the resulting information across the firm and industry.

16.2 CAPITAL AND THE CRISIS

The main body of financial regulations in place when the crisis started was Basel I, but most jurisdictions and banks had already made a significant step towards Basel II. It quickly became apparent that many of the criticisms of Basel II, which had been dismissed by the BCBS prior to the crisis, were indeed valid. Perhaps the largest failure of the Basel Accords was demonstrated by bank capital.

Banks around the world found themselves confronted with an unexpected problem when the crisis started. At the time, they seemed generally to be highly capitalised, comfortably exceeding the Basel II capital adequacy ratio (CAR), many at 12–13%. However, when the crisis was underway, this turned out to be insufficient, not because a CAR of 13% is not respectable, but rather because the markets did not believe that 13% represented the banks' true CAR. What happened was that banks were faced with a twin problem, *toxic assets* and *capital fragility*, aided by the practice of *capital structure optimisation*.

16.2.1 The undermining of capital

Recall the Basel CAR from Definition 13.5:

$$\text{CAR} = \frac{C = T_1 + T_2}{w_1 \times A_1 + w_2 \times A_2} \geq 8\% \tag{16.1}$$

It is in the interest of any bank to make the CAR look as large as possible, for a given set of assets and liabilities. To this end, a bank might employ capital structure optimisation to maximise the numerator of (16.1) whilst minimising the denominator.

Toxic assets in the denominator

There are two categories of variables in the denominator in (16.1), the assets and the risk weights. It can be difficult to identify the value of assets because only a fraction of them are actively traded on the open market and consequently have a market price. The rest are illiquid, without a market price, so the only way to obtain valuation is by using a financial model to find the most likely price given the nature of assets and general market conditions.

It is even harder to calculate the risk weights because, unlike prices, risk cannot be measured. Instead, it has to be inferred from historical information about the assets, their inherent properties and general market conditions. In the language of statistics, *risk is a latent variable*. The only way to identify risk is by using a statistical model to forecast the risk. Since every model is incorrect by definition, every risk forecast is incorrect and highly sensitive to the underlying assumptions of the model.

An example of an asset that has both problems is collateralised debt obligation (CDO) tranches, since both the valuation and risk assessment come from a pricing model that is highly sensitive to the underlying assumptions. Before 2007, both the banks and the rating agencies were too optimistic in their assumptions, assigning too high values and too low risk to the CDO tranches.

As a consequence, many of the assets held by banks were referred to colloquially as *toxic*, meaning that their market value was highly uncertain and their risk weights understated. This meant the markets did not trust the quality of the denominator, and often ignored the risk weights during the crisis from 2007, assuming the worst.

Capital fragility and the numerator

The numerator in (16.1) was also mistrusted. It is composed of the two main categories of capital, tier 1 and tier 2. Of those, tier 1 is closer to the ideal qualities of bank capital, especially the equity part. By contrast, tier 2 capital is imperfect, especially the *hybrid capital instruments*.

Hybrids are financial instruments that, at least in theory, provide almost the same protection as equity but at a lower cost. They broadly define a range of securities which are positioned between equity and senior debt, being long-term bonds with a special feature enabling the issuing bank to convert them into equity or defer payments in times of difficulty. This means that such instruments are able to absorb losses without triggering the financial institution into liquidation.

In principle, hybrid instruments sound like a good idea. They provide stable long-term funding to a bank, whilst providing protection when things get rough. They are, of course, inferior to equity. Not only is equity the banks' own money while hybrids are just borrowed money; equity also is money owned by the banks' owners, which presumably incentivises them to behave prudently.

The main problem with hybrids is how they were set up; in particular, it was generally at the discretion of the bank when a payment could be deferred or the bond converted. In other words, there was no explicit trigger for conversion, and the experience during the crisis showed that banks were quite reluctant to trigger conversion.

An important reason seems to have been that banks sold these instruments to preferred clients with the promise of a high return, and were reluctant to see them suffer losses. In other words, *reputation risk* held them back. The banks converted only when forced to do so by the supervisors during the crisis.

Another key reason was that a conversion into equity is dilutive and thus runs against shareholder and perhaps management interests.

Finally, doing a conversion signals that the financial institution is in difficulty and, therefore, creates the potential for a run, not only on the bank converting but also on other banks.

This meant that the protection afforded by the hybrid capital instruments turned out to be illusory for the most part; the markets recognised this and ignored hybrids when calculating bank capital and evaluating the strength of financial institutions.

Capital structure optimisation

The banks are directly to blame for this predicament. Before the crisis, they wanted to demonstrate they were highly capitalised, and to achieve that they used capital structure optimisation to maximise the visible part of their capital whilst at the same time keeping the cost of capital as low as possible. In effect, the number representing capital was maximised and the protection minimised.

Both the regulators and the banks seem to have assumed that such optimisation was benign, or at least not damaging given other sources of protection, such as management expertise, lending of last resort (LOLR), modern risk management, diversification, the secular decline in risk, and the like. In other words, capital structure optimisation was condoned, not because the potentially adverse consequences were not understood, but rather because other protection factors were thought to be in place.

16.2.2 Case study: European banks in the crisis

When the crisis started in 2007, the financial markets became increasingly concerned about banks failing, and started to look for signs of weakness. The markets dismissed the optimistic reported assessments of bank capital and instead focused on the most conservative way to calculate bank capital. The banks with the biggest disparity between the loose and strict ways of calculating capital were deemed most at risk. In turn, this caused difficulties for institutions that were highly capitalised by the Basel ratio but not by the conservative measures. These problems were the subject of many studies by financial institutions, and we draw on numbers from Lehman Brothers (2008).

Four capital adequacy ratios

We focus on four different ways of calculating a CAR, where going down this list we find increasingly restrictive or conservative measures of the capital ratio:

- **Tier 1/RWA** This is the more strict Basel ratio, tier 1 capital divided by risk-weighted assets (RWA).
- **Core tier 1/RWA** This focuses only on the equity part of tier 1, since core tier 1 is composed of shareholders' equity and retained earnings.
- **Tier 1/TA** This replaces RWA with total assets (TA).
- **Tangible equity/TA** This replaces tier 1 with tangible common equity, the subset of shareholders' equity that is not preferred equity and not intangible assets.

Aggregate results

Figure 16.3 shows the four ratios. Of those, tier 1/RWA is trending upwards, therefore, the Basel capital ratio was sending the signal that the banks were becoming more capitalised and, hence, safer over time. However, we see that from 2002 equity has been reduced and other forms of tier 1 have become an increasing part of tier 1 capital.

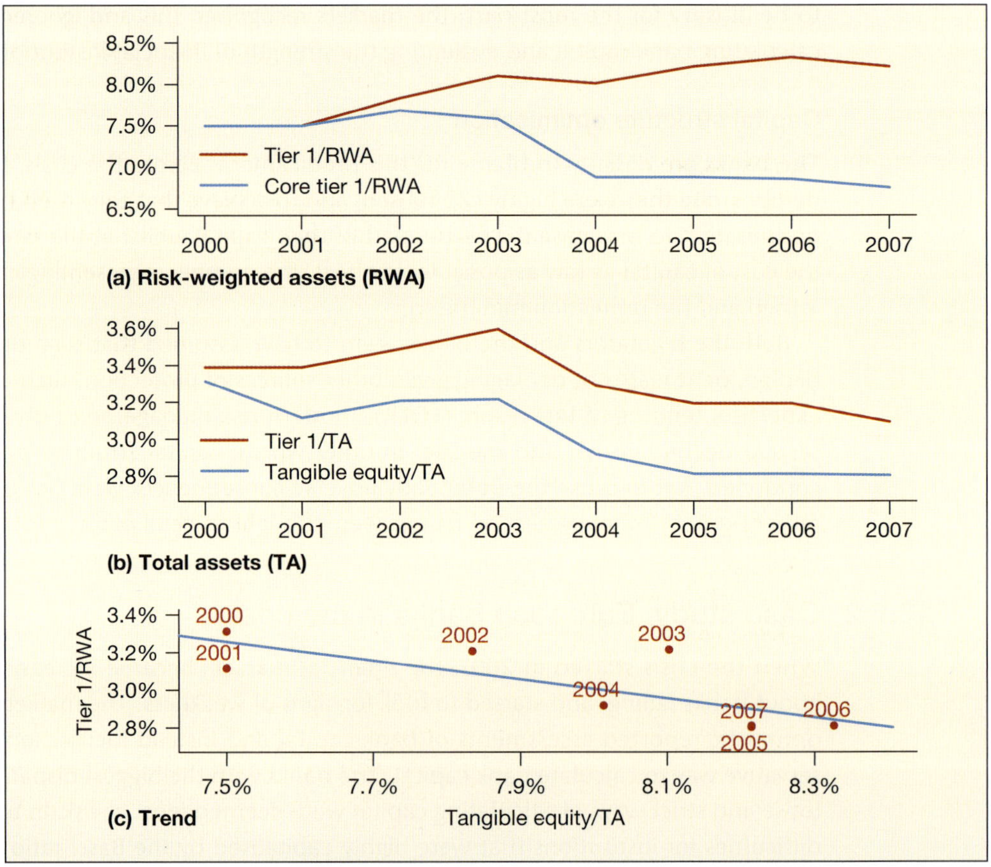

Figure 16.3 Capital ratios over time

Data source: Lehman Brothers (2008)

This is in line with Figure 16.3(b); tier 1/TA first increases sharply but then starts dropping from 2004, whilst the most conservative capital measure, tangible equity over TA, is steadily dropping throughout the sample period. These results support the analysis of the impact of financial engineering on the capital structure; the visible reported component is increasing, but a look at the components that are harder to manipulate shows that the banks' capitalisation was getting worse over time.

Finally, Figure 16.3(c) shows a cross-plot of tangible equity/TA to tier 1/RWA, along with a regression line. We see here the relationship is trending downwards, albeit with a high degree of uncertainty. This demonstrates how Basel capital and conservatively calculated capital were evolving at a different rate.

Individual results

A similar picture emerges by looking at individual European institutions in Table 16.1 during the first quarter of 2008, when the crisis was becoming serious and considerable focus was on bank capital. What is interesting is the change in rankings of different institutions when we switch from using the Basel ratio all the way to tangible equity/TA. Figure 16.4 shows the ranking of capital, identifying four categories of banks.

CS went from being the best capitalised bank to below average, whilst UBS went from being the tenth lowest capitalised bank in the sample to the lowest. Both of these banks, especially the latter, experienced significant difficulties in the crisis. DB, similarly, went from 35 to 2. Banks like HSBC maintained a fairly consistent ranking across all the measures.

The sample contains some institutions that ran into difficulties. Interestingly, AIB, which was now in serious trouble with the sovereign debt crisis in Ireland, was looking relatively healthy, whilst RBS was showing clear signs of financial engineering.

Figure 16.4 shows this same information in a different way, as a cross-correlation between tier1/RWA and tangible equity/TA, where we identify banks that have received some government assistance. There seems to be little or no connection between needing help and having a weak capital base; if anything, the most highly capitalised banks with the best capital were more likely to get into trouble.

Table 16.1 Capital ratios and rank amongst peers in Q1 2008

	$\frac{\text{Tier 1}}{\text{RWA}}$	$\frac{\text{Tangible equity}}{\text{TA}}$	Distress
Allied Irish Bank (AIB)	7.6% (23)	5.8% (43)	Fatal
Credit Suisse (CS)	11.5% (50)	3.6% (22)	Considerable
Deutsche Bank (DB)	8.7% (35)	1.3% (2)	Considerable
HSBC	9.1% (37)	4.2% (33)	Moderate
Royal Bank of Scotland (RBS)	7.3% (19)	2.2% (7)	Fatal
Santander	7.77% (28)	5.3% (39)	Moderate
SocGen	6.7% (8)	2.3% (10)	Moderate
UBS	6.9% (10)	0.4% (1)	Considerable

Note. Ranks: 1 worst capitalised, 50 best capitalised

Data source: Capital Advisory Group: Current topics, Technical Report (Lehman Brothers 2008), Epiq Systems, Inc.

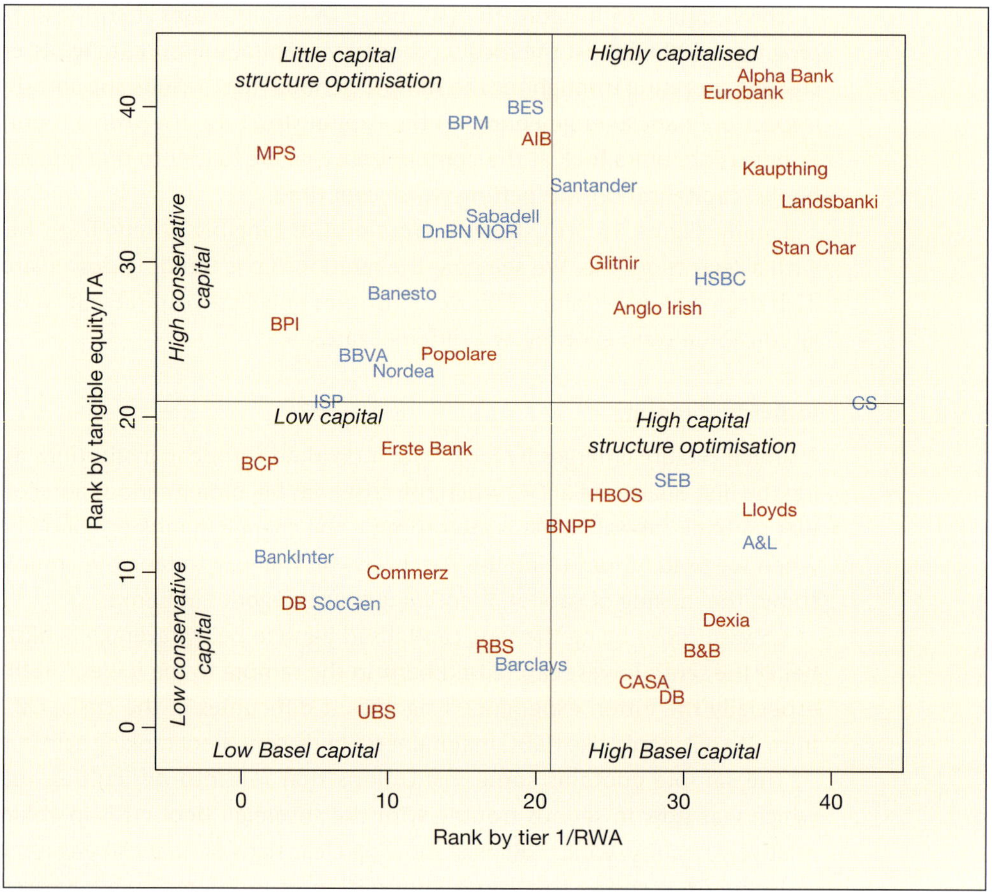

Figure 16.4 **Capital rankings of European banks in Q1 2008. Those that failed or got significant government help between 2007 and July 2012 in red**

Data source: Lehman Brothers (2008). Note: 1 worst capitalised, 42 best capitalised

Analysis

These results do not provide much indication that bank capital is doing what is expected of it; at least, it is hard to reconcile the fact that many of the most highly capitalised institutions failed, while many of the low capitalised banks survived the crisis, and amongst those that seemed most active in capital structure optimisation, most survived.

However, using TA, as in the leverage ratio is also problematic. After all, if two banks have the same amount of capital and one buys government bonds and the other junk bonds, both would have the same leverage ratio, but the second bank is a lot more risky. For this reason, it is better to have banks meet multiple capital ratios at the same time, which is indeed what Basel III aims to do.

These results are consistent with those of Blundell-Wignall and Atkinson (2010) who contend that banks' ability to arbitrage the capital weights to reduce capital and expand leverage is very extensive. They give a simple example showing that the Basel risk-weighting approach has allowed banks to expand their leverage almost without limit for all practical purposes.

Ultimately, this provides a good argument for transparency. Instead of trusting the bank to put assets into the right risk bucket and apply the correct formula for diversification and unlikely events, the market could make that judgement independently. What the crisis demonstrated is that if the market is not given information, it is likely to make crude worst-case assumptions, which does not benefit anybody.

16.3 SUMMARY

While there are many reasons for the crisis that started in 2007, failures in financial regulations and risk management were a direct contributor.

If regulations and risk management function as intended, risk-taking by banks is contained and bank failures, and certainly near-systemic crises, are highly unlikely. A key reason why the crisis happened in 2007 is that financial regulations and risk management at the time focused on frequent non-extreme events, neglecting tail risk, whilst ignoring endogenous risk and the systemic aspect of bank activities.

Perhaps the single most identifiable failure of regulations was in the Basel Accords and especially bank capital regulations. Prior to the crisis, banks appeared to be highly capitalised, but this was mostly illusory, because banks used capital structure optimisation to manipulate their CAR.

Questions for discussion

1 Was excessive deregulation and liberalisation of financial markets a key contributor to the crisis from 2007?

2 It is sometimes said that the outcome of active risk management is to lower volatility and fatten the tails. What does this mean, and do you agree?

3 Does the focus of prudential regulations potentially increase systemic risk?

4 How did financial engineering undermine the integrity of bank capital?

5 What is the problem of toxic assets in bank capital?

6 Did the hybrid capital instruments work effectively in the early stages of the crisis from 2007?

7 What you think about the assumption in the Basel accords and EU laws that sovereigns are risk free?

References

Blundell-Wignall, A. and Atkinson, P. (2010). Thinking beyond Basel III: necessary solutions for capital and liquidity. *OECD Journal: Financial Market Trends,* Volume 2010, Issue 1.

Danielsson, J. (2011). *Financial Risk Forecasting*. John Wiley & Sons.

Financial Services Authority (2009b). The Turner review: a regulatory response to the global banking crisis. Technical report, European Central Bank. www.fsa.gov.uk/pubs/other/turner_review.pdf.

Financial Times (2007). Goldman pays the price of being big. *Financial Times,* 13 August.

Goodhart, C. (2009). *The Regulatory Response to the Financial Crisis*. Edward Elgar, Cheltenham, UK.

Greenspan, A. (1997). Discussion at symposium: *Maintaining Financial Stability in a Global Economy,* p. 54. Federal Reserve Bank of Kansas City.

Larosiere, J. (2009). The high-level group report on financial supervision in the EU. Technical report. http://ec.europa.eu/commission_barroso/president/pdf/statement_20090225_en.pdf.

Lehman Brothers (2008). Capital advisory group: current topics. Technical report, Lehman Brothers.

UBS (2008). Shareholder report on UBS's write-downs. Technical report.

Wall Street Journal (2007). One 'quant' sees shakeout for the ages – '10,000 years'. *Wall Street Journal,* 11 August.

17 THE ONGOING CRISIS: 2007–2009 PHASE

The worst global financial crisis since the Great Depression started in August 2007, reached a peak in the second part of 2008 and seemed to be over by 2009. However, that turned out to be wrong – a second phase started in 2010 and, at the time of writing, it is getting worse by the day. In this chapter the focus is on the first phase, whilst Chapter 19 addresses the European sovereign debt crisis.

The underlying causes of the crisis are familiar. Banks took on too much debt whilst not recognising the increasing underlying risks, in the short run making everybody feel better off. The complexity and the hidden risk and the shadow banking system enabled those desiring to ignore problems to continue investing.

It all ended in tears. Crises require people to sell assets below the price at which they bought them. Market participants came to realise that their assumptions were wrong, that valuations had been too high, so out of sync with reality that a correction became inevitable. This happened in 2007.

This chain of events is well known to policymakers who had set in place safeguards both to prevent such excesses building up and to protect us from the eventual failure. The safeguards failed. Developments in the financial system had outpaced the regulatory and supervisory structure. Financial institutions were increasingly taking advantage of globalised markets, the structure of banks was changing and they were increasingly dependent on models and complexity for profits whilst relying more and more on short-term wholesale funding. All of this meant that financial institutions were becoming more interconnected and dangerous. Regulations did not keep up; the Basel II Accord, implemented in 2007, represents state-of-the-art regulatory thinking from the late 1990s.

As financial institutions became ever more international, the potential for cross-border banking failures was mostly ignored, with no effective internationally

coordinated supervision or resolution regimes. Even in Europe, with its common market in financial services, supervision was a strictly national affair, and the supervisors in different countries did not speak much with each other. The regulatory and supervisory structure in place in 2007 was inadequate for the banking system at the time.

Links to other chapters

Many aspects of the crisis have been discussed in detail in other specialised chapters. There are parallels with Chapter 2 (the Great Depression, 1929–1933), Chapter 14 (bailouts), Chapter 15 (dangerous financial instruments) and Chapter 16 (failures in risk management and regulation). Chronologically, the discussion here builds directly on those chapters and does not repeat their content.

Key concepts

- **First and second globalisms**
- **Hidden risk**
- **How banking has changed**
- **Investors' strike**
- **Liquidity and bailouts**
- **Bear Stearns, AIG and Lehman**
- **The fall of 2008**
- **Subprime**
- **Response to the crises**

Readings for this chapter

Many books and papers have been written about the crisis. We made especial use of the following. Murphy (2009) provides a good discussion of the role played by credit instruments in the crisis, Bitner (2008) discusses the role of subprime mortgages, Lewis (2011) discusses the overvaluation of structured credit products, while Huertas (2010) gives a perspective of a senior official of the FSA. Brunnermeier (2008) has a blow-by-blow description of early events.

17.1 BUILD-UP TO A CRISIS

It is difficult to identify the causes of the crisis of 2007–2009 because of the number of different factors that came together. Commentators will invariably disagree about the causes. We are still debating the causes of the Great Depression 70 years after it ended, and are likely to debate the causes of this crisis for decades to come. This is a measure of the complexity of the financial system and the heterogeneity of commentators.

17.1.1 Globalism

The crisis was a product of the relatively liberalised economic environment that followed the collapse of the Bretton Woods system in the early 1970s. The global economy has been gradually opening, with increasingly free trade and capital flows, along with deregulation and privatisation. If there is one defining term for the general economic environment, it is *globalism*. This is not, however, the first but the second time globalism has been the prevailing philosophy.

Throughout this period of ever increasing globalism, we did not suffer a global financial crisis, and when this crisis happened, everybody was ill-prepared.

The first globalism

In understanding what went wrong, it is useful to draw lessons from the *first globalism*, from the second part of the nineteenth century up until the first World War (WWI). Globalism was even more prevalent in many aspects in that epoch. The exchange rates of the major currencies were fixed because of the gold standard, capital flows between countries were mostly unhindered, and passports had yet to be invented.

Then, as now, in a highly interconnected financial system, a relatively small liquidity crisis could trigger significant and widespread losses, simply because of the two key vulnerabilities in a financial system: confidence and interconnectedness. This was at the heart of three crises discussed earlier, in 1866, 1906 and 1914, and many others. The problem of liquidity was well understood by bankers and policymakers, and policy responses reflected that understanding.

The second globalism

Throughout the Bretton Woods era, the global economy was heavily regulated, with trade and capital flows restricted. While this did not prevent economic crises, it was more effective in preventing financial crisis, as noted by Reinhart and Rogoff (2009), with crises mostly national affairs. If links between countries are limited, crises stay within national borders.

The break-up of the Bretton Woods system in the early 1970s signalled the start of the *second era of globalism*, both trade and capital flows were liberalised, countries became ever more interconnected and banking truly international. This created new challenges for policymakers, challenges that were not adequately recognised.

Money was being made in new places, in the Middle East, whose *petrodollars* were 'recycled' to countries seeking capital inflows, typically Latin America. From 1975 to 1982 Latin American borrowings from abroad increased from \$75 billion to \$313 billion. This meant that finance became much more important than before, and the financial system had become a major source of systemic risk for the first time since before the second World War (WWII).

History was forgotten

The lessons of the first globalism, in particular the potential for international liquidity crises, seem to have been forgotten by many of the architects of financial regulation and financial stability policies in the era of the second globalism. In particular, the design of financial regulations and our approach to financial stability did not adequately recognise the dangers inherent in the global economy. Financial regulations remained focused on the prudent behaviour of individual institutions, and central banks were more concerned with monetary than financial stability. It is almost as if international liquidity crises were thought impossible. History was forgotten.

The Washington consensus and anti-globalism

Two conflicting philosophies defined the attitude towards the second globalism, the *Washington consensus* and *anti-globalism*. The International Monetary Fund (IMF) was in charge of global currency arrangements during the Bretton Woods era, and after it collapsed, the Fund became the champion of the Washington consensus. As capital flows surged in the 1970s, sovereign debt problems became increasingly common but individual banks felt ill-equipped to deal with them. During the first globalism, this problem was solved by gunboat diplomacy, but during the second globalism, the IMF assumed the role of debt enforcer. It provided emergency loans for countries in difficulty, demanding in return what it called *structural adjustment programmes*. Generally, these programmes followed the Washington consensus. While the structural adjustment programmes might have been sensible, the way they were implemented became quite controversial and often counterproductive, as we saw in the discussion of the Asian crisis. That set the stage for a backlash against the Washington consensus – anti-globalism.

Whilst the prevailing economic orthodoxy until 2007 was quite consistent with the Washington consensus, the crisis has changed that, and we are increasingly seeing the various elements of anti-globalism impacting on policy. Even the IMF has referred to itself as 'new and cuddly', eschewing old policies, for example, by advocating capital controls.

17.1.2 Monetary policy and bubbles

The financial system was heavily regulated in the 1970s; the big enemy was inflation. In order to conquer it, central bankers, encouraged by academic research, developed the doctrine of central bank independence and the primacy of monetary policy. The problem is that the success in fighting inflation, and the importance of maintaining stable monetary policy, let central banks drop their guard and neglect financial stability.

We now see, with the benefit of hindsight, that the central bankers became a little like generals who dwell on the winning tactics of the last battle and thus get blindsided by a new enemy. They became complacent because they were able to maintain low interest rates and enjoy low inflation.

The factors enabling this success were not properly recognised, not least the impact of China. Its production costs were steadily falling, not only making China a strong competitor but also keeping prices low. In effect, *China was exporting deflation*. This worked to counteract the inflationary impacts of the low interest rates.

The Greenspan put

After inflation was conquered, some central banks, especially the Federal Reserve System (Fed), proceeded to use monetary policy as a means to contract financial shocks by providing massive amounts of liquidity. Just two examples are the reaction to the LTCM crisis and 11 September 2001.

Those liquidity injections became known as the *Greenspan put* – after Alan Greenspan, then chairman of the Fed – as the Fed stood by to bail out the financial markets when a shock hit, providing a put option. The impact was to increase moral hazard and stimulate asset bubbles, both in equities but perhaps more importantly in American real estate.

Risk-averse short-term investors

There was another impact from the low-interest policy. Significant amounts of money are held by traditional risk-averse short-term investors, such as municipalities and other government authorities facing asynchronous tax revenues and expenditures, money market mutual funds, and the like.

While this type of investor traditionally might have placed its funds in government paper, the low interest rate and low perceived risk environment encouraged such investors to seek more yield in still 'very low risk' assets, which in turn stimulated the market for the various highly rated structured credit products. When the crisis hit in the summer of 2007, the first manifestation was the withdrawal of those investors from the asset backed securities markets. It was said that they '*went on strike*', but more accurately they simply rebalanced back to their traditional investments – short-term government securities.

17.1.3 Savings glut

It was quite easy prior to 2007 to raise very large amounts of money on the capital markets, and some commentators have claimed that this is due to the fact that there were more savings in the world than could be invested wisely. Two ingredients are the expansion of pension funds and the massive build-up of currency reserves, for example, in the East Asian countries reacting to the crisis of 1997. Governor Ben Bernanke in 2005 coined the term *global savings glut*, which indicates that worldwide there is too much saving relative to available investment opportunities. This means that the global savings glut directly contributed to the problem of *global imbalances*.

This assertion was challenged by Borio and Disyatat (2011) who argue against the presumption that net capital flows from current account surplus countries to deficit nations helped finance credit booms there and that a rise in saving relative to investment in surplus countries depressed world interest rates. Their argument is that available data give only a partial picture of capital flows, revealing little about financing and excluding financial asset-based transactions which are the main part of cross-border activities. They further argue that the impact of interest rates is based on the stock of debt, reflecting the interaction between central bank rates, expectations about future policy rates and risk premiums.

17.1.4 Efficient markets

Some observers have argued that the efficient market hypothesis (EMH) is one of the causes of the crisis. It is a theory developed by financial economists, saying that market prices are efficient in the sense that one cannot on average achieve systematic excess profits by forecasting prices with available data and technology.

A narrow notion of the EMH captures the inability to systematically make money by forecasting. This is not problematic and is supported by empirical evidence. After all, if markets were not efficient in that sense, one could easily make almost infinite profits. This is the view that is most prevalent in academic studies referring to efficient markets.

There is, however, another interpretation of the EMH which is the view that a belief in efficient markets makes people blind to the faults of the market. For example, former Fed chairman, Paul Volcker, said in 2011 that it was 'clear that among the causes of the recent financial crisis was an unjustified faith in rational expectations [and] market efficiencies'. This view is more common amongst non-economists, who often attribute the wider meaning to those using it formally in the narrow sense.

17.2 HIDDEN AND IGNORED RISK

Prior to the crisis, it is almost as if all of the relevant stakeholders had what we could call the *2003–2006 mindset*. The general perception was that we had solved the problem of financial risk, by applying ever more sophisticated statistical models, modelling the financial system on an almost atomistic level, where risk was understood and controlled. This period is sometimes called *the great moderation*.

Underneath, the situation was different: the very fact that risk was perceived as low motivated market participants to assume ever more risk. The authorities charged with overseeing risk did not understand what was going on. This is a clear example of Hyman Minsky's observation that *stability is destabilising*. The very fact that we perceive the situation as being stable motivates us to take on more risk, which then destabilises the system.

Why risk was undetected

Recall a quote from the first chapter of this book by Andrew Crockett in 2000:

> 'The received wisdom is that risk increases in recessions and falls in booms. In contrast, it may be more helpful to think of risk as increasing during upswings, as financial imbalances build up, and materialising in recessions.'

These words were very prescient, written seven years before the crisis erupted. But what are the mechanisms that allow risk to build up whilst hidden away?

Pro-cyclicality and endogenous risk

Perhaps the strongest factor is pro-cyclicality, capturing the tendency of the components of some system to amplify cyclical behaviour, be it the business cycle or the valuation cycle. It makes booms bigger and busts deeper. Pro-cyclicality is fundamentally a manifestation of endogenous risk.

Pro-cyclicality is an inevitable part of finance. Banks have a tendency to over-extend themselves when things are going well, lending too much to borrowers engaged in speculation and contributing to an asset price bubble. A virtuous feedback loop is formed between credit expansion, speculative investments and rising prices. Eventually, the bubble bursts.

The complexity of finance and the use of models add to the pro-cyclicality. The complexity enables financial institutions to create ever more categories of instruments, supposedly increasing efficiency, but often this complexity just serves to hide risk-taking. A clear example of this is shown by the postmortem analysis done by UBS into its losses at the beginning of the crisis (UBS, 2008). Amongst the many findings is inappropriate use of value-at-risk (VaR) models for credit exposures.

Financial models contribute to pro-cyclicality. They are generally based on short price histories, and so long as prices are going up and risk is perceived as low, the models give a signal to buy, creating a bubble. Risk estimates are always influenced by recent experience, which can be especially dangerous when the pace of innovation is high. At that time, new products are introduced that did not exist in more stable times; innovation is aimed at avoiding perceived risks and gives a pretext for the idea that this time is different and risks are really lower.

Leverage and capital

The 8% regulatory minimum capital adequacy ratio (CAR) allows banks significant leverage. During normal times this is not a problem, but it does make them vulnerable to shocks affecting their capital and assets. One reason is that one would usually expect individual losses to be relatively uncorrelated, so that a full loss of the 8% capital would seem quite unlikely. However, an assumption of diversification is crucial for this assumption to work. In a crisis, correlations between assets tend to increase sharply, and diversification does not work as well – an example of *non-linear dependence*. That makes it much more likely that a bank will suffer losses large enough to lose most or all of its capital, as did happen to some in the crisis.

17.3 THE CHANGING NATURE OF BANKING

After most financial crises, the postmortem analysis identifies the failures allowing the crisis to happen, often resulting in safeguards preventing a repeat of events. Considering the long history of banking crises, we might have expected the underlying risks in banking to be sufficiently well understood so that large-scale failures are prevented. One reason why this turned out to be incorrect in 2007 is that banking had been changing in nature in a way that was poorly understood, creating hidden risks, whilst regulations did not keep up.

Funding

The most expensive way for a bank to fund itself is via capital, followed by long-term borrowing. The shorter the maturity of funds, the cheaper they are. For that reason, prior to the crisis, financial institutions, driven by competitive pressures, were increasingly resorting to the shortest possible funding – overnight (Brunnermeier, 2008, reports up to 40% for large American banks). Of course, any bank's assets have much longer maturities, so that such a funding strategy gives rise to a significant maturity mismatch. We see the funding options in the following table:

Capital *(very expensive)*
Long-term financing *(expensive)*
Short-term financing *(cheap)*
Three-month commercial paper
Repo (one day) *cheapest*

While overnight funding is the cheapest for banks in normal times, it *maximises liquidity risk*. One of the first things to happen when the crisis started in 2007 was a drying up of the interbank market, causing banks relying on overnight funding to face a significant liquidity squeeze.

In principle, borrowing overnight from the interbank market is not much different from depending on retail deposits, which are payable on demand. In practice, the differences are significant: overnight repos are much more dangerous.

While both sorts of funding are subject to bank runs, sophisticated investors in the interbank market are much more likely to do a run than retail depositors. The reason is that they monitor their counterparties very carefully, and spot problems quickly. By contrast, retail depositors tend only to react after the problems hit the news. A good example of this was the failure of Northern Rock, where the institutional run took place over a month before the retail run.

Shadow banking

A traditional, even caricature, view of a bank has it collecting demand deposits and making long-term loans. While such a picture has always been over-simplistic, in recent years it is increasingly outdated, not least as banks have embraced what is called *shadow banking*. This enables banks to move risk into entities directly under their control but not a part of the balance sheet. This can help in tax and risk management, and aid in capital structure optimisation. One example of this is conduits as banks as discussed in Example 15.2.

Shadow banking is not a term with a single precise meaning, but generally refers to institutions and banking practices that exist outside the traditional regulated banking sector.

Shadow banking enabled regulated financial institutions to conduct business outside the glaring eye of bank supervisors, shareholders, accountants and other stakeholders, in a way that was legal and compliant with extant regulations.

The move towards shadow banking is a clear example of Goodhart's Law. By putting heavy regulations on bank capital and assets, regulators created the incentives that made bank capital and assets poor measures of financial solidity. Shadow banks were one of the mechanisms used.

It is worth noting that many structures such as SIVs and conduits that were off-balance sheet and, hence, a part of the shadow banking system, under regulations prior to 2007, no longer enjoy that status under the Basel II Accord, which took effect in 2007 in many countries.

Given the long time it took to move Basel II from proposal to implementation – seven years – if that process had been faster, some of the problems causing the crisis might have been prevented, since banks would not have been able to take on so much risk without it being noticed.

17.4 CRISIS, 2007–2008

There were increasing signs that something was underfoot early in 2007. HSBC revealed losses of $10.5 billion on mortgage-backed securities in February 2007, soon to be followed by other firms. The first financial institution to fail – the canary in the coalmine – was IKB in July 2007.

The impact was predictable and major deleveraging was soon underway. Investors converted risky assets into cash, inevitably creating a downward pressure on prices. As always happens at the onset of crisis, historical correlations began to increase sharply, exactly what endogenous risk predicts.

The VIX, often called the 'markets fear gauge', started increasing in early 2007, as seen in Figure 17.1, but the volatility levels remained below those of earlier in the decade.

The quant event of 2007

The IKB failure was quickly followed by a quant crisis, where many prop desks and hedge funds using statistical arbitrage methods saw very large losses. One reason is that they underestimated the non-linear dependence in return distributions, whereby correlations sharply increase in a crisis. The high dependence across trading strategies and funds meant that trades got crowded, and the heterogeneity in behaviour wasn't all that high.

In July 2007, shares began to move in ways that were the opposite of those predicted by computer models. Trigger selling by the funds as they attempted to cover their losses and meet margin calls exacerbated the share price movements. Just one example is Goldman's flagship Global Alpha fund which lost 27% of its value. It was eventually closed in the autumn of 2011 after sustaining more losses.

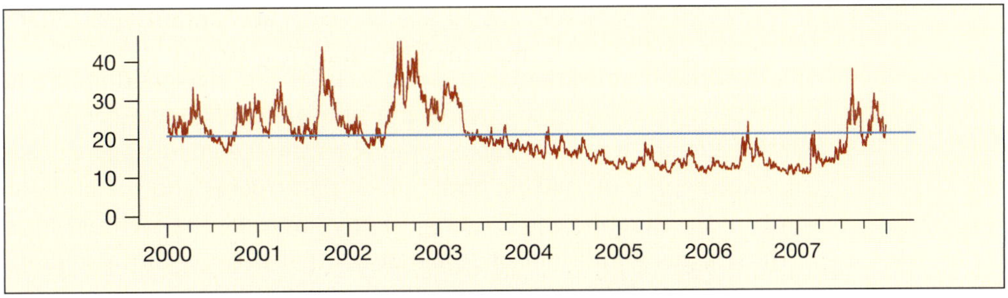

Figure 17.1 Intraday high VIX in 2000–2007 and long-run mean

Data source: finance.yahoo.com

The eye of the storm

After the main crisis event in August 2007, it appeared that the worst was over. However, fundamental problems had been exposed. Investors went on strike. In the autumn of 2007 and the winter of 2008, more and more financial institutions started to face liquidity problems.

Bear Stearns

The weakest of the American investment banks, Bear Stearns, started facing serious difficulties in early 2008. As losses mounted, in March 2008 the New York Federal Reserve Bank (NYFed) gave a $29 billion loan to JP Morgan to facilitate its takeover of Bear Stearns, buying it at $10 a share. Bear traded at $172 in January 2007, and at $93 in February 2008. The Chairman of the Fed, Ben Bernanke, defended the bailout in the Senate Banking Committee, saying 'Given the exceptional pressures on the global economy and financial system, the damage caused by a default by Bear Stearns could have been severe and extremely difficult to contain.'

Temporary calm

While the bailout temporarily prevented widespread disruption in financial markets, it was highly controversial and created the expectation that the authorities should similarly bail out other banks that were considered too big to fail (TBTF). This temporarily calmed the markets, but by September 2008 two important financial institutions were facing difficulties, Lehman Brothers and AIG.

17.4.1 Lehman Brothers

Perhaps the most disruptive event of the crisis was the failure of Lehman Brothers on 15 September 2008. It was one of the largest financial institutions in the world, an investment bank under US rules, and suffered large losses on real estate. Its bankruptcy was a turning point in the crisis. It triggered a collapse in asset prices and an almost complete drying up of liquidity. The US came under heavy pressure to bail Lehman out, but it did not do so, maintaining that there was no legal authority for a bailout. It remains controversial whether that was a mistake.

DILEMMA 17.1 The controversial decision not to bail out Lehman Brothers

Those arguing that this was the right decision maintain that if Lehman had been bailed out, it would have cemented expectations by the markets that any bank would be bailed out, encouraging risk-taking and simply creating ingredients for a larger failure down the road – a pure example of moral hazard. Lehman's failure crystallised a problem already present, making both market participants and the authorities realise the gravity of the situation and creating the conditions for the eventual crisis response.

Those arguing in favour of a bailout say that because of the failure, global liquidity almost completely dried up, with interbank lending, trade financing and the like falling to zero, setting the world economy on the road to collapse. The failure created unnecessary uncertainty, not only causing the severe crisis of the last part of 2008, but also leading to the European sovereign debt crisis. By bailing out Lehman, the authorities would have been given more time to implement measured, negotiated and less damaging crisis-fighting methods.

17.4.2 AIG

The day after Lehman Brothers failed, one of the world's largest insurance companies, AIG, received a bailout from the NYFed. It was considered more systematically important than Lehman Brothers because it was the largest writer of CDSs in the world, and it was feared that its default would trigger a systemic crisis, especially coming right after the failure of Lehman. For an overview of how AIG got into such problems with CDSs, see, for example, Lewis (2009).

AIG and CDSs

> 'It is hard for us, without being flippant, to even see a scenario within any kind of realm of reason that would see us losing one dollar in any of those transactions.'
>
> Joseph J. Cassano, the AIG executive in charge of the credit default swap (CDS) unit, August 2007

AIG was one of the world's largest insurance companies with a trillion-dollar balance sheet, 116,000 employees and operations in 130 countries. It set up a London-based bank that quickly became the world's largest seller of CDSs. The reason why AIG was able to become such a large writer of CDSs was that it had an AAA rating, making it the safest possible counterparty, requiring the smallest haircuts. It wrote about $450 billion worth of corporate CDSs, which suffered small losses, and about $75 billion of subprime-mortgage CDSs which suffered more losses after the crisis started. This eventually caused AIG to be downgraded, increasing its funding costs and haircuts, in a typical vicious feedback loop.

Given the danger posed by the failure of AIG, the authorities felt they had no choice but to provide a bailout, eventually amounting to $130 billion. Note, however, that the losses to taxpayers will be much smaller, even though the final amount will not be known for some time. The US taxpayer also gave tens of billions of dollars to financial institutions that were counterparties to AIG, most to Goldman Sachs and Deutsche Bank.

While the collapse of AIG could be handled more surgically by avoiding bailing out its counterparties, the existing resolution regime did not allow for that option. Given the alternatives, the bailout was the lesser of two evils, as the failure of AIG might have triggered a systemic crisis.

17.4.3 The fall of 2008

The failure of Lehman and the bailout of AIG triggered the worst phase of the crisis in the autumn of 2008. Global liquidity dried up and financial institutions depending on the interbank market found themselves without funding. This was the high point of the global credit crunch. The extreme risk levels are clearly visible in the VIX, seen in Figure 17.2, which shot up in September.

The crisis threatened to cause a repeat of the Great Depression, however, as we discussed in Section 2.4, the authorities took on board the lessons from the Depression and did the necessary to stop the liquidity crisis in its tracks.

A clear manifestation of the determination of the authorities was the scale of the various bailouts provided to the financial sector, as discussed in Section 14.5. In the absence of these bailouts, it seems likely that large parts of the European and American banking systems would have failed, with catastrophic consequences for the real economy.

Figure 2.6 showed the collapse in world trade during the Great Depression. We add to that figure current trade data in Figure 17.3, and show both time periods scaled to begin at 100. World trade fell significantly in the second half of 2008, but quickly recovered.

17.4.4 The crisis appeared over by 2009

By the middle of 2009, it seemed that the worst was over, the VIX returned to its long mean by year end, as seen in Figure 17.2, and the stock markets were improving, as indicated in Figure 17.4.

Banks were no longer in difficulty, the economy started to recover and the stock markets were rising. This, however, was just the eye of the storm; the second round was coming.

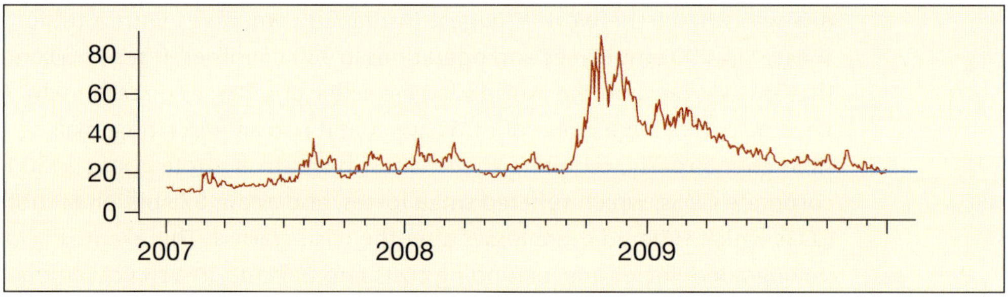

Figure 17.2 Intraday high VIX in 2007–2009 and long-run mean

Data source: finance.yahoo.com

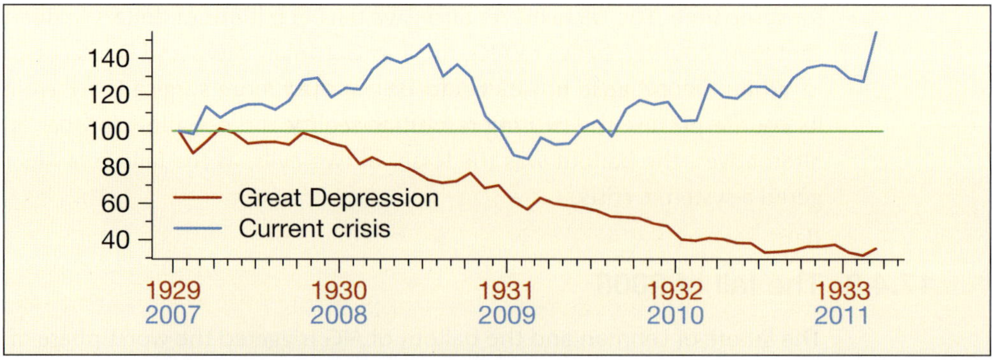

Figure 17.3 World trade (USD), scaled to start at 100

Data source: World Trade Organization (WTO) and League of Nations

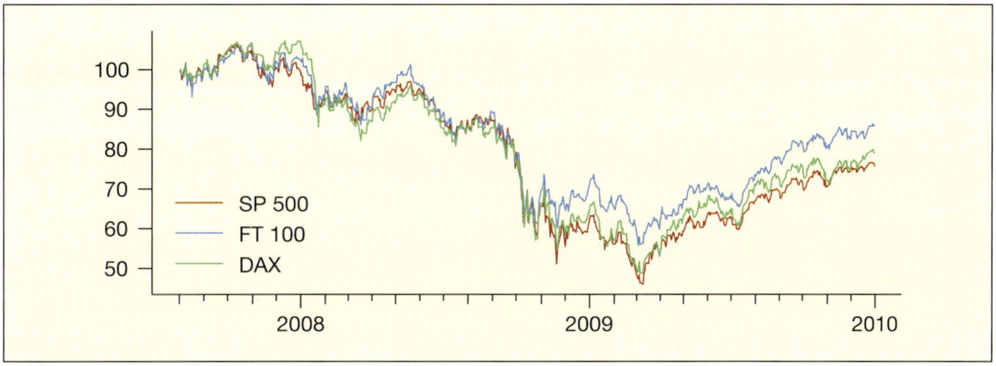

Figure 17.4 Major stock indices, 1 August 2007 = 100
Data source: finance.yahoo.com

17.5 WAS IT A SUBPRIME CRISIS?

In the early stages of the crisis, it was often called a '*subprime crisis*' because of the prevalence of US subprime mortgages in the most infamous structured credit products. This begs the question of whether the subprime mortgages were to blame or whether their role in the crisis was coincidental.

In 2007, total credit in the US was $50 trillion; $14 trillion was owed by the household sector, of which $11 trillion were mortgages. However, subprime mortgages constituted only $1.3 trillion and their delinquency rate hit 13% at the height of the crisis in 2008, or $170 billion. Therefore, the subprime mortgage sector accounted for only 2.6% of US debt and subprime delinquencies for only 0.3% of overall debt. By comparison, a 3% change in the US stock market amounts to perhaps $500 billion.

The amount of damage apparently caused by such a small sector was quite impressive, and to understand how that happened one has to look at how the subprime mortgages were used and the acceleration effects created by the resulting instruments. One mechanism was the $4.5 trillion of derivative contracts linked to subprime mortgages.

The role of subprime was only ancillary; the banks demanded high-risk assets during the bull market prior to the crisis. This did not seem all that worrying because the falls in risk premiums made historical returns look excellent. Perceived risk was low. One of the most obvious ways to exploit this was through structured credit products containing subprime mortgages. If it had not been subprimes, the market would have used something else. The real destruction was caused by the accelerator effects inherent in these products.

Conduits, structured investment vehicles (SIVs) and the assumption of diversification gave banks the opportunity to expand their exposures to extreme levels, whilst simultaneously hiding the underlying risks. The sudden vast amounts of capital invested in risky assets forced up prices, whilst lowering perceived risk, creating a classic bubble and laying the groundwork for the crisis.

The crisis itself was inevitable because the structured products gave the appearance of low risk – low enough to fool both the banks and their supervisors. Because of the tendency of the industry to extrapolate such low-risk environments to infinity, eventually the underlying risk would have been so high and the valuations so unrealistic that the crisis was bound to occur. The fact that it happened to involve subprime mortgages or structured credit products was ancillary.

17.6 POLICY RESPONSE

After the crisis started, it took the authorities some time to realise what was happening. The first authority to respond was the Fed, but the European authorities, both central banks and supervisors, were much slower to act. While we can only guess as to the reason, an important reason seems to be that the European authorities did not understand the various financial instruments that played a central role in the crisis.

In the UK, the Bank of England (BoE) had been downplaying the importance of financial stability in the preceding years, whilst the Financial Services Authority (FSA) was more concerned with micro-prudential regulations. In Europe, the European Central Bank (ECB) did not have any supervisory mandate, with no European supervisor or agency concerned with financial stability.

EXAMPLE 17.1 The United Kingdom

One example is from Alistair Darling (2011), the then UK Chancellor (minister of finance) who described the governor of the BoE, Mervyn King, as 'impish' and 'incredibly stubborn' and excessively focused on moral hazard, maintaining that 'a penalty interest rate must apply to any help given by the Bank', reflecting Bagehot's rules. Darling further quotes King as saying 'He regretted not having confronted these issues before', referring to the need for liquidity in the second part of 2007.

Lessons from history

Most financial crises are fundamentally the same, only the details differ. This crisis is no different. There are many historical parallels, where events have often been eerily similar – the wilful ignorance of risk build-up, the failure of protection mechanisms, and early fumbling policy responses. Financial crises always have liquidity as a central theme.

The historical event that resonates most with this crisis is the Great Depression. Even though it had faded from memory, the institutional safeguards put in place after the Depression are, for the most part, still in place and policymakers were quick to brush up on their Depression lessons. In this, we are fortunate that the governor of the Fed, Ben Bernanke, has written extensively about the Depression.

When the authorities finally woke up to the seriousness of the crisis, it was as if they started with a list of mistakes made in the 1930s and said 'we are going to do the correct thing this time around'.

17.7 SUMMARY

The focus in this chapter has been on the first part of the ongoing global crisis, 2007 to 2009. The background to the crisis is the era of the second globalism following the collapse of the Bretton Woods system, with ever increasing international capital flows, especially to the US, helping to maintain very low interest rates. This was not a cause for concern because large countries exported deflation, keeping inflation low.

The central theme is that it was a classical financial crisis, but with many unique ingredients such as inadequacies in financial regulations and excessive amounts of financial engineering.

The visible crisis was the manifestation of inappropriate investment decisions, poor risk estimates and mistaken assumptions on liquidity, all made over the preceding years. Subprime was the trigger, but its role was only ancillary.

Fortunately, the authorities had studied the policy mistakes during the Great Depression, and been determined not to repeat them.

Questions for discussion

1 Identify the main economic factors leading to the crisis.

2 Describe a typical crisis/bubble and analyse the 2007–2009 crisis in the context of that.

3 What is the role of 'accelerators' in crisis?

4 What was the role of complex assets and marking to market/model/magic in the crisis?

5 How has banking changed over the past decades and how did that make banks more vulnerable?

6 What were the initial signs of the crisis in the summer of 2007?

7 What were the main symptoms of the crisis when it reached its peak?

8 Was it correct to bail AIG out?

9 Many commentators maintain the failure to bail Lehman out was the main factor in the crisis becoming so severe. Today, European authorities use the example of Lehman as a justification for supporting European banks. Do you agree?

10 Was the crisis response of the authorities appropriate?

References

Bernanke, B. S. (2005). The global saving glut and the US current account deficit. Speech delivered at the Sandridge Lecture, Virginia Association of Economists, Richmond, VA.

Bitner, R. (2008). *Confessions of a Subprime Lender: an Insider's Tale of Greed, Fraud, and Ignorance*. John Wiley & Sons.

Borio, C. and Disyatat, P. (2011). Global imbalances and the financial crisis: link or no link? Technical report, BIS. Working Paper 346.

Brunnermeier, M. (2008). Deciphering the 2007–08 liquidity and credit crunch. *J. Econ. Perspect.*, 23(1): 77–100.

Crockett, A. (2000). Marrying the micro- and macro-prudential dimensions of financial stability. The General Manager of the Bank for International Settlements, www.bis.org/review/rr000921b.pdf.

Darling, A. (2011). *Back from the Brink: 1,000 Days at Number 11*. Atlantic Books, London.

Huertas, T. F. (2010). *Crisis: Cause, Containment and Cure*. Palgrave Macmillan.

Lewis, M. (2009). The man who crashed the world. *Vanity Fair,* August.

Lewis, M. (2011). *The Big Short: Inside the Doomsday Machine*. Penguin.

Murphy, D. (2009). *Unravelling the Credit Crunch*. CRC Press.

Reinhart, C. M. and Rogoff, K. (2009). *This Time Is Different: Eight Centuries of Financial Folly*. Princeton University Press.

UBS (2008). Shareholder report on UBS's write-downs. Technical report.

Volcker, P. (2011). Financial reform: Unfinished business. www.nybooks.com/articles/archives/2011/nov/24/financial-reform-unfinished-business.

18 ONGOING DEVELOPMENTS IN FINANCIAL REGULATION

Reforms of financial regulations tend to come after crises. Then, after some decades have passed and those who stood watch during the crises have retired, standards relax, until it all starts over again.

We have already seen some examples of this in this book. The Overend and Gurney (O&G) crisis of 1866 led to lending of last resort (LOLR) policies, and the Great Depression motivated a number of new regulations like deposit insurance and the Glass–Steagall Act, while regulatory failures in the United States in the early 1980s led that country to develop prompt corrective action. Such crisis response is not always positive, as there is great political pressure on policymakers to 'do something now' and quick policymaking is often bad policymaking.

One of the main causes of the crisis from 2007 was the failure of financial regulations. In response, G20 member countries, represented by the Financial Stability Forum (FSF), issued an influential report in 2008, identifying five priority areas of what it saw as the post-crisis regulatory reform process: 'Strengthened prudential oversight of capital, liquidity and risk management. Enhancing transparency and valuation. Changes in the role and uses of credit ratings. Strengthening the authorities' responsiveness to risks. Robust arrangements for dealing with stress in the financial system.'

Not surprisingly, a large number of initiatives have been launched since 2007 by various nation states, government organisations, financial institutions, lobbying groups, academics and other assorted pundits. The mother of all reform battles has been launched, and we are seeing the most substantial restructuring of financial regulations since at least the 1930s.

At a risk of overgeneralisation, there are three different approaches being discussed. Some claim that the entire financial system is unsound, requiring a root and branch reform, perhaps even to the extent of being moved to state hands. Opposed to that are those who argue the system is fine as it is, even identifying state interference as the cause of the crisis. Such views, whilst not common in the early stages of the crisis, have gained increased traction more recently. The mainstream view is between those extremes, maintaining that financial regulations need significant reform, and the structure of the financial industry needs to be altered, but without fundamentally altering the landscape.

It is often very difficult to disentangle the motives of those participating in the debate, and frequently debate participants are more motivated by personal gain or deep-seated ideologies than a desire to improve the system. For some, the crisis is an opportunity to press some agenda, succinctly described by Rahm Emanuel, former White House Chief of Staff to President Barack Obama, in 2007: 'You don't ever want a crisis to go to waste; it's an opportunity to do important things that you would otherwise avoid.'

The two main parties to the regulatory debate are the authorities and the industry. Regulators and supervisors have come under intense pressure from their political masters to 'do something about the financial system' and in response have launched a number of initiatives. The G20 has taken a lead on the international stage in guiding the regulatory developments, with the Basel Committee for Banking Supervision (BCBS) playing a key role.

The governmental responses have been far from uniform, exposing national differences. Countries with large financial centres – large exporters of financial services – want to protect their financial sectors, whilst others may prefer to cut the financial sector down in size. The way the various governments approach the reform process shows a lot of opportunistic behaviour, since a particular regulatory initiative may adversely affect a competing financial centre and favour the sponsoring country. Within Europe, the crisis has provided opportunities for state aid to national champions that might under more normal circumstances not be allowed.

The financial industry has responded with a furious lobbying effort, arguing that the various initiatives increase complexity, are not effective, are unfair, are discriminatory, or prevent financial institutions from fulfilling their role of supporting the economy, for example, because of the adverse impact of new capital regulations on the small and medium-sized enterprise (SME) sector.

Underneath it are fears about new regulations adversely affecting profitability and the competitive landscape. Regulations do not affect banks uniformly. A bank finding that its competitors will be more strongly and adversely affected by new regulations than it will, is likely to support those regulations. This has exposed the different preferences of various parts of the system, with banks and non-banks, large and small institutions, and institutions in different countries all having different agendas. For example, the main technical advocacy group of large internationally active banks, the Institute of International Finance (IIF), has a very different agenda than smaller banks.

Regulatory reform is technical, and the language often impenetrable. Add to that the multiple agendas being pursued, the many special interests being protected, and the fact that the discussion tends to take place in closed meetings, and it is clear that the debate is complex and difficult to follow.

However, at the time of writing, half a decade has passed since the 2007 crisis started and a picture is starting to emerge on the post-crisis regulatory landscape. For a roadmap, see Baudino (2011).

New government agencies have been tasked with the study of systemic risk, eventually to develop regulations and strategies for addressing systemic risk. This falls under the general heading of *macro-prudential regulations*. The Basel Accord has been identified as needing significant reform, and it will see changes in the calculation of capital and the introduction of liquidity constraints. Enhanced monitoring and crisis response is a central plank of the new regime. Individual countries have also launched important initiatives, and we have seen a reshuffle of supervisory agencies.

Unfortunately, it appears that some areas identified as key contributors to the crisis from 2007 are unlikely to be effectively addressed. The most important of these is the too big to fail (TBTF) problem. TBTF institutions played a central role in attenuating market discipline and breeding excess confidence before the crisis. A significant effort is going into this area by the various authorities, but the core problem is likely to remain. In fact, it has been made worse, by encouraging mergers and further entrenching the assumption that national champions will receive national support.

Less clarity exists on risk-taking. We hear politicians complain in one sentence about excessive risk-taking and the need to do something about risk, and in the next sentence demanding more lending to the politically sensitive SME sector. The view of the policymakers, reasonably enough, is that the financial system should be taking risk primarily in areas that benefit the economy rather than just speculating. In practice, no such clear delineation exists.

At the moment, chastened by recent and painful experience, financial institutions are content to run with modest amounts of risk. However, past experience indicates that this reticence is unlikely to survive competitive pressures for long, nor that regulators will be very effective in enforcing it against the will of market participants.

Different regulatory initiatives may sometimes be in conflict with each other. Since insurance companies need to invest large amounts of reserves, they are a large traditional buyer of bank bonds. One issue has arisen with Solvency II, the European insurance regulations to be implemented in 2014. It will induce insurance companies to hold shorter-dated instruments, while banks will need to issue longer instruments. This interferes with the insurers' ability to fulfil their social role, and raises questions where bank funding is going to come from. However, this remains controversial and several studies, such as that by Gorter and Bijlsma (2012), maintain that the impact will be relatively small.

Such conflicting views highlight the difficulty in quantifying the impact of new regulatory initiatives, as debate participants often have compelling arguments, backed up by detailed studies, but with widely different conclusions and even methodological approaches.

We have already discussed several regulatory initiatives in Chapter 9, in particular, central counterparties (CCPs), financial transaction tax (FTT), restrictions on bonuses and narrow banking, and will not repeat that discussion here.

The online chapter at www.GlobalFinancialSystems.org contains the latest developments in the regulations debate.

Links to other chapters

This chapter directly builds on the previous two chapters on financial regulations, Chapter 13 (financial regulations) and Chapter 16 (failures in risk management and regulations), as well as Chapter 9 (trading and speculation). The motivation for these reforms is the ongoing crisis, discussed in Chapter 17 (the ongoing crisis: 2007–2009 phase) and Chapter 19 (sovereign debt crises).

Key concepts

- **Post-crisis regulatory reform**
- **New institutions and the changing role of old institutions**
- **Basel III**
- **Flexible capital buffers**
- **SIFIs, G-SIBs and too big to fail**

Readings for this chapter

A large number of proposals and studies for regulatory reform have been made over the past few years and we have drawn on these reports, many of which can be found on the websites of the various agencies, for the BIS www.bis.org, the BCBS www.bis.org/bcbs/, the FSA www.fsa.gov.uk, the Fed www.federalreserve.gov/, the FSB www.financialstabilityboard.org and the IIF www.iif.com. A good collection of articles on the ongoing developments is Quagliariello and Cannata (2011).

18.1 NEW AND CHANGED INSTITUTIONS

The crisis that started in 2007 demonstrated that the institutional setup of the various government agencies charged with overseeing the financial system was inadequate. Many agencies seemed to live in their own silos, focusing on narrow mandates and ignoring the overall objectives of financial regulations, perhaps inevitably for bureaucratic institutions established with specific legal mandates.

18.1.1 National institutions

Central banks and supervisors

The role of central banks has changed significantly. Before the crisis, the central banks tended to focus on monetary policy, with supervision moved to separate institutions. Financial stability was a low priority and the concept of central bank independence sacrosanct. After the crisis started, some central banks, most prominently the Bank of England (BoE), were initially quite reluctant to engage with a broader mandate of financial stability, but in the end did not have much choice.

The crisis demonstrated that the central banks have to play a key role in financial stability because they have a monopoly on printing money, one of the vital instruments in support and resolution operations. However, they can play this role effectively only if they also have appropriate supervisory information and powers, and the willingness to use them. The result is that the central banks have been gaining new responsibilities.

This is the case in the United Kingdom, where many of the functions of the Financial Services Authority (FSA) are to be merged with the BoE, leaving only micro-prudential regulations. Similarly, in the US, the Securities and Exchange Commission (SEC) used to supervise investment banks, but the remaining investment banks have become bank holding companies and, hence, are subject to prudential regulation by the Federal Reserve System (Fed). The SEC remains a significant regulator in issues relating to securities markets and trading.

However, the central banks have also lost some power to the treasury/ministries of finance, as any bailouts need government approval, and the new systemic risk institutions enshrine the role of the treasury, especially in the US.

The treasury

The crisis demonstrated the key role played by the treasury because it manages the public purse. Vast amounts of public money were allocated to fighting the crisis and, since the treasury is ultimately responsible for public money, it necessarily took a pivotal role. This does not mean the treasury is better equipped to do this than the central banks or the supervisors; far from it, the technical expertise lies with the latter. One could say that the treasury has regained some of its historical role lost the when the central banks became independent.

While it is inevitable that the treasuries are intimately involved in the regulatory reform process, and need to take the lead in any bailout operation, this does not come without cost. The role of the treasury has led to an unfortunate politicisation of financial regulation. The reason is that government agencies like the supervisor or central bank are one step removed from the political process. The treasury is directly under political control. This inevitably means that the treasury is more populist, more susceptible to lobbying. The political leanings of the minister, and the political advisers he or she makes use of, can directly affect the regulatory reform agenda. Not only can this lead to sharp differences between various countries, it may also contribute to regulation risk since we may expect rapid policy shifts when governments change.

18.1.2 International institutions

Financial regulations have been designed and coordinated internationally at least since the early 1970s. This is mostly done under the auspices of the BCBS, most importantly with the Basel Accords.

G20 and FSB

Since the crisis, the lead in coordinating the international efforts in financial regulations and crisis response has been taken by the G20. In a summit in 2009, the G20 called for the establishment of the Financial Stability Board (FSB) based on an older body called the FSF. The mandate of the FSB is to monitor the global financial system, coordinate with other relevant bodies like the International Monetary Fund (IMF) and make recommendations to member states.

IMF

One international organisation has taken on a new life with the crisis, the IMF. By early 2007, the Fund was in serious financial difficulties, laying off staff, and there was speculation it might be shut down altogether. Its reputation had been damaged by the previous crises it engaged with, in Asia in 1997, and in Turkey and Argentina in the early 2000s. No large economy had requested Fund assistance after Argentina, and because interest on loans to countries in crisis is the major source of revenue for the IMF, it was suffering financially from the lack of crises. By 2006, it had found itself without a mission or money.

All of this changed in 2007. As individual countries got into serious difficulties, it was felt that the only body with sufficient expertise, authority and funds to help those countries was the IMF. It has taken a pivotal role in the European crisis, being involved with Cyprus, Iceland, Hungary, Greece and other countries, and has become one of the main players in formulating the crisis response. It has a very limited role, however, in formulating regulatory policy.

EU

The crisis exposed significant weaknesses in the approach of the European Union (EU) to financial regulation and supervision. Financial regulations are to a significant extent designed and implemented on a Union level, but implemented only on a state level. Before the crisis, different national supervisors had limited interaction with each other and often applied widely differing standards to regulations. The European Central Bank (ECB) was focused only on monetary stability, and there was almost no macro-prudential policymaking within the EU. The EU has been addressing this problem since 2007, and has taken major steps towards more centralised European supervision via new institutions like the European Systemic Risk Board (ESRB), the European Banking Authority (EBA) and the European Securities and Markets Authority (ESMA). The EU is currently planning the Single Supervisory Mechanism (SSM) as an embyonic pan-EU supervisor.

18.1.3 New systemic risk institutions

The crisis has led to the creation of new types of institutions explicitly responsible for systemic risk. The US established the Financial Stability Oversight Council (FSOC) in 2010, whose mandate is to identify and monitor risk to the US financial system and respond to threats to financial stability. The chairperson is from the Treasury. The counterparty in the UK is the Financial Policy Committee (FPC), with a different institutional setup because the Treasury has only a non-voting role.

The situation is somewhat different in the EU because it is unable to create a systemic risk body with the same powers as its counterparts in the UK and the US. Therefore, the EU version, the ESRB set up in 2010, has a much more limited role. It is supposed to prevent or mitigate systemic risk, taking into account macroeconomic developments and contributing to the smooth functioning of the internal market. The ESRB is hosted and supported by the ECB.

This does leave a vacuum, and at the time of writing it is unclear how it will be filled. The EU would like to fill it with a new powerful institution tasked with Union-wide supervision and macro-prudential regulations, but this has run into significant opposition from various member states. If the EU is unsuccessful, the power vacuum will probably be filled by the ECB at Union level and various state bodies like the FPC.

18.1.4 European banking union

To overcome the problems caused by the lack of a single European supervisor, the EU established the EBA in 2011, to increase transparency in the European banking system by identifying capital structure weaknesses. It is best known for the stress tests it runs on European banks. Those have been somewhat hampered by the problem of sovereign debt, which as we noted in Chapter 13 is considered risk-free by the EU for the purpose of bank capital calculations, when the debt is funded and issued in the currency of the issuer. This means that sovereign debt is not included in the stress tests, undermining their credibility.

The EU announced in June 2012 its intention to establish a banking union in Europe, creating a pan-European supervisor, and explicitly link discipline and control from the EU to assistance to individual member states. The ECB is involved with the mechanism, implying that it will be to some extent separate from it. The motivation for the establishment of the banking union is to maintain financial stability, preserve the single market in financial services and avoid competitive distortions in the single market.

The EU would want the banking union to have at least four key elements. The first is what is known in European Union jargon as *the single rulebook*, meaning that the same rules are to be applied uniformly throughout the Union. Second, banking supervision will be pan-European. The third element is a pan-European resolution regime, and finally a harmonised deposit insurance scheme. The SSM is a step towards this goal.

It remains unclear at the time of writing what the banking union will look like, when it will be established, or even if it will be established. At the moment, each member state maintains its own supervisor, and establishing a new supervisory agency is not a trivial undertaking.

The notion of a banking union has run into significant opposition, led by Germany. A banking union might lead to stronger states having to pay for deposit insurance payoffs or provide bailouts to banks in weaker member states. This means that an effective banking union requires a *transfer union*, a political step many countries are reluctant to take.

18.1.5 International cooperation and colleges of supervisors

Many regulations are harmonised internationally to some extent, for example via the activities of the International Organisation of Securities Commissions (IOSCO) and the BCBS, and various other similar arrangements. Within the EU, a significant number of regulations are pan-European, even if there are important national differences in specific implementations.

The situation is different for the enforcement of banking regulations, and the crisis from 2007 demonstrated the fragmented nature of banking supervision. Until that point, supervision was essentially a national affair. Supervisors in different countries had a limited overview of the overseas activities of financial institutions operating in their jurisdiction. This even extended to the EU, where it became especially problematic because banks were able to operate throughout the Union because of the common market, but without any centralised overview of their activities.

In response to this, various initiatives are underway to coordinate the activities of supervisors. An important example of this is the activities of the Senior Supervisors Group, representing 10 major banking nations. Within this work, *colleges of supervisors* have regained a renewed importance, referring to multilateral working groups of relevant supervisors working together to ensure consolidated supervision of internationally active banking groups. Colleges of supervisors have become one of the key components in the ongoing reform of financial regulation. However, enforcement is the last frontier of coordination and cooperation, and there is some way to go.

While cooperation among supervisors has improved considerably since the crisis, there have been some hiccups, most famously in the case of UK bank Standard Chartered, accused by the New York Department of Financial Services of money laundering. It informed the FSA only 90 minutes before announcing the allegations, and appears not to have cooperated much with other US supervisory agencies, even though some of them had supervisory powers over the bank.

18.2 BASEL III

The most important changes in financial regulations are in the Basel Accords. After the start of the crisis, the BCBS moved with surprising speed and in short order introduced the next revision of the capital accords, called Basel III, at the end of 2009 in a series of consultative documents, which have been steadily updated since then. The Committee identifies the system as a main priority:

> 'The objective of the [regulatory] reforms is to improve the banking sector's ability to absorb shocks arising from financial and economic stress, whatever the source, thus reducing the risk of spillover from the financial sector to the real economy.'
>
> Basel Committee on Banking Supervision (2011b)

These priorities are consistent with the definitions of systemic risk in Section 12.1.

The main impetus of the reforms is on capital, prioritising equity and introducing several categories of capital buffers. In addition, the proposals include liquidity regulations and the management of counterparty risk. At the time of writing, the latest version of the Basel III was published by the BCBS in June 2011, and we follow that here.

18.2.1 Capital

The Basel III proposals make several important changes to how capital is calculated. Under Basel II, the main parts of capital are tier 1 and tier 2, and since most of the direct problems caused by capital relate to tier 2, it is not surprising that it is to be significantly reduced in importance and most emphasis put on tier 1, especially equity.

Types of capital

Regular bank capital will continue to be split into tier 1 and tier 2, and the minimum capital adequacy ratio (CAR) will remain at 8%. However, the relative amount of tier 1 will increase, with especially more emphasis put on equity, that is the common equity tier 1 (CET1). For technical details on the terminology of the capital regulations, see BCBS (2011c).

Several new categories of equity are to be introduced. A *capital conservation buffer* can be used to absorb losses during stress, while a *countercyclical buffer* fluctuates with the general state of the economy, and global systemically important banks (G-SIBs) are to get a separate capital charge. Therefore:

$$\begin{aligned}\text{total regulatory capital} = {} & \text{tier 1} + \text{tier 2}\\ & + \text{conservation buffer}\\ & + \text{countercyclical buffer}\\ & + \text{G-SIB surcharge}\end{aligned}$$

By 2019, if all goes according to schedule, the capital ratios will be as indicated in Table 18.1, with the transition in steps over the coming years as seen in Table 18.2.

Table 18.1 Eventual components of capital

Category	Ratio
Tier 1	6%(CET1 = 4.5%)
Total capital (does not include those below)	8%
Add-ons, all CET1:	
Conservation buffer	2.5%
Countercyclical buffer	0%–2.5%
Systemically important banks	1%–2.5% (+ 1%)

Data source: Basel III: a global regulatory framework for more resilient banks and banking systems, Technical Report, 2011b, Annex 4 (Basel Committee on Banking Supervision 2011), Bank for International Settlements

Table 18.2 Timing of the transition

Year of introduction	Common equity	Conservation buffer	Minimum tier 1	Minimum total + buffers
2013	3.5%		4.5%	8%
2014	4.0%		5.5%	8%
2015	4.5%		6.0%	8%
2016	–	0.625%	–	8.625%
2017	–	1.25%	–	9.25%
2018	–	1.875%	–	8.875%
2019	–	2.5%	–	10.5%

Data source: Basel III: a global regulatory framework for more resilient banks and banking systems, Technical Report, 2011b, Annex 4 (Basel Committee on Banking Supervision 2011), Bank for International Settlements

Conservation buffer

The idea behind the conservation buffer is to solve one of the worst problems with capital buffers. They do not provide any protection if they cannot be used in times of crisis. It therefore makes sense for financial institutions to be able to reduce their capital levels in times of difficulty, and that is the purpose of the conservation buffer, allowing for up to a 2.5% reduction in capital when needed.

Drawing down the buffers is not without consequences. Banks are restricted in providing distributions to shareholders, other capital providers and employees, because these stakeholders are supposed to bear the risk that recovery will not be forthcoming. Furthermore, the banks are likely to be given a deadline for rebuilding their buffers.

Countercyclical capital buffer

The risk sensitivity of capital amplifies the problem of pro-cyclicality in banking. This has become especially pertinent after the crisis in the debate of risk-taking by banks and lending to SMEs. This problem is partly addressed in Basel III by the introduction of a countercyclical buffer that should be maintained when the economy is doing well but is reduced during recessions.

While such a buffer is sensible in theory, in practice, it can be difficult to decide on what measure should be used to signal where we are in the business cycle. Many proposals have been made, such as credit/GDP, various asset prices, funding spreads and credit default swap (CDS) spreads, credit conditions surveys, real GDP growth and data on the ability of non-financial entities to meet their debt obligations on a timely basis. There is a difficult trade-off in implementing those. The most accurate, and the hardest to put numbers to, are based on national accounts, such as GDP, but that is measured only with a significant lag: it takes many months for the state of the economy to be known and such numbers may even be revised for a number of years. As a consequence, a GDP-based buffer might not be very countercyclical; it might even become procyclical, allowing for a reduction in capital when the economy started to grow, or requiring an increase in capital as the economy is heading for a recession.

While other measures are more up-to-date, they are still lagging behind the state of the economy and, hence, may have unforeseen consequences for cyclicality. In addition, such measures are likely to be more noisy, not least because they achieve shorter lags by relying on data from markets, and these may not always reflect the broader economy in the desired manner.

It is not surprising, therefore, that the formulation of the countercyclical buffer has been controversial – see Borio *et al.* (2010) for more discussion, and Repullo and Saurina (2011) for critical analysis. The BCBS converged to a credit-to-GDP ratio with respect to its trend. This has problems of its own, and we can look forward to banks arguing that trend rates have increased during future upswings, reducing their need for capital.

Systemically important financial institutions (SIFIs)

Financial institutions that are so large that their failure threatens a systemic crisis are denoted in the Basel jargon as systemically important financial institutions (SIFIs). When applied only to banks, we use the term global systemically important banks (G-SIBs).

The reason why AIG was bailed out, and why the failure of Lehman was so damaging, is exactly because they were systemically important.

Not surprisingly, G-SIBs are singled out in the Basel process:

> 'The assessment methodology for global systemically important banks [incorporates] an indicator-based approach and comprises five broad categories: size, interconnectedness, lack of substitutability, global activity and complexity.'
>
> BCBS (2011c)

G-SIBs are to have an extra buffer of 1–3.5% of CET1, though the last 1% of that is currently an empty bucket designed to be a disincentive for banks to get bigger.

The G-SIB surcharge is intended, at least in part, to reflect the extra risk created by G-SIBs and to neutralise the advantage the TBTFs are felt to enjoy. This is part of several policy initiatives aimed at this category of banks, discussed in Section 18.6 below.

Table 18.3 shows the latest list of institutions deemed to be G-SIBs, along with their capital charges.

CoCos

The problems associated with hybrid bank capital, as discussed in the last chapter, have led to the introduction of capital instruments with a more explicit trigger called contingent convertibles (CoCos). While there are several different versions of CoCos, one of the most common is bonds that turn into equity if a bank's capital ratio becomes too low, while another type involves write-downs. A key distinction between CoCos and other capital instruments is that the former focuses on explicit early triggers and hence early interventions, while the latter is more related to resolution and disincentives.

Several banks have already issued CoCos, but the only nation requiring their use is Switzerland, where UBS has issued write-down CoCos and Credit Suisse (CS) convertible CoCos.

While CoCos are not a direct part of the Basel III proposals, there are some indications that they may become included in some form, as hinted by the statement that 'all classes of capital instruments fully absorb losses at the point of non-viability before taxpayers are exposed to loss' (Basel Committee on Banking Supervision, 2011a).

If CoCos are to become a key part of bank capital, the interesting question is who holds them. If it is only other financial institutions, systemic risk is not reduced, and may

Table 18.3 G-SIBs as of November 2012

Bucket	CAR	Banks
5	3.5%	(Empty)
4	2.5%	Citigroup, Deutsche Bank, HSBC, JP Morgan Chase
3	2.0%	Barclays, BNP Paribas
2	1.5%	Bank of America, Bank of New York Mellon, Credit Suisse, Goldman Sachs, Mitsubishi UFJ FG, Morgan Stanley, Royal Bank of Scotland, UBS
1	1.0%	Bank of China, BBVA, Groupe BPCE, Group Crédit Agricole, ING Bank, Mizuho FG, Nordea, Santander, Société Générale, Standard Chartered, State Street, Sumitomo Mitsui FG, Unicredit Group, Wells Fargo

Data source: Update of group of global systemically important banks (G-SIBs) Annex 1 (Financial Stability Board 2012), Bank for International Settlements

even increase because of cross-exposures. It is important, therefore, to have restrictions on CoCo ownership, and to ensure that the owners are willing and able to hold the equity if the conversion takes place.

A major issue is whether there would be a market interest in CoCos, given their possible conversion, legal-investment issues, and the like. For example, natural buyers of bank debt, such as insurance companies and pension funds, might find the potential for conversion unpalatable at a time when their other assets are already under stress. However, banks have found little difficulty placing CoCos in the market, suggesting that these fears are misplaced.

18.2.2 Leverage ratio

One of the reasons why many banks got into so much difficulty in 2008 was a general mistrust of the risk weights on assets in the calculation of the Basel CAR, as discussed in Section 16.2. One way this can be addressed is by doing away with the risk weights in the calculation of the CAR. The resulting ratio is known as the leverage ratio (LR):

$$\text{LR} = \frac{\text{equity}}{\text{assets}} = \frac{\text{tier 1 capital}}{\text{total assets}} \geq 3\%$$

The 3% is a rule introduced by Basel III with a phased-in implementation.

Before the crisis, the LR was the preferred way of specifying capital requirements in the US, whilst Basel-regulated banks elsewhere used the risk-weighted ratio.

The LR does have some advantages over the Basel CAR, in particular, that by disregarding the risk weights, there is less model risk in the calculation of the ratio, and less scope for manipulation and capital structure optimisation aiming at maximising the visible ratio whilst minimising the cost and protection afforded by the ratio.

There are also considerable disadvantages to the LR. Because it does not distinguish between the most safe government bonds (like those of the UK, Germany and the US) and junk bonds, it creates a disincentive to hold safe assets. This also puts LR in conflict with the objectives of the liquidity coverage ratio (LCR) aiming at encouraging banks to hold liquid government bonds. The LR is especially problematic for banks in countries holding very large structural positions in government bonds, like Japanese banks.

If the choice was between either the LR or the Basel ratio, it would be hard to decide between the two. Both ratios are flawed, but do meet a useful objective. Therefore, the decision by the Committee to require both ratios simultaneously is sensible, providing a useful compromise between the various issues, and reducing the scope for gaming.

18.3 LIQUIDITY

Some national jurisdictions, like the UK, have long required banks to hold liquidity buffers, but such requirements have not extended to international regulations. In particular, Basel II is essentially silent on the question of liquidity.

Events from 2007 have demonstrated the fallacy of such complacency, because the sudden disappearance of liquidity was at the heart of the crisis, and remains a major problem in the ongoing sovereign debt crisis.

First, it was assumed that banks could always obtain *funding liquidity*, which meant that they naturally migrated to the cheapest forms of liquidity, overnight repos. When the interbank market dried up in 2007, banks that relied heavily on short-term funding found themselves in significant difficulty. Because funding problems happen very quickly – literally overnight – the banks, the authorities and everybody else were caught unprepared, and governments had to rapidly provide bailouts. Longer and more stable funding would have made it easier to deal with these problems.

Second, it was assumed that some types of funding were more stable than they turned out to be. For example, bank deposits coupled with deposit insurance have historically represented funding that was considered unlikely to evaporate quickly. Deposit insurance schemes were thought to provide sufficient assurance to depositors, and hence prevent bank runs. However, the limitations of deposit insurance schemes have made depositors more skittish, especially those holding high-interest Internet savings accounts. Events in the crisis demonstrated that depositors were sensible enough to withdraw large amounts of money at the slightest whiff of trouble.

For these reasons, liquidity regulations have became a priority in the Basel III proposals, and the Committee has proposed two liquidity ratios, the 30-day LCR and the one-year net stable funding ratio (NSFR).

18.3.1 Liquidity coverage ratio

The LCR is based on the idea that banks should have sufficient *high quality liquid assets* to survive an acute stress scenario lasting *one month*:

$$\text{LCR} = \frac{\text{Stock of high quality liquid assets}}{\text{Net cash outflows over a 30-day time period}} \geq 100\%$$

Numerator

The assets need to be *unencumbered*, meaning that they have not been pledged or allocated to other purposes, and hence are ready to be monetised.

A key challenge lies in the definition of high quality liquid assets. Two categories of assets are defined, level 1 and level 2. Level 1 assets are traditionally highly safe and liquid assets, such as cash, demand deposits with central banks and marketable government and international agency securities that meet certain conditions. Level 2 assets contain marketable government and international agency securities that are more risky than their level 1 counterparts as well as low-risk liquid corporate bonds.

The included assets should be monetisable, at a low cost, providing a relatively certain amount to a bank facing funding problems.

Denominator

It is harder to define what to include in the denominator. The basic idea is that banks have certain amounts of outflows and expect to receive some amounts of money. The difference between the two, the net cash outflow, needs to be sufficiently low. There are several challenges in the determination of net flows. A bank may have a reasonably clear idea of outflows, but less of potential inflows, especially in times of stress. For example, while it may have positions that are fully netted out, actually receiving funds depends on the solvency of the counterparty.

Other problems include how to account for net flows from derivative positions and other complex assets, where valuations may be model driven and assets only traded over-the-counter (OTC).

At the time of writing, it is unclear how these issues will be resolved.

National discretion

National supervisors have significant discretion in how they implement the ratio, giving rise to fears of inconsistent implementation, regulatory arbitrage and a race to the bottom.

Costs

Maintaining a large buffer of liquid assets is costly for the banks. These assets cannot be used for other, more lucrative, purposes and the LCR, therefore, will directly affect the banks' profitability. They maintain that this will reduce their lending capacity, especially in the context of the LR, with the sectors most affected presumably the SMEs.

This leads to one of the typical dilemmas in the regulatory reform process. More liquid assets make the banks more resilient, but at the expense of less lending.

Sovereign bonds as liquid assets

The liquidity ratios are subject to the same problem as bank capital in that government bonds are considered safe assets. Because some of the distressed European sovereign bonds are considered riskless for the purpose of the ratios, a bank complying could actually end up being more risky than a bank holding safer liquid assets that do not count as safe liquid assets in LCR calculations.

Dilemma

The dilemma for the policymakers is that true stability is strongly associated with high costs. When banks are the most overconfident – right before a crisis happens – they are least willing to pay the premium associated with stable sources of funding, and prefer to take more risk by funding short term. Whatever definition of 'stable funding' is adopted, in the next crisis banks will be meeting this requirement from the cheapest available sources. This funding will be cheapest because it is the least stable.

While seeking stable sources of funding is a sensible idea, like liquidity it seems almost certain to disappoint when tested in the next crisis, because banks' incentive to reduce their funding cost is too strong.

Gaming

Perhaps the main concern about the LCR is the same as worries about the integrity of bank capital. Banks were able to use capital structure optimisation to significantly game their capital levels. There is no reason to believe that there is any less scope for gaming when it comes to liquidity. If anything, the problem might be worse because with capital we have three decades of observations on how it can be gamed and, hence, have an understanding of how to minimise the problem. The worry is that the banks would be more inventive and more nimble in the gaming process than the supervisors.

There are many ways to undermine the LCR. A bank might enter into contracts that effectively encumber a large part of its liquid resources, but not in a way considered encumbering by the supervisors.

Another way might be contracts that give rise to large cash requirements when a bank comes under stress. So long as these do not give rise to any net cash flows (however defined) under normal circumstances, these might leave the LCR intact, but also mean that at the onset of a crisis liquid resources would collapse much faster than anticipated.

While these loopholes are obvious, there are many ways to achieve the same purpose in a less visible way.

18.3.2 Net stable funding ratio

The NSFR is designed for longer time horizons, creating incentives for banks to better maturity-match liabilities to investments.

$$\text{NSFR} = \frac{\text{Available amount of stable funding}}{\text{Required amount of stable funding}} \geq 100\%$$

Stable funding is defined as the fraction of equity and liability financing expected to be reliable sources of funds over a one-year horizon, during extended stress. At the time of writing, the definition is still quite vague, but more details are expected when the final version of Basel III is published.

Issues

The NSFR demonstrates the common dilemma between safety and credit creation. One of the main functions of banks is maturity transformations, simultaneously providing savers with demand deposit accounts and making long-term loans. Therefore, maturity mismatches are inherent in any bank, and not something that should be eliminated, or even significantly reduced.

Therefore, a strict interpretation of the NSFR might seriously undermine the maturity transformation function of banks, to the detriment of society.

Another concern relates to cliff effects. One result from the Basel capital ratios was the creation of 364-day loans, one day short of one year, triggering capital requirements. A one-year NSFR might do the same, with banks preferring 364-day loans.

This has two important disadvantages. First, it increases liquidity risk because borrowers will have to worry about rolling over loans every 364 days. This is the type of risk that is most likely to manifest itself during turmoil, at exactly the worst time. The second problem is that it disrupts business planning, because companies cannot count on long-term funding for long-term projects. It might lead to funding migrating away from banks onto the capital markets, where larger companies can issue longer-term bonds. This in turn disadvantages the SMEs, because their access to the capital markets is more limited than that of their larger competitors.

18.3.3 Danger

Perhaps the main worry about the liquidity ratios is that they may create an impression of protection that is not veridical. This would endogenously encourage more risk-taking and therefore undermine financial stability. It would be disastrous if the authorities assumed the liquidity ratios were successful, and hence that liquidity crises could not happen. In the next crisis the authorities should be prepared for reported liquidity to prove just as illusory as reported capital. The ratios came under heavy criticism from the industry and in response an amended, less strict, version was announced at the start of 2013.

18.4 HOW MUCH CAPITAL?

Individual countries have drawn different conclusions from the crisis. Some have said that banking was excessively risky and that it is important to increase capital to reduce risk-taking. Others have taken a different view, arguing that banks are currently weak and by increasing capital their banks might be pushed into more difficulties or even default.

Dilemma

There are two main problems for the authorities. First, there is the classical one whereby a safe and resilient financial system may be over-conservative when it comes to lending. Second, for a country with weak banks to make the rules stricter may perversely cause banks to collapse, whilst maintaining weak regulations and low capital levels may give the banks sufficient breathing room to improve their financial positions over time. The various national positions on capital levels can be understood in the context of those two concerns.

National positions

Perhaps surprisingly, the countries that most advocate more restrictive Basel III rules, including more capital, are the US, the UK and Switzerland. The last two are countries with particularly large financial sectors and all three share in a relatively *laissez-faire* tradition on financial regulation. They are joined by Sweden, Denmark and the Netherlands within the EU, and by Canada and Australia among other BCBS members.

Even more surprisingly, the countries that most strongly advocate weak regulations and low capital are Germany and France, especially the latter. If we consider the public statements of the leaders of those countries, one would get the impression that they are against risk-taking and speculation, advocating strict regulations, but in the committees in which the rules are being drafted, those countries advocate the opposite.

The difference in national attitudes can partly be explained by the fact that countries with relatively stronger banks, and countries whose banks have been more forthcoming in recognising problem assets and recapitalising, find it easier to require more capital. If banks are weak and have been allowed to hide losses, they will find it more difficult to increase capital. The attitude of the Germans and the French depends in large part on the role of banks in their economies, and for the French the amount of *dirigiste* influence the state has over banks' lending and general economic activity.

The Basel III proposals are the outcome of an agreement amongst all member countries of the BCBS, and in the end, the capital levels were much lower than desired by certain members. For some countries, this is not necessarily that problematic, because they can simply unilaterally insist on more capital, a position taken by several countries, including the US and Canada. The situation is different in Europe, because of the *maximum harmonisation principle*, and as usual is more complex.

18.4.1 Maximum harmonisation principle

Amongst the European members of the BCBS, some want more capital than eventually agreed to. Of those, the most vocal are the UK, Sweden, the Netherlands and others. Initially, they aimed to follow the non-European members and unilaterally increase their capital requirements. That ran into significant opposition, especially from the European Commission, and to a lesser extent France and Germany, who claim it runs counter to the so-called maximum harmonisation principle.

Besides a desire for more capital, the opposition to maximum harmonisation is generally rooted in a preference for national flexibility for macro-prudential policies, and many member states, and even the ECB, have expressed a desire for such flexibility.

Single rulebook

This principle is well stated by Andrea Enria (2011), head of the EBA, who highlights the great importance, when implementing European regulations, of consistent implementation and of the *single rulebook*. This obviously makes sense because inconsistent rules and implementation can be a cloak for protectionism, encourage regulatory arbitrage and increase frictional costs.

This has implications for the enthusiasm for more capital, because the single rulebook implies that all member states need to have 'exactly the same rules on the definition of capital and maintain them up to date in a coordinated fashion in light of financial innovation'. This means that member countries should not be allowed to require more capital for their banks than agreed to by the EU, and cannot seek to establish an independent brand based on higher regulatory standards.

Main dilemma

Maximum harmonisation is quite important for the EU, not least because of the importance of the common rulebook. It is also a defence against further tiering of the market, which happens when the stronger countries rush ahead, undermining the market image of the weaker ones.

The eventual outcome is problematic, however, especially if the eventual capital requirements in Europe will be lower than outside the Union. This will send a signal that North American and Asian BCBS member countries will have more resilient banking systems. It is possible that this will cause higher-quality clients to migrate to these banks, leaving poorer-quality clients and riskier activities to the EU. Lower capital requirements will at least suggest that Europe has a more fragile banking system than the rest of the world.

Perhaps the real problem is that it signals both a deep current malaise and an unwillingness to tackle it, guaranteeing the crisis will fester.

Eventually, enough wiggle room was found to allow member countries to adopt any minimum capital ratios they desire.

18.4.2 Economic costs

Basel III significantly increases the direct cost of doing banking but hopefully will make the banking system more resilient, and perhaps reduce the total cost to society from banking. The question of which of these factors dominates remains highly controversial, and whilst many studies have been made, the conclusions are not consistent.

The main dilemma for policymakers is the elusive cost and benefit problem that is so hard to analyse, especially the growth versus stability trade-offs.

Studies

Admati *et al.* (2010) argue that increased bank equity brings with it significant economic benefits, whilst lowering leverage and the risk of bank failures. Other studies find that Basel III will be costly, for example studies by the New York Federal Reserve Bank (NYFed) (Angelini *et al.*, 2011) and the BIS (2010). The latter finds that a 1% increase in equity will lead to a 0.19% reduction in GDP over four years. An FSA study (de Ramon *et al.*, 2012) finds that quantifying the pros and cons is difficult. The Institute of International Finance (2010) finds a much stronger impact, where a 2% increase in capital, along with other elements of Basel III, will cost 3.1% of GDP over five years.

GDP impact

It is very hard to identify the costs and benefits of Basel III. By a first approximation, increased capital increases the cost of doing business, reducing lending and increasing the cost of lending. However, if the banking systems become more resilient, requiring fewer and smaller bailouts and, hence, are less prone to boom and bust cycles, these costs are partially, and even fully, offset.

In addition, standard Modigliani–Miller analysis would predict that reduced funding costs because of higher capital would provide greater security for well-capitalised banks. This implies that the GDP impact of higher capital would be very small. After all, every time a bank issues new capital, the economic impact is non-detectable.

It is hard to see how a relatively modest increase in bank capital, tiny compared to GDP, could have anything but a very moderate economic impact. This suggests that the studies with the low impact numbers are more credible.

GDP and stability trade-off

It is important how the main issues are compared. Are we comparing the question of short-term growth against more short-term resiliency, or multi-decade growth compared to the potential for systemic crisis?

The empirical studies tend to focus on the former, not least because it is easier to analyse. The main question for society is the second. Systemic crises are so costly that we would do almost anything to prevent them. More capital would be a cheap way to prevent systemic crises, so long as it was effective.

And herein lies the relevant question. What is the best way to prevent systemic risk, taking into account the effectiveness and cost? If the answer is capital, it is obvious that capital requirements should be increased. If the answer is not necessarily capital, then the capital increases are harder to justify.

To this day, this question has not been answered in a satisfactory way.

18.5 RECOVERY AND RESOLUTION

In response to the crisis, the authorities have put significant emphasis on crisis resolution, as discussed in Bassani and Trapanese (2011). For an industry view, see Institute of International Finance (2012). Resolving the failure of an individual financial institution is difficult in the best of times.

Resolving bank failures within existing bankruptcy laws

Bankruptcy law moves very slowly and intends to protect the interests of the creditors. In any bankruptcy, the clients of the failed company will suffer, but when a bank fails the effects may be particularly severe.

This provides the motivation for special bank resolution regimes, for example the FSB Key Attributes, the Federal Deposit Insurance Corporation (FDIC) resolution regime and the Dodd–Frank orderly liquidation authority. The objective is to take bank insolvencies out of the usual bankruptcy procedures and make quick administrative action possible.

18.5.1 Resolution regimes

Every financial centre has some resolution regime in place. These are most routinely applied to domestic failures, and work reasonably well, provided the institution is small and operates only in the home country.

Definition 18.1 Resolution regimes These refer to the mechanisms implemented when a financial institution fails, like bankruptcy proceedings, dealing with creditors and debtors, provision of continuous banking services and the like.

When financial institutions become large, the problems of resolution become much harder, and even more so when they involve multiple jurisdictions.

Before the crisis, the problem of cross-border resolution had been to a large extent ignored because of the many inherent complexities. It is hard to see how an international agreement could effectively override markedly different national regimes. The failure of Lehman Brothers demonstrated the complacency inherent in the extant resolution regimes.

EXAMPLE 18.1 Lehman Brothers

When Lehman brothers failed, there was a scramble to file for bankruptcy. The bankruptcy filing in New York occurred just after midnight on Monday 15 September, beating the London filing by a few minutes. Even if London had been first, it would not have made much difference, because liquidity in Lehman Brothers was handled centrally in New York. It swept to New York each night, only to be released to the regional operations the next day. The Friday sweep took $8 billion out of London.

At the point of failure, a single integrated operation with a common treasury function, the situation on Friday, was replaced by around 100 discrete entities, all insolvent and with their bankruptcies being handled by their respective national regimes. Each administrator has a duty to maximise recovery for the creditors to its entity, which places them in a competitive situation, and four years after the bankruptcy there are still fresh, multi-billion-dollar claims being made by one administrator against another. As most of these will need to be addressed in court, it is clear that for most creditors substantial repayment remains a distant prospect, and also that the frictional costs of the bankruptcy will be very high.

While the scramble for filing was not all that important, the bigger problem was that proceedings in the US, UK and other jurisdictions all went on independently, without adequate legal grounds to establish one, consolidated proceeding.

Source: based on information from *Financial Times* (2008) and Sorkin (2010)

Lehman Brothers was international in life but national in death, as noted by Thomas Huertas.

The administrators of a single bankrupt entity are not allowed to place cooperation with other administrators above the interests of the creditors whose money they are spending, so it is sometimes difficult for them to justify cooperative information sharing unless it is clear that their creditors will benefit. An external entity could assist in promoting efficient information sharing and cooperation and reduce duplicated effort.

In 2009, the FSB announced principles for cross-border and crisis management. Based on the Lehman experience, this should be of some help. Building on supervisory colleges, a new entity called a crisis management group (CMG) should be in place, ready to handle crisis management. The CMGs are meant to improve information sharing, build-up of trust and cooperation between various authorities.

However, beyond that it is not clear how much a CMG can achieve, in practice, as the fundamental problem is one of conflicting fiduciary duty. By law, administrators are not allowed to give preference to the interests of other group companies over those of their creditors, so while better information sharing would perhaps save time it would not prevent the attempts by administrators to maximise their outgoing claims against other group companies, and to minimise the incoming claims they accept. Intragroup arrangements will be complex, so this will remain a recipe for lengthy wrangling even if a CMG can provide improved access to company data.

18.5.2 Living wills

One way to reduce the danger created by the failure of banks is by the concept of *living wills*. The objective of living wills is to require banks to demonstrate how they could be wound up during financial turmoil without requiring bailouts. In effect, living wills serve to provide a manual to deal with difficulties and, if necessary, unwind failed banks painlessly without recourse to public funds.

Living wills were originally proposed by the FSA in October 2009 and have two phases, recovery and resolution. The recovery plans are managed by the firm and the resolution plans by the authorities. The recovery plans are put into effect before insolvency or resolution, involving perhaps the sales of businesses, the winding down of exposures, and the like. The resolution plans address how to handle a bank in resolution. A lot of that is just collecting information so that all concerned can understand the legal entity structure, IT issues, business exposures, where assets are in the group, etc.

The idea of living wills is sensible, but it remains to be seen how it can be executed effectively. Furthermore, they may create interesting legal problems because bankruptcy law tends to take precedence over pre-existing contracts and can even unwind recent management decisions if these are deemed improper. This will be especially relevant across jurisdictions, and one could imagine a court in one country refusing to recognise some of the steps and demanding that their own rules take precedence when their subsidiaries are involved.

It also seems likely, given management incentives, that supervisors will be slow to recognise that resolution is required. It would be unwise to assume that, in practice, resolution will commence swiftly enough to prevent the requirement of public funds.

18.6 WHAT ABOUT TOO BIG TO FAIL?

An important failure of financial regulations before 2007, and one that has been getting worse since then, is the problem of TBTF financial institutions, especially the G-SIBs.

A bank that is TBTF is a bank whose failure would be so catastrophic that it would probably trigger a systemic crisis. The economic and political consequences of the failure of a TBTF institution are so big that a government has no choice but to try to bail it out, even if it may be beyond the government's means to do so.

Bank incentives

Banks have direct incentives to become TBTF. Any bank that is perceived as TBTF is more likely to be bailed out than smaller banks. Creditors notice this, and provide funds to the TBTFs at lower costs than to their smaller competitors, because those loans are implicitly underwritten by the government. This funding cost advantage gives the TBTFs a competitive advantage over their competitors. After all, if your failure triggers a systemic crisis, you will be bailed out. Your funding costs will reflect that bailout and so your competitive situation is improved. Finally, in order to become TBTF, it helps to be seen as big, interconnected and dangerous. If a bank is badly run, it is more dangerous and more likely to become seen as TBTF. This creates perverse incentives for bank management.

18.6.1 The view until 2007

Having financial institutions of this type does not seem very sensible. Regardless, prior to the crisis, banks were allowed and often encouraged to grow and merge, eventually creating many TBTF institutions. This happened without much public scrutiny, and with the acquiescence, or even direct encouragement, of the authorities.

Supervisors

In the past, banking supervisors have not been very concerned about the TBTF institutions. They were not subject to more stringent prudential requirements, nor was their range of activities restricted. On the contrary, if anything, the tendency of policymakers was to treat TBTF banks more lightly than other banks, reflecting the perceived benefits of diversification and management sophistication. In other words, because of their size, they were considered safer than smaller institutions.

Government

Politicians are also to blame for the TBTF problem. Countries often like to have national champions, big and powerful banks, visible on the global stage, demonstrating the prowess of the country. Therefore, governments actively encourage banks to become large, to become TBTF.

A view frequently expressed by governments before 2007, and even to this day, is that what is good for the *national banking champion* is good for finance and hence the country. National champions are, almost by definition, TBTF, and frequently identified as a major contributory factor to the crisis from 2007. They are one of the main reasons why we have so far been unable to resolve the banking crisis in Europe.

An interesting observation from Table 18.3 is how many European countries are represented. The US has its fair share of G-SIBs, eight, but it is within the means of such a large economy to bail out one or even more of its G-SIBs. Banking assets in the US are much smaller than in the EU. Furthermore, of the top banks in Table 18.3, JP Morgan's assets equal 15% of GDP and Citigroup's 13%. Overall, the assets of US banks aggregate to less than the country's GDP.

The same cannot be said for the European countries; for example, the UK and France each have four G-SIBs. Two European countries facing a sovereign debt crisis have some banks in the G-SIB group, Spain with two and Italy with one. The European banks are also much larger relative to their national GDP than in the US: Deutsche Bank has 84% of Germany's GDP, Santander 92% of Spain's GDP, and RBS, Barclays and HSBC together have 337% of the British GDP.

Summary

The crisis demonstrated the problem of TBTF institutions by identifying the importance of systemic risk compared to idiosyncratic risk. In principle, a large, globally diversified firm may be less likely to fail than smaller and more concentrated firms. Problems in one business line are offset by profits elsewhere, and diversification may in principle protect a large financial institution against idiosyncratic risk, so long as its idiosyncratic risk was different from that of other financial institutions.

Instead, the crisis showed that financial institutions were exposed to the same risk to a much greater extent than envisioned and, therefore, exposed to similar self-reinforcing collapses in confidence as their counterparts. If the markets have doubts about the institution's solvency, diversification will not protect it. Lehman was but one example.

18.6.2 What is being done?

Emergency measures in crisis

The problem of TBTF has become worse since 2007 because several institutions that were already very large were allowed to merge, because that was thought to be the best emergency response at the time. Some examples from the US include Bank of America with Merrill Lynch, JP Morgan Chase with Bear Stearns, and Wells Fargo with Wachovia, and in the UK, HBOS with Lloyds TSB. In all of these cases, the TBTF problem was made worse and competition was reduced. For example, post-merger, Lloyds has 21% in SME banking and provides one in five mortgages to new borrowers in the UK.

New initiatives

The authorities have recognised that crisis mergers were unfortunate, and have proposed a range of new measures intended to avoid them in the future.

A number of initiatives are aimed at the TBTF problem, most within the FSB. This includes special resolution regimes, additional regulations and increased intensity of supervision, and the G-SIB capital surcharges.

18.6.3 The problem is not really getting better

Whilst many of the initiatives aimed at the TBTFs make significant contributions towards mitigating some of the worst aspects of the problem, even to the extent of preventing more TBTFs from being created in the future, the signs do not point to the problem getting better.

First, the main reason why the problem exists in the first place is that governments like to have large, internationally known banks that demonstrate the prowess of the country. That means they implicitly agree to have TBTF banks.

Second, large national banks are ideally placed as lobbyists, being few, wealthy, and with similar interests. Because state support is so valuable to banks, they devote a great deal of effort to 'maintaining close links' with governments, via various forms of influence and lobbying. We have seen senior managers of large banks migrate to equally senior jobs in government, and some governments employing bankers as senior advisors. Similarly, senior government officials often migrate to high-level bank jobs.

Finally, we can expect competition for G-SIB status to be intense because of the lower funding costs it will bring. The G-SIB designation officially identifies the banks as such. It sends a signal that the banks are under a special watch, and most likely would not be allowed to fail. In turn, it makes them a preferred counterparty, lowering their cost of funding and giving them a competitive advantage. In other words, the G-SIB surcharge institutionalises the category of institutions that were perhaps the main contributor to the crisis, and are most likely to be bailed out in the future.

18.7 SUMMARY

Following the crisis that started in 2007, a significant revamp of financial regulations has been underway. One large set of changes relates to the Basel process and the work of the FSB. The next iteration of the capital accords, Basel III, is expected to be implemented from 2013, tightening the calculation of bank capital, introducing drawdown buffers, countercyclical buffers and special charges for G-SIBs. The accord also specifies new regulations on liquidity.

Several government regulatory institutions have been created as a consequence of the crisis; some have acquired more responsibility and others less. The relationship between the central banks, the supervisors and the treasuries has been altered, with the central banks taking on more responsibility but also losing some of their independence to the treasury.

Many other ideas have been discussed but have not made it into the reform process. Some problems, most importantly what to do about TBTFs, are not being dealt with in a satisfactory manner.

Chapter 9 discussed several regulatory initiatives, CCPs, FTT, restrictions on bonuses and narrow banking, and we have not repeated that discussion here.

Until a new crisis emerges, the initiatives discussed here, and in Chapter 9, are likely to be the final word on the financial regulatory process, as there seems to be insufficient political will to tackle more fundamental issues.

Questions for discussion

1 How has the role of the central banks changed in the crisis?

2 How has the role of the treasury changed in the crisis?

3 How has the role of the supervisor changed in the crisis?

4 Compare contrast the systematic risk institutions in the US, UK and EU.

5 What is the problem the European banking union is meant to solve and what is the main reason why it may not happen?

6 What are the main changes to capital in Basel III?

7 Which do you prefer, the risk-weighted Basel CAR or the leverage ratio?

8 Do you expect the LCR to be effective?

9 Does the NSFR positively or negatively affect the problem of maturity mismatches?

10 What is the maximisation harmonisation principle, and do you think it should be used to set European capital levels?

11 What are the main legal problems in resolution?

12 Do you think that the problem of too big to fail is being adequately addressed?

References

Admati, A. R., DeMarzo, P. M., Hellwig, M. F. and Pfleiderer, P. (2010). Fallacies, irrelevant facts, and myths in the discussion of capital regulation: why bank equity is not expensive. Working Paper, Graduate School of Business, Stanford University.

Angelini, P. L., Clerc, L., Curdia, V., Gambacorta, L., Gerali, A., Locarno, A., Motto, R., Roeger, W., den Heuvel, S. V. and Vlcek, J. (2011). Basel III: long-term impact on economic performance and fluctuations. Technical report, Federal Reserve Bank of New York.

Basel Committee on Banking Supervision (2011a). Basel Committee issues final elements of the reforms to raise the quality of regulatory capital. www.bis.org/press/p110113.pdf.

Basel Committee on Banking Supervision (2011b). Basel III: a global regulatory framework for more resilient banks and banking systems. Technical report.

Basel Committee on Banking Supervision (2011c). Global systemically important banks: assessment methodology and the additional loss absorbency requirement. www.bis.org/publ/bcbs207.pdf.

Bassani, G. and Trapanese, M. (2011). Crisis management and resolution. In Quagliariello, M. and Cannata, F., editors, *Basel III and Beyond*. Riskbooks, London.

Baudino, P. (2011). The policy response: from the G20 requests to the FSB roadmap; working towards the proposals of the Basel Committee. In Quagliariello, M. and Cannata, F., editors, *Basel III and Beyond*. Riskbooks, London.

BIS (2010). Assessing the macroeconomic impact of the transition to stronger capital and liquidity requirements. www.bis.org/publ/othp10.pdf.

Borio, C., Drehmann, M., Gambacorta, L., Jimenez, G. and Trucharte, C. (2010). Countercyclical capital buffers: exploring options. Technical report, BIS. Working Paper 317.

de Ramon, S., Iscenko, Z., Osborne, M., Straughan, M. and Andrews, P. (2012). Measuring the impact of prudential policy on the macroeconomy. A practical application to Basel III and other responses to the financial crisis. Technical report, FSA. Occasional Paper Series 42.

Enria, A. (2011). The future of EU regulation. www.eba.europa.eu/cebs/media/aboutus/Speeches/The-Future-of-EU-Regulation–British-Bankers-Association–29-June-2011.pdf.

Financial Stability Forum (2008). Report of the financial stability forum on enhancing market and institutional resilience. Technical report.

Financial Times (2008). Winding up Lehman Brothers. *Financial Times*, 7 November.

Gorter, J. and Bijlsma, M. (2012). Strategic moves. www.risk.net/life-and-pension-risk.

Institute of International Finance (2010). Interim report on the cumulative impact of proposed changes in the banking regulatory framework. Technical report.

Institute of International Finance (2012). Making resolution robust. Technical report.

Quagliariello, M. and Cannata, F. (2011). *Basel III and Beyond*. Riskbooks, London.

Repullo, R. and Saurina, J. (2011). The countercyclical capital buffer of Basel III: a critical assessment. CEMFI Working Paper 1102, June 2011.

Sorkin, A. R. (2010). *Too Big to Fail: Inside the Battle to Save Wall Street*. Penguin.

19 SOVEREIGN DEBT CRISES

Sovereign debt crises happen when a national government – the sovereign – is unable to service its debt. This form of crisis was common in the developed world until the second World War (WWII), but after that has mostly been consigned to emerging markets countries.

The reason is that developed countries are able to borrow in their own currency, and so can usually find ways to avoid defaulting, perhaps by inflating the debt away. Recently, however, sovereign debt has become a serious policy issue for some members of the euro zone.

This chapter focuses on giving a general background to sovereign debt crises in general, as well as the causes of the European sovereign debt crisis. The crisis in Europe is still ongoing, and because of the rapid developments, we maintain a separate chapter on that crisis online at www.GlobalFinancialSystems.org.

Links to other chapters

This chapter mostly stands on its own, but the most direct connections are to Chapter 17 (the ongoing crisis: 2007–2009 phase).

Key concepts

- Newfoundland
- External and domestic debt
- Sovereign defaults and corporate defaults
- Enforcement of sovereign debt
- Currency unions and sovereign debt crises
- European sovereign debt crisis

Readings for this chapter

For a good overview of debt crises, see Sturzenegger and Zettelmeyer (2007). Reinhart and Rogoff (2009) present a comprehensive collection of facts and figures. For legal analysis, see, for instance, Gulati and Triantis (2007), and for a legal view on how to do restructuring, see Buchheit (2011). For statistical analysis of the cost of sovereign default, see Borensztein and Panizza (2008). For an overview of the euro, Marsh (2010) is comprehensive.

19.1 NEWFOUNDLAND

In the long history of sovereign debt crises, creditors have resorted to a variety of extreme means to enforce their claims. However, they have never used liquidation, in the same way as a corporation is liquidated, except in the case of Newfoundland. We follow this story as told by Hale (2003).

Newfoundland is the extreme easternmost part of Canada. The British established a settlement there in 1497 and the economy was primarily based on fishing. It became the first self-governing part of the British Empire in 1855 and by the end of the nineteenth century it enjoyed most of the trappings of sovereignty.

The Newfoundland government borrowed heavily to finance its military expenditures in the first World War (WWI), and continued increasing its debt throughout the 1920s. By 1933, its public debt was about three times GDP. By that time the economy had collapsed, not least because the Catholic countries of Latin America stopped buying fish because of the Great Depression.

The government of Newfoundland asked the British government for help, which obliged by sending a Royal Commission to investigate the situation. While Newfoundland preferred to default, this was not considered palatable to the Commission, which declared: 'No part of the British Empire has ever yet defaulted on its loan obligations [. . .] bankruptcy is at best an ugly word and carries a stigma which a nation even more than an individual would do well to avoid.'

The Deputy Leader of the (opposition) Labour Party, Clement Attlee, suggested that default was preferable to giving up democracy. Referring to Britain's own default on its wartime loans from the United States (US), he said: 'All the best countries default nowadays' (Hansard 1933). But in the early 1930s it was impossible to imagine a British dominion defaulting.

The Commission's proposal was that Newfoundland temporarily give up its independence to a UK-appointed administration – a dictatorship in all but name – and this was agreed to by Newfoundland's population in 1933.

Following WWII, the UK government felt compelled to resolve the issue. The alternatives were for Newfoundland to become a part of the UK, to become a part of the United States (US), to become independent or to merge with Canada. The first choice was unpalatable to the UK, and the second disliked by Canada, so only the last two were considered.

The UK-run administration held a referendum, and a slim majority rejected confederation with Canada. The administration repeated the referendum several weeks later, this time getting a majority vote for confederation. The British North America Act required that the local parliament solicit the federation with Canada, but as Newfoundland had no parliament, the British government chose to overlook this requirement. It appointed a negotiations team in short order and by 1949 Newfoundland had became a part of Canada. The confederation treaty was an act of Canada and Britain, not of Newfoundland.

In dealing with the crisis, the British government opted to liquidate Newfoundland, the only case in modern history where a sovereign nation has suffered that fate.

19.2 SOVEREIGN DEBT

Sovereign debt is owed by a sovereign authority, often including government entities such as the central bank. It does not include the debt of regional and local governments, nor the debt of government-owned agencies or enterprises, unless explicitly guaranteed by the central government. A sovereign default occurs when the government fails to meet payments on its sovereign debt.

Historically, governments were the biggest borrower from banks, and the success and failure of financial institutions was directly dependent on the ability of the sovereign to meet its obligations, often in turn dependent on its success in war. As noted by Homer and Sylla (1996), during the Renaissance, important financial institutions, including the Medici's, failed because of the inability or unwillingness of the kings to repay their loans. In turn, those sovereigns who were more likely to wage wars were considered more risky, paying a spread over those more peaceful. After all, if the king loses, the creditor will not be repaid.

Sovereign default has been a part of virtually every country's history. France defaulted eight times from 1500, but eventually managed to emerge from its status as a serial defaulter, and has not defaulted since 1788. Spain defaulted seven times in the nineteenth century after having defaulted six times in the preceding three centuries.

The UK defaulted frequently a few centuries back. It defaulted indirectly in the late 1800s by unilaterally adjusting the coupons on its debt, and did not fully repay its WWI war debt to government and private investors in the US, owing $4.4 billion in 1934. Updating to current prices,[1] this is $74 billion if adjusted by the consumer price index (CPI) and $1,010 billion if measured as a share of GDP.

As the developed nations stopped defaulting on their debt in the twentieth century, countries that had recently gained independence started to have trouble with their debt burden. For example, India has defaulted four times and practically every newly independent African country has defaulted at least once. The most defaults in any continent is in Latin America where every country has defaulted at least twice. China also defaulted twice in the twentieth century.

19.2.1 External and domestic debt

Governments can issue debt in either domestic or foreign currency. Generally, *domestic debt* is issued in local currency, under local law and held by local citizens, whilst *external debt* is issued in foreign currency, under foreign law and held by foreigners. Many exceptions exist, and this distinction does not apply to debt issued by euro zone governments.

[1]See www.measuringworth.com.

External defaults get much more attention than domestic defaults. One reason is that they are more common, but it is also because external defaults are highly visible in international capital markets and, hence, the international press; whereas domestic defaults are less visible, and often more indirect.

External debt

Most countries prefer to issue domestic currency debt, but this is often not a viable option, perhaps because the domestic debt market is underdeveloped and not very deep. In this case, a country might resort to issuing foreign currency debt to overseas investors. We refer to this as external debt. Of course, anything will sell if priced appropriately, so the implication is that the yield at which domestic debt can be sold appears unattractively high compared to that of foreign debt.

Countries default regularly on external debt, often because of adverse external factors, such as falling commodity prices, increases in interest rates or the sudden stop or reversal of capital flows. External borrowing, not surprisingly, is strongly pro-cyclical. High commodity prices are often correlated with increased borrowing, setting the stage for a debt crisis when commodity prices eventually drop.

Many emerging markets countries prefer short-term borrowing because it is cheaper than longer maturities. Investors also prefer shorter maturities, both because that minimises their risk and also because it gives them more ability to discipline borrowers. However, short-term borrowing introduces roll-over risk and makes a country more vulnerable to a liquidity crisis, as we have seen in the East Asian case.

Domestic debt

Domestic currency debt, mostly held by local citizens, has traditionally been the major part of the overall stock of public debt, perhaps averaging at around two-thirds of total debt. This proportion is much higher for developed economies. Unlike external debt, outright defaults of domestic debt are much less common than defaults on external debt. Governments, however, have numerous indirect options for reducing the domestic debt burden, for example inflation, the forced conversion of debt to lower coupon rates, and a unilateral reduction in principal. Both the UK and the US have resorted to such measures. Another possibility is financial repression in the form of an interest rate ceiling with a simultaneous rise in inflation. India, for example, introduced interest rate ceilings in the wake of its external debt restructuring in 1972–1976.

The many alternatives for reducing the debt burden mean that it is often difficult to determine exactly what constitutes a default and what is just an event that happens to reduce the debt burden. The extensive 'wiggle-room' this provides borrowers is one reason why foreign lenders tend to prefer foreign-currency debt, issued in developed countries' jurisdictions.

Debt reduction through inflation

Perhaps the most common way for a government to reduce its debt burden is by reducing the value of its currency by inflation. Before the advent of paper money, governments would regularly debase their coinage, which was usually based on silver or gold, by mixing in cheaper metals, shaving down coins or reissuing smaller coins in the same denomination. For example, between 1542 and 1547 the pound lost 83% of its silver content. The tools of inflating away debt have changed over the years and the introduction of fiat money made it much easier for governments to create inflation.

High inflation by itself does not have to imply default, so long as interest rates compensate or the debt is inflation indexed, but a rapid increase in inflation when debt is not indexed strongly signifies that a government is deliberately deflating debt away. Some commentators have claimed that the inflation in the US in 1947–1948 was deliberately created to reduce WWII debt, and once that debt had reached manageable levels, the government slowed down the inflation. One could argue that the various quantitative easings (QEs) are a form of inflating debt away.

What about European sovereign debt?

While the distinction between internal and external debt has never been absolute, the boundaries were further blurred with the euro zone. Is Greek debt, issued in euros, external or internal debt? Since a significant portion of the debt is held by foreigners, it is external, but it is issued in the Greek domestic currency and, therefore, domestic. Furthermore, 86% of Greek debt is subject to Greek law, with the rest mostly issued in euros in London and, hence, subject to UK law.

This means that in the case of the euro zone, the distinction between domestic and external debt depends very much on context.

19.2.2 Difference from corporate defaults

Sovereign defaults are inherently different from corporate defaults. A company goes broke when it breaches a covenant with its creditors, perhaps by failing to pay interest, so that creditors petition a court for a formal bankruptcy process. In that process, a company may be restructured or in a worst case *liquidated*. The creditors can draw on a well-defined legal framework providing them with clearly drawn-up rights, and rely on bankruptcy courts to enforce their claims.

Countries do not generally go out of business and get liquidated, the single exception being Newfoundland. The creditors cannot use a formal legal process to enforce their claims against a country in the same way as they can use the legal system in a corporate bankruptcy, because there is no proper supranational legal framework for enforcing sovereign debt contracts across borders.

However, the trigger is the same: default means failure to honour a contract, perhaps through failure to repay principal or to make an interest payment or through some unilateral adjustment in contract terms.

Unlike a corporation, a country defaults because the government has made a strategic decision to default, presumably after cost–benefit analysis, weighing the cost of debt service against the losses incurred because of default. It could perhaps better be compared to the US 'Chapter 7' reorganisation because the existing management may well remain in place. Consequently, countries generally default long before they run out of the ability to service debt. This means that in sovereign defaults the lenders depend on both the ability and the willingness of the government to honour its debt.

19.2.3 Why repay sovereign debt?

Defaulting on foreign currency debt held by foreigners imposes costs on the foreigners and saves the nation-state money. So why pay back at all? The reason is that it is costly to default. Not only does it adversely affect the reputation of a country, but creditors often have a variety of means to enforce their claims, relying on carrots and sticks.

Reputation risk

A country that defaults suffers a loss to its reputation, which may hamper its access to international capital markets or increase future costs of borrowing. Since the ability to tap the international capital markets at a low cost is quite valuable, it provides direct incentives not to default.

One example of this was provided by South Africa repaying apartheid-era debt. *The Economist* (1999) had strong opinions about the consequences: '[South Africa's] credit rating would be wrecked as it came to be lumped in with other deadbeats. Foreign investors would be deterred and South Africa would have to pay more for future borrowing.'

Analysis of default costs

A country that defaults on its obligations is also likely to suffer disruption in international trade. Access to trade financing might seize, and creditors may attempt to enforce their claims in friendly jurisdictions. Similarly, loss of reputation may discourage foreign direct investment, since a country that defaults may appear more likely to seize the assets of foreigners or cause difficulties for their operations.

Borensztein and Panizza (2008) analyse the costs of sovereign defaults, considering reputational costs, international trade exclusion costs, costs to the domestic economy through the financial system, and political costs to the authorities. They find that reputational costs are significant but short lived. There is little impact on trade, growth in the domestic economy suffers, default episodes seem to cause banking crises and not vice versa, and finally governments suffer a significant political cost from the consequences of debt crises.

Contagion

In Europe, banks are exposed to high-risk European sovereigns, and this may trigger their default and transmit a sovereign debt crisis to their home country. This works as a channel for contagion.

Default immunity and economic development

The impact of sovereign defaults varies greatly between countries: some seem quite immune whilst others are strongly affected. Less developed countries generally are not as sensitive to sovereign defaults than their more developed counterparts. After all, if a country is relatively self-sufficient and most consumers buy from domestic companies, where the export sector is small, a sovereign default on external debt might not have a huge impact.

For example, one reason why the Latin American countries have defaulted so frequently is that such an event affects the population only indirectly, perhaps because they have adapted their economies to become default immune, a classic case of a self-fulfilling prophecy.

However, the more exposed a country is to the global economy, the better its previous reputation, and the less its citizens are prepared for the event, the bigger the impact of a sovereign default. This is why it is so difficult for European countries to contemplate a default. The costs can be expected to be much larger than, say, for Argentina which defaulted in 2002.

19.2.4 Debt (in)tolerance

Definition 19.1 Debt intolerance Even though a lot of commentary focuses on debt/GDP, that is not as relevant as some other variables indicating the ability to service debt, for example debt/foreign income.

Some countries manage easily with very high debt levels, perhaps exceeding 240% of GDP as in Japan, whilst others default with debt levels of 40%. The inability to maintain high debt levels was called *debt intolerance* by Reinhart *et al.* (2003). This happens when a weak institutional structure, and a problematic political system, make external borrowing a tempting way to avoid tough decisions regarding fiscal spending and taxing.

What matters is the point at which lenders cease to lend, which depends on their belief on whether the loan will be repaid. This will be influenced mainly by how much damage they perceive the borrower is exposed to if they default. If this is high for whatever reason, for example because the lender has a big army, the borrower does a lot of international trade, or the borrower has a big reputation to protect for some other reason, then the debt/GDP ratio can get high.

Debt intolerance manifests itself in the extreme duress many emerging markets experience at external debt levels that would seem quite manageable by the standards of more developed countries. Default can occur in emerging markets at levels of debt well below the 60% ratio of debt to GDP that is enshrined in the Maastricht Treaty, though the comparison is not entirely fair. Maastricht applies to highly developed countries and some less developed countries that receive credit enhancement via the euro and associated political machinery; as a result its signatories can be expected to be highly debt tolerant.

Mexico defaulted in 1982 with a ratio of debt to GNP of 47% and Argentina in 2001 at around 50%. Reinhart and Rogoff (2009) find that external debt exceeded 100% of GNP in only 16% of defaults of emerging markets during 1970–2008. More than half the defaults occurred at levels *below* 60%, and 20% occurred below 40%. The threshold level is determined by the history of the country. A serial defaulter with persistent inflation and weak institutions and in which citizens are inured to crises will have a lower threshold than a country that appears to have lower credit risk.

EXAMPLE 19.1 Japan

The country that successfully manages the world's highest debt level is Japan, where the government debt reached 230% in 2011. The reason such a high debt level is sustainable is that all of the debt is in domestic currency, interest rates are almost zero and most of the debt is held by domestic agents. This high debt is not without problems. The Japanese economy has been stagnating for two decades, often suffering from borderline deflation. If the government attempts to stimulate the economy, it may cause interest rates to increase, sharply increasing the debt burden. Any attempt to inflate the debt away would be opposed by the electorate, an unusually high proportion of whom are beyond retirement age and consequently living primarily on savings.

Vulnerabilities

As a country's debt gets closer to the intolerance level, it becomes increasingly vulnerable to shocks. It may not have the funds for a fiscal stimulus, and any negative shock will reduce tax revenues and, hence, increase the relative debt burden. Even though policymakers may find that their debt levels appear manageable under the current – favourable – economic situation, high debt may mean the country is unable to respond to a crisis. We see some of this in the European sovereign debt crisis.

This means that it can take very little to trigger a sovereign debt crisis, and it can happen without any significant changes in wealth or income. All that is needed is a change in confidence. This means that many of the same forces are at work in a sovereign debt crisis as in a currency crisis, and we can easily analyse them with one of the second-generation (2G) currency crisis models discussed earlier.

If the market begins to suspect that a government may not be able to pay back its debt, it will demand a higher compensation for taking on the higher risk of default. A spike in bond yields, driven by fear that a government will fail to honour its debt, makes debt refinancing for a country difficult to impossible. This is a sovereign debt crisis. We illustrate the mechanisms in Figure 19.1.

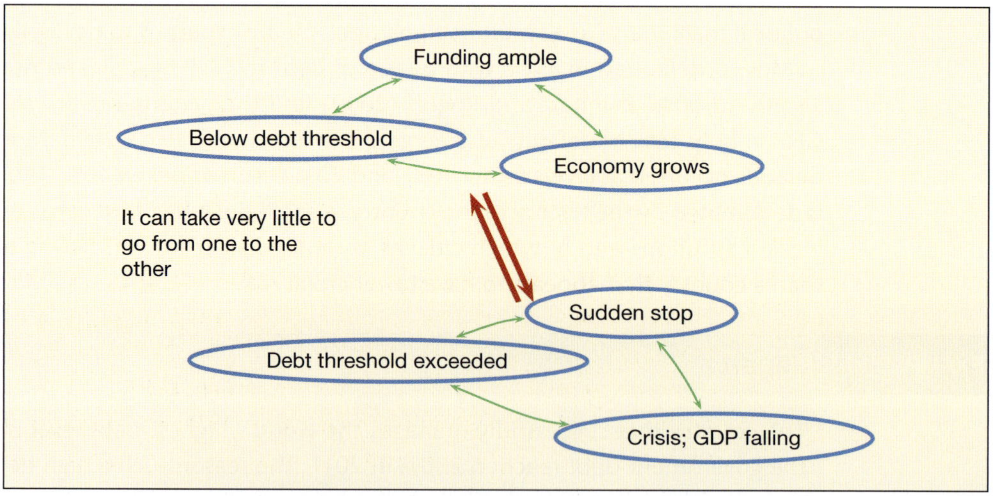

Figure 19.1 Towards a sovereign debt crisis

19.3 ENFORCEMENT

Even though it is just not possible to legally enforce sovereign debt as efficiently as corporate debt, creditors have a wide variety of means at their disposal to compel governments to repay.

Institutions

There are several supranational mechanisms for addressing sovereign debt. Perhaps the most prominent of those is the Paris Club, which is a group of finance officials from 19 of the world's largest economies, meeting in the French Ministry of Economy, Finance and Industry. They provide specialised financial services such as war funding, debt restructuring, debt relief and debt cancellation. Resorting to the Paris Club is often the last course of action for highly indebted poor countries. Recent examples include the cancelling of some of the debt of Nigeria, Liberia and the Democratic Republic of Congo.

The International Monetary Fund (IMF) (see Krueger, 2002) proposed a formal legal mechanism for dealing with sovereign debt restructuring. This would have established similar legal structures for sovereign debt as exist for corporate debt. However, this initiative was rejected by almost everybody.

Military enforcement

In centuries past, some states resorted to rather extreme measures to guarantee their claims. Egypt reneged on its obligations to France and Britain in 1882 and as a response both countries invaded Egypt, making it a British 'protectorate'. Just a few years before, the British invaded Istanbul in 1876 in the wake of one of Turkey's defaults.

Similarly, the US interventions in Venezuela in the 1890s and the Dominican Republic in 1916 and the occupation of Haiti in 1915 were at least partly motivated by debt repayment concerns. Haiti was effectively run as a military dictatorship by the US Marines, who used their control of the country's institutions, such as the customs house, to enforce US interests.

The French and Belgian occupation of the Ruhr region in Germany between 1923 and 1925 was motivated by German difficulties in making war reparations. The formal pretext was that Germany was 10 days late in delivering 100,000 telegraph poles!

Vulture funds and extreme legal steps

Claims on governments can live on for a long time, even centuries, as the examples of Haiti and Russia show. If the prospects of repayment appear low, such debt may trade on the secondary market for pennies to the dollar, attracting so-called *vulture funds* which specialise in buying sovereign debt at very large discounts and pursuing impoverished countries in international courts.

One example was reported in *The Guardian* newspaper in 2007 (Kaseki, 2007): 'billionaire Paul Singer, who in 1996 paid $11m for discounted Peruvian debt and then threatened to bankrupt the country unless they paid him $58m [. . .] In order to keep a good standing in international financial markets Peru paid. Singer and his New York-based investment fund, Elliot Associates, have since sued the Republic of Congo (Congo Brazzaville) for $400m for a debt bought at $10m.' Peru was forced to pay because it sent funds to Euroclear to pay bond holders participating in its restructuring, and the Court of Appeals in Brussels enjoined Euroclear from making the payments because they violated *pari passu* clauses. A similar case was reported by the BBC (2012a) in which Ghana impounded an Argentinian naval vessel at the request of Elliot Capital Management, to enforce the fund's claim against Argentina arising from that country's sovereign default in 2002.

Induce restructuring – carrots and sticks

Buchheit (2011) identifies two ways for a debtor to restructure sovereign debt, labelled carrots and sticks.

- **Carrots.** The creditor can offer to stretch out maturities or raise interest rates to counteract the costs of a haircut. The sovereign can also offer credit enhancements, such as collateral securities or guarantees. This is quite costly for the sovereign, perhaps even removing the advantages of defaulting in the first place. Also these sweeteners may run foul of existing covenants and may violate *pari passu* clauses.
- **Sticks.** If the sovereign is unable or unwilling to fund a restructuring plan, it can employ a variety of encouragements to get maturity extensions, interest rate reductions or haircuts. The sovereign can either threaten default or actually default. In every sovereign restructuring over the past 30 years until the Greek restructuring, the sovereign either suspended payments or threatened default on debt that was not a part of the restructuring.

Encouraging lenders to agree

One problem in debt restructuring is to get all of the creditors to agree to a settlement, and several features have been introduced into restructuring processes to facilitate agreement.

Exit consents have become a common feature of debt restructuring, after Ecuador in 2000. Bondholders that agree to restructuring give the sovereign a proxy vote that may strip away valuable features of old bonds, making them less attractive to holdouts. This often requires only a simple majority of bondholders.

Bonds may have collective action clauses (CAC) that permit the majority or supermajority of creditors to modify key features of the terms of bonds, including principal and interest payments.

If sovereign debt is governed by local law, the government may just change the law to facilitate restructuring. While emerging market borrowers often are not able to issue bonds governed by their own law, European sovereign debt generally is governed by local law.

19.3.1 History lessons

Buchheit (2011) draws the following six lessons from history.

First, don't let a sovereign debt problem become a banking crisis. Sovereign debt is frequently held by domestic or foreign banks, and there is always the potential that a large sovereign default may trigger a banking crisis domestically and even abroad. The restructuring process should aim to prevent this. One simple approach would be to discourage banks from buying government debt, something most governments find hard to resist.

Second, don't delay recognising that debt levels are unsustainable. The longer governments try to prevent an inevitable restructuring, the higher the costs. Mexico in 1982 and Argentina in 2001 are good examples of such mistakes. Of course, with governments usually out of power following restructuring, it can be tempting for them to hold on as long as possible.

Third, keep track of government obligations. In most cases, the government has a relatively clear idea of its own direct liabilities, but the problem is caused by unmonitored borrowing by other government entities, like local governments or state-owned enterprises, enjoying a sovereign guarantee. Such borrowing can often explode under the radar. This was a major problem for Argentina, and is now emerging as a problem for Spain and China.

Fourth, ask for enough relief. If a country comes out of a restructuring process with debt levels that are too high, the problem remains, and the country may have to go through many rounds of debt restructuring. A cautionary tale is the repeated debt restructuring of Latin American countries in the 1980s, and the ongoing problems with Greece.

Fifth, be ruthlessly efficient. Sovereign debt crises don't come alone, but are usually the final part of significant underlying problems and are often accompanied by other crises. It is in everybody's interests to resolve the crisis as quickly as possible. This is likely to require dealing with some uncomfortable underlying causes (such as reduced competitiveness or unsustainable expenditure) as well as the crises that result from them.

Finally, be even-handed and treat all creditors the same way. Creditors will always jockey for advantage. Commercial banks may say they have always provided funds and government creditors may use geopolitics. Debtors should not discriminate amongst its creditors, unless absolutely necessary. One exception might be trade and supplier debt. However, for every creditor accorded preferential treatment, the remainder must be treated more harshly, and overall resentment will be increased by any perceived lack of fairness.

19.4 BACKGROUND TO THE EUROPEAN SOVEREIGN DEBT CRISIS

The global crisis that started in 2007 seemed to some commentators to be mostly over by 2009, but towards the end of that year the second phase of the crisis started, the European sovereign debt crisis. It started with Greece, but soon Portugal and Ireland were also in crisis, to be followed by Spain and Cyprus. As these problems remain unresolved, it is worth examining the historical precedents.

19.4.1 The Faroese crisis of 1992

The first sovereign debt crisis in the European Union (EU) is not the current one; several member states have been in serious difficulties and have even received bailouts, such as Britain from the IMF in 1976. There is, however, one sovereign debt crisis from 20 years ago that has many parallels with the current problems of some countries in the Union, the Faroese crisis of 1992. We follow the story as told by Danielsson and Oskarsson (2012) and show key statistics in Figure 19.2.

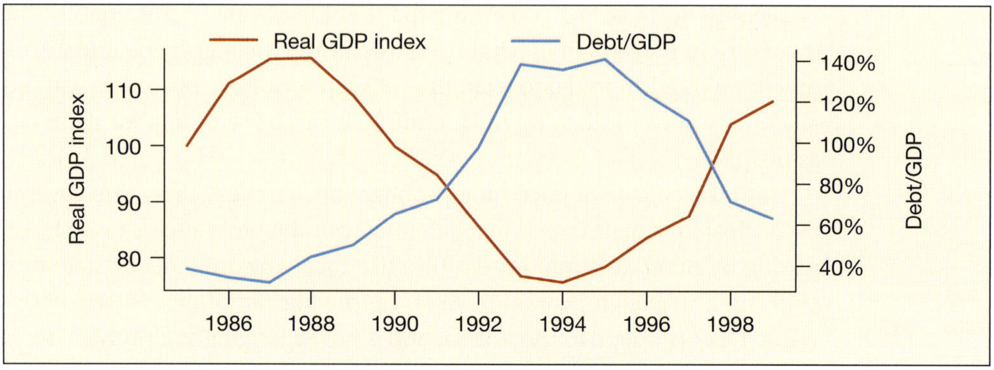

Figure 19.2 **Real Faroese GDP and government debt/GDP**

The Faroe Islands are a Danish possession situated between Iceland and Scotland. Even though they are part of Denmark, and use the Danish currency, they are not a member of the EU. The economy of the Faroes is primarily based on fishing. As the neighbouring countries expanded their economic zones to 200 miles, the Faroese fishing fleet lost access to its traditional fishing grounds, and profits plummeted. In response, the government of the Faroes resorted to subsidising its only export sector – fishing – to the tune of 34% of total exports throughout the 1980s.

Prior to the crisis in 1990, government net debt never exceeded 50% of GDP. Private debt, however, had been increasing rapidly, reaching 125% of GDP in 1990. The private borrowing was facilitated by government guarantees, capital subsidies and production guarantees. Some of the loan guarantees were deliberately kept secret from the Faroese parliament, the Danish government and the general public, while bad book-keeping shielded other support from scrutiny.

The guarantees meant the foreign creditors only worried about the ability of the Faroese government to repay the loans. Creditors implicitly assumed the Faroese sovereign debt was underwritten by the Danish government, with its AAA rating, even though no explicit guarantees were issued. The Danish government did not seem all that concerned and did nothing to disabuse the creditors.

The money was not put to good use, export subsidies directly added to the debt burden and many, if not most, investments turned out to be sour. In addition to financial intermediation, the local banks actively engaged in interest rate and tax arbitrage between the Faroe Islands and Denmark, reaping significant profits.

Eventually, it all got too much, and as the economy was hit by exogenous shocks due to a slowdown in the global economy and reduced fishing catch, a sovereign debt crisis ensued. The first affected were the banks, and the Danish financial supervisor became concerned and demanded that the banks shut down their arbitrage schemes and sharply increase loan provisions. This was the final straw for the banks. They defaulted and the Danish government forced the Faroese government to take the banks over at its own expense. This caused debt to reach 140% of GDP, mostly borrowed from the Danish government.

To the chagrin of the Faroese, the Danish deposit insurance fund and foreign banks, like Danske Bank, got off relatively scot-free. As the domestic banks defaulted, the GDP contracted by 40%, and 15% of the population emigrated. The crisis soured relations between the Faroese and their colonial masters. The Faroese maintained that Denmark had acted with malice in forcing them to assume too much debt in the crisis and imposing too much austerity, a view vindicated by the Danish state commission report on the crisis in January 1998 and a Danish parliamentary decision to ask the government to renegotiate the settlement terms in favour of the Faroese. The Danes worried about moral hazard and claimed the Faroese had been irresponsible and should not have an open-ended claim on the Danish treasury.

The conflict simmered until March 1998, when the Social Democrats won a majority in the Danish parliament, provided that the Faroese Social Democratic MP supported them, which he did, securing a settlement of the dispute worth DKK 1.5 billion to the Faorese authorities, or 20% of the islands' GDP.

After the crisis, the Faroese economy recovered swiftly, with an annual growth of 4% between 1995 and 2010. The Faroese ran a capital account surplus amounting to 13% of GDP per year for a decade, eliminating the sovereign debt. This was helped by the re-exports of the excess investment goods acquired prior to the crisis, and a sharp fall in imports, not least because of widespread emigration.

There are many parallels between the Faroese crisis and the ongoing European sovereign debt crisis, especially for Greece. Both countries got into difficulty because of excess borrowing, facilitated by belonging to a currency union with an AAA-rated partner. The creditors implicitly assumed that the debt was somehow underwritten, and that fiscal misconduct was prevented by the rules of the greater community. In neither case did the senior partner seem all that concerned, even as the sovereign debt spiralled upwards.

In the Faroese case, the crisis in state relations was eventually resolved when political necessities outweighed the cost of the bailout. It did help to have representation in the parliament of the main protagonist.

19.4.2 Currency union

The origins of the European sovereign debt crisis can be found two decades earlier in the formulation of the Economic and Monetary Union (EMU) and the euro.

History of monetary unions in Europe

There is a long history of monetary unions in Europe. For example, in the nineteenth century, we had the Latin Monetary Union, established in 1866 with Belgium, France, Italy and Switzerland as members, soon to be joined by Spain and Greece, and others later. This was not a true monetary union because each country issued its own currency, but they maintained pegged exchange rates with each other. The Latin union survived until 1914. The UK discussed joining, but two stumbling blocks prevented it. First, it had to devalue slightly, to make one pound sterling equivalent to 25 French francs. The second was that it had to decimalise, giving up shillings and pence. Another nineteenth-century attempt was the Scandinavian monetary union between Denmark, Sweden and Norway, established in 1873 and also lasting until 1914. These two attempts were just the last in a long chain of monetary unions, mostly doomed to failure.

The German monetary union in 1857 was a success. It replaced the currencies of the many German states with a dual system that lasted until the German unification of 1870, with the two currencies themselves replaced by the mark in 1875.

The other main success was the Belgium–Luxembourg monetary union of 1922. This came under stress on occasion, especially in the 1980s when Belgium unilaterally devalued the franc, infuriating the Luxembourgers. In response, Luxembourg set up a standby central bank, ready to switch over to Luxembourg francs within 24 hours if Belgium misbehaved again.

19.4.3 Why do monetary unions succeed and why do they fail?

Transfer unions

Definition 19.1 Transfer union A transfer union is an arrangement whereby a number of countries come together in some organisation, where the stronger members of the group directly and significantly subsidise the weaker members on a long-term continuous basis, and where the member countries have strong political connections between them.

Intergovernmental transfers are very common, as, for example, in development aid. Most of these do not imply that the countries involved are members of a transfer union. For example, development aid fails both of the tests in the definition above.

Is the EU a transfer union or not? If we look at the EU budget for 2010 (European Union, 2011, Annex 2c, p. 75), we see that the net amount received by member countries is around 0.3% of the GDP of the Union, even though for some member countries it might be as high as 4%. It is harder to identify net transfers within individual countries, but one report attempts to do that for Spain for 2005 (Spanish government, 2008, table 1, p. 13), finding that intra-region transfers amount to 2.2% of the GDP of Spain, in some regions amounting to 16% of that region's GDP.

This suggests that a transfer union is defined by the magnitude of the transfers. Individual nation states transfer an order of magnitude more funds between regions than the EU. Consequently, individual nation states are generally transfer unions, but the EU is not.

Success and failure

Whilst there is no set formula for why monetary unions succeed, they tend to bring together people who belong together culturally, in a single nation state, where people move freely between different parts of the country, the same rules and regulations apply generally across the union, economic development is not deeply out of sync and there is general acceptance of the notion of a transfer union. The main exception to this relates to situations in which small countries use the currency of a much bigger one, like Luxembourg and Belgium or Panama and the US. This directly relates to analysis of optimum currency areas, first discussed by Mundell (1961).

Monetary unions fail when these things are not in place. In times past, different members might be prone to war between themselves, activity not conducive to running joint monetary policy. Also, over time, it is likely that some countries prosper and others are left behind. If so, they will come to require different monetary policies. This suggests that unless a transfer union is in place, currency unions among near equal parties are unstable.

19.4.4 European currency arrangements since Bretton Woods

The EU has gone through several attempts at currency arrangements. The first was the 'snake in the tunnel' in the 1970s. This was followed by the European Monetary System (EMS), whereby a new virtual currency was created, the European Currency Unit (ECU). Exchange rates were supposed to fluctuate within a 2.25% target zone, except 6% for Italy. The German mark was the effective reserve currency of the arrangement. This caused the EMU crisis in the early 1990s as discussed in Section 12.4.

The European authorities decided to adopt a common currency in 1995 – the euro – to be implemented as an accounting currency on 1 January 1999, with coins and banknotes entering circulation on 1 January 2002. For an overview of the euro, see Marsh (2010). The area where the euro is the legal currency, and whose members are a part of the European Central Bank (ECB), is referred to as the euro zone, currently consisting of 17 members.[2] The euro is also used in six other countries,[3] but they are not represented at the ECB.

The motivation for setting up a monetary union need not be primarily economic. The reason the EU was set up in the first place is because it was felt that if Europe became integrated, war would be prevented. Based on that metric, the Union has been a success, the past 60 years having been about the most peaceful in European history. The establishment of the EMU was the next logical step in the integration process. This means that the motivation for the euro was more political than economic.

The Maastricht criteria

The designers of the euro did recognise the danger facing monetary unions and, in response, established the Maastricht criteria, which have four requirements. Two are related to restrictions on exchange rates and interest rates prior to joining.

Definition 19.2 Maastricht debt criteria The deficit must not exceed 3% annually, with the possibility of temporary suspension in exceptional cases. Government debt must not exceed 60% of GDP, and if it is higher, must approach the 60% at a satisfactory pace.

Table 19.1 shows the debt and deficits of member countries in the year they joined. More than half violated Maastricht criteria that year, and of those that qualified, two are now in a state of crisis.

---

[2]Austria, Belgium, Cyprus, Estonia, Finland, France, Germany, Greece, Ireland, Italy, Luxembourg, Malta, the Netherlands, Portugal, Slovakia, Slovenia and Spain.

[3]Montenegro, Andorra, Monaco, San Marino, Vatican City and Kosovo.

Table 19.1 Euro zone deficit and debt in first year of euro membership and Maastricht compliance

Country	Year of joining	Deficit	Debt	Primary balance	Compliance with Maastricht
Austria	1999	−2.3%	66.8%	1.1%	×
Belgium	1999	−0.6%	113.6%	6.2%	×
Cyprus	2008	0.9%	48.9%	3.8%	✓
Estonia	2011	1.0%	6.0%	1.1%	✓
Finland	1999	1.7%	45.7%	4.7%	✓
France	1999	−1.8%	58.9%	1.2%	✓
Germany	1999	−1.6%	61.3%	1.6%	×
Greece	2001	−4.5%	103.7%	2.0%	×
Ireland	1999	2.7%	46.6%	5.0%	✓
Italy	1999	−1.9%	113.0%	4.6%	×
Luxembourg	1999	3.4%	6.4%	3.7%	✓
Malta	2008	−4.6%	62.3%	−1.4%	×
Netherlands	1999	0.4%	61.1%	4.7%	×
Portugal	1999	−3.1%	51.4%	−0.2%	×
Slovakia	2009	−8.0%	35.6%	−6.6%	×
Slovenia	2007	0.0%	23.1%	1.2%	✓
Spain	1999	−1.2%	62.4%	2.3%	×

Data source: Eurostat, http://epp.eurostat.ec.europa.eu/portal/page/portal/eurostat/home/ © European Union

19.4.5 Evolution of European debt

Table 19.2 shows that debt levels vary quite significantly across the euro zone. Greece and Italy have the highest debt, with Estonia the least. Only three countries satisfied the Maastricht criteria in 2011.

Figure 19.3 shows the change in debt over the past decade and a half. Two countries in crisis, Greece and Portugal, have had the biggest increase in debt, while Belgium has been the most successful in reducing its debt.

The figures indicate that the level of debt tolerance varies widely across Europe. Table 19.2 shows that there is not a particularly strong correspondence with debt levels and credit rating, otherwise Estonia would be the most highly rated country in Europe and Belgium and Italy would be rated much lower, with even the AAA ratings of France and Germany under threat. This is a clear example of how debt tolerance varies across the Union.

Figure 19.4 shows the evolution of the ratings of the main crisis countries. Deficits seem to do a good job in predicting ratings, suggesting that a debt tolerance concept based solely on debt/GDP ratio is incomplete.

Total (public plus private) gross external debt/GDP is reported in www.reinhartandrogoff.com for a number of countries, and we report the results for the euro zone members in Figure 19.5, where available. Ireland has the highest level of external debt, exceeding

Table 19.2 Euro zone debt to GDP, Maastricht compliance, and ratings in August 2012

Country	1995 debt	2007 debt	2011 debt	2011 deficit	2011 primary balance	Rating, August 2012	Compliance with Maastricht
Austria	68%	60%	72%	−2.6%	0.0%	AAA	×
Belgium	130%	84%	98%	−3.7%	−0.4%	AA	×
Cyprus	52%	59%	72%	−6.3%	−3.8%	BB+	×
Estonia	8%	4%	6%	1.0%	1.1%	A+	✓
Finland	57%	35%	49%	−0.5%	0.6%	AAA	✓
France	56%	64%	86%	−5.2%	−2.6%	AAA	×
Germany	56%	65%	81%	−1.0%	1.6%	AAA	×
Greece	97%	107%	165%	−9.1%	−2.2%	CCC	×
Ireland	80%	25%	108%	−13.1%	−9.7%	BBB+	×
Italy	121%	103%	120%	−3.9%	1.0%	A−	×
Luxembourg	7%	7%	18%	−0.6%	−0.1%	AAA	✓
Malta	35%	62%	72%	−2.7%	0.4%	A+	×
Netherlands	76%	45%	65%	−4.7%	−2.6%	AAA	×
Portugal	59%	68%	108%	−4.2%	−0.4%	BB+	×
Slovakia	22%	30%	43%	−4.8%	−3.2%	A+	×
Slovenia	19%	23%	48%	−6.4%	−4.5%	A	×
Spain	63%	36%	68%	−8.5%	−6.1%	BBB	×

Data source: Eurostat and Fitch

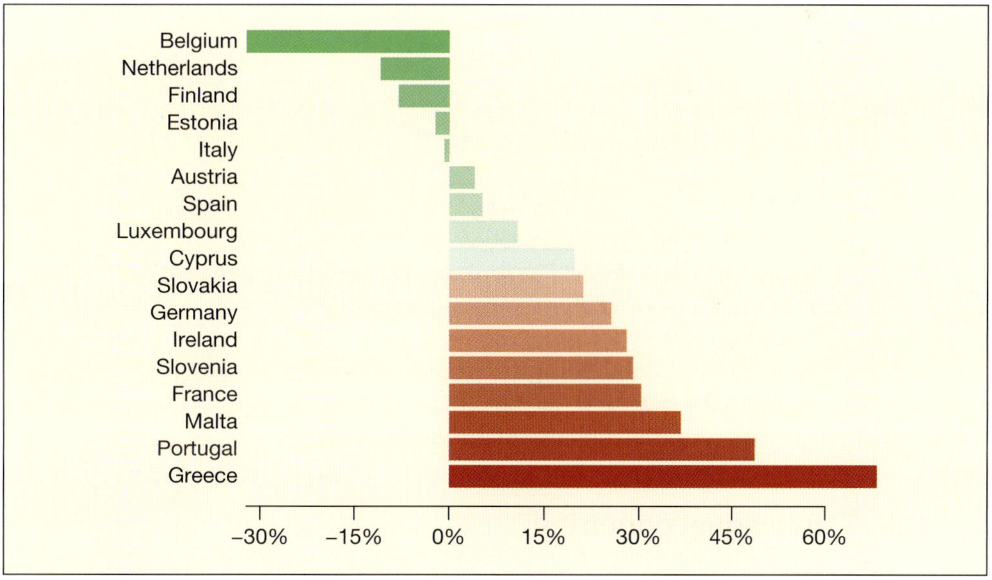

Figure 19.3 Change in debt to GDP in the euro zone, 1995–2011

Data source: Eurostat

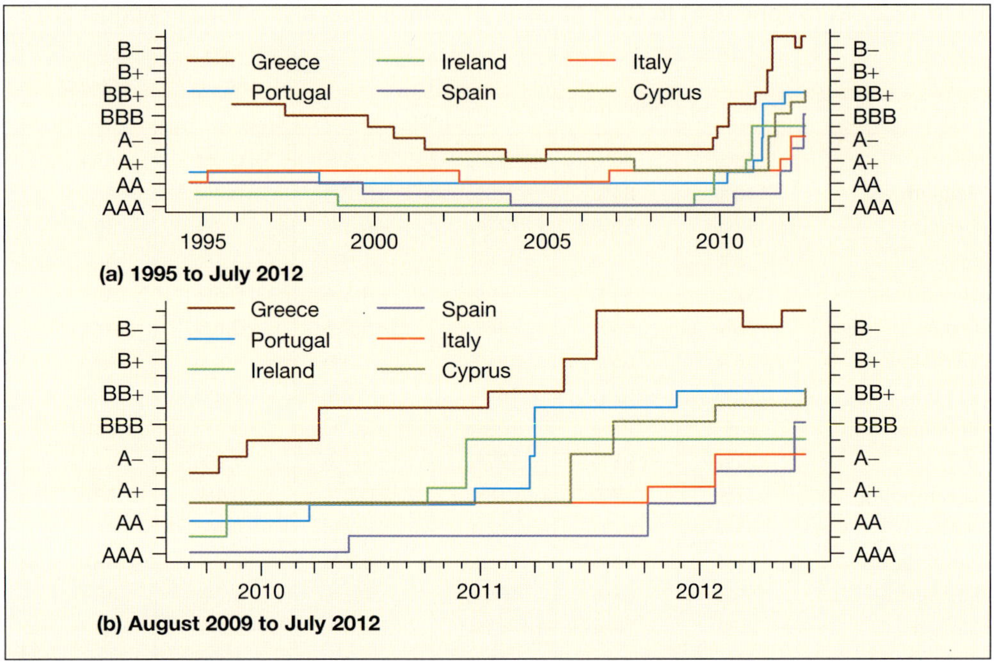

Figure 19.4 Ratings

Data source: Fitch

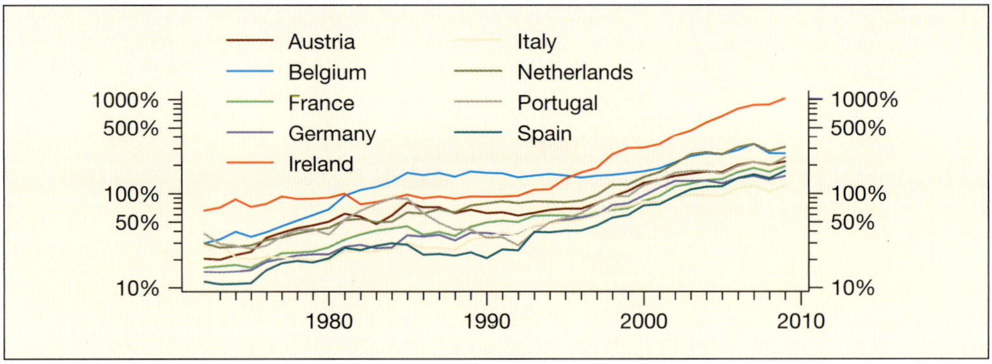

Figure 19.5 Total (public plus private) gross external debt/GDP

Data source: Eurostat and www.reinhartandrogoff.com

10 times the GDP, and Italy the smallest at 1.2. In round terms, external debt has increased 10 times since the collapse of Bretton Woods.

19.4.6 Individual countries

Of the member states of the euro zone, six countries are in particular difficulties. Three have already received bailouts – Ireland, Greece and Portugal. Cyprus may be next, while Spain got a bailout for its banks and a government bailout may follow. The biggest worry is Italy, which has received only indirect assistance via the ECB liquidity facility but is

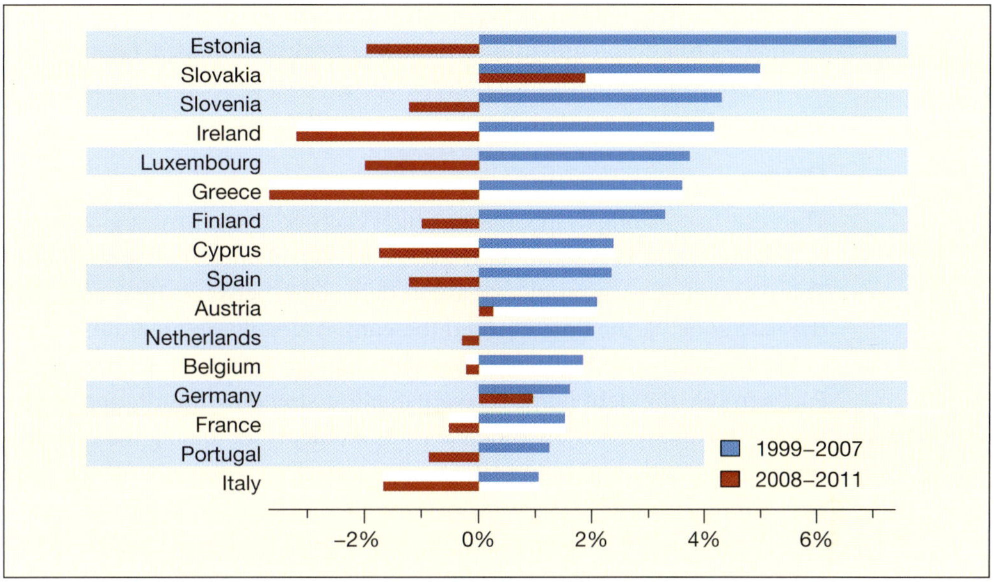

Figure 19.6 Real average annual economic growth

Data source: Eurostat. No data available for Malta

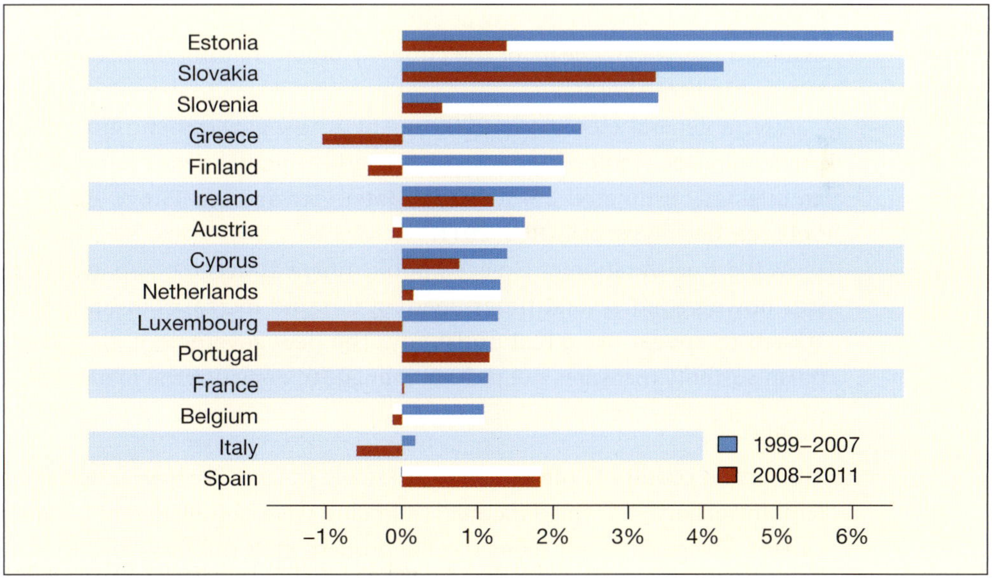

Figure 19.7 Average annual productivity growth

Data source: Eurostat. No data available for Malta

in a precarious position. We can see economic and productivity growth in Figures 19.6 and 19.7, respectively.

It is important to note that the benefits of the euro zone do not all flow in one direction. The presence of uncompetitive countries in the euro zone has over many years weakened the euro and so improved external (to EU) terms of trade for the most competitive;

these have also benefited from growth at the expense of their less competitive neighbours. Germany's full employment and relatively healthy domestic finances are due in part to the currency union. Below we present background analysis on main crisis countries. More information is in the online chapter at www.GlobalFinancialSystems.org.

Greece

The crisis had its origins in Greece, which was one of the fastest growing economies in the euro zone in the 1990s and early 2000s, averaging an annual growth rate of close to 4%. This was fuelled by a rapid increase in debt, 68% between 1995 and 2011, the highest in the euro zone. At the time it joined the euro, it already violated the Maastricht criteria, but unlike the other two high-debt countries, Italy and Belgium, its primary balance was low. Furthermore, the debt numbers were manipulated downwards, and are reported as provisional. To comply with the monetary requirements for joining the euro, the Greek government consistently and deliberately misreported the country's official economic statistics. For example, Greece paid several investment banks to execute deals that moved a high level of debt off-balance sheet in order to conceal the actual level of debt. Greece never enjoyed a high credit rating; still, until 2009 its rating was A, and as recently as 2004 it was A+.

While there are many reasons for the crisis in Greece, prior to joining the euro its ability to borrow too much was limited by its high inflation and perceived structural weaknesses. The governments would use devaluations to stimulate the economy when needed. After it joined, it was able to borrow at almost the same interest rate as Germany, as investors assumed in the early years of the currency union that bonds of various euro zone countries carried equal risks.

After a general election in 2009 swept a new government into office, the incoming prime minister, George Papandreou, revised the actual deficit figures of the country from an originally estimated 6% to 12.7%, later increased to 13.6%. Accumulated sovereign debt reached 165% of GDP in 2011.

As the true situation of Greece's public finances became apparent, Greek public debt was downgraded several times, leading to rapid increases in bond yields as a default started to appear like a real possibility. The new government embarked on a course of harsh austerity measures but did not manage to convince the markets.

Ireland

The second country to run into difficulties was Ireland. We have already discussed its problems in Section 14.1. The difficulties in Ireland were quite different in nature from those in Greece. The government seemed quite prudent in its public financing; the problems were in the banking sector, mostly financed with borrowing from abroad. After the government failed in its attempt to use sovereign liquidity guarantees to the banks as means to restore confidence, the Irish debt levels increased from 25% in 2007 to 108% in 2011, and are still rising. The Irish government obtained an €85 billion bailout from the EU in 2010.

Portugal

Soon after Greece got into difficulty, Portugal followed, for many of the same reasons but not on as extreme a scale as Greece. Eventually, it got a €78 billion bailout from the EU and the IMF in 2011. In return, it has to implement austerity measures, such as privatisation, increasing sales taxes, freezing or cutting benefits, cutting school spending, freezing pensions and reducing the number of civil servants. Unemployment reached 14.8% in the beginning of 2012. To date, Portugal has been able to comply with the requirements, and the current consensus suggests that its problems are less profound than those of Greece.

Cyprus

Cyprus is the latest country to get into difficulty, caused primarily by the exposure of its banks to Greece. It requested a bailout from the EU in the summer of 2012, but delays in coming to an agreement led to a banking crisis in March 2013, which ended with a bailout agreement with the EU and the IMF, with large haircuts imposed on bank creditors and depositors.

Spain

The situation in Spain is in many ways similar to that of Ireland. In both cases the government had low debt, and the problems were created in the banking sector. In both countries, real-estate speculation played an important part, especially in Spain.

The Spanish government was slow to wake up to its problems; as problems in the banking sector mounted, and as unemployment sharply increased, it was perceived as sitting on its hands. This undermined investor confidence in the government, in spite of its low debt levels at the time, and the cost of borrowing increased sharply, along with debt downgrades. In 2012, finally recognising the problems in the banking sector, the government got a banking bailout from the EU. In exchange, Spain gave up some supervisory control over its banking sector, the first step towards a banking union. After all, 'he who pays the piper calls the tune'!

Italy

If we had been studying the statistics presented here in 2007, none of the crisis countries would have shown particular weaknesses compared to other member states. The only exception is Italy. It was not compliant with the Maastricht criteria when it joined, with debt of 113%, and its debt levels are essentially the same now as they were in 1995. It had the lowest economic growth in the euro zone in the first eight years of the euro, the second lowest productivity growth after Spain (almost zero) and is ageing rapidly. The main positive factor is that Italian debt is mostly held domestically.

Italy so far has avoided a sovereign debt crisis, but there are considerable fears that it might get to that state if it is not able to effectively address its structural problems.

19.4.7 The causes of the sovereign debt crisis

If there is one single cause it is the euro. Before the European countries had a common currency, each country borrowed in its own currency, where the borrowing rates reflected the fundamentals of the country. If the country got into difficulty, it always had the option of devaluing, which simultaneously made its economy more competitive and reduced the real value of its sovereign debt, because of the resulting inflation. In this situation, the sovereign debt of the country was its own affair, not spilling over to other European countries.

This all changed with the euro. When a country has a common currency, weaker countries no longer have the ability to devalue their currency or inflate away their debt, while at the same time their borrowing rates are likely to improve. Initially, such countries find it easier to borrow, while at the same time they have less ability for dealing with a crisis. It seems optimistic of the designers of the euro in the 1990s to discount such an eventuality.

The problem has become so extreme because no member country (supposedly) can leave the euro zone, so that the fate of the weakest member automatically becomes a direct concern of the strongest number. Lenders' belief in this proposition was the reason for the sharp reduction in interest rates enjoyed by the weaker countries, contributing greatly to the economic booms preceding the crisis.

19.4.8 Why is it so difficult to solve the crisis?

Unfortunately, the resulting integration of the economies of member states now poses substantial problems. If a country leaves, it will cause huge economic disruption for other member countries. Politicians' credibility will suffer, and the benefits of currency union to the remaining members will be reduced.

This gives the potential leavers a strong negotiating position. If they are unable to survive in the currency union, they can point out that a transfer union is necessary to prevent them from leaving.

The problem is that the wealthier countries find the transfer union unpalatable. Even though the political leaders may be contemplating it, it is less clear whether they have the support of their voters.

The differing agendas and incentives of the European authorities make it impossible for them to speak with one voice on the crisis and, hence, directly contribute to the instability. There is also an element of brinkmanship at work: if the crisis gets bad enough, perhaps a transfer union will be seen as the only solution, taking Europe directly towards unification – a desirable outcome for many. To the extent that wealthy countries are committed to no country leaving the union, they cede negotiating power to poor countries that can threaten to do so.

Whilst this is opposed by voters in wealthy countries (and whilst the loss of sovereignty is opposed by voters in poor countries), this opposition is not entirely clear-cut. If the question is posed slightly differently, there is also strong support for 'solidarity' with other European countries, suggesting that the current state of indecision and muddled compromise could persist for a long time.

19.4.9 Global impact

In principle, there is no reason why a sovereign debt crisis in a handful of countries should threaten a global crisis. Even in a European context, the GDP of the crisis countries is still relatively small, and it would cost the euro only zone about 2% of its GDP to do a complete bailout of Greece.

This suggests that in order to understand the nature of the problem we should not focus on the detail of what is happening in Greece but rather how it affects the rest of the global economy. As with other crises discussed in this book, the trigger event for a crisis is less important than the mechanism allowing it to spiral out of control. In Europe, the enabling factor is the euro, the cross-border economic activity it (by design) increased, and the result that a major crisis in any member country can cause a crisis of confidence elsewhere.

This is why the crisis response of the European authorities is so important. To date, the response has not been sufficient to stop the crisis, and the situation is at best stable but in a very unsatisfactory state. More probably it will continue to deteriorate, as the fundamental problems remain unaddressed. It seems likely that some trigger may be required to bring about fundamental change.

19.5 SUMMARY

We started by discussing one of the extreme cases of dealing with the sovereign debt crisis, when the country of Newfoundland was liquidated.

The topic of this chapter is sovereign debt crises, perhaps the most common form of crisis throughout history. We discussed the nature of sovereign debt crises, what makes sovereign debt special and different from corporate debt, how the interests of creditors can be protected, and how a country should respond when faced with a sovereign debt crisis.

Even though there is no international court that enforces sovereign debt, creditors have a variety of means at their disposal, historically military intervention and more recently a range of sanctions.

We followed this by a discussion of the European sovereign debt crisis, starting with the first sovereign debt crisis in the EU, and analysis of monetary unions, why they succeed and why they fail. This is key to understanding the European sovereign debt crisis, and we analysed to what extent the necessary conditions for a successful monetary union have been present in the euro zone. Finally, we discussed some of the European countries that are experiencing economic difficulty, why it is so difficult to solve the crisis, and the global impact.

We leave a detailed analysis of current events to a chapter that is published online at www.GlobalFinancialSystems.org.

Questions for discussion

1 Is it too strong to say Britain liquidated Newfoundland?

2 How can a government default on its debt without actually declaring default?

3 Yields on government bonds of the US are currently trading at record lows. How can this be reconciled with the fact that the US is approaching its greatest level of debt to GDP in its history, apart from in wartime?

4 Do you think a return to gunboat diplomacy would be useful in dealing with sovereign debt crises?

5 The role of entities buying sovereign bonds on the secondary market at a big discount is controversial, especially the so-called 'vulture funds'. Do you agree with their methods and, more generally, what is your view on the enforcement mechanisms that should exist for sovereign debt?

6 What is the main reason why the euro zone was established?

7 What are main conditions for a successful monetary union, and did the euro zone fulfil those criteria?

8 What is the cause of the European sovereign debt crisis?

9 Would Greece be better off if it left the euro zone?

10 Would the euro zone be better off if Greece left?

11 Does a country suffer more when it experiences a currency crisis or when it experiences a banking crisis or a sovereign debt crisis?

12 Many commentators talk of contagion when it comes to sovereign debt crises. Identify how this could happen.

References

BBC (2012a). Argentina ship in Ghana seized over loans default. www.bbc.co.uk/news/world-africa-19827562.

Borensztein, E. and Panizza, U. (2008). The costs of sovereign default. Technical Report WP/08/238, IMF.

Buchheit, L. C. (2011). Sovereign debt restructuring – the legal context. Cleary Gottlieb Steen & Hamilton LLP, New York.

Daníelsson, J. and Oskarsson, H. (2012). The first sovereign debt crisis in the EU. *Vox EU*, 11 September. www.voxeu.org/article/europe-s-pre-eurozone-debt-crisis-faroe-islands-1990s.

European Union (2011). EU budget 2010 financial report. Technical report.

Gulati, M. and Triantis, G. (2007). Contracts without law: sovereign versus corporate debt. *University of Cincinnati Law Review*, 75: 977–1004.

Hale, D. (2003). The Newfoundland lesson. *The International Economy*, 17(3): 52–61.

Hansard (1993) http://hansard.millbanksystems.com/commons/1933/dec/12/newfoundland-bill#S5CV0284PO_19331212_HOC_267.

Homer, S. and Sylla, R. (1996). *A History of Interest Rates*. Rutgers University Press.

Kaseki, J.-R. (2007). Preying on the poor. *The Guardian*, 27 September.

Krueger, A. O. (2002). A new approach to sovereign debt restructuring. Technical report, IMF.

Marsh, D. (2010). *The Euro: the Politics of the New Global Currency*. Yale University Press.

Mundell, R. A. (1961). A theory of optimum currency areas. *Amer. Econ. Rev.*, 51: 657–65.

Reinhart, C. M. and Rogoff, K. (2009). *This Time Is Different: Eight Centuries of Financial Folly*. Princeton University Press.

Reinhart, C. M., Rogoff, K. and Savastano, M. A. (2003). Debt intolerance. Technical report, NBER.

Spanish government (2008). Las balanzas fiscales de las CC.AA. españolas con las AA. Públicas Centrales 2005. Technical report, Ministerio de Economía y Hacienda.

Sturzenegger, F. and Zettelmeyer, J. (2007). *Debt Defaults and Lessons from a Decade of Crises*. MIT Press.

The Economist (1999). South Africa's debt: unforgivable. *The Economist* (US), 24 April.

GLOSSARY

1G first-generation currency crisis model.

2G second-generation currency crisis model.

ABCP asset-backed commercial paper is a short-term debt instrument, typically with a maturity between 90 and 180 days, backed by physical assets such as trade receivables.

ABS asset-backed securities derive their value and income payments from a pool of underlying assets.

ADR American depositary receipts.

AIB Allied Irish Bank is an Irish bank that got bailed out by its government.

AIG American International Group, a US insurance company that failed in 2008 because of its CDS writing activities.

Basel I the first international capital accords, in effect from 1992 until 2007.

Basel II the second international capital accords, in effect from 2007.

Basel III the next version of the international capital accords, intended to be implemented from 2013 but being delayed.

BCBS Basel Committee for Banking Supervision is a group of senior officials that design international financial regulations, best known for the Basel Accords.

BCCI Bank of Credit and Commerce International, a Luxembourg-registered bank, with head offices in Karachi and London. It was established in 1972 and collapsed in 1991 after massive fraud.

BIS Bank for International Settlements.

BoE Bank of England.

BoJ Bank of Japan.

CAC collective action clauses permit the majority or supermajority of creditors to modify key features of the terms of bonds, including principal and interest payments.

CAPM capital asset pricing model.

CAR capital adequacy ratio.

CBT computer based trading.

CCP central counterparty.

CDO collateralised debt obligation.

CDS credit default swap.

CEO chief executive officer.

CET1 common equity tier 1, a part of bank capital.

CFTC Commodity Futures Trading Commission is an independent agency of the United States government that regulates futures and option markets.

CIO Chief Investment Office.

CMG Crisis Management Group, a cooperative multinational and multi-organisational set up to deal with the failures of large cross-border financial institutions.

CoCo contingent convertibles.

CPI consumer price index.

CRA credit rating agencies are international firms that provide evaluations of the creditworthiness of various types of borrowers.

CS Credit Suisse is a large Swiss bank.

DAX the main German stock market index.

DB Deutsche Bank is a large German bank.

DJIA the Dow Jones industrial average index is a popular United States stock market index.

EBA European Banking Authority.

ECB European Central Bank.

ECU European Currency Unit.

EEA European Economic Area.

EMH the efficient market hypothesis maintains that one cannot systematically earn excessive profits from exploiting public information.

EMS European Monetary System.

EMU synonymous with the euro zone.

ERM European Exchange Rate Mechanism.

ESMA European Securities and Markets Authority.

ESRB European Systemic Risk Board.

EU European Union.

EURIBOR Euro Interbank Offered Rate, a reference rate calculated from the averaged interest rates at which euro zone banks offer to lend unsecured funds to other banks.

FDIC Federal Deposit Insurance Corporation.

Fed the Federal Reserve System is the central bank of the United States.

FPC Financial Policy Committee.

FSA Financial Services Authority.

FSB Financial Stability Board.

FSF Financial Stability Forum, a group of financial authorities of the G7 countries. It is superseded by the FSB.

FSOC Financial Stability Oversight Council.

FT100 the main British stock market index.

FTT financial transaction tax.

FX foreign exchange.

GATT General Agreement on Tariffs and Trade.

G-SIB global systemically important banks that have been identified by the FSB as being especially large and whose failure poses a special danger to the world economy.

G20 a group of large countries that include Argentina, Australia, Brazil, Canada, China, France, Germany, India, Indonesia, Italy, Japan, Mexico, Russia, Saudi Arabia, South Africa, South Korea, Turkey, the United Kingdom, the United States and collectively the European Union.

GDP gross domestic product.

GNP gross national product.

HBOS a large British bank that failed in the crisis from 2007.

HFT high-frequency trading.

HSBC a large British bank.

IIF the Institute of International Finance is the main advocacy group (lobbyists) of internationally active banks.

IKB a German bank that was the first financial institution to fail in the crisis in 2007.

ILOLR international lender of last resort.

IMF International Monetary Fund.

IOSCO International Organization of Securities Commissions is an association of organisations that regulate the world's securities and futures markets.

IRB internal rating based refers to banks developing their own methodologies for assessing risk.

LCR liquidity coverage ratio.

LIBOR London Interbank Offered Rate, average interest rate from banks calculated by the British Bankers' Association.

LOLR lending of last resort.

LR leverage ratio.

LTCM Long Term Capital Management, a celebrated hedge fund that failed in 1998, triggering a global crisis.

MPT modern portfolio theory.

NSFR net stable funding ratio.

NYFed the New York Federal Reserve bank is the most important branch of the Fed. It is the Fed's main interface with financial markets.

O&G Overend and Gurney.

OECD Organisation for Economic Cooperation and Development, a Paris-based international organisation.

OTC over-the-counter.

PPP purchasing power parity.

QE quantitative easing.

RBS Royal Bank of Scotland is a large British bank that got bailed out by the government in the crisis from 2007.

RFC Reconstruction Finance Corporation.

RWA risk-weighted assets of a bank, used in capital calculations.

S&L savings and loans, a part of the United States financial system that was in a crisis in the 1980s.

S&P Standard & Poor.

S&P-500 the Standard & Poor's 500 index is the most representative United States stock market index.

SDR special drawing rights, a virtual currency created by the IMF.

SEC Securities and Exchange Commission.

SIC Special Investigation Commission.

SIFI systemically important financial institution.

SIV structured investment vehicle.

SME small and medium-sized enterprise.

SNB Swiss National Bank.

SPV special purpose vehicle.

SSM Single Supervisory Mechanism, the embryonic pan-EU supervisor.

TA total assets of a bank, used in capital calculations.

TARP Troubled Asset Relief Program.

TBTF too big to fail.

UBS a large Swiss bank.

UIP uncovered interest rate parity.

UK United Kingdom.

US United States.

USD US dollar.

VaR Value-at-Risk is a common statistical technique for forecasting market risk.

VIX implied volatility of the S&P-500 index.

WTO World Trade Organization.

WWI First World War.

WWII Second World War.

BIBLIOGRAPHY

Abdelal, R. (2007). *Capital Rules: The Construction of Global Finance*. Harvard University Press.

Acharya, V. and Pedersen, L. H. (2005). Asset pricing with liquidity risk. *J. Finan. Econ.*, 77: 375–410.

Admati, A. R., DeMarzo, P. M., Hellwig, M. F., and Pfleiderer, P. (2010). Fallacies, irrelevant facts, and myths in the discussion of capital regulation: why bank equity is not expensive. Working Paper, Graduate School of Business, Stanford University.

Adrian, T. and Shin, H. S. (2010). Liquidity and leverage. *J. Finan. Intermed.*, 19: 418–37.

Ahamed, L. (2009). *Lords of Finance, The Bankers Who Broke the World*. The Penguin Group.

Akerlof, G. (1970). The market for 'lemons': quality uncertainty and the market mechanism. *Quart. J. Econ.*, 84(3): 488–500.

Alba, P., Bhattacharya, A., Claessens, S., Ghosh, S. and Hernandez, L. (1998). Volatility and contagion in a financially-integrated world: lessons from East Asia's recent experience. Paper presented at the PAFTAD 24 Conference, 'Asia Pacific Financial Liberalization and Reform', 1998.

Alessandri, P. and Haldane, A. G. (2009). Banking on the state. Mimeo, Bank of England.

Allen, F. and Gale, D. (1994). Limited market participation and volatility of asset prices. *Amer. Econ. Rev.*, 84: 933–55.

Allen, F. and Gale, D. (2005). From cash-in-the-market pricing to financial fragility. *J. Eur. Econ. Assoc.*, 3: 535–46.

Anderson, G. M., Shughart, W. F., II and Tollison, R. D. (1988). A public choice theory of the great contraction. *Public Choice*, 59: 3–23.

Angelini, P. L., Clerc, L., Curdia, V., Gambacorta, L., Gerali, A., Locarno, A., Motto, R., Roeger, W., den Heuvel, S. V. and Vlcek, J. (2011). Basel III: long-term impact on economic performance and fluctuations. Technical report, Federal Reserve Bank of New York.

Arnason, R. and Danielsson, J. (2011). Capital controls are exactly wrong for Iceland. *Vox EU*, 14 November. www.voxeu.org/article/iceland-and-imf-why-capital controls-are-entirely-wrong.

Bagehot, W. (1873). *Lombard Street: a Description of the Money Market*. H.S. King, London.

Bandt, D. and Hartmann, P. (2000). Systemic risk: a survey. Working paper no. 35, European Central Bank.

Barnier, M. (2011) quoted in Barker, A., EU ban on 'naked' CDS to become permanent. *Financial Times*, 19 October, www.ft.com/cms/s/0/cc9c5050-f96f-11e0-bf8f-00144feab49a.html.

Basel Committee on Banking Supervision (1996). Amendment to the Capital Accord to Incorporate Market Risks. www.bis.org/publ/bcbs24.pdf.

Basel Committee on Banking Supervision (2004). Bank failures in mature economies. Working paper no. 13, Bank of International Settlements.

Basel Committee on Banking Supervision (2006). The management of liquidity risk in financial groups. Technical report, pp. 1–25.

Basel Committee on Banking Supervision (2011a). Basel Committee issues final elements of the reforms to raise the quality of regulatory capital. www.bis.org/press/p110113.pdf.

Basel Committee on Banking Supervision (2011b). Basel III: a global regulatory framework for more resilient banks and banking systems. Technical report.

Basel Committee on Banking Supervision (2011c). Global systemically important banks: assessment methodology and the additional loss absorbency requirement. www.bis.org/publ/bcbs207.pdf.

Bassani, G. and Trapanese, M. (2011). Crisis management and resolution. In Quagliariello, M. and Cannata, F., editors, *Basel III and Beyond*. Riskbooks, London.

Baudino, P. (2011). The policy response: from the G20 requests to the FSB roadmap; working towards the proposals of the Basel Committee. In Quagliariello, M. and Cannata, F., editors, *Basel III and Beyond*. Riskbooks, London.

BBC (2012a). Argentina ship in Ghana seized over loans default. www.bbc.co.uk/news/world-africa-19827562.

BBC (2012b). Barclays' widening Libor-fixing scandal. www.bbc.co.uk/news/ business-18671255.

Benediktsdottir, S., Danielsson, J. and Zoega, G. (2011). Lessons from a collapse of a financial system. *Economic Policy*, 26: 183–231.

Bernanke, B. (1995). The macroeconomics of the Great Depression: a comparative approach. *J. Money Credit and Banking*, 27(1): 1–28.

Bernanke, B. S. (2005). The global saving glut and the US current account deficit. Speech delivered at the Sandridge Lecture, Virginia Association of Economists, Richmond, VA.

BIS (2010). Assessing the macroeconomic impact of the transition to stronger capital and liquidity requirements. www.bis.org/publ/othp10.pdf.

Bitner, R. (2008). *Confessions of a Subprime Lender: an Insider's Tale of Greed, Fraud, and Ignorance*. John Wiley & Sons.

Black, F. (1971). Toward a fully automated exchange, part I. *Financial Analysts J.*, 27: 28–35.

Black, F. (1995). Hedging, speculation, and systemic risk. *J. Derivatives*, 2: 6–8.

Black, F. and Scholes, M. (1973a). The pricing of options and corporate liabilities. *J. Polit. Econ.*, 81(3): 637–54.

Black, F. and Scholes, M. (1973b). The valuation of option contracts and a test of market efficiency. *J. Finance*, 27: 399–418.

Bloomberg (2011). Secret Fed loans undisclosed to Congress gave banks $13 billion in income. www.bloomberg.com/news/2011-11-28/secret-fed-loansundisclosed-to-congress-gave-banks-13-billion-in-income.html.

Blundell-Wignall, A. and Atkinson, P. (2010). Thinking beyond Basel III: necessary solutions for capital and liquidity. *OECD Journal: Financial Market Trends*, Volume 2010, Issue 1.

Board of Governors of the Federal Reserve System (2009). Revenge of the steamroller: ABCP as a window on risk choices. Unpublished paper, Division of International Finance.

Borensztein, E. and Panizza, U. (2008). The costs of sovereign default. Technical Report WP/08/238, IMF.

Borio, C. (2009). Ten propositions about liquidity crisis. Working paper no. 293, Bank of International Settlements.

Borio, C. and Disyatat, P. (2011). Global imbalances and the financial crisis: link or no link? Technical report, BIS. Working Paper 346.

Borio, C., Drehmann, M., Gambacorta, L., Jimenez, G. and Trucharte, C. (2010). Countercyclical capital buffers: exploring options. Technical report, BIS. Working Paper 317.

Brady Commission (1988). Report of the presidential task force on market mechanisms. Technical report, Government Printing Office, Washington, DC.

Brown, W. A. (1940). The international gold standard reinterpreted, 1914–1934. Technical report, National Bureau of Economic Research.

Bruner, R. F. and Carr, S. D. (2007). *The Panic of 1907: Lessons Learned from the Market's Perfect Storm*. John Wiley & Sons.

Brunnermeier, M. (2008). Deciphering the 2007–08 liquidity and credit crunch. *J. Econ. Perspect.*, 23(1): 77–100.

Brunnermeier, M. and Pedersen, L. H. (2009). Market liquidity and funding liquidity. *Rev. Finan. Stud.*, 22(6): 2201–38.

Buchheit, L. C. (2011). Sovereign debt restructuring – the legal context. Cleary Gottlieb Steen & Hamilton LLP, New York.

Buffett, W. (2003). Avoiding a mega-catastrophe. *Fortune*, 24 March.

Buffett, W. (2012). Why stocks beat gold and bonds. *Fortune*, 27 February.

Bussiere, M., Saxena, S. C. and Tovar, C. E. (2010). Chronicle of currency collapses re-examining the effects on output. Technical report, ECB. Working paper series no. 1226, July.

Cagan, P. (1956). The monetary dynamics of hyperinflation. In Friedman, M., editor, *Studies in the Quantity Theory of Money*. University of Chicago Press.

Calello, P. and Ervin, W. (2010). From bail-out to bail-in. *The Economist*, 28 January.

Capie, F. and Wood, G. E. (2006). *The Lender of Last Resort*. Routledge.

Caprio, G. and Honohan, P. (2009). Banking crises. In Berger, A., Molyneux, P., and Wilson, J., editors, *The Oxford Handbook of Banking*. Oxford University Press.

Committee on the Global Financial System (1999). A review of financial market events in autumn 1998. Technical report, Bank for International Settlements.

Copeland, L. (2000). *Exchange Rates and International Finance*. Prentice Hall.

Coval, J., Jurek, J. and Stafford, E. (2008a). The economics of structured finance. Harvard Business School Working Paper 09-060.

Coval, J. D., Jurek, J. W. and Stafford, E. (2008b). Economic catastrophe bonds. Mimeo, Harvard University.

Crockett, A. (2000). Marrying the micro- and macroprudential dimensions of financial stability. The General Manager of the Bank for International Settlements, www.bis.org/review/rr000921b.pdf.

Crouhy, M., Galai, D. and Mark, R. (2000). *Risk Management*. McGraw-Hill.

Danielsson, J. (2011). *Financial Risk Forecasting*. John Wiley & Sons.

Danielsson, J. and Keating, C. (2009). Bonus incensed. *Vox EU*, 25 May. http://voxeu.org/index.php?q=node/3602.

Danielsson, J. and Oskarsson, H. (2012). The first sovereign debt crisis in the EU. *Vox EU*, 11 September. www.voxeu.org/article/europe-s-pre-eurozone-debt-crisis-faroe-islands-1990s.

Danielsson, J. and Shin, H. S. (2003). Endogenous risk. In *Modern Risk Management - a History*. Risk Books, London. www.riskresearch.org.

Danielsson, J., Embrechts, P., Goodhart, C., Keating, C., Muennich, F., Renault, O. and Shin, H. S. (2001). An academic response to Basel II. www.bis.org/bcbs/ca/fmg.pdf.

Danielsson, J., Shin, H. and Zigrand, J.-P. (2012a). Endogenous and systemic risk. In Haubrich, J. G. and Lo, A. W., editors, *Quantifying Systemic Risk*. University of Chicago Press for NBER; Download from www.riskresearch.org.

Danielsson, J., Shin, H. and Zigrand, J.-P. (2012b). Endogenous extreme events and the dual role of prices. *Ann. Rev. Econ.,* 4(1): 111–129; download from www.riskresearch.org.

Danielsson, J., Shin, H. and Zigrand, J.-P. (2012c). Procyclical leverage and endogenous risk. Mimeo, LSE, www.riskresearch.org.

Darling, A. (2011). *Back from the Brink: 1,000 Days at Number 11*. Atlantic Books, London.

Davis, E. P. (1999). A reappraisal of market liquidity risk in the light of the Russian/LTCM global securities markets crisis. Bank of England.

de Ramon, S., Iscenko, Z., Osborne, M., Straughan, M. and Andrews, P. (2012). Measuring the impact of prudential policy on the macroeconomy. A practical application to Basel III and other responses to the financial crisis. Technical report, FSA. Occasional Paper Series 42.

de Soto, J. H. (2009). *Money, Bank Credit, and Economic Cycles*. Ludwig von Mises Institute, Auburn, AL.

Dewatripont, M. and Tirole, J. (1994). *The Prudential Regulation of Banks*. MIT Press.

Diamond, D. and Dybvig, P. (1983). Bank runs, deposit insurance, and liquidity. *J. Polit. Econ.,* 91: 401–19.

Duffie, D. (2007). Innovations in credit risk transfer: implications for financial stability. Mimeo, Stanford University.

Duffie, D. (2010). Is there a case for banning short speculation in sovereign bond markets? *Financial Stability Review,* 14, Banque de France.

Duffie, D. and Singleton, K. (2003). *Credit Risk*. Princeton University Press.

Duffie, D. and Zhu, H. (2011). Does a central clearing counterparty reduce counterparty risk? Stanford University Working Paper.

Eichengreen, B. (1996). *Golden Fetters: the Gold Standard and the Great Depression, 1919-1939*. Oxford University Press.

Eichengreen, B. and Irwin, D. (2009). The slide to protectionism in the Great Depression: who succumbed and why? NBER Working Paper 15142.

Elliot, G. (2006). *Overend & Gurney, a Financial Scandal in Victorian London*. Methuen.

Enria, A. (2011). The future of EU regulation. www.eba.europa.eu/cebs/media/aboutus/Speeches/The-Future-of-EURegulation–British-Bankers-Association–29-June-2011.pdf.

Epstein, G. and Ferguson, T. (1984). Monetary policy, loan liquidation, and industrial conflict: the Federal Reserve and open market operations of 1932. *J. Econ. His.,* 44: 957–83.

European Union (2011). EU budget 2010 financial report. Technical report.

Fabozzi, F. J. (2009). *Bond Markets, Analysis, and Strategies,* 7th edition. Pearson.

Ferguson, N. (2008). *The Ascent of Money*. The Penguin Group.

Financial Services Authority (2009a). Reforming remuneration practices in financial services. Technical report.

Financial Services Authority (2009b). The Turner review: a regulatory response to the global banking crisis. Technical report, European Central Bank. www.fsa.gov.uk/pubs/other/turner review.pdf.

Financial Services Authority (2012). Final notice. Technical report. www.fsa.gov.uk/static/pubs/final/barclays-jun12.pdf.

Financial Stability Board (2012) Update of global systemically important banks (G-SIBS) Annex 1, Bank for International Settlements.

Financial Stability Forum (2008). Report of the financial stability forum on enhancing market and institutional resilience. Technical report.

Financial Times (2007). Goldman pays the price of being big. *Financial Times,* 13 August.

Financial Times (2008). Winding up Lehman Brothers. *Financial Times,* 7 November.

Financial Times (2010a). The benefits of naked CDS. *Financial Times,* 2 March.

Financial Times (2010b). HSBC in clearest warning over relocation. *Financial Times,* 3 September.

Financial Times (2012a). DoJ probes $2bn JPMorgan trading loss. *Financial Times,* 15 May.

Financial Times (2012b). JPMorgan whale harpooned. *Financial Times,* 11 May.

Flood, R. P. and Garber, P. M. (1984). Collapsing exchange rate regimes: some linear examples. *J. Int. Econ.,* 17: 223–34.

Frankel, J. A. (1999). No single currency regime is right for all countries at all times. Working paper 7338, National Bureau of Economic Research.

Friedman, M. (1969). The optimum quantity of money. In Friedman, M., editor, *The Optimum Quantity of Money and Other Essays,* chapter 1, pp. 1–50. Adline Publishing Company, Chicago.

Friedman, M. and Schwartz, A. (1963). *A Monetary History of the United States: 1867-1960*. Princeton University Press.

Goldstein, M. (1998). *The Asian Financial Crisis: Causes, Cures, and Systemic Implications*. Institute for International Economics, Washington, DC.

Goodhart, C. (1999). Myths about the lender of last resort. Technical report FMG SP 120, London School of Economics. http://fmg.lse.ac.uk/pdfs/sp120.pdf.

Goodhart, C. (2002). The organizational structure of banking supervision. *Economic Notes,* 31(1): 1–32.

Goodhart, C. (2009). *The Regulatory Response to the Financial Crisis*. Edward Elgar, Cheltenham, UK.

Goodhart, C. (2011). *The Basel Committee on Banking Supervision: a History of the Early Years 1974-1997*. Cambridge University Press.

Goodhart, C. and Schoenmaker, D. (1995). Should the functions of monetary policy and banking supervision be separated? *Oxford Economic Papers,* 47(4): 539–60.

Gorter, J. and Bijlsma, M. (2012). Strategic moves. www.risk.net/life-and-pension- risk.

Gosh, A. R., Gulde, A.-M. and Wolf, H. C. (2002). *Exchange Rate Regime: Choices and Consequences*. MIT Press.

Graeber, D. (2011). *Debt: The First 5,000 Years*. Melville House Publishing, New York.

Graham, B. and Dodd, D. (1934). *Security Analysis*. Whittlesey House (McGraw-Hill).

Greenspan, A. (1997). Discussion at symposium: *Maintaining Financial Stability in a Global Economy,* p. 54. Federal Reserve Bank of Kansas City.

Gulati, M. and Triantis, G. (2007). Contracts without law: Sovereign versus corporate debt. *University of Cincinnati Law Review,* 75: 977–1004.

Hale, D. (2003). The Newfoundland lesson. *The International Economy,* 17(3): 52–61.

Hanke, S. H. and Kwok, A. K. F. (2009). On the measurement of Zimbabwe's hyperinflation. *Cato J.,* 29(2): 353–64.

Hansard (1933). http://hansard.millbanksystems.com/commons/1933/dec/12/newfoundland-bill#S5CV0284PO_19331212_HOC_267.

Herring, R. J. and Litan, R. E. (1995). *Financial Regulation in the Global Economy*. The Brookings Institution, Washington, DC.

Homer, S. and Sylla, R. (1996). *A History of Interest Rates*. Rutgers University Press.

Honohan, P. and Klingebiel, D. (2003). The fiscal cost implications of an accommodating approach to banking crises. *J. Banking Finance,* 27(8): 1539–60.

Huertas, T. F. (2010). *Crisis: Cause, Containment and Cure*. Palgrave Macmillan.

Hull, J. C. (2011). *Options, Futures, and Other Derivatives,* 8th edition. Prentice Hall.

Hull, J. C. (2012). *Risk Management and Financial Institutions,* 3rd edition. Prentice Hall.

Hume, D. (1752). On the balance of trade. In *Essays, Moral, Political and Literary*. Edinburgh and London.

Institute of International Finance (2010). Interim report on the cumulative impact of proposed changes in the banking regulatory framework. Technical report.

Institute of International Finance (2012). Making resolution robust. Technical report.

International Monetary Fund (1997). Camdessus announces IMF support for Indonesia's economic program. News brief no. 97/19, 8 October 1997, www.imf.org/external/np/sec/nb/1997/nb9719.htm.

International Monetary Fund (1998). World economic outlook and international capital markets: interim assessment. Financial turbulence and the world economy. Technical report. www.imf.org/external/pubs/ft/weo/weo1298/index.htm.

International Monetary Fund (2008). Global financial stability report: containing systemic risks and restoring financial soundness. April 2008, pp. 1–211.

International Monetary Fund, Bank for International Settlements, Financial Stability Board (2009). Report to G20 finance ministers and governors. Guidance to assess the systemic importance of financial institutions, markets and instruments: Initial considerations. Technical report.

Ito, T. (2007). Asian currency crisis and the International Monetary Fund, 10 years later: Overview. *Asian Econ. Policy Rev.,* 2: 16–49.

Kaminsky, G. L. and Reinhart, C. M. (1999). The twin crises: the causes of banking and balance-of-payments problems. *Amer. Econ. Rev.,* 89: 473–500.

Kane, E. J. (1989). The S&L insurance mess: how did it happen? Technical report, Urban Institute Press.

Kaseki, J.-R. (2007). Preying on the poor. *The Guardian,* 27 September.

Kashyap, A. K., Rajan, R. G. and Stein, J. C. (2008). Rethinking capital regulation. http://online.wsj.com/public/resources/documents/Fed-JacksonHole.pdf.

Kaufman, G. G. (1996). Bank failures, systemic risk, and bank regulation. *Cato J.,* 16(1): 17–46.

Keynes, J. M. (1920). *The Economic Consequences of the Peace*. Harcourt Brace, New York.

Keynes, J. M. (1924). *A Tract on Monetary Reform*. Macmillan.

Keynes, J. M. (1936). *The General Theory of Interest, Employment and Money*. Macmillan.

Kindleberger, C. (1986). *The World in Depression, 1929-1939,* 2nd edition. University of California Press.

Kindleberger, C. P. (1996). *Manias, Panics, and Crashes: a History of Financial Crises*, 3rd edition. John Wiley & Sons.

Kohn, M. (1999). Early deposit banking. Mimeo, Dartmouth College, Hanover, NH.

Kohn, M. (2003). *Financial Institutions and Markets*, 2nd edition. Oxford University Press.

Kovacevich, R. M. (1996). Deposit insurance: It's time to cage the monster. www.minneapolisfed.org/publications papers/pub display.cfm?id=2682.

Krueger, A. O. (2002). A new approach to sovereign debt restructuring. Technical report, IMF.

Krugman, P. (1979). A model of balance-of-payments crises. *J. Money Credit Banking*, 11(3): 311–25.

Krugman, P. (1998). What happened to Asia? Mimeo, MIT.

Krugman, P. R. and Obstfeld, M. (2006). *International Economics: Theory and Policy*, 7th edition. Pearson.

Kupiec, P. H. and Ramirez, C. D. (2009). Bank failures and the cost of systemic risk: Evidence from 1900–1930. Technical report, FDIC.

Kyle, A. (1985). Continuous auctions and insider trading. *Econometrica*, 53(6): 1315–36.

Laeven, L. and Valencia, F. (2008). Systemic banking crises: a new database. Technical report, IMF. IMF Working Paper.

Larosiere, J. (2009). The high-level group report on financial supervision in the EU. Technical report. http://ec.europa.eu/commission barroso/president/pdf/statement 20090225 en.pdf.

Lavigne, R. (2008). Sterilized intervention in emerging-market economies: trends, costs and risks. Discussion paper 2008-4, Bank of Canada.

Leeson, N. (1999). *Rogue Trader*. Sphere, London.

Lehman Brothers (2008). Capital advisory group: current topics. Technical report, Lehman Brothers.

Lewis, M. (2009). The man who crashed the world. *Vanity Fair*, August.

Lewis, M. (2011). *The Big Short: Inside the Doomsday Machine*. Penguin.

Lewis, M. K. and Mizen, P. D. (2000). *Monetary Economics*. Oxford University Press.

Li, D. X. (2000). On default correlation: a copula function approach. *J. Fixed Income*, 9: 43–54.

Liikanen, E. (2012). High-level expert group on reforming the structure of the EU banking sector. Technical report, European Union.

Lowenstein, R. (2000). *When Genius Failed – the Rise and Fall of Long-Term Capital Management*. Random House, New York.

Macrae, R. and Watkins, C. (1998). A disaster waiting to happen. Mimeo, www.cs.rhul.ac.uk/home/chrisw/Disaster.pdf.

Madura, J. (2010). *Financial Institutions and Markets*, 9th edition. South Western College, Cincinnati, OH.

Marsh, D. (2010). *The Euro: the Politics of the New Global Currency*. Yale University Press.

McCallum, B. T. (1996). *International Monetary Economics*. Oxford University Press.

Merton, R. (1995). A functional perspective of financial intermediation. *Financial Management*, 24: 23–41.

Merton, R. C. (1974). On the pricing of corporate debt: the risk structure of interest rates. *J. Finance*, 29: 449–70.

Miller, G. P. (1996). Is deposit insurance inevitable? Lessons from Argentina. *Int. Rev. Law Econ.*, 16: 211–32.

Minsky, H. (1992). The financial instability hypothesis. Working paper, Mimeo, Yale University.

Mishkin, F. S. and Eakins, S. (2011). *Financial Markets and Institutions*, 6th edition. Pearson.

Moe, T. G., Solheim, J. A., and Vale, B. (2004). The Norwegian banking crisis. Technical report, Norges Bank. Occasional Paper no. 33.

Morris, S. and Shin, H. S. (1998). Unique equilibrium in a model of self-fulfilling currency attacks. *Amer. Econ. Rev.*, 88: 587–97.

Morris, S. and Shin, H. S. (1999). Risk management with interdependent choice. *Oxford Review of Economic Policy*, 15: 52–62, reprinted in *Bank of England Financial Stability Review*, 7, 141–150. www.bankofengland.co.uk/fsr/fsr07art5.pdf.

Moysich, A. (2000). The savings and loan crisis and its relationship to banking. In Federal Deposit Insurance Corporation, *History of the 80s – Lessons for the Future. Volume I: an Examination of the Banking Crises of the 1980s and Early 1990s*, Chapter 4. FDIC, Washington, DC.

Mundell, R. A. (1961). A theory of optimum currency areas. *Amer. Econ. Rev.*, 51: 657–65.

Murphy, D. (2009). *Unravelling the Credit Crunch*. CRC Press.

Mussa, M. (2002). *Argentina and the Fund: From Triumph to Tragedy*. Institute for International Economics, Washington, DC.

Obstfeld, M. (1996). Models of currency crises with self-fulfilling features. *Eur. Econ. Rev.*, 40(3–5): 1037–47.

Obstfeld, M. and Rogoff, K. (1996). *Foundations of International Macroeconomics*. MIT Press.

OECD (2002). Forty years' experience with the OECD code of liberalisation of capital movements. Technical report.

Quagliariello, M. and Cannata, F. (2011). *Basel III and Beyond*. Riskbooks, London.

Radelet, S. and Sachs, J. (2000). The onset of the East Asian financial crisis. In Krugman, P., editor, *Currency Crises*. University of Chicago Press. www.nber.org/chapters/c8691.

Reinhart, C. M. and Rogoff, K. (2009). *This Time Is Different: Eight Centuries of Financial Folly*. Princeton University Press.

Reinhart, C. M., Rogoff, K. and Savastano, M. A. (2003). Debt intolerance. Technical report, NBER.

Repullo, R. and Saurina, J. (2011). The countercyclical capital buffer of Basel III: a critical assessment. CEMFI Working Paper 1102, June.

Santos, J. A. C. (2000). Bank capital regulation in contemporary banking theory: A review of the literature. Technical Report 90, Bank for International Settlements. www.bis.org/publ/work90.pdf?noframes¯1.

Sarno, L. and Taylor, M. P. (2003). *The Economics of Exchange Rates*. Cambridge University Press.

Schumpeter, J. (1942). *Capitalism, Socialism and Democracy*. Harper, New York.

SEC and CFTC (2010). Findings regarding the market events of May 6, 2010. Technical report.

Selgin, G. (2003). Adaptive learning and the transition to fiat money. *Econ. J.*, 113(484): 147–65.

Shin, H. S. (2008). Reflections on modern bank runs: A case study of Northern Rock. Mimeo, Princeton University.

Shin, H. S. (2010). *Risk and Liquidity. Clarendon Lectures in Finance*. Oxford University Press.

Sicsic, P. (1992). Was the Franc Poincaré deliberately undervalued? *Explorations in Economic History*, 29: 69–92.

Sorkin, A. R. (2010). *Too Big to Fail: Inside the Battle to Save Wall Street*. Penguin.

Spanish government (2008). Las balanzas fiscales de las CC.AA. españolas con las AA. Públicas Centrales 2005. Technical report, Ministerio de Economía y Hacienda.

Stiglitz, J. (2009). Obama's ersatz capitalism. www.nytimes.com/2009/04/01/opinion/01stiglitz.html?r=1&scp=2&sq=stiglitz&st=cse.

Stoler, P. and Kalb, J. B. (1982). The great Vatican bank mystery. http://time.com/time/magazine/article/0,9171,951806,00.html.

Sturzenegger, F. and Zettelmeyer, J. (2007). *Debt Defaults and Lessons from a Decade of Crises*. MIT Press.

Sullivan, R., Timmermann, A. and White, H. (1999). Dangers of data mining: the case of calendar effects in stock returns. *J. Econometrics*, 105(1): 249–86.

Taylor, J. B. (1993). Discretion versus policy rules in practice. *Carnegie-Rochester Conference Series on Public Policy*, 39: 195–214.

The Economist (1999). South Africa's debt: unforgivable. *The Economist* (US), 24 April.

The Economist (2009). No empty threat. Credit-default swaps are pitting firms against their own creditors. *The Economist* (US), 18 June.

Tobin, J. (1996). A currency transactions tax, why and how? *Open Economies Review*, 7: 493–9.

Truell, P. and Gurwin, L. (1992). *False Profits: the Inside Story of BCCI, the World's Most Corrupt Financial Empire*. Houghton Mifflin, Boston, MA.

UBS (2008). Shareholder report on UBS's write-downs. Technical report.

Volcker, P. (2011). Financial reform: Unfinished business. www.nybooks.com/articles/archives/2011/nov/24/financial-reformunfinished-business.

Wall Street Journal (2007). One 'quant' sees shakeout for the ages – '10,000 years'. *Wall Street Journal*, 11 August.

Wall Street Journal (2009a). Action on AIG unit may cost taxpayers. *Wall Street Journal*, 13 April. online.wsj.com/article/SB123957925343711995.html.

Wall Street Journal (2009b). Paul Volcker: think more boldly. *Wall Street Journal*, 14 December. online.wsj.com/ article/SB10001424052748704825504574586330960597134.html.

Washington Post (2004). Credit raters' power leads to abuses, some borrowers say. *Washington Post*, 24 November. www.washingtonpost.com/wp-dyn/articles/A8032-2004Nov23.html.

Weisbrot, M. (2007). Ten years after: the lasting impact of the Asian financial crisis. Technical report. http://www.cepr.net/documents/publications/asia_crisis_2007_08.pdf.

Zigrand, J.-P. (2010). What do network theory and endogenous risk theory have to say about the effects of CCPs on systemic stability? *Financial Stability Review*, 14, Banque de France.

INDEX